A SUBJECT BIBLIOGRAPHY
OF THE FIRST WORLD WAR

Also by A. G. S. Enser

FILMED BOOKS AND PLAYS 1928-1986

A SUBJECT BIBLIOGRAPHY OF THE SECOND WORLD WAR:
BOOKS IN ENGLISH 1939-1974

A SUBJECT BIBLIOGRAPHY OF THE SECOND WORLD WAR:
BOOKS IN ENGLISH 1975-1987

A SUBJECT BIBLIOGRAPHY OF THE FIRST WORLD WAR

Books in English 1914-1987

A. G. S. Enser

FLA FRSA

Gower

First published in 1979 by André Deutsch Ltd
This edition published by
Gower Publishing Company Limited
Gower House
Croft Road
Aldershot
Hants   GU11 3HR
England

Gower Publishing Company
Old Post Road
Brookfield
Vermont 05036
USA

British Library Cataloguing in Publication Data

Enser, Alfred George Sidney
  A subject bibliography of the First World War.
  1. European War, 1914–1918–Bibliography
  I. Title   II. Series
  016.9403   Z6207.E8

  ISBN 0 566 05619 4

Typeset in Great Britain by Lazerset, Aldershot.
Printed in Great Britain by Billing & Sons Ltd, Worcester.

CONTENTS

Preface	*vii*
List of Abbreviations	*ix*
Subject Bibliography	1
Author Index	333
Subject Index	405
Index of Titled Books only	409

PREFACE

The First World War was a truly shattering event. Its consequences were global, and affected social and political life as never before. Empires were destroyed; dynasties ended; new dimensions of warfare evolved; and casualties on a horrific scale sustained. Since 1914 life has never been the same, and what the world gained in the advancement of scientific and technical knowledge, cannot equate the loss to the world of the flower of mankind.

Books on the First World War continue to be published, and interest has been revived and widened considerably, recently, by films and television programmes. For many years there has been no general bibliography published on books in English on the Great War. This compilation is intended to fill the gap, as a guide both to the general reader, and to the researcher in any type of library – public, special, polytechnic or university.

SCOPE

This subject index covers the years 1914 to 1987, omitting, in general, works of less than forty pages, as well as poetry, fiction, juvenile books, humour, rolls of honour and the publications of the War Graves Commission.

In the main the entries have been taken from the *British Museum Subject Catalogue;* the *United States Catalogue,* later the *Cumulative Book Index;* the *British National Bibliography; Whitaker;* and the bibliographies compiled by *Falls; Lange & Berry;* and *Protheroe.* Place, publisher, date of first publication and number of pages is given where known, as is any change of title in the United Kingdom, United States of America, or in subsequent editions. In this revised edition previous omissions are now included where possible.

ARRANGEMENT

The subject headings are arranged in alphabetical order. As a general rule, within each subject heading the entries are also arranged alphabetically by author or title. Exceptions to this are BRITISH ARMY; MEMOIRS; UNITED STATES; and UNITED STATES ARMY. For these the arrangements are as follows:

BRITISH ARMY (general): Fourth Army; Fifth Army; Divisions (in numerical order); Brigades (in numerical order); Regiments (in alphabetical order); Corps (in alphabetical order); Cavalry; Royal Artillery; Royal Engineers; and British Expeditionary Force.

MEMOIRS are arranged alphabetically under the name of the subject except for major personalities such as Churchill, Lloyd George, Pershing and Woodrow Wilson, who have separate subject headings.

UNITED STATES (general); American-Germans; Intervention; Neutrality; Preparedness.

UNITED STATES ARMY (general); Divisions (in numerical order); Infantry (in numerical order); Engineers (in numerical order); Field Artillery (in numerical order); Machine Gunners; Air Division.

Major events are given separate subject headings (Cambrai; Marne; Passchendaele; Somme; Verdun) with *see also* references to related or wider subject material.

Bibliographical information is sufficient for identification but is kept to a minimum. Of course, general agreement in the placing of every entry under a subject cannot be expected in a compilation of this nature on such a complex event such as the First World War; but I have aimed to place each entry where the majority of users would expect to find it, bearing in mind the subject arrangement. It must be emphasized that no claim is made for the entries to be exhaustive, and I shall be pleased to be informed of omissions and errors.

ACKNOWLEDGEMENTS

I wish to express my thanks for help, so willingly given to me by Miss A. Duhig of the National Army Museum; John W. Hunt, Librarian, the Royal Military Academy, Sandhurst; Terence J. Rix, Borough Librarian of Hammersmith; Godfrey Thompson, City Librarian of the City of London; the Staff of East Sussex County Libraries, especially Miss M. L. Butler, Mrs S. M. Beck, Miss W. V. Baulcomb, and Mr E. W. Watkins; C. P. Ravilious of Sussex University Library; and Brian Holden Reid of the Institute of Historical Research, University of London.

In particular, my thanks to my wife for her constant care, encouragement and practical help.

In this revised edition I wish to thank Roger Joye, and Peter T. Scott for their invaluable help. Also Sue McNaughton of Gower for her support of my various books, and Dr I. Webb and Mrs. Conyers of Brighton Polytechnic.

A. G. S. ENSER
Eastbourne, February, 1988

ABBREVIATIONS

Ariz	Arizona
Ark	Arkansas
Aus	Austria
Austr	Australia
Berks	Berkshire
BC	British Columbia
bib	Bibliography
Bucks	Buckinghamshire
Cal	California
Camb	Cambridgeshire
Chesh	Cheshire
CI	Channel Islands
Co	Colorado
comp	compiler
Conn	Connecticut
Corn	Cornwall
CUP	Cambridge University Press
Derbys	Derbyshire
ed(s)	editor(s)
Fla	Florida
Ga	Georgia
Hants	Hampshire
Herts	Hertfordshire
HMS	His/Her Majesty's Ship
HMSO	His/Her Majesty's Stationery Office
Humb	Humberside
Ill	Illinois
Ind	Indiana
Inter	International
Io	Iowa
jr	junior
Kan	Kansas
Kty	Kentucky
Lancs	Lancashire
LI	Long Island
Mass	Massachusetts
Md	Maryland
Mich	Michigan
Middx	Middlesex

Minn	Minnesota
Mo	Missouri
Mon	Monmouth
NC	North Carolina
nd	no date
NH	New Hampshire
NJ	New Jersey
North	Northumberland
Northants	Northamptonshire
NS	Nova Scotia
NSW	New South Wales
NY	New York State
NZ	New Zealand
Okl	Oklahoma
Ont	Ontario
Ore	Oregon
OTC	Officers' Training Corps
OUP	Oxford University Press
Oxon	Oxford
P	Press
p	pages
Pa	Pennsylvania
pl	plates
pseud	pseudonym
pts	parts
RAF	Royal Air Force
RFC	Royal Flying Corps
rev. ed.	revised edition
RI	Rhode Island
RNAS	Royal Naval Air Service
Scot	Scotland
Soc	Society
Som	Somerset
SPCK	Society for Promoting Christian Knowledge
Staffs	Staffordshire
Sx	Sussex
Sy	Surrey
Tas	Tasmania
Tenn	Tennessee
Tex	Texas
UK	United Kingdom
UMI	University Microfilms International
Un of America	University Publications of America
UP	University Press
US	United States of America
unp	unpaged

Va	Virginia
VAD	Voluntary Aid Detachment
Vol(s)	Volume(s)
Washington DC	Washington District of Columbia
Wilts	Wiltshire
Wis	Wisconsin
Yorks	Yorkshire

SUBJECT BIBLIOGRAPHY

ADDRESSES AND SPEECHES

AFTER two years: messages and speeches of eminent men on the second anniversary of the declaration of war *(London: Hodder & Stoughton 1916), 59p.*

BAKER, N D
 Frontiers of freedom *(New York: Doran 1918), 335p.*

BUCKELL, A C
 The greatest war: six addresses *(London: Skeffington 1915), 102p.*

BUTLER, N M
 A world in ferment: interpretations of the war for a new world *(New York: Scribner 1917), 254p.*

GINSBURG, B W *ed*
 War speeches, 1914-1917 *(New York: OUP 1917), 194p.*

GREAT speeches of the war *(London: Hazell Watson & Viney 1915), 311p.*

LANE, F K
 The American spirit: addresses in war-time *(New York: Stokes 1918), 131p.*

LODGE, H C
 War addresses, 1915-1917 *(Boston, Mass: Houghton Mifflin 1917), 303p.*

PLOWDEN-WARDLAW, J
 The test of war: war addresses given at Cambridge *(London: R. Scott 1916), 202p.*

RALEIGH, *Sir* W
 England and the war: speeches and addresses *(London: OUP 1918), 144p.*

SMITH, *Sir* GEORGE A
 Our common conscience: addresses delivered in America, 1918 *(London: Hodder & Stoughton 1919), 293p.*

WEBB, C
 In time of war (London: Blackwell 1918), 105p.

[*See also outstanding personalities under their names, e.g.* WILSON]

AFGHANISTAN

JAMES, F H
 Faraway campaign *(London: Grayson 1934), 281p.*

AFRICA

AFRICANUS *pseud*
 The Prussian lash in Africa *(London: Hodder & Stoughton 1918), 143p.*

CAMBRIDGE, T R
In the land of Turkana *(London: Heath Cranton 1921), 80p.*
DANE, E
British campaigns in Africa and the Pacific *(London: Hodder & Stoughton 1919), 215p.*
FARWELL, B
The great War in Africa 1914-1918 *(New York: Norton 1986), 382p.*
O'NEILL, H C
The War in Africa, 1914-1917 *(London: Longmans 1919), 113p.*
PAGE, M E *ed.*
Africa and the First World War *(London: Macmillan 1987), 270p; bib.*
SHORTHOUSE, W J T
Sport and adventure in Africa *(London: Seeley 1923), 316p.*
WHITTALL, W
With Botha and Smuts in Africa *(London: Cassell 1917), 280p.*
[*See also* EAST AFRICA, SOUTH AFRICA. SOUTH-WEST AFRICA]

AGRICULTURE

AUGE-LARIBE, M
Agriculture and food supply in France during the war *(New Haven, Conn: Yale UP 1927), 328p.*
CANADA Department of Agriculture
Production and thrift: agricultural war book *(Ottawa: 1916), 250p.*
HALL, A D
Agriculture after the war *(London: Murray 1916), 146p.*
HIBBARD, B H
Effects of the Great War upon agriculture in the United States and Great Britain *(New York: OUP 1919), 232p.*
League of Nations
Agricultural production in Continental Europe during the 1914-1918 war and reconstruction period *(London: 1943), 122p.*
WIBBERLEY, T
War-time farming *(London: Pearson 1916), 47p.*
[*See also* FOOD]

AIRCRAFT PRODUCTION

KNAPPEN, T M
Wings of war: an account of the important contribution of the United States to aircraft invention, engineering, development and production during the World War *(New York: Putnam 1920), 289p.*
MIXTER, G W *and* EMMONS, H H
U.S. Army aircraft production facts *(Washington DC: 1919), 106p.*

AIR WARFARE (general)

ABBOT, W J
Aircraft and submarines *(New York: Putnam 1918), 388p.*
B W T
Plane tales from the skies *(London: Cassell 1918), 181p.*
BARRETT, W E
The first war planes *(New York: Fawcett 1964), 112p.*
BENN, W W
In the side shows: observations of a flier on five Fronts *(New York: Doran 1920), 310p.*
BIDDLE, C J
Way of an eagle *(New York: Scribner 1919), 297p.*
BINGHAM, H
Explorer in the air service *(New Haven, Conn: Yale UP 1920), 260p.*
BRUCE, E S
Aircraft in war *(London: Hodder & Stoughton 1914), 177p.*
BRUCE, J M
Britain's first war planes *(Poole, Dorset: Arms & Armour 1987), 128p*
War planes of the First World War *(New York: Doubleday 1972), 2 vols.*
BUIST, H M
Aircraft in the German war *(London: Methuen 1914), 248p.*
CAMPBELL, C *and* WOOD J, W
Aces and aircraft of World War I *(Poole, Dorset: Blandford 1981), 144p.*
CAMPBELL, G F
A soldier in the sky *(Chicago: Davis 1918), 232p.*
CASTLE, H G
Fire over England: the German air raids of World War I *(London: Secker & Warburg 1982), 254p.*
CHRISTY, J *and* SHAMBURGER, P
Aces and planes of World War I *(East Norwark, Conn: Sports Car 1968), 120p.*
CLARK, A
Aces high: the war in the air over the Western Front, 1914-18 *(London: Weidenfeld & Nicolson 1973), 191p.*
CLAXTON, W J
The mastery of the air *(London: Blackie 1915), 256p.*
CLIFFORD, G R
My experiences as an aviator in the World War *(Boston, Mass: Badger 1928), 276p.*
CODMAN, C R
Contact *(Boston, Mass: Little, Brown 1937), 248p.*
CONTACT *pseud*
Cavalry of the clouds *(New York: Doubleday 1918), 266p. U.K. title:* An airman's outings.
CUNEO, J R
Winged Mars *(Harrisburg, Pa: Military Service 1947), 2 vols.*
DAVIES, G C
World War I aeroplanes *(London: Ward Lock 1974), 144p.*
DOMMETT, W E
Aeroplanes and airships *(London: Whittaker 1915), 106p.*

DRAKE, V
Above the battle *(New York: Appleton 1918), 322p.*

DRIGGS, L la T
Heroes of aviation: authentic stories of the great aviators in the war *(Boston, Mass: Little, Brown 1918), unp.*

ELLIOTT, S E
Wooden crates and gallant pilots *(Philadelphia, Pa: Dorrance 1974), 275p.*

FARRÉ, H
Sky fighters of France: aerial warfare, 1914-1918 *(Boston, Mass: Houghton Mifflin 1919), 143p.*

FITCH, W S
Wings in the night *(Boston, Mass: Jones, Marshall 1938), 302p.*

FITZSIMONS, B *ed*
Warplanes and air battles of World War I *(London: Phoebus 1973), 150p.*

GILCHRIST, J W S
An aerial observer in World War I *(Richmond, Va: Gilchrist 1966), 134p.*

GRAHAME-WHITE, C *and* HARPER, H
Aircraft in the Great War *(London: Fisher Unwin 1915), 346p.*

GREY, C G
Tales of the flying services: the adventures and humour of aerial warfare *(London: Newnes 1915), 124p.*

GRIDER, J M
War birds: diary of an unknown aviator *(London: Hamilton 1927), 277p.*

GUTTERSEN, G
Granville tales and tail spins from a flyer's diary *(New York: Abingdon Press 1919), 176p.*

HALL, J N
High adventure: a narrative of air fighting in France *(London: Constable 1918), 236p.*

HARTNEY, H E
Wings over France *(Folkestone, Kent: Bailey 1974), 360p; previously published as:* Up and at 'em.

HASLETT, E
Luck on the wing: thirteen stories of a sky spy *(New York: Dutton 1920), 303p.*

HASTINGS, H D *and* PARKER, P
War planes in battle dress, 1914-18 *(New York: Walker 1964), unp.*

HERMES *pseud*
The hornets: tales of the air *(London: Nash 1917), 186p.*

HICKS, W J
The command of the air *(London: Nisbet 1916), 192p.*

HOLLEY, I B
Ideas and weapons: exploitation of the aerial weapon by the United States during World War I *(London: OUP 1953), 222p.*

JABLONSKI, E
The knighted skies: a pictorial history of World War I in the air *(London: Nelson 1964), 241p; bib.*

JONES, H A
The official history of the war in the air *(Oxford: Clarendon 1928), 6 vols.*
Sir Walter Raleigh and the air history: a personal recollection *(London: Arnold 1922), 48p.*

KERSHAW, A
The first war planes *(London: Phoenix 1972), 65p; bib.*
LANCHESTER, F W
Aircraft in warfare: the dawn of the fourth army *(London: Constable 1915), 222p.*
LAWSON, D
Great air battles: World War I and II *(New York: Lothrop 1958), 223p.*
LEIGH, H
Planes of the Great War *(London: Hamilton 1934), 111p.*
LEONING, G C
Military aeroplanes *(San Diego, Cal: Frye & Smith 1915), 169p.*
LONGSTREET, S
The canvas falcons: the story of the men and the planes of World War I *(Cleveland. Ohio: World Publishing 1970); 365p.*
MCKEE, A
The friendless sky: the story of air combat in World War I *(London: Souvenir Press 1962), 256p.*
MACMILLAN, N
Offensive patrol: the story of the RNAS, RFC, and RAF in Italy *(London: Jarrolds 1973), 264p.*
Tales of two air wars *(London: Bell 1953), 272p.*
MIDDLETON, E C
Glorious exploits of the air *(London: Simpkin, Marshall 1917), 255p.*
The Great War in the air *(London: Waverley 1920), 4 vols.*
The way of the air: incidents in the air service in the north of France *(London: Heinemann 1917), 192p.*
MONEY, R R
Flying and soldiering *(London: Nicholson & Watson 1937), 319p*
MONTGOMERY-MOORE, C
That's my bloody plane: World War I experiences *(Chester, Conn: Pequot Press 1975),157p.*
MORISON, F
War on great cities: a study of the facts *(London: Faber 1937), 245p.*
MORTANE, J
Special missions of the air: an exposition of some of the mysteries of aerial warfare *(London: Aeroplane 1919), 131p.*
MUNSON, K
Aircraft of World War I *(London: Ian Allan 1967), 175p.*
NORMAN, A
The great air war *(London: Collier-Macmillan 1968), 558p; bib.*
OUGHTON, F
The aces *(London: Spearman 1961), 390p; bib.*
PHELAN, J A
Aircraft and flyers of the First World War *(London: Stephens 1974), 128p; previously published as:* Heroes and aeroplanes of the Great War, 1914- 1918.
PLATT, F C *comp*
Great battles of World War I (in the air) *(London: New English Library 1966), 206p.*

PULITZER, R
Over the front in an aeroplane *(New York: Harper 1915), 158p.*
RAFBIRD *pseud*
Zooms and spins: an Army pilot's light and shade impressions *(London: Sampson Low 1919), 120p.*
RALEIGH, *Sir* W
The war in the air *(Oxford: Clarendon 1922-28), 6 vols.*
REYNOLDS, Q J
They fought for the sky: the story of the First World War in the air *(New York: Rinehart 1957), 298p; bib.*
ROBSON, W A
Aircraft in war and peace *(London: Macmillan 1916), 176p.*
ROWE J P *jr*
Letters from a World War I aviator *(Wellesley Mass: Sinclair 1986), 151p.*
SIMKINS, P
Air fighting 1914-18: the struggle for air superiority over the Western Front *(London: Imperial War Museum 1978), 80p.*
SMITH, MYRON J *jr*
World War I in the air: a bibliography and a chronology *(New York: Scarecrow Press 1977), 271p.*
SPAIGHT, J M
Aircraft in war *(London: Macmillan 1914), 184p.*
SPRINGS, E W
Above the bright blue sky: more about the war birds *(New York: Doubleday 1928), 275p.*
STARK, R
Wings of war: an airman's diary of the last year of World War One *(London: Hamilton 1933), 227p.*
SUTHERLAND, L W *and* ELLISON, N
Aces and kings *(Sydney, Aust: Angus & Robertson 1935), 275p.*
TALBOT, F A
Aeroplanes and dirigibles of war *(London: Heinemann 1915), 296p.*
THETFORD, O G *and* RIDING, E J
Aircraft of the 1914-18 war *(Leicester: Harborough 1946), 126p.*
WADE, W L
The aeroplane in the Great War: a record of achievement *(London: Virtue 1920), 229p.*
WALCOTT, S
Above the French lines: letters of an American aviator, July 4, 1917 to December 8, 1917 *(Princeton, NJ: Princeton UP 1918): 93p.*
WALTERS, E W
Heroic airmen and their exploits *(London: Kelly 1917), 270p.*
WAR IN THE AIR *(London: OUP 1922-1937), 6 vols.*
WHITEHOUSE, A *pseud*
Decisive air battles of the First World War *(New York: Duell 1963), 360p.*
Heroes of the sunlit skies *(New York: Doubleday 1967), 384p.*
The years of the sky kings *(London: Macdonald 1960), 334p.*

WOODHOUSE, J *and* EMBLETON, G
  The war in the air, 1914-1918 *(London: Almark 1974), 95p.*
[*See also BOMBERS, FIGHTERS, FRENCH AIR FORCE, GERMAN AIR FORCE, ROYAL FLYING CORPS,
  ROYAL AIR FORCE, US AIR FORCE*]

AISNE

GREAT BRITAIN War Office
  The battle of the Aisne, 13-15th September 1914 *(London: HMSO 1935), 56p.*
MILLS, A H
  With my regiment from the Aisne to La Bassée *(London: Soldiers' Tales of the Great War
  1915), 231p.*
ROGERSON, S
  The last of the ebb *(London: Barker 1937), 147p.*

ALLENBY

A BRIEF record of the advance of the Egyptian Expeditionary Force under General Allenby,
  July 1917-October 1918 *(London: HMSO 1919), unp.*
BULLOCK, D
  Allenby's war: the road to Damascus 1916-1918 *(Poole, Dorset: Blandford 1987), 160p;
  bib.*
FALLS, C
  Armageddon, 1918 *(London: Weidenfeld & Nicolson 1964), 216p.*
GARDNER, B
  Allenby *(London: Cassell 1965), 314p; bib.*
GILBERT, V
  The romance of the last Crusade *(New York: Appleton 1924), 235p.*
SAVAGE, R
  Allenby of Armageddon *(London: Diamond 1928), 314p.*
WAVELL, *Sir* A P
  Allenby *(London: Harrap 1940-1943), 2 vols.*
[*See also MESOPOTAMIA, PALESTINE*]

ALSACE-LORRAINE

BLUMENTHAL, D
  Alsace-Lorraine: a study of the relations of Alsace-Lorraine to France and Germany
  (London: Putnam 1918), 67p.
CHURCH, L F
  The story of Alsace-Lorraine *(London: Kelly 1915), 176p.*
DUHEM, J
  The question of Alsace-Lorraine *(London: Hodder & Stoughton 1918), 206p.*
HARRISON, M
  The stolen lands: a study in Alsace-Lorraine *(London: Kegan Paul 1918), 206p.*
HAZEN, C D
  Alsace-Lorraine under German rule *(New York: Holt 1917), 246p.*

PHILLIPSON, C
  Alsace-Lorraine: past, present and future *(London: Fisher Unwin 1918), 327p.*
VIZETELLY, E A
  The true story of Alsace-Lorraine *(London: Chatto & Windus 1918), 323p.*

AMBULANCES

ALDRICH, M
  On the edge of the war zone *(London: Constable 1918), 279p.*
BLACK, D
  Red dust: an Australian trooper in Palestine *(London: Cape 1931), 303p.*
BRADLEY A O
  Back of the front in France *(London: Butterfield 1918), 155p.*
BRYAN, J H
  Ambulance 464 *(New York: Macmillan 1918), 220p.*
BUSWELL, L
  Ambulance No. 10: personal letters from the front *(London: Constable 1917), 177p.*
CATCHPOOL, T C
  On two fronts *(London: Headley 1918), 176p.*
CHASE, H L
  The 2/lst London Field Ambulance: an outline of the 4 1/2- years service at home and abroad, 1914-1918 *(London: Morton, Burt 1924). 104p.*
COYLE, E R
  Ambulancing on the French front *(New York: Britton 1918), 243p.*
CUTLER, G R
  Of battles long ago: memoirs of an American ambulance driver in World War I *(New York: Exposition 1979), 280p.*
FIELD ambulance sketches *(London: Lane 1919), 157p.*
FLOREZ, C de
  No. 6: a few pages from the diary of an ambulance driver *(New York: Dutton 1918), 150p.*
FRIENDS of France: the field service of the American ambulance *(Boston, Mass: Houghton Mifflin 1916), 297p.*
GLEASON, A H
  With the first war ambulance in Belgium *(New York: Burt 1918), 213p.*
IMBRIE, R W
  Behind the wheel of a war ambulance *(New York: McBride 1918), 248p.*
JOBSON, A
  Via Ypres: the story of the 39th Divisional Field Ambulance *(London: Westminster City, 1935), 236p.*
LENG, W St Q
  S.S.A.10: notes on the work of a British Volunteer Ambulance convoy with the French Army *(Sheffield: 1918), 71p.*
MITCHELL, C van S
  With a military ambulance in France, 1914-1915 *(Princeton, NJ: Princeton Banner P 1915), 97p.*
ORCUTT, P D
  White road of mystery: the note-book of an American ambulancier *(London: Lane 1918), 173p.*

RICE, P S
   An American crusader at Verdun *(Princeton: Princeton UP 1918), 103p; previously published as:* An ambulance driver in France.
ROBINSON, W J
   My fourteen months at the front: an American's baptism of fire *(London: Hodder & Stoughton 1916), 286p.*
SHIVELY, G J *ed*
   Record of the S.S.U.585 Yale ambulance unit with the French Army, 1917-1919 *(New York: Brick Row 1920), 286p.*
SINCLAIR, M
   A journal of impressions: record of experiences with a field ambulance in the autumn of 1914 *(London: Hutchinson 1915), 348p.*
[*see also* HOSPITALS, NURSING]

AMIENS

AMIENS before and during the war *(Milltown, NJ: Michelin Tire 1919), 55p.*
BLAXLAND, G
   Amiens, 1918 *(London: Muller 1968), 274p; bib.*
KEARSEY, A
   The battle of Amiens, 1918, and operations 8th August-3rd September: the turn of the tide on the Western Front *(Aldershot, Gale & Polden 1950), 79p.*

ANIMALS

BAKER, P S
   Animal war heroes *(London: Black 1933), 129p.*
BAYNES, E H
   Animal heroes of the Great War *(New York: Macmillan 1927), 307p.*
RICHARDSON, E H
   British war dogs *(London: Skeffington 1920), 288p.*
ROHAN, J
   Rags: the story of a dog who went to war *(New York: Harper 1930), 242p.*

ANTHOLOGY

THOMPSON, T *comp*
   Coming dawn: a war anthology *(London: Lane 1918), 289p.*

ANTWERP

FOSTER, H C
   At Antwerp and the Dardanelles *(London: Mills & Boon 1918), 162p.*

ARABIA [SEE MESOPOTAMIA]

ARCHANGEL

HALLIDAY, E M
  The ignorant armies: the Anglo-American Archangel Expedition, 1918-1919 *(New York: Harper 1960), 232p; bib.*
IRONSIDE, W E *1st baron Ironside*
  Archangel, 1918-1919 *(London: Constable 1953), 220p.*
[*See also* RUSSIAN ALLIED CAMPAIGN]

ARMENIA

BANKER, M S
  My beloved Armenia *(Chicago: Bible Trust 1936), 205p.*
CARAMAN, E
  Daughter of the Euphrates *(New York: Harper 1939), 277p.*
CHALLAND, G
  From genocide to resistance *(London: Zed 1983), 144p.*
FA-IZ AL-GHUSAN
  Martyred Armenia *(London: Pearson 1917), 56p.*
GATES, H L
  The auction of souls: the story of Aurora Mardiganian *(London: Odhams 1920), 272p.*
GERMANY, Turkey and Armenia: a selection of documentary evidence relating to the Armenian atrocities *(London: Keliher 1917), 127p.*
GIBBINS, H A
  The blackest page of modern history: events in Armenia *(New York: Putnam 1916), 71p.*
HACOBIAN, A P
  Armenia and the war: an Armenian's point of view *(London: Hodder & Stoughton 1917), 200p.*
HARTILL, L R
  Men are like that *(Indianapolis: Bobbs-Merrill 1928), 305p.*
KERR, S E
  The lions of Marash *(Albany, NY: State University of New York 1973), 318p.*
KNAPP, G H
  The tragedy of Bitlis *(New York: Revell 1919), 160p.*
MEGERDICHIAN, E
  From Turkish toils: the narrative of an Armenian family's escape *(London: Pearson 1918), 51p.*
NA IM, *Bey*
  The memoirs of NA IM Bey: Turkish official documents relating to the deportation and massacres of Armenians *(London: Hodder & Stoughton 1920), 83p.*
PAPAZIAN, B S
  The tragedy of Armenia *(Boston, Mass: Pilgrim Press 1918), 164p.*

TOYNBEE, A J
Armenian atrocities: the murder of a nation *(London: Hodder & Stoughton 1915), 119p.*
The treatment of Armenians in the Ottoman Empire *(London: Hodder & Stoughton 1916), 684p.*

ARMISTICE

BARCLAY, C N
Armistice, 1918 *(London: Dent 1968), 155p.*
BROWN, M *and* SEATON, S
Christmas truce *(London: Cooper & Secker & Warburg 1984), 228p; bib.*
MAURICE, *Sir* F B
The Armistices of 1918 *(London: Royal Institute of International Affairs 1943), 104p.*
MOTTRAM, R H
Ten years ago: Armistice and other memories *(London: Chatto & Windus 1928), 179p.*
RUDIN, H R
Armistice, 1918 *(New Haven, Conn: Yale UP 1944), 442p.*

ARMS AND ARMOUR

CHARTERIS, N K
Some lectures and notes on machine-guns *(London: W. H. Smith 1915), 106p.*
DOOLY, W G *jr*
Great weapons of World War I *(New York: Walker 1969), 340p.*
ELLIS, J
The social history of the machine-gun *(London: Croom Helm 1975), 186p; bib.*
FORTY, G
A photo history of armoured cars in two World Wars *(Poole, Dorset: Blandford 1984), 190p.*
HOGG, I V
The machine-gun *(London: Phoebus 1976), 64p.*
HOGG, I V *and* WEEKS, J
Military small arms of the twentieth century *(London: Arms & Armour Press 1974), 284p.*
HOLLEY, I B
Ideas and weapons *(London: OUP 1953), 222p; bib.*
LONGSTAFF, F V *and* ATTERIDGE, A H
The book of the machine-gun *(London: Rees 1917), 435p.*
MACHINE-GUNNERS pocket book *(London: Graham & Latham 1915), 55p.*
OMMUNDSEN, H *and* ROBINSON, E H
Rifles and ammunition, and rifle shooting *(London: Cassell 1915), 354p.*
PEARCE, C E
War up-to-date: a vade mecum of modern methods of warfare *(London: Stanley Paul 1915), 132p.*
SIMPLEX *pseud*
Instructions on the Lewis automatic machine-gun *(London: Forster Groom 1916), 156p.*

TRACY, C D
Revolver shooting in war *(London: Sifton Praed 1915), 54p.*
WILKINSON, F
World War I weapons and uniforms *(London: Ward Lock 1978),128p.*

ARRAS

ARRAS: Lens-Douai and the battles of Artois *(Milltown, NJ: Michelin Tire 1921), 128p.*
FOX, F
The battles of the ridges: Arras-Messines, March-June 1917 *(London: Pearson 1918), 111p.*

ART AND ARTISTS

BONE, M
War drawings *(London: Country Life 1917-18), 5pts.*
Western Front *(London: Country Life 1916-17), 10 pts.*
With the Grand Fleet *(London: Country Life 1917), unp.*
CANNELL, W 0
Fighting types *(London: Lane 1918), unp.*
COLERIDGE, J D
The Grand Fleet: a sketch book *(London: Warner 1920), 46p.*
EBERLE, M
World War I and the Weimar artists: Dix, Grosz, Beckmann, Schlemmer *(New Haven, Conn: Yale 1985), 134p.*
GALLATIN, A E
Art and the Great War *(New York: Dutton 1919), 288p.*
GEORGE C MARSHALL Research Foundation
Posters of World War I and World War II *(Charlottesville, Va: UP 1979), 127p.*
GREAT BRITAIN Imperial War Museum
War pictures *(London: HMSO 1919), 112p.*
GREAT BRITAIN Ministry of Information
War paintings and drawings by British artists *(New York: Carnegie Institute 1919), 21p.*
HALE, W
By motor to the firing line: an artist's notes and sketches with the armies of Northern France June-July 1915 *(New York: Century 1916), 283p.*
HARDIE, M *and* SABIN, A K *eds*
War posters issued by belligerent and neutral nations, 1914-1919 *(London: Black 1920), 275p.*
HARVEY, H
A soldier's sketches under fire *(London: Sampson Low 1916), 190p.*
HOLME, C
The war depicted by distinguished British artists *(London: The Studio 1918), 98p.*
IMPERIAL War Museum
A concise catalogue of paintings, drawings and sculpture of the First World War 1914-18 *(London: Imperial War Museum 1963), 366p.*

JONES, B *and* HOWELL, B
Popular arts of the First World War *(London: Studio Vista 1972), 176p.*
JONES, M
The dance of death: medallic art of the First World War *(London: British Museum 1979), 32p.*
KAHN, E L
The neglected majority: les camoufleurs, art history and World War I *(Lanham, Md: Un of America 1984), 276p.*
MAXWELL, D
A dweller in Mesopotamia: being the adventures of an official artist in the garden of Eden *(London: Lane 1920), 124p.*
The last crusade *(London: Lane 1920), 144p.*
NEVINSON, C R W
British artists at the front *(London: Country Life 1918), 4 pts.*
Modern war paintings *(London: Grant Richards 1917), 79p.*
The Great War fourth year *(London: Grant Richards 1918), 25p + 24 pls.*
NEW ENGLAND AVIATORS 1914-1918
Their portraits and their records *(Boston, Mass: Houghton Mifflin 1919), 2 vols.*
ORPEN, *Sir* W
An onlooker in France, 1917-1919 *(London: Williams & Norgate 1921), 123p.*
PENNELL, J
Pictures of war work in America *(Philadelphia: Lippincott 1918), 51p.*
Pictures of war work in England *(London: Heinemann 1916), 51p.*
ROTHENSTEIN, J
British artists and the war *(London: Davies 1931), 31p.*
TREVES, *Sir* F *and* GOODCHILD, G eds
Made in the trenches *(London: Allen & Unwin 1916), 240p.*
WILKINSON, N L
The Dardanelles: colour sketches from Gallipoli *(London: Longmans 1915), 118p.*

ARTILLERY (GENERAL)

GIBBS, A H
The grey wave *(London: Hutchinson 1920), 271p.*
GOODCHILD, G
Behind the barrage: the story of a siege battery *(London: Jarrolds 1918), 232p.*
GORDON, H
The unreturning army: a field-gunner in Flanders, 1917-18 *(London: Dent 1967), 133p.*
HOGG, I V
The guns, 1914-18 *(New York: Ballantine 1971), 160p; bib.*
HOGG, I V *and* THURSTON, L F
British artillery weapons and ammunition, 1914-1918 *(London: Ian Allan 1973), 255p.*
LINTIER, P
My .75: reminiscences of a gunner of a .75 m/m battery in 1914 *(New York: Grosset 1919), 320p.*
LOWE, C E B
Siege battery 94 during the World War *(London: Werner Laurie 1919), 159p.*

MERRILL, W
A college man in khaki: letters of an American in the British artillery *(New York: Doran 1918), 234p.*
O, F O
With the guns *(London: Nash 1916), 222p.*
SEVERN, M
The Gambardier: giving some account of the heavy and siege artillery in France, 1914-18 *(London: Benn 1930), 224p.*
SULZBACH, H
With the German guns: four years on the Western Front, 1914-1918 *(London: Cooper 1973), 256p.*
TAYLOR, G W
The boy with the guns *(London: Lane 1919), 197p.*
TYTLER, N F
Field guns in France *(London: Hutchinson 1929), 255p.*
WADE, A
The war of the guns *(London: Batsford 1936), 192p; later published as:* Gunner on the Western Front.
WAGGER *pseud*
Battery flashes *(London: Murray 1916), 133p.*

ASQUITH

ASQUITH, H H *1st earl of Oxford & Asquith*
The genesis of war *(London: Cassell 1923), 304p.*
The great shell shortage: Mr. Asquith's reply to Lord French *(London: Cassell 1919), 45p.*
Memories and reflections *(London: Cassell 1928), 2 vols.*
JENKINS, R
Asquith *(London: Collins 1964), 372p.*
KOSS, S E
Asquith *(London: Lane 1976), 310p.*
SPENDER, H
Herbert Henry Asquith *(London: Newnes 1915), 177p.*
SPENDER, J A *and* ASQUITH, C
Life of Herbert Henry Asquith, Lord Oxford & Asquith *(London: Hutchinson 1932), 2 vols.*

ATROCITIES [see WAR CRIMES]

AUSTRALIA

ADCOCK, A St J
Australasia triumphant *(London: Simpkin Marshall 1915), 99p.*

AH KOW, A
  William McKenzie ... Anzac padre *(London: Salvationist Press 1949), 74p.*
BASSETT, J
  The home front 1914-1918 *(Oxford: OUP 1983), 90p.*
BEAN, C E W
  The official history of Australia in the war of 1914-1918 *(Sydney: Angus & Robertson 1921), 12 vols.*
BOWDEN, S H
  The history of the Australian Comforts Fund *(Sydney: 1922), 421p.*
BROINOWSKI, L
  Tasmania's war record, 1914-1918 *(Hobart, Tas: Watch 1921), 370p.*
JENNINGS, M J
  Australia in the Great War *(Melbourne: Hill of Content 1970), 94p.*
KEMPE, H
  Participation *(Melbourne: Hawthorn 1973), 200p.*
SCOTT, E
  Australia during the war *(Sydney: Australian War Memorial 1938), unp.*
SMART, H C
  Australia in the Great War: the story told in pictures *(London: Cassell 1916-18), 192p.*
SOUTER, C
  Lion and Kangaroo: the initiation of Australia, 1901-1919 *(Sydney: Collins 1976), 344p.*
STRONG, A T
  Australia and the war *(Melbourne: Robertson 1915), 158p.*
WILKINS, G H
  Australian war photographs: a pictorial record from Nov. 1917 to the end of the war *(London: Australia House 1919), 144p.*

AUSTRALIAN AIR FORCE

CUTLACK, F M
  Australian Flying Corps in the Western and Eastern theatres of war, 1914-1918 *(Sydney: Angus & Robertson 1923), 485p.*
WALL, A G N
  Letters of an airman *(Melbourne: Robertson 1918), 248p.*
WHITE, T W
  Guests of the unspeakable: the odyssey of an Australian airman - being a record of captivity and escape in Turkey *(London: Hamilton 1928), 320p.*

AUSTRALIAN ARMY

BARRETT, *Sir* J W *and* DEANE, P E
  The Australian Army Medical Corps in Egypt, 1914-1915 *(London: Lewis 1918), 259p.*
BEAN, C E W
  Anzac to Amiens: a shorter history of the Australian fighting services in the First World War *(Canberra: Australian War Memorial 1946), 567p.*

The Australian Imperial Force in France, 1916 *(Sydney: Angus & Robertson 1929)*, *1036p.*
The Australians in France and the story of Anzac: the official history *(Sydney: Angus & Robertson 1929-1942), 6 vols.*
Letters from France on the achievements of the Australian Imperial Force in 1916 *(London: Cassell 1917), 231p.*
Two men I knew: William Bridges and Brudenell White, founders of the Australian Imperial Force *(London: Angus & Robertson 1957), 234p.*
BEDFORD, C W
Legs eleven: history of the 11th Battalion, A.I.F. *(Perth: Imperial 1940).*
BELL, A D ed.
Sergeant Richardson's war: an Australian in World War I *(Adelaide: Rigby 1980), 98p.*
BERRIE, G
Morale: a story of Australian Light Horsemen *(Sydney: Holland & Stephenson 1949), 252p.*
BLOCKSIDGE, W J
An Anzac muster *(Sydney: 1921), 288p.*
BROWN, J
Turkish days and ways *(Sydney: Angus & Robertson 1940), 288p.*
BRUGGER, S M
Australians and Egypt 1914-1915 *(Melbourne: Melbourne UP 1980), 178p.*
BULEY, E C
Glorious deeds of Australasians in the Great War *(London: Meltrose 1915), 337p.*
BUTLER, A G
The official history of the Australian Army Medical Services in the war of 1914-1918 *(Sydney: Angus & Robertson 1938), unp.*
CAVILL, H W
Imperishable Anzacs *(Sydney: Brooks 1916).*
CHARLTON, P
Australians on the Somme Pozieres 1916 *(London: Cooper & Secker & Warburg 1986), 318p.*
COLLETT, H B
The 28ths: a record of war service with the A.I.F. *(Perth 1922), unp.*
CUTLACK, F M
The Australians: their final campaign in France, 1918 *(London: Sampson Low 1918), 336p.*
CUTTRISS, G P
'Over the top' with the Third Australian Division *(London: Kelly 1918), 139p.*
DARLINGTON, *Sir* H
Letters from Helles *(London: Longmans 1936), 154p.*
DENNY, W J
The Diggers: the Australian Forces in the European War *(London: Hodder & Stoughton 1919), 300p.*
DIEPPE, C ed
As it was: a graphic frontline record in the pictures of our Diggers and their foe on the Western Front, 1916-1918 *(Surrey Hills, NSW: Wentworth 1973), 136p.*

DINNING, H
By-ways on service: notes from an Australian Journal *(London: Constable 1918), 281p.*

DONNELL, A
Letters of an Australian Army Sister *(New York: OUP 1920), 292p*

DUNN, E A
Three Anzacs in the war *(London: Skeffington 1918), 246p.*

DYSON, W
Australia at war: drawing at the Front *(London: Palmer & Hayward 1918), 52p.*

ELLIS, A D
The story of the Fifth Australian Division *(Sydney; Angus & Robertson 1920), 468p.*

FIGHTING Australia: a souvenir record of the Australian Forces in the war *(London: The Throne 1917), 94p.*

GAMMAGE, W L
The broken years: Australian soldiers in the Great War *(Canberra: Australian National UP 1974), 301p.*

GORMAN, E
With the 22nd: a history of the 22nd Battalion A.I.F. *(Melbourne: Champion 1919), unp.*

GREEN, F C
The Fortieth: a record of the 40th Battalion, A.I.F. *(Hobart, Tas: 1922), 247p.*

GREEN, J
News from No Man's Land *(London: Kelly 1917), 144p.*

GULLETT, *Sir* H S
The Australian Imperial Force in Sinai and Palestine, 1914–1918 *(Sydney: Angus & Robertson 1937), 844p.*

GULLETT, *Sir* H S and BARRETT, C L
Australia in Palestine *(Sydney: Angus & Robertson 1919), 153p.*

HAMMOND, E W
History of the 11th Light Horse Regiment *(Brisbane: Brooks 1942), unp.*

HANMAN, E F
Twelve months with the Anzacs *(Brisbane: 1916), 160p.*

HISTORY of the 11th Field Company, Australian Engineers *(London: War Narratives 1919), 75p.*

HOGAN, *Mrs* G F
Experiences of a Dinki Di R.R.C. nurse *(Glebe, NSW: 1933), 121p.*

HOGUE, W D
Love letters of an Anzac *(London: Melrose 1916), 219p.*

IDRIESS, I O
Desert column: leaves from the diary of an Australian Trooper in Gallipoli, Sinai and Palestine *(London: Angus & Robertson 1951), 312p.*

JOYNT, W D
Saving the Channel ports *(Melbourne: Wren 1975), 223p; bib.*

KNYVETT, R H
'Over there' with the Australians *(London: Hodder & Stoughton 1918), 289p.*

LOCKE, C R L
The fighting 10th *(Adelaide: Webb 1936).*

LONGMORE, C
The old Sixteenth: being a record of the 16th Battalion, A.I.F. during the Great War, 1914–1918 *(Perth: Imperial 1921), unp.*

MCCARTHY, D
Gallipoli to the Somme: the story of C.E.W. Bean *(London: Cooper 1983), 400p.*

MACGILL, P
The Diggers: the Australians in France *(London: Jenkins 1919), 120p.*

MACKENZIE, K W
The story of the 17th Battalion, A.I.F. in the Great War *(Sydney: Chipping 1946), unp.*

MACKENZIE, S S
The Australians at Rabaul: the capture and administration of the German possession in the Southern Pacific *(Sydney: 1927), 412p.*

MCNICOL, N G
Thirty-seventh: history of the 37th Battalion A.I.F. *(Melbourne: Robertson & Mullens 1936), 355p.*

MAXWELL, J
Hell's bells and Mademoiselles *(Sydney: Angus & Robertson 1932), 267p.*

MITCHELL, G D
Backs to the wall *(Sydney: Angus & Robertson 1937), 268p.*

MONASH, *Sir* J
The Australian victories in France in 1918 (London: Hutchinson 1920), 351p.
War letters *(Sydney: Angus & Robertson 1935), 299p.*

MORROW, E
Iron in the fire *(Sydney: Angus & Robertson 1934), 268p.*

NEWTON, L W
The story of the 12th *(Hobart, Tas: Walch 1925), unp.*

OLDEN, A C N
Western cavalry in the war: the story of the 10th Light Horse *(Melbourne, McCubbin nd.), unp.*

PAGE, G *ed*
Shadows from wire: poems and photographs of Australians in the Great War *(Canberra: Australian War Memorial nd), 111p.*

PEARL, C
Anzac newsreel *(Sydney: Ure Smith 1963), unp.*

ROBSON, L L
The first Australian Imperial Force *(Melbourne: Melbourne UP 1970), unp.*

ROSS, J
The myth of the Digger: the Australian soldier in two world wars *(Sydney: Hale 1985), 251p.*

ROSS, M *and* ROSS, N
Light and shade in war *(London: Arnold 1916), 271p.*

RULE, E J
Jacka's mob *(Sydney: Angus & Robertson 1933), 346p.*

SCHULER, P F E
Australia in arms *(London: Fisher Unwin 1916), 328p.*

SCRYMGEOUR, J T
Blue eyes: a true romance of the Desert column *(Ilfracombe: Stockwell 1961), 83p.*

SMITH, P A
  The Anzacs *(Melbourne: Nelson 1978), 372p.*
SMITHERS, A J
  Sir John Monash *(London: Cooper 1973), 303p.*
STEPHEN, A C
  An Australian in the RFA: being letters and diary of Adrien Consett Stephen *(Sydney: Penfold 1918), 200p.*
THE STORY of the Anzacs *(Melbourne: Ingram 1971), unp.*
THORNTON, G
  With the Anzacs in Cairo: the tale of a great fight *(London: Allenson 1918), 159p.*
THORPE, C H
  A handful of Ausseys *(London: Lane 1919), 296p.*
TILTON, M
  The grey battalion *(Sydney: Angus & Robertson 1933), 310p.*
TIVEYCHOC, A
  There and back: the story of an Australian soldier, 1915-1935 *(Sydney: Angus & Robertson 1935), 285p.*
TWELVE months with the Australian Expeditionary Force *(London: Newnes 1916), 122p.*
WILLIAMS, H R
  Comrades of the great adventure *(Sydney: Angus & Robertson 1935), 307p.*
  The gallant company: an Australian soldier's story of 1915-1918 *(Sydney: Angus & Robertson 1933), 275p.*
WREN, E
  Randwick to Hargicourt: history of the 3rd Battalion Australian Imperial Force *(Sydney: Mc Donald 1935), 399p.*
[*See also* DARDANELLES. GALLIPOLI, MESOPOTAMIA. PALESTINE, WESTERN FRONT]

AUSTRALIAN NAVY

JOSE, A W
  The Royal Australian Navy 1914-1918 *(Sydney: Angus & Robertson 1928): 649p.*
[*See also* ROYAL NAVY]

AUSTRIA

BULLITT, E D
  An uncensored diary from the Central Empires *(London: Stanley Paul 1918), 282p.*
BURIAN von RAJECZ, S
  Austria in dissolution *(New York: Doran 1925), 455p.*
GRATZ, G *and* SCHUELLER, R
  The economic policy of Austria-Hungary during the war in its external relations *(New Haven, Conn: Yale UP 1928), 286p.*
GREGER, R
  Austro-Hungarian warships of World War I *(London: Ian Allan 1976), 192p.*

HANSSEN, H P
 Diary of a dying empire *(Bloomington, Ind: Indiana UP 1955), 409p.*
KASSOWITZ, K E
 Around a world on fire: exploits and escapes of an Austrian World War surgeon *(Milwaukee, Kan: Gutenberg 1935), 197p.*
LUCAS, J S
 Austro-Hungarian infantry, 1914-1918 *(London: Almark 1973), 112p.*
LUDWIG, E
 Austria-Hungary and the war *(New York: Ogilvie 1915), 220p.*
MACHAR, J S
 The jail: experiences in 1916 *(Oxford: Clarendon 1922), 218p.*
MAGLIC, K
 The dandy Hun: the adventures and escapes of K. Maglic *(London: Lane 1932), 200p.*
MANTEYER, G de
 Austria's peace offer, 1916-1917 *(London: Constable 1921), 360p.*
MAY, A J
 The passing of the Hapsburg monarchy, 1914-1918 *(London: OUP 1966): 2 vols; bib.*
NAUMANN, F
 Central Europe *(London: King 1916), 354p.*
O'CONNOR, M D
 Air aces of the Austro-Hungarian Empire 1914-1918 *(Mesa, Ariz: Champlin 1986), 336p.*
PICK, R
 The last days of Imperial Vienna *(New York: Dial Press 1976), 261p.*
PRIBRAM, A F
 Austrian foreign policy 1908-1918 *(London: Allen & Unwin 1923), 128p.*
REDLICH, J
 Austrian war government *(New Haven, Conn: Yale UP 1929), 175p.*
SCHREINER, G A
 Iron ration: three years in warring Central Europe *(New York: Harper 1918), 385p.*
SHANAFELT, G W
 The secret enemy: Austria Hungary and the German Alliance, 1914-1918 *(Boulder, Co: East European Monographs 1985), 272p.*
SPENCER, F
 Battles of a bystander *(New York: Liveright 1941), 260p*
TASLAUANU, O C
 With the Austrian Army in Galicia *(London: Skeffington 1918), 255p.*
TREADWAY, J D
 The falcon and the eagle: Montenegro and Austria-Hungary, 1908-1914 *(Lafayette, Ind: Pardue UP 1983), 349p.*
VOSNJAK, B
 A dying Empire: Central Europe, Pan-Germanism, and the downfall of Austria-Hungary *(London: Allen & Unwin 1918), 198p.*
ZANARDI LANDI, C F *Countess*
 Is Austria doomed? *(London: Hodder & Stoughton 1916), 187p.*
ZEMAN, Z A B
 The break-up of the Habsburg Empire, 1914-1918: a study in national and social revolution *(London: OUP 1961), 274p; bib.*

BALFOUR

BALFOUR, A J *1st earl Balfour*
Essays, speculative and political *(New York: Doran 1921), 241p.*
TOWNE, C H *ed*
The Balfour visit, and the significance of the conferences in the United States in 1917 *(New York: Doran 1917), 87p.*

BALKANS

ABRAHAM, J J
My Balkan log *(London: Chapman & Hall 1921), 311p.*
ALDRIDGE, O M
The retreat from Serbia through Albania *(London: Minerva 1916), 113p.*
BROWN, D
In the heart of German intrigue *(Boston, Mass: Houghton Mifflin 1918), 377p.*
BUXTON, L
The black sheep of the Balkans *(London: Nisbet 1920), 191p.*
BUXTON, N *and* BUXTON, C R
The war and the Balkans *(London: Allen 1915), 112p.*
DURHAM, M E
Twenty years of Balkan tangle *(London: Allen & Unwin 1920), 295p.*
GESHEV, L E
The Balkan league *(London: Murray 1915), 141p.*
GORDON, J *and* Gordon, C J
The luck of thirteen: wanderings and flight through Montenegro and Serbia *(London: Smith, Elder 1916), 378p.*
GORDON, *Mrs* W
A woman in the Balkans *(London: Hutchinson 1916), 404p.*
HAY, I *pseud*
A ship of remembrances: Galliopoli-Salonika *(London: Hodder & Stoughton 1926), 43p.*
LAKE, H
Campaigning in the Balkans *(New York: McBride 1918), 229p.*
NAPIER, H D
The experiences of a military attaché in the Balkans *(London: Drane's 1924), 293p.*
NEWBIGIN, M I
Geographical aspects of Balkan problems in their relations to the great European War *(London: Constable 1915), 243p.*
SETON-WATSON, R
The Balkans, Italy and the Adriatic *(London: Nisbet 1916), 79p.*
The rise of nationality in the Balkans *(London: Constable 1917), 303p.*
[*See also MACEDONIA, RUMANIA, SERBIA, YUGOSLAVIA*]

BALLOONS

HALL, N S
 Balloon buster: Frank Luke of Arizona *(New York: Doubleday 1928), 191p.*
HODGES, G
 Memoirs of an old balloonatic *(London: Kimber 1972), 175p.*
MORRIS, A
 The balloonatics *(London: Jarrolds 1970), 212p; bib.*
WIDNER, E J
 Military observation balloons *(London: Crosby Lockwood 1918), 158p.*
WILKINSON, S
 Lighter than air *(London: Stockwell 1939), 203p.*

BATTLEFIELDS

B, B
 Over there: a Little guide for pilgrims to Ypres: the Salient and Talbot House, Poperinghe *(London: Talbot House 1935), 45p.*
BATTLEFIELDS of the World War *(Milltown, NJ: Michelin Tire 1919), 2 vols.*
BODLEY, J E C
 Romance of the battle-line in France *(New York: Dutton 1920), 369p.*
COOMBS, R E B
 Before endeavours fade: a guide to the battlefields of the First World War *(London: Battle of Britain, 1976), 136p.*
COOP, J O
 A short guide to the battlefields: where to go and how to see them *(Liverpool: 1921), 96p.*
FIELDS and battlefields, by no. 31540 *(New York: McBride 1918),260p.*
FLEMING, A
 How to see the battlefields *(London: Cassell 1919), 124p.*
GAREY, E B
 American guide book to France and its battlefields *(New York: Macmillan 1920), 331p.*
HAMMERTON, J A
 Wrack of war *(London: Murray 1918), 236p.*
HANDBOOK to Belgium and the battlefields *(London: Ward Lock 1921), 304p.*
HUTCHISON, G S
 Pilgrimage *(London: Rich & Cowan 1935), 270p.*
JOHNSON, D W
 Battlefields of the World War: Western and Southern fronts, a study in military geography *(New York: OUP 1921), 648p.*
LOWE, T A
 The Western battlefields: a guide to the British lines *(Aldershot: Gate & Polden 1921), 61p.*
MOSS, J A *and* HOWLAND, H S
 America in battle: with guide to the American battlefields in France and Belgium *(Menasha, Wis: Banta 1920), 615p.*

MOTTRAM, R H
Journey to the Western Front twenty years after *(London: Bell 1936), 292p.*
MUIRHEAD, F *ed*
Belgium and the Western Front, British and American *(London: Macmillan 1920), 368p.*
OXENHAM, J
High altars: the battle-fields of France and Flanders as I saw them *(London: Methuen 1918), 78p.*
PRACTICAL guide to the British war area in France and Belgium *(London: Vickery, Kyrle 1920), 116p.*
SOMMERVILLE. F *pseud*
Present day Paris and the battlefields *(New York: Appleton 1920), 170p.*
SWINTON, *Sir* E D
Twenty years after: the battlefields of 1914-18, then and now *(London: Newnes 1936-38), 3 vols.*
TAYLOR, H A
Good-bye to the battlefields, today and yesterday on the Western Front *(London: Stanley Paul 1930), 288p.*
UNITED STATES American Battle Monuments Commission
American Armies and battlefields in Europe: a history, guide and reference book *(Washington DC: 1938), 547p.*
WEST, R J
A guide to the battlefields of the Western Front *(New York: McBride 1920), unp.*

BATTLES (general)

DAVIS, H W C *ed*
Battles of the Marne and Aisne *(London: OUP 1914), 56p.*
Battles of Ypres-Armentières *(London: OUP 1915), 59p.*
GREAT battles of the Great War *(London: Daily Chronicle 1914), 186p.*
HILDITCH, A N
Battle sketches 1914-15 *(Oxford: Milford 1915), 206p.*
KEEGAN, J
The face of battle *(London: Cape 1976), 352p.*
OFFICIAL names of the battles and other engagements fought by the military Forces of the British Empire during the Great War *(London: HMSO 1921), unp.*
PEN pictures of British battles *(London: Eyre & Spottiswoode 1917), 71p.*
SLOWE, P *and* WOODS, R
Fields of death: battle scenes of the First World War *(London: Hale 1986), 256p; bib.*
A SOUVENIR OF THE BATTLEFIELDS
Pilgrimage, August 1928 *(London: British Legion 1928), 152p.*
WREN, J
The great battles of World War I *(London: Hamlyn 1972), 434p.*
[See also individual battles, E.G. CAMBRAI, MONS, SOMME, VERDUN]

BATTLESHIPS

HAYWARD, V
HMS *Tiger* at bay: a sailor's memoir, 1914-18 *(London: Kimber 1977), 190p.*
PRESTON, A
Battleships of World War I: an illustrated encyclopaedia of the battleships of all nations, 1914-1918 *(London: Arms & Armour Press 1972), 260p; bib.*
WILSON, H W
Battleships in action *(London: Sampson Low 1926), 2 vols.*
[*See also* JUTLAND AND THE NAVIES OF INDIVIDUAL COUNTRIES]

BEATTY

RAWSON, G
Earl Beatty *(London: Jarrolds 1930), 256p.*

BELGIUM

ASTON, *Sir* G G
The triangle of terror in Belgium *(London: Murray 1918), 105p.*
BASSOMPIERRE, A de
The night of August 2-3, 1914 at the Belgian Foreign Office *(London: Hodder & Stoughton 1916), 43p.*
BELGIUM and Germany: texts and documents *(London: Nelson 1915), 132p.*
BERDEN, L
Pictures of ruined Belgium *(London: Lane 1917), 245p.*
A BOOK of Belgium's gratitude *(London: Lane 1915), 412p.*
BUFFIN, C *baron, ed*
Brave Belgians *(New York: Putnam 1918), 377p.*
CAMMAERTS, E
Through the iron bars: two years of German occupation in Belgium *(London: Lane 1917), 72p.*
CAMPBELL, H
Belgian soldiers at home in the United Kingdom *(London: Saunders & Cullingham 1918), 95p.*
CARTON DE WIART, H
The way of honour *(London: Allen & Unwin 1918), 256p.*
CRAM, R A
Heart of Europe *(New York: Scribner 1915), 325p.*
D'YDEWALLE, C
Albert and the Belgians *(London: Methuen 1935), 314p.*
ESSEN, L van der
The invasion and the war in Belgium from Liège to the Yser *(London: Fisher Unwin 1917), 356p.*
A short account of the German invasion and occupation of Belgium *(London: Fisher Unwin 1918), 104p.*

FELSTEAD, S T
  Under the German heel: revelations of life in Belgium under the German occupation, 1914-1918 *(London: Newnes 1940), 228p.*
FOX, F
  The agony of Belgium *(London: Hutchinson 1915), 317p.*
FUEHR, A
  The neutrality of Belgium *(New York: Funk 1915), 248p.*
GALET, E J
  Albert, King of the Belgians in the Great War *(London: Putnam 1931), 341p.*
GERLACHE DE GOMERY, A de
  The unconquerable soul: Belgium in wartime *(London: Hodder & Stoughton 1918), 253p.*
GIBSON, H
  A diplomatic diary *(London: Hodder & Stoughton 1917), 296p.*
GRASSHOFF, R
  The tragedy of Belgium: an answer to Professor Waxweiler *(New York: Dillingham 1915), 244p.*
GRAY, E M
  Belgium under the German sword *(London: Hodder & Stoughton 1915).*
GREAT BRITAIN Foreign Office
  Reply of the Belgian Ministries of justice and Foreign Affairs to the German White Book of the 10th May 1915 *(London: HMSO 1918), 375p.*
  Second Belgian Grey Book *(London: HMSO 1915), 88p.*
GRELLING, R
  Belgian documents: a companion volume to 'The Crime' *(London: Hodder & Stoughton 1919), 308p.*
GRONDIJS, L H
  The Germans in Belgium *(London: Ammunition for Civilians 1915), 95p.*
HALASI, O
  Belgium under the German heel *(London: Cassell 1917), 257p.*
HOUTTE, P van
  The Pan-Germanic crime *(London: Hodder & Stoughton 1915), 192p.*
HUNTE, E T E
  War bread: a personal narrative of the war and relief in Belgium *(New York: Holt 1916), 374p.*
IN the trail of the German Army *(London: Daily Chronicle 1914), 47p.*
JORGENSEN, J
  False witness: an examination of the German accusations against Belgium *(London: Hodder & Stoughton 1916), 234p.*
KAUFFMAN, R W
  In the moment of time: things seen on the bread-line of Belgium *(New York: Moffat 1915), 272p.*
KEEGAN, J
  Opening moves: August 1914 *(New York: Ballantine 1971), 160p.*
KELLOGG, V L
  Fighting starvation in Belgium *(New York: Doubleday 1918), 219p.*
KING Albert's book: a tribute to the Belgian King and people *(London: Hodder & Stoughton 1914), 187p.*

LA BARRE, G

Captive of the Kaiser in Belgium; with the fall of Namur *(London: Mills & Boon 1914)*, *96p.*

LANGENHOVE, F van

The growth of a legend *(New York: Putnam 1916), 321p.*

LIBERT DE FLEMALLE, G de

Fighting with King Albert *(London: Hodder & Stoughton 1915), 327p.*

LIDDELL, R S

The track of the war *(London: Simpkin, Marshall 1915), unp.*

MACK, L

A woman's experiences in the Great War especially in Antwerp and Brussels during the German occupation *(London: Fisher Unwin 1915), 304p.*

MACNAUGHTAN, *Miss* S

A woman's diary of the war: experiences in Belgium *(London: Nelson 1915), 168p.*

MAETERLINCK, M

The wrack of the storm *(London: Methuen 1916), 277p.*

MARKLAND, R

The glory of Belgium *(London: Erskine Macdonald 1915), 137p.*

MASSART, J

Belgians under the German eagle *(London: Fisher Unwin 1916), 368p.*

The secret Press in Belgium *(London: Fisher Unwin 1918), 105p.*

MERCIER, D J *cardinal*

A shepherd among wolves: war-time letters of Cardinal Mercier *(London: Faith Press 1921), 213p.*

The voice of Belgium: the war utterances of Cardinal Mercier *(London: Burns & Oates 1917) 329p.*

MILLARD, O E

Burgomaster Max *(London: Hutchinson 1936), 287p.*

Uncensored: the true story of the clandestine newspaper 'La Libre Belgique' published in Brussels during the German occupation *(London: Hale 1937), 287p.*

MOKVELD, L

The German fury in Belgium *(London: Hodder & Stoughton 1917), 247p.*

NOTHOMB, P

The barbarians in Belgium *(London: Jarrolds 1915), 294p.*

NYROP, K

The imprisonment of the Ghent professors Paul Fredericq and Henri Pirenne: a question of might and right *(London: Hodder & Stoughton 1917), 91p.*

OSSIAN-NILSSON, K G

Militarism at work in Belgium and Germany *(London: Fisher Unwin 1917), 91p.*

PASSELECQ, F

Truth and travesty: an analytical study of the reply of the Belgian Government to the German White Book *(London: Causton 1916), 86p.*

RANDOLPH, J A

The call of Belgium *(London: Architect P 1915), 82p.*

SAROLEA C

How Belgium saved Europe *(London: Heinemann 1915), 226p.*

SINCLAIR, M
   A journal of impressions in Belgium *(London: Hutchinson 1915), 332p.*
SOMVILLE, G
   The road to Liège *(London: Hodder & Stoughton 1916), 296p.*
TOYNBEE A J
   The German terror in Belgium *(London: Hodder & Stoughton 1917), 157p.*
TWELLS, J H
   In the prison city: Brussels 1914-1918 *(London: Melrose 1919), 293p.*
VAUGHAN, G E M
   The flight of Mariette: a story of the siege of Antwerp *(London: Chapman & Hall 1916), 147p.*
VERHAEREN, E
   Belgium's agony *(London: Constable 1915), 131p.*
VISSCHER, C de
   Belgium's case: a juridical enquiry *(London: Hodder & Stoughton 1916), 164p.*
WAR of 1914: military operations in Belgium, July 31 to Dec. 31, 1914 *(London: Collingridge 1915), 96p.*
WAXWEILER, E
   Belgium and the Great Powers: her neutrality explained and vindicated *(New York: Putnam 1916), 186p.*
   Belgium neutral and loyal: the war of 1914 *(New York: Putnam 1915), 338p.*
WHITEHOUSE, J H
   Belgium in war *(Cambridge: CUP 1915), 40p.*
WHITLOCK, B
   Belgium under the German occupation *(London: Heinemann 1919), 2 vols; U.S. title: Belgium.*
WITHINGTON, R
   In occupied Belgium *(Boston, Mass: Cornhill 1921), 173p.*
YERTA, G *and* YERTA, M
   Six women and the invasion *(New York: Macmillan 1917), 377p.*

BIBLIOGRAPHIES

BINGHAM, A *ed*
   Handbook of the European war *(White Plains, NY: Wilson 1916), 2 vols.*
BRITISH MUSEUM Department of Printed Books
   Subject index of books relating to the European war, 1914-1918, acquired by the British Museum, 1914-1920 *(London: British Museum 1922).*
BULKLEY, M E
   Bibliographical survey of contemporary sources for the economical and social history of the war *(London: Milford 1922), 648p.*
FALLS, C
   War books: a critical guide *(London: Davies 1930), 315p.*
HALL, H
   British archives and the sources for the history of the World War *(Oxford: Milford 1925), 445p.*

HART, A B *ed*
America at war: a handbook of patriotic education references *(New York: Doran 1918), 425p.*
LANGE, F W T *and* BERRY, W T
Books on the Great War *(London: Grafton 1915-16), 4 vols.*
PROTHEROE, G W
Catalogue of war publications: comprising works published to June 1923 *(London: Murray 1923), 431p.*
SCHAFFER, R
The United States in World War I: a select bibliography *(Oxford: Clio 1978), 224p.*
SMITH, M J *jr*
World War I in the air: a bibliography and chronology *(New York: Scarecrow 1977), 271p.*
Two World Wars: a selective bibliography *(Oxford: Pergamon Press 1964), 246p.*
WOODWARD, D R
America and World War I: a selected annotated bibliography of English language sources *(New York: Garland 1985), 368p.*

BLOCKADE

BANE, S L *and* LUTZ, R H *eds*
Blockade of Germany after the Armistice, 1918-1919 *(Stanford, Cal: Stanford UP 1942), 874p.*
CHATTERTON, E K
The big blockade *(London: Hurst & Blackett 1932), 287p.*
CONSETT, M W
The triumph of unarmed forces, 1914-1918: an account of the transactions by which Germany, during the Great War was able to obtain supplies *(London: Williams & Norgate 1923), 334p.*
EISENMENGER, *Frau* A
Blockade; the diary of an American middle-class woman, 1914-1924 *(London: Constable 1932), 273p.*
GUICHARD, L
The naval blockade, 1914-1918 *(London: Allan 1930), 324p.*
HAMPSHIRE, A C
The blockaders *(London: Kimber 1980), 274p.*
MENNE, B
Armistice and Germany's food supply, 1918-19: a study of conditional surrender *(London: Hutchinson 1944), 96p.*
MUNRO, D J
Convoys, blockades and mystery towers *(London: Sampson Low 1932), 208p.*
PARMALEE, M
Blockade and sea power: the blockade 1914-1919, and its significance for a world state *(London: Hutchinson 1925), 449p.*
RICHTER, L
Family life in Germany under the blockade *(London: National Labour 1919), 59p.*

RITCHIE, H
The 'Navicert' system during the World War *(Washington DC: Carnegie Endowment 1938), 83p.*
SCHREINER, G A
The iron ration: the economic and social effects of the Allied blockade on Germany and the German people *(London: Murray 1918), 380p.*
SINEY, M C
The Allied blockade of Germany, 1914-1916 *(Minneapolis, Minn: Michigan UP 1957), 339p; bib.*
VINCENT, C P
The politics of hunger: the Allied blockade of Germany 1915-1919 *(Athens, Miss: Ohio UP 1985), 191p.*

BOMBERS

BARTLETT, C P O
Bomber pilot, 1916-1918 *(London: Ian Allan 1974), 80p.*
BEWSHER, P
'Green balls': the adventures of a night bomber *(London: Blackwood 1919), 309p.*
JONES, N
The origins of strategic bombing: a study of the development of British air strategic thought and practice up to 1918 *(London: Kimber 1973), 240p.*
MUNSON, K
Bombers 1914-19: patrol and reconnaissance aircraft *(Poole, Dorset: Blandford 1968), 187p.*
REECE, R H
Night bombing with the Bedouins *(Boston, Mass: Houghton Mifflin 1919), 99p.*
[*See also* AIR WARFARE, THE AIR FORCES OF INDIVIDUAL COUNTRIES, *e.g.* ROYAL AIR FORCE]

BOTHA

MORRIS, K
A great soldier of the Empire: Botha's wonderful conquests *(London: Stevens 1917), 150p.*
Louis Botha; or, Through the Great Thirst Land *(London: Stevens 1915), 150p.*
RITCHIE, M
With Botha in the field *(London: Longmans 1915), 68p.*
TREW, H F
Botha treks *(London: Blackie 1936), 190p.*
[*See also* EAST AFRICA, SMUTS, SOUTH AFRICA, SOUTH WEST AFRICA]

BOY SCOUTS

FINNEMORE, J
A Boy Scout with the Russians *(London: Chambers 1915), 400p.*

ROLAND, PHILIPPS
Boy Scout *(London: Roland House 1933), 75p.*

BREST-LITOVSK

BREHM, B
That was the end *(London: Hurst & Blackett 1934), 333p.*
MAGNES, J L
Russia and Germany at Brest-Litovsk: a documentary history of the peace negotiations *(New York: Rand 1919), 192p.*
PROCEEDINGS of the Brest-Litovsk Peace Conference: the peace negotiations between Russia and the Central Powers, 21 Nov. 1917 - 3 Mar. 1918 *(Washington DC: 1918), 187p.*
TEXTS of the Russian 'Peace' *(Washington DC: 1918), 233p.*
WHEELER-BENNETT, J W
Brest-Litovsk: the forgotten peace, March 1918 *(London: Macmillan 1938), 478p; bib.*

BRITAIN

ADCOCK, A St J
Seeing it through: how Britain answered the call *(London: Hodder & Stoughton 1915), 191p.*
ARMITAGE, F P
Leicester, 1914-1918: the war-time story of a Midland town *(Leicester: Backus 1933), 364p.*
ARMSTRONG, G G
Our ultimate aim in the war *(London: Allen & Unwin 1916), 233p.*
BAVIN, W D
Swindon's war record *(Swindon: Drew 1922), 352p*
BENNETT, E A
Liberty: a statement of the British case *(London: Hodder & Stoughton 1914), 58p.*
BRAZIER, R H *and* SANDFORD, E
Birmingham and the Great War, 1914-1919 *(Birmingham: 1921), 350p.*
BUCKROSE, J E
War time in our street *(London: Hodder & Stoughton 1917), 158p.*
BUNSELMEYER, R E
The cost of the war, 1914-1919: British economic war aims and the origin of reparation *(Hamden, Conn: Archon 1975), 249p.*
CAMPBELL, A
Crieff in the Great War *(Edinburgh: 1925), 279p.*
CARTMELL, H
For remembrance: an account of the part played by Preston in the war *(Preston: 1919), 280p.*
CASTLE, A *and* CASTLE, E
Little hours in great days *(London: Constable 1919), 272p.*
CHESTERTON, G K
The crimes of England *(London: Palmer & Hayward 1915), 127p.*

CHEVRILLON, A
  Britain and the war *(London: Hodder & Stoughton 1917), 258p.*
CLARKE, A O T
  Transport and sport in the Great War period *(London: Garden City Press 1938), 212p.*
CROYDON and the war *(Croydon: 1920), 437p.*
DAVIES, *Sir J*
  The Prime Minister's secretariat, 1916-1920 *(Newport, Mon: Johns 1951), 199p.*
DAVRAY, H D
  Through French eyes: Britain's effort *(London: Constable 1916), 263p.*
DESTREE, J
  Britain in arms *(London: Lane 1917), 292p.*
FAIRLIE, J A
  British war administration *(New York: OUP 1919), 302p.*
FARNOL, J
  Great Britain at war *(Boston, Mass: Little, Brown 1918), 167p.*
FORMBY, C W
  The soul of England; or, A great Empire at the cross roads *(London: Wells, Gardner, Darton 1916), 174p.*
FUSSELL, P
  The great war and modern memory *(London: OUP 1975), 363p.*
GLEASON, A H
  Inside the British Isles *(New York: Century 1917), 434p.*
GRANT, R
  Their spirit: some impressions of the English and French during the summer of 1916 *(Boston, Mass: Houghton Mifflin 1916), 100p.*
GREAT BRITAIN Foreign Office
  Great Britain and the European crisis: correspondence and statements in Parliament *(London: HMSO 1914), 177p.*
  The Great War and how it arose *(London: HMSO 1915), 56p.*
  The outbreak of the war of 1914-18: based mainly on British official documents *(London: HMSO 1919), 146p.*
GREAT BRITAIN National Council for Civil Liberties
  British freedom, 1914-1917 *(London: Headley 1917), 93p.*
GUINN, P S
  British strategy and politics, 1914 to 1918 *(New York: OUP 1965), 359p.*
HALLOWES, F S
  Mothers of men and militarism *(London: Headley 1915), 128p.*
HINSLEY, F H
  British foreign policy under Sir Edward Grey *(London: CUP 1977), 702p.*
HOLLOWAY, W H
  Northamptonshire and the Great War *(Northampton: 1921), 229p.*
HUGUET, V J M
  Britain and the war *(London: Cassell 1928), 243p.*
HURWITZ, S J
  State intervention in Great Britain: a study of economic control and social response, 1914-1919 *(New York: Columbia UP 1949), 321p.*

INGRAM, A F W
Rebuilding the walls *(London: Wells, Gardner 1922), 234p.*
KENNEDY, W A
As Britons see it *(London: Good 1914), 122p.*
KNIGHT, W S M
History of Britain during the Great War: the anarchy before the outbreak *(London: Ridd Masson 1915), 280p.*
LEE, J A
Todmorden and the Great War *(Todmorden: 1922), 233p.*
LE QUEUX, W
Britain's deadly peril *(London: Stanley Paul 1915), 176p.*
LIDDLE, P ed.
British social and military experience in the First World War *(London: Brassey's 1985), 233p.*
LONGBOTTOM, F W
Chester in the Great War *(Chester: 1920), 78p.*
LOWE, C J and DOCKRILL, M L
The mirage of power: British foreign policy, 1900-22 *(London: Routledge & Kegan Paul 1967), 3 vols.*
MACKIE, D M
Forfar and district in the war *(Forfar: 1921), 199p.*
MACVEAGH, E C and BROWN, L D
Yankee in the British zone *(New York: Putnam 1920), 418p.*
MAIR, C
Britain at war 1914-1919 *(London: Murray 1982), 122p.*
MARWICK, A
The deluge: British society and the First World War *(London: Bodley Head 1965), 336p; bib.*
MASTERMAN, C F G
England after the war *(London: Hodder & Stoughton 1922), 215p.*
MIRRORS of Downing Street: some political reflections *(London: Mills & Boon 1920), 216p.*
MOLESWORTH, Sir G L
Democracy and war *(London: Spon 1919), 191p.*
MORRIS, J
The German air raids on Great Britain, 1914-1918 *(London: Sampson Low 1925), 306p.*
MOYNIHAN, M ed
People at war, 1914-1918 *(Newton Abbot, Devon: David & Charles 1973), 224p.*
MULLINS, C F
Shocked and disillusioned: being some observations of an Englishman who came home *(London: Griffith 1919), 68p.*
OSBORNE, J M
The voluntary recruiting movement in Britain 1914-1916 *(New York: Garland 1982), 160p.*
PANKHURST, E S
The Home Front: a mirror to life in England during the war *(London: Hutchinson 1932), 46p.*

PARKER, P
The old lie: the Great War and the public school ethos *(London: Constable 1987), 288p.*

PEEL, *Mrs* C D E
How we lived then, 1914-1918: a sketch of social and domestic life in England during the war *(London: Lane 1929), 235p.*

PEEL, D C S
A year in public life *(London: Constable 1919), 296p.*

PERFECT, C T
Hornchurch during the Great War *(Colchester, Essex: 1920), 340p.*

PLAYNE, C E
Britain holds on, 1917-1918 *(London: Allen & Unwin 1933), 440p.*
Society at war, 1914-1916 *(London: Allen & Unwin 1931), 380p.*

REVENTLOW, E *count*
The vampire of the Continent *(New York: Jackson Press 1916), 225p.*

RICHARDSON, E M E
Remembrance wakes *(London: Heath Cranton 1934), 210p.*

RIMELL, R L
Air war over Great Britain 1914-1918 *(London: Arms & Armour 1987), 64p.*

ROBERTSON, W
Middlesborough's effort in the Great War *(Middlesborough: 1922), 333p.*

ROTHWELL, V H
British war aims and peace diplomacy, 1914-1918 *(Oxford: Clarendon Press 1971), 315p; bib.*

ROWSON, J W
Bridport and the Great War *(London: Werner Laurie 1923), 224p.*

RUDKIN, M S
Inside Dover, 1914-1918: a woman's impression *(London: Stockwell 1933), 216p.*

RURAL Scotland during the war *(Oxford: Milford 1926), 311p.*

RUSSELL, G W E
The spirit of England: papers written in 1914 and 1915 *(London: Smith, Elder 1915), 314p.*

SANDAY, W
The meaning of the war for Germany and Great Britain *(Oxford: Milford 1915), 124p.*

SMITH, ANNIE S
An Englishwoman's home *(New York: Doran 1918), 173p.*

STONE, G F *and* WELLS, C
Bristol and the Great War, 1914-1919 *(Bristol: 1920), 399p.*

STREET, G S
At home in the war *(London: Heinemann 1918), 134p.*

SWART, P C
England in war-time: a three week's visit to England, October 1917 *(Rotterdam: Nieuwe Rotterdamsche Courant 1918), 94p.*

TENNENT, R J
Red herrings of 1918 *(Tunbridge Wells, Kent: Midas 1980), 114p.*

TERRAINE, J
Impacts of war, 1914-1918 *(London: Hutchinson 1970), 227p; bib.*

TONNIES, F
Warlike England, as seen by herself *(New York: Dillingham 1915), 202p.*

TOWNE, C H
Shaking hands with England *(New York: Doran 1919), 119p.*

VEDETTE
Britain and Armageddon: what we are fighting for *(London: Rees 1914), 60p.*

WALBROOK, H M
Hove and the Great War *(Hove, Sussex: 1920), 160p.*

WALSH, C
Mud, songs and blighty: a scrapbook of the First World War *(London: Hutchinson 1975), 176p.*

WARD, *Mrs* H
England's effort *(London: Smith, Elder 1916), 228p.*

Towards the goal: letters on Great Britain's efforts in the war *(London: Murray 1917), 246p.*

WHITE, C M
The Gotha summer: the German daytime raids on England May to August 1917 *(London: Hale 1986), 258p; bib.*

WHY we are at war *(London: OUP 1914), 264p.*

WILE, F W
The assault: Germany before the outbreak, and England in Wartime *(London: Heinemann 1916), 394p.*

Explaining the Britishers: the story of England's mighty effort in liberty's cause, as seen by an American *(London: Heinemann 1919), 126p.*

WILLIS, I C
England's Holy War: how we went into the war - how we got on with the war - how we came out of the war *(New York: Knopf 1928), 398p.*

WILSHER, L
Britain in World War I *(Edinburgh: Holmes-McDougall 1933), 80p; bib.*

WILSON, T
The myriad faces of war: Britain and the Great War 1914-1918 *(Cambridge: Polity 1986), 864p.*

WINTER, J M
The Great War and the British people *(Cambridge, Mass: Harvard 1986), 360p.*

WOLFF, H W
Rural reconstruction *(London: Selwyn & Blount 1921), 363p.*

WOODWARD, *Sir* LI
Great Britain and the war of 1914-1918 *(London: Methuen 1967), 610p.*

WRENCH, *Sir* J E L
Struggle, 1914-1920 *(London: Nicholson & Watson 1935), 504p.*

BRITISH ARMY (general)

ADAMS, J B P
Nothing of importance: eight months at the front with a Welsh battalion *(New York: McBride 1918), 334p.*

ALLINSON, S
The Bantams: the untold story of World War I *(London: Baker 1981), 287p.*

ANDREWS, W L
  Haunting years: the commentaries of a War Territorial *(London: Hutchinson 1930), 288p.*
BARNES, R M
  The British Army of 1914 *(London: Seeley 1968), 296p.*
BARR, J C
  Home service: the recollections of a Commanding Officer serving in Great Britain, 1914-1919 *(Paisley, Scot: Gardner 1920), 365p.*
BECKE, A F
  The order of battle of Divisions *(London: HMSO 1935-1945), 6 vols.*
BECKETT, F W *and* SIMPSON, K *eds.*
  A nation in arms: a social study of the British Army in the First World War *(Manchester: Manchester UP 1985), 276p.*
BENT, J
  From training camp to fighting line *(London: Kelly 1915), 55p.*
BIGWOOD, G
  The Lancashire fighting Territorials *(London: Country Life 1916), 163p.*
BRADLEY, S
  More adventures of an A.D.C. *(London: Lane 1915), 254p.*
BURRAGE, A
  War is war *(London: Gollancz 1930), 288p.*
CATTO, A
  With the Scottish troops in France *(Aberdeen: 1918), 83p.*
CENTURION *pseud*
  Gentlemen at arms *(London: Heinemann 1918), 296p.*
CHARTERIS, J
  At G.H.Q. *(London: Cassell 1931), 363p.*
CRAVATH, P D
  Great Britain's part: observations of an American visitor to the British Army in France at the beginning of the third year of the war *(New York: Appleton 1917), 127p.*
CROZIER, F P
  A brass hat in No Man's Land *(London: Cape 1930), 254p.*
  The men I killed *(London: Joseph 1937), 288p.*
CUMMING, H R
  A brigadier in France, 1917-1918 *(London: Cape 1922), 272p.*
DAVIS, A H
  Extracts from the diary of a Tommy, 1916-1919 *(London: Palmer 1932), 292p.*
DOUIE, C O G
  The weary road: recollections of a subaltern of infantry *(London: Murray 1929), 226p.*
DOYLE, *Sir* A C
  The British campaigns in France and Flanders *(London: Hodder & Stoughton 1916-20, 6 vols.*
DUGDALE, G
  'Langemark' and 'Cambrai': a war narrative, 1914-1918 *(Shrewsbury: Wilding 1932), 132p.*
DUNCAN, J
  With the Church Lads Brigade Battalion in France *(London: Skeffington 1916), 120p.*

EDMONDS, C
A subaltern's war *(London: Davies 1929), 224p.*
EDMONDS, J E
Military operations of the British Army in the Western theatre of war in 1914-1918 *(London: HMSO 1922-1949), 16 vols.*
EMPEY, A G
From the fire step: the experiences of an American soldier in the British Army *(New York: Burt 1917), 256p.*
'Over the top' *(New York: Burt 1917), 315p.*
FAY, *Sir* S
The War Office at war *(London: Hutchinson 1937), 288p.*
FOX, F
The British Army at war *(London: Fisher Unwin 1917), 143p.*
'GSO' *pseud*
G.H.Q. (Montreuil-sur-Mer) *(London: Philip Allan 1920), 306p.*
GAULD, H D
'Scotland yet!' *(London: Hutchinson 1930), 336p.*
GERMAINS, V W
The Kitchener armies: the story of a national achievement *(London: Davies 1930), 306p.*
GILL, D *and* DALLAS, G
The unknown army *(London: Verso 1985), 178p.*
GRAHAM, S
The challenge of the dead *(London: Cassell 1921), 176p.*
GREAT BRITAIN War Office
Battle honours awarded for the Great War *(London: HMSO 1925), 76p.*
GREEN, H
The British Army in the First World War: the Regulars, the Territorials and Kitchener's army, with some of the campaigns into which they fitted *(London: Clowes 1968), 116p.*
GROOM, W H A
Poor bloody infantry: a memoir of the First World War *(London: Kimber 1976), 185p.*
HALL, J N
Kitchener's mob: the adventures of an American in the British Army *(London: Constable 1916), 200p.*
HARBOTTLE, G
Civilian soldier 1914–1919: a period relived *(Newcastle-upon-Tyne: Arthur 1981), 132p.*
HARDY, E J
The British soldier: his courage and humour *(London: Unwin 1915), 248p.*
HARRIS, H
The Irish Regiments in the First World War *(Cork: Mercier Press 1968), 230p.*
HASLAM, A D
Cannon fodder *(London: Hutchinson 1930), 285p.*
HAWKINS, F
From Ypres to Cambrai: the diary of an infantryman, 1914-1919 *(Morley, Yorks: Elmfield 1974), 144p.*
HAY, I *pseud*
Carrying on after the first hundred thousand *(London: Blackwood 1917), 316p.*
The first hundred thousand *(London: Blackwood 1915), 342p.*

HEAD, C O
No great shakes *(London: Hale 1943), 252p.*
HESKETH-PRITCHARD, H
Sniping in France *(London: Hutchinson 1920), 269p.*
HOWELL, R
Phillip Howell: a staff officer in Flanders and Salonika *(London: Allen & Unwin 1942), 251p.*
HURD, P H
The fighting Territorials *(London: Country Life 1915), 2 vols.*
HUTCHISON, G S
Warrior: a record of the part played by the infantryman in the war *(London: Hutchinson 1932), 316p.*
IRON times with the Guards *(London: Murray 1918), 373p.*
JAMES, E A
A record of the battles and engagements of the British Armies in France and Flanders, 1914-1918 *(Aldershot: Gale & Polden 1924), 48p.*
British regiments 1914–1918 *(London: Samson 1978), 140p.*
KEIR, *Sir* J L
A soldier's eye-view of our Armies *(London: Murray 1919), 245p.*
KERR, S P
What the Irish Regiments have done *(London: Fisher Unwin 1916), 201p.*
KIPLING, R
The new army in training *(London: Harrap 1916), 66p.*
LATHAM, B
A Territorial soldier's war *(Aldershot: Gale & Polden 1967), 133p.*
LAVERY, F
Irish heroes in the war *(London: Everett 1917), 335p.*
LEGARD, *Sir* J D
The North Riding of Yorkshire Volunteers, 1914-1919 *(York: Yorkshire Herald 1919), 95p.*
LEVEY, J H
Lectures to regimental officers on the western campaigns *(London: Forster, Groom 1915), 87p.*
LOGAN, L
On the King's service: inward glimpses of men at arms *(London: Hodder & Stoughton 1917), 141p.*
McDERMOTT, F
Confessions of an old soldier *(Worthing, Sx: Churchman 1984), 146p.*
MACDONAGH, M
The Irish at the Front *(London: Hodder & Stoughton 1916), 158p.*
The Irish on the Somme: being the second series of 'The Irish at the Front' *(London: Hodder & Stoughton 1917), 197p.*
MACECHERN, D
The sword of the North: Highland memories of the Great War *(Inverness: Carruthers 1923), 671p.*
MATTHEWS, E C
With the Cornwall Territorials on the Western Front *(Cambridge: Spalding 1922), unp.*

MAURICE, *Sir* F

The Maurice case: from the papers of Major-General Sir F. Maurice *(London: Cooper 1972), 245p.*

MUNRO, I S

Youth of yesteryear: campaigns, battles, services and exploits of the Glasgow Territorials in the last Great War *(London: Hodge 1939), 117p.*

MURRAY, J

Call to arms: from Gallipoli to the Western Front *(London: Kimber 1980), 191p.*

NEWBOLT, *Sir* H

Book of the thin red line *(London: Longmans 1915), 320p.*

NOAKES, A

Distant drum: the personal history of a Guardsman in the Great War *(Tunbridge Wells, Kent: Noakes 1952), 241p.*

OFFICERS died in the Great War 1914–1919 *(London: HMSO 1919), 262p.*

OREX *pseud*

Three chevrons *(London: Lane 1919), 240p.*

O'TOOLE, T

The way they have in the Army *(London: Lane 1915), 263p.*

REGIMENTAL nicknames and traditions of the British Army *(Aldershot: Gale & Polden: 1916), 118p.*

RUFFIN, H *and* TUDESQ, A

The square jaw: sketches of the British Armies on the Western Front *(London: Nelson 1918) 103p.*

SEELEY, J E B

My horse Warrior *(London: Hodder & Stoughton 1934), 160p.*

SETON, *Sir* B G *and* GRANT, J

The pipes of war: a record of the achievements of pipers of Scottish and overseas Regiments during the war *(Glasgow: Maclehose 1920), 291p.*

SHEPHARD, E

A sergeant-major's war from Hill 60 to the Somme *(Marlborough, Wilts: Crowood 1987).*

SMITH, Rodney

Your boys *(London: Hodder & Stoughton 1918), 91p.*

SOMMERS, C

Temporary crusaders *(London: Lane 1919) 143p.*

Temporary heroes *(London: Lane 1917), 244p.*

SWINTON, *Sir* E D

Eye-witness: being personal reminiscences of certain phases of the Great War including the genesis of the tank *(London: Hodder & Stoughton 1932), 321p.*

TALBOT, K R B

A subaltern's odyssey: memories of the Great War 1915–1917 *(London: Kimber 1980), unp.*

TALE of a Territorial: experiences at home and abroad during the years, 1914, 1915 and 1916 *(Wellingborough, Northants: 1918), 165p.*

THOMAS, A

A life apart *(London: Gollancz 1968), 160p.*

THURBURN, R G
A record of awards of battle honours for the Great War, 1914–1919 *(London: Army Museums Ogilvy Trust 1978), 146p.*

TURNER, P W
Not for glory *(London: Maxwell 1969), 113p; bib.*

VAUGHAN, E C
Some desperate glory: diary of a young officer 1917 *(London: Cooper 1981), 232p.*

VIVIAN, E C H
With the Scottish Regiments at the Front *(London: Hodder & Stoughton 1914), 182p.*

WALLACE, E
Kitchener's Army and the Territorial Forces: the full story of a great achievement *(London: Newnes 1915), 194p.*

WARR, C L
Echoes of Flanders: stories of the Scottish Regiments in the war *(London: Simpkin, Marshall 1916), 307p.*

WHATES, H R
Midland Regiments in France *(Birmingham: 1917), 58p.*

WILLIAMS, A F B
Raising and training the new armies *(London: Constable 1918), 312p.*

WINTER, D
Death's men: soldiers of the Great War *(London: Lane 1978), 283p; bib.*

WYNDHAM, H
Soldiers on service *(London: Nash 1915), 65p.*

YEO, *pseud*
Soldier men *(London: Lane 1917), 239p.*

(Fourth Army)
MONTGOMERY, *Sir* A A
The story of the Fourth Army in the battle of the hundred days, August 8th to November 11th 1918 *(London: Hodder & Stoughton 1920), 370p.*

(Fifth Army)
BENSTEAD, C R
The Fifth Army fell back *(London: Mellifont Library 1937), 255p.*

GOUGH, *Sir* H de la P
The Fifth Army *(London: Hodder & Stoughton 1931) 355p.*
The March retreat *(London: Cassell 1934), 216p.*

READ, H E
In retreat: experiences in the British Fifth Army, in March 1918 *(London: Woolf 1925), 42p.*

SPARROW, W S
The Fifth Army in March 1918 *(London: Lane 1921), 333p.*

(Divisions)
HAMILTON, E W
The first seven divisions: being a detailed account of the fighting from Mons to Ypres *(London: Hurst & Blackett 1916), 318p.*

HEADLAM, C
  History of the Guards Division in the Great War *(London: Murray 1924), 2 vols.*
STIRLING, J
  The Territorial Divisions, 1914-1918 *(London: Dent 1922), 224p.*
BOLWELL, F A
  With a Reservist in France: a personal account of all the engagements in which the 1st
  Division, 1st Corps took part *(London: Routledge 1917), 156p.*
WYRALL, E
  History of the Second Division, 1914-1918 *(London: Nelson 1921), 2 vols.*
MCNISH, R
  Iron Division: the history of the Third Division *(London: Allen 1978), 190p.*
HUSSEY, A H
  Narrative of the 5th Divisional Artillery 1914–1918 *(Woolwich: R.A.Institute 1919),55p.*
HUSSEY, A H *and* INMAN, D S
  The Fifth Division in the Great War *(London: Nisbet 1921), 278p.*
MARDEN, T O
  A short history of the 6th Division, Aug. 1914-March 1919 *(London: Rees 1920), 120p.*
ATKINSON, C T
  The Seventh Division, 1914-1918 *(London: Murray 1927), 529p.*
CROSSE, E C
  The defeat of Austria: as seen by the 7th Division *(London: Deane 1919), 129p.*
FORBES, H E
  The saga of the Seventh Division *(London: Lane 1920), 74p.*
KENNEDY, E J
  With the immortal Seventh Division *(London: Hodder & Stoughton 1916), 198p.*
BORASTON, J H *and* BAX, C E O
  The Eighth Division in war *(London: Medici Society 1926), 359p.*
EWING, J
  History of the 9th-Scottish-Division, 1914-1919 *(London: Murray 1921), 435p.*
CROFT, W D
  Three years with the 9th Division *(London: Murray 1919), 303p.*
COOPER, B
  The Tenth (Irish) Division in Gallipoli *(London: Jenkins 1918), 296p.*
SCOTT, *Sir* A B *and* BRUMWELL, P M
  History of the 12th (Eastern) Division in the Great War *(London: Nisbet 1923), 272p.*
STEWART, J *and* BUCHAN, J
  The Fifteenth (Scottish) Division, 1914-1919 *(London: Blackwood 1926), 489p.*
ATTERIDGE, A H
  History of the 17th-Northern-Division *(Glasgow: Maclehose 1929), 482p.*
NICHOLS, G H F
  The 18th Division in the Great War *(London: Blackwood 1922), 485p.*
A SHORT history of the 19th (Western) Division 1914–1918 *(London: Murray 1919), 112p.*
WYRALL, E
  History of the 19th Division, 1914-1918 *(London: Arnold 1932), 254p.*
EARLE, E G
  History of the 20th Divisional artillery 1914–1918 *(Woolwich: R A Inst. 1919), unp.*

INGLEFIELD, V E
 History of the Twentieth (Light) Division *(London: Nisbet 1921), 319p.*
SANDILANDS, H R
 The 23rd Division, 1914-1919 *(London: Blackwood 1925), 389p.*
KINCAID-SMITH, M
 The 25th Division in France and Flanders *(London: Harrison 1920), 429p.*
DAVIDSON, G
 The incomparable 29th and the 'River Clyde' *(Aberdeen: Bisset 1920), 238p.*
GILLON, S
 Story of the 29th Division *(London: Nelson 1925), 276p.*
JOHNSON, R M
 29th Divisional artillery war record and honours book 1915–1918 *(Woolwich: R A Inst. 1921), unp.*
MURE, A H
 With the incomparable 29th *(London: Chambers 1919), 206p.*
BRIEF history of the 30th Division from July to November 1918 *(London: War Narratives 1919), 64p.*
WHINYATES, R *ed*
 Artillery and Trench mortar memories 32nd Division *(Eastbourne, Sx: Whinyates, 1932), 684p.*
FILGATE, J V M
 History of the 33rd Division Artillery in the war, 1914-1918 *(London: Vacher 1921), 212p.*
HUTCHISON, G S
 The Thirty-Third Division in France and Flanders, 1915-1919 *(London: Waterloo 1921), 178p.*
SHAKESPEAR, J
 The Thirty-Fourth Division, 1915-1919 *(London: Witherby 1921), 328p.*
DAVSON, H M
 The history of the 35th Division in the Great War *(London: Sifton Praed 1927), unp.*
FALLS, C
 History of the Thirty-Sixth (Ulster) Division *(London: M'Caw Stevenson & Orr 1922), 297p.*
THE GOLDEN Horseshoe: 37th Division, B.E.F. *(London: Cassell 1919), 112p.*
BEAUMAN, A B
 With the 38th in France and Italy: a record of the doings of the 1st Bn South Staffordshire Regiment 1916-1918 *(Lichfield, Staffs: Lomax 1920), 48p.*
MUNBY, J E
 A history of the 38th Division *(London: Rees 1920), 84p.*
WISBKIN, H W
 A short history of the 39th (Deptford) Divisional artillery 1915–1918 *(London: Berryman 1923), 80p.*
WHITTON, F E
 History of the 40th Division *(Aldershot: Gale & Polden 1926), 315p.*
GIBBON, F P
 The 42nd East Lancashire Division, 1914-1918 *(London: Country Life 1920), 246p.*

PRIESTLEY, R E
   Breaking the Hindenburg Line: the story of the 46th Division *(London: Fisher & Unwin 1919), 200p.*
MAUDE, A H
   The 47th London Division, 1914-1918 *(London: Stapleton 1922), 359p.*
WILLIAMSON, B
   'Happy days' in France and Flanders with the 47th and 48th Divisions *(London: Harding & More 1921), 196p.*
BARNETT, G H
   With the 48th Division in Italy *(Edinburgh: Blackwood 1923), 162p.*
HUGHES, F K
   A short history of the 49th West Riding and Midland Infantry Division TA *(Barnet, Middx: Stellar 1957), 48p.*
WYRALL, E
   The history of the Fiftieth Division, 1914-1919 *(London: Lund Humphries 1939), 376p.*
BEWSHER, F W
   History of the 51st (Highland) Division, 1914-1918 *(Edinburgh: Blackwood 1921), 411p.*
FARRELL, F A
   The 51st Division war sketches *(Edinburgh: Jack 1970), 63p.*
ROSS, R B
   The Fifty-First in France *(London: Hodder & Stoughton 1918), 313p.*
THOMPSON, R R
   The Fifty-Second (Lowland) Division, 1914-1918 *(Glasgow: 1923), 610p.*
YOUNG, J
   With the 52nd Division in three continents *(Edinburgh: Blackwood 1920), 112p.*
WARD, C H D
   History of the 53rd (Welsh) Division, 1914-1918 *(Cardiff: Western Mail 1927), 288p.*
COOP, J O
   The story of the 55th Division *(Liverpool: Daily Post 1919), 184p.*
WARD C H D
   The 56th Division-1st London Territorial Division *(London: Murray 1921), 331p.*
BRADBRIDGE, E U *ed*
   Record of the 59th Division, 1915-1918 (North Midland) *(Chesterfield, Derbys: Edmunds 1928), 186p.*
VINCE, C
   England in France: sketches mainly with the 59th Division *(London: Constable 1919), 182p.*
DALBIAC, P H
   History of the 60th Division-2/2nd London Division *(London: Allen & Unwin 1927), 255p.*
WYRALL, E
   The history of the 62nd (West Riding) Division, 1914-1919 *(London: Lane 1924-25), 2 vols.*
WARD, C H D
   The 74th (Yeomanry) Division in Syria and France *(London: Murray 1922), 288p.*

(Brigades)

FOULKES, C H
  'Gas!': the story of the Special Brigade *(Edinburgh: Blackwood 1934), 361p.*

KEATING, J *and* LAVERY, F
  Irish heroes in the war: the story of the Tyneside Irish Brigade *(London: Everett 1917), unp.*

OMMANNEY, C H
  The war history of the 1st Northumbrian Brigade, RFA *(Newcastle-upon-Tyne: Hindson 1927), 350p.*

HALDANE, *Sir* J A L
  A Brigade of the old Army, 1914: 10th Infantry Brigade, Aug.-Nov. 1914 *(London: Arnold 1920), 149p.*

GLEICHEN, A E W *count*
  The doings of the Fifteenth Infantry Brigade, August 1914 to March 1915 *(London: Blackwood 1917), 283p.*

HISTORY of the 15th Infantry Brigade 1914–1919 *(Oxford: OUP 1919), 124p.*

HISTORY of the 50th Infantry Brigade, 1914-1919 *(London: 1919), 175p.*

THE 54th Infantry Brigade 1914–1918: some records of battle and laughter in France *(Aldershot, Hants: Gale & Polden 1919), 207p.*

GRANT, D F
  History of 'A' Battery, 84th Army Brigade, R.F.A., 1914-19 *(London: Marshall 1922), 85p.*

DICKSON, W K
  War record of the 2nd City of Edinburgh Battery, First Lowland Brigade-C Battery 86th Army Brigade, 1914-1918 *(Edinburgh: Blackwood 1923), 114p.*

STANLEY, F C
  The history of the 89th Brigade, 1914-1918 *(Liverpool: Daily Post 1919), 295p.*

JAMIE, J P W
  'The 177th Brigade', 1914-1918 *(Leicester: Thornley 1931), 73p.*

(Regiments)

Argyll and Sutherland Highlanders HAWORTH, C
  March to Armistice, 1918 *(London: Kimber 1968), 172p.*
  MORRISON, A D *ed*
  Summarised war diary of the 7th Battalion Argyll and Sutherland Highlanders *(Alve, Scot: Cunningham nd), 103p.*
  FORRESTER, J *and* WATSON, C *eds*
  Argyll and Sutherland Highlanders, 9th Battalion: Dunbartonshire men at the Front *(Glasgow: Jordanhill 1978), 67p.*

The Black Watch CASSELLS, J
  With the Black Watch, 1914 *(London: Melrose 1919), 248p.*
  WAUGHOPE, A G
  History of the Black Watch–Royal Highlanders, 1914-1918 *(London: Medici Society 1922-1926), 3 vols.*

The Border Regiment WYLLY, H C
  The Border Regiment in the Great War *(Aldershot: Gale & Polden 1924), 272p.*

The Cambridgeshire Regiment RIDDELL, E P A *and* CLAYTON, M C
The Cambridgeshires, 1914-1919 *(Cambridge: Bowes & Bowes 1934), 292p.*
The Cameronians Fifth Battalion, the Cameronians (Scottish Rifles), *1914-1919 (Glasgow: Jackson 1936), 256p.*
LAWSON, J B
A Cameronian officer *(Glasgow: Smith 1921), 263p.*
STORY, H H
History of the Cameronians (Scottish Rifles), 1910-1933 *(Aylesbury, Bucks: Hazell Watson & Viney 1961), 430p.*
WHITE, J
With the Cameronians in France *(Glasgow: White 1917), 122p.*
The Cheshire Regiment CHURTON, W A V
War record of the 1/5th (Earl of Chester's) Battalion, the Cheshire Regiment, 1914-1919 *(Chester: The Cheshire Regiment 1920), 130p.*
CROOKENDEN, A
The history of the Cheshire Regiment in the Great War *(Chester: Crookenden 1939), 358p.*
SIMPSON, F
The Cheshire Regiment: or, 22nd Regiment of Foot: the First Battalion at Mons *(Chester: Simpson 1929), 75p.*
The Coldstream Guards ROSS-OF-BLADENSBURG, *Sir* J F G
The Coldstream Guards, 1914-1918 *(London: OUP 1928), 3 vols.*
The Devonshire Regiment ATKINSON, C T
The Devonshire Regiment, 1914-1918 *(Exeter: Eland 1926), 767p.*
COLWILL, R A
Through hell to victory, from Passchendaele to Mons with the 2nd Devons in 1918 *(Torquay: Colwill 1927), 272p.*
The Dorsetshire Regiment HISTORY of the Dorsetshire Regiment 1914-1919 *(Dorchester: Ling 1933), 3 pts.*
Durham Light Infantry AINSWORTH, R B
The story of the 6th Battalion, Durham Light Infantry, France, April 1915-November 1918 *(London: St. Catherine 1919), 59p.*
LOWE, W D
War history of the 18th (S) Battalion, Durham Light Infantry *(Oxford: Milford 1920), 203p.*
RAIMES, A L
The Fifth Battalion, Durham Light Infantry, 1914-1918 *(Darlington: DLI HQ 1931), 227p.*
East Kent Regiment (The Buffs) MOODY, R S H
Historical records of the Buffs, East Kent Regiment *(London: Medici Society 1923), unp.*
PONSONBY, C
The Buffs, 1914-1919 *(London: Melrose 1920), 205p.*
East Lancashire Regiment HOPKINSON, E C
1st Battalion, the East Lancashire Regiment, August and September, 1914 *(Cambridge: Hopkinson 1926), 73p.*

NICHOLSON, *Sir* C L *and* MACMULLEN, H
History of the East Lancashire Regiment in the Great War, 1914-1918 *(Liverpool: Littlebury 1936), 568p.*
East Surrey Regiment PEARSE, H W *and* SLOMAN, H S
History of the East Surrey Regiment *(London: Medici Society 1924), 2 vols.*
East Yorkshire Regiment HISTORY of the 10th (Service) Battalion the East Yorkshire Regiment (Hull Commercials), 1914-1919 *(Hull: Brown 1937), 204p.*
WHITE, W L
Records of the East Yorkshire Volunteer Force, 1914-1919 *(Hull: Brown 1920), 82p.*
WYRALL, E
The East Yorkshire Regiment in the Great War, 1914-1918 *(London: Harrison 1918), 486p.*
The Essex Regiment BANKS, T M *and* CHELL, R A
With the 10th Essex in France *(London: Gay & Hancock 1924), 334p.*
BURROWS, J W
The Essex Regiment: 1st Battalion *(Southend-on-Sea: Burrows 1931) 293p.*
The Essex Regiment: 2nd Battalion (56th) (Pompadours) *(Southend-on-Sea: Burrows 1937), 232p.*
CRONEY, P
Soldier's luck: memoirs of a soldier in the Great War *(Ilfracombe: Stockwell 1965), 319p.*
GIBBONS, T
With the 1/15th Essex in the East *(Colchester: Benham 1921), 210p.*
The Glasgow Highlanders M' D R
A silver lining: the Glasgow Highlanders in France *(London: Simpkin Marshall 1916), 91p.*
The Gloucestershire Regiment BARNES, A F
The story of the 2/5th Battalion Gloucestershire Regiment, 1914-18 *(Gloucester: Crypt House 1930), 192p.*
GRAZEBROOK, R M
The Gloucestershire Regiment: war narratives, 1914-1915 *(Gloucester: Crypt House 1928), 84p.*
PAGAN, A W
Infantry: an account of the 1st Gloucestershire Regiment during the war, 1914-1918 *(Aldershot: Gale & Polden 1951), 2 vols.*
WOOD, W J
With the 5th Glo'sters at home and overseas from 3rd August 1914 to 21st March 1918 *(Gloucester: Crypt House 1925), 115p.*
WYRALL, E
The Gloucestershire Regiment in the war, 1914-1918: the records of the 1st (28th), 2nd (61st), 3rd (Special Reserve), and 4th, 5th and 6th (First Line T.A.) Battalions *(London: Methuen 1931), 357p.*
The Gordon Highlanders LIFE of a regiment: vol. 4 The Gordon Highlanders in the First World War, 1914-1919 *(Aberdeen: Aberdeen UP 1958), 276p.*
MACKENZIE, D
The Sixth Gordons in France and Flanders, with the 7th and 51st Divisons *(Aberdeen: Rosemount 1921), 241p.*

THOMSON, P D
The Gordon Highlanders: a short record of the services of the Regiment *(Devonport: Swiss 1921), 172p.*
The Green Howards WYLLY, H C
The Green Howards in the Great War *(privately printed 1926), 419p.*
The Grenadier Guards CHANDOS, O L *viscount*
From peace to war: a study in combat 1857-1918 *(London: Bodley Head 1968), 208p.*
CRASTER, J M
Fifteen rounds a minute!: the Grenadiers at war, August to December, 1914 *(London: Macmillan 1976), 186p.*
FRYER, E R M
Reminiscences of a Grenadier *(London: Digby, Long 1921), 241p.*
GRAHAM, S
A Private in the Guards *(London: Macmillan 1919), 356p.*
PONSONBY, *Sir* F
The Grenadier Guards in the Great War, 1914-1918 *(London: Macmillan 1920), 3 vols.*
The Hampshire Regiment ATKINSON, C T
The Royal Hampshire Regiment: vol. 2, 1914-1918 *(Winchester: Regimental HQ 1952), 515p.*
STEVENS, F E
The battle story of the Hampshire Regiment *(Southampton: Hampshire Advertiser 1920), 65p.*
COWLAND, W S
Some account of the 10th and 12th Battalions, the Hampshire Regiment, 1914-1918 *(Winchester: Warren 1930), 78p.*
The Highland Light Infantry FIFTH battalion Highland Light in the war, 1914-1918 *(Glasgow: Maclehose 1921), 250p.*
The Honourable Artillery Company LAMBERT, A
Over-the-top: a 'P.B.I.' in the H.A.C. *(London: Long 1930), 244p.*
WALKER, G G
The Honourable Artillery Company in the Great War, 1914-1919 *(London: Seeley 1930), 592p.*
The Irish Guards KIPLING, R
The Irish Guards in the Great War *(London: Macmillan 1923), 2 vols.*
Irish Regiments HARRIS, H
The Irish Regiments in the First World War *(Dublin: Mercier Press 1968), 230p.*
The King's Own Scottish Borderers BROWN, W S
War record of the 4th Battalion King's Own Scottish Borderers and Lothian and Border Horse *(Galashiels: McQueen 1920), 215p.*
ELLIOT, G F S
War history of the 5th Battalion the King's Own Scottish Borderers *(Dumfries: Dinwiddie 1928), 328p.*
GILLON, S A
The King's Own Scottish Borderers in the Great War *(Berwick-on-Tweed: Regimental HQ 1930), 488p.*

Goss, J
A Border Battalion: the history of the 7/8th Battalion King's Own Scottish Borderers *(Edinburgh: Foulis 1920), 366p.*

The King's Own Yorkshire Light Infantry BOND, R C
The history of the King's Own Yorkshire Light Infantry in the Great War *(London: Percy Lund, Humphries 1930), vol. 3.*

The King's Regiment BURKE-GAFFNEY, J J
The story of the King's Regiment, 1914-1918 *(Formby, Lancs: Regimental HQ 1954), 203p.*

ROBERTS, E H G
The study of the '9th' King's in France *(Liverpool: Northern 1922), 133p.*

WURTZBURG, C E
The history of the 2/6th Battalion, 'The King's Own' (Liverpool Regiment), 1914-1919 *(Aldershot: Gale & Polden 1920), 368p.*

WYRALL, E
The history of the King's Regiment (Liverpool) *(London: Arnold 1928-30), 2 vols.*

The King's Shropshire Light Infantry WOOD, W de B ed
The history of the King's Shropshire Light Infantry in the Great War *(London: Medici Society 1925), 470p.*

The Lancashire Fusiliers LATTER, J C
The history of the Lancashire Fusiliers, 1914-1918 *(Aldershot: Gale & Polden 1949), 2 vols.*

ASHURST, G
My bit: a Lancashire Fusilier at war 1914–18 *(Marlborough, Wilts: Bird 1987), 240p.*

The Leicestershire Regiment KELLY, D V
39 months with the 'Tigers' (the 110th Infantry Brigade), 1915-1918 *(London: Benn 1930), 160p.*

MILNE, J
Footprints of the 1/4th Leicestershire Regiment, August 1914 to November 1918 *(Leicester: Backus 1935), 158p.*

THOMPSON, E J
The Leicestershires beyond Baghdad *(London: Epworth 1919), 156p.*

WYLLY, H C
History of the 1st and 2nd Battalions, the Leicestershire Regiment in the Great War *(Aldershot: Gale & Polden 1928), 215p.*

The Lincolnshire Regiment SIMPSON, C R
The history of the Lincolnshire Regiment, 1914-1918 *(London: Medici Society 1931), 510p.*

The London Regiment ELLIOT, W R
The Second Twentieth: being the history of the 2/20th Battalion London Regiment *(Aldershot: Gale & Polden 1920), 314p.*

MAY, E
Signal Corporal: the story of the 2nd London Irish Rifles (2/18th Battalion London Regiment), 1914-1918 *(London: Johnson 1972), 180p.*

ASHLEY, R S
War diary of Private R S (Jock) Ashley 2472, 7th London Regiment 1914–1918 *(Buckhurst Hill, Essex: Stone 1982), 103p.*

WAR record of the 21st London Regiment, First Surrey Rifles, 1914-1919 *(London: Skinner 1928), 277p.*

The London Scottish Regiment LINDSAY, J H
The London Scottish in the Great War *(London: Regimental HQ 1925), 423p.*

The Loyal North Lancashire Regiment WAR history of the 1st/4th Battalion the Loyal North Lancashire Regiment *(Preston: Toulmin 1921), 205p.*

The Manchester Regiment HURST, G B
With the Manchesters in the East *(London: Longmans 1918), 104p.*

The Manchesters since their formation: with a record of the honours and casualties of the war of 1914-1916 *(London: Picture Advertising 1916), 179p.*

WILSON, S J
The Seventh Manchesters, July 1916 to March 1919 *(Manchester: Manchester UP 1920), 161p.*

The Middlesex Regiment GRAIN, H W W
The 16th (Public Schools) Service Battalion (The Duke of Cambridge's Own) Middlesex Regiment in the Great War, 1914-18 *(London: Lewington, 1935), 105p.*

WARD, J
With the 'Die-Hards' in Siberia *(London: Constable 1920), 313p.*

WYRALL, E
The Die-Hards (Middlesex Regiment) in the Great War *(London: Harrison 1926-1930), 2 vols.*

The Monmouthshire Regiment SOMERSET, W H B
On the Western Front, 1/3rd Battalion Monmouthshire Regiment *(Abergavenny: Sergeaunt 1926), 127p.*

The Northamptonshire Regiment KING, H B
7th (S) Battalion Northamptonshire Regiment, 1914-1919 *(Nottingham: Mark 1919), 123p.*

MOORE, C *comp*
Kitchener's pioneers *(Huntingdon, Northants: Author, 1978), 66p.*

The North Staffordshire Regiment HISTORY of the 1st and 2nd Battalions the North Staffordshire Regiment (The Prince of Wales's), 1914-1923 *(Longton, Staffs: Hughes & Harber 1933), 120p.*

MEAKIN, W
The Fifth North Staffords and the North Midland Territorials (the 46th and 59th Divisions), 1914-1919 *(Longton, Staffs: Hughes and Harber 1920), 175p.*

MISSEN, L R
The history of the 7th Service Battalion Prince of Wales North Staffordshire Regiment, 1914-1919 *(Cambridge: Heffer 1920), 149p.*

The Northumberland Fusiliers BUNBURY, W J
A diary of an officer with the 4th Northumberland Fusiliers, 1915 *(Hexham, North: Catherall 1918), 63p.*

CALLIN, R W
When the lantern of hope burned low: the story of the 1/4th Northumberland Fusiliers (TF) during the German offensives of March, April, May 1918 *(Hexham, North: Catherall 1919), 87p.*

COOKE, C H
Historical records of the 16th Battalion Northumberland Fusiliers, 1914-1918 *(Newcastle-upon-Tyne: Chamber of Commerce 1923), 235p.*
Historical records of the 19th Service Bn. Northumberland Fusiliers *(Newcastle-upon-Tyne: 1920), 306p.*
SHAKESPEAR, J
A record of the 17th and 32nd Service Battalions, Northumberland Fusiliers, N.E.R. Pioneers, 1914-1919 *(Newcastle-upon-Tyne: Northumberland Press 1926), 183p.*
Historical records of the 18th (Service Battalion) Northumberland Fusiliers (Pioneers) *(Newcastle-upon-Tyne: Chamber of Commerce 1920), 211p.*
The Oxfordshire & Buckinghamshire Light Infantry HISTORY of the 43rd and 52nd (Oxfordshire and Bucks) Light Infantry in the Great War, 1914-1919 *(Aldershot: Gale & Polden 1938).*
PICKFORD, P
War record of the 1/4th Battalion Oxfordshire & Buckinghamshire Light Infantry *(Banbury, Oxon: Banbury Guardian 1919), 127p.*
ROSE, G K
The story of the 2/4th Oxfordshire and Buckinghamshire Light Infantry *(Oxford: Blackwell 1920), 241p.*
WHEELER, C *ed*
Memorial record of the Seventh (Service) Battalion the Oxfordshire and Bucks. Light Infantry *(Oxford: Blackwell 1922), 224p.*
WRIGHT, P L
The First Buckinghamshire Battalion, 1914-1919 *(London: Hazell, Viney 1920), 216p.*
The Queen's Own Cameron Highlanders SANDILANDS, J W *and* MACLEOD, N
The history of the 7th Battalion Queen's Own Cameron Highlanders *(Stirling: Mackay 1922), 207p.*
DAVIES, W
The compassionate war *(London: Abbotsbury 1980), 81p.*
The Queen's Own London Regiment LIVERMORE, B
Long 'un: a damn bad soldier *(Batley, Yorks: Hayes 1974), 179p.*
The Queen's Own Royal West Kent Regiment ATKINSON, C T
The Queen's Own Royal West Kent Regiment, 1914-1919 *(London: Simpkin Marshall 1924), 629p.*
HISTORY of the Eighth Battalion the Queen's Own Royal West Kent Regiment, 1914-1919 *(London: Hazell, Viney, 1921), 285p.*
MOLONY, C V
'Invicta' : with the First Battalion the Queen's Own Royal West Kent Regiment in the Great War *(London: Nisbet 1923), 326p.*
The Queen's Westminster Rifles HENRIQUES, J Q
War history of the 1st Battalion, Queen's Westminster Rifles, 1914-1918 *(London: Medici Society 1923), 348p.*
The Rifle Brigade BERKELEY, R
The history of the Rifle Brigade in the war of 1914-1918 *(London: Rifle Bde Club 1927), vol, 1: 1914-1916, 245p.*

ROWLANDS, D H
For the duration: the story of the Thirteenth Battalion the Rifle Brigade *(London: Simpkin Marshall 1932), 158p.*

The Royal Berkshire Regiment CRUTTWELL, C R M
The war service of the 1/4 Royal Berkshire Regiment (T.F.) *(Oxford: Blackwell 1922), 160p.*

The Royal Dublin Fusiliers WYLLY, H C
Neill's 'Blue Caps,': 1st Battalion the Royal Dublin Fusiliers *(Dublin: Maunsell 1925), 259p.*

The Royal Fusiliers GREY, W E
The 2nd City of London Regiment (Royal Fusiliers) in the Great War *(London: Regimental HQ 1929), 463p.*

GRIMWADE, F C
The war history of the 4th Battalion, the London Regiment (Royal Fusiliers), 1914-1919 *(London: Regimental HQ 1922), 544p*

HISCOCK, E
The bells of Hell go ting-a-ling-a-ling *(London: Arlington 1976), 149p.*

HISTORY of the Royal Fusiliers University and Public Schools Brigade *(London: The Times 1917), 128p.*

O'NEILL, H C
The Royal Fusiliers in the Great War *(London: Heinemann 1922), 436p.*

WARD, F W
The 23rd Battalion Royal Fusiliers *(London: Sidgwick & Jackson 1920), 166p.*

WYRALL, E
The 17th-S-Battalion, Royal Fusiliers, 1914-1918 *(London: Methuen 1930), 312p.*

The Royal Guernsey Light Infantry BLICQ, A S
Norman Ten Hundred: a record of the 1st (Service) Battalion Royal Guernsey Light Infantry *(Guernsey,CI: Guernsey Press 1920), 104p.*

The Royal Inniskilling Fusiliers FOX, *Sir* F
The Royal Inniskilling Fusiliers in the Great War *(London: Constable 1928), 318p.*

The Royal Irish Fusiliers BURROWS, A R
The 1st Battalion, the Faufg-a-Ballaghs, Irish Fusiliers in the Great War *(Aldershot: Gale & Polden 1926), 182p.*

The Royal Irish Regiment GEOGHEGAN, S
The campaigns and history of the Royal Irish Regiment *(Edinburgh: Blackwood 1927), unp.*

The Royal Munster Fusiliers JERVIS, H S
The 2nd Munsters in France *(Aldershot: Gale & Polden 1922), 71p.*

RICKARD, *Mrs* L
The story of the Munsters *(London: Hodder & Stoughton 1918), 132p.*

The Royal Scots EWING, J
The Royal Scots, 1914-1919 *(Edinburgh: Oliver & Boyd 1925), 2 vols.*

9th Royal Scots (TF) B Company on active service *(Edinburgh: Turnbull & Spears 1916), 94p.*

The Royal Ulster Rifles FALLS, C
The history of the first seven Battalions, the Royal Irish Rifles (now the Royal Ulster Rifles) in the Great War *(Aldershot: Gale & Polden 1925) unp.*

The Royal Warwickshire Regiment BILL, C A
The 15th Battalion Royal Warwickshire Regiment (2nd Birmingham Battalion) in the Great War *(Birmingham: Cornish 1932), 151p.*
CARRINGTON, C E
The war record of the 1/5th Battalion, the Royal Warwickshire Regiment *(Birmingham: Cornish 1922), 97p.*
CHIDGEY, H T
Black square memories: an account of the 2/8th Battalion The Royal Warwickshire Regiment, 1914-1918 *(Oxford: Blackwell 1924), unp.*
COLLINSON, C S
The 11th Royal Warwicks in France, 1915-16 *(Birmingham, Cornish 1928), 134p.*
FAIRCLOUGH, J E B
The First Birmingham Battalion in the Great War, 1914-1919: being a history of the 14th Service Battalion of the Royal Warwickshire Regiment *(Birmingham: Cornish 1933), 210p.*
HISTORY of the 1/6th Battalion, The Royal Warwickshire Regiment, 1914-1919 *(Birmingham: Cornish 1922), 91p.*
HISTORY of the 2/6th Battalion, The Royal Warwickshire Regiment 1914-19 *(Birmingham: Cornish 1929), 117p.*
KINGSFORD, C L
The story of the Royal Warwickshire Regiment *(London: Newnes 1921), 235p.*
The Royal Welch Fusiliers BURTON, F N
The war diary, 1914-1918 of the 10th-Service-Battalion Royal Welch Fusiliers *(Plymouth: Brendon 1926), 100p.*
DAVIES, E
Taffy went to war *(Knutsford, Chesh: Davies 1976), 87p; bib.*
DUNN, J C
The war the infantry knew 1914–1919: a chronicle of service in France and Belgium *(London: Jane's 1987), 613p.*
ELLIS, C
The 4th-Denbighshire-Battalion Royal Welch Fusiliers in the Great War *(Wrexham, Wales: Woodall 1926), 148p.*
RICHARDS, F
Old soldiers never die *(London: Faber 1933), 324p.*
WAR the infantry knew, 1914-1919; a chronicle of service in France and Belgium with the Second Battalion His Majesty's Twenty-Third Foot, the Royal Welch Fusiliers *(London: King 1938), 613p.*
WARD, C H D
Regimental records of the Royal Welch Fusiliers *(London: Forster Groom 1928-1929), 4 vols.*
The Scots Guards, DUNDAS, H L N
Henry Dundas, Scots Guards: a memoir *(Edinburgh: Blackwood 1921), 253p.*
EWART, W H G
Scots Guard *(London: Rich & Cowan 1934), 304p.*
PETRE, F L *and others*
The Scots Guards in the Great War, 1914-1918 *(London: Murray 1925), 349p.*

The Scottish Rifles FINDLAY, J M
  With the 8th Scottish Rifles, 1914-1919 *(London: Blackie 1926), 240p.*
The Seaforth Highlanders HALDANE, M M
  A history of the Fourth Battalion the Seaforth Highlanders *(London: Witherby 1928), 372p.*
  SUTHERLAND, D
  War diary of the Fifth Seaforth Highlanders, 51st (Highland) Division *(London: Lane 1920), 179p.*
The Sherwood Foresters FRYER, P
  The men from Greenwood: being the war history of the 11th-Service-Battalion Sherwood Foresters *(Nottingham: Cresswell 1921), 170p.*
  GERRING, C
  A record of the early Volunteer Movement, and of the Notts Volunteer Regiment (The Sherwood Foresters), 1914-1919 *(Nottingham: Sisson & Parker 1920), 68p.*
  HALL, W G
  The Green triangle: being the history of the 2/5th Battalion the Sherwood Foresters, 1914-1918 *(London: Garden City Press 1920), 197p.*
  OATES, W C
  The Sherwood Foresters in the Great War, 1914-1918: the 2/8th Battalion *(Nottingham: Bell 1920), 230p.*
  WEETMAN, W C C
  The Sherwood Foresters in the Great War, 1914–1919: 1/8th Battalion *(Nottingham: Foreman 1920), 323p.*
  WYLLY H C
  The 1st and 2nd Battalions, the Sherwood Foresters in the Great War *(Aldershot: Gale & Polden 1926), 224p.*
The Somerset Light Infantry FOLEY, H A
  Scrap book of the 7th Battalion Somerset Light Infantry: being a chronicle of their experiences in the Great War *(Aylesbury: 1933), 156p.*
  MAJENDIE, V H B
  A history of the 1st Battalion the Somerset Light Infantry (Prince Albert's), July 1st 1916 to the end of the war *(Taunton, Som: Goodman 1921), 127p.*
  WYALL, E
  The history of the Somerset Light Infantry, Prince Albert's, 1914-1919 *(London: Methuen 1927), 419p.*
The South Wales Borderers ATKINSON, C T
  The history of the South Wales Borderers, 1914-1918 *(London: Medici Society 1931), 613p.*
The South Staffordshire Regiment ANDERSON A L K
  The unbreakable coil: the 3rd Battalion, South Staffordshire Regiment in the European war *(Wolverhampton: Whitehead 1924), 86p.*
  WAR history of the Sixth Battalion the South Staffordshire Regiment (TF) *(London: Heinemann 1925), 258p.*
The Suffolk Regiment MURPHY, C C R
  The history of the Suffolk Regiment, 1914-1927 *(London: Hutchinson 1928), 431p.*
The Welsh Guards WARD, C H D
  History of the Welsh Guards *(London: Murray 1920), 515p.*

EVANS, M St H *pseud*
Going across: or, With the 9th Welsh in the Butterfly Division *(Newport, Mon: Johns 1952), 228p.*
The Welsh Regiment WARD, C H D
The Welsh Regiment of Foot Guards, 1915-1918 *(London: Murray 1936), 147p.*
The West Riding Regiment BALES, P G
The history of the 1/4th Battalion Duke of Wellington's Regiment, 1914-1918 *(Halifax, Yorks: Mortimer 1920), 324p.*
FISHER, J J
History of the Duke of Wellington's West Riding Regiment during the first three years of the Great War *(Halifax, Yorks: Fisher 1918), 152p.*
MAGNUS, L
The West Riding Territorials in the Great War *(London: Kegan Paul 1920), 324p.*
The West Yorkshire Regiment WYRALL, E
The West Yorkshire Regiment in the war, 1914-1918 *(London: Lane 1924), 2 vols.*
The Wiltshire Regiment BLICK, G
The 1/4th Wiltshire Regiment, 1914-1919 *(Trowbridge: Blick 1933), 142p.*
The Worcestershire Regiment CORBETT, E C
The Worcestershire Regiment: war story of the 1/8th (Territorial) Battalion *(Worcester: 'Herald' 1921), 155p.*
STACKE, H F
The Worcestershire Regiment in the Great War *(Kidderminster: Cheshire 1929), 667p.*
TAYLOR, F A J
The bottom of the barrel *(London: Regency 1978), 174p.*
The York and Lancaster Regiment GRANT, D P
The 1/4th Hallamshire Battalion York and Lancaster Regiment, 1914-1919 *(London: Arden 1926), 164p.*
SPARLING, R A
History of the 12th Service Battalion York and Lancaster Regiment *(Sheffield: Northend 1920), 143p.*

(Corps)
Machine-Gun Corps COPPARD, G
With a machine gun to Cambrai: the tale of a young Tommy in Kitchener's Army, 1914-1918 *(London; HMSO 1969), 135p.*
CRUTCHLEY, C E *ed*
Machine-gunner, 1914-1918 *(Northampton: Crutchley 1973), 175p.*
HISTORY and memoir of the 33rd Battalion Machine-Gun Corps and of the 19th, 98th, 100th and 248th Machine-Gun Companies *(London: Waterhouse 1919), 118p.*
HUTCHISON, G S
Machine-guns: a history of the Machine-Gun Corps *(London: Macmillan 1938), 365p.*
RUSSELL, A
The Machine Gunner *(Kineton, Warwicks: Roundwood 1977), 172p.*
With the Machine-Gun Corps from Grantham to Cologne *(London: Dranes 1923), 218p.*
War diary of First Machine-Gun Squadron *(London: Straker 1922), 67p.*
Royal Army Medical Corps BRERETON, F S
The Great War and the R.A.M.C. *(London: Constable 1919), 300p.*

Doc *pseud*
Letters from somewhere *(London: Heath Cranton 1918), 139p.*
'SERGEANT-MAJOR R.A.M.C.'
With the R.A.M.C. in Egypt *(New York: Funk 1918), 328p.*
VIVIAN, E C H
With the R.A.M.C. at the Front *(London: Hodder & Stoughton 1914), 180p.*

Royal Army Service Corps ABBOTT-BROWN, C
How to do it: the A.S.C. subaltern's and N.C.O.'s vade mecum *(London: Forster Groom 1916), 97p.*
AGATE, J E
The letters of a temporary officer in the Army Service corps *(London: Constable 1917), 288p.*
BADCOCK, G E
History of the Transport Services of the Egyptian Expeditionary Force *(London: Rees 1925), 388p.*
BEATSON, A M
The motor-bus in war: being the impressions of an A.S.C. officer during the two years and a half at the Front *(London: Fisher Unwin 1918), 223p.*
GIBBON, M
Inglorious soldier *(London: Hutchinson 1968), 335p.*
HODY, E H
With the mad 17th to Italy: the 17th Divisional Supply Column and its move from France to Italy in 1917 *(London: Allen & Unwin 1920), 160p.*
MARCOSSON, L F
The business of war: the A.S.C. *(London: Lane 1918), 213p.*
SHELTON, A C
On the road from Mons with an Army Service Corps train *(London: Hurst & Blackett 1916), 172p.*
STEWART, H.A.
From Mons to Loos: being the diary of a supply officer *(London: Blackwood 1916), 306p.*

Royal Army Veterinary Corps BLENKINSOP, *Sir* L J *and* RAINEY, K *eds*
History of the Great War based on official documents: Veterinary Services *(London: HMSO 1925).*

Royal Corps of Signals SCRIVENOR, J B
Brigade signals *(Oxford: Clarendon 1932), 176p.*

Royal Tank Corps BROWNE, D G
The tank in action *(London: Blackwood 1920), 517p.*
THE TANK CORPS honours and awards 1916–1919 *(Birmingham: Midland Medals 1982), 402p.*
CARR, C D'A
From chauffeur to Brigadier *(London: Benn 1930), 323p.*
COOPER, B
Tank battles of World War I *(London, Ian Allan 1974), 95p.*
ELLIS, C W *and* ELLIS, A W
The Tank Corps *(London: Country Life 1919), 288p.*
FOLEY, J
The boilerplate war *(London: Muller 1963), 195p; bib.*

FULLER, J F C
Tanks in the Great War, 1914-1918 *(London: Murray 1920), 331p.*
HAIGH, R
Life in a tank *(London: Hodder & Stoughton 1918), 182p.*
HICKEY, D E
Rolling into action: memories of a Tank Corps Section Commander *(London: Hutchinson 1936), 288p.*
JENKIN, A
A tank driver's experiences; or, Incidents in a soldier's life *(London: Elliot Stock 1922), 190p.*
MACINTOSH, J C
Men and tanks *(London: Lane 1920), 142p.*
WATSON, W H L
A company of tanks *(London: Blackwood 1920), 296p.*
WILSON, G M
Fighting tanks: an account of the Royal Tank Corps in action 1916-1919 *(London: Seeley 1929), 250p.*
The Officer Training Corps ERRINGTON, F H L
The Inns of Court Officer Training Corps during the Great War *(London: Inns of Court HQ 1922), 375p.*
HAIG-BROWN, A R
The O.T.C. and the Great War *(London: Country Life 1915), 258p.*

(Cavalry)
ADDERLEY, H A
The Warwickshire Yeomanry in the Great War *(Warwick: W.H. Smith 1922), 224p.*
AQUILA *pseud*
With the Cavalry in the West *(London: Lane 1922), 246p.*
ARTHUR, *Sir* G *and* SHENNAN, P
The story of the Household Cavalry *(London: Heinemann 1926), vol. 3, 283p.*
BICKERSTETH, J B
History of the 6th Cavalry Brigade, 1914-1919 *(London: Baynard 1920), 124p.*
BOYLE, R C
Record of the West Somerset Yeomanry, 1914-1919 *(London: St. Catherine 1922), 188p.*
C, *pseud*
The Yeomanry Cavalry of Worcestershire, 1914-1922 *(Stourbridge, Worcs: Mark & Moody 1926) 251p.*
CAVALRY Combat *(Harrisburg, Pa: Military Service 1937), 524p.*
CHARRINGTON, H V S
The 12th Royal Lancers in France *(Aldershot: Gale & Polden 1919), 207p.*
COLEMAN, F
With Cavalry in 1915: the British Trooper in the trench line, through the second battle of Ypres *(London: Sampson Low 1916), 318p.*
DARLING, J C
The 20th Hussars in the Great War *(Lyndhurst, Hants: Darling 1923), 131p.*
DURAND, *Sir* H M
The Thirteenth Hussars in the Great War *(London: Blackwood 1921), 392p.*

EDWARDS, H I P

The Sussex Yeomanry and the 16th (Sussex Yeomanry) Battalion, Royal Sussex Regiment, 1914-1919 *(London: Melrose 1921), 398p.*

EVANS, H K D

The 4th (Queen's Own) Hussars in the Great War *(Aldershot: Gale & Polden 1920), 198p.*

FOX, F

History of the Royal Gloucestershire Hussars Yeomanry, 1898-1922 *(London: Philip Allan 1923), 336p.*

GALTREY, S

The horse and the war *(London: Country Life 1918), 131p.*

HARDY, S J

History of the Royal Scots Greys - the Second Dragoons - August 1914-March 1919 *(No imprint: 1928), 216p.*

HATTON, S F

The yarn of a yeoman: an account of the Middlesex Yeomanry during the Great War *(London: Hutchinson 1930), 286p.*

JESSEL, *Sir* H M

The story of Romsey Remount Depot *(London: Abbey 1920), 117p.*

KEITH-FALCONER, A W

The Oxfordshire Hussars in the Great War *(London: Murray 1927), 391p.*

KEMP, P K

The Staffordshire Yeomanry (Q.O.R.R.) in the First and Second World Wars, 1914-1918 and 1939-1945 *(Aldershot: Gale & Polden 1950), 168p.*

OGILVIE, D D

The Fife and Forfar Yeomanry, and 14th Fife and Forfar Yeomanry Battalion R.H., 1914-1919 *(London: Murray 1921), 212p.*

PEASE, H

History of the Northumberland Hussars Yeomanry, 1819-1919 *(London: Constable 1924), 296p.*

PEEL, S C

O.C. Bedfordshire Yeomanry *(London: OUP 1935), 101p.*

PRESTON, R M P

Desert mounted corps: an account of the Cavalry operations in Palestine and Syria, 1917-1918 *(London: Constable 1921), 356p.*

ROWE, Edward

2nd County of London (Westminster Dragoons) Yeomanry: the first twenty years *(London: Clowes 1962), 154p.*

SCOTT, F J

Records of the Seventh Dragoon Guards during the Great War *(Sherborne, Dorset: Bennett 1923), 210p.*

SOUTHERN, L J C

The Bedfordshire Yeomanry in the Great War *(London: OUP 1935), 146p.*

TALLENTS, H

The Sherwood Rangers Yeomanry in the Great War *(London: Allan 1926), 186p.*

THOMPSON, C W

Records of the Dorset Yeomanry, 1914-1919 *(Sherborne, Dorset: Bennett 1921), 164p.*

WHITMORE, F D H
The 10th Royal Hussars and the Essex Yeomanry during the war *(Colchester, Benham 1920), 326p.*
WILLCOX, W T
The 3rd (King's Own) Hussars in the Great War, 1914-1919 *(London: Murray 1925), 387p.*

(Royal Artillery)
ANDERSON, A T
War services of the 62nd West Riding Divisional Artillery *(Cambridge: CUP 1920), 142p.*
ASSHER, B
A nomad under arms: the chronicle of an artilleryman from 1914 to the Armistice *(London: Witherby 1931), 368p.*
BECKE, A F
The Royal Regiment of Artillery at Le Cateau, Wednesday 26th August, 1914 *(Woolwich: R.A. HQ 1919), 87p.*
BEHREND, A F
Nine days: adventures of a Heavy Artillery Brigade, 90th Brigade R.G.A. of the Third Army during the German offensive of March 21-29, 1918 *(Cambridge: Heffer 1921), 115p.*
BERDINNER, H F
With the Heavies in Flanders: a record of the 24th Heavy Battery R.G.A. *(London: Botolph 1922), 143p.*
BIDWELL, S
Gunners at war: a tactical study of the Royal Artillery in the Twentieth Century *(London: Arms & Armour Press 1970), 256p; bib.*
BLACK, J
Around the guns: Sundays in camp *(London: Clarke 1915), 90p.*
BLACKWELL, E *and* AXE, E C
Romford to Beirut: the war record of 'B' Battery, 271st Brigade RFA *(Clacton-on-Sea, Essex: Humphries 1926), 193p.*
BROWNLOW, C A L
The breaking of the storm *(London: Methuen 1918), 232p.*
BUCKLAND, C S B
The 25th Army Brigade R.G.A. on the Western Front in 1918 *(Oxford: Clarendon 1940), 110p.*
BURNE, A H
Some pages from the history of 'Q' Battery, R.H.A., in the Great War *(Woolwich: R.A. Institute 1922), 51p.*
CARR, W
A time to leave the ploughshares: a gunner remembers *(London: Hale 1985), 223p.*
DAVSON, H M
Memoirs of the Great War *(Aldershot: Gale & Polden 1964), 172p.*
The story of 'G' Troop, Royal Horse Artillery *(Woolwich: R.A. HQ 1914), 106p.*
DEPEW, A N
Gunner Depew *(London: Cassell 1918), 296p.*

FRASER-TYLTER, N

With Lancashire lads and field guns in France, 1915-1918 *(Manchester: Heywood 1922), 287p.*

GEE, A E *and* SHAW A

A record of D245 Battery, 1914–1919 *(London: Renwick 1931), 182p.*

KINGHAM, W R

London gunners: the story of the H.A.C. Siege Battery in action *(London: Methuen 1919), 279p.*

MARR, J L

The 142nd Heavy Battery R.G.A.: their work in France and Belgium *(Sunderland: Rutter & King 1920), 64p.*

MUNDY, P C D

History of the 1/1st Hants Royal Horse Artillery during the Great War *(Southampton: Hampshire Advertiser 1922), 81p.*

OSWALD, O C W

How some wheels went round: the 61st Heavy Artillery Group in the Great War *(London: Dranes 1929), 218p.*

THE ROYAL Artillery war commemoration book *(London: Bell 1920), 432p.*

SIEPMAN, H

Echo of the guns: recollections of an artillery officer *(London: Hale 1987), vol. I.*

SMITH, J

The City of Aberdeen Royal Field Artillery, 157th Brigade *(Aberdeen: 1917), 123p.*

THORBURN, A D

Amateur gunners: the adventures of an ordinary soldier in France, Salonika and Palestine in the Royal Field Artillery *(Liverpool: Porter 1934), 199p.*

'TWO ELEVEN': being the history of 211 Siege Battery R.G.A. on the Western Front *(Portsmouth: Royal Garrison Artillery 1925), 86p.*

WADSWORTH, W W

War diary of the 1st West Lancashire Brigade R.F.A. *(Liverpool: Daily Post 1923), 159p.*

WEBBER, J J

178 Siege Battery R.G.A. France 1916-1918 *(Leeds: Chorley 1919), 127p.*

WEBER, W H F

A Field Artillery Group in battle: a tactical study based on the action of 2nd Brigade, R.F.A., during the German offensive 1918, the 100 days' battle, and the battle of Cambrai *(Woolwich: R.A. HQ 1923), 164p.*

(Royal Engineers)

BRAGG, *Sir* W L

Artillery survey in the First World War *(Elstree, Herts: Field Survey Association 1971), 43p*

COLLECTIONS and recollections of 107th Field Company Royal Engineers *(Darlington: Dresser 1918), 144p.*

DOPSON, F W

The 48th Divisional Signal Company in the Great War *(Bristol: Arrowsmith 1938), 143p.*

EBERLE, V F

My sapper venture *(London: Pitman 1973), 208p.*

Fox, M S
'Corporals all': with the Special Brigade Royal Engineers, 1915-1919 *(West Worthing, Sx: Harman 1967), 145p.*

FURTHER recollections of 107th Field Company Royal Engineers *(Darlington: Dresser 1920), 227p.*

GRIEVE, W G *and* NEWMAN, B
Tunnellers: the story of the Tunnelling Companies, Royal Engineers, during the World War *(London: Jenkins 1936), 334p.*

HISTORY of the 520th (Field) Company Royal Engineers (T.F.), 1914-1918 *(London: War Narratives 1919), 89p.*

INNES, J R
Flash spotters and sound rangers: how they lived, worked and fought in the Great War *(London: Allen & Unwin 1935), 308p.*

LAWRENCE, D
Sapper Dorothy Lawrence, the only English woman soldier, late Royal Engineers *(London: Lane 1919), 190p.*

LAYTHAM, J H
Chronicles of the 20th Light Railway Train Crews Company, Royal Engineers, 1917-1919 *(Bath: Coward & Gradwell 1919), 52p.*

PRIESTLEY, R E
The Signal Service in the European War of 1914 to 1918 *(Chatham, Kent: R.E., HQ 1921), 359p.*

65 R.E.: a short record of the service of the 65th Field Company, Royal Engineers *(Cambridge: Heffer 1920), 156p.*

SYNTON, E
Tunnellers all *(London: Grant Richards 1918), 255p.*

WORK of the Royal Engineers in the European War, 1914-19 *(Chatham, Kent: R.E., HQ 1921) unp.*

BRITISH EMPIRE

BROUGHTON, U H
The British Empire at war *(Edinburgh: Morrison & Gibb 1916), 50p.*

BUCHAN, J
Days to remember: the British Empire in the Great War *(London: Nelson 1923), 200p.*

DAVENPORT, B
What the British Empire is doing in the war *(London: Fisher Unwin 1916), 54p.*

DUCHESNE, A E
Democracy and the Empire *(London: OUP 1916), 126p.*

THE EMPIRE and the future *(London: Macmillan 1916), 128p.*

GREAT BRITAIN War Office
Statistics of the military effort of the British Empire during the Great War 1914-1920 *(London: HMSO 1922), 880p.*

HURD, P *and* HURD, A
New Empire partnership: defence, commerce, policy *(London: Murray 1915), 400p.*

KEITH, A B
   War government of the British Dominions *(Oxford: Clarendon 1921), 353p.*
LUCAS, *Sir C ed*
   The Empire at war *(London: OUP 1921-26), 6 vols.*
LUKE, C H
   The war and the parting of the ways: the future of the British Empire in relation to the Great War *(London: Sampson Low 1915), 115p.*
POLLARD, A F
   The Commonwealth at war *(London: Longmans 1917), 256p.*
RUTHERFORD, V H
   Commonwealth or Empire *(London: Headley 1917), 135p.*
WEBSTER, R G
   The awakening of an Empire *(London: Murray 1917), 648p.*

BRITISH EXPEDITIONARY FORCE

THE B.E.F. Times: a facsimile reprint of the trench magazine *(London: Jenkins 1918), unp.*
CAFFREY, K
   Farewell Leicester Square: the Old Contemptibles *(London: Deutsch 1980), 288p; bib.*
CAREW, T
   The vanished army *(London: Kimber 1964), 239p; bib.*
CASUALTY *pseud*
   Contemptible *(London: Heinemann 1916), 232p.*
GAUNT, F
   The immortal first: a private soldier's diary of his experiences with the original B.E.F., France *(London: Macdonald 1917), 56p.*
MOORE, W
   Notes on the operations of the B.E.F., August 22nd to September 9th, 1914 *(Hythe, Chesh: 1925), 62p.*
NEWTON, W D
   Undying story: the work of the British Expeditionary Force on the Continent, from Mons, Aug. 23, 1914 to Ypres, Nov. 15, 1914 *(London: Jarrold 1915), 384p.*
SIMPSON, K
   The Old Contemptibles *(London: Allen & Unwin 1981), 143p.*
VIVIAN, A P G
   The Phantom Brigade; or, The contemptible adventurers *(London: Benn 1930), 256p.*

CALAIS

MONTAGUE, C E
   Notes from Calais base *(London: Fisher Unwin 1918), 38p.*

CAMBRAI

COOPER, B
The ironclads of Cambrai *(London: Souvenir 1967)*, *243p.*
COPPARD, G
With a machine gun to Cambrai *(London: HMSO 1969)*, *174p.*
DE PREE, H D
The battle of Cambrai, November 20th to 30th, 1917 *(Woolwich: R.A. HQ 1928)*, *50p.*
EVEREST, J H
The first battle of the tanks: Cambrai, November 20th, 1917 *(Ilfracombe, Devon: Stockwell 1942)*, *96p.*
GIBBS, P
Open warfare: from Cambrai to the Marne *(London: Heinemann 1918)*, *552p.*
MILES, W
Military operations France and Belgium, 1917: the battle of Cambrai *(London: HMSO 1949)*, *399p.*
WOOLLCOMBE, R
The first tank battle: Cambrai 1917 *(London: Barker 1967)*, *232p; bib.*
[See also ROYAL TANK CORPS, TANKS]

CAMOUFLAGE

ROBERTSON, B
Bombing colours: British bomber camouflage and markings, 1914-1937 *(London: Stephens 1972)*, *176p.*
SOLOMON, S J
Strategic camouflage *(London: Murray 1920)*, *62p.*
THETFORD, O G
Camouflage '14-'18 aircraft *(Leicester: Harborough 1943)*, *77p.*

CANADA (general)

ARMSTRONG, E H
The crisis of Quebec, 1914-1918 *(New York: Columbia UP 1937)*, *270p.*
BELL, R W
Canada in war paint *(London: Dent 1917)*, *208p.*
BORDEN, *Sir* R L
The war and the future *(London: Hodder & Stoughton 1917)*, *164p.*
BRUCE, H A
Politics and the Canadian Army Medical Corps *(Toronto: Briggs 1919)*, *321p.*
CANADA Department of Secretary of State
Copies of Proclamation Orders in Council and documents relating to the European War *(Ottawa: 1915)*, *350p.*
CANADIAN Jews in World War I *(Montreal: Jewish Congress 1947–8)*, *2 vols.*

DUNCAN-CLARKE, S J *and* PLEWMAN, W R
  Pictorial history of the Great War: Canada in the Great War *(Toronto: Hertel 1919), 320p.*
FALCONER, R A
  The German tragedy and its meaning for Canada *(Toronto: Univ. of Toronto Press 1915)*,
  90p.
GARDAM, J
  Seventy years after, 1914–1984 *(Stittsville, Ont: Canada Wings 1983), 99p.*
GLAZEBROOK, G P
  Canada at the Paris Peace Conference *(Toronto: OUP 1942), 156p.*
GROVES, H
  Toronto does her 'Bit' *(Toronto: 1918), 72p.*
HAYDON, W
  Canada and the war *(Bristol: Arrowsmith 1915), 90p.*
HOPKINS, J C
  Canada at war, 1914-1918 *(New York: Doran 1919), 448p.*
HUNT, M S
  Nova Scotia's part in the Great War *(Halifax, NS: 1920), 432p.*
KERR, W B
  Historical literature on Canada's participation in the Great War *(Toronto: 1933-34), 2 pts.*
McCLUNG, N L
  Next of kin: those who wait and wonder *(Boston: Houghton Mifflin 1917), 257p.*
MENZIES, J H
  Canada and the war *(Toronto: 1916), 117p.*
MERRITT, W H
  Canada and National Service *(Toronto: 1917), 247p.*
NASMITH, G G
  Canada's sons and Great Britain in the World War *(Toronto: Winston 1919), 607p.*
RICHARDSON, G *and others*
  The Great War and Canadian society *(Toronto: Toronto UP 1978), 2 vols.*
SCOTT, F G
  The Great War as I saw it *(Toronto: Goodchild 1922), 327p.*
THOMPSON, J H
  The harvest of war: the prairie west 1914–1918 *(New York: Mclelland & Stewart 1978)*,
  207p.

CANADIAN AIR FORCE

COSGROVE, E C
  Canada's fighting pilots *(Toronto: Clarke, Irwin 1965), 190p.*
DREW, G A
  Canada's fighting airmen *(Toronto: Ryerson 1931), 305p.*
MACLENNAN, R W
  The ideals and training of a flying officer *(Kingston, Ontario: 1918), 60p.*
SULLIVAN, A
  Aviation in Canada, 1917-1918: the work of the R.A.F., Canada *(Toronto: 1920), 318p.*

CANADIAN ARMY

AITKEN, W M
Canada in Flanders: the official story of the Canadian Expeditionary Force *(London: Hodder & Stoughton 1916-17), 2 vols.*
BENNETT, S G
The 4th Canadian Mounted Rifles, 1914-1919 *(Toronto: 1926), 336p.*
BLACK, E G
I want one volunteer *(Toronto: Ryerson 1965), 183p.*
CADENHEAD, J F
The Canadian Scottish *(Aberdeen: Rosemount Press 1915), unp.*
CAMERON, K
History of No. 1 General Hospital Canadian Expeditionary Force, 1914-1919 *(Ottawa: 1938), 667p.*
CANADA Field Comforts Commission
With the first Canadian contingent *(Toronto 1915), 119p.*
CANADA in khaki: a tribute to the officers and men now serving in the Canadian Expeditionary Force *(London: Pictorial 1917), 172p.*
CARREL, F
Impressions of war *(Quebec: 1919), 248p.*
CORRIGALL, D J
History of the Twentieth Canadian Battalion (Central Ontario Regiment) Canadian Expeditionary Force in the Great War, 1914-1918 *(Toronto: Rogers 1936), 323p.*
CRAMM, R
The first five hundred: being a historical sketch of the military operations of the Royal Newfoundland Regiment in Gallipoli and on the Western Front during the Great War, 1914-1918 *(New York: Williams 1921), 315p.*
CURRIE, J A
'The Red Watch': with the First Canadian Division in Flanders *(Toronto: 1916), 294p.*
CURRY, F C
From the St Lawrence to the Yser: with the 1st Canadian Brigade *(London: Smith, Elder 1916), 166p.*
DAFOE, J W
Over the Canadian battlefields: notes of a journey in March 1919 *(Toronto: 1919), 89p.*
DINESEN, T
Merry hell!: a Dane with the Canadians *(London: Jarrolds 1930), 254p.*
DUGUID, A F
Official history of the Canadian Forces in the Great War, 1914-1919 *(Ottawa: Dept. of National Defence 1938), 1 vol.*
FETHERSTONHAUGH, R C
No. 3 Canadian General Hospital (McGill), 1914-1919 *(Montreal: Gazette 1928), 274p.*
24th Battalion Canadian Expeditionary Force Victoria Rifles of Canada, 1914-1919 *(Montreal: Gazette 1930), 318p.*
FROST, L M
Fighting men *(Toronto: Clarke, Irwin 1967), 267p.*
GOODSPEED, D J
The road past Vimy: the Canadian Corps, 1914-1918 *(Toronto: Macmillan 1969), 185p.*

GOULD, L M
  From British Columbia to Baiseux: being the narrative history of the 102nd Canadian Infantry Brigade *(Victoria, BC: 1919), 134p.*
GRANT, R
  S.O.S. Stand to!: three years' experience with the First Canadian Division in the European War *(New York: Appleton 1918), 296p.*
GRAVES, H S
  Lost diary: being an eye-witness account of the service of the First Canadian Corps (1914-1917) and pioneer fighter plane service (1917-1918) *(Victoria BC: Graves 1941), 131p.*
HAHN, J E
  The Intelligence Service within the Canadian Corps, 1914-1918 *(Toronto: 1930), 263p.*
HAYNES, H
  Midst shot and shell in Flanders *(London: Collins 1916), 223p.*
HAYES, J
  The Eighty-Fifth in France and Flanders *(Halifax NS: 1920), 362p.*
HODDER-WILLIAMS, R
  Princess Patricia's Canadian Light Infantry, 1914-1919 *(London: Hodder & Stoughton 1923), 2 vols.*
KERR, W B
  Arms and the maple leaf: memories of Canada's Corps, 1918 *(Seaforth, Ottawa: McLean 1943), 90p.*
  Shrieks and crashes: being memories of Canada's Corps, 1917 *(Toronto: 1929), 218p.*
LIST of officers and men serving in the First Canadian contingent of the British Expeditionary Force, 1914 *(London: BEF 1915), 353p.*
LIVESAY, J F B
  Canada's hundred days: from Amiens to Mons, 1918 *(Toronto: Allen 1919), 421p.*
LYNCH, J W
  Princess Patricia's Canadian Light Infantry, 1917-1919 *(Hicksville, NY: Exposition 1976), 208p.*
MCBRIDE, H W
  Rifleman went to war *(Marines, NC: Small Arms 1935), 398p.*
MACINTYRE, D E
  Canada at Vimy *(Toronto: Peter Martin 1967), 229p.*
MCKENZIE, F A
  Canada's day of glory *(Toronto: Ryerson 1918), 342p.*
  Through the Hindenburg Line: crowning days on the Western Front: the Canadian Expeditionary Force in 1917 and 1918 *(London: Hodder & Stoughton 1918), 429p.*
MACKENZIE, J J
  Number 4 Canadian Hospital *(Toronto: Macmillan 1933), 247p.*
MACPHAIL, *Sir* A
  Official history of the Canadian Forces in the Great War: the Medical Services *(Ottawa: King's Printers 1923), unp.*
MILLAR, W C
  From Thunder Bay through Ypres with the fighting 52nd (Canada) *(Fort William, Ont: 1918), 101p.*
NASMITH, G G
  On the fringe of the great fight *(Toronto: McClelland 1917), 263p.*

NICHOLSON, G W L
Official history of the Canadian Army in the First World War: Canadian Expeditionary Force 1914–1919 *(Ottawa: Queen's Printer 1962), 621p.*

NOMINAL rolls of officers, non-commissioned officers and men *(Ottawa: Govt. PO 1914–1918), 2 vols.*

NOYES, F W
Stretcher bearers - at the double!: history of the fifth Canadian Field Ambulance *(Toronto: 1936), 315p.*

OFFICIAL list of casualties to members of the Canadian Expeditionary Force *(Ottawa: Govt. PO 1914–1919), 5 vols.*

PLUMMER, M ed
With the first Canadian contingent *(London: Hodder & Stoughton 1915), 120p.*

RAE, H
Maple leaves in Flanders fields *(London: Smith, Elder 1916), 268p.*

ROBERTS, C G D
Canada in Flanders: official story of the Canadian Expeditionary Force *(London: Hodder & Stoughton 1918), 3 vols.*

ROSEN, A *and* MARTIN, P
Canadian Expeditionary Force military cap badges of World War I *(Toronto: Alternative Graphics 1985), 124p.*

RUSSENHOLT, E S
Six thousand Canadian men: being the history of the 44th Battalion Canadian Infantry, 1914-1919 *(Winnipeg: 1932), 364p.*

SCUDAMORE, T V
A short history of the 7th Battalion Canadian Expeditionary Force *(Montreal: 1931), unp.*
2nd Canadian Heavy Battery in the World War, 1914-1919 *(Montreal, 1932), 117p.*

SHELDON-WILLIAMS, R F L
Canadian Front in France and Flanders *(New York: Macmillan 1921), 208p.*

SNELL, A E
The C.A.M.C.: with the Canadian Corps during the last hundred days *(Toronto: 1924), 292p.*

STEELE, H
The Canadians in France, 1915-18 *(London: Fisher Unwin 1920), 364p.*

STORY of the Sixty-Sixth Canadian Field Artillery *(Edinburgh: 1919), 148p.*

SUNNY Subaltern: Billy's letters from Flanders *(Toronto: 1916), 175p.*

SWETTENHAM, J A
To seize the victory: the Canadian Corps in the World War *(Toronto: Ryerson 1965), 265p.*

THIRTY Canadian V.C.'s *(London: Skeffington 1918), unp.*

TOPP, C B
The 42nd Battalion, Canadian Expeditionary Force Royal Highlanders of Canada in the Great War *(1931), 412p.*

TUCKER, A B
The battle glory of Canada *(London: Cassell 1915), 168p.*

UNKNOWN soldiers, by one of them *(New York: Vantage 1959), 170p.*

URQUART, H M
   History of the 16th Battalion - The Canadian Scottish – Canadian Expeditionary Force in the Great War *(New York: Macmillan 1933), 853p.*
WHITTON, F E
   The history of the Prince of Wales's Leinster Regiment, Royal Canadians *(Aldershot: Gale & Polden 1926), 2 vols.*
WILLIAMS, R F L
   The Canadian Front in France and Flanders *(London: Black 1920), 208p.*
WILLSON, B
   From Quebec to Piccadilly and other places: some Anglo-Canadian memories *(London: Cape 1929), 366p.*
   In the Ypres Salient: the story of a fortnight's Canadian fighting, June 2-16, 1916 *(London: Simpkin Marshall 1916), 79p.*

CANTEENS

BALDWIN, M
   Canteening overseas *(New York: Macmillan 1920), 200p.*
CULLING, E V H
   Arms and the woman: a canteen worker with the French *(London: Murray 1932), 227p.*
DIXON, A M
   Canteeners *(New York: Dutton 1918), 175p.*
UNCENSORED letters of a canteen girl *(New York: Holt 1920), 265p.*
VREDENBURG, E
   West and East with the Expeditionary Force canteens *(London: Tuck 1919), 96p.*

CAPORETTO

FALLS, C
   Caporetto, 1917 *(London: Weidenfeld & Nicolson 1966), 200p; bib.*
SETH, R
   Caporetto: the scapegoat battle *(London: Macdonald 1965), 208p; bib.*

CARMANIA

SIMPSON, C
   The ship that hunted itself *(London: Weidenfeld & Nicolson 1977), 207p.*
   [See also GERMAN SURFACE RAIDERS]

CARTOONS

BAIRNSFATHER, B
   Bullets and billets *(London: Grant Richards 1917), 201p.*
   From mud to mufti *(London: Grant Richards 1919), 313p.*

CROSBY, P L
   That rookie from the 13th Squad *(New York: Harper 1918), 54p.*
DAY, K H
   Camion cartoons *(Boston, Mass: Jones, Marshall 1919), 119p.*
DYSON, W
   Australia at war: winter on the Somme and at Ypres, 1916 and 1917 *(London: Palmer &*
   Hayward 1918), 52p.
   Kultur cartoons *(London: Stanley Paul 1915), unp.*
   War cartoons *(London: Hodder & Stoughton 1916), unp.*
HADJICH, T D
   The world's war cartoons *(London: Palmer & Hayward 1916), 48p.*
HECHT, G J *comp*
   The war in cartoons *(New York: Dutton 1919), 207p.*
LEETE, A
   The Bosch book *(London: Duckworth 1916), 48p.*
MR PUNCH's history of the Great War *(New York: Stokes 1919), 304p.*
POY *pseud*
   Poy's war cartoons *(London: Simpkins, Marshall 1915), 64p.*
RAEMAEKERS, L
   America in the war *(New York: Century 1918), 207p.*
   'Land and Water' edition of Raemaeker's cartoons *(London: Land &Water 1916-17), 2*
   vols.
   Raemaeker's cartoons *(London: Hodder & Stoughton 1916), 40p.*
ROBINSON, B
   Cartoons on the war *(London: Dent 1915), 73p.*
ROBINSON, W H
   Hunlikely! *(London: Duckworth 1916), 53p.*
   The saintly Hun *(London: Duckworth 1916), 48p.*
   Some 'frightful' war pictures *(London: Duckworth 1915), unp.*
SACRE *pseud*
   Sidelights: an official series of caricature portraits: military *(London: Constable 1918),*
   1st series.
SULLIVAN, E J
   The Kaiser's garland *(London: Heinemann 1915), 96p.*
THOMAS, B *and* WILLIAMS, W
   One hundred war cartoons *(London: London Opinion 1919), 208p.*

CASEMENT

INGLIS, B
   Roger Casement *(London: Hodder & Stoughton 1973), 448p; bib.*
KNOTT, G H *ed*
   The trial of Sir Roger Casement *(London: Hodge 1917), 344p.*
MACCALL, R
   Roger Casement: a new judgment *(London: Hamilton 1956), 328p.*

NOYES, A
The accusing ghost of justice for Casement *(London: Gollancz 1957), 191p.*
PARMITER, G de C
Roger Casement *(London: Barker 1936), 376p.*
REDMOND-HOWARD, L G
Sir Roger Casement *(Dublin: Maunsel 1916), 64p.*
SPINDLER, K
Gun running for Casement: in the Easter Rebellion, 1916 *(London: Collins 1921), 250p.*
[See also EASTER RISING, IRELAND]

CATHOLICISM

BRENNAN, A
Pope Benedict XV and the war *(London: King 1917), 63p.*
CATHOLICS of the British Empire and the war *(London: Burns & Oates 1917), 70p.*
CHAMPNEYS, A C
Tekel: the Papacy and the war *(London: Bell 1919), 55p.*
JOHNSON, H J T
Vatican diplomacy in the war *(Oxford: Clarendon 1933), 46p.*
KENSIT, J A
Rome behind the Great War *(London: Protestant Truth Society 1919), 63p.*
MAGAN, P T
The Vatican and the war *(Nashville, Tenn: Southern 1915), 128p.*
A SIMPLE prayer book for soldiers *(London: Catholic Truth Society 1915), 85p.*
WAR addresses for Catholic pulpit and platform *(New York: Wagner 1918), 313p.*
WATCHMAN *pseud*
Rome and Germany: the plot for the downfall of Britain *(London: Dranes 1916), 386p.*
Rome and the war, and coming events in Britain *(London: McBride 1916), 291p.*

CAUCASUS

KAYALOFF, J
The battle of Sardarabad *(The Hague, Holland: Mouton 1973), 230p.*

CAVELL

BLACKBURN, D
The martyr nurse *(London: Ridd, Masson 1915), 88p.*
CAVELL, E
Nurse Cavell: the story of her life and martyrdom *(London: Pearson 1915), 64p.*
CHARLTON, R *and* LASCOT, F R
Edith Cavell *(London: Hodder & Stoughton, 1915), unp.*
FELSTEAD, S T
Edith Cavell: the crime that shook the world *(London: Newnes 1940), 211p.*

GOT, A
  The case of Miss Cavell, from the unpublished documents of the trial *(London: Hodder & Stoughton 1920), 198p.*
HILL, W
  The martyrdom of Nurse Cavell: the life story of the victim of Germany's most barbarous crime *(London: Hutchinson 1915), 44p.*
HOEHLING, A A
  The whisper of eternity *(New York: Yoseloff 1957), 161p; U.K. title:* Edith Cavell.
JUDSON, H
  Edith Cavell *(New York: Macmillan 1940), 288p.*
LEEDS, H
  Edith Cavell *(London: Jarrold 1915), 92p.*
PROTHEROE, E
  Edith Cavell: nurse and martyr *(London: Epworth 1928), 94p.*
  A noble woman: the life story of Edith Cavell *(London: Kelly 1916), 170p.*
SAROLEA, C
  The murder of Nurse Cavell *(London: Allen 1915), 78p.*

CEMETERIES

HURST, S C
  The silent cities: an illustrated guide to the war cemeteries and memorials to the 'missing' in France and Flanders *(London: Methuen 1929), 407p.*

CENSORSHIP

BELL, E P
  The British censorship *(London: Unwin 1915), unp.*
BROWNRIGG, *Sir* D E R
  Indiscretions of the Naval censor *(London: Cassell 1920), 315p.*
BUSCH, T *pseud*
  Secret service unmasked *(London: Hutchinson 1950), 272p.*
LYTTON, N S
  The Press and the General Staff *(London: Collins 1921), 231p.*
MOCK, J R
  Censorship, 1917 *(Princeton, NJ: Princeton UP 1941), 250p.*

CEYLON

ABHAYASURIYA, S
  Ceylon and the war *(Colombo, Ceylon: 1919), 232p.*

CHAPLAINS

AYSCOUGH, J
French windows: experiences of a chaplain at the Front *(London: Arnold 1917), 302p.*

BEAMAN, A
The squadroon *(London: Lane 1920), 306p.*

BIRMINGHAM, G A
A padre in France *(London: Hodder & Stoughton 1918), 302p.*

BLACKBURNE, H W
This also happened on the Western Front: the padre's story *(London: Hodder & Stoughton 1932), 189p.*

BOULLIER, J A
Jottings by a gunner and chaplain *(London: Kelly 1917), 96p.*

BURY, H
Here and there in the war zone *(London: Mowbray 1916), 338p.*

CAMPBELL, R J
With our troops in France *(London: Chapman & Hall 1916), 95p.*

CAREY, B
Leaves from the diary of a Catholic chaplain in the Great World War *(Pittsburgh, Pa: Murdock Kerr 1919), 151p.*

CARNBEE, G T
War memories and sketches *(Paisley, Scot: Gardner 1916), 182p.*

A CHAPLAIN
Vermelles: notes on the Western Front *(Edinburgh: Scottish Chronicle 1918), 88p.*

CHAPLAINS in council *(London: Arnold 1917), 63p.*

CREIGHTON, O
With the Twenty-Ninth Division in Gallipoli: a chaplain's experiences *(London: Longmans 1916), 191p.*

DAY, H C
An Army chaplain's war memories *(London: Burns & Oates 1917), 182p.*
A Cavalry chaplain *(London: Heath Cranton 1922), 188p.*

DEVAS, D
From a cloister to camp: being reminiscences of a priest in France, 1915-1918 *(London: Sands 1919), 199p.*

DIGBY, E
Tips for padres: a handbook for chaplains *(Aldershot: Gale & Polden 1917), 43p.*

DRURY, W E
Camp follower: a padre's recollections of Nile, Somme and Tigris during the First World War *(Dublin: Exchequer 1968), 352p.*

GAELL, R
Priests in the firing line *(London: Longmans 1916), 243p.*

GEARE, W D
Letters of an Army chaplain *(London: Wells, Gardner 1918), 93p.*

HUMPHREY, F
The experiences of a temporary C.F. *(London: Hunter & Longhurst 1916), 89p.*

IN the Northern mists: a Grand Fleet chaplain's note book *(London: Hodder & Stoughton 1916), 241p.*

JONES, B D
  The diary of a padre at Suvla Bay *(London: Faith 1916), 112p.*
KENNEDY, G A S
  Rough talks by a padre *(London: Hodder & Stoughton 1918), 268p.*
KLEIN, F
  Diary of a French Army chaplain *(London: Melrose 1915), 288p.*
McKERNAM, M
  Padre: Australian chaplain in Gallipoli and France *(London: Allen & Unwin 1987), 206p.*
MOYNIHAN, M *ed.*
  God on our side *(London: Secker & Warburg nd), 230p.*
PERKINS, A M
  Between battles at a base in France *(London: Fisher Unwin 1918), 127p.*
PRENTICE, S
  Padre: a Red Cross chaplain in France *(New York: Dutton 1919), 328p.*
PYM, T W *and* GORDON, G
  Papers from Picardy, by two chaplains *(London: Constable 1917), 227p.*
SMITH, G V
  The Bishop of London's visit to the Front *(London: Longmans 1915), 94p.*
SPURR, F C
  Some chaplains in khaki *(London: Allenson 1915), 158p.*
STEUART, R H J
  March, kind comrade *(London: Sheed & Ward 1931), 261p.*
THOMPSON, G
  War memories and sketches *(Paisley, Scot: Gardner 1916), 182p.*
THORNTON, G
  With the Anzacs in Cairo *(London: Allenson 1917), 159p.*
TIPLADY, T
  The Cross at the Front: a chaplain's experiences *(London: Epworth 1939), 95p.*
  The soul of the soldiers *(London: Methuen 1918), 176p.*
WAKEFIELD, H R *bishop*
  A fortnight at the Front *(London: Longmans 1915), 43p.*
WATKINS, O S
  With French in France and Flanders: being the experiences of a chaplain attached to a field
  ambulance *(London: Kelly 1915), 192p.*
WATT, L M
  In France and Flanders with the fighting men *(London: Hodder & Stoughton 1917), 220p.*
  In the land of war: a padre with the bagpipes *(Edinburgh: Turnbull & Spence 1915), 108p.*
WESTERDALE, T L B
  Messages from Mars: a chaplain's experiences at the Front *(London: Kelly 1917), 89p.*
WINNIFRITH, D P
  The Church in the fighting line: experiences of an Army chaplain *(London: Hodder &
  Stoughton 1915), 199p.*

CHILDREN

LEESON, C
 The child and the war: being notes on juvenile delinquency *(London: King 1917), unp.*
 [*See also EDUCATION, REFUGEES*]

CHINA

HOYT, E P
 The fall of Tsingtao *(London: Barker 1975), 149p.*
JONES, J
 The fall of Tsingtao, with a study of Japan's ambitions in China *(Boston, Mass: Houghton Mifflin 1915), 214p.*
KLEIN, D
 With the Chinks *(New York: Lane 1919), 258p.*
LA FARGUE, T E
 China and the Great War *(Stanford, Cal: Stanford UP 1937), 278p.*
LA MOTTE, E N
 Peking dust *(New York: Century 1919), 240p.*
MYRON, P *pseud*
 Our Chinese chances through Europe's war *(Chicago: Caspar 1915), 220p.*
PLUESCHOW, G
 My escape from Donington Hall, preceded by an account of the siege of Kiao-Chow in 1915 *(London: Lane 1922), 243p.*
SUMMERSKILL, M
 China: on the Western Front: Britain's Chinese work force in the First World War *(London: Author 1982), 236p.*
WHEELER, W R
 China and the Great War *(New York: Macmillan 1919), 263p.*

CHRONOLOGIES

GREAT BRITAIN Committee of Imperial Defence Historical Section
 History of the Great War based on official documents: principal events 1914-1918 *(London: HMSO 1922), 394p.*
GREAT BRITAIN Ministry of Information
 Chronology of the war *(London: Constable 1918-20), 4 vols.*

CHURCHILL

CHURCHILL, W S
 Traveller in wartime *(New York: Macmillan 1918), 172p.*
 The world crisis, 1911-1918 *(London: Butterworth 1923-31), 6 vols.*

GERMAINS, V W
  The tragedy of Winston Churchill *(London: Hurst & Blackett 1931), 288p.*
GILBERT, M
  Winston S. Churchill: vol. 3; 1914-1916 *(London: Heinemann 1971), 988p.*
HIGGINS, T
  Winston Churchill and the Dardanelles *(London: Heinemann 1964), 239p; bib.*
HOUGH, R
  Former naval person: Churchill and the wars at sea *(London: Weidenfeld & Nicolson 1985), 244p.*
THE WORLD crisis by Winston Churchill: a criticism by Lord Sydenham and others *(London: Hutchinson 1927), 192p.*
X, Captain *pseud*
  With Winston Churchill at the Front *(London: Gowans 1924), 111p.*

CLEMENCEAU

BRUUN, G
  Clemenceau *(Cambridge, Mass: Harvard UP 1943), 225p.*
CLEMENCEAU, G E B
  France facing Germany: speeches and articles *(New York: Dutton 1919), 396p.*
  Grandeur and misery of victory *(London: Harrap 1930), 400p.*
DUCRAY, C
  Clemenceau *(London: Hodder & Stoughton 1919), 181p.*
GEFFROY, G
  Clemenceau *(London: Nutt 1919), 217p.*
HYNDMAN, H M
  Georges Clemenceau: the man and his times *(London: Grant Richards 1919), 307p*
LECOMTE, G
  Georges Clemenceau, the tiger of France *(New York: Appleton 1919), 298p.*
MacCABE, J
  Georges Clemenceau, France's grand old man *(London: Watts 1919), 88p.*

COAL

REDMAYNE, *Sir* R A S
  The British coal-mining industry during the war *(Oxford: Clarendon 1923), 348p.*

CONFERENCES [see under name, e.g. VERSAILLES]

CONGRESSIONAL MEDAL OF HONOR

HOPPER, J M
  Medals of honor *(New York: Day 1929), 381p.*

UNITED STATES Department of War
Congressional Medal of Honor, the Distinguished Service Cross and the Distinguished Service Medal issued by the War Department since April 6th, 1917 up to and including Nov. 11, 1919 *(Washington DC: 1920), 1054p.*

CONSCIENTIOUS OBJECTORS

BAKER, G
The soul of a skunk: the autobiography of a conscientious objector *(London: Partridge 1930), 274p.*

BAXTER, A
We will not cease *(London: Gollancz 1939), 286p.*

BELL, J *ed*
We did not fight: 1914-1918 experiences of war resisters *(London: Cobden-Sanderson 1935), 392p.*

CATCHPOOL, T C
On two fronts: letters of a conscientious objector *(London: Allen & Unwin 1940), 160p.*

CHAMBERLAIN, W J
A C.O. in prison *(London: No-Conscription Fellowship 1916), 62p.*

DUCKERS, J S
Handed over: prison experiences of a conscientious objector *(London: Daniel 1917), 159p.*

GRAHAM, J W
Conscription and conscience: a history 1916-1919 *(New York: Kelley 1969), 388p.*

HOBHOUSE, *Mrs* H
I appeal to Caesar: the case of the conscientious objector *(London: Allen & Unwin 1917), 106p.*

HOVELL, H
Rebel prophets and 'Assassins Anglais' *(London: Housman's Bookshop 1975), 65p; bib.*

JAMES, S B
The man who dared *(London: Daniel 1917), 100p.*

KELLOGG, W G
The conscientious objector *(New York: Garland 1972), 141p.*

MASON, E W
Made free in prison *(London: Allen & Unwin 1918), 221p.*

MEYER, E L
'Hey! Yellowbacks!': the war diary of a conscientious objector *(New York: Day 1930), 209p.*

PEAKE, A S
Prisoners of hope: the problem of the conscientious objector *(London: Allen & Unwin 1918), 127p.*

PETERSON, H C *and* FITE, G C
Opponents of war, 1917-1918 *(Madison, Wis: University of Wisconsin P 1957), 412p.*

PETRE, M D
Reflections of a non-combatant *(London: Longmans 1915), 142p.*

PRICE, T
Crucifiers and crucified *(Alvechurch, Worc: Price 1917), 167p.*
RAE, J
Conscience and politics: the British Government and the conscientious objector to military service, 1916-1919 *(London: OUP 1970), 280p; bib.*
UNITED STATES Department of War
Statement concerning the treatment of conscientious objectors in the Army *(Washington DC: 1919), 71p.*

CONSCRIPTION

ADAMS, R J Q *and* POIRIER, P P
The conscription controversy in Great Britain 1900-18 *(London: Macmillan 1987), 286p.*
CASE, C M
Non-violent coercion: a study in methods of social pressure *(London: Allen & Unwin 1923), 423p.*
COULTON, G G
The case for compulsory military service *(London: Macmillan 1918), 388p.*
GRAHAM, J W
Conscription and conscience: a history, 1916-1919 *(London: Allen & Unwin 1922), 388p.*
KENNEDY, T C
The hound of conscience: a history of the No-Conscription Fellowship 1914-1918 *(Fayetterville, Ark: Kansas UP 1981), 322p.*
LAMBERT, R C *ed*
The Parliamentary history of conscription in Great Britain *(London: Allen & Unwin 1917), 367p.*
MOORE, H W
Plowing my own furrow *(New York: Norton 1985), 225p.*

CORONEL

BENNETT, G
Coronel and the Falklands *(London: Batsford 1962), 192p; bib.*
HILDITCH, A N
Coronel and Falkland Islands *(London: OUP 1915), 37p.*
HIRST, L
Coronel and after *(London: Davies 1934), 277p.*
HOUGH, R
The pursuit of Admiral von Spee *(London: Allen & Unwin 1969), 180p.*
IRVING, J
Coronel and the Falklands *(London: Philpot 192/), 247p.*
MIDDLEMAS, K
Command the far seas: a naval campaign of the First World War *(London: Hutchinson 1961), 255p.*

PITT, B
  Coronel and Falkland *(London: Cassell 1960), 184p.*
POCHHAMMER, H
  Before Jutland: Coronel and the battle of the Falklands *(London: Jarrolds 1931), 255p.*

CRUISERS

BROCKLEBANK, H C R
  Tenth Cruiser Squadron northern patrol *(Dorchester: Brocklebank 1974), 57p.*
BUCHAN, W
  The log of HMS *Bristol*: May 13, 1914-Dec 17, 1915 in American waters and the Mediterranean *(London: Westminster 1916), 164p.*
BURT, R A
  British cruisers in World War I *(London:Arms & Armour 1986), 164p.*
BYWATER, H C
  Cruisers in battle: naval 'light cavalry' under fire, 1914-1918 *(London: Constable 1939), 276p.*
YOUNG; A B F
  With the battle cruisers *(London: Cassell 1921), 296p.*
[*See also the* NAVIES OF INDIVIDUAL COUNTRIES]

CZECHOSLOVAKIA

BAERLEIN, H P B
  The march of the seventy thousand *(New York: Arno 1926), 287p.*
CAPEK, T *ed*
  Bohemia under Hapsburg misrule: ideals and aspirations of the Bohemian and Slovak peoples as affected by the European war *(New York: Revell 1915), 188p.*
HOYT, E P
  The army without a country *(New York: Macmillan 1967), 243p.*

DARDANELLES

ASHMEAD BARTLETT, E
  Ashmead Bartlett's despatches from the Dardanelles *(London: Newnes 1916), 164p.*
  The uncensored Dardanelles *(London: Hutchinson 1928), 286p.*
BRIDGES, T C
  On land and sea at the Dardanelles *(London: Collins 1915), 198p.*
BRODIE, C G
  Forlorn hope, 1915: the submarine passage of the Dardanelles *(London: Frederick 1956), 91p.*
CALLWELL, *Sir* C E
  The Dardanelles *(London: Constable 1919), 361p.*

CASSAR, G H
  The French and the Dardanelles: a study of failure in the conduct of war *(London: Allen & Unwin 1971), 276p; bib.*
CHATTERTON, E K
  Dardanelles dilemma: the story of the naval operations *(London: Rich & Cowan 1935), 320p.*
THE DARDANELLES : an epic told in pictures; a hundred photographs, many taken under fire *(London: Alfieri 1916), 110p.*
THE DARDANELLES, their story and their significance in the Great War *(London: Melrose 1915), 168p.*
DARLINGTON, *Sir* H C
  Letters from Helles *(London: Longmans 1936), 153p.*
DELAGE, E
  The tragedy of the Dardanelles *(London: Lane 1932), 268p.*
DE LOGNE, S
  The Straits impregnable *(London: Murray 1917), 301p.*
DENHAM, H M
  Dardanelles: a midshipman's diary 1915-16 *(London: Murray 1981), 200p.*
FORTESCUE, G
  What of the Dardanelles: an analysis *(London: Hodder & Stoughton 1915), 91p.*
GREEN, J
  News from no-man's-land *(London: Allen & Unwin 1918), 144p.*
HAMILTON, *Sir* I S M
  Ian Hamilton's despatches from the Dardanelles *(London: Newnes 1917), 254p.*
  Ian Hamilton's final despatches *(London: Newnes 1916), 128p.*
HERBERT, A P
  The secret battle *(London: Methuen 1919), unp.*
HOGUE, O
  Trooper Bluegum at the Dardanelles *(London: Melrose 1916), 287p.*
HOYT, E P
  Disaster at the Dardanelles *(London: Barker 1976), 166p.*
KEARSEY, A H C
  Notes and comments on the Dardanelles campaign *(Aldershot: Gale & Polden 1934), 147p.*
LAFFIN, J
  Damn the Dardanelles *(London: Osprey 1980), 224p.*
MOSELEY, S A
  The truth about the Dardanelles *(London: Cassell 1916), 267p.*
NEVINSON, H W
  The Dardanelles campaign *(London: Nisbet 1918), 449p.*
PRICE, W H
  With the Fleet in the Dardanelles during the campaign in the Spring of 1915 *(London: Melrose 1916), 124p.*
SHANKLAND, P *and* HUNTER, A
  Dardanelles patrol *(London: Collins 1964), 194p.*
SILAS, E
  Crusading at Anzac, anno domini, 1915 *(London: The British Australasian 1916), unp.*

UNCENSORED letters from the Dardanelles *(London: Soldier's Tales of the Great War 1916),*
293p.
WESTER-WEMYSS, R *baron*
   The Navy in the Dardanelles campaign *(London: Hodder & Stoughton 1924), 288p.*
WILKINSON, N L
   The Dardanelles: colour sketches from Gallipoli *(London: Longmans 1915), 118p.*
[*See also* AUSTRALIAN ARMY, BRITISH ARMY, GALLIPOLI, NEW ZEALAND, ROYAL NAVY, TURKEY]

DENMARK

ERICHSEN, E
   Forced to fight: the tale of a Schleswig Dane *(London: Heinemann 1917), 184p.*
JORGENSEN, J
   False witness *(London: Hodder & Stoughton 1916), 227p.*
   The war pilgrim *(London: Burns & Oates 1917), 120p.*

DEPORTATIONS

CELARIE, H
   Slaves of the Huns: the experiences of two girls of Lille *(London: Cassell 1918), 243p.*
DESTREE, J
   The deportations of Belgian workmen *(London: Fisher Unwin 1917), 44p.*
FRANCE Ministry of Foreign Affairs
   The deportation of women and girls from Lille *(London: Hodder & Stoughton 1916), 81p.*
HEUVEL, J van der
   Slave raids in Belgium: the facts about the deportations *(London: Fisher Unwin 1917),*
   42p.
TOYNBEE, A J
   The Belgian deportations *(London: Fisher Unwin 1916), 72p.*

DESPATCH RIDERS

CORCORAN, A P
   Daredevil of the Army: experiences as a buzzer and despatch rider *(New York: Dutton*
   1918), 206p.
WATSON, W H L
   Adventures of a despatch rider *(Edinburgh: Blackwood 1915), 272p.*

DESTROYERS

BELL, J J
   Little grey ships *(London: Murray 1916), 183p.*

BROOKES, E
  Destroyer *(London: Jarrolds 1962), 212p; bib.*
BURT, R A
  British destroyers in World War I *(London: Arms & Armour 1986), 164p.*
CHAMBERS, H R *jr*
  United States submarine chasers in the Mediteranean, Adriatic, and the attack on Durazzo *(New York: Putnam 1920), 91p.*
CONNOLLY, J B
  U-boat hunters *(New York: Scribner 1918), 263p.*
DAWSON, L
  Flotillas *(London: Rich & Cowan 1933), 271p.*
FREEMAN, L R
  Sea-Hounds *(New York: Dodd 1919), 309p.*
KEMP, P K
  H.M. Destroyers *(London: Jenkins 1956), 237p.*
PAINE, R D
  The fighting fleets: five months of active service with the American destroyers and their allies in the war zone *(London: Constable 1918), 392p.*
TAFFRAIL *pseud*
  Endless story: being an account of the work of the destroyers, flotilla leaders, torpedo boats and patrol boats in the Great War *(London: Hodder & Stoughton 1931), 451p.*
  A little ship *(London: Chambers 1918), 337p.*
THE TENEDOS Times: a monthly journal of the Mediterranean destroyer flotilla in the early part of the war *(London: Allen & Unwin 1917), 144p.*
[See also NAVAL WARFARE (general), ROYAL NAVY, UNITED STATES NAVY]

DICTIONARIES

ATKINSON, C F
  Dictionary of English and French military terms and other words useful to officers *(London: Rees 1916–17), 2 vols.*
  Dictionary of English and German military terms and other words useful to officers *(London: Rees 1915–16), 2 vols.*
DEARLE, N B
  Dictionary of official wartime organisations *(London: Mitford 1928), 322p.*
GREAT BRITAIN War Office
  French-English dictionary of military terms and of other words useful to officers *(London: HMSO 1919), 616p.*
HERWIG, H H *comp*
  Biographical dictionary of World War I *(Westport, Conn: Greenwood 1982), 424p; bib.*
MAUNSELL, M C
  English-French and French-English military and naval technical dictionary *(London: Vickers, 1918), 591p.*
  English-Italian, Italian-English artillery and naval technical terms *(London: Vickers 1918), 227p.*

TWENEY, C F

Dictionary of naval and military terms *(London: Fisher Unwin 1914), 232p.*

VIZETELLY, F H

The soldier's service dictionary of English and French terms *(New York: Funk & Wagnalls 1918), 188p*

DIPLOMATIC HISTORY

ABBOTT, G F

Turkey, Greece and the Great Powers: a study in friendship and hate *(London: Scott 1917), 384p.*

ANDRASSY, J *count*

Diplomacy and the war *(London: Bale 1921), 323p.*

BAILEY, T A

The policy of the United States towards the neutrals, 1917–1918 *(New York: Arno 1979), 520p.*

BARKER, J E

The great problems of British statesmanship *(London: Murray 1917), 456p.*

BULLARD, A

The diplomacy of the Great War *(New York: Macmillan 1916), 344p.*

CALDER, K J

Britain and the origins of the new Europe, 1914-1918 *(Cambridge: CUP 1976), 268p; bib*

CALHOUN, F S

Power and principle: armed intervention in Wilsonian foreign policy *(Kent, Ohio: Kent State UP 1986), 333p.*

CARNEGIE ENDOWMENT FOR INTERNATIONAL PEACE

Diplomatic documents relating to the outbreak of the European war *(New York: 1916), 2 vols.*

DILLON, E J VON

A scrap of paper: the inner history of German diplomacy *(London: Hodder & Stoughton 1914), 220p.*

DIPLOMATIC correspondence between the U.S. and Germany, Aug 1, 1914-April 6, 1917 *(New York: OUP1918), 378p.*

FEST, W

Peace or partition: the Habsburg monarchy and British policy, 1914-1918 *(London: St.Martin's 1978), 276p.*

FINCH, G A

The treaty of peace with Germany in the United States Senate: an exposition and review *(New York: American Association for International Conciliation 1920), 64p.*

FISH, C R

American diplomacy *(New York: Holt 1915), 541p.*

FLOTO, I

Colonel House in Paris: a study of American policy at the Paris Peace Conference 1919 *(Princeton, NJ: Princeton UP 1981), 374p.*

GAJDA, P A
  Postscript to victory: British policy and the German-Polish borderlands *(New York UP of America 1982), 232p.*
GOOCH, G P
  Recent revelations of European diplomacy *(London: Longmans 1928), 218p.*
GOTTLIEB, W W
  Studies in secret diplomacy during the First World War *(London: Allen & Unwin 1957), 431p; bib.*
GRAYSON, B L
  Russian American relations in World War 1 *(New York Ungar 1979), 151p.*
GREAT BRITAIN Foreign Office
  Collected diplomatic documents relating to the outbreak of the European war *(London: HMSO 1915), 561p.*
HANAK, H
  Great Britain and Austria-Hungary during the First World War: a study in the formation of public opinion *(London: OUP 1962), 312p; bib.*
  How diplomats make war *(New York: Huebsch 1915), 376p.*
HUDSON, W J
  Billy Hughes in Paris: the birth of Australian diplomacy *(London: Nelson 1978), 147p.*
KENNAN, G F
  The fateful alliance: France, Russia and the coming of the First World War *(New York Pantheon 1984), 300p.*
KERNEK, S J
  Distractions of peace during war: the Lloyd George Government's reactions to Woodrow Wilson, Dec 1916-Nov 1918 *(Philadelphia: American Philosophical Soc., 1975), 117p.*
LEE, D E
  Europe's crucial years: the diplomatic background of World War I *(Hanover, NH: University P of New England 1974), 482p.*
LINK, A S
  Wilson: the struggle for neutrality, 1914-1915 *(London: OUP nd) vol. 3, 736p; bib.*
MURRAY, A C
  At close quarters: a sidelight on Anglo-American diplomatic relations *(London: Murray 1946), 106p.*
NABOKOV, K
  The ordeal of a diplomat *(London: Duckworth 1921), 320p.*
NEILSON, K
  Strategy and supply: the Ango-Russian alliance 1914-17 *(London: Allen & Unwin 1984), 338p, bib.*
NEKLUDOFF, A
  Diplomatic reminiscences before and during the World War, 1911–17 *(London: Murray 1920), 554p.*
PARSONS, E B
  Wilsonian diplomacy: Allied-American rivalries in war and peace *(St Louis, Mo: Forum 1978), 213p.*
PRICE, M P
  Diplomatic history of the war *(London: Allen & Unwin 1915). 770p.*

RUSSELL, F M
  The Saar: battleground and pawn *(New York: Russell & Russell 1970), 204p.*
SCOTT, J B
  A survey of international relations between the United States and Germany, Aug. 1, 1914 to April 6, 1917 *(London: OUP 1918), 506p.*
SEYMOUR, C
  American diplomacy during the war *(Baltimore:Johns Hopkins 1934), 417p.*
  The diplomatic background of the war 1870-1914 *(New Haven, Conn: Yale UP 1916), 311p.*
STEVENSON, D
  French war aims against Germany, 1914-1919 *(Oxford: OUP 1982), 283p.*
STOWELL, E C
  The diplomacy of the war of 1914 *(Boston, Mass: Houghton Mifflin 1915), 3 vols.*
U.S. Department of State
  Declarations of war: severances of diplomatic relations, 1914-1918 *(Washington DC: 1919), 99p.*
U.S. Special Diplomatic Mission to Russia
  America's message to the Russian people *(Boston, Mass: Jones, Marshall 1918), 154p.*
WALWORTH, A C
  America's moment: 1918: American diplomacy at the end of the war *(New York: Norton 1977), 309p.*
  Wilson and his peacemakers:American diplomacy at the Paris Peace Conference 1919 *(New York Norton 1986), 618p.*
WARTH, R D
  The Allies and the Russian revolution: from the fall of the Monarchy to the peace of Brest-Litovsk (London: CUP 1954), 294p.
WASHINGTON and Berlin, 1916-17: originals of the correspondence exchanged between Count Bernstorff and Berlin with documents on the German peace proposal of 1916 *(New York: Reilly 1920), 128p.*
WEBER, F G
  Eagles on the Crescent: Germany, Austria and the diplomacy of the Turkish alliance *(Ithaca., NY: Cornell UP 1970), 284p; bib.*
WEST, R
  The Department of State on the eve of the First World War *(Athens, Ga: UP of Georgia 1978), 183p.*
WILLERT, *Sir* A
  The road to safety: a study in Anglo-American relations *(New York: Praeger 1953), 184p.*
WOOD, E F
  The notebook of an Attaché: seven months in the war zone *(London: Grant Richards 1915), 358p.*
YATES, L A R
  United States and French security, 1917-1921: a study in American diplomatic history *(New York: Twayne 1957), 252p.*
YOUNG, G
  Nationalism and war in the Near East *(London: OUP 1915), 460p.*

ZEMAN, Z A B
A diplomatic history of the First World War *(London: Weidenfeld & Nicolson 1971)*, *402p. U.S. title:* The gentlemen negotiators.
[See also HISTORY *(general),* INDIVIDUAL COUNTRIES, POLITICS]

DISABLED EX-SERVICEMEN

CLIFFORD, W G
The ex-soldier *(London: Black 1916), 300p.*
GOODCHILD, G *ed*
Blinded soldiers and sailors gift book *(New York: Putnam 1916), 231p.*
HATT, C W
The future of the disabled soldier *(London: Bale 1917), 209p.*
HOWSON, G
Handbook for the limbless *(London: Disabled Soc. 1922), 225p.*
MACMURTRIE, D C
The disabled soldier *(New York: Macmillan 1919), 232p.*
MAWSON, T H
An Imperial obligation: industrial villages for partially disabled soldiers *(London: Grant Richards 1917), 124p.*
RECALLED to life: return to civil life of disabled soldiers and sailors *(London: Bale 1918), 204p.*
SLADE, G H
Two sticks *(London: Mills & Boon 1923), 127p.*
[See also HOSPITALS, MEDICAL, NURSING]

DISARMAMENT

JAFFE, L S
The decision to disarm Germany: British policy towards post-war German disarmament 1914-1919 *(London: Allen & Unwin 1985), 286p.*

DIXMUDE

LE GOFFIC, C
Dixmude: the epic of the French Marines *(London: Heinemann 1916), 164p.*

DOVER PATROL

BACON, *Sir* R H S
The concise story of the Dover Patrol *(London: Hutchinson 1932), 320p.*
The Dover Patrol, 1915-1917 *(London: Hutchinson 1919), 2 vols.*

BENNETT, J J
   The Dover Patrol *(London: Grant Richards 1919), 214p.*
COXON, S W
   Dover during the dark days *(London: Lane 1919), 296p.*
EVANS, E R G R
   Keeping the seas *(London: Sampson Low 1919), 326p.*

DRAMA

McGUINESS, F
   Observe the sons of Ulster marching towards the Somme *(Harlow, Essex: Faber 1986), 80p.*
MAETERLINCK, M
   The Burgomaster of Stilemonde *(New York: Dodd 1918), 148p.*
SHERRIFF, R C
   Journey's end *(London: Gollancz 1929), 128p.*
SHERWOOD, R E
   Waterloo Bridge *(New York: Scribner 1929), unp.*
WILSON, J
   Hamp *(London: Evans 1963), unp.*

DRINK

CARTER, H
   The control of the drink trade in Britain *(London: Longmans 1919), 343p.*
CARVER, T N
   Government control of the liquor business in Great Britain and the United States *(New York: OUP 1919), 192p.*
MURRAY, M
   Drink and the war, from the patriotic point of view *(London: Chapman & Hall 1915), 156p.*

EAST AFRICA

BUCHANAN, A
   Three years of war in East Africa (London: Murray 1919), 247p.
C, F
   On safari: experiences of a gunner in the East African campaign *(Cape Town: 1917), 90p.*
CAMPBELL, W W
   East Africa by motor lorry: recollections of an ex-motor transport driver *(London: Murray 1928), 318p.*
COLLYER, J J
   The South Africans: with General Smuts in German East Africa, 1916 *(Pretoria: 1939), 2 pts.*

CROWE, J H V
  General Smut's campaign in East Africa *(London: Murray 1918), 280p.*
DOLBEY, R V
  Sketches of the East Africa campaign *(London: Murray 1918), 219p.*
FENDALL, C P
  The East African Field Force *(London: Witherby 1921), 238p.*
GARDNER, B
  German East Africa: the story of the First World War in East Africa *(London: Cassell 1963), 213p; bib.*
HODGES, G
  The carrier corps: military labor in the East African campaign 1914-1918 *(Westport, Conn: Greenwood 1986), 244p.*
HORDERN, C
  Military operations in East Africa, Aug. 1914-Sept. 1916 *(London: HMSO 1941), vol 1.*
HOYT, E P
  Guerilla: Colonel von Lettow-Vorbeck and Germany's East African Empire *(New York Macmillan 1981), 216p,bib.*
KOCK, N
  Blockade and Jungle *(London: Hale 1941), 256p.*
LETTOW-VORBECK, P E von
  East African campaigns *(New York: Speller 1957), 303p.*
  My reminiscences of East Africa *(London: Hurst & Blackett 1920), 335p.*
MILLER, C
  Battle for the bundu: the 1st World War in East Africa *(London: Macdonald & Jane's 1974), 353p.*
MOSLEY, L
  Duel for Kilimanjaro; an account of the East African campaign, 1914-1918 *(London: Weidenfeld & Nicolson 1963), 244p; bib.*
REID, F
  Footslogging in East Africa: sketches of the East African campaign *(Cape Town: 1918), 140p.*
REITZ, D
  Trekking on *(London: Faber 1933), 351p.*
SAMPSON, F J
  The conquest of German East Africa *(Cape Town: 1917), 71p.*
SHACKLETON, C W
  East African experiences 1916: a private's story of the war in German East Africa *(Richmond, Va: Knox 1940), 136p.*
SIBLEY, J R
  Tanganyikan guerrilla: East African campaign, 1914-18 *(New York: Ballantine 1971), 160p; bib*
SPANTON, E F
  In German gaols: a narrative of two years' imprisonment in German East Africa *(London: SPCK 1917), 123p.*
THOMAS, E W
  Bivouac and baobab: campaign notes in German East Africa *(Maritsburg: 1917), 70p.*

THORNHILL, C J
  Taking Tanganyika: experiences of an Intelligence officer, 1914-1918 *(London: Stanley Paul 1917), 288p.*
  Two years'captivity in German East Africa *(London: Hutchinson 1918), 239p.*
WALMSLEY, L
  Flying and sport in East Africa *(London: Blackwood 1920), 306p.*
WOOD, G
  I was there *(Ilfracombe, Devon: Stockwell 1984), 70p.*
WYNN, A H W
  Ambush *(London: Hutchinson 1937), 256p.*
YOUNG, F B
  Marching on Tanga: with General Smuts in East Africa *(London: Collins 1919), 264p.*
  [See also BOTHA, SMUTS]

EASTERN EUROPE

CLARK, A
  Suicide of the Empires: the battles on the Eastern Front, 1914-18 *(London: BPC Unit 75 1971), 127p; bib.*
EVANS, *Sir* G
  Tannenberg, 1410 and 1914 *(London: Hamilton 1970), 182p; bib.*
FORTESCUE, G
  Russia, the Balkans and the Dardanelles *(London: Melrose 1915), 284p.*
GOLOVIN, N N
  Russian campaign of 1914: the beginning of the war and operations in East Prussia *(Fort Leavenworth, Kan: Rees 1934), 410p.*
IRONSIDE, *Sir* W E
  Tannenberg: the first thirty days in East Prussia *(Edinburgh: Blackwood 1925), 306p.*
JUKES, G
  Carpathian disaster: death of an army *(New York: Ballantine 1971), 160p; bib.*
KEARSEY, A H C
  A study of the strategy and tactics of the East Prussian campaign *(London: Sifton Praed 1932), 66p.*
KIRALY, B K and DREISZIGER, F *eds.*
  East Central European society in World War 1 *(Highland Lakes, Ohio: Atlantic 1985), 623p.*
KIRSCHTEIN, A J
  Lullaby of guns *(Denver, Co: Western Jewish Advocate 1936), 188p.*
MURRAY, M
  The Russian advance *(London: Hodder & Stoughton 1914), 192p.*
REED, J
  The war in Eastern Europe *(London: Nash 1916), 334p.*
STANDING, P C
  The campaign in Russian Poland *(London: Hodder & Stoughton 1914), 185p.*
STONE, N
  The Eastern Front, 1914-1917 *(London: Hodder & Stoughton 1975), 348p; bib.*

THURSTAN, V
 The hounds of war unleashed (St Ives, Cornw: United Writers 1978), 93p.
WASHBURN, S
 Field notes from the Russian Front *(London: Melrose 1915), 291p.*
THE RUSSIAN campaign, April to August 1915 *(London: Melrose 1915), 347p.*
[See also GERMAN ARMY, POLAND, RUSSIAN ARMY]

EASTER RISING

KELLY, S P
 Pictorial review of 1916: a complete ... account of the events which occurred in Dublin in
 Easter Week *(Dublin: Parkside P 1946), 68p.*
[See also IRELAND]

ECONOMICS

ANGELL, N
 The Peace Treaty and the economic chaos of Europe *(London: Swarthmore 1919), 143p.*
BARKER, J E
 Economic statesmanship: the great industrial and financial problems arising from the war
 (London: Murray 1918), 408p.
BARRON, C W
 A world remaking; or, Peace finance *(New York: Harper 1920), 242p.*
BOWLEY, A L
 Prices and wages in the United Kingdom, 1914-1920 *(London: OUP 1921), 228p.*
 Some economic consequences of the Great War *(London: Butterworth 1930), 251p.*
BRAILSFORD, H N
 The war of steel and gold *(London: Bell 1915), 340p.*
BURK, K
 Britain, America and the sinews of war 1914-1918 *(London: Allen and Unwin 1984),*
 287p.
CLAPP, E J
 Economic aspects of the war *(New Haven, Conn: Yale UP 1915), 340p.*
CROWELL, J F
 Government war contracts *(New York: OUP 1920), 357p.*
CULBERTSON, W S
 Commercial policy in war time and after *(New York: Appleton 1919), 478p.*
D'ACOSTA, U
 Peace problems in economics and finance *(London: Routledge 1918), 165p.*
DEARLE, N B
 An economic chronicle of the Great War for Britain and Ireland, 1914-1919 *(London:*
 OUP 1929), 397p.
DICKSEE, L R
 Business methods and the war *(Cambridge: CUP 1915), 71p.*

EDSALL, E W

The coming scrap of paper *(London: Allen 1915), 187p.*

GARVIN, J L

Economic foundations of peace; or, World partnership as the truer basis of the League of Nations *(New York: Macmillan 1919), 574p.*

GORE-BROWNE, F

The effect of war on commercial engagements *(London: Jordan 1914), 103p.*

GREAT BRITAIN Tariff Commission

The war and British economic policy *(London: HMSO 1915), 174p.*

GREBLER, L

The cost of the World War to Germany and to Austria-Hungary *(New Haven, Conn: Yale UP 1940), 192p.*

HALE, W B

American rights and British pretensions on the seas *(New York: McBride 1915), 172p.*

HANNA, H S *and* LAUCK, W

Wages and the war: a summary of recent wage movements *(Washington DC: Bureau of Applied Economics 1918), 356p.*

HARDACH, G

The First World War, 1914-1918 *(Berkeley,Cal: UP of California 1981), 328p.*

HIRST, F W

The political economy of war *(London: Dent 1915), 327p.*

KEYNES, J M

The economic consequences of the peace *(London: Macmillan 1919), 279p.*

A revision of the Treaty: being a sequel to 'The economic consequences of the peace' *(London: Macmillan 1922), 233p.*

KIRKALDY, A W *ed*

Industry and finance *(New York: Pitman 1918-1920), 2 vols.*

Labor, finance and the war *(New York: Pitman 1917), 344p.*

LAUCK, W

The cost of living and the war *(Washington DC: Bureau of Applied Economics 1918) 196p.*

LITMAN, S

Prices and price control in Great Britain and the United States during the World War *(New York: OUP 1920), 331p.*

LYDDON, W G

British war missions to the United States, 1914-1918 *(London: OUP 1938), 233p.*

MACFARLANE, C W

The economic basis of an enduring peace *(Philadelphia, Pa: Jacobs 1918), 74p.*

MANTOUX, E

Carthaginian peace; or, The economic consequences of Mr. Keynes *(New York: Scribner 1952), 210p.*

MAPPIN, G E

Can we compete?: Germany's assets in trade finance *(London: Skeffington 1918), 159p.*

MARCOSSON, I F

The war after the war *(London: Lane 1917), 272p.*

MOULTON, H F

The business man's guide to the Peace Treaty *(London: Allen & Unwin 1919), 81p.*

SCOTT, W R
  Economic problems of peace after the war *(Cambridge: UP 1917-1918), 2 series.*
SMITH, L B *and* COLLINS, H T
  The economic position of Argentine during the war *(Washington DC: Bureau of Foreign & Domestic Commerce 1920), 140p.*
SMITH, *Sir* S
  The real German rivalry *(London: Fisher Unwin 1918), 87p.*
SNOW, C D and KRAL, J J
  German trade and the war *(Washington DC: Bureau of Foreign & Domestic Commerce 1918), 236p.*
STEIN, H
  Government price policy in the United States during the World War *(Williamstown, Mass: Williams College 1939), 138p.*
VANDERLIP, F A
  What happened to Europe *(New York: Macmillan 1920), 188p.*
WHITMAN, S
  The war on German trade *(London: Ammunition for Civilians 1914), 123p.*
WHYTE, A G and ELDER, T G
  The under-war *(London: Electrical 1914), 126p.*
[See also FINANCE]

EDUCATION

ADAMS, J W B
  A pedagogue's fatigues *(London: Ocean 1932), 87p.*
BADLEY, J H
  Education after the war *(London: Blackwell 1917), 125p.*
BRITISH Universities and the war: a record and its meaning *(London: The Field & Queen 1917), 103p.*
BROCKINGTON, W A
  Elements of military education *(London: Longmans 1916), 379p.*
BURNET, J
  Higher education and the war *(London: Macmillan 1917), 248p.*
DEAN, A D
  Our schools in wartime and after *(New York: Ginn 1918), 335p.*
GRAY, H B *and* TURNER, S
  Eclipse or Empire *(London: Nisbet 1916), 326p.*
HOVRE, F de
  German and English education (London: Constable 1917), 108p.
KOLBE, P R
  Colleges in war time and after: a contemporary account of the effect of the war upon higher education in America *(New York: Appleton 1919), 320p.*
MAIS, S P B
  A public school in war time: on the effect the war has had and will have on public schools *(London: Murray 1916), 178p.*

MOORE, E C
　What the war teaches about education *(New York: Macmillan 1919), 334p.*
ODUINETS, D M
　Russian schools and universities in the World War *(New Haven, Conn: Yale UP 1929),
　239p.*
PELLATT, T
　Public school education and the war *(London: Duckworth 1917), 127p.*
THWING, C F
　American colleges and universities in the Great War, 1914-1919 *(New York: Macmillan
　1920), 276p.*
WEST, A F
　War and education *(London: Milford 1921), 86p.*

EGYPT

BADCOCK, G E
　History of the Transport Services of the Egyptian Expeditionary Force *(London: Rees
　1925), 388p.*
BRIGGS, M S
　Through Egypt in wartime *(London: Fisher Unwin 1919), 280p.*
CHIROL, *Sir* V
　The Egyptian problem *(London: Macmillan 1920), 343p.*
DOULL, D
　With the Anzacs in Egypt: life and scenes in the land of the Pharoahs *(Sydney: Angus &
　Robertson 1916), 143p.*
ELGOOD, P G
　Egypt and the Army *(London: Milford 1924), 382p.*
GWATKIN-WILLIAMS, *Mrs*
　In the hands of the Senussi *(London: Pearson 1916), 112p.*
MASSEY, W T
　The desert campaigns: Suez Canal, Libya *(London: Constable 1918), 178p.*
MURRAY, *Sir* A J
　Sir Archibald Murray's despatches June 1916-June 1917 *(London: Dent 1920), 229p.*
PIRIE-GORDON, H *ed*
　A brief record of the advance of the Egyptian Expeditionary Force *(London: HMSO
　1919), unp.*

EMDEN

FRANCIS JOSEPH, *prince*
　Emden: my experiences in S.M.S.Emden *(London: Jenkins 1928), 293p.*
HOEHLING, A A
　Lonely command: a documentary *(London: Cassell 1957), 191p.*

HOYT, E P
  The last cruise of the 'Emden' *(London: Deutsch 1967), 242p; bib. U.S. title:* Swan of the
  East.

ENTERTAINMENT

ASHWELL, L
  Modern troubadours: a record of the concerts at the Front *(London: Gyldendal 1922),*
  245p.
EVANS, J W *and* HARDING, G L
  Entertaining the American Army: the American stage and lyceum in the World War *(New*
  York: Associated P 1921), 259p.
MAYO, M
  Trouping for the troops: fun-making at the Front *(New York: Doran 1919), 149p.*

EQUIPMENT

AZAN, P J L
  Warfare of today *(Boston, Mass: Houghton Mifflin 1918), 351p.*
BOND, A R
  Inventions of the Great War *(New York: Century 1919), 344p.*
FITZSIMONS, B
  Heraldry and regalia of war *(London: Phoebus 1973), 160p.*
FUNCKEN, L *and* FUNCKEN, F
  The First World War: arms and uniforms *(London: Ward Lock 1974), 2 vols; bib.*
ROUVIER, J
  Present day warfare: how an Army trains and fights *(New York: Scribner 1918), 195p.*
STOCKBRIDGE, F P
  Yankee ingenuity in the war *(New York: Harper 1920), 372p.*
WILKINSON, F
  Cavalry and Yeomanry badges of the British Army 1914 *(London: Arms and Armour*
  Press 1973), 64p.
WILLIAMS H S *and* WILLIAMS, E H
  Modern warfare *(London: Grant Richards 1915), 328p.*
[*See also* ARMS AND ARMOUR]

ESCAPES

ARMSTRONG, H C
  On the run: escaping tales *(London: Rich & Cowan 1934), 330p.*
BOTT, A J
  Eastern flights: a record of escape *(London: Penguin 1940), 160p.*
CAUNTER, J A L
  13 days: the chronicle of an escape from a German prison *(London: Bell 1918), 224p.*

COOK, G
Break out!: great wartime escape stories *(London: Hart-Davis, Macgibbon 1974), 191p.*
DUNCAN, W
How I escaped from Germany *(Liverpool: 1919), 108p.*
DURNFORD H G E
The tunnellers of Holzminden *(London: CUP 1930), 199p.*
ELLISON, W
Escaped!: adventures in German captivity *(London: Blackwood 1918), 311p; later published as:* Escapes and adventures.
ESCAPERS all: being the personal narratives of fifteen escapers from war-time prison camps *(London: Lane 1932), 302p.*
ETTIGHOFFER, P C
Tovarish *(London: Hutchinson 1935), 288p.*
EVANS, E J
The escaping club *(London: Lane 1921), 267p.*
GRINNELL-MILNE, D
An escaper's log *(London: Lane 1926), 192p.*
HARDING, G P
Escape fever *(London: Hamilton 1932), 224p.*
HARDY, J L
I escape *(London: Lane 1927), 260p.*
HARRISON, M C C
Within four walls: accounts of escapes from German prison camps *(London: Arnold 1930), 306p.*
HERVEY, H E
Cage-birds *(London: Penguin 1940), 155p.*
HILL, C W
The spook and the commandant *(London: Kimber 1975), 201p.*
JOHNSTON M A B *and* YEARSLEY, K D
Four-fifty miles to freedom *(London: Blackwood 1919), 295p.*
JONES, E H
The road to En-dor: being an account of how two P.O.W.'s at Yozgad in Turkey won their way to freedom *(London: Lane 1920), 351p.*
KEELING, E H
Adventures in Turkey and Russia (London: Murray 1924), 240p.
KEITH, E A
My escape from Germany *(London: Nisbet 1918), 285p.*
KNIGHT, F
'Brother Bosch': an airman's escape from Germany *(London: Heinemann 1919), 175p.*
KOEHL, H
Airman's escape: being the record of a German airman's escape from France in 1918 *(London: Lane 1933), 236p.*
KRIST, G
Prisoner in the Forbidden Land *(London: Faber 1938), 353p.*
MCMULLEN, F *and* EVANS, J
Out of the jaws of Hunland *(New York: Putnam 1918), 248p.*

MARTIN, J
Captivity and escape *(London: Murray 1917), 193p.*
MILNE, D G
An escaper's log *(London: Lane 1926), 306p.*
O'BRIEN, P A
Outwitting the Hun: my escape from a German prison camp *(London: Heinemann 1918), 266p.*
PAGE, E
Escaping from Germany *(London: Melrose 1919), 387p.*
PEARSON, G E
The escape of a Princess Pat: capture, fifteen months' imprisonment and final escape *(London: Heinemann 1918), 223p.*
PLUESCHOW, G
My escape from Donington Hall, preceded by an account of the siege of Kiao-Chow in 1915 *(London: Lane 1922), 243p.*
STOFFA, P
Round the world to freedom *(London: Lane 1933), 286p.*
THERESE, J *pseud*
With Old Glory in Berlin: the story of a young American girl who went to Germany ... lived in Berlin for thirteen months and made her escape eight months after America had entered the conflict *(Boston, Mass: Page 1918), 319p.*
THOMAS, C
They also served: experiences of a private soldier as prisoner of war in German camp and coal mine, 1916-18 *(London: Hurst & Blackett 1939), 383p.*
TIERCE, A
Between two fires: being a true account of how the author sheltered four escaped British prisoners of war in Lille *(London: Lane 1931), 301p.*
WINCHESTER, B
Beyond the tumult *(London: Allison & Busby 1971), 207p.*

ESPIONAGE [see SECRET SERVICE]

ESSAYS

BARRIE, J M
Echoes of the war *(London: Hodder & Stoughton 1918), 168p.*
BRANDES, G
The world at war *(New York: Macmillan 1917), 272p.*
BRYCE, J
Essays and addresses in war time *(London: Macmillan 1918), 197p.*
CANBY, H S
Education by violence: essays on the war and the future *(New York: Macmillan 1919), 233p.*
COLLIN, C C R
War against war and the enforcement of peace *(New York: Macmillan 1917), 163p.*

DAWSON, W H ed
  After-war problems *(London: Allen & Unwin 1916), 366p.*
EASTMAN, M
  Understanding Germany: the only way to end war *(New York: Kennerley 1916), 169p.*
ELLIS, H
  Essays in war time *(London: Constable 1916), 352p.*
EWART, W H G
  When Armaggedon came: studies in peace and war *(London: Rich & Cowan 1933), 368p.*
FOAKES-JACKSON, F J ed
  The Faith and the war *(London: Macmillan 1915), 278p.*
GALSWORTHY, J
  A sheaf: papers on the European war *(London: Heinemann 1916), 308p.*
GOSSE, E
  Inter arma *(London: Heinemann 1916), 264p.*
HANKEY, D
  The beloved captain *(London: Bles 1956), 127p.*
LYND, R
  If the Germans conquered England and other essays *(Dublin: Maunsel 1917), 166p.*
MACNABB, V J
  Europe's ewe-lamb, and other essays of the Great War *(London: Washbourne 1915), 278p.*
MAEZTU, R de
  Authority, liberty and function in the light of the war *(London: Allen & Unwin 1916),
  288p.*
MURRAY, G
  Faith, war and policy: addresses and essays on the European war *(Boston, Mass:
  Houghton Mifflin 1918), 298p.*
TRIANA, S P
  Some aspects of the war *(London: Fisher Unwin 1915), 226p.*

EX-SERVICEMEN

CLIFFORD, W G
  The ex-soldier, by himself *(London: Black 1916), 308p.*
MAYO, K
  Soldiers what next! *(London: Cassell 1934), 476p.*
SHERREN, W
  The rights of the ex-Service man and woman *(London: Gooding 1921), 111p.*
  [See also DISABLED EX-SERVICEMEN].

FALKLAND ISLANDS

COOPER, H E H
  The battle of the Falkland Isles *(London: Cassell 1919), 224p.*

VERNER, R H C
The battle cruisers at the action of the Falkland Islands *(London: Bale 1920), 85p.*
[See also CORONEL, GERMAN NAVY, ROYAL NAVY]

FAR EAST

MILLARD, T F F
Democracy and the Eastern question: the problem of the Far East as demonstrated by the
Great War *(New York: Century 1919), 446p.*
O'NEILL, H C
The war in the Far East, 1914 *(London: Longmans 1919), 113p.*
PRATT, A
The judgment of the Orient *(London: Dent 1916), 71p.*
[See also CHINA, JAPAN]

FIGHTERS

BACON, W S *ed*
Sky fighters of World War I *(London: Fawcett 1960), 144p.*
BATCHELOR, J
Fighting aircraft of World War One and Two *(London: Phoebus 1976), 255p.*
BIDDLE, C J
Fighting airman: the way of an eagle *(New York: Doubleday 1968), 286p.*
BISHOP, W A
The courage of early morning: the story of Billy Bishop *(London: Heinemann 1966),
206p.*
Winged warfare: hunting the Huns in the air *(London: Hodder & Stoughton 1918), 301p.*
BORDEAUX, H
Georges Guynemer, knight of the air *(New Haven, Conn: Yale UP 1918), 256p.*
BOWEN, E
Knights of the air *(Alexandria Va: Time Life 1980), 192p.*
BOWYER, C
Albert Ball, V.C. *(London: Kimber 1977), 208p; bib.*
Sopwith Camel: king of combat *(Falmouth, Cornw: Glasney 1978), 192p.*
BRISCOE, W A *and* STANNARD, H R
Captain Ball, V.C. *(London: Jenkins 1918), 320p.*
COLE, C
McCudden, V.C. *(London: Kimber 1967), 224p.*
CONNORS, J F
Albatross: fighters in action *(Carrolton, Tex: Squadron Signal 1981), 49p.*
CRUNDALL, E D
Fighter pilot on the Western Front *(London: Kimber 1975), 192p.*
FUNDERBURK, T R
The early birds of war: the daring pilots and fighter aeroplanes of World War I *(London:
Barker 1968), 154p; U.S. title: The fighters.*

GRIBBLE, L R
Heroes of the fighting RAF *(London: Harrap 1941), 204p.*
GURNEY, G
Five down and glory: a history of the American air ace *(New York: Putnam 1958), 302p.*
Flying aces of World War I *(New York: Random House 1965), 185p.*
HALLION, R
Rise of the fighter aircraft 1914-18 *(Baltimore, Mo: Nautical & Aviation 1984), 200p.*
JACKSON, R
Fighter pilots of World War I *(London: Barker 1977), 152p.*
JOHNS, W G
Fighter planes and aces *(London: Hamilton 1932), 90p.*
JONES, J I T
An air-fighter's scrap-book *(London: Nicholson & Watson 1938), 322p.*
King of air-fighters: biography of Major 'Mick' Mannock, V.C., D.S.O., M.C. *(London: Nicholson & Watson 1934), 303p.*
KINNEY, C *and* TITLER, D M
I flew a Camel *(Philadelphia, Pa: Dorrance 1972), 122p.*
KNIGHT, G F
A knight of the air *(London: Stockwell 1940), 160p.*
LEE, A G
No parachute: a fighter pilot in World War I *(London: Jarrolds 1968), 234p.*
Open cockpit: a pilot of the Royal Flying Corps *(London: Jarrolds 1969), 184p.*
McCUDDEN, J T B
Flying fury: 5 years in the Royal Flying Corps *(Folkestone, Kent: Bailey 1973), new ed. 356p.*
MacSCOTCH *pseud*
Fighter pilot *(London: Routledge 1936), 248p.*
MANNOCK, E
The personal diary of Major Edward 'Mick' Mannock *(London: Spearman 1966), 221p.*
MOLTER, B A
Knights of the air *(New York: Appleton 1918), 243p.*
MORTANE, J
Guynemer, the ace of aces *(New York: Moffat 1918), 267p.*
NOBLE, W
With a Bristol fighter squadron *(London: Melrose 1920), 186p.*
REVELL, A
British fighter units, Western Front 1917–18 *(London: Osprey 1978), 48p.*
The vivid air: Gerald and Michael Constable Maxwell, fighter pilots in both wars *(London: Kimber 1978), 255p.*
RICKENBACKER, E V
Fighting the flying circus *(New York: Doubleday 1965), 296p.*
ROBERTS, E M
Flying fighter: an American above the lines in France *(New York: Harper 1918), 338p.*
ROBERTSON, B *ed*
Air aces of 1914–1918 war *(Letchworth, Herts: Harleyford 1964), 211p.*
SIMS, E H
Fighter tactics and strategy, 1914-1970 *(London: Cassell 1972), 266p; bib.*

SMITHERS, A J
   Wonder aces of the air *(London: Gordon & Cremonesi 1979), 192p.*
TAYLOR, *Sir* G
   Sopwith Scout 7309 *(London: Cassell 1968), 177p.*
TODD, R M
   Sopwith Camel Fighter ace *(Falls Church, Va: Ajay 1978), 112p.*
VOSS, V
   Flying minnows: memories of a World War I fighter pilot *(London: Arms & Armour Press 1977), 318p.*
WALLACE, M
   Pilots of World War I *(London: Macdonald 1979), 361p.*
WINTER, D
   The first of the few: fighter pilots of the First World War *(London: Lane 1982), 223p*
WHITEHOUSE, A *pseud*
   The Zeppelin fighter *(New York: Doubleday 1966), 290p.*
[See also AIR WARFARE, AIR FORCES OF INDIVIDUAL COUNTRIES]

FILMS

BROWNLOW, K
   The war, the west and the wilderness *(New York: Knopf 1979), 602p.*
MOULD, D H
   American newsfilm *(New York: Garland 1983), unp.*
PENDO, S
   Aviation in the cinema *(Metuchen, NJ: Scarecrow 1985), 402p.*
WARD, L W
   The motion picture goes to war: the United States Government film effort during World War I *(Ann Arbor, Mich: UMI 1985), 176p.*

FINANCE

ALLEN, J E
   The war debt and how to meet it *(London: Methuen 1919), 150p.*
ANDERSON, B M
   Effects of the war on money, credit and banking in France *(New York: OUP 1919), 227p.*
BARRON, C W
   War finance: as viewed from the roof of the world in Switzerland *(Boston, Mass: Houghton Mifflin 1919), 368p.*
BENSON, R
   State credit and banking during the war and after *(London: Macmillan 1918), 53p.*
BOGART, E L
   Direct and indirect costs of the great World War *(New York: OUP 1919), 338p.*
   War costs and their financing: a study of the financing of the war and the after-war problems of debt and taxation *(New York: Appleton 1921), 509p.*

CASSEL, G
  Money and foreign exchange after 1914 *(London: Constable 1922), 287p.*
COLLMAN, C A
  The war plotters of Wall Street *(New York: 1915), 140p.*
COST of the World War to Germany and Austria-Hungary *(New Haven, Conn: Yale UP 1940), 192p.*
DEARLE, N B
  Labour cost of the World War to Great Britain, 1914-1922 *(New Haven, Conn: Yale UP 1940), 260p.*
DULLES, E L
  The French franc, 1914-1918: the facts and the interpretation *(New York: Macmillan 1929), 570p.*
EDGEWORTH, F Y
  Currency and finance in time of war *(Oxford: Clarendon 1917), 48p.*
ENGLAND's financial supremacy *(London: Macmillan 1917), 121p.*
FARROW, T *and* CROTCH, W W
  How to win the war: the financial solution *(London: Werner Laurie 1916), 98p.*
FINANCIAL mobilization for war *(Cambridge: CUP 1918), unp.*
FISK, H E
  French public finance in the Great War and today *(New York: Bankers Trust 1922), 363p.*
  The inter-Ally debts *(New York: Bankers Trust 1924), 369p.*
FLIER, M J van der
  War finances in the Netherlands up to 1918 *(Oxford: Clarendon 1923), 150p.*
GARRETT, P W
  Government control over prices *(Washington DC: 1920), 834p.*
GIBSON, A H *and* KIRKALDY, A W
  British finance 1914-21 *(London: Pitman 1921), 481p.*
GILBERT, C
  American financing of World War I *(Westport, Conn: Greenwood 1970), 259p.*
GRADY, H F
  British war finance, 1914-1919 *(New York: Columbia UP 1927), 316p.*
GREAT BRITAIN British Association
  Credit, Industry and the war *(London: British Association 1915), 268p.*
  Industry and finance: war expedients and reconstruction *(London: British Association 1918), 371p.*
  Labour, finance and the war *(London: British Association 1916), 344p.*
HIRST, F W *and* ALLEN, J E
  British war budgets *(London: Milford 1926), 495p.*
HOLLANDER, J H
  War borrowing: a study of Treasury certificates of indebtedness of the United States *(New York: Macmillan 1919), 215p.*
JEZE, G
  The war finance of France: the war expenditure of France *(New Haven, Conn: Yale UP 1927), 344p.*
KAHN, O H
  Reflections of a financier *(London: Hodder & Stoughton 1921), 438p.*

KIERNAN, T J
  British war finance and the consequences *(London: King 1921), 132p.*
LAUGHLIN, J L
  Credit of the nations: a study of the European war *(New York: Scribner 1918), 406p.*
LAWSON, W R
  British war finance, 1914-15 *(London: Constable 1915), 367p.*
MacVEY, F L
  The financial history of Great Britain, 1914-1918 *(New York: OUP 1918), 101p.*
MALLOCK, W H
  Capital, war and wages: three questions in outline *(London: Blackie 1918), 93p.*
MASON, D M
  Monetary policy, 1914-1918 *(London: Hopkinson 1928), 113p.*
NICHOLSON, J S
  War finance *(London: King 1918), 504p.*
NOYES, A D
  Financial chapters of the war *(London: Macmillan 1916), 255p.*
  The war period of American finance *(New York: Putnam 1926), 459p.*
PIGOU, A C
  The disorganization of commerce and finance: the problems to be faced *(Oxford: Clarendon 1916), 85p.*
  The economy and finance after the war *(London: Dent 1916), 76p.*
RADCLYFFE, R
  The war and finance *(London: Dawson 1914), 54p.*
RUSSIAN public finance during the war *(New Haven, Conn: Yale UP 1928), 461p.*
SCHWABE, W S *and* GUEDALLA, P
  Effect of war on Stock Exchange transactions *(London: E. Wilson 1915), 140p.*
SCURR, J
  Casting the silver bullets *(London: Limit 1915), 127p.*
SHAW, W A
  Currency, credit and the Exchanges during the Great War and since -1914-26, more particularly with reference to the British Empire *(London: Harrap 1927), 202p.*
SHIRRAS, G F
  Some effects of the war on gold and silver *(London: Royal Statistical Society 1920), 56p.*
SMITH, H H
  How to pay for the war by developing the latent resources of the Empire *(London: Bale 1918), 186p.*
SONNE, H C
  The City: its finance, July 1914-July 1915 and future *(London: E. Wilson 1915), 308p.*
SPRINGER, L
  Some aspects of financial and commercial after-war conditions *(London: King 1918), 118p.*
STAMP, *Sir* J C
  Taxation during the war *(London: Milford 1932), 249p.*
STILLWELL, A E
  The great plan: how to pay for the war *(London: Hodder & Stoughton 1918), 184p.*
STOLL, O
  The people's credit *(London: Nash 1915), 243p.*

WALL, W W
  The war and our financial fabric *(London: Chapman & Hall 1915), 224p.*
WAR Finance Acts of 1914 to 1917 *(London: Gee 1918), 187p.*
WEBB, S *ed*
  How to pay for the war *(London: Fabian Society 1917), 278p.*
WHITE, B
  The currency of the Great War *(London: Waterlow 1921), 104p.*
WHITE, *Sir* T
  The story of Canada's war finance *(Montreal: 1921), 70p.*
WITHERS, H
  War and Lombard Street *(London: Smith, Elder 1915), 171p.*
  War-time financial problems *(London: Murray 1919), 306p.*

FINLAND

HALTER, H
  Finland breaks the Russian chains *(London: Hamilton 1940), 232p.*
HANNULA, J O
  Finland's war of independence *(London: Faber 1939), 229p.*
HARMAJA, L
  Effects of the war on economic and social life in Finland *(New Haven, Conn: Yale UP 1933), 125p.*

FISHING

GREAT BRITAIN Board of Agriculture and Fisheries
  Fisheries in the Great War: being the report on sea fisheries for the years 1915, 1916, 1917 and 1918 *(London: HMSO 1920), 194p.*
WOOD, W
  The fisherman in war-time *(London: Sampson Low 1918), 240p.*

FIUME

ANNUNZIO, G d'
  The rally *(Milan: 1919), 175p.*
LUCCHI, L de
  By the waters of Fiume: a story of love and patriotism *(London: Longmans 1919), 105p.*
MACDONALD, J N
  A political escapade: the story of Fiume and D'Annunzio *(London: Murray 1921), 176p.*

FLANDERS

ARMSTRONG, W J M
  My first week in Flanders *(London: Smith, Elder 1916), 40p.*
BAGGS, T A
  Back from the Front: an eye-witness's narrative of the beginnings of the Great War of 1914 *(London: Palmer 1914), 128p.*

BARTLETT, V
Mud and khaki: sketches from Flanders and France *(London: Simpkin Marshall 1917)*, *187p.*

BERTRAND, A
The victory of Lorraine, August 24-September 12, 1914 *(London: Nelson 1918), 136p.*

DANE, E
The battles in Flanders from Ypres to Neuve Chapelle *(London: Hodder & Stoughton 1915), 192p.*
Hacking through Belgium *(London: Hodder & Stoughton 1914), unp.*

EYE-WITNESS *pseud*
Narrative of the war from the Marne to Neuve Chapelle, September 1914-March 1915 *(London: Arnold 1915), 303p.*

GIBBS, *Sir* P H
The struggle in Flanders *(New York: Doran 1919), 464p; previously published as:* From Bapaume to Passchendaele.

GILLESPIE, A D
Letters from Flanders *(London: Smith, Elder 1916), 326p.*

HAMILTON, E W
The first seven Divisions: being a detailed account of the fighting from Mons to Ypres *(London: Hurst & Blackett 1916), 312p.*

HYNDSON, J G W
From Mons to the first battle of Ypres *(London: Wyman 1932), 128p.*

INGPEN, R
Fighting retreat to Paris *(New York: Doran 1914), 192p.*

KEEGAN, J
Opening moves *(New York: Ballantine 1971), 160p; bib.*

LLOYD, T
The blazing trail of Flanders *(London: Heath Cranton 1933), 254p.*

PERRIS, G H
Campaign of 1914 – France and Belgium *(New York: Holt 1915), 395p.*

POWELL, E A
Fighting in Flanders *(London: Heinemann 1914), 227p.*

R, L F
Naval guns in Flanders, 1914-1915 *(New York: Dutton 1920), 184p.*

RAYMOND, E
Tell England *(London: Cassell 1930).*

RICKARD, *Mrs* L
The story of the Munsters at Etreux *(London: Hodder & Stoughton 1918, 132p.*
The story of the Munsters at Festubert, Rue de Bois and Hulluch *(London: Hodder & Stoughton 1918), 116p.*

SIMONDS, F H
The greatest war, the second phase: from the fall of Antwerp to the second battle of Ypres *(New York: Kennerley 1915), 284p.*

THURLOW, E G L
The pill-boxes of Flanders *(London: Nicholson & Watson 1933), 47p.*

TUCHMAN, B W
August 1914 *(London: Constable 1962), 499p; bib.*

WARR, C L
Echoes of Flanders *(London: Simpkin Marshall 1916), 307p.*
WILLIAMS, G V
With our Army in Flanders *(London: Arnold 1915), 347p.*
WILLIAMSON, H
The wet Flanders Plain *(London: Faber 1929), 147p.*
WOLFF, L
In Flanders fields: the 1917 campaign *(New York: Viking 1958), 313p; bib,*
YOUNG, G W W
From the trenches: Louvain to the Aisne: the first record of an eye-witness *(London: Fisher Unwin 1914), 318p.*
[See also AISNE, DIXMUDE, LOOS, MONS, YPRES]

FLYING BOATS

X, P L
The spider's web: the romance of a flying-boat war flight *(London: Blackwood 1919), 278p.*

FOCH

ASTON, *Sir* G
The biography of the late Marshal Foch *(London: Hutchinson 1929), 318p.*
ATTERIDGE, A H
Marshal Ferdinand Foch: his life and theory of modern war *(London: Skeffington 1918), 256p.*
BUGNET, *Commandant*
Foch talks *(London: Gollancz 1929), 288p.*
FOCH, F
The memoirs of Marshal Foch *(London: Heinemann 1931), 594p.*
JOHNSTON, R M
General Foch: an appreciation *(Boston, Mass: Houghton Mifflin 1918), 53p.*
LAUGHLIN, C E
Foch the man *(New York: Revell 1918), 155p.*
LIDDELL HART, B H
Foch, the man of Orleans *(London: Eyre & Spottiswoode 1933), 532p.*
MARSHALL-CORNWALL, *Sir* J
Foch as military commander *(London: Batsford 1972), 268p; bib.*
PUAUX, R
Marshal Foch: his life, his work, his faith *(London: Hodder & Stoughton 1918), 208p.*
RECOULY, R
Foch: his character and leadership *(London: Fisher Unwin 1920), 267p.*
Marshal Foch: his own words on many subjects *(London: Butterworth 1929), unp.*
UNITED STATES Department of War
The Allied Armies under Marshal Foch in the Franco-Belgian theatre of operations *(Washington DC: 1924-25), 3 vols.*

FOOD

BEVERIDGE, *Sir* W H
   British food control *(London: Milford 1928), 447p.*
BYRON, M
   How to save cookery: a war-time cookery book *(London: Hodder & Stoughton 1915), 256p.*
COLLER, F H
   A State trading adventure *(London: Milford 1925), 360p.*
DICKSON, M R
   The food front in World War I *(Washington DC: American Council on Public Affairs 1944), 194p.*
ELTZBACHER, P
   Germany's food: can it last? *(London: University of London P 1915), 232p.*
GUERRIER, E
   We pledged allegiance: the U.S. food administration *(Stanford, Cal: Stanford UP 1941), 170p.*
LISSA, N R de
   War-time cookery: three weeks' meals for a family of eight at 2s. per day *(London: Simpkin Marshall 1915), 56p.*
LLOYD, E M H
   Experiments in State control at the War Office and Ministry of Food *(Oxford: Clarendon 1924), 460p.*
MIDDLETON, *Sir* T H
   Food production in war *(Oxford: Clarendon 1923), 373p.*
MILES, H E
   Economy in war time; or, Health without meat *(London: Methuen 1915), 144p.*
MULLENDORE, W C
   History of the United States Food Administration, 1917-1919 *(Stanford, Cal: Stanford UP 1941), 399p.*
OLDMEADOW, E
   Home cookery in war time *(London: Grant Richards 1914), 270p.*
PHILIP, A
   Rations, rationing and food control *(London: Book World 1918), 161p.*
SENN, C H
   Meals without meat *(London: Food & Cookery 1916), 138p.*
STRUVE, P B
   Food supply in Russia during the World War *(New Haven, Conn: Yale UP 1930), 469p.*
SURFACE, F M
   The grain trade during the World War: being a history of the Food Administration Grain Corporation and the United States Grain Corporation *(New York: 1928), 679p.*
TURNOR, C
   Our food supply: perils and remedies *(London: Country Life 1916), 182p.*
[See also AGRICULTURE]

FORT VAUX

BORDEAUX, H
  The deliverance of the captives *(London: Nelson 1919), 301p.*
  The last days of Fort Vaux *(London: Nelson 1917), 227p.*
[See also VERDUN]

FOURTEEN POINTS

HANSEN, H
  The adventures of the Fourteen Points *(New York: Century 1919), 385p.*
HARDY, G M G
The Fourteen Points and the Treaty of Versailles *(Oxford: Clarendon 1939), 40p.*
[See also WOODROW WILSON]

FRANCE

ACHIEVEMENT of France *(London: Methuen 1915), 79p.*
AYSCOUGH, J
  French windows *(London: Arnold 1917), 296p.*
BALDWIN, J M
  France and the war *(New York: Appleton 1916), 62p.*
BAUSMAN, F
  Let France explain *(London: Allen & Unwin 1923), 264p.*
BECKER, J J
  The Great War and the French people *(New York: St. Martin's 1986), 343p.*
BELL, W
  A scavenger in France: extracts from the diary of an architect, 1917-1919 *(London: Daniel 1920), 353p.*
BOULNOIS, H M
  Some soldiers and little Mamma *(London: Lane 1919), 203p.*
BRINGOLF, H
  I have no regrets: the strange life of a diplomat vagrant *(London: Jarrolds 1933), 286p.*
BURKE, K
  Little heroes of France *(New York: Doubleday 1920), 223p.*
COBB, R
  French and German, German and French: a personal interpretation of France under two occupations, 1914–1918/1940–1944 *(Hanover, NH: New England UP 1983), 188p; bib.*
CROISILLES, H
  The flaming sword of France *(London: Dent 1918), 191p.*
DARK, S
  The glory that is France *(London: Nash 1916), 150p.*
DAWBARN, C
  France at bay *(London: Mills & Boon 1915), 236p.*

DAY, S R
Round about Bar-le-Duc *(London: Skeffington 1918), 256p.*
DE PRATZ, C
A Frenchwoman's notes on the war *(London: Constable 1916), 290p.*
DODD, *Mrs* A B
Heroic France (New York: Poor 1915), 214p.
DORR, *Mrs* R
A soldier's mother in France *(Indianapolis, Ind: Bobbs, Merrill 1918), 252p.*
DRUMONT, *Mme* E A
A French mother in war time *(London: Arnold 1916), 167p.*
DUNSANY, E J *18th baron*
Unhappy far off things *(Boston, Mass: Little, Brown 1919), 104p.*
FORTESCUE, G
France bears the burden *(New York: Macmillan 1917), 214p.*
FRANCE, A
The path of glory *(London: Lane 1915), 170p.*
FRANCE Ministry of Foreign Affairs
Germany's violation of the laws of war *(London: Heinemann 1915), 342p.*
FRANKLIN, J H
In the track of the storm: a report of a visit to France and Belgium *(Philadelphia, Pa: American Baptist 1919), 140p.*
THE FRENCH Yellow Book *(London: The Times 1914), 220p.*
FRIGHTFULNESS in retreat: an account of the devastation caused by the German Army in the retreat from the Somme *(London: Hodder & Stoughton 1917), 76p.*
GIBBONS, H A
France and ourselves: interpretive studies, 1917-1919 *(New York: Century 1920), 286p.*
GIDE, C
Effects of the war upon French economic life *(Oxford: Clarendon 1923), 197p.*
GOMEZ CARRILLO, E
Among the ruins *(London: Heinemann 1915), 346p.*
GRANT, R
Their spirit: some impressions of the English and French during the summer of 1916 *(Boston, Mass: Houghton Mifflin 1916), 100p.*
HAMILTON, C
Senlis *(London: Collins 1917), 137p.*
HERRICK, R
The world decision *(Boston, Mass: Houghton Mifflin 1916), 252p.*
HOGGSON, N F
Just behind the Front in France *(New York: Lane 1918), 171p.*
JARVES, *Mrs* E D
War days in Brittany *(Washington DC: Jackson 1920), 151p.*
JERROLD, L
France today *(London: Murray 1916), 236p.*
JOHNSON, O M
The spirit of France *(Boston, Mass: Little, Brown 1916), 256p.*

JOHNSON, S
Enemy within: hitherto unpublished details of the great conspiracy to corrupt and destroy France *(New York: McCann 1919), 297p.*

KING, J C
Generals and politicians: conflict between France's High Command, Parliament and Government, 1914-1918 *(London: CUP 1951), 294p; bib.*

KIPLING, R
France at war *(London: Macmillan 1915), 72p.*

LANDRIEUX, M
The cathedral of Reims: the story of a German crime *(London: Kegan Paul 1920), 197p.*

LAPRADELLE, A de ed
War letters from France *(New York: Appleton 1916), 107p.*

LAUGHLIN, C E
The martyred towns of France *(New York: Putnam 1919), 469p.*

LAUZANNE, S J
Fighting France *(New York: Appleton 1918), 230p.*

LILLE before and during the war *(Milltown, NJ: Michelin Tire 1919), 64p.*

MACKAY, H
Journal of small things, 1914-1916 *(London: Melrose 1917), 284p.*

MALCOLM, I Z
Scraps of paper: German proclamations in Belgium and France *(New York: Doran 1916), 37p.*

MALHERBE, F de
The flame that is France *(New York: Century 1918), 182p.*

MAUD, C E
My French year *(London: Mills & Boon 1919), 272p.*

MERIWETHER, L
The war diary of a diplomat *(New York: 1919), 303p.*

MITCHELL, F
Tried and tempted in every shape and form *(London: Larby 1921), 226p.*

NAVARRO, A de
France afflicted: France serene *(London: Chapman & Hall 1920), 211p.*

NEEDHAM, M M
Shall angels weep again? *(London: Joseph 1936), 311p.*

O'SHAUGHNESSY, E L
My Lorraine journal *(New York: Harper 1918), 195p.*

PICKHARD, M F S
France in war time, 1914-1915 *(London: Methuen 1915), 201p.*

PRYSE, G S
Four days: an account of a journey in France between August 28th and 31st, 1914 *(London: Lane 1932), 305p.*

RANDOLPH, W
French churches in the war zone *(London: Kegan Paul 1916), 59p.*

RENOUVIN, P
The forms of war government in France *(New Haven, Conn: Yale UP 1927), 166p.*

RHEIMS and the battles for its possession *(Milltown, NJ: Michelin Tire 1920), 176p.*

ROLLAND, R
Above the battle *(London: Allen & Unwin 1916), 193p.*
SABATIER, P
A Frenchwoman's thoughts on the war *(London: Fisher Unwin 1915), 164p.*
ST JOHN, I
A journey in wartime *(London: Lane 1919), 192p.*
SAILLENS, R
The soul of France *(London: Morgan & Scott 1917), 274p.*
SMITH, F B
Observations in France *(New York: Associated P 1918), 83p.*
STEPHENS, W
The book of France in aid of the French Parliamentary Committee's Fund for the relief of the invaded Departments *(London: Macmillan 1915), 272p.*
The France I knew *(New York: Dutton 1919), 255p.*
STODDARD, F R
War time France: the story of an American Commission abroad *(New York: Moffat 1918), 201p.*
STRONG, R
Diary of an English resident in France during twenty-two weeks of war time *(London: Nash 1915), 357p.*
TOWNE, C H
Shaking hands with England *(New York: Doran 1919), 119p.*
TOYNBEE, A J
The German terror in France *(New York: Doran 1917) 220p.*
VIVIANI, R
As we see it: France and the truth about the war *(London: Hodder & Stoughton 1923), 269p.*
WADDINGTON, M K
My war diary *(London: Murray 1917), 370p.*
WARREN, *Mrs* M R
The white flame of France *(Boston, Mass: Small 1918), 358p.*
WHARTON, E N
Fighting France, from Dunkerque to Belfort *(New York: Scribner 1915), 238p.*
WHITAKER, J P
Under the heel of the Hun: an Englishwoman's two and a half years in Roubaix and Lille *(London: Hodder & Stoughton 1917), 114p.*
WISTER, O
Neighbours henceforth: a survey of conditions in France after the war *(London: Macmillan 1922), 423p.*
WRAY, W F
Across France in war time *(London: Dent 1916), 182p.*

FRENCH AIR FORCE

BERAUD-VILLARS, J M E
Notes on a lost pilot *(Hamden, Conn: Shoe String 1975), 285p.*

COPPENS DE HOULTHULST, W
Days on the wing: war memoirs *(London: Hamilton 1934), 290p.*
FONCK, R
Ace of aces *(New York: Doubleday 1967), 164p.*
GENET, E C C
An American for Lafayette: the diaries of... Lafayette Escadrille *(Charlottesville, Va: Virginia UP 1981), 224p.*
HALL, B *and* NILES, J J
One man's war: the story of the Lafayette Escadrille *(London: Hamilton 1929), 352p.*
HALL, J N *and* NORDHOFF, C B *eds*
Lafayette flying corps *(Boston, Mass: Houghton Mifflin 1920), 2 vols.*
McCONNELL, J R
Flying for France: with the American Escadrille at Verdun *(New York: Grosset 1918), 176p.*
MASON, H M
High flew the falcons: the French aces of World War I *(Philadelphia. Pa: Lippincott 1965), 172p.*
PARSONS, E C
Flight into hell: the story of the Lafayette Escadrille *(London: Long 1938), 255p; U.S. title:* Great adventure.
VIGILANT *pseud*
French war birds *(London: Hamilton 1937), 256p.*
WINSLOW, C D
With the French Flying Corps *(London: Constable 1917), 226p.*
[See also FIGHTERS]

FRENCH ARMY

ALLEN, H W
The unbroken line: along the French trenches from Switzerland to the North Sea *(London: Smith, Elder 1916), 328p.*
ARNAUD, R
Tragédie bouffe: a Frenchman in the First World War *(London: Sidgwick & Jackson 1966), 154p; U.S. title:* My funny little war.
BARBUSSE, H
Under fire: the story of a squad *(New York: Dutton 1917), 344p.*
BELMONT, F
A crusader of France: lettres d'un officier de Chasseurs Alpins *(London: Melrose 1917), 365p.*
BERGER, M
The ordeal by fire *(New York: Putnam 1917), 532p.*
BOURCIER, E
Under German shells *(New York: Scribner 1918), 217p.*
BRACQ, J C
The provocation of France: fifty years of German aggression *(New York: OUP 1916), 209p.*

BROOKS, A
As I saw it *(New York: Knopf 1930), 299p; previously published as:* Battle in 1918.
COBLENTZ, P
The silence of Sarrail *(London: Hutchinson 1930), 288p.*
CORNET-AUQUIER, A
Soldier unafraid: letters from the trenches on the Alsatian Front *(Boston, Mass: Little, Brown 1918), 110p.*
DAVIS, R H
With the French in France and Salonika *(London: Duckworth 1916), 240p.*
DAWBARN, C
Joffre and his Army *(London: Mills & Boon 1916), 233p.*
DAWSON, A J
For France: some impressions of the French Front *(London: Hodder & Stoughton 1917), 176p.*
DESAGNEAU, H
A French soldier's war diary, 1914-1918 *(Morley, Yorks: Elmfield 1975), 112p.*
DUPONT, M
In the field, 1914-1915 *(London: Heinemann 1916), 307p.*
FERREE, B
The bombardment of Reims *(New York: Scott 1917), 128p.*
GREY, W E
With the French Eastern Army *(London: Hodder & Stoughton 1915), 187p.*
HARDEN, E S
An American poilu *(Boston, Mass: Little, Brown 1919), 244p.*
HARMON, F S
Keep 'em rolling: letters about French ammunition trucks *(New York: Harmon 1975), 282p.*
IN the fire of the furnace, by a sergeant in the French Army *(London: Smith, Elder 1916), 414p.*
KING, D W
L. M.8046: the war diary of a legionnaire *(London: Arrowsmith 1929), 211p.*
LAFOND, G
Covered with mud and glory: a machine-gun company in action *(Boston, Mass: Small 1918), 265p.*
LE ROUX, R C H
On the field of honour *(Boston, Mass: Houghton Mifflin 1918), 281p.*
LETTERS of a soldier, 1914-15 *(London: Constable 1917), 211p.*
LEWYS, G *pseud*
Charmed American: a story of the Iron Division in France *(New York: Lane 1919), 328p.*
LINTIER, P
My seventy-five: journal of a French gunner *(August-September 1914) (London: Davies 1929), 230p.*
MACDONALD, M
Under the French flag: a Britisher in the French Army *(London: Scott, 1917), 207p.*
MALLET, C
Impressions and experiences of a French trooper, 1914-1915 *(London: Constable 1916), 144p.*

MAZE, P
A Frenchman in khaki *(London: Heinemann 1934)*, *353p.*
MILLET, P
Comrades in arms *(London: Hodder & Stoughton 1916)*, *272p.*
NADEL, H *pseud*
Down the red lane *(Indianapolis, Ind: Bobbs-Merrill 1930)*, *270p.*
NICOLAS, R
Campaign diary of a French officer, Feb-May, 1915 *(Boston, Mass: Houghton Mifflin 1917)*, *163p.*
PIERREFEU, J de
French Headquarters, 1915-1918 *(London: Bles 1924)*, *319p.*
RADIGUET, R
The making of a modern army, and its operations in the field *(London: Putnam 1918)*, *178p.*
REDIER, A
Comrades in courage *(New York: Doubleday 1918)*, *260p.*
RIMBAUD, I
In the whirlpool of war *(London: Fisher Unwin 1918)*, *256p.*
RION, G
The diary of a French private *(London: Fisher Unwin 1916)*, *315p.*
ROUGES, J *pseud*
Bourru: soldier of France *(New York: Dutton 1919)*, *383p.*
ROUJON, J
Battles and bivouacs: a French soldier's note-book *(London: Allen & Unwin 1916)*, *255p.*
RUFFIN, H *and* TUDESQ, A
Brother Tommy *(London: Fisher Unwin 1918)*, *160p.*
SHEAHAN, H
A volunteer poilu *(Boston, Mass: Houghton Mifflin 1916)*, *217p.*
SPEARS, *Sir* E
Two men who saved France: Pétain and De Gaulle *(London: Eyre & Spottiswoode 1966)*, *222p.*
WARD, H
Mr. Poilu: notes and sketches with the fighting French *(London: Hodder & Stoughton 1916)*, *158p.*

FRENCH NAVY

COUHAT, J L
French warships of World War I *(London: Ian Allan 1974)*, *304p.*
MILAN, R *pseud*
Vagabonds of the sea: the campaign of a French cruiser *(New York: Dutton 1919)*, *248p.*

FRENCH, SIR JOHN

CASSAR, G H
The tragedy of Sir John French (Newark, Del: Delaware *UP* 1985), 324p.

CHISHOLM, C
Sir John French: an authentic biography *(London: Jenkins 1914), 160p.*
COLEMAN, F
From Mons to Ypres with French *(London: Sampson Low 1916), 323p.*
FRENCH, E G
French replies to Haig *(London: Hutchinson 1936), 266p.*
The Kitchener-French dispute: a last word *(Glasgow: MacClellan 1960), 77p.*
FRENCH, *Sir* J D F *1st viscount*
The despatches of Lord French, and a complete list of the officers and men mentioned *(London: Chapman & Hall 1917), 607p.*
1914 *(London: Constable 1919), 414p.*
Some war diaries, addresses and correspondence of F.M. the Rt. Hon. the Earl of Ypres *(London: Jenkins 1937), 360p.*
JERROLD, W
Field Marshal Sir John French: the story of his life and battles *(London: Hammond 1915), 272p.*
WATKINS, O S
With French in France and Flanders *(London: Kelly 1915), 192p.*

FRONTIERS

KALTENBACH, F W
Self-determination, 1919: a study in frontier-making between Germany and Poland *(London: Jarrolds 1938), 150p.*
MORROW, I F D
The peace settlement in the German-Polish borderlands: a study of conditions today in the pre-war Prussian Provinces of East and West Prussia *(London: Royal Institute of International Affairs 1936), 558p.*

GALLANTRY

BARRON, E A
Deeds of heroism and daring *(New York: Harper 1920), 402p.*
A BOOK of British Heroes *(London: Richards 1914), 171p.*
DEEDS that thrill the Empire *(London: Hutchinson 1917), 2 vols.*
ELLIOT, H *ed*
Snapshot of valor *(New York: Grosset 1918), 303p.*
FEVYER, W H *comp.*
The Distinguished Service Medal 1914-1920 *(Polstead: Hayward 1982), 121p.*
FIELDING-HALL, H
The field of honour *(London: Constable 1915), 140p.*
FRASER, J F *ed*
Deeds that will never die: stories of heroism in the Great War *(London: Constable 1914), 230p.*

HONOURS and awards of the Old Contemptibles, the officers and men of the British Army and Navy mentioned in despatches, 1914-1915 *(London: Arms and Armour Press 1971)*, *58p.*

LEASK, G A
Golden deeds of heroism *(London: Johnson 1919)*, *246p.*

MACKENZIE, D A
Heroes and heroic deeds of the Great War *(London: Blackie 1915)*, *192p.*

O'CONNOR, T P *ed*
T.P.'s journal of great deeds of the Great War *(London: Hodder & Stoughton 1915)*, *3 vols.*

OUR gallant Guards *(Aldershot: Gale & Polden 1916)*, *unp.*

OUR heroic Highlanders *(Aldershot: Gale & Polden 1916)*, *unp.*

SWETLAND, M J *and* SWETLAND, L
These men: for conspicuous bravery above and beyond the call of duty *(Harrisburg, Pa: Military Service 1940)*, *312p.*

THRILLING deeds of valour: stories of heroism in the Great War *(London: Blackie 1916)*, *unp.*

WALLACE, E
Heroes all: gallant deeds of the war *(London: Newnes 1914)*, *255p.*

[See also CONGRESSIONAL MEDAL OF HONOUR, VICTORIA CROSS]

GALLIPOLI

ALEXANDER, H M
On two fronts: France and Gallipoli *(London: Heinemann 1917)*, *255p.*

ANZAC Book: written and illustrated in Gallipoli *(London: Cassell 1916)*, *169p.*

ANZAC memorial: soldiers' stories of Gallipoli *(London: Fisher Unwin 1916)*, *303p.*

ASPINALL-OGLANDER, C F
Official history of the Great War, military operations: Gallipoli *(London: Heinemann 1929-1932)*, *2 vols.*

BEAN, C E W
Gallipoli mission *(Sydney: Australian War Memorial 1948)*, *406p.*
Gallipoli correspondent *(London: Allen & Unwin 1983)*, *217p, bib.*

BEHREND, A
Make me a soldier: a platoon commander in Gallipoli *(London: Eyre & Spottiswoode 1961)*, *156p.*

BENSON, *Sir* I
The man with the donkey: John Simpson Kirkpatrick, the Good Samaritan of Gallipoli *(London: Hodder & Stoughton 1965)*, *96p.*

BIGWOOD, G
The Lancashire fighting Territorials in Gallipoli *(London: Newnes 1916)*, *155p.*

BRIDGES, R
The immortal dawn: the Australians at Gallipoli *(London: Hodder & Stoughton 1917)*, *279p.*

BUSH, E W
Gallipoli *(London: Allen & Unwin 1975)*, *335p.*

CRAVEN, D
  Peninsula of death *(London: Sampson Low 1937), 256p.*
CREIGHTON, O
  With the 29th Division in Gallipoli: a chaplain's experiences *(London: Longmans 1916), 191p.*
FALLON, D
  The big fight: Gallipoli to the Somme *(London: Cassell 1918), 271p.*
GALLISHAW, J
  Trenching at Gallipoli: the personal narrative of a Newfoundlander *(New York: Century 1916), 241p.*
GILL, E W B
  War, wireless and wangles *(Oxford: Clarendon 1934), 88p.*
GRAHAM, J G
  Gallipoli diary *(London: Allen & Unwin 1918), 328p.*
HAMILTON, *Sir* I S M
  Gallipoli diary *(London: Arnold 1920), 2 vols.*
HANNA, H
  The pals of Suvla Bay: being the record of 'D' Company of the 7th Royal Dublin Fusiliers *(Dublin: Maunsell 1917), 243p.*
HEAD, C O
  A glance at Gallipoli *(London: Eyre & Spottiswoode 1931), 203p.*
JAMES, R R
  Gallipoli *(London: Batsford 1965), 384p; bib.*
KANNENGIESSER, H
  The campaign in Gallipoli *(London: Hutchinson 1928), 280p.*
KEYES, *Sir* R J B
  The fight for Gallipoli *(London: Eyre & Spottiswoode 1941), 360p.*
LIDDLE, P
  Men of Gallipoli: the Dardanelles and Gallipoli experience, August 1914 to January 1916 *(London: Lane 1976), 320p; bib.*
  Gallipoli 1915: pens, pencils and cameras at war *(London: Brassey 1985), 157p.*
MacCUSTRA, L
  Gallipoli days and nights *(London: Hodder & Stoughton 1916), 149p.*
MACKENZIE, E M C
  Gallipoli memories *(London: Cassell 1929), 405p.*
MASEFIELD, J
  Gallipoli *(London: Heinemann 1916), 191p.*
MOOREHEAD, A
  Gallipoli *(London: Hamilton 1956), 383p; bib.*
MURRAY, J
  Gallipoli as I saw it *(London: Kimber 1965), 192p.*
NOLAN, S
  Nolan's Gallipoli *(Kent Town, Aust: Rigby 1963), 118p.*
NORTH, J
  Gallipoli: the fading vision *(London: Faber 1936), 390p.*
PATTERSON, J H
  With the Zionists in Gallipoli *(London: Hutchinson 1916), 315p.*

PEMBERTON, T J
  Gallipoli today *(London: Benn 1926), 117p.*
PRIESTMAN, E Y
  With a Baden Powell Scout in Gallipoli: a record of the Belton Bulldogs *(London: Routledge 1916), 311p.*
PUGSLEY, C
  Gallipoli: New Zealand story *(London: Hodder & Stoughton 1985), 384p.*
STUDENT *pseud*
  The Gallipoli campaign: an outline of the military operations *(London: Sifton Praed 1923), 87p.*
WRIGHT, S S
  Of that fellowship: the tragedy, humour and pathos of Gallipoli *(London: Stockwell 1931), 128p.*
[See also AUSTRALIAN ARMY, DARDENALLES, NEW ZEALAND, TURKEY]

GAS WARFARE

ADDISON, J T
  The story of the first Gas Regiment *(Boston, Mass: Houghton Mifflin 1919), 326p.*
AULD, S J M
  Gas and flame in modern warfare *(New York: Doran 1918), 201p.*
HABER, L F
  The poisonous cloud: chemical warfare in the First World War *(Oxford: Clarendon 1985), 770p, bib.*
HOGG, I V
  Gas *(New York: Ballantine 1975), 160p.*
LANGER, W L
  Gas and flame in World War I *(New York: Knopf 1965), 120p.*
LANGER, W L and MACMULLIN, R B
  With E of the First Gas *(New York: MacMullin 1919), 111p.*
ROBERTS, A A
  The poison war *(London: Heinemann 1915), 143p.*

GENOA

FINK, C
  The Genoa Conference: European diplomacy,1921-1922 *(Chapel Hill, NC: North Carolina UP 1984), 365p.*
WHITE, S
  The origins of detente: the Genoa Conference and Soviet-Western relations 1921-1922 *(Cambridge: CUP 1985), 255p, bib.*

GERMANY (general)

ACKERMAN, C W
  Germany the next republic *(London: Hodder & Stoughton 1917), 288p.*
AJAX *pseud*
  The German pirate: his methods and record *(New York: Doran 1918), 124p.*
ANGELL, N
  Prussianism and its destruction *(London: Heinemann 1914), 240p.*
BALLARD, F
  Plain truths versus German lies *(London: Kelly 1915), 143p.*
BANG, J P
  Hurrah and hallelujah: the spirit of new Germanism *(London: Hodder & Stoughton 1916), 288p.*
BARKER, J E
  Foundations of Germany: a documentary account revealing the causes of her strength, wealth and efficiency *(London: Smith, Elder 1916), 288p.*
BENSON, E F
  Crescent and Iron Cross *(London: Hodder & Stoughton 1918), 268p.*
BERGER, M
  Germany after the Armistice *(New York: Putnam 1920), 337p.*
BEVAN, E R
  German social democracy during the war *(London: Allen & Unwin 1918), 280p.*
  German war aims *(London: Longmans 1917), 48p.*
  The method in the madness *(London: Arnold 1917), 309p.*
BLATCHFORD, R
  General von Sneak: a little study of the war *(London: Hodder & Stoughton 1918), 179p.*
BLUECHER, E M *princess of Wahlstadt*
  An English wife in Berlin: a private memoir of events, politics and daily life in Germany throughout the war *(London: Constable 1920), 336p.*
BRAILSFORD, H N
  Across the blockade: travels in enemy Europe *(London: Allen & Unwin 1919), 157p.*
BROWN, C
  Germany as it is today *(New York: Doran 1918), 337p.*
BROWN, D
  In the heart of German intrigue *(Boston, Mass: Houghton Mifflin 1918), 377p.*
BUTLER, T
  Boche land before and during the war *(London: Heinemann 1916), 205p.*
CAN Germany win? *(London: Pearson 1914), 160p.*
CARSTEN, F L
  War against war *(London: Batsford 1982), 336p.*
CHAMBERLAIN, H S
  The ravings of a renegade *(London: Jarrolds 1915), 207p.*
CHERADAME, A
  The Pangerman plot unmasked *(London: Murray 1916), 235p.*
CHESTERTON, C E
  The Prussian hath said in his heart – *(London: Chapman & Hall 1914), 240p.*

CHESTERTON, G K
The barbarism of Berlin *(London: Cassell 1914)*, *94p.*
COOK, *Sir* T A
Kultur and catastrophe *(London: Murray 1915)*, *131p.*
CURTIN, D T
Edge of the quicksands *(New York: Doran 1918)*, *321p.*
The land of deepening shadow: Germany 1916 *(London: Hodder & Stoughton 1917)*, *379p.*
DARK, S
Thou art the man: the story of a great crime *(London: Werner Laurie 1915)*, *94p.*
DE BEAUFORT, J M
Behind the German veil: a record of a journalistic war pilgrimage *(London: Hutchinson 1917)*, *367p.*
DOTY, M Z
Short rations: an American woman in Germany, 1915-16 *(London: Methuen 1917)*, *252p.*
DROSTE, C L
Germany's Golgotha: a reply to Owen Wister's Pentecost of calamity *(New York: German University League 1917)*, *143p.*
EGAN, M F
Ten years near the German frontier: a retrospect and a warning *(London: Hodder & Stoughton 1919)*, *291p.*
FARRAR, L L
The short war illusion: German policy, strategy and domestic affairs, Aug-Dec 1914 *(Santa Barbara, Cal: ABC-CLIO 1973)*, *207p.*
FEDYSHYN, O S
Germany's drive to the East and Ukranian revolution, 1917-1918 *(New Brunswick, NJ: Rutgers UP 1971)*, *401p.*
FELDMAN, G D
Army, industry and labor in Germany, 1914-1918 *(Princeton, NJ: Princeton UP 1966)*, *572p.*
German imperialism, 1914-1918 *(New York: Wiley 1972)*, *221p; bib.*
FERNAU, H
The coming democracy *(London: Constable 1917)*, *320p.*
Fischer, F
Germany's aims in the First World War *(London: Chatto & Windus 1967)*, *692p; bib.*
World power or decline: the controversy over Germany's aims in the First World War *(New York: Norton 1974)*, *131p.*
FOX, E L
Behind the scenes in warring Germany *(New York: McBride 1915)*, *333p.*
William Hohenzollern & Co. *(London: Hurst & Blackett 1918)*, *254p.*
FREYTAG-LORINGHOVEN, H F P
Deductions from the World War *(New York: Putnam 1918)*, *212p.*
FRIEDEL, V H
The German school as a war nursery *(New York: Macmillan 1919)*, *270p.*
FULLERTON. G S
Germany today *(Indianapolis, Ind: Bobbs-Merrill 1915)*, *181p.*

GARDINER, J B W
  German plans for the next war *(New York: Doubleday 1918), 139p.*
GATZKE, H W
  Germany's drive to the West: a study of Germany's Western war aims during the First
  World War *(Baltimore: Johns Hopkins UP 1950), 316p; bib.*
GERARD, *Sir* J W
  Face to face with Kaiserism *(London: Hodder & Stoughton 1918), 324p; U.S. title:* My
  four years in Germany.
GERMAN war proclamations *(London: Allen & Unwin 1915), 88p.*
THE GERMAN White Book *(London: OUP 1914), 48p.*
GERMANY Auswartiges Amt
  German White Book concerning the responsibility of the authors of the war *(Washington
  DC: 1924), 178p.*
GERMANY Nationalversammlung
  Official German documents relating to the World War *(Washington DC: 1923),* 2 vols.
GERMANY'S great lie: the official German justification of the war exposed *(London:
  Hutchinson 1914), 195p.*
GERMANY'S war mania *(London: Shaw 1914), 272p.*
GRAVES, A K
  The red secrets of the Hohenzollerns *(London: McBride 1915), 212p.*
GRAY, A
  The upright sheaf: Germany's intentions after the war *(London: Methuen 1915), 76p.*
GRUMBACH, S
  Germany's annexionist aims *(London: Murray 1917), 158p.*
HAFKESBRINK, H
  Unknown Germany: an inner chronicle of the First World War, based on letters and diaries
  (New Haven, Conn: Yale UP 1948), 164p.
HANSSEN, H P
  Diary of a dying Empire *(Bloomington, Ind: Indiana UP 1955), 409p.*
HAR DAYAL
  Forty-four months in Germany and Turkey, February 1915 to October 1918 *(London:
  King 1920), 103p.*
HARRISON, F
  The German peril *(London: Fisher Unwin 1915), 300p.*
HAU, G W
  War echoes; or, Germany and Austria in the crisis *(Chicago: Open Court 1915), 352p.*
HENDERSON, E F
  Germany's fighting machine: her Army, her Navy, her air-ships, and why she arraigned
  them against the Allied Powers of Europe *(Indianapolis, Ind: Bobbs-Merrill 1914), 47p.*
HERVIER, P L
  The super-Huns *(London: Nash 1917), 205p.*
HILLGRUBER, A
  Germany and the two world wars *(Cambridge, Mass: Harvard 1981), 120p; bib.*
HOLMES, E
  The nemesis of docility: a study of German character *(London: Constable 1916), 270p.*
HOPE, A
  The new German-testament: some texts and a commentary *(London: Methuen 1916), 61p.*

HOUGHTON, M
In the enemy's country: being the diary of a little tour in Germany during the early days of the war *(London: Chatto & Windus 1915), 279p.*

HUBATSCH, W
Germany and the Central Powers in the World War, 1914-1918 *(Lawrence, Kan: University of Kansas P 1963), 133p.*

HUBERICH, C H *and* KING, R *eds*
The prize code of the German Empire, as in force July 1, 1915 *(New York: Voorhis 1915), 177p.*

HUGINS, R
Germany misjudged: an appeal to international goodwill *(Chicago: Open Court 1916), 111p.*

J'ACCUSE by a German *(London: Hodder & Stoughton 1915), 448p.*

JANNASCH, L
German militarism at work: a collection of documents *(London: Cayme 1926), 116p.*

JEPHSON, *Lady* H J
A war-time journal: Germany 1914 *(London: Melrose 1915), 99p.*

JOHANNET, R
Pan-Germanism versus Christendom *(London: Hodder & Stoughton 1916), 193p.*

KAHN, O H
Right above race: an indictment of Germany *(New York: Century 1918), 182p.*

KELLOGG, V L
Germany in the war and after *(New York: Macmillan 1919), 101p.*

KESSLER, H *graf von*
Germany and Europe *(New Haven, Conn: Yale UP 1923), 150p.*

KITCHEN, M
The silent dictatorship: the politics of the German High Command under Hindenburg and Ludendorff, 1916-1918 *(New York: Holmes & Meier 1976), 301p.*

KOCKA, J
Facing total war: German society 1914-1918 *(Cambridge, Mass: Harvard 1984), 278p.*

KRAUSE, C L
What is the German nation dying for? *(New York: Boni & Liveright 1918), 303p.*

KUNZ, A
Civil servants and the politics of inflation in Germany 1914-1924 *(Berlin: De Gruyte 1986), 427p.*

LE SUEER, G
Germany's vanishing colonies *(London: Everett 1915), 190p.*

LEWIN, E
The German road to the East *(London: Heinemann 1916), 340p.*

LICHNOWSKY, C M *prince*
Heading for the abyss: reminiscences *(London: Constable 1928), 471p.*

LIEBKNECHT, K P
'The future belongs to the people': speeches *(New York: Macmillan 1918), 144p.*

LITTLEFAIR, M
An English girl's adventures in hostile Germany *(London: Long 1915), 128p.*

LUGARD, E
An Emperor's madness; or, National aberration *(London: Routledge 1916), 135p.*

MCAULEY, M E
   Germany in war time: what an American girl saw and heard *(Chicago: Open Court 1917)*, *297p.*

MCCABE, J
   Treitsche and the Great War *(London: Fisher Unwin 1914), 288p.*

MCFALL, H
   Germany at bay *(London: Cassell 1917), 304p.*

MACLAREN, A D
   Germanism from within *(London: Constable 1916), 363p.*

MACLEOD, G H
   The blight of kultur *(London: Sampson Low 1918), 238p.*

MACCAS, L
   German barbarism: a neutral's indictment *(London: Hodder & Stoughton 1916), 240p.*

MACH, E von
   Germany's point of view *(Chicago: McClung 1915), 443p.*

MENDELSSOHN-BARTHOLDY, A
   The war and German society: the testament of a liberal *(New Haven, Conn: Yale UP 1937), 299p.*

MENNE, B
   Armistice and Germany's food supply, 1918-19: a study of conditional surrender *(London: Hutchinson 1944), 96p.*

MILLIOUD, M
   The ruling caste and frenzied trade in Germany *(London: Constable 1916), 158p.*

MORRISON, M A
   Sidelights on Germany: studies on German life and character during the Great War, based on the enemy Press *(London: Hodder & Stoughton 1918), 150p.*

MUHLON, W
   Vandal of Europe *(New York: Putnam 1918), 335p.*

MULLER, G A von
   The Kaiser and his Court: the diaries, notebooks and letters of Georg A. von Muller, Chief of the Naval Cabinet, 1914-1918 *(London: Macdonald 1961), 430p.*

MUNRO, R
   From Darwinism to Kaiserism: origin, effects and collapse of Germany's attempt at world dominion *(Glasgow: Maclehose 1918), 194p.*

NEUTRAL *pseud*
   In Germany today *(London: Methuen 1915), 120p.*

NIEMOLLER, M
   From U-boat to concentration camp *(London: Hodge 1939), 281p.*

NIPPOLD, O
   The awakening of the German people *(London: Allen & Unwin 1918), 60p.*

NOTESTEIN, W and STOLL, E E *comps*
   Conquest and kultur: aims of the Germans in their own words *(Washington DC: Committee on Public Information 1918), 160p.*

ORTH, S P
   The Imperial impulse: background studies of Germany and Russia *(New York: Century 1916), 234p.*

OUT of their own mouths: utterances of German rulers *(New York: Appleton 1917), 254p.*

PACKER, S
Prussia's bid for world power *(London: Fisher Unwin 1915), 110p.*
PERRIS, G H
Germany and the German Emperor *(London: Melrose 1914), 530p.*
PIERMARINI *pseud*
What I saw in Berlin and other European capitals during wartime *(London: Nash 1915), 332p.*
POWYS, J C
The menace of German culture *(London: Rider 1915), 127p.*
PRINCE, M
The creed of Deutschtum *(Boston, Mass: Badger 1918), 311p.*
PYKE, E L
Desperate Germany *(London: Hodder & Stoughton 1918), 300p.*
RAYMOND, A
Intimate Prussia *(London: Black 1918), 286p.*
ROBERTSON, C J M
Britain versus Germany *(London: Unwin 1917), 124p.*
The Germans; controversial and polemical *(London: Williams & Norgate 1916), unp.*
RODDIE, W S
Peace patrol *(London: Christophers 1932), 327p.*
RUMBOLD, *Sir* H
War crisis in Berlin, July-August 1914 *(London: Constable 1944), new ed. 372p.*
SADLER, W S
Long heads and round heads; or, What's the matter with Germany *(Chicago: McClurg 1918), 157p.*
SAROLEA, C
The curse of the Hohenzollern *(London: Allen 1915), 101p.*
German problems and personalities *(London: Chatto & Windus 1917), 271p.*
SEIBERT, W A
A trip to Germany during wartime *(New York: Seibert 1915), 126p.*
SELOTE, F
Through a lens darkly *(London: Hutchinson 1933), 283p.*
SILBERSTEIN, G E
The troubled alliance: German-Austrian relations, 1914-1917 *(Lexington, Ky: Kentucky UP 1970), 366p.*
SMITH, Munro
Militarism and statecraft *(London: Putnam 1918), 305p.*
SMITH, Thomas F A
The soul of Germany *(London: Hutchinson 1916), 354p.*
What Germany thinks *(London: Hutchinson 1915), 330p.*
SPRAGUE, F M
Made in Germany *(Boston, Mass: Pilgrim 1916), 218p.*
STEWART, H L
Nietzsche and the ideals of modern Germany *(London: Arnold 1915), 250p.*
SUTER-LERCH, H J
Germany her own judge *(Boston, Mass: Houghton Mifflin 1918), 145p.*

Swope, H B
  Inside the German Empire in the third year of the war *(New York: Burt 1917), 366p.*
Talbot, H
  After the day: Germany unconquered and unrepentant *(Philadelphia, Pa: Lippincott 1920), 301p.*
Thayer, W R
  The collapse of superman *(Boston, Mass: Houghton Mifflin 1918), 77p.*
  Germany versus civilisation *(London: Constable 1916), 238p.*
Thompson, R J
  England and Germany in the war *(Boston, Mass: Chapple 1915), 127p.*
Trumpener, U
  Germany and the Ottoman Empire, 1914-1918 *(Princeton, NJ: Princeton UP 1968), 433p.*
Villard, O G
  Germany embattled: an American interpretation *(London: Sampson Low 1915), 181p.*
Waldstein, *Sir* C
  What Germany is fighting for *(London: Longmans 1917), 116p.*
Wesselitsky, G de
  The German peril and the Grand Alliance *(London: Fisher Unwin 1916), 65p.*
Wetterle, *L'Abbé F*
  Behind the scenes in the Reichstag *(London: Hodder & Stoughton 1918), 208p.*
Whalen, R W
  Bitter wounds: German victims of the Great War, 1914-1939 *(Ithica, NY: Cornell 1984), 245p.*
Wister, O
  The Pentecost of calamity *(London: Macmillan 1915), 128p.*
Wolff, T
  Eve of 1914 *(London: Gollancz 1935), 655p.*
Zimmerman, E
  The German Empire of Central Africa as the basis of a new German world policy *(London: Longmans 1918), 62p.*

GERMAN AIR FORCE

Haddow, G W *and* Grosz, P M
  The German giants: the story of the R-planes, 1914-1919 *(New York: Funk 1969), 310p.*
Haupt-Heydemarck, G
  Double-decker C666 *(London: Hamilton 1931), 207p.*
  Flying Section 17 *(London: Hamilton 1934), 178p.*
  War flying in Macedonia *(London: Hamilton 1935), 196p.*
Immelmann, F
  Immelmann, the eagle of Lille *(London: Hamilton 1935), 223p.*
Imrie, A
  The German Army Air Service *(London: Ian Allan 1971), 176p.*
  German air aces of World War One *(London: Arms & Armour 1987), 64p.*
  German fighter units June 1917-1918 *(London: Osprey), 48p.*
  Fokker fighters in World War I *(London: Arms & Armour 1986), 64p.*

KILDUFF, P
  Germany's last knight of the air: memoirs of Major Carl Degelow *(London: Kimber 1979), 218p; bib.*
MORRIS, J
  The German air raids on Great Britain, 1914-1918 *(London: Pordes 1969), 306p.*
MUSCIANO, W A
  Eagles of the black cross *(New York: Obolensky 1966), 301p.*
NEUMANN, G P
  The German Air Force in the Great War *(London: Hodder & Stoughton 1921), 297p.*
RIMELL, R L *comp.*
  The German Army Air Service in World War One *(London: Arms & Armour 1985), 64p.*
SCHROEDER, H
  An airman remembers *(London: Hamilton 1936), 320p.*
STARK, R
  Wings of war: an airman's diary of the last year of the war *(London: Hamilton 1933), 227p.*
UDET, E
  Ace of the black cross *(London: Newnes 1937), 251p.*
VIGILANT *pseud*
  German war birds *(London: Hamilton 1931), 264p.*
WERNER, J
  Knight of Germany: Oswald Boelcke, German ace *(London: Hamilton 1933), 241p.*
[See also RICHTHOFEN]

GERMAN ARMY

BENSEN, W
  Hindenburg's soldier *(New York: Vantage 1965), 177p.*
BINDING, R G
  A fatalist at war *(London: Allen & Unwin 1929), 246p.*
BUCHER, G
  In the line, 1914-1918 *(London: Cape 1932), 325p.*
COBB, I S
  The red glutton: an account of the earlier phases of the war, by an American journalist with the German Army *(London: Hodder & Stoughton 1915), 414p; U.S. title:* Paths of glory.
DOMELIER, H
  Behind the scenes at German Headquarters *(London: Hurst & Blackett 1920), 271p.*
FALKENHAYN, E G S
  General Headquarters, 1914-1916, and its critical decisions *(London: Hutchinson 1919), 299p; U.S. title:* German General Staff and its decisions.
A GERMAN deserter's war experience *(New York: Huebsch 1917), 192p.*
GERMANY Auswärtiges Amt
  The German Army in Belgium: the White Book of May 1915 *(London: Swarthmore 1921), 282p.*

GOERLITZ, W
 History of the German General Staff, 1657-1945 *(New York: Praeger 1953), 508p; U.K. title:* German General Staff.
GREAT BRITAIN War Office
 Handbook of the German Army in war, January 1917 *(London: HMSO 1917), 125p.*
HEDIN, S A
 With the German Armies in the West *(London: Lane 1915), 402p.*
HEINZ, M
 Loretto: sketches of a German war volunteer *(New York: Liveright 1930), 316p.*
HOFFMANN, O F C
 The war of lost opportunities *(London: Kegan Paul 1924), 246p.*
JUENGER, E
 Copse 125: a chronicle from the trench warfare of 1918 *(London: Chatto & Windus 1918), 264p.*
 The storm of steel *(London: Chatto & Windus 1929), 319p.*
KOEPPEN, E
 Higher Command *(London: Faber 1931), 427p.*
MARTIN, A G
 Mother country – Fatherland: the story of a British-born German soldier *(London: Macmillan 1936), 390p.*
MIDDLEBROOK, M
 The Kaiser's battle: 21 March 1918, the first day of the German Spring offensive *(London: Lane 1978), 431p; bib.*
NASH, D
 German infantry, 1914-1918 *(London: Almark 1971), 56p.*
ORGILL, D
 German armour *(New York: Ballantine 1974), 159p.*
POSECK, M von
 German cavalry in Belgium and France 1914 *(Washington DC: US Cavalry Association 1923), 237p.*
RITTER, G
 The Schlieffen Plan: critique of a myth *(London: Wolff 1958), 195p.*
ROSINSKI, H
 The German Army *(London: Hogarth 1939), 267p.*
STEPHENS, F J *and* MADDOCKS, G
 The organization and uniforms of the Imperial German Army, 1900-1918 *(London: Almark 1975), 80p.*
UNITED STATES Department of War
 Histories of two hundred and fifty-one Divisions of the German Army which participated in the war, 1914-1918 *(Washington DC: 1920), 748p.*
WESTMAN, S K
 Surgeon with the Kaiser's Army *(London: Kimber 1968), 185p.*
WITKOP, P *ed*
 German students' war letters *(London: Methuen 1929), 376p.*

GERMAN NAVY

DIXON, T B
The enemy fought splendidly: being the 1914-1915 diary of the battle of the Falklands and its aftermath *(Poole, Dorset: Blandford 1983), 96p; bib.*

FREIDWALD, L
Last days of the German Fleet *(London: Constable 1932), 318p.*

GIBBON, P
The triumph of the Royal Navy: official record of the surrender of the German Fleet *(London: Hodder & Stoughton 1919), 48p.*

HORN, D
The German Naval mutinies of World War I *(New Brunswick, NJ: Rutgers UP 1969), 346p; U.K. title:* Mutiny on the high seas.

HOYT, E P
Defeat at the Falklands: Germany's East Asian Squadron 1914 *(London: Hale 1981), 240p, bib.*
The elusive seagull: the adventures of the World War I German minelayer the 'Moewe' *(London: Frewin 1970), 208p.*
The Germans never lost *(New York: Funk 1968), 239p.*
The Karlsruhe affair *(London: Barker 1976), 156p.*
Kreuzerkrieg *(Cleveland, Ohio: World 1968), 340p.*

HURD, A S
The German Fleet *(London: Hodder & Stoughton 1915), 190p.*

JANE, F T
All about the German Navy *(London: Sampson Low 1915), 58p.*

KONIG, P
The voyage of the Deutschland *(London: Pearson 1917), 126p.*

KOPP, G
Two lone ships: Goeben and Breslau *(London: Hutchinson 1931), 288p.*

McLAUGHLIN, R
The escape of the Goeben: prelude to Gallipoli *(London: Seeley 1974), 180p; bib.*

MILNE, *Sir* A B
The flight of the 'Goeben' and the 'Breslau' *(London: Nash 1921), 160p.*

PLIVIER, T
Kaiser's coolies *(London: Faber 1931), 308p.*

RUGE, F
Scapa Flow 1919: the end of the German Fleet *(London: Ian Allan 1973), 175p; bib.*

SCHEER, R
Germany's High Seas Fleet in the World War *(London: Cassell 1920), 375p.*

SCHUBERT, P *and* GIBSON, L
Death of a Fleet, 1917-1919 *(New York: Coward-McCann 1932), 278p.*

STUMPF, R
War, mutiny and revolution in the German Navy *(New Brunswick, NJ: Rutgers UP 1967), 422p; U.K. title:* The private war of Seaman Stumpf.

VAN DER VAT, D
The grand scuttle: the sinking of the German Fleet at Scapa Flow in 1919 *(London: Hodder*

& *Stoughton 1982), 240p.*

The ship that changed the world: the escape of the Goeben to the Dardanelles in 1914 *(London: Hodder & Stoughton 1985), 252p.*

WOODWARD, D

The collapse of power: mutiny in the High Seas Fleet *(London: Barker 1973), 240p.*

[See also U-BOATS]

GERMAN SURFACE RAIDERS

ALEXANDER, R

The cruise of the raider Wolf *(London: Cape 1939), 320p.*

BURDICK, C B

The frustrated raider: the story of the German cruiser 'Cormoran' in World War 1 *(Carbondale, III: Southern Illinois UP 1979), 119p; bib.*

CAMERON, J S

Ten months in a German raider: a prisoner of war aboard the 'Wolf' *(New York: Doran 1918), 178p.*

CHATTERTON, E K

The 'Konigsberg' adventure *(London: Hurst & Blackett 1932), 287p.*

The sea raiders *(London: Hurst & Blackett 1931), 285p.*

CLARKE, A H F

To Kiel in the German raider Wolf – and after: being an account of the experiences of an English civilian captured in the Indian Ocean *(Colombo, Ceylon: 1920), 174p.*

HOYT, E P

Ghost of the Atlantic: the Kronprinz Wilhelm *(London: Barker 1974), 160p.*

The raider Wolf *(London: Barker 1975), 150p.*

LANGMAID, K

The sea raiders *(London: Jarrolds 1963), 240p.*

MUECKE, H von

The 'Ayesha' *(Boston, Mass: Houghton Mifflin 1917), 229p.*

NIEZYCHOWSKI, A von *count*

The cruise of the Kronprinz Wilhelm *(London: Selwyn & Blount 1929), 285p.*

SCHMALENBERG, P

German raiders: a history of auxiliary cruisers of the German Navy,1895-1945 *(Annopolis, Md: Naval Inst. 1979), 144p.*

THOMAS, L J

Lauterbach of the China Sea: the escapes and adventures of a sea-going Falstaff *(New York: Doubleday 1930), 302p.*

TRAYES, F G

Five months on a German raider: the adventures of an Englishman captured by the 'Wolf' *(London: Headley 1919), 187p.; U.S. title:* Captive on a German raider.

VAN DER VAT, D

The last corsair: the story of the Emden *(London: Hodder & Stoughton 1983), 205p.*

[See also CARMANIA, Q SHIPS]

GOLD COAST

CLIFFORD, *Sir* H C
   The Gold Coast Regiment in the East African campaign *(London: Murray 1920), 306p.*
LUCAS, *Sir* C P
   The Gold Coast and the war *(London: Milford 1920), 56p.*
[See also EAST AFRICA]

GOUGH

FARRAR-HOCKLEY, A
   Goughie: the life of General Sir Hubert Gough *(London: Hart-Davis 1975), 416p.*
[See also BRITISH ARMY (FIFTH ARMY)]

GREECE

ABBOTT, G F
   Greece and the Allies, 1914-22 *(London: Methuen 1922), 242p.*
BROWN, D
   Constantine: King and traitor *(London: Lane 1918), 300p.*
   In the heart of German intrigue *(Boston, Mass: Houghton Mifflin 1918), 377p.*
THE GREEK Army and the recent Balkan offensive *(London: Allen & Unwin 1919), 59p.*
HIBBEN, P
   Constantine I and the Greek people *(New York: Century 1920), 592p.*
LAWSON, J C
   Tales of Aegean intrigue *(London: Chatto & Windus 1920), 271p.*
MELAS, G M
   Ex-King Constantine and the war *(London: Hutchinson 1920), 296p.*
PALLES, A A
   Greece's Anatolian venture – and after: a survey of the diplomatic and political aspects
   of the Greek expedition to Asia Minor, 1915-1922 *(London: Methuen 1922), 239p.*
PHOCAS-COSMETATOS, S P
   The tragedy of Greece *(London: Kegan Paul 1928), 327p.*
PRICE, W H C
   Venizelos and the war *(London: Simpkin Marshall 1917), 200p.*
TRAPMANN, A H
   The Greeks triumphant *(London: Forster Groom 1915), 294p.*
WILLMORE, J S
   The story of King Constantine as revealed in the Greek White Book *(London: Longmans
   1919), 83p.*

GREY

GREY, E *1st viscount*
   Twenty-five years, 1892-1916 *(London: Hodder & Stoughton 1925), 2 vols.*

LUTZ, H
Lord Grey and the World War *(London: Allen & Unwin 1928), 346p.*
ROBBINS, K
Sir Edward Grey *(London: Cassell 1970), 438p; bib.*
SIR EDWARD Grey: the man and his work *(London: Newnes 1915), 192p.*
TREVELYAN, G M
Grey of Fallodon: the life of Sir Edward Grey, afterwards Grey of Fallodon *(London: Longmans 1937), 407p.*

HAIG

ARTHUR, *Sir* G
Lord Haig *(London: Heinemann 1928), 164p.*
BEVAN, T
With Haig at the Front *(London: Collins 1916), 224p.*
CHARTERIS, J
Field Marshal Earl Haig *(London: Cassell 1929), 400p.*
COOPER, D
Haig *(London: Faber 1935-36), 2 vols.*
DAVIDSON, *Sir* J
Haig: master of the field *(London: Nevill 1953), 158p.*
DEWAR, G A B *and* BORASTON, J H
Sir Douglas Haig's command *(London: Constable 1922), 2 vols.*
DUNCAN, G S
Douglas Haig as I knew him *(London: Allen & Unwin 1966), 141p.*
HAIG, DOROTHY *countess*
The man I knew *(Edinburgh: Moray 1936), 335p.*
HAIG, *Sir* Douglas *1st earl*
Sir Douglas Haig's despatches, December 1915-April 1919 *(London: Dent 1919), 2 vols.*
The private papers of Douglas Haig, 1914-1919: being selections from the private diary and correspondence *(London: Eyre & Spottiswoode 1952), 383p.*
MARSHALL-CORNWALL, *Sir* J
Haig as military commander *(London: Batsford 1973), 324p.*
SECRETT, T
Twenty-five years with Earl Haig *(London: Jarrolds 1929), 288p.*
SIXSMITH, E K G
Douglas Haig *(London: Weidenfeld & Nicolson 1976), 212p*
TERRAINE, J
Douglas Haig: the educated soldier *(London: Hutchinson 1963), 508p.*

HARWICH

CARR, W G
Brasshats and bell-bottomed trousers: unforgettable and splendid feats of the Harwich Patrol *(London: Hutchinson 1939), 272p.*

KNIGHT, E F
  The Harwich naval forces: their part in the Great War *(London: Hodder & Stoughton 1919), 236p.*
WOOLARD, C L A
  With the Harwich naval forces, 1914-1918; or, Under Commodore Tyrwhitt in the North Sea *(London: HMSO 1934), 114p.*

HELIGOLAND BIGHT

JANE, L C
  The action off Heligoland, August 1914 *(Oxford: Clarendon 1915), 38p.*

HINDENBURG

BENECKENDORFF UND HINDENBURG, P L
  Out of my life *(London: Cassell 1920), 458p.*
LUDWIG, E
  Hindenburg and the saga of the German revolution *(London: Heinemann 1935), 389p.*
WHEELER-BENNETT, *Sir* J
  Hindenburg – wooden titan (London: Macmillan 1936), unp.

HINDENBURG LINE

JENKINS, B A
  Facing the Hindenburg Line: personal observations at the Fronts and in the camps of the British, French, American and Italians during the campaigns of 1917 *(New York: Revell 1917), 256p.*
MACKENZIE, F A
  Through the Hindenburg Line: crowning days on the Western Front *(London: Hodder & Stoughton 1918), 437p.*
[See also WESTERN FRONT]

HISTORY (general)

ALINGTON, A F
  The lamps go out: 1914, and the outbreak of war *(London: Faber 1962), 140p; bib.*
ALLEN, G H *and others*
  The Great War *(Philadelphia, Pa: Barrie 1916), 5 vols.*
ALTING, J H *and* BUNING, W de C
  Effect of the war upon the Colonies *(New Haven, Conn: Yale UP 1928), 140p.*
AMERICAN HOSTAGE *(periodical)*
  The American Heritage history of World War I *(New York: American Heritage 1964), 384p.*

ARNOUX, A
   The European war *(Boston, Mass: Houghton Miffllin 1915-17), 3 vols.*
ASTON, *Sir* G G
   The Great War of 1914-1918 *(London: Butterworth 1930), 251p.*
ATTERIDGE, A H
   The first phase of the Great War *(London: Graphic 1914), 244p.*
   The second phase of the Great War *(London: Hodder & Stoughton 1915), 218p.*
   The world wide war: first stage *(London: Philip Allan 1915), 184p.*
BALDWIN, E F
   The World War: a sketch of the different nations now at war *(London: Macmillan 1915), unp.*
BALDWIN, H W
   World War I: an outline history *(London: Hutchinson 1963), 181p.*
BANSE, E
   Germany, prepare for war *(London: Lovat Dickson 1934), 427p.*
BARNETT, C
   The Great War *(London: Park Lane 1979), 192p; bib*
BATTINE, C
   Military history of the war: the campaign of 1914 *(London: Hodder & Stoughton 1916), vol 1.*
BELLOC, J H P
   A general sketch of the European war: the first phase *(London: Nelson 1916), 284p.*
   A general sketch of the European war: the second phase *(London: Nelson 1916), 404p.*
   The two maps of Europe and some aspects of the Great War *(London: Pearson 1915), 128p.*
BENEDICT, B
   History of the Great War *(New York: Bureau of National Lit 1919), 2 vols.*
BEVERIDGE, A J
   What is back of the war *(Indianapolis, Ind: Bobbs-Merrill 1915), 430p.*
BOOTH, A H
   The true book about the First World War *(London: Muller 1958), 144p.*
BORER, M C
   The First World War *(London: Hamilton 1970), 64p.*
BRAITHWAITE, W S B
   Story of the Great War *(New York: Stokes 1919), 373p.*
BRIDGE, F M
   A short history of the Great World War *(London: Deane 1920), 274p.*
BROOK-SHEPHERD, G
   November 1918 *(London: Collins 1981), 300p.*
   Royal Sunset: the European dynasties and the Great War *(New York: Doubleday 1987), 357p.*
BROPHY, J
   The five years: a conspectus of the Great War *(London: Barker 1936), 320p.*
BUCHAN, J
   A history of the Great War *(London: Nelson 1921-22), 4 vols.*
   The long road to victory *(London: Nelson 1920), 366p.*

BUCHAN, J *ed*
  Nelson's history of the war *(London: Nelson 1915-19), 24 vols.*
CAINE, T H H
  The drama of the three hundred and sixty-five days: scenes in the
  Great War *(London: Heinemann 1915), 126p.*
CAMERON, J
  1914 *(London: Cassell 1959), 210p; bib.*
CANA, F R *ed*
  The Great War in Europe *(London: Virtue 1915-20), 8 vols.*
CANNING, J
  Living history: 1914 *(London: Odhams 1968), 269p.*
CAREY, G V *and* SCOTT, H S
  An outline history of the Great War *(Cambridge: CUP 1929), 279p.*
COLLIER'S history of the war *(New York: Collier 1919), 8 vols.*
COOLIDGE, A C
  The origins of the Triple Alliance *(New York: Scribner 1917), 236p.*
CRUTTWELL, C R M F
  A history of the Great War, 1914-1918 *(Oxford: Clarendon 1934), 649p.*
CUNNINGTON, S
  The world in arms, 1914-1918 *(London: Arnold 1921), 184p.*
DANIELL, D S
  World War I: an illustrated history *(London: Benn 1965), 128p.*
D'AUVERGNE, E B F
  An ABC guide to the Great War *(London: Werner Laurie 1914), 46p.*
DAVENPORT, B
  A history of the Great War to Aug. 1915 *(New York: Putnam 1916), 545p.*
DAVID, D
  The 1914 campaign, August-October 1914 *(Spelhurst: Spellmount 1987), 208p.*
DUPUY, T N
  The military history of World War I *(New York: Watts 1967), 12 vols.*
EASUM, C V
  Half-century of conflict *(New York: Harper 1952), 929p.*
EATON, W D *and* READ, H C
  A complete history of the World War *(Chicago: Thomas 1919), 5 vols.*
EDEN, A *Ist earl of Avon*
  Another world 1897-1917 *(London: Lane 1976), 156p.*
EDMONDS, *Sir* J E
  Military operations *(London: Macmillan 1933), 592p.*
  A short history of World War I *(London: OUP 1951), 454p.*
ESPOSITO, V J *ed*
  A concise history of World War I *(London: Pall Mall 1964), 414p.*
ESSAME, H
  The battle for Europe, 1918 *(London: Batsford 1972), 216p.*
EVERETT, S
  World War I: an illustrated history *(London: Hamlyn 1980), 256p.*
FALLON, D
  The big fight (Gallipoli to the Somme) *(New York: Watts 1918), 301p.*

FALLS, C
   The First World War *(London: Longmans 1960), 421p; bib.*
FERRO, M
   The Great War, 1914-1918 *(London: Routledge & Kegan Paul 1973), 239p; bib.*
FIEBEGER, G J
   World War: a short account of the principal land operations on the Belgian, French, Russian, Italian, Greek and Turkish Fronts *(West Point, NY: U.S. Military Academy 1921), 272p.*
FIELD, G L
   The First World War *(Exeter: Wheaton 1966), 112p.*
   The First World War *(Edinburgh: Scottish Record Office 1986), 52p.*
FLETCHER, C R L
   The Great War: a brief sketch *(London: Murray 1920), 199p.*
FLOWER, N
   The history of the Great War *(London: Waverley 1915-21), 14 vols.*
FLOWERS, M *ed*
   What every American should know about the war *(New York: Doran 1918), 368p.*
FRANCE Ministry of War
   The French official view of the first six months of the war *(London: Constable 1915), 88p.*
FROTHINGHAM, T G
   Guide to the military history of the World War, 1914-1918 *(London: Fisher Unwin 1921), 367p.*
G,
   The last lap of the European war *(London: Melrose 1917), 140p.*
GARVIN, J L
   The coming of the Great War *(London: Chapman & Hall 1915), 148p.*
GEISS, I *comp*
   July 1914: the outbreak of the First World War: selected documents *(London: Batsford 1967), 400p; bib.*
GIBBONS, S R *and* MORICAN, P
   World War One *(London: Longmans 1965), 144p; bib.*
GIBBS, P H
   The soul of the war *(London: Heinemann 1914), 362p.*
   The way to victory *(New York: Doran 1919), 2 vols.*
GIBSON, M
   Spotlight on the First World War *(Hove Sx: Horizon 1985), 76p.*
GIES, J
   Crisis 1918: the leading actors, strategies and events in the German gamble for total victory on the Western Front *(New York: Norton 1974), 288p.*
GOODSPEED, D J
   The German wars 1914-1945 *(Boston, Mass: Houghton Mifflin 1977), 561p.*
GREAT BRITAIN
   Committee of Imperial Defence: Historical Section History of the Great War, based on official documents, principal events, *1914-1918 (London: HMSO 1922-25), 9 vols.*
GREW, E S
   The Great War *(London: Gresham 1920), 361p.*

GRIFFITHS, W R
   The Great War *(Garden City, NY: Avery 1986), 224p.*
HALÉVY, E
   The world crisis of 1914-1918: an interpretation *(Oxford: Clarendon 1930), 57p.*
HALLAM, G H
   Notes on the war: a short history from month to month *(Sidcup, Kent: Hallam 1914-19), 395p.*
HALSEY, F W
   The Literary Digest history of the World War *(New York: Literary Digest 1919-20), 10 vols.*
HAMILTON, D E
   How the fight was won: a general sketch of the Great War *(Toronto: 1920), 85p.*
HAMMERTON, *Sir* J A
   The Great War: I was there *(London: Amalgamated 1938-39), 3 vols.*
   Popular history of the Great War *(London: Fleetway House 1934), 6 vols.*
   The war illustrated album de luxe *(London: Amalgamated 1915-17), 8 vols.*
HANSON, J M *ed*
   World War through the telebinocular *(Meadville, Pa: Keystone View 1931), 494p.*
HARDACH, G
   The First World War *(London: Lane 1977), 328p.*
HAYES, C J H
   A brief history of the Great War *(New York: Macmillan 1920), 461p.*
HAYES, G P
   World War I: a compact history *(New York: Hawthorn 1972), 338p; bib*
HENDERSON, J H
   Soldier country *(Wellington, NZ: Millwood 1978), 216p.*
HERDMAN, T
   Some geographical factors in the Great War *(London: Brown 1915), 71p.*
HIGONNET, M *and others*
   Behind the lines: gender and the two world wars *(New Haven, Conn: Yale 1987), 310p.*
HISTORY of the World War *(New York: O'Connor 1920), 800p*
HOARE, R J
   World War One: an illustrated history in colour, 1914-1918 *(London: Macdonald 1973), 64p; bib.*
HOARE, S
   Fighting in World War I *(London: Batsford 1986), 48p.*
HOBLEY, L F
   The First World War *(Glasgow: Blackie 1972), 117p; bib.*
HODGES, T O
   Short history of the Great War for young people *(London: Macmillan 1921), 223p.*
HOOBLER, D *and* HOOBLER, T
   An album of World War I *(London: Watts 1976), 96p.*
HOOPER, F H
   These eventful years *(London: Encyclopaedia Britannica 1924), 2 vols.*
HORNE, C F *and* AUSTIN, W F *eds*
   Great events of the Great War *(Indianapolis, Ind: American Legion nd), 7 vols.*

HOWLAND, C R
  Military history of the World War *(Fort Leavenworth, Kansas: General Service School 1923), 2 vols.*
JERROLD, D
  The war on land, 1914-1918 *(London: Benn 1928), 80p.*
JOHN BULL *(periodical)*
  John Bull's diary of the war *(London: John Bull 1915), 214p.*
KENNEDY, J M
  How the nations waged war *(London: Hodder & Stoughton 1914), 190p.*
KING, J C *comp*
  The First World War *(New York: Harper 1972), 350p; bib.*
KIRBY, D
  War, peace and revolution: international socialism at the crossroads 1914-1918 *(New York: St. Martin's 1986), 497p.*
KNIGHT, W S M
  History of the great European war, its causes and effects *(London: Caxton 1914-20), 10 vols.*
LE QUEUX, W
  The war of the nations: a history of the great European conflict *(London: Newnes 1914), vol 1.*
LIDDLE, P *ed.*
  Testimony of war, 1914-1918 *(Salisbury,Wilts: Russell 1979), 96p.*
LIDDELL HART, H B
  History of the World War, 1914-1918 *(London: Faber 1934), 635p.*
  The real war, 1914-1918 *(London: Faber 1930), 539p.*
  The war in outline *(London: Faber 1936), 259p.*
LIPSON, E
  Europe, 1914-1939 *(London: Black 1957), 7th ed. 494p.*
LOCK, B S
  Right against might: the Great War of 1914 *(Cambridge: CUP 1914), 43p.*
LOW, S J *ed*
  Spirit of the Allied nations *(New York: Macmillan 1915), 214p.*
LUCAS, J
  The world fight for freedom *(Glasgow: Gibson 1919), 133p.*
LYON, L
  Pomp of power *(London: Hutchinson 1922), 291p.*
MCCLELLAN, G B
  The heel of war *(New York: Dillingham 1916), 177p.*
MACDONALD, L
  1914 *(London: Joseph 1987), 446p; bib.*
MACENTEE, G
  Military history of the World War *(New York: Scribner 1937), 583p.*
MACKENZIE, D A
  The story of the Great War *(London: Blackie 1920), 288p.*
MACKINDER, *Sir* H J
  The World War and after *(London: Philip Allan 1924), 286p.*

MACPHERSON, W L
 Short history of the Great War *(New York: Putnam 1920), 410p.*
MAGNUS, L
 The third great war in relation to modern history *(Bristol: 1914), 187p.*
MANCHESTER GUARDIAN *(newspaper)*
 History of the war, 1914-15 *(Manchester: Heywood 1915), 2 vols.*
MARCH, F A
 History of the World War *(Philadelphia, Pa: Winston 1918), 736p.*
MARSHALL, L
 The story of Europe and the nations at war *(Philadelphia, Pa: International 1914), 464p.*
 World War *(Philadelphia, Pa: Winston 1915), 349p.*
MARSHALL, S A
 World War I *(New York: American Heritage 1985), 512p.*
MARTIN, E S
 The war week by week as seen from New York *(New York: Martin 1914), 217p.*
MASTERS, J
 Fourteen eighteen *(London: Joseph 1965), 176p.*
MAURICE, *Sir* F B
 Forty days in 1914 *(London: Constable 1919), 212p.*
 The last four months: the end of the war in the West *(London: Cassell 1919), 251p.*
MILLER, J M *and* CANFIELD, H S
 The people's war book: history, cyclopaedia and chronology of the Great War *(Detroit: Dickerson 1919), 520p.*
MORRISON, D
 The Great War, 1914-1918 *(Edinburgh: Oliver & Boyd 1981), 41p; bib.*
MUMBY, F A
 The Great World War: a history *(London: Gresham 1915-1920), 9 vols.*
MURRAY, A M
 The 'Fortnightly' history of the war: to July 1916 *(London: Chapman & Hall 1916), 403p.*
MUSMAN, R
 The First World War *(London: Chatto & Windus 1968), 110p; bib.*
NOWAK, C F
 The collapse of Central Europe *(London: Kegan Paul 1924), 365p.*
O'NEILL, H C
 A history of the war *(London: Jack 1920), 1064p.*
OPEN UNIVERSITY
 World War I *(Milton Keynes: Open UP 1973), 180p.*
OWEN, E
 Glory departing *(London: Buchan & Enright 1983), 288p; bib.*
PANICHAS, G A
 Promise of greatness: the war of 1914-1918 *(London: Cassell 1968), 572p.*
PARKER, *Sir* G
 The world in the crucible *(London: Murray 1915), 423p.*
PEARCE, B
 How Haig saved Lenin *(London: Macmillan 1987), 144p; bib.*
PIMLOTT, J
 The First World War *(London: Watts 1986), 62p; bib.*

PITT, B
1918: the last act *(New York: Norton 1964), 318p.*
POLLARD, A F
A short history of the Great War *(London: Methuen 1920), 411p.*
PRIOR, R
Churchill's 'World Crisis' as history *(London: Croom Helm 1983), 339p.*
REINERS, L
The lamps went out in Europe *(Toronto: McClelland 1955), 310p.*
REPINGTON, C à'C
The First World War *(London: Constable 1920), 2 vols.*
REYNOLDS, F J *and* CHURCHILL, A L *eds*
World's War events recorded by statesmen, commanders, historians and by men who fought or saw the great campaign *(New York: Collier 1919), 3 vols.*
RIBBONS, I
Tuesday 4 August 1914 *(London: OUP 1970), 80p.*
RICHARDS, I
A sketch-map history of the Great War and after, 1914-1935 *(London: Harrap 1943), 136p.*
RICKARDS, M *and* MOODY, M
The First World War: ephemera, mementos, documents *(London: Jupiter 1975), 246p.*
ROBBINS, K
The First World War *(Oxford: OUP 1984), 186p; bib.*
ROBERTSON, *Sir* W
Soldiers and statesmen, 1914-1918 *(London: Cassell 1926), 2 vols.*
ROLT-WHEELER, F W *and* DRINKER, F E *eds*
World War for liberty: a comprehensive and authentic history of the war by land, sea and air *(New York: National 1919), 551p.*
ROTH, J J
World War I: a turning point in modern history *(New York: Knopf 1967), 137p.*
ROWE, J G
A popular history of the Great War *(London: Sharp 1919), 656p.*
SAGE, W N *and* RUSH, E E
World War for democracy: a complete history giving an account of the cause and events of the World War *(Kansas, Mo: McIndoo 1919), 283p.*
SANDERSON, J D
Behind enemy lines *(London: Van Nostrand 1959), 327p.*
SCHMITT, B E *and* VEDELER, H C
The world in the crucible 1914-1919 *(New York: Harper 1984), 553p.*
SCHOONMAKER, E D
World storm and beyond *(New York: Century 1915), 294p.*
SEDGEWICK, F R
The Great War in 1914: a sketch of the operations in Europe and Asia *(London: Forster, Groom 1921), 186p.*
SHEIP, S S
Handbook of the European war *(New York: H. W. Wilson 1914), 334p.*
SHERMER, D R
World War I *(London: Octopus 1973), 256p.*

SILVERMAN,D P
  Reconstructing Europe after the Great War *(Cambridge, Mass: Harvard 1982), 347p.*
SIMONDS, F H
  History of the World War *(New York: Doubleday 1917-1920), 5 vols.*
SNYDER, L L
  Historic documents of World War I *(Princeton, NJ: Van Nostrand 1958), 191p.*
SOUZA, C *and* MACFALL, C H C
  Germany in defeat: a strategic history of the war *(London: Kegan Paul 1915-19), 4 vols.*
SPEARS, E L
  Liaison, 1914 *(London: Heinemann 1931), 597p.*
STOKESBURY, J L
  A short history of World War I *(New York: Morrow 1981), 348p.*
SYNGE, M B
  The story of the world at war *(Edinburgh: Blackwood 1926), 219p.*
TAYLOR, A A
  The First World War *(London: LUTP 1972), 71p.*
TAYLOR, A J P
  The First World War: an illustrated history *(London: Hamilton 1963), 224p.*
  The struggle for mastery in Europe, 1848-1918 *(Oxford: Clarendon 1954), 638p.*
TERRAINE, J
  The Great War, 1914-1918: a pictorial history *(London: Hutchinson 1965), 400p.*
  To win a war: 1918 the year of victory *(London: Sidgwick & Jackson 1978), 284p.*
THOMAS, *Sir* W B
  Events of the Great War *(London: Routledge 1930), 78p.*
THOMSON, C B
  Old Europe's suicide: an account of certain events during the period 1912-1919
  (Manchester: 1920), 188p.
TILLEY, E H
  The loud echo of thunder *(New York: Pageant 1969), 159p.*
THE TIMES *(London newspaper)*
  Documentary history of the war: military, naval, diplomatic *(London: The Times 1917-20), 2 vols.*
  The Times history of the war *(London: The Times 1914-20), 22 vols.*
THOUMIN, R *comp*
  The First World War *(London: Secker & Warburg 1963), 544p; bib.*
TOLAND, J W
  No man's land: the last year of the Great War *(New York: Doubleday 1980), 651p;bib.*
TREVELYAN, G M
  The war and European revolution in relation to history *(London: University of London P 1920), 48p.*
TUOHY, F
  The crater of Mars *(London: Heinemann 1929), 325p.*
ULANOFF, S M
  Illustrated history of World War I in the air *(New York: Arco 1971), 171p.*
USHER, R G
  The story of the Great War *(New York: Macmillan 1919), 350p.*

VAN ZILE, E S
A game of empires: a warning to America *(New York: Moffat 1915), 302p.*

VAST, H
A little history of the Great War *(New York: Holt 1920), 262p.*

VERROY,C
The European War *(New York: Rich 1915), 48p.*

VIERECK, G S
As they saw us: Foch, Ludendorff and other leaders write our war history *(New York: Doubleday 1929), 379p.*

WALLACE, E
Standard history of the war, comprising the official despatches from General French *(London: Newnes 1914-15), 4 vols.*

WEINTRAUB, S
A stillness heard round the world: the end of the Great War, November 1918 *(New York: Dutton 1985), 467p.*

WELLS, H G
The war of the future: Italy, France and Britain at war *(London: Cassell 1917), 297p.*

WERSTEIN, I
The many faces of World War I *(New York: Messner 1963), 191p.*

WHITE, J W
Text-book of the war for Americans *(Philadelphia, Pa: Winston 1915), 551p.*

WHY Germany capitulated on November 11, 1918: a brief study *(London: Hodder & Stoughton 1919), 68p.*

WILKINSON, S
August 1914 *(London: Milford 1914), 90p.*

WILLIAMS, A F B
The campaigns of 1917 *(London: HMSO 1918), 96p.*

WILLIAMS, J
The Home Fronts: Britain, France and Germany, 1914-1918 *(London: Constable 1972), 326p; bib.*

WILSON, H W *and* HAMMERTON, J A *eds*
The Great War: the standard history of the world wide conflict *(New York: H. W. Wilson 1914-19), 13 vols.*

WILSON, P W
The unmaking of Europe: the first phase of the Hohenzollern war *(London: Nisbet 1915), 332p.*

WILSON, T
The myriad faces of war: Britain and the Great War, 1914-1918 *(Cambridge: Polity 1985), 762p.*

WINGFIELD-STRATFORD, E C
The harvest of victory, 1918-1926 *(London: Routledge 1935), 472p.*

WINTER, D
Deaths men: soldiers of the Great War *(London: Penguin 1985), 283p*

WOHL, R
The generation of 1914 *(Cambridge, Mass: Harvard 1979), 307p.*

WOOD, L *and others eds*
The history of the First World War *(New York: Grolier 1965), 4 vols.*

WYNNE, C W
    If Germany attacks *(London: Faber 1940), 343p.*
WYRALL, E
    Europe in arms: a concise history *(London: Wright 1915), 3 vols.*

HOLLAND [see NETHERLANDS]

HOSPITALS

ANDERSON, I W
    Zigzagging *(Boston, Mass: Houghton Mifflin 1918), 269p.*
BAGNOLD, E
    Diary without dates *(New York: Luce 1918), 145p.*
BLACK, E W
    Hospital heroes *(New York: Scribner 1919), 223p.*
BRADFORD, M
    A hospital letter writer in France *(London: Methuen 1920), 108p.*
BRUCE, C
    Humour in tragedy: hospital life behind three Fronts *(London: Skeffington 1918), 66p.*
CATOR, D
    In a French military hospital *(London: Longmans 1915), 99p.*
CLYMER, G *ed*
    History of United States Army Base Hospital No. 6, and its part in the American
    Expeditionary Forces, 1917-1918 *(Boston, Mass: Clymer 1924), 263p.*
DAVIES, E C
    Ward tales *(London: Lane 1920), 211p.*
DUHAMEL, G
    The new book of martyrs *(London: Heinemann 1918), 215p.*
EYDOUX-DEMAINS, M
    In a French hospital *(London: Fisher Unwin 1915), 170p.*
FENN C R
    Middlesex to wit: being a brief record of the work performed at the Auxiliary Military
    Hospitals in Middlesex during the war, 1914-1918 *(London: St. Catherine 1919), 46p.*
GEISINGER, J F
    History of the U.S. Army Base Hospital No. 45 in the Great War *(Richmond, Va: Levy
    1924), 464p.*
GRAY, T
    Hospital days in Rouen *(London: Gowans & Gray 1919), 96p.*
HAPPY – though wounded: the book of the 3rd London Hospital *(London: Country Life
    1917), 141p.*
HUTTON, I E
    With a woman's unit in Serbia, Salonika and Sebastopol *(London: Williams & Norgate
    1928), 302p.*
LA MOTTE, E N
    Backwash of war *(New York: Putnam 1934), 204p.*

LETTERS from a French hospital *(London: Constable 1917), 96p.*
LEWIS, T E
    Twelve months in an Army Hospital *(Washington DC: Gruver 1921), 227p.*
LORD, J R
    The story of the war hospital, Epsom *(London: Heinemann 1920), 264p.*
MALCOLM, I Z
    War pictures behind the lines *(New York: Dutton 1915), 226p.*
MILLS, A H
    Hospital days *(London: Fisher Unwin 1916), 187p.*
MOON, E R P
    Four weeks as acting Commandant at the Belgian Field Hospital *(London: Humphreys 1915), 78p.*
MUIR, W
    The happy hospital *(London: Simpkin Marshall 1918), 155p.*
    Observations of an orderly in an English war hospital *(London: Simpkin Marshall 1917), 249p.*
NAVAROO, A de
    The Scottish women's hospital at the French Abbey of Royaumont *(London: Allen & Unwin 1917), 223p.*
O'BRIAN, A L
    No glory: letters from France, 1917-1919 *(Buffalo, NY: Airport 1936), 184p.*
PLATOON COMMANDER *pseud*
    Hospital days *(London: Unwin 1916), 188p.*
POOTLE, F A
    Stretchers: the story of a hospital unit on the Western Front *(London: OUP 1930), 366p.*
RECKITT, H J
    V.R.76: a French military hospital *(London: Heinemann 1921), 292p.*
SERGEANT, E S
    Shadow-shapes: the journal of a wounded woman, October 1918-May 1919 *(Boston, Mass: Houghton Mifflin 1920), 236p.*
SMITH, L N
    Four years out of life *(London: Allan 1931), 302p.*
SPEAKMAN, M A V
    Memories: experiences of American hospital service in France *(Wilmington, Del: 1937), 191p.*
STIMSON, J C
    Finding themselves: the letters of an American Army Chief Nurse in a British Hospital in France *(New York: Macmillan 1918), 231p.*
THURSTON, V
    Field hospital and flying column *(London: Putnam 1915), 183p.*
THE WARDS in war time *(London: Blackwood 1916), 343p.*
WAR nurse's diary: sketches from a Belgian field hospital *(New York: Macmillan 1918), 115p.*
WIGHT, O B *ed*
    On active service with Base Hospital U.S. Army, March 20, 1918, to May 25, 1919 *(Portland, Ore: Arcady 1919), 191p.*
[See also MEDICAL, NURSES]

HOSPITAL SHIPS

FIFTY thousand miles on a hospital ship *(London: RTS 1917), 284p.*
FLEMING, J A
   The last voyage of H.M. Hospital Ship 'Britannic' *(London: Simpkin Marshall 1917), 43p.*
PLUMRIDGE, J H
   Hospital ships and ambulance trains *(London: Seeley Service 1975), 203p.*

HOUSE, COLONEL

FLOTO, I
   Colonel House in Paris *(Aarhus, Denmark: Universitets, 1973), unp.*
GRANT, A *pseud*
   The real Colonel House *(New York: Doran 1918), 306p.*
HOUSE, E M
   The intimate papers of Colonel House *(Boston, Mass: Houghton Mifflin 1926), 2 vols.*
VIERECK, G S
   The strangest friendship in history: Woodrow Wilson and Colonel House *(London: Duckworth 1932), 375p.*

HUNGARY

APPONYI, A *count and others*
   Justice for Hungary: review and criticism of the effect of the Treaty of Trianon *(London: Longmans 1928), 376p.*
BANDHOLTZ, H H
   An undiplomatic diary *(New York: Columbia UP 1933), 394p.*
BIRINYI, L K
   The tragedy of Hungary *(Cleveland: Birinyi 1924), 340p.*
DEAK, F
   The Hungarian-Rumanian land dispute: a study of the Hungarian property rights in Transylvania under the Treaty of Trianon *(New York: 1928), 272p.*
DEMPSEY, J J *and* JOY, W L
   Storms over the Danube: adventures in Central Europe in war and revolution *(London: Selwyn & Blount 1938), 288p.*
DONALD, *Sir* R
   The tragedy of Trianon: Hungary's appeal to humanity *(London: Butterworth 1928), 348p.*
HORVATH, J
   Responsibility of Hungary for the war *(Budapest: Hungarian Frontier Readjustment League 1933), 98p.*
KAROLYI, M *count*
   Fighting the world: the struggle for peace *(London: Kegan Paul 1924), 464p.*

MACDONALD, M
Some experiences in Hungary, Aug. 1914 to Jan. 1915 *(London: Longmans 1916), 135p.*
MOCSY, I J
The effects of World War I: the uprooted Hungarian refugees *(New York: Brooklyn College 1983), 252p.*
SETON WATSON, R W
Treaty revision and the Hungarian frontiers *(London: Eyre & Spottiswoode 1934), 75p.*
VOLK, K M
Buddies in Budapest *(Los Angeles, Cal: Kellaway-Ide-Jones 1936), 253p.*
[See also AUSTRIA, TRIANON]

INDIA

INDIA and the war *(London: Hodder & Stoughton 1915), 77p.*
INDIA's services in the war *(Lucknow: 1922), 5 vols.*
LEIGH, M S
The Punjab and the war *(Lahore: 1922), 285p.*
PRASAD, Y D
The Indian Muslims and World War I: a phase of disillusionment with British Rule 1914-1918 *(Patna: India Janaki Prakasham 1985), 202p.*
SAMS, H A
The Post Office of India in the war *(Bombay: 1922), 430p.*
SYDENHAM, G *1st baron*
India and the war *(London: Hodder & Stoughton 1915), 90p.*
VENKATA-NARASAYYA, T K
The war and the British Raj *(Madras: 1915), 100p.*

INDIAN ARMY

ALEXANDER, H M
On two fronts: adventures of an Indian Mule Corps in France and Gallipoli *(London: Heinemann 1917), 248p.*
BIBIKOFF, M
Our Indians at Marseilles *(London: Smith, Elder 1915), 172p.*
GRIMSHAW, R
Indian cavalry officer 1914-15 *(Northport, N Y: Costello 1986), 223p.*
HARPER, R W E
Singapore mutiny *(Singapore: OUP 1984), 254p; bib.*
MEREWETHER, J W B *and* SMITH, Sir F
The Indian Corps in France *(London: Murray 1918), 550p.*
SINGH, S N
The King's Indian Allies: The Rajahs and their India *(London: Sampson Low 1916), 320p.*
WILLCOCKS, Sir J
With the Indians in France *(London: Constable 1920), 406p.*

INDUSTRY

BAKER, C W
Government control and operation of industry in Great Britain and the United States during the World War *(London: Milford 1921), 138p.*

BING, A M
War-time strikes and their adjustment *(New York: Dutton 1921), 329p.*

BOWLEY, A L
The effect of the war on the external trade of the United Kingdom *(Cambridge: CUP 1915), 55p.*

CARTER, H *ed*
Industrial reconstruction *(New York: Dutton 1918), 295p.*

CLARKSON, G B
Industrial America in the World War: the strategy behind the line, 1917-1918 *(Boston, Mass: Houghton Mifflin 1923), 138p.*

COLE, G D H
Labour in the coal-mining industry *(Oxford: Clarendon 1923), 274p.*
Workshop organization *(Oxford: Clarendon 1923), 186p.*

FONTAINE, A
French industry during the war *(New Haven, Conn: Yale UP 1926), 477p.*

GRAY, H L
War time control of industry: the experience of England *(New York: Macmillan 1918), 307p.*

HAMMOND, M B
British labor conditions and legislation during the war *(New York: OUP 1919), 335p.*

HATCH, F H
The iron and steel industry of the United Kingdom under war conditions *(London: Harrison 1920), 167p.*

HENDERSON, H D
The Cotton Control Board *(Oxford: Clarendon 1922), 74p.*

KELLER, C
The power situation during the war *(Washington DC: Engineer Dept. 1921), 300p.*

LANGNER, L *and* WHITE, W W
Basic patent and trade-mark laws of the principal belligerent powers, together with war legislation, ordnances and edicts since August 1, 1914 to January 1, 1919, affecting patents, trade marks and designs *(Washington DC: 1919), 475p.*

LESCABOURA, A C *and* BIRD, J M
The inventive and industrial triumphs of the war *(New York: Harper 1920), 399p.*

PEDDIE, J T
British industry and the war *(London: Longmans 1914), 102p.*

POYNTER, A
The coming war *(London: Murray 1916), 180p.*

UNITED STATES Bureau of Labor Statistics
British industrial experience during the war *(Washington DC: 1918), 2 vols.*

UNITED STATES Department of War
A report on the activities of the War Department in the field of industrial relations during the war *(Washington DC: 1919), 90p.*

UNITED STATES National War Labor Board
 National War Labor Board: a history of its formation and activities, together with its awards *(Washington DC: 1922), 234p.*
WARNE, F J
 The workers at war *(New York: Century New World 1920), 250p.*
WATKINS, G S
 Labor problems and labor administration in the United States during the war *(Urbana, Ill: University of Illinois P 1920), 2 vols.*
WOLFE, H
 Labour supply and regulation *(Oxford: Clarendon 1923), 422p.*
ZAGORSKY, S O
 State control of industry in Russia during the war *(New Haven, Conn: Yale UP 1928), 351p.*

INSURANCE

GEPHART, W F
 Effects of the war upon insurance *(New York: OUP 1918), 302p.*

INTELLIGENCE

BEESLY, P
 Room 40: British naval intelligence 1914-18 *(London: Hamilton 1982), 320p.*

INTERNATIONAL LAW

ANGELL, N
 The world's highway: on the so-called freedom of the seas *(New York: Doran 1916), 361p.*
BATY, T *and* MORGAN, J H
 War: its conduct and legal results *(London: Murray 1915), 606p.*
CABABE, M
 The freedom of the seas *(London: Murray 1918), 159p.*
DAMPIERRE, J *de marquis*
 German imperialism and international law *(London: Constable 1916), 285p.*
DIPLOMATIC correspondence between the United States and belligerent Governments relating to neutral rights and commerce *(New York: American Journal of Int. Law, 1915), vol. 9, 405p.*
EGERTON, W A
 Contraband of war *(Portsmouth: Gieve 1915), 57p.*
FRANCE Ministry of Foreign Affairs
 Germany's violations of the laws of war, 1914-15 *(London: Heinemann 1915), 379p.*
GANTENBEIN. J W
 The doctrine of continuous voyage *(Portland, Ore: 1929), 207p.*

GARNER, J W
  International law and the Great War *(London: Longmans 1920), 2 vols.*
  Prize law during the World War *(New York: Macmillan 1917), 712p.*
GRAHAM, M W
  The controversy between the United States and the Allied Governments respecting neutral rights and commerce during the period of American neutrality 1914-17 *(Austin: University of Texas P 1923), 192p.*
GRIERSON, F D
  The ABC of military law *(London: Fisher Unwin 1916), 96p.*
GROTIUS, H
  The freedom of the seas *(London: OUP 1917), 179p.*
HALL, J A
  The law of naval warfare *(London: Chapman & Hall 1914), 176p.*
HIGGINS, A P
  Armed merchant ships *(London: Stevens 1914), unp.*
  Defensively-armed merchant ships and submarine warfare *(London: Stevens 1917), 56p.*
MORRISSEY, A M
  The American defense of neutral rights, 1914-1917 *(Cambridge, Mass: Harvard UP 1939), 230p.*
PHILLIPSON, C
  International law and the Great War *(London: Fisher Unwin 1915), 407p.*
PIGGOTT, *Sir* F
  The neutral merchant in relation to the law of contraband of war and blockade *(London: London UP 1915), 128p.*
PYKE, H R
  Law of contraband of war *(London: OUP 1915), 354p.*
RENAULT, L
  First violations of International law by Germany: Luxembourg and Belgium *(London: Longmans 1917), 87p.*
[See also WAR CRIMES]

INTERNMENT

MAHONEY, H C
  Interned in Germany *(New York: McBride 1918), 390p.*

IRELAND

BOYLE, J F
  The Irish Rebellion of 1916: a brief history of the revolt and its suppression *(London: Constable 1916), 298p.*
CARTER, B R
  Another part of the platform *(Boston, Mass: Houghton Mifflin 1931), 237p.*
ESCOUFLAIRE, R C
  Ireland an enemy of the Allies? *(London: Murray 1919), 268p.*

HAMILTON, E W *baron*
   The soul of Ulster *(London: Hurst & Blackett 1917), 200p.*
LAW, H A
   Why is Ireland at war? *(Dublin: Maunsel 1915), 42p.*
MCCARTHY, D E
   The Irish in the Great War *(New York: American Irish Historical Society 1931), 102p.*
MCGUIRE, J K
   The King, the Kaiser and Irish freedom *(New York: Devin-Adair 1915), 313p.*
   What would Germany do for Ireland? *(New York: Wolfe 1916),309p.*
MCKENZIE, F A
   The Irish Rebellion: what happened and why *(London: Pearson 1916), 112p.*
NORWAY, *Mrs* H
   The Sinn Fein rebellion as I saw it *(London: Smith, Elder 1916), 111p.*
PHILLIPS, W A
   The revolution in Ireland, 1906-1923 *(London: Longmans 1923), 343p.*
REDMOND-HOWARD, L G
   Six days of the Irish Republic *(Dublin: Maunsel l 1916), 139p.*
STEPHENS, J
   The insurrection in Dublin: a diary *(Dublin: Maunsel 1916), 125p.*
WELLS, W B *and* MARLOWE, N
   A history of the Irish Rebellion of 1916 *(Dublin: Maunsel 1917), 279p.*

ISLE OF MAN

BLACKBURN, C J
   How the Manx fleet helped in the Great War *(Douglas, I.O.M.: 1923), 61p.*
SARGEAUNT, B E
   The Isle of Man and the Great War *(Douglas, L O.M.: 1922), 214p.*

ITALY

BAUNVILLE, J
   Italy and the war *(London: Hodder & Stoughton 1916), 267p.*
CATELLANI, E L
   Italy and Austria at war *(Florence: 1918), 155p.*
COLLINS, J
   Italy re-visited, 1917-1918 *(London: Fisher Unwin 1919), 306p.*
DILLON, E J von
   From the Triple to the Quadruple Alliance: why Italy went to war *(London: Hodder & Stoughton 1915), 242p.*
DOUGLAS, G N
   Alone: travels in Italy during the war of 1914-19 *(London: Chapman & Hall 1921),280p.*
EDELSTON, R H
   Italian neutrality *(London: CUP 1915), 72p.*

FERRERO, G
  Europe's fateful hour *(New York: Dodd 1918), 243p.*
GAY, H N
  Italy's great war, and her national aspirations *(Milan: 1917), 267p.*
GUARD, W J
  The spirit of Italy *(New York: Rogowski 1916), 268p.*
HALES, A G
  Where angels fear to tread: sketches of Italy during the European war *(London: Hodder & Stoughton 1918), 314p.*
THE ITALIAN Green Book: diplomatic documents *(London: Hodder & Stoughton 1915), 96p.*
ITALY and the war *(London: Bell 1917), 268p.*
LE QUEUX, W
  Devil's spawn: how Italy will defeat them *(New York: Brentano 1915), 187p.*
LOW, S J M
  Italy in the war *(London: Longmans 1916), 316p.*
MACCLURE, W K
  Italy's part in the war *(Florence: 1918), 106p.*
MACENTEE, G L
  Italy's part in winning the World War *(Princeton, NJ: Princeton UP 1934), 114p.*
ORLANDO, V E
  War speeches *(Rome: 1919), 322p.*
PAGE, T N
  Italy and the World War *(London: Chapman & Hall 1921), 422p.*
PITT, W O
  Italy and the unholy alliance *(London: Melrose 1915), 223p.*
SALANDRA, A
  Italy and the Great War: from neutrality to intervention *(London: Arnold 1932), 382p.*
SPERANZA, G C
  Diary: Italy 1915-1919 *(New York: Columbia UP 1941), 2 vols.*
THOMPSON, B
  Four months in Italy in wartime *(London: Lane 1920), 111p.*
VIVIAN, H
  Italy at war *(London: Dent 1917), 370p.*
WALLACE, W K
  Greater Italy *(London: Constable 1917), 322p.*
WANNAMAKER, O D
  With Italy in her final war of liberation *(New York: Revell 1923), 294p.*
WOODHOUSE, E J *and* WOODHOUSE, C G
  Italy and the Jugoslavs *(Boston, Mass: Badger 1920), 394p; bib.*
ZIMMERN, H
  Italian leaders of today *(London: Williams & Norgate 1915), 336p.*

ITALY (Italian Army)

ANGELI, D
  Sword and plough *(London: Constable 1918), 157p.*
DESTRÉE, J *and* DUPIERREUX, R
  To the Italian Armies *(London: Fisher Unwin 1917), 87p.*
IRWIN, W
  The Latin at war *(London: Constable 1917), 330p.*
ITALY Army Commando Supremo
  The battle of the Piave, June 15-23, 1918 *(London: Hodder & Stoughton 1921), 82p.*
LUSSU, E
  Sardinian Brigade *(New York: Grove 1970), 274p.*
STEEGE, K R
  We of Italy: letters of Italian soldiers *(London: Dent 1917), 278p.*

ITALY (Italian Front)

ALLEN, W
  Our Italian Front *(London: Black 1920), 203p.*
DALTON, H
  With British guns in Italy *(London: Methuen 1919), 267p.*
EDMONDS, *Sir* J E *and* DAVIES, H R
  Military operations: Italy 1915-1919 *(London: HMSO 1949), 450p.*
GLADDEN, E N
  Across the Piave: a personal account of the British Forces in Italy, 1917-1919 *(London: HMSO 1971), 220p.*
GOLDSMID, C H
  Diary of a liaison officer in Italy *(London: Williams & Norgate 1920), 178p.*
HARDIE, M
  Our Italian Front *(New York: Macmillan 1920), 203p.*
POWELL, E A
  With the Italians *(London: Heinemann 1917), 239p.*
PRICE, J M
  Six months on the Italian Front, 1915-1916 *(London: Chapman & Hall 1917), 300p.*
TREVELYAN, G M
  Scenes from the Italian war *(London: Nelson 1919), 255p.*
VILLARI, L
  The war on the Italian Front *(London: Cobden-Sanderson 1932), 308p.*

ITALY (Italian Navy)

HURD, A S
  Italian sea-power and the Great War *(London: Constable 1918), 124p.*

JAPAN

KOBAYASHI, U
The basic industries and social history of Japan, 1914-1918 *(New Haven, Conn: Yale UP 1930), 280p.*
MCCORMICK, F
The menace of Japan to America *(Boston, Mass: Little, Brown 1917), 372p.*
POOLEY, A M
Japan at the cross roads *(London: Allen & Unwin 1917), 362p.*
SUNDERLAND, J T
Rising Japan: is she a menace or a comrade? *(London: Putnam 1918), 231p.*
UNITED STATES Tariff Commission
Japan: trade during the war *(Washington DC: 1919), 147p.*

JELLICOE

APPLIN, A
Admiral Jellicoe *(London: Pearson 1915), 112p.*
JELLICOE, J R *1st earl*
The crisis of the naval war *(London: Cassell 1920), 331p.*
The Jellicoe papers: selections from the private and official correspondence of Admiral of the Fleet Earl Jellicoe of Scapa *(Shortlands, Hants: Navy Records Society 1966), 1 vol.*
MOORE, H C
Under Jellicoe's command *(London: Collins 1916), 224p.*
PATTERSON, A T
Jellicoe: a biography *(London: Macmillan 1969), 272p.*
[See also JUTLAND, ROYAL NAVY]

JEWS

ADLER, M
Prayer book for Jewish sailors and soldiers *(London: Eyre & Spottiswoode 1915), 73p.*
FREULICH, R
Soldiers in Judea: stories and vignettes of the Jewish Legion *(New York: Herzi 1965), 216p.*
LEVINGER, L J
A Jewish chaplain in France *(New York: Macmillan 1921), 220p.*
LEVISON, L
The Jewish problem and the World War *(London: Morgan & Scott 1916), 68p.*
LONDON Committee of Deputies of the British Jews
The Peace Conference, Paris 1919: report of the delegation of the Jews of the British Empire on the Treaties of Versailles, Saint Germain-en-Laye and Neuilly *(London: 1920), 115p.*
NEW YORK American Jewish Committee
The Jews in the Eastern war zone *(New York: 1916), 120p.*

RAVAGE, M E
  The jew pays: a narrative of the consequences of the war to the Jews of Eastern Europe *(New York: Knopf 1919), 152p.*
ROHOLD, S B
  The war and the Jew *(Toronto: 1915), 98p.*
SZAJKOWSKI, Z
  The attitude of American Jews to World War I, the Russian Revolution of 1917, and Communism *(New York: Ktav 1972), 714p.*
ZHABOTINSKY, V E
  The story of the Jewish Legion *(New York: Ackermann 1945), 191p.*

JOFFRE

DAWBARN, C
  Joffre and his army *(London: Mills & Boon 1916), 233p.*
FRENCH GUNNER *pseud*
  General Joffre *(London: Simpkin, Marshall 1915), 64p.*
JOFFRE, J J C
  Memoirs *(London: Bles 1932), 2 vols.*
KAHN, A
  Life of General Joffre: the cooper's son who became Commander-in-Chief *(London: Heinemann 1915), 123p.*

JUTLAND

ALEXANDER, A C B
  Jutland: a plea for a Naval General Staff *(London: Rees 1923), 63p.*
BACON, *Sir* R H S
  The jutland scandal *(London: Hutchinson 1924), 159p.*
BELLAIRS, C W
  The battle of Jutland *(London: Hodder & Stoughton 1920). 312p.*
BENNETT,G
  The battle of Jutland *(London: Batsford 1964), 208p; bib.*
BUCHAN, J
  The battle of Jutland *(London: Nelson 1917), 44p.*
COSTELLO, J *and* HUGHES, T
  Jutland, 1916 *(London: Weidenfeld & Nicolson 1976), 240p; bib.*
FAWCETT, H W *and* HOOPER, G W
  The fighting at Jutland *(London: Hutchinson 1929), 255p.*
FROST, H H
  The battle of Jutland *(Annapolis: (U.S. Naval Institute 1936), 571p.*
FROTHERINGHAM, T G
  A true account of the battle of Jutland *(Cambridge, Mass: Bacon & Brown 1920), 62p.*
GIBSON, L *and* HARPER, J E T
  The riddle of Jutland *(London: Cassell 1934), 416p.*

GILL, C C
   What happened at Jutland *(New York: Doran 1921), 187p.*
GREAT BRITAIN Admiralty
   Narrative of the battle of Jutland *(London: HMSO 1924), 121p.*
HARPER, J E T
   The truth about Jutland *(London: Murray 1917), 200p.*
HASE, G von
   Kiel and Jutland *(London: Skeffington 1927), 128p.*
HOUGH, R
   The battle of Jutland *(London: Hamilton 1964), 64p.*
IRVING, J
   The smoke screen of Jutland *(London: Kimber 1966), 256p.*
JELLICOE, J R *1st earl*
   The battle of Jutland Bank, May 31 – June 1, 1916: the despatches of Admiral Sir John
   Jellicoe and Vice-Admiral Sir David Beatty *(London: Milford 1916), 100p.*
LEGG, S *comp*
   Jutland: an eye-witness account of a great battle *(London: Hart-Davis 1966), 152p; bib.*
MACINTYRE, D
   Jutland *(London: Evans 1957), 210p.*
MALDEN, R H
   The battle of Jutland, May 31, 1916 *(Leeds: Jackson 1918), 47p.*
OAKESHOTT, E
   The blindfold game: 'The Day' at Jutland *(Oxford: Pergamon 1969), 128p.*
POLLEN, A
   The great gunnery scandal: the mystery of Jutland *(London: Collins 1980), 280p.*
TERRY, C S *ed*
   The battle of Jutland Bank, May 31-June 1, 1916 *(London: OUP 1916), 100p.*
WALLACE, C
   From jungle to Jutland *(London: Nisbet 1932), 343p.*
WYLLIE, W L
   More sea fights of the Great War including the Battle of Jutland *(London: Cassell 1919),
   171p.*
[See also JELLICOE, ROYAL NAVY]

KAISER WILHELM II

ADAM, *Mme* J
   The schemes of the Kaiser *(London: Heinemann 1917), 226p.*
BALFOUR, M
   The Kaiser and his times *(London: Cresset 1964), 524p.*
BAUMONT, M
   The fall of the Kaiser *(London: Allen & Unwin 1931), 256p.*
CATLING, A H
   The Kaiser under the searchlight *(London: Fisher Unwin 1914), 138p.*
DAVIS, A N
   The Kaiser as I know him *(New York: Harper 1918), 301p. U.K. title:* The Kaiser I knew.

HILL, D J
Impression of the Kaiser *(London: Chapman & Hall 1918)*, 288p.
KAUTSKY, C
The guilt of William Hohenzollern *(London: Skeffington 1920)*, 272p.
KURENBURG, J von
The Kaiser: a life of Wilhelm II, last Emperor of Germany *(London: Cassell 1954)*, 370p.
THE LAST of the War Lords *(London: Grant Richards 1918)*, 293p.
LEGGE, E
The public and private life of Kaiser Wilhelm II *(London: Nash 1915)*, 226p.
LE QUEUX, W
The secret shame of the Kaiser: his dastardly plots at Amerongen *(London: Hurst & Blackett 1919)*, 187p.
LUDWIG, E
Wilhelm Hohenzollern *(New York: Putnam 1926)*, 495p.
MIDDLEBROOK, M
The Kaiser's battle: the first day of the German Spring Offensive *(London: Lane 1983)*, 433p.
PALMER, A
The War Lord of the First Reich *(London: Weidenfeld & Nicolson 1978)*, 276p; bib.
TOPHAM, A
Memories of the Kaiser's Court *(New York: Dodd 1914)*, unp.
WHITE, A
Is the Kaiser insane?: a study of the great outlaw *(London: Pearson 1915)*, 169p.
WILLIAM II *emperor of Germany*
Letters to the Tsar *(London: Hodder & Stoughton 1920)*, 300p.
My memoirs *(London: Cassell 1922)*, 348p.
WILSON, L
The incredible Kaiser: a portrait of William II *(London: Hale 1963)*, 196p.

KITCHENER

ARTHUR, *Sir* G C A
The life of Lord Kitchener *(London: Macmillan 1920)*, 3 vols.
CASSAR, G H
Kitchener, architect of victory *(London: Kimber 1977)*, 573p; bib.
DAVRAY, H D
Lord Kitchener *(London: Fisher Unwin 1917)*, 96p.
ESHER, R *viscount*
The tragedy of Lord Kitchener *(London: Murray 1921)*, 235p.
GERMAINS, V W
The truth about Kitchener *(London: Lane 1925)*, 344p.
GREW, E S *and others*
Field Marshal Lord Kitchener: his life and work for the Empire *(London: Gresham 1916)*, 3 vols.
JERROLD, W
Earl Kitchener of Khartoum *(London: Hammond 1915)*, 250p.

LE BAS, *Sir* H *ed*
  The Lord Kitchener memorial book *(London: Hodder & Stoughton 1917), unp.*
MCCORMICK, D
  The mystery of Lord Kitchener's death *(London: Putnam 1959), 223p; bib.*
MAGNUS, P
  Kitchener: portrait of an Imperialist *(London: Murray 1958), 410p.*
MENPES, M
  Lord Kitchener *(London: Black 1915), 64p.*
PHILLIPS, W C
  The loss of HMS 'Hampshire' and the death of Lord Kitchener *(Tunbridge Wells, Kent: Hepworth 1930), 56p.*
PROTHEROE, E
  Lord Kitchener *(London: Kelly 1916), 336p.*
RYE, J B *and* GROSNER, H G
  Kitchener in his own words *(London: Fisher Unwin 1917), 588p.*

KUT

BARBER, C H
  Besieged in Kut and after *(London: Blackwood 1917), 344p.*
BARKER, A J
  Townshend of Kut *(London: Cassell 1967), 265p; bib.*
BISHOP, H C W
  A Kut prisoner *(London: Lane 1920), 243p.*
BRADDON, R
  The siege *(London: Cape 1969), 352p; bib.*
KEELING, E H
  Adventures in Turkey and Russia *(London: Murray 1924), 250p.*
LONG, P W
  Other ranks of Kut *(London: Williams & Norgate 1938), 379p.*
MILLAR, R
  Kut: the death of an Army *(London: Secker & Warburg 1969), 323p; bib.*
MOUSLEY, E O
  The secrets of a Kuttite: an authentic story of Kut, adventures in captivity and Stamboul intrigue *(London: Lane 1921), 392p.*
NEAVE, D L
  Remembering Kut *(London: Barker 1937), 321p.*
SANDES, E W C
  In Kut and captivity with the Sixth Indian Division *(London: Murray 1919), 496p.*
SHERSON, E
  Townshend of Chitral and Kut: based on his diaries and private papers *(London: Heinemann 1928), 411p.*

LANGUAGE

BROPHY, J *and* PARTRIDGE, E
The long trail: what the British soldier sang and said in the Great War, 1914-1918 *(London: Deutsch 1965), 239p; previously published as:* Songs and slang of the British soldier.
FRASER, E *and* GIBBONS, J *comps*
Soldier and sailor words and phrases *(Detroit: Gale 1958), 372p.*
SMITH, C A
New words self-defined *(New York: Doubleday 1919), 215p.*

LATIN AMERICA

KIRKPATRICK, F A
South America and the war *(New York: Putnam 1919), 79p.*
MARTIN, P A
Latin America and the war *(Baltimore: 1925), 582p.*

LAW

ARMSTRONG, J W S
War and treaty legislation, 1914-1922, affecting British property in Germany and Austria *(London: Hutchinson 1922), 594p.*
CAMPBELL, H
The law of war and contract including the present war decisions at home and abroad *(New York: OUP 1918), 365p.*
CHARTRES, J S
Judicial interpretations of the Munitions of War Acts *(London: Stevens 1917), 76p.*
The Munitions of War Acts 1915 and 1916 *(London: Stevens 1916), 123p.*
COSTELLO, L W J *and* O'SULLIVAN, R
The Profiteering Act 1919 *(London: Stevens 1919), 75p.*
NATHAN, M
The influence of war on contracts and other liabilities *(London: Sweet & Maxwell 1916), 130p.*
PAGE, A
War and alien enemies *(London: Stevens 1915), 223p.*
RUSSELL, B A W *3rd earl*
Justice in war time *(New York: Haskell 1974), 2nd ed. 229p.*
[See also INTERNATIONAL LAW]

LAWRENCE OF ARABIA

ALDINGTON, R
Lawrence of Arabia: a biographical inquiry *(London: Collins 1969), 504p.*

BRENT, P
T. E. Lawrence *(London: Weidenfeld & Nicolson 1975), 232p; bib.*
EDMONDS, C *pseud*
T. E. Lawrence *(London: Davies 1935), 191p.*
GLEN, D
In the steps of Lawrence of Arabia *(London: Rich & Cowan 1939), 320p.*
GORMAN, J T
With Lawrence to Damascus *(London: OUP 1940), 44p.*
GRAVES, Richard P
Lawrence of Arabia and his world *(London: Thames & Hudson 1976), 127p; bib.*
GRAVES, Robert
Lawrence and the Arabs *(London: Cape 1927), 179p.*
HYDE, H M
Solitary in the ranks: Lawrence of Arabia as airman and private soldier *(London: Constable 1977), 288p; bib.*
KNIGHTLEY, P
Lawrence of Arabia *(London: Sidgwick & Jackson 1976), 84p.*
KNIGHTLEY, P *and* SIMPSON, C
The secret lives of Lawrence of Arabia *(London: Nelson 1969), 331p; bib.*
LAWRENCE, T E
Evolution of a revolt: early postwar writings of T. E. Lawrence *(University Park, Pa: Pennsylvania State UP 1968), 175p.*
The letters of T. E. Lawrence *(London: Cape 1938), 896p.*
Secret despatches from Arabia *(London: Golden Cockerel 1939), 173p.*
Seven pillars of wisdom: a triumph *(London: Cape 1935), 700p.*
T. E. Lawrence to his biographers *(New York: Doubleday 1963), 260p.*
LIDDELL HART, B H
'T. E. Lawrence' in Arabia and after *(London: Cape 1934), 454p.*
LONNROTH, E
Lawrence of Arabia: an historical appreciation *(London: Vallentine Mitchell 1956), 102p.*
MACK, J E
A prince of our disorder *(Boston, Mass: Little, Brown 1975), 561p; bib.*
MEYERS, J
The wounded spirit: a study of 'Seven Pillars of Wisdom' *(London: Martin Brian & O'Keefe 1973), 200p; bib.*
MOUSA, S
T. E. Lawrence: an Arab view *(London: OUP 1966), 301p; bib.*
NUTTING, A
Lawrence of Arabia: the man and the motive *(London: Hollis & Carter 1961), 256p; bib.*
PEARMAN, D G
The Imperial Camel Corps with Colonel Lawrence, and Lawrence and the Arab revolt *(London: Nelson 1928), 44p.*
RICHARDS, V
Portrait of T. E. Lawrence *(London: Cape 1936), 254p.*
ROBINSON, E
Lawrence *(London: OUP 1935), 250p.*
Lawrence the rebel *(London: Lincolns-Prager 1946), 228p.*

ROLLS, C S
Steel chariots in the desert: the story of an armoured-car driver with the Duke of Westminster in Libya and in Arabia with T. E. Lawrence *(London: Cape 1937), 285p.*
SHUMWAY, H L
War in the desert *(London: Collins 1938), 256p.*
STEWART, D
T. E. Lawrence *(London: Hamilton 1977), 352p.*
STORRS, *Sir* R H A
Lawrence of Arabia *(London: Penguin 1940), 128p.*
THOMAS, L
With Lawrence in Arabia *(London: Hutchinson 1925), 256p.*
YARDLEY, M
Backing into the limelight *(London: Harrap 1985), 267p.*

LEAGUE OF NATIONS

ASHBEE, C R
The American League to enforce peace *(London: Allen & Unwin 1916), 92p.*
BARCLAY, *Sir* T
New methods of adjusting international disputes and the future *(London: Constable 1918), 220p.*
BARKER, E
A confederation of the nations: its powers and constitution *(London: Milford 1918), 54p.*
BASSETT, J S
Lost fruits of Waterloo: views on a League of Nations *(New York: Macmillan 1919), 289p.*
BRAILSFORD, H N
A League of Nations *(London: Headley 1918), 349p.*
DE BARY, R
The international king: a war appeal for federal union *(London: Longmans 1918), 80p.*
DICKINSON, G L
The choice before us *(London: Allen & Unwin 1917), 286p.*
ERZBERGER, M
League of Nations: the way to the world's peace *(New York: Holt 1919), 331p; bib.*
GOLDSMITH, R
A League to enforce peace *(New York: Macmillan 1917), 331p.*
GORE, C
The League of Nations: the opportunity of the Churches *(London: Hodder & Stoughton 1918), 78p.*
HYDE, H E
The international solution *(London: Allen & Unwin 1918), 93p.*
The two roads: international government or militarism *(London: King 1916), 155p.*
LODGE, H C
Senate and the League of Nations *(New York: Scribner 1925), 424p.*
MINOR, R C
A republic of nations: a study of the organization of a federal League of Nations *(London: OUP 1918), 345p.*

OPPENHEIM, L
  The League of Nations and its problems *(London: Longmans 1919), 96p.*
PAISH, *Sir* G
  A permanent League of Nations *(London: Fisher Unwin 1918), 144p.*
PARES, B
  The League of Nations and other questions of peace *(London: Hodder & Stoughton 1918)*, *155p.*
STALLYBRASS, W T S
  A society of states; or, Sovereignty, Independence and equality in a League of Nations *(London: Kegan Paul 1918), 176p.*
WOOLF, L S ed
  The framework of a lasting peace *(London: Allen & Unwin 1917), 154p.*
[See also PEACE]

LENIN

FOX, R
  Lenin *(London: Gollancz 1933), 320p.*
SHUB, D
  Lenin *(New York: Doubleday 1951), unp.*
SHUKMAN, H
  Lenin and the Russian Revolution *(London: Batsford 1967), 224p; bib.*

LETTERS

BENTINCK, H D
  The letters of Major Henry Bentinck *(London: Scott 1919), 138p.*
BICKERSTAFFE-DREW, F ed
  John Ayscough's letters to his mother during 1914, 1915 and 1916 *(London: Chatto & Windus 1919), 323p.*
CALLAWAY, R F
  Letters from two Fronts *(Brighton, Sx: 1917), 98p.*
CASALIS, A E
  A young soldier of France and of Jesus Christ *(Eastbourne, Sx: Strange 1916), 86p.*
CHAPIN, H
  Soldier and dramatist: being his letters *(London: Lane 1916), 328p.*
DAWSON, C W
  Khaki courage: letters in war-time *(London: Lane 1917), 185p.*
DAWSON, N P ed
  Good soldier: a selection of soldiers' letters, 1914-1918 *(New York: Macmillan 1918), 177p.*
DEVENISH, G W
  A subaltern's share in the war: letters *(London: Constable 1917), 177p.*

DOUGHTY, H
  An actor-soldier, Henry Doughty: extracts from his letters, 1914-1919 *(London: Hutchinson 1926), 86p.*
ELLICE, A
  War diary and letters *(Inverness: 1920), 88p.*
ENGALL, J S
  A subaltern's letters, 1915-16 *(London: Griffiths 1917), 131p.*
FARRER, R J
  The void of war: letters from three Fronts *(London: Constable 1918), 271p.*
FEILDING, R
  War letters to a wife: France and Flanders, 1915-1919 *(London: Medici Society 1929), 384p.*
FROM dug-out and billet: an officer's letters to his mother *(London: Hurst & Blackett 1916), 194p.*
G, H L
  Meanwhile: a packet of war letters *(London: Murray 1916), 168p.*
GILLESPIE, A D
  Letters from Flanders written to his home people *(London: Smith, Elder 1916), 332p.*
GOW, K
  Letters of a soldier; killed in action October 17th, 1918 *(Broadway, NY: Covert 1920), 457p.*
GRANT, A G
  Letters from Armageddon *(Boston, Mass: Houghton Mifflin 1930), 295p.*
GREENWELL, G H
  An infant in arms: war letters of a company officer, 1914-1918 *(London: Dickson & Thompson 1935), 304p.*
HAMMOND, J M
  A living witness: letters 1914-1917 *(London: Morgan & Scott 1925), 187p.*
HANKEY, D
  A student in arms: letters to the *Spectator* from the Front *(London: Melrose 1916), 233p.*
HEATH, A G
  Letters *(Oxford: Clarendon 1917), 222p.*
HENDERSON, K
  Letters to Helen: impressions of an artist on the Western Front *(London: Chatto & Windus 1917), 110p.*
HEWETT, S H
  A scholar's letters from the Front *(London: Longmans 1918), 114p.*
HOUSMAN, L
  War letters of fallen Englishmen *(London: Gollancz 1930), 318p.*
JOHNSTON, A
  At the Front *(London: Constable 1917), 130p.*
JONES, H P M
  War letters of a public school boy *(London: Cassell 1918), 280p.*
KAUTZ, J I
  Trucking to the trenches: letters from France, June-November 1917 *(Boston, Mass: Houghton Mifflin 1918), 172p.*

KEELING, F H
  Keeling's letters and recollections *(London: Allen & Unwin 1918), 329p.*
KILPATRICK, J A
  Atkins at war, as told in his own letters *(London: Jenkins 1914), 126p.*
LAFFIN, J ed
  Letters from the Front, 1914-1918 *(London: Dent 1973), 135p.*
LAWSON, H S
  Letters of a headmaster soldier *(London: Allenson 1919), 142p.*
MANWARING, G B
  If we return: letters of a soldier of Kitchener's Army *(London: Lane 1918), 165p.*
MASEFIELD, J
  John Masefield's letters from the Front 1915–1917 *(London: Constable 1984), 320p.*
MERTON, J
  Love letters under fire *(London: Duckworth 1916), 271p.*
MOYNIHAN, M ed
  Greater love: letters home 1914-1918 *(London: Allen 1980), 211p.*
  A place called Armageddon: letters from the Great War *(Newton Abbot, Devon: David & Charles 1975), 191p.*
NEVILLE, J E H
  The war letters of a light infantry-man *(London: Sifton Praed 1930), 201p.*
OLIVER, F S
  The anvil of war: letters *(London: Macmillan 1936), 351p.*
OWEN, W
  Selected letters *(Oxford, OUP 1986).*
SANSOM, N J
  Letters from France, June 1915-July 1917 *(London: Melrose 1921), 383p.*
SEEGER, A
  Letters and diary of Alan Seeger *(London: Constable 1917), 211p.*
SLATER, G ed
  My warrior sons: the Boston family diary, 1914-1918 *(London: Davies 1973), 228p.*
SORLEY, C H
  Letters from Germany and the Army *(Cambridge: CUP 1916), 191p.*
  The letters of Charles Sorley *(Cambridge: CUP 1919), 320p.*
SPICER, L D
  Letters from France, 1915-1918 *(London: York 1979), 131p.*
STANLEY, A A
  College man in khaki: letters of an American in the British artillery *(New York: Doran 1918), 234p.*
STEARNS, G
  From Army camps and battle fields: 76 weekly letters *(Minniapolis: Augsburg 1919), 381p.*
A TEMPORARY gentleman in France: love letters *(London: Cassell 1916), 197p.*
TIPPETT, E J
  Who won the war?: letters and notes of an M.P. in Dixie, England and France and Flanders *(Toledo, Ore: Toledo Type Setting 1920), 222p.*

TYNDALE-BISCOE, J
Gunner subaltern: letters written by a young man to his father during the Great War *(London: Cooper 1971), 192p.*
VAN VORST, M
War letters of an American woman *(London: Lane 1916), 352p.*
VERNEDE, R E
Letters to his wife *(London: Collins 1917), 219p.*
WHYTE, G H
Glimpses of the Great War: letters from Three Fronts *(London: Theosophical Society 1919), 133p.*

LIBRARIES

ELLIS, A
Public libraries and the First World War *(Upton, Wirral: Ffynnon 1975), 75p.*
KOCH, T W
Books in war: the romance of library war service in the American Army *(Boston, Mass: Houghton Mifflin 1919), 388p.*
ROUNDS, O M
Buck privates on Parnassus *(Boston, Mass: Meador 1933), 217p.*

LIÈGE

BIGELOW, G L
Liège on the line of march: an American girl's experience when the Germans came through Belgium *(New York: Lane 1918), 156p.*
HAMELIUS, P
The siege of Liège *(London: Werner Laurie 1914), 79p.*
HILDITCH, A N
The stand of Liège *(Oxford: Clarendon 1915), 40p.*
KENNEDY, J M
The campaign round Liège *(London: Hodder & Stoughton 1914), 188p.*
[See also BELGIUM, FLANDERS]

LIGGETT

LIGGETT, H
A. E. F., ten years ago in France *(New York: Dodd 1928), 335p.*
Commanding an American Army: recollections of the Great War *(Boston, Mass: Houghton Mifflin 1925), 207p.*

LLOYD GEORGE

DILNOT, F
  Lloyd George: the man and his story *(London: Fisher Unwin 1917), 192p.*
DU PARCQ, H
  David Lloyd George *(London: Newnes 1915), 176p.*
EDWARDS, J H
  The life of David Lloyd George *(London: Waverley 1914-1918), 4 vols. U.S. title:* David
  Lloyd George.
HAZLEHURST, C
  Politicians at war: a prologue to the triumph of Lloyd George *(London: Cape 1971), 1 vol.*
LLOYD GEORGE, D
  The great crusade: extracts from speeches delivered during the war *(London: Hodder &
  Stoughton 1918), 215p.*
  Through terror to triumph: speeches and pronouncements since the beginning of the war
  (London: Hodder & Stoughton 1915), 187p.
  The truth about reparations and war debts *(London: Heinemann 1932), 150p.*
  The truth about the peace treaties *(London: Gollancz 1938), 2 vols.*
  War memoirs *(London: Nicholson & Watson 1933), 6 vols.*
LLOYD GEORGE and the war *(London: Hutchinson 1917), 159p.*
MILLS, J S
  David Lloyd George: War Minister *(London: Cassell 1924), 313p.*
ROCH, W F
  Mr Lloyd George and the war *(London: Chatto & Windus 1920), 222p.*
ROSS, S
  Lloyd George and the First World War *(Hove: Wayland 1987), 48p; bib.*

LONDON

JONES, C S
  London in war-time *(London: Grafton 1917), 129p.*
MACDONAGH, M
  In London during the Great War *(London: Eyre & Spottiswoode 1935), 336p.*
METCHIM, D B
  Our own history of the war: from a South London view *(London: Stockwell 1918), 71p.*
MILES, H
  Untold tales of war-time London *(London: Palmer 1930), 173p.*
MILNE, J
  A new tale of two cities, calling up the life adventures of the Great War-time in London
  and Paris *(London: Lane 1923), 172p.*
MORRISS, H F
  Bermondsey's 'Bit' in the Greatest War *(London: James 1923), 252p.*
NEWTON, J F
  Preaching in London: a diary of an Anglo-American friendship *(London: Allen & Unwin
  1922), 140p.*

PAGET, H L
Records of the raids *(London: SPCK 1918), 47p.*
RAWLINSON, A
The defence of London, 1915-1918 *(London: Melrose 1923), 267p.*
[See also BRITAIN, ZEPPELINS]

LOOS

MACGILL, P
The great push: an episode of the Great War *(London: Jenkins 1916), 254p.*
The red horizon *(London: Jenkins 1916), 306p.*
WARNER, P
The battle of Loos *(London: Kimber 1976), 245p.*

LOUVAIN

CHAMBRY, R
The truth about Louvain *(London: Hodder & Stoughton 1915), 95p.*
GERMANS at Louvain *(London: Hodder & Stoughton 1916), 115p.*
NOEL, L
Louvain, 1891-1914 *(Oxford: Clarendon 1915), 241p.*
O'KAVANAGH, J
Gethsemane of a little child and its sequel in Louvain *(Cleveland, Ohio: Stratford 1919), 124p.*
[See also BELGIUM]

LUDENDORFF

GOODSPEED, D J
Ludendorff: soldier, dictator, revolutionary *(London: Hart-Davis 1966), 272p.*
LUDENDORFF, E
The General Staff and its problems *(London: Hutchinson 1920), 721p.*
My war memoirs *(London: Hutchinson 1919), 2 vols.*
PARKINSON, R
Tormented warrior: Ludendorff and the Supreme Command *(London: Hodder & Stoughton 1978), 251p; bib.*
TSCHUPPIK, C
Ludendorff: the tragedy of the specialist *(London: Allen & Unwin 1932), 282p.*
[See also GERMAN ARMY]

LUSITANIA

ADAMS, A H
The Lusitania crime and the escape of the Orduna *(Winnipeg: 1915), 90p.*
BAILEY, T A *and* RYAN, P B
The Lusitania disaster: an episode in modern warfare and diplomacy *(London: Cassell 1975), 33p.*
DROSTE, C L
The Lusitania case *(London: Stephen 1972), 224p.*
ELLIS, F D
The tragedy of the Lusitania *(Philadelphia, Pa: National 1915), 320p.*
HICKEY D *and* SMITH G
Seven days to disaster: the sinking of the Lusitania *(London: Collins 1981), 336p; bib.*
HISTORICUS *pseud*
The 'Lusitania' case: was Bryan's resignation justified? *(New York: Masterson 1915), 71p*
JONES, J P
The German spy in America: the secret plotting of German spies in the United States, and the inside story of the sinking of the Lusitania *(London: Hutchinson 1917), 256p.*
LAURIAT, C E
Lusitania's last voyage *(Boston, Mass: Houghton Mifflin 1915), 159p.*
PROCEEDINGS on a formal investigation into the the the of the S.S. *Lusitania,* 1st to 5th days *(London: Wyman 1915), 5 pts.*
SIMPSON, C
Lusitania *(London: Longmans 1972), 295p; bib.*
STILGEBAUER, E
Ship of death *(New York: Brentano 1918), 232p.*

LUXEMBURG

GRIBBLE, F H
In Luxemburg in war time *(London: Headley 1916), 216p.*
[See also BELGIUM*]*

MACEDONIA

CASSON, S
Steady drummer *(London: Bell 1935), 281p.*
DAY, H C
Macedonian memories *(London: Heath Cranton 1930), 196p.*
FALLS, C
Military operations Macedonia *(London: HMSO 1933-35), 2 vols.*
GEORGEVITCH, T R
Macedonia *(London: Allen & Unwin 1918), 300p.*

MATHER, W D
'Muckydonia,' 1917–1918: being adventures of a one time pioneer in Macedonia and Bulgaria during the First World War *(Ilfracombe: Stockwell 1979), 754p.*
NICOL, G
Uncle George: Field Marshal Lord Milne of Salonika and Rubisland *(London: Reedminster 1976), 341p; bib.*
SELIGMAN, V J
Macedonian musings *(London: Allen & Unwin 1918), 188p.*
SMITH, R S
A subaltern in Macedonia and Judea, 1916-17 *(London: Mitre 1930), 183p.*
VILLARI, L
The Macedonian campaign, 1915-1919 *(London: Fisher Unwin 1922), 285p.*
[See also BALKANS, SERBIA]

MANDATES

MAANEN-HELMER, E
The Mandates system in relation to Africa and the Pacific Islands *(London: King 1929), 331p.*
WHITE, F
Mandates *(London: Cape 1926), 196p.*
WRIGHT, P Q
Mandates under the League of Nations *(Chicago: Chicago UP 1930), 634p.*

MAPS

BANKS, A
A military atlas of the First World War *(London: Heinemann 1975), 344p*

MARNE

ALDRICH, M
A hilltop on the Marne *(London: Constable 1915), 159p.*
Peak of the load: the waiting months on the hilltop *(Boston, Mass: Small 1918), 277p.*
ASPREY, R B
The first battle of the Marne *(London: Weidenfeld & Nicolson 1962), 212p; bib.*
BERGER, M
Secret of the Marne: how Sergeant Fritsch saved France *(New York: Putnam 1918), 361p.*
BLOND, G
The Marne *(London: Macdonald 1965), 256p.*
CORBETT-SMITH, A
The Marne - and after *(London: Cassell 1917), 324p.*

CUVRU-MAGOT, H
  Beyond the Marne: Quincy, Hulry, Voisins before and during the battle *(Boston, Mass: Small 1918), 111p.*
GREAT BRITAIN War Office
  Battle of the Marne, 8th-10th September 1914: tour of the battlefield *(London: HMSO 1935), 50p.*
HORN, T
  Lancer dig in: 1914 diary–the Marne *(Orwell, Camb: Ellisons 1983), 47p.*
HUARD, F W
  My home in the field of honour: experiences of a resident near the River Marne in 1914 *(London: Hodder & Stoughton 1916), 302p.*
ISSELIN, H
  The battle of the Marne *(London: Elek 1965), 296p; bib.*
KLUCK, A von
  The march on Paris and the battle of the Marne, 1914 *(New York: Longmans 1920), 175p.*
LE GOFFIC, C
  General Foch at the Marne: the fighting in and near the marshes of Saint Goud *(London: Dent 1918), 223p.*
PERRIS, G H
  The battle of the Marne *(London: Methuen 1920), 274p.*
THE MARNE battlefields 1914 *(Miltown, NJ: Michelin 1917), 264p.*
THE Two battles of the Marne *(London: Butterworth 1927), 255p.*
TYNG, S T
  The campaign of the Marne, 1914 *(New York: Longmans 1935), 413p.*
WHITTON, F E
  The Marne campaign *(London: Constable 1917), 311p.*
WISE, J C
  Turn of the tide: American operations at Cantigny, Chateau Thiery and the second battle of the Marne *(New York: Holt 1920), 255p.*
[See also FLANDERS, WESTERN FRONT]

MATA HARI

COULSON, T
  Mata Hari, courtesan and spy *(London: Hutchinson 1934), 256p.*
HOWE, R W
  Mata Hari, the true story *(New York: Dodd Mead 1986), 292p.*
KEAY, J
  The spy who never was: the life and loves of Mata Hari *(London: Joseph 1987), 214; bib.*
OSTROVOSKY, E
  Eve of dawn: the rise and fall of Mata Hari *(London: Macmillan 1978), 273p.*
WAAGENAR, S
  The murder of Mata Hari *(London: Barker 1964), 286p.*

MEDALS

DORLING, S
  Ribbons and medals: naval, military and civil *(London: Philip 1916), 80p.*
  Ribbons and medals of the Great War *(London: Philip 1920), 35p.*
GREAT BRITAIN War Office
  A review of new Orders, Decorations and Gallantry Medals instituted by His Majesty during the war, 1914-1920, of changes made in existing Orders, Decorations and Gallantry Medals *(London: HMSO 1920), 22p.*
JOHNSON, S C
  The medals of our fighting men *(London: Black 1916), 120p.*
SERVICE medals, ribbons, badges and flags *(London: Philip 1916), unp.*
[See also CONGRESSIONAL MEDAL OF HONOUR, VICTORIA CROSS]

MEDICAL

ALLISON, R S
  The surgeon probationer *(Belfast: Blackstaff 1979), 142p.*
ALPORT, A C
  Malaria and its treatment in the line and at base *(Baltimore: Wood 1919), 279p.*
ASH, E L
  Nerve in wartime: causes and cure of nervous breakdown *(London: Mills & Boon 1915), 126p.*
BAINBRIDGE, W S
  Report on medical and surgical developments of the war *(Washington DC: Naval Medical Bulletin 1919), 250p.*
BAYLY, H W
  Triple challenge; or, War, whirligigs and windmills: a doctor's memoirs *(London: Hutchinson 1935), 396p.*
BAYNE, J B
  Bugs and bullets *(New York: R. R. Smith 1944), 256p.*
BEGG, R C
  Surgery on trestles: a saga of suffering and triumph *(Norwich: Jarrold 1967), 259p.*
BENSON, S C
  'Back from hell' *(Chicago: McClurg 1918), 250p.*
BINYON, R L
  For dauntless France: an account of Britain's aid to the French wounded *(London: Hodder & Stoughton 1918), 372p.*
BLENKINSOP, *Sir* L J *and* RAINEY, J W
  Veterinary services *(London: HMSO 1915), 782p.*
BRITISH medicine in the war *(London: B.M.A. 1917), 138p.*
BRITNIEVA, M
  One woman's story *(London: Barker 1934), 286p.*
BROCA, A *and* DUCROQUET, J
  Artificial limbs *(London: University of London P 1918), 178p.*

BROWN, M W
Neuropsychiatry and the war *(New York: Arno nd), 117p.*
CALL, A P
Nerves and the war *(Boston, Mass: Little, Brown 1918), 220p.*
CAMPBELL, P
Back of the Front *(London: Newnes 1915), 126p.*
CAMUS, J
Physical and occupational re-education of the maimed *(London: Baillière-Tindall 1918), 206p.*
CARBERY, A R D
The New Zealand medical service in the Great War *(Auckland, NZ: Whitcombe & Tombs 1924), 567p.*
CARREL, A *and* DEHELLY, G
The treatment of infected wounds *(London: Baillière 1915), unp.*
CHURCH, J R
The doctor's part: what happens to the wounded in war *(New York: Appleton 1918), 283p.*
COLLIE, *Sir* J
The management of neurasthenia and allied disorders contracted in the Army *(London: Bale & Danielsson 1917), unp.*
CRESWICK, P *and others*
Kent's care for the wounded *(London: Hodder & Stoughton 1915), 212p.*
CUMMINS, S L
Studies of influenza in hospitals of the British Armies in France, *1918 (London: Medical Research Committee 1919), 112p.*
CUSHING, H
From a surgeon's journal, 1915-1918 *(London: Constable 1936), 534p.*
DAVENPORT, C B *and* LOVE, A G
Army anthropology *(Washington DC: Dept. of Army 1921), 635p.*
DEARBORN, F M *ed*
American homeopathy in the World War *(New York: Globe 1923), 447p.*
DEARDEN, H
Medicine and duty: a war diary *(London: Heinemann 1928), 234p.*
Time and chance *(London: Heinemann 1940), 226p.*
DELORME, E
War surgery *(London: Lewis 1915), 256p.*
DERBY, R
'Wade in, Sanitary!': the story of a Division Surgeon in France *(New York: Putnam 1919), 260p.*
DOLBEY, R V
A regimental surgeon in war and prison *(London: Murray 1917), 248p.*
DUDGEON, L S
Studies of bacillary dysentery occurring in the British Forces in Macedonia *(London: Medical Research Committee 1919), 83p.*
EDER, M D
War shock: the psycho-neuroses in war *(London: Heinemann 1917), 162p,*
FARMBOROUGH, F
Russian album *(Salisbury, Wilts: Russell 1979), 96p.*

FENTON, N
Shell shock and its aftermath *(St. Louis: Mosby 1926), 173p.*
FISHER, D F
Day of glory *(New York: Holt 1919), 149p.*
FOX, R F
Physical remedies for disabled soldiers *(London: Baillière 1917), 287p.*
GERVIS, H
Arms and the doctor: being the military experiences of a middle-aged medical man *(London: Daniel 1920), 85p.*
GORDON, M H
Cerebrospinal fever: studies in the bacteriology, preventive control, and specific treatment of ... among the military forces, 1915-19 *(London: Medical Research Committee 1920), 205p.*
GOSSE, P
Memoirs of a camp follower: adventures and impressions of a doctor in the Great War *(London: Longmans 1934), 299p.*
GREAT BRITAIN War Office
Report of enquiry into 'Shell shock' *(London: HMSO 1922).*
GROVE, E W H
Gunshot injuries of bones *(London: OUP 1915), 128p.*
GROW, M C
Surgeon Grow: an American in the Russian fighting *(New York: Stokes 1918), 304p.*
HANES, E L
Minds and nerves of soldiers *(Altadena, Cal: Hanes 1941), 221p.*
HARMER, M
The forgotten hospital *(Chichester, Sx: Springwood 1982), 170p.*
HARRIS, W
Nerve injuries and shock *(London: OUP 1915), 128p.*
HASTINGS, S
First aid for the trenches: simple instructions for saving life *(London: Murray 1916), 63p.*
HAYS, H M
Cheerio!: an American medical officer with the British Army *(New York: Knopf 1919), 291p.*
HERRINGHAM, *Sir* W P
A physician in France *(London: Arnold 1919), 293p.*
HIS, W
German doctor at the Front *(Harrisburg, Pa: National Service 1933), 230p.*
HOWE, M A D
The Harvard Volunteers in Europe: personal records of experiences in military, ambulance and hospital service *(Cambridge, Mass: Harvard UP 1916), 263p.*
HUGHES, B and BANKS, H S
War surgery from firing line to base *(Baltimore: Wood 1919), 623p.*
HULL, A J
Surgery in war *(London: Churchill 1916), 496p.*
HURST, *Sir* A F *and others*
Medical diseases of war *(Baltimore: Williams & Welkins 1944), 507p.*

HUTCHINSON, W
 Doctor in war *(Boston, Mass: Houghton Mifflin 1918), 481p.*
INDEX MEDICUS
 War supplement: a classified record of literature on military medicine and surgery, 1914–1917 *(New York: Carnegie Institute 1918), 260p.*
IRELAND, M W
 The Medical Department of the United States Army in the World War *(Washington DC: 1923), unp.*
JONES, R
 Injuries of the joints *(London: OUP 1915), 190p.*
KRIPPNER, M
 The quality of mercy: women at war, Serbia 1915–18 *(Newton Abbot, Devon: David & Charles 1980), 223p.*
LAGARDE, L A
 Gunshot injuries *(London: Bale 1914), unp.*
LA MOTTE, E N
 The backwash of war *(New York: Putnam 1916), 186p.*
LAWSON, *Sir* A
 War blindness at St. Dunstan's *(London: Oxford Med. 1922), 148p.*
LEJARS, F
 Urgent surgery *(London: Wright 1915), 2 vols.*
LELEAN, P S
 Sanitation in war *(London: Churchill 1917), 344p.*
L'ETANG, H
 The pathology of leadership *(London: Heinemann 1969), 256p*
LEWIS, T
 The soldier's heart and the effort syndrome *(New York: Hoeber 1920), 439p.*
LLOYD, L
 Lice and their menace to man, with a chapter on trench fever *(London: Hodder & Stoughton 1919), 150p.*
McCOMBE, J *and* MENZIES, A F
 Medical service at the Front *(Philadelphia, Pa: Lea 1918), 128p.*
McDILL, J R
 Lessons from the enemy: how Germany cares for her war disabled *(Philadelphia, Pa: Lea 1918), 262p.*
McKENZIE, R T
 Reclaiming the maimed: a handbook of physical therapy *(New York: Macmillan 1918), 128p.*
MACDONALD, L
 The roses of no man's land *(London: Joseph 1980), 318p.*
MACLEAN, H
 Albuminuria and war nephritis among British troops in France *(London: Medical Research Committee 1919), 113p.*
MACNAUGHTON, S
 My war experiences in two continents *(London: Murray 1919), 286p.*
MACPHERSON, *Sir* W G
 History of the Great War: medical services *(London: HMSO 1921), 12 vols.*

MACQUEEN, J M
  Our war: being the experiences in France of a specialist sanitary officer *(Halesowen, Worcs: MacQueen 1931), 188p.*
MAKINS, G H
  Gunshot injuries of the arteries *(London: OUP 1914), unp.*
MANION, R J
  A surgeon in arms *(New York: Appleton 1918), 309p.*
MARR, H C
  Psychoses of the war, including neurasthenia and shell shock *(New York: OUP 1919), 292p.*
MARTIN, A A
  A surgeon in khaki *(London: Arnold 1915), 279p.*
MAXWELL-LEFROY, H
  Measures for avoidance and extermination of flies, mosquitoes, lice and other vermin *(London: Thacker 1915), unp.*
MILITARY medical manuals *(London: London UP 1918), 7 vols.*
MITTON, G E
  The cellar-house of Pervyse *(London: Black 1916), 277p.*
MOORE, W
  The thin yellow line *(London: Cooper 1974), 270p; bib.*
MORISON, R *and* RICHARDSON, W G
  Abdominal injuries *(London: OUP 1915), unp.*
  Bipp treatment of war wounds *(London: Frowde & Hodder 1918), 72p.*
MUIR, J R
  Years of endurance *(London: Allan 1936), 292p.*
MUNTHE, A
  Red Cross and Iron Cross *(London: Murray 1916), 158p.*
MURPHY, J K
  Wounds of the thorax in war *(London: OUP 1915), 156p.*
MURRAY, F
  Women as army surgeons; being the history of the Women's Hospital Corps in Paris, Wimereux and Endell Street, September 1914-October 1919 *(London: Hodder & Stoughton 1920), 263p.*
MYERS, C S
  Shell shock in France, 1914-1918 *(London: CUP 1940), 146p.*
NASMITH, G G
  On the fringe of the great fight *(New York: Doran 1918), 263p.*
OSBURN, A C
  Unwilling passenger *(London: Faber 1932), 415p.*
PENHALLOW, D P
  Military surgery *(New York: OUP 1918), 555p.*
PLOWMAN, C F *and* DEARDEN, W F
  Fighting the fly peril *(London: Unwin 1915), 128p.*
POWER, *Sir* d'A
  Wounds in war: their treatment and results *(London: OUP 1915), 108p.*
PRINZING, F
  Epidemics resulting from wars *(Oxford: Clarendon 1916), unp.*

RAMSAY, A M *and others*
Injuries of the eyes, nose, throat and ears *(London: OUP 1915), 160p.*

RAWLING, L B
Surgery of the head *(London: OUP 1915), 150p.*

RORIE, D
A medico's luck in the war: being reminiscences of R.A.M.C. work with the 51st Highland Division *(Aberdeen: Milne & Hutchison 1929), 264p.*

ROTH, P B
Notes on military orthopaedics *(London: Kimpton 1916), unp.*

ROUSSY, G *and* L'HERMITTE, J
Psychoneuroses of war *(London: London UP 1918), 226p.*

SHIPLEY, A E
Minor horrors of war *(London: Smith, Elder 1916), 208p.*
More minor horrors *(London: Smith, Elder 1916), 178p.*

SHIPLEY, A M
The officers and nurses of Evacuation Eight *(New Haven, Conn: Yale UP 1929), 190p.*

SINCLAIR, M
A journal of impressions in Belgium *(London: Hutchinson 1915), 332p.*

SMITH, G E *and* PEAR, T H
Shell shock and its lessons *(London: Longmans 1917), unp.*

SMITH, L N
Four years out of life *(London: Allan 1931), 302p.*

SOUTHARD, E E
Shell-shock and other neuropsychiatric problems presented in five hundred and eighty-nine case histories from the war literature, 1914-1918 *(Boston, Mass: Leonard 1919), 982p; bib.*

SOUTTAR, H S
A surgeon in Belgium *(London: Arnold 1915), 217p.*

SQUIRE, J E
Medical hints for the use of medical officers temporarily employed with troops *(London: Milford 1915), 128p.*

STEWART, P *and* EVANS, A
Nerve injuries and their treatment *(London: Frowde & Hodder 1916), 220p.*

STRONG, R P
Trench fever *(London: OUP 1918), 453p.*
Typhus fever, with particular reference to the Serbian epidemics *(Cambridge, Mass: Harvard UP 1920), 273p.*

THE TALE of a casualty clearing station *(London: Blackwood 1917), 306p.*

TEICHMAN, O
Diary of a Yeomanry M.O., Egypt, Gallipoli, Palestine and Italy *(London: Fisher Unwin 1921), 283p.*

THURSTON, V
The hounds of war unleashed *(St. Ives, Corn: United Writers 1978), 93p.*

TOPLEY, W W C
A report on the probable proportion of enteric infections among the undiagnosed febrile cases invalided from the Western Front since October 1916 *(London: Medical Research Committee 1920), 88p.*

TUBBY, A H
A consulting surgeon in the Near East *(London: Christophers 1920), 279p.*
VEDDER, E H
The medical aspects of chemical warfare *(London: Baillière 1925), unp.*
WALKER, H F B
A doctor's diary in Damaraland *(London: Arnold 1917), 207p.*
WALLACE, *Sir* C S
War surgery of the abdomen *(New York: Blakiston 1918), 152p.*
WALLACE, *Sir* C S *and* FRASER, J
Surgery at a casualty clearing station *(New York: Macmillan 1919), 320p.*
WENZEL, M *and* CORNISH, J
Auntie Mabel's war *(London: Lane 1980), 128p.*
WILMER, W H
Aviation medicine in the A.E.F. *(Washington DC: Dept. of Army 1920), 322p.*
WRIGHT, *Sir* A E
Wound infections and some new methods for the study of the various factors which come
into consideration in their treatment *(London: London UP 1915), 100p.*
YEALLAND, L R
Hysterical disorders of warfare *(New York: Macmillan 1918), 252p.*
[See also AMBULANCES, HOSPITALS, NURSES]

MEDITERRANEAN

USBORNE, C V
Smoke on the horizon: Mediterranean fighting, 1914-1918 *(London: Hodder & Stoughton 1933), 327p.*

MEMOIRS

ADDISON, C
Four and a half-years: personal diary from June 1914 to January 1919 *(London: Hutchinson 1934), 2 vols.*
ALBERT I *King of the Belgians*
The war diaries of Albert I, King of the Belgians *(London: Kimber 1954), 228p.*
(BAKER, S H) BAKER, J
A leader of men: Major Sydney Harold Baker *(London: Lane 1920), 359p.*
(BAKER, Newton D) HAYES, R A
Secretary Baker at the Front *(New York: Century 1918), 185p.*
PALMER, F
Newton D Baker: America at war *(New York: Dodd 1931), 2 vols.*
BARROW, *Sir* G
The fire of life *(London: Hutchinson 1942), unp.*
BENES, E
My war memoirs *(London: Allen & Unwin 1928), 512p.*

BERNSTORFF, J H A
  My three years in America *(London: Skeffington 1920), 359p.*
BERTIE, F L *viscount*
  The diary of Lord Bertie of Thame, 1914-1918 *(London: Hodder & Stoughton 1924), 2 vols.*
BETHMAN-HOLLWEG, T T F
  Reflections on the World War *(London: Butterworth 1920), 172p.*
  Seven war speeches *(Zurich: 1916), 87p.*
(BINCKLEY, R C) FISCH, M H
  Selected papers of Robert C. Binckley *(Cambridge, Mass: Harvard UP 1948), 426p.*
(BLACKBURNE, C H) BLACKBURNE, L E
  Lieut. Col. C. H. Blackburne: a memoir *(London: Allenson 1919), 197p.*
BRIDGES, *Sir* T
  Alarms and excursions: reminiscences of a soldier *(London: Longmans 1938), 361p.*
BRYAN, W J *and* BRYAN, M
  The memoirs of William Jennings Bryan *(Philadelphia, Pa: Winston 1925), 560p.*
BULOW, B von *prince*
  Memoirs *(Boston, Mass: Little, Brown 1931), 4 vols.*
BUXTON, A R
  Andrew R. Buxton: a memoir *(London: Scott 1918), 292p.*
CALLWELL, *Sir* C E
  Experiences of a dug-out *(London: Constable 1920), 339p.*
CHILDS, *Sir* W
  Episodes and reflections *(London: Cassell 1930), 304p.*
(COWANS, *Sir* John) CHAPMAN-HUSTON, W D M
  General Sir John Cowans, the Quarter-Master General of the Great War *(London: Hutchinson 1924), 2 vols.*
CROY, M de *princess*
  War memoirs *(London: Macmillan 1932), 309p.*
CZERNIN, O *count*
  In the World War *(London: Cassell 1919), 387p.*
(DEEDES, *Sir* Wyndham) PRESLAND, J *pseud*
  Deedes Bey: a study of Sir Wyndham Deedes, 1883-1923 *(London: Macmillan 1942), 359p.*
DOUGLAS, S *1st baron Douglas of Kirtleside*
  Years of combat: the first volume of the autobiography *(London: Collins 1963), 384p; bib.*
DUMBA, C
  Memoirs of a diplomat *(Boston, Mass: Houghton Mifflin 1932), unp.*
ESHER, R *viscount*
  Journals and letters; vol. 3: 1910-1915 *(London: Nicholson & Watson 1938), 320p.*
(FISHER, John A *1st baron*)
  Memories and records *(London: Hodder & Stoughton 1919-1920), 2 vols.*
BACON, *Sir* R
  Life of Lord Fisher *(London: Hodder & Stoughton 1929), 2 vols.*
MARDER, A J *ed*
  Fear God and dread nought *(London: Cape 1952-59), 3 vols.*

(FORBES, J K) TAYLOR, W *and* DIACK, P
  Student and sniper sergeant: a memoir of J. K. Forbes *(London: Hodder & Stoughton 1916), 182p.*
(FULLER, J F C)
  Memoirs of an unconventional soldier *(London: Nicholson & Watson 1936), 506p.*
TRYFALL, A J
  'Boney' Fuller: the intellectual General *(London: Cassell 1977), 314p; bib.*
(GARNETT, K G) GARNETT, R
  Kenneth Gordon Garnett *(London: Chiswick 1918), 64p.*
GERARD, *Sir* J W
  My four years in Germany *(London: Hodder & Stoughton 1917), 320p.*
GLUBB, *Sir* J B
  Into battle: a soldier's diary of the Great War *(London: Cassell 1978), 223p.*
GOUGH, *Sir* H
  Soldiering on: the memoirs of General Sir Hubert Gough *(London: Barker 1954), 260p.*
GRAVES, R
  Goodbye to all that *(London: Cape 1929), 448p.*
(HALDANE, R B *viscount*)
  Autobiography *(London: Hodder & Stoughton 1929), 376p.*
KOSS, S E
  Lord Haldane: scapegoat for liberalism *(New York: Columbia UP 1969), 263p.*
MAURICE, *Sir* F
  Haidane *(London: Faber 1937-1939), 2 vols.*
SOMMER, D
  Haldane of Cloan *(London: Allen & Unwin 1960), 448p.*
(HALL, *Sir* Reginald) JAMES, *Sir* W
  The eyes of the Navy: a biographical study of Admiral Sir Reginald Hall *(London: Methuen 1955), 212p.*
(HAMILTON, *Sir* Ian) HAMILTON, I B M
  The happy warrior: a life of General Sir Ian Hamilton *(London: Cassell 1966), 487p.*
HAMILTON, R G A
  The war diary of the Master of Belhaven, 1914-1918 *(London: Murray 1924), 472p.*
HARINGTON, *Sir* C H
  Tim Harington looks back *(London: Murray 1941), 288p.*
HARMSWORTH, A C W *1st baron Northcliffe*
  At the war *(London: Hodder & Stoughton 1917), 323p.*
(HAYASHI, Tadusu *count*) POOLEY, A M
  Secret memoirs of Count Tadusu Hayashi *(London: Nash 1915), 315p.*
HICKLING, H
  Sailor at sea *(London: Kimber 1965), 224p.*
(HIPPER, Franz von) WALDEYER-HARTZ, H
  Admiral von Hipper *(London: Rich & Cowan 1933), 276p.*
HOFFMANN, M
  War diaries and other papers *(London: Secker 1929), 2 vols.*
(HOOVER, Herbert) KELLOGG, V L
  Herbert Hoover: the man and his work *(New York: Appleton 1920), 375p.*

(HUGHES, William M) SLADEN, D
From boundary rider to Prime Minister: Hughes of Australia, the man of the hour *(London: Hutchinson 1916), 224p.*
JACK, J L
General Jack's diary, 1914-1918: the trench diary of Brigadier-General J. L. Jack *(London: Eyre & Spottiswoode 1964), 320p.*
JAMAL, *Pasha*
Memories of a Turkish statesman, 1913-1919 *(London: Hutchinson 1922), 302p.*
KAROLYI, M *count*
Fighting the world *(London: Kegan Paul 1924), 420p.*
(KEMAL, Ismail) STORY, S *ed*
The memoirs of Ismail Kemal Bey *(London: Constable 1920), 530p.*
KERENSKY, A F
The catastrophe *(New York: Appleton 1927), 376p.*
KERR, M
Land, sea and air *(London: Longmans 1927), 416p.*
KREISLER, F
Four weeks in the trenches: the war story of a violinist *(Boston, Mass: Houghton Mifflin 1915), 86p.*
LANSING, R
War memoirs *(Indianapolis, Ind: Bobbs-Merrill 1935), 383p.*
(LICHNOWSKY, Karl M *prince*) YOUNG, H F
Prince Lichnowsky and the Great War *(Athens, Ga: University of Georgia P 1977), 281p.*
LIDDELL HART, *Sir* B H
Memoirs *(London: Cassell 1965), 2 vols.*
MACMILLAN, H
Winds of change *(London: Macmillan 1966), 668p.*
MANSFIELD, W *viscount Sandhurst*
Day to day, 1914-1915 *(London: Arnold 1928), 357p.*
MARSHALL, *Sir* W
Memories of four Fronts *(London: Benn 1929), 340p.*
MASARYK, T G
The making of a State: memories and observations, 1914-1918 *(London: Allen & Unwin 1927), 461p.*
(MAUDE, *Sir* Stanley) CALLWELL, *Sir* C E
The life of Lieut.-General Sir Stanley Maude *(London: Constable 1920), 360p.*
MAXIMILIAN ALEXANDER, F W *prince of Baden*
The memoirs of Prince Max of Baden *(London: Constable 1928), 2 vols.*
MAXWELL, G A
Swan song of a rustic moralist: the recollections – humorous and tragic of a private soldier during World War I *(New York: Exposition 1975), 162p.*
MEINERTZHAGEN, R
Army diary, 1899-1926 *(Edinburgh: Oliver & Boyd 1960), 301p.*
MERCIER, D J *cardinal*
Cardinal Mercier's own story *(London: Hodder & Stoughton 1920), 441p.*
KELLOGG, C
Mercier: the fighting Cardinal of Belgium *(New York: Appleton 1920), 248p.*

(MILNE, G F *1st baron*) NICOL, G
   Uncle George: Field Marshal Lord Milne of Salonika and Rubislan *(London: Reedminster 1976), 341p; bib.*
MITCHELL, W
   Memoirs of World War I: from start to finish of our greatest war *(New York: Random House 1960), 312p.*
MORGENTHAU, H
   Ambassador Morgenthau's story *(London: Hodder & Stoughton 1918), 407p.*
MUSSOLINI, B
   My diary, 1915-17 *(Boston, Mass: Small nd), 195p.*
NABOKOFF, C
   Ordeal of a diplomatist: four years' personal recollections at the Russian Embassy in London *(London: Duckworth 1921), 320p.*
NEVINSON, H W
   Last changes last chances *(London: Nisbet 1928), 378p.*
NICHOLAS *prince of Greece*
   Political memoirs, 1914-1917 *(London: Hutchinson 1928), 319p.*
ORPEN, *Sir* W
   An onlooker in France *(London: Williams & Norgate 1924), 127p.*
OSBORN, E B
   The new Elizabethans: a first selection of the lives of young men who have fallen in the Great War *(London: Lane 1919), 311p.*
(PAGE Walter H) GREGORY, R
   Walter Hines Page: ambassador to the Court of St James's *(Lexington, Ky: University of Kentucky P 1970), 236p.*
   HENDRICK, B J
   Life and letters of Walter H. Page *(New York: Doubleday 1925), 3 vols.*
PALEOLOGUE, G M
   An ambassador's memoirs, 1914-1917 *(London: Hutchinson 1973), 945p.*
PARES, *Sir* B
   My Russian memoirs *(London: Cape 1935), 623p.*
PILSUDSKI J
   The memories of a Polish revolutionary and soldier *(New York: AMS P 1971), 377p.*
(PLUMER, Herbert *1st viscount*) HARINGTON, *Sir* C H
   Plumer of Messines *(London: Murray 1935), 351p.*
(PRICHARD, H) PARKER, E
   Hesketh Prichard: a memoir *(London: Fisher Unwin 1924), 271p.*
POINCARÉ, R
   The memoirs of Raymond Poincaré *(London: Heinemann 1926-1929), 3 vols.*
   HUDDLESTON, S
   Poincaré: a biographical portrait *(London: Allen & Unwin 1924), 192p.*
(POLLARD, G B *and* POLLARD, R T) POLLARD, A W
   Two brothers *(London: Sidgwick & Jackson 1917), 61p.*
(POULTON, R) POULTON, E B
   The life of Ronald Poulton *(London: Sidgwick & Jackson 1919), 410p.*
(RAWLINSON, Arthur *1st Baron of Trent*) MAURICE, *Sir* F
   The life of General Lord Rawlinson of Trent *(London: Cassell 1928).*

REITH, J C W *1st baron*
Wearing spurs *(London: Hutchinson 1966), 223p.*
RIDDELL, G A *baron*
Lord Riddell's war diary, 1914-1918 *(London: Nicholson & Watson 1933), 367p.*
ROBERTSON, *Sir* W
From Private to Field Marshal *(London: Constable 1921), 415p.*
Soldiers and statesmen *(London: Cassell 1926), 2 vols.*
The life story of the Chief of the Imperial General Staff *(London: Cassell 1916), 150p.*
RODD, *Sir* J R
Social and diplomatic memories, 1902-1919 *(London: Arnold 1925), 401p.*
(ROLLS, C S) MORRISS, H F
Two brave brothers *(London: James 1918), 212p.*
ROSS, N
Noel Ross and his work *(London: Arnold 1919), 210p.*
SALTER, J A *1st baron*
Slave of the lamp: a public servant's notebook *(London: Weidenfeld & Nicolson 1967), 302p.*
SASSOON, S
Memoirs of an infantry officer *(London: Faber 1930), 334p.*
Siegfried's journey, 1916-1920 *(London: Faber 1945), 224p.*
SCHOEN, W E *baron*
The memoirs of an ambassador *(London: Allen & Unwin 1922), 254p.*
SEELY, J E B
Adventure *(London: Heinemann 1930), 326p.*
SHARP, W G
The war memoirs of W. G. Sharp: American Ambassador to France, 1914-19 *(London: Constable 1931), 431p.*
(SHAW-STEWART, P) KNOX, R A
Patrick Shaw-Stewart *(London: Collins 1920), 205p.*
SMITH, F E *1st viscount Birkenhead*
My American visit *(London: Hutchinson 1918), 288p.*
(SPRING-RICE, *Sir* Cecil) GWYNN, S *ed*
The letters and friendships of Sir Cecil Spring-Rice *(Boston, Mass: Houghton Mifflin 1929), unp.*
(STARR, D P) STARR, L
The war story of Dillwyn Parrish Starr *(New York: Putnam 1917), 136p.*
STEIN, Hermann von
A War Minister and his work: reminiscences of 1914-18 *(London: Skeffington 1920), 260p.*
SWINTON, *Sir* E D
Eye-witness: being personal reminiscences of certain phases of the Great War, including the genesis of the tank *(London: Hodder & Stoughton 1932), 332p.*
SYKES, *Sir* F
From many angles *(London: Harrap 1943), 592p.*
TIRPITZ, A P F
My memoirs *(London: Hurst & Blackett 1919), 2 vols.*

(VANAMEE, P) VANAMEE, M C
  Vanamee: a biography of Parker Vanamee *(London: Faber 1929), 313p.*
WHEATLEY, D
  Officer and temporary gentleman, 1914-1919 *(London: Hutchinson 1977), 254p.*
(WILSON, *Sir* Henry) ASH, B
  The last dictator: a biography of Field Marshal Sir Henry Wilson *(London: Cassell 1968) 308p; bib.*
  CALLWELL, *Sir* C E
  Sir Henry Wilson: his life and diaries *(London: Cassell 1927), 2 vols.*
  COLLIER, B
  Brasshat *(London: Secker & Warburg 1961), 362p.*
(WILSON, *Mrs* Woodrow) WILSON, E B
  The memoirs of Mrs. Woodrow Wilson *(London: Putnam 1939), 461p.*
WINDISCHGRAETZ, L A *prince*
  My memoirs *(London: Allen & Unwin 1921), 356p.*
(WOOD, W B) BYGOTT J
  Two soldier brothers *(London: Jarrolds 1919), 176p.*

MERCHANT NAVY

BATEMAN, C T
  U-boat devilry: illustrating the heroism and endurance of merchant seamen *(London: Hodder & Stoughton 1918), 175p.*
BEAUMONT, J C H
  The British Mercantile Marine during the war *(London: Gay & Hancock 1919), 54p.*
BONE, D W
  Merchantmen-at-arms: the British Merchant service in the war *(London: Chatto & Windus 1919), 259p.*
BRITISH
  Vessels lost at sea, 1914-1918 *(Cambridge: Stephens 1977), 184p.*
CORNFOD, L C
  The Merchant seaman in war *(London: Hodder & Stoughton 1917), 320p.*
DIXON, W M
  The fleets behind the Fleet: the work of the Merchant seamen and fishermen in the war *(London: Hodder & Stoughton 1917), 131p.*
ELEY, C V A
  How to save a big ship from sinking even though torpedoed *(London: Simpkin Marshall 1915), 207p.*
FAYLE, C E
  History of the Great War sea-borne trade *(London: Murray 1920-1924), 3 vols.*
GREAT BRITAIN Admiralty
  Merchant shipping losses *(London: HMSO 1919), 164p.*
HOOK, F A
  Merchant adventurers, 1914-1918 *(London: Black 1920), 314p.*

HOPKINS, C P
 'National Service'of British merchant seamen, 1914-1919 *(London: Routledge 1920),*
 206p.
HURD, A S
 A merchant fleet at war *(London: Cassell 1920), 139p.*
 The Merchant Navy *(London: HMSO 1921-1929), 3 vols.*
 Ordeal at sea: the story of the British seaman's fight for freedom *(London: Jarrolds 1918),*
 227p.
KNIGHT, E F
 The Union-Castle and the war, 1914-1919 *(London: Union-Castle 1920), 63p.*
LESLIE, H W
 'The Royal Mail' war book: being an account of the operations of the ships of the Royal
 Mail Steam Packet Co., 1914-19 *(London: Heinemann 1920), 207p.*
PATTERSON, J E
 A war-time voyage: being the itinerary of an ocean-tramp from port to port, 1916-17
 (London: Dent 1918), 280p.
POOLMAN, K
 Armed merchant cruisers *(London: Cooper & Secker & Warburg 1985), 228p.*
SALTER, J A
 Allied shipping control *(Oxford: Clarendon 1921), 372p.*
SMITH, *Sir* F E *1st earl of Birkenhead*
 The destruction of merchant ships under international law *(London: Dent 1917), 110p.*
SMITH, J R
 Influence of the Great War upon shipping *(New York: OUP 1919), 357p.*
WHEELER, H F B
 Daring deeds of merchant seamen in the Great War *(London: Harrap 1918), 319p.*
Y.
 The odyssey of a torpedoed tramp *(London: Constable 1918), 284p.*
[See also Q SHIPS, U-BOATS]

MESOPOTAMIA CAMPAIGN

BARKER, A J
 The neglected war: Mesopotamia, 1914-1918 *(London: Faber 1967), 534p; bib;*
 U.S. title: The bastard war.
BELL, G M L
 The Arab war: confidential information for General Headquarters *(London: Golden*
 Cockerel 1940), 50p.
BETTS, E
 The bagging of Baghdad *(London: Lane 1920), 238p.*
BIRD, W D
 A chapter of misfortunes: the battles of Ctesiphon, and of the Dujailah in Mesopotamia
 (London: Forester, Groom 1923), 288p.
BLACKLEDGE, W J
 The legion of marching madmen *(London: Sampson Low 1936), 244p.*

BLACK TAB *pseud*
  On the road to Kut: an officer's story of the Mesopotamia campaign *(London: Hutchinson 1917), 304p.*
BRAY, N N E
  A Paladin of Arabia: the biography of Brevet Lieut.-Col. G. E. Leachman *(London: Heritage 1936), 429p.*
  Shifting sands *(London: Unicorn 1934), 312p.*
BROWNE, K M
  'Pot luck' - with the E.E.F. *(London: Stockwell 1920), 96p.*
BUCHANAN, *Sir* G C
  The tragedy of Mesopotamia *(Edinburgh: Blackwood 1938), 287p.*
BURNE, A H
  Mesopotamia: the last phase *(Aldershot: Gale & Polden 1938), 134p.*
THE CAMPAIGN of the British Army in Mesopotamia, 1914-1918 *(London: Pitman 1930), 179p.*
CANDLER, E
  The long road to Baghdad *(London: Cassell 1919), 2 vols.*
CLARK, A T
  To Baghdad with the British *(New York: Appleton 1918), 295p.*
DANE, E
  British campaign in the Nearer East *(London: Hodder & Stoughton 1917-19), 2 vols.*
DAVIES, D W
  A Welshman in Mesopotamia *(Aberystwyth, Wales: Gwasg Cambria 1986), 120p.*
DINNING, H
  Nile to Aleppo: with the Light Horse in the M.E. *(London: Allen & Unwin 1920), 287p.*
DUNSTERVILLE, L C
  The adventures of Dunsterforce *(London: Arnold 1920), 323p.*
EGAN, E F
  The war in the cradle of the world: Mesopotamia *(New York: Harper 1918), 371p.*
EVANS, R
  A brief outline of the campaign in Mesopotamia, 1914-1918 *(London: Sifton Praed 1926), 135p.*
EWING, W
  From Gallipoli to Baghdad *(London: Hodder & Stoughton 1917), 306p.*
HALL, L J
  The Inland Water Transport in Mesopotamia *(London: Constable 1921), 253p.*
HURGRONJE, C S
  The Holy War, made in Germany *(New York: Putnam 1917), 82p.*
IDRIESS, I L
  Lurking death: true stories of snipers in Gallipoli, Sinai and Palestine *(Sydney: Angus & Robertson 1942), 87p.*
JOATAMON *pseud*
  A mug in Mesopotamia *(Poona, India: 1918), 62p.*
KEARSEY, A H C
  Notes and lectures on the campaign in Mesopotamia *(London: Rees 1927), 106p.*
  A study of the strategy and tactics of the Mesopotamia campaign *(Aldershot: Gale & Polden 1934), 192p.*

LAWLEY, *Sir* A
A message from Mesopotamia *(London: Hodder & Stoughton 1917), 131p.*
LELAND, F W G
With the M.T. in Mesopotamia *(London: Forster, Groom 1920), 253p.*
MARSHALL, *Sir* W R
Memories of four Fronts *(London: Benn 1929), 340p.*
MESOPOTAMIA COMMISSION
Report of the Commission appointed to inquire into the origin, inception and operations of war in Mesopotamia *(London: HMSO 1917), unp.*
MOBERLY, F J
Official history of the Great War; military operations: the campaign in Mesopotamia *(London: HMSO 1923-1927), 4 vols.*
MORE, J N
With Allenby's crusaders *(London: Heath Cranton 1923), 232p.*
NUNN, W
Tigris gunboats: a narrative of the Royal Navy co-operation with the military forces in Mesopotamia *(London: Melrose 1932), 288p.*
PARKER, A G
The diaries of Pasha Parker: war in the desert 1914–1918 *(London: Quartet 1983), 223p.*
REYNARDSON, H B
Mesopotamia, 1914-15 *(London: Melrose 1919), 272p.*
ROOSEVELT, K
War in the garden of Eden *(London: Murray 1920), 253p.*
SHAHBAZ, Y H
Rage of Islam: an account of the massacre of Christians by the Turks in Persia *(Philadelphia, Pa: American Baptist 1918), 182p.*
SWAYNE, M L
In Mesopotamia *(London: Hodder & Stoughton 1917), 166p.*
SYKES, C
Wassmuss, 'the German Lawrence' *(London: Longmans 1936), 271p.*
TOROSSIAN, S
From Dardanelles to Palestine: a true story of five battle Fronts *(Boston, Mass: Meador 1947), 219p.*
TOWNSHEND, *Sir* C V F
My campaign in Mesopotamia *(London: Butterworth 1920), 400p.*
WILSON, *Sir* A T
Loyalties, Mesopotamia, 1914-1917: a personal and historical record *(London: OUP 1930), 340p.*
Mesopotamia, 1917-1920 *(London: OUP 1931), 420p.*
WINSTONE, H V F
Leachman *(London: Quartet 1982), 256p.*
WITH a Highland Regiment in Mesopotamia, 1916-1917 *(Bombay, India: 1918), 165p.*
YOUNG, *Sir* H
The independent Arab *(London: Murray 1933), 344p.*
[See also LAWRENCE OF ARABIA, NEAR EAST, PALESTINE, TURKEY]

MINES AND MINE-SWEEPING

BARRIE, A
  War underground *(London: Muller 1962)*, 272p.
BELKNAP, R R
  Yankee mining squadron; or, Laying the North Sea mine barrage *(Annapolis, Md: U.S. Naval Institute 1920)*, 110p.
CORNFORD, L C
  The paravane adventure *(London: Hodder & Stoughton 1919)*, 278p.
CORRIGAN, J P
  Tin ensign: mine planting the North Sea *(Jericho, NY. Exposition 1971)*, 202p.
COWIE, J S
  Mines, minelayers and minelaying *(Toronto: OUP 1949)*, 216p.
DORLING, H T
  Swept channels: being an account of the work of minesweepers in the Great War *(London: Hodder & Stoughton 1935)*, 388p.
LANGMAID, K
  The approaches are mined *(London: Jarrolds 1965)*, 256p.
TROUNCE, H D
  Fighting the Boche underground *(New York: Scribner 1918)*, 236p.
UNITED STATES Office of Naval Records
  Northern barrage and other mining activities *(Washington DC: 1920)*, 146p.
  Northern barrage: taking up the mines *(Washington DC: 1920)*, 79p.

MISCELLANEOUS WRITINGS

BLAKESLEE, G H
  The problems and lessons of the war *(New York: Putnam 1916)*, 381p.
BODLEY, J E C
  The romance of the battle line in France *(London: Constable 1919)*, 255p.
CABLE, B
  Grapes of wrath *(London: Smith, Elder 1917)*, 268p.
CAMPBELL, R W
  The mixed division *(London: Hutchinson 1916)*, 320p.
CANDLER, E
  The year of chivalry *(London: Simpkin Marshall 1916)*, 308p.
CAPEL, A
  Reflection on victory and a project for the federation of governments *(London: Werner Laurie 1917)*, 135p.
CHAPMAN, G
  Vain glory: a miscellany of the Great War, 1914-1918 *(London: Cassell 1937)*, 762p; bib.
CHAPPLE, J M
  'We'll stick to the finish!': people and places visited in the war zones *(Boston, Mass: Chapple 1918)*, 303p.
COOK, *Sir* T A
  The last lap *(London: Murray 1916)*, 116p.

FOLKS, H
  The human costs of the war *(New York: Harper 1920), 325p.*
GIBBS, *Sir* P H
  Realities of war *(London: Heinemann 1920), 455p.*
GRAHAM, S
  The challenge of the dead *(London: Benn 1930), 160p.*
GRIERSON, F
  Illusions and realities of the war *(New York: Lane 1918), 192p.*
HAMON, A F
  Lessons of the World War *(London: Fisher Unwin 1918), 438p.*
HART, A B *and others*
  Problems of readjustment after the war *(New York: Appleton 1915), 185p.*
HODSON, J
  The soul of a soldier *(London: Routledge 1918), 127p.*
HOLLAND, W L
  Final call to arms; or, Armageddon *(Worthing, Sx: Jones 1915), 106p.*
HUDSON, S
  War-time silhouettes *(London: Allen & Unwin 1916), 224p.*
JEFFERSON, C E
  What the war is teaching *(New York: Revell 1916), 218p.*
KEABLE, R
  Standing by: war-time reflections *(London: Nisbet 1919), 260p.*
LOTI, P
  War *(London: Werner Laurie 1917), 228p.*
LOYSON, P H
  The gods in battle *(London: Hodder & Stoughton 1917), 317p.*
MACCABE, J
  The soul of Europe *(London: Fisher Unwin 1915), 156p.*
MACGILL, P
  The red horizon *(London: Jenkins 1916), 306p.*
MACKINTOSH, E W
  War, the liberator *(London: Lane 1918), 156p.*
MASEFIELD, J
  St. George and the dragon: the war and the future *(London: Heinemann 1919), 104p.*
MUEHLON, W
  Dr Muehlon's diary: notes written early in the war *(London: Cassell 1918), 247p.*
ROLLAND, R
  The forerunners *(London: Allen & Unwin 1920), 215p.*
THAYER, W R
  Volleys from a non-combatant *(London: Curtis Brown 1919), 322p.*
TROTTER, W
  Instincts of the herd in peace and war, 1916-1919 *(London: OUP 1953), 219p.*
USHER, R G
  The winning of the war *(New York: Harper 1918), 381p.*
WILKINS, H T
  Mysteries of the Great war *(London: Allan 1935), 412p.*

MISSIONARIES

IN the whirlpool of the races: missionaries at the battle Fronts *(London: London Missionary Society 1920), 102p.*
[See also CHAPLAINS]

MONS

ASCOLI, D
The Mons Star: the British Expeditionary Force, 5th Aug–22nd Nov 1914 *(London: Harrap 1981), 250p.*
BLOEM, W
The advance from Mons, 1914 *(London: Davies 1930), 211p.*
COLEMAN, F A
From Mons to Ypres *(London: Sampson Low 1919), 343p.*
CORBETT-SMITH, A
The retreat from Mons *(London: Cassell 1916), 256p.*
GORDON, G S
Mons and the retreat *(London: Constable 1918), 94p.*
HERBERT, A N H
Mons, Anzac and Kut *(London: Arnold 1919), 251p.*
LUCY, J
There's a devil in the drum *(London: Faber 1938), 393p.*
TERRAINE, J
Mons: the retreat to victory *(London: Batsford 1960), 224p.*
[See also BRITISH EXPEDITIONARY FORCES, FLANDERS]

MORALS

COLLINGS, J
The Great War: its lessons and its warnings *(London: Rural World 1916), 113p.*
HIRSCHFELD, M *and* GASPAR, A *eds*
Sexual history of the World War *(New York: Panurge 1934), 350p.*

MOTOR LAUNCHES

CHATTERTON, E K
The auxiliary patrol *(London: Sidgwick & Jackson 1923), 332p.*
GRANVILLE, W *and* KELLY, R A
Inshore heroes: the story of H.M. Motor Launches in two World Wars *(London: W. H. Allen 1961), 320p; bib.*
MAXWELL, G S
The motor launch patrol *(London: Dent 1920), 303p.*

MUHLHAUSER, G H P
Small craft *(London: Lane 1920), 268p.*

MUNITIONS

CABLE, B
Doing their bit: war work at home *(London: Hodder & Stoughton 1916), 134p.*
CANADA Munition Resources Commission
Final report on the work of the Commission *(Toronto 1920), 260p.*
CARNEGIE, D
History of munition supply in Canada, 1914-1918 *(New York: Longmans 1925), 336p.*
COLE, G D H
Trade Unionism and munitions *(Oxford: Clarendon 1923), 251p.*
COSENS, M
Lloyd George's munition girls *(London: Hutchinson 1916), 160p.*
CROWELL, B
American munitions, 1917-18 *(Washington DC: Dept. of Army 1919), 592p.*
DEWAR, G A B
The great munitions feat, 1914-1918 *(London: Constable 1921), 343p.*
FARROW, E S
American guns in the war with Germany *(New York: Dutton 1920), 223p.*
FOXWELL, A E
Munition lasses: six months as principal overlooker in danger buildings *(London: Hodder & Stoughton 1918), 63p.*
FROST, G H
Munitions of war: a record of the B.S.A. and Daimler Companies during the war *(Birmingham: B.S.A. & Daimler 1921), 222p.*
GREAT BRITAIN Ministry of Munitions
History of the Ministry of Munitions *(London: HMSO 1922), 12 vols.*
HAMILTON, M L *Lady*
Three years of the duration: memoirs of a munition worker 1914–1918 *(Wellington, NZ: Reed 1978), 125p.*
HIGH explosive shell *(New York: American Mechanist 1915), 70p.*
JONES, B E
Workshop hints for munition workers *(London: Cassell 1916), 160p.*
PULL, E
The munition worker's handbook: a guide for persons taking up munition work *(London: Crosby Lockwood 1916), 142p.*
RAMSEY, A R J *and* WESTON, H C
A manual of explosives *(London: Routledge 1916), 128p.*
WRIGLEY, C
Lloyd George and the British Labour Movement in peace and war *(Hassocks. Sx: Harvester P 1976), 298p; bib.*
YATES, L K
The woman's part: a record of munition work *(London: Hodder & Stoughton 1918), 63p.*

MUTINIES

ALLISON, W *and* FAIRLEY, J
  The monocled mutineer *(London: Quartet 1978), 206p.*
HORN, D
  The German naval mutinies of World War I *(New Brunswick, NJ: Rutgers 1969), 346p.*
WATT, R M
  Dare call it treason *(New York: Simon & Schuster 1963), 285p.*
WILLIAMS, J
  Mutiny, 1917 *(London: Heinemann 1962), 257p; bib.*
[See also FRENCH ARMY, GERMAN NAVY]

NAVAL WARFARE (General)

BATCHELOR, J
  Fighting ships of World War One and Two *(London: Phoebus 1976), 255p.*
BENNETT, G
  Naval battles of the First World War *(London: Batsford 1968), 320p; bib.*
BUCHAN, J
  Naval episodes of the Great War *(London: Nelson 1938), 325p.*
BYWATER, H C
  Their secret purposes: dramas and mysteries of the naval War *(London: Constable 1932), 311p.*
CHATTERTON, E K
  Gallant gentlemen *(London: Hurst & Blackett 1931), 296p.*
  Seas of adventures: the story of the naval operations in the Mediterranean, Adriatic and Aegean *(London: Hurst & Blackett 1936), 319p.*
CORBETT-SMITH, *Sir* J
  Naval operations *(London: Longmans 1938-1940), 3 vols.*
THE DECLARATION of London and Naval Prize Bill: national starvation in war and paralysis of Britain's power and rights at sea *(London: Imperial Maritime League 1920), 248p.*
FITZSIMONS, B *ed*
  Warships and sea battles of World War I *(London: Phoebus 1973), 160p.*
FLEETS of the world, 1915 *(London: Nash 1915), 198p.*
FROTHINGHAM, T G
  The naval history of the World War *(Cambridge, Mass: Harvard UP 1925), 3 vols.*
GIBSON, R H
  Three years of naval warfare *(London: Heinemann 1918), 326p.*
GILL, C C
  Naval power in the war *(1914-1918) (New York: Doran 1919), 302p.*
GILL, C C *and* STEVENS, W O
  The war on the sea *(New York: Harper 1920), 402p.*
GRIFF *pseud*
  Surrendered: some naval war secrets *(London: Griff 1926), 246p.*
HALL, S K
  The war at sea, 1914-1918 *(London: Benn 1929), 80p.*

HOEHLING, A A
  The Great War at sea: a history of naval action, 1914-1918 *(London: Barker 1965), 336p; bib.*
HUNTER, F T
  Beatty, Jellicoe, Sims and Rodman: Yankee gobs and British tars as seen by an Anglomaniac *(New York: Doubleday 1919), 204p.*
HURD, A S
  The Fleets at war *(London: Hodder & Stoughton 1915), 227p.*
HURD, A S *and* BYWATER, H C
  From Heligoland to Keeling Island: 100 days of naval war *(London: Hodder & Stoughton 1915), 216p.*
JELLICOE, J R *1st viscount*
  The crisis of the naval war *(London: Cassell 1920), 331p.*
KIPLING, R
  Sea warfare *(London: Macmillan 1916), 222p.*
KOCK, N
  Blockade and jungle *(London: Hale 1940), 256p.*
LANGMAID, K J R
  The blind eye *(London: Jarrolds 1972), 166p.*
LE FLEMING, H M
  ABC of warships of World War I *(New Rochelle, NY: Soccer 1962), 352p.*
MACINTYRE, D
  Fighting ships and seamen *(London: Evans 1963), 192p.*
MAXWELL, G S
  The naval Front *(London: Black 1920), 203p.*
MILLER, W H
  Sea fighters: Navy years of the Great War *(New York: Macmillan 1920), 216p.*
NEWBOLT, *Sir* H J
  A naval history of the war, 1914-1918 *(London: Hodder & Stoughton 1920), 350p.*
PAINE, R D
  Corsair in the war zone *(Boston, Mass: Houghton Mifflin 1920), 303p.*
ROLT-WHEELER, F W
  Wonder of war at sea *(New York: Lothrop 1919), 376p.*
ROSE, H W
  Brittany patrol: the story of the suicide fleet *(New York: Norton 1937), 367p.*
WYLLIE, W L *and* WREN, M F
  Sea fights of the Great War: naval incidents during the first nine months *(London: Cassell 1918), 167p.*
[See also NAVIES OF INDIVIDUAL COUNTRIES]

NEAR EAST

ALLEN, T
  The tracks they trod: Salonika and the Balkans, Gallipoli, Egypt and Palestine revisited *(London: Joseph 1932), 191p.*

BATES, J V
  Our Allies and enemies in the Near East *(London: Chapman & Hall 1918), 234p.*
BRIDIE, J
  Some talk of Alexander: a revue with interludes *(London: Methuen 1926), 180p.*
BROWN, W S
  My war diary, 1914-1919: recollections of Gallipoli, Lemnos, Egypt and Palestine *(Galashiels, Scot: Border Standard 1941), 134p.*
DANE, E
  British campaigns in the Nearer East, 1914-1918 *(London: Hodder & Stoughton 1919), 2 vols.*
DICKSON, W E R
  East Persia: a backwater of the Great War *(London: Arnold 1924), 279p.*
DYER, R E H
  The raiders of the Sarhad: being the account of a campaign against the brigands of the Persian-Baluchi border during the Great War *(London: Witherby 1921), 223p.*
FUSILIER Bluff: the experiences of an unprofessional soldier in the Near East, 1918-1919 *(London: Bles 1934), 283p.*
GIBBONS, H A
  The reconstruction of the Near East *(New York: 1917), 228p.*
HALL, J R
  The desert hath pearls *(Melbourne: Hawthorn 1975), 219p.*
HALL, W H
  Near East: crossroads of the world *(London: Interchurch World Movement 1920), 230p.*
KEARSEY, A H C
  The operations in Egypt and Palestine, 1914 to June 1917 *(Aldershot: Gale & Polden 1932), 88p.*
LAWSON, J C
  Tales of Aegean intrigue *(New York: Dutton 1921), 271p.*
MACKINNON, I
  Garroot: adventures of a Clydeside apprentice *(London: Cape 1933), 250p.*
MURRAY, *Sir* A J
  Sir Archibald Murray's despatches, June 1916-June 1917 *(London: Dent 1920), 229p.*
PARFIT, J T
  Serbia to Kut: an account of the war in Bible lands *(London: Hunter & Longhurst 1917), 55p.*
RAWLINSON, A
  Adventures in the Near East, 1918-1922 *(London: Melrose 1923), 377p.*
TENNANT, J E
  In the clouds above Baghdad: being the records of an air commander *(London: Palmer 1920), 289p.*
TOROSSIAN, S
  From Dardanelles to Palestine: a true story of five battle Fronts of Turkey and her Allies and a harem romance *(Boston, Mass: Meador 1947), 219p.*
WOODS, H C
  Cradle of the war: the Near East and Pan-Germanism *(Boston, Mass: Little, Brown 1918), 360p; bib.*

YEATS-BROWN, F C C
Golden Horn *(London: Gollancz 1932), 287p.*

NEGROES

BARBEAU, A E *and* HENRI, F
The unknown soldiers: black American troops in World War I *(Philadelphia, Pa: Temple UP 1974), 279p.*
BUCHANAN, A
Three years of war in East Africa *(Westport, Conn: Negro UP 1969), 247p.*
COMPLETE history of the colored soldiers in the war *(Brooklyn, NY: Bennett & Churchill 1919), 159p.*
HEYWOOD, C D
Negro combat troops in the World War: the story of the 371st Infantry *(Worcester, Mass: Commonwealth P 1929), 310p.*
HUNTON, *Mrs* A D *and* JOHNSON, K M
Two colored women with the American Expeditionary Forces *(Brooklyn, NY: Hunton 1921), 256p.*
JOHNSTON, *Sir* H
The black man's part in the war *(London: Simpkin Marshall 1911), 128p.*
LITTLE, A W
From Harlem to the Rhine: the story of New York's colored volunteers *(New York: Covici 1936), 382p.*
LYNK, M V
Negro pictorial review of the Great World War: a visual narrative of the Negro's glorious part in the world's greatest war *(Memphis, Tenn: Twentieth Century 1919), 65p.*
MASON, M *and* FURR, A
The American Negro soldier with the Red Hand of France *(New York: Cornhill 1921), 180p.*
MILLER, K
Kelly Miller's history of the World War for human rights *(Westport, Conn: Negro UP 1969), 495p; previously published as:* Our war for human rights.
ROSS, W A
My colored battalion *(Menasha, Wis: Banta 1920), 119p.*
SCOTT, E J
Scott's official history of the American Negro in the World War *(New York: Arno 1969), 511p.*
UNITED STATES Division of Negro Economics
The Negro at work during the World War and during reconstruction *(Washington DC: 1921), 144p.*
WILLIAMS, C
Sidelights on Negro soldiers *(Boston, Mass: Brimmer 1923), 248p.*

NETHERLANDS

NETHERLANDS and the World War *(New Haven, Conn: Yale UP 1928), 4 vols.*
VANDENBOSCH, A
The neutrality of the Netherlands during the World War *(Grand Rapids, Mich: Eerdmans 1927), 349p.*
VAN DYKE, H
Fighting for peace *(London: Hodder & Stoughton 1917), 256p.*

NEUTRALS

BREWER, D C
Rights and duties of neutrals *(New York: Putnam 1916), 260p.*
EDLESTON, R H
Italian neutrality *(Cambridge: CUP 1915), 72p.*
NEUTRALITY, its history, economics and law *(New York: Farrar 1935-1936), 4 vols.*
RAPPAPORT, A
The British Press and Wilsonian neutrality *(London: OUP 1951), 162p.*
RISTE, O
The neutral Ally: Norway's relations with belligerent Powers in the First World War *(London: Allen & Unwin 1965), 295p; bib.*
SWEDEN, Norway, Denmark and Iceland in the World War *(New Haven, Conn: Yale UP 1930), 593p.*
UNITED STATES Department of State
Neutrality proclamations, 1914-1918 *(Washington DC: 1919), 64p.*

NEUVE CHAPELLE

BAYNES, J
Morale: a study of men and courage: the Second Scottish Rifles at the battle of Neuve Chapelle *(London: Cassell 1967), 286p; bib.*

NEW GUINEA (GERMAN)

BURNELL, F S
Australia versus Germany: the story of the taking of German New Guinea *(London: Allen 1915), 254p.*
REEVES, L C
Australians in action in New Guinea *(Sydney: Angus & Robertson 1915), 97p.*

NEW ZEALAND

AITKEN, A C
  Gallipoli to the Somme: recollections of a New Zealand infantryman *(London: OUP 1963), 177p.*
ALLEN, S S
  2/Auckland, 1918: a record of service in France *(Auckland: Whitcombe & Tombs 1920), 188p.*
BRERETON, C B
  Tales of three campaigns: experiences with the 12th (Nelson) Company, N.Z.E.F. *(London: Selywn & Blount 1926), 290p.*
BURTON, O E
  The Auckland Regiment: being an account of the doings on active service of the First, Second and Third Battalions *(Auckland: Whitcombe & Tombs 1922), 323p.*
  Silent Division: New Zealanders at the Front, 1914-1918 *(Sydney: Angus & Robertson 1935), 326p.*
BUTTERWORTH, H M
  Letters written in the trenches near Ypres between May and September 1915 *(Wellington, NZ: Whitcombe & Tombs 1916), 84p.*
BYRNE, A E
  Official history of the Otago Regiment New Zealand Expeditionary Force in the Great War 1914–1918 *(Dunedin, NZ: Wilkie nd), 407p.*
BYRNE, J R
  New Zealand Artillery in the field, 1914-18 *(Auckland: Whitcombe & Tombs 1922), 314p.*
CARTER, F L
  The conflagration in Europe *(Christchurch: Whitcombe & Tombs 1914), 86p.*
COWAN, J
  The Maoris in the Great War *(Auckland: Whitcombe & Tombs 1928), 184p.*
DREW, H T B
  The war effort of New Zealand *(Auckland: Whitcombe & Tombs 1923), vol. 4.*
DYER, H G
  Ma Te Reinga; by way of Reinga: the way of the Maori soldier *(Ilfracombe, Devon: Stockwell 1953), 96p.*
FERGUSON, D
  History of the Canterbury Regiment, N.Z.E.F., 1914-1919 *(Auckland: Whitcombe & Tombs 1921), 364p.*
HAND-NEWTON, C T
  A physician in peace and war *(Christchurch, NZ: Peryer 1967), unp.*
HYDE, R
  Passport to hell: the story of John Douglas Stark, bomber, Fifth Regiment New Zealand Expeditionary Force *(London: Hurst & Blackett 1936), 288p.*
LEARY, L P
  New Zealanders in Samoa *(London: Heinemann 1918), 248p.*
LUXFORD, J H
  With the machine gunners in France and Palestine: the official history of the New Zealand Machine Gun Corps *(Wellington: Whitcombe & Tombs 1923), 255p.*

MACKENZIE, C N
The tale of a trooper: experiences of a New Zealand trooper in the European war *(London: Lane 1921), 200p.*
MALTHUS, C
Anzac: a retrospect *(Auckland: Whitcombe & Tombs 1965), 159p.*
MILLER, E
Camps, tramps and trenches: the diary of a New Zealand sapper, 1917 *(Dunedin: Reed 1939), 207p.*
MOORE, A B
The mounted riflemen in Sinai and Palestine: the story of New Zealand's crusaders *(Auckland: Whitcombe & Tombs 1920), 175p.*
NEILL, J C
The New Zealand Tunnelling Company, 1915-1919 *(Auckland: Whitcombe & Tombs 1922), 159p.*
NEW ZEALAND at the Front *(London: Cassell 1917), 196p.*
NEW ZEALAND EXPEDITIONARY FORCE
The Great War, 1914–1918 roll of honour *(Wellington, NZ: Govt PO, 1924), 358p.*
List of casualties and a summary of casualties in order of units *(Wellington, NZ: Govt PO 1915-1919), 2 vols.*
ON the Anzac trail: being extracts from the diary of a New Zealand sapper *(London: Heinemann 1916), 210p.*
POWLES, C G
The history of the Canterbury Mounted Rifles, 1914-1919 *(Auckland: Whitcombe & Tombs 1928), 267p.*
The New Zealanders in Sinai and Palestine *(Auckland: Whitcombe & Tombs 1922), 284p.*
REGIMENTAL history of New Zealand Cyclist Corps in the Great War, 1914-1918 *(Auckland: Whitcombe & Tombs 1922), 139p.*
ROBERTSON, J
With the cameliers in Palestine *(Dunedin: Reed 1938), 243p.*
SHELL shocks: New Zealanders in France *(London: Jarrolds 1917), 68p.*
STEWART, H
The New Zealand Division, 1916-1919: a popular history *(Auckland: Whitcombe & Tombs 1921), 634p.*
STUDHOLME, J
New Zealand Expeditionary Force: a record of personal services during the war of officers, nurses and first-class warrant officers; and other facts relating to the N.Z.E.F. *(Wellington: 1928), 563p.*
WAITE, F
The New Zealanders at Gallipoli *(Auckland, Whitcombe & Tombs 1919), vol 1.*
WESTON, C H
Three years with the New Zealanders *(London: Skeffington 1918), 255p.*
WILKIE, A H
Official war history of the Wellington Mounted Rifles Regiment, 1914-1919 *(Wellington: 1924), 259p.*

NICHOLAS II TSAR

ALEXANDRA Empress of Russia
Letters of the Tsaritsa to the Tsar, 1914-16 *(London: Duckworth 1923), unp.*
BULYGIN, P *and* KERENSKY, A
The murder of the Romanovs *(London: Hutchinson 1935), 286p.*
COWLES, V
The last Tsar and Tsarina *(London: Weidenfeld & Nicolson 1977), 232p; bib.*
THE FALL of the Romanoffs: how the ex-Empress and Rasputin caused the Russian Revolution *(London: Jenkins 1917), 312p.*
HANBURY-WILLIAMS, *Sir* J
The Emperor Nicholas II as I knew him *(London: Humphreys 1922), 271p.*
MASSIE, R
Nicholas and Alexandra *(London: Gollancz 1968), 584p; bib.*
RADZIWILL, C *princess*
Nicholas II: the last of the Tsars *(London: Cassell 1931), 320p.*
RIVET, C
The last of the Romanoffs *(London: Constable 1917), 246p.*
SUMMERS, A *and* MANGOLD, T
The file on the Tsar *(London: Gollancz 1976), 352p.*
WILTON, R
Last days of the Romanoffs *(London: Butterworth 1920), 320p.*
[See also RASPUTIN, RUSSIA, RUSSIAN REVOLUTION]

NIGERIA

OSUNTOKUN, A
Nigeria in the First World War *(London: Longman 1979), 336p; bib.*

NORWAY

VIGNESS, P G
The neutrality of Norway in the World War *(Stanford, Cal: Stanford UP 1932), 188p.*
[See also NEUTRALS, SCANDINAVIA]

NURSES AND NURSING

ARNOLD, G
Sister Anne! Sister Anne!: stories of hospital work in France during the war *(Toronto: 1919), 235p.*
BAGNOLD, E
A diary without dates: thoughts and impressions of a V.A.D. *(London: Heinemann 1918), 146p.*

BEAUCHAMP, P
Fanny goes to war *(London: Murray 1919), 290p.*
BILLINGTON, M F
The roll-call of serving women *(London: RTS 1915), 227p.*
BORDEN, M
The forbidden zone: experiences as a nurse attached to the French Army *(London: Heinemann 1929), 199p.*
BOYLSTON, H D
'Sister': the war diary of a nurse *(New York: Washburn 1927), 292p.*
CAMPBELL, P
Back of the Front: experiences of a nurse *(London: Newnes 1915), 126p.*
DEXTER, M
In the soldier's service *(Boston, Mass: Houghton Mifflin 1918), 209p.*
DIARY of a Nursing Sister on the Western Front *(Edinburgh: Blackwood 1915), 300p.*
FITZWILLIAMS, D C L
A nursing manual for nurses and nursing orderlies *(London: Hodder & Stoughton 1915), 446p.*
GLEICHEN, *Lady* H
Contacts and contrasts: experiences of a nurse with the Italian Armies *(London: Murray 1940), 344p.*
GOWER, M F *duchess of Sutherland*
Six weeks at the war *(London: The Times 1914), 116p.*
HALDANE, E S
The British nurse in peace and war *(London: Murray 1923), 282p.*
HARDEN, H S S
Faenza Rest Camp: a story of the Mediterranean L. of C. *(London: Hutchinson 1920), 111p.*
LUARD, K E
Unknown warriors *(London: Chatto & Windus 1930), 306p.*
McDOUGALL, G
A nurse at the war: nursing adventures in Belgium and France *(New York: McBride 1917), 203p.*
MACNAUGHTAN, S
A woman's diary of the war *(London: Nelson 1915), 168p.*
MARTIN-NICHOLSON, *Sister*
My experiences on three Fronts *(London: Allen & Unwin 1916), 288p.*
MILLARD, S
I saw them die *(London: Harrap 1936), 127p.*
NURSING adventures: a F.A.N.Y. in France *(London: Heinemann 1917), 203p.*
REMINISCENT sketches 1914 to 1919; by members of Her Majesty's Queen Alexandra's Imperial Military Nursing Service *(London: HMSO 1922), 80p.*
STIMSON, J C
Finding themselves: the letters of an American Army Chief Nurse in a British Hospital in France *(New York: Macmillan 1919), 231p.*
TAYLER, H
A Scottish nurse at work *(London: Lane 1920), 156p.*

WAR Nurse's diary: sketches from a Belgian field hospital *(New York: Macmillan 1918)*, *115p.*

[See also HOSPITALS, MEDICAL]

OCCULT

ALLAN, A
Armageddon! before and after *(London: Potter-Solvent 1914), 111p.*
ALTSHELER, J A
The hosts of the air: the story of a quest in the Great War *(New York: Appleton 1915), 338p.*
ANCIENT Babylon and modern Germany versus the new Jerusalem *(London: Stockwell 1916), 176p.*
BAILLIE, W
History in prophecy *(London: Thynne 1915), 88p.*
BARKER, E
War letters from the living dead *(New York: Kennerley 1915), 318p.*
BARTLETT, W T
The world's crisis in the light of prophecy *(Watford, Herts: 1915), 156p.*
BEGBIE, H
On the side of the angels: a reply to Arthur Machen *(London: Hodder & Stoughton 1915), 126p.*
BERRY, J M
European history foretold *(London: Thynne 1915), 271p.*
BLATCHFORD, R
The war that was foretold *(London: Associated Newspapers 1915), 48p.*
BOND, F B
The hill of vision: a forecast of the war gathered from automatic writings *(London: Constable 1918), 134p.*
CHURCHWOMAN *pseud*
The chariots of God *(London: Stockwell 1916), 119p.*
COMMENTITIUS *pseud*
The Great War for the greater peace *(London: Murby 1915), 131p.*
CRAFER, T W
A prophet's visions and the war *(London: Skeffington 1916), 83p.*
CROSLAND, T W H
Find the angels *(London: Werner Laurie 1915), 95p.*
CROSS, J
Christendom's impending doom *(Bristol: 1915), 580p.*
D, F
The war and the prophets *(London: Morgan 1915), 94p.*
DAWSON, W B
The close of the present age in the light of the periods predicted in prophecy *(London: Marshall 1917), 67p.*
DENISON, H P
The Lord in his temple: the message of Habakkuk to a world at war *(London: Scott 1916), 67p.*

De Saint Dalmas, H G E
The time of the end and the 'Weeks' of Daniel: a discovery and restatement *(London: Thynne 1917), 163p.*
Dod, T A
Notes on the present age *(London: Murray 1916), 252p.*
Einstein, L
A prophecy of the war, 1913-1914 *(New York: Columbia UP 1918), 94p.*
Fair, F
Momentous events *(London: Roberts 1915), 130p.*
Fox, R J
Revelation on revelation and these latter days *(London: Kegan Paul 1916), 413p.*
Unexpected tidings of the war *(London: Kegan Paul 1915), 128p.*
Giraud, S L
Ghosts in the Great War, and true tales of haunted houses *(London: Fleetway 1927), 120p.*
Gordon, G
An interpreter of war: Habakkuk *(London: Longmans 1915), 63p.*
Graebner, T C
Prophecy and the war *(St. Louis, Missouri: Concordia 1918), 112p.*
Hoare, E
Palestine, Russia and the present *(London: Thynne 1915), 91p.*
Jones, C S
W. T. Stead and the war: prophecies that have come true *(London: Review of Reviews 1917), 120p.*
Lancaster, G H
Prophecy, the war, and the Near East *(London: Marshall 1919), 272p.*
Lavington, H *pseud*
Psychical phenomena and the war *(New York: Dodd 1918), 362p.*
Machen, A
The angels of Mons *(London: Simpkin Marshall 1915), 133p.*
Manley, W F
Galaxy of coming events: meaning and outcome of this European war *(Los Angeles, Cal: Manley 1918), 263p.*
Messenger, F M
World war, four horses of Revelation *(Chicago: Messenger 1918), 135p.*
Morrison, H C
World war in prophecy: the downfall of the Kaiser and the end of the dispensation *(Louisviille, Ky: Pentecost 1917), 95p.*
Murray, M
Bible prophecies and the plain man, with special reference to the present war *(London: Hodder & Stoughton 1915), 319p.*
Nurse, E J
Prophecy and the war *(London: Skeffington 1915), 93p.*
P, E
The hidden side of war: some revelations and prophecies *(London: Elliot Stock 1918), 134p.*
Rawson, F L
How the war will end *(London: Crystal 1914), 65p.*

SHIRLEY, R
  Prophecies and omens of the Great War *(London: Rider 1914), 64p.*
SULLEY, H
  Is it Armageddon? *(London: Simpkin Marshall 1915), 107p.*
TAYLOR, I E
  Angels, Saints and Bowmen at Mons *(London: Theosophical Society 1916), unp.*
THURSTON, H
  The war and the prophets: notes on certain popular predictions current in this latter age *(London: Burns & Oates 1915), 202p.*
TIARKS, H C
  Eternal certainties; or, The war, the world, and the future *(London: Marshall 1918), 147p.*
TROTTER, A
  The great world drama *(London: Elltiot Stock 1915), 116p.*
WATSON, A S
  The flashing sword and its significance *(London: Roberts 1917), 73p.*
WYNN, W
  Revelation in the light of the war and modern events *(London: Thynne 1916), 202p.*

OCCUPATION

ALLEN, H T
  My Rhineland journal *(London: Hutchinson 1924), 611p.*
  The Rhineland occupation *(Indianapolis, Ind: Bobbs-Merrill 1927), 347p.*
THE OCCUPATION of the Rhineland 1918–1929 *(London: HMSO 1987)*
APEX *pseud*
  The uneasy triangle: four years of the occupation *(London: Murray 1931), 276p.*
HINKSON, K
  Life in the occupied area *(London: Hutchinson 1925), 274p.*
MARKHAM, V R
  A woman's watch on the Rhine: sketches of the occupation *(London: Hodder & Stoughton 1921), 301p.*
TUOHY, F
  Occupied, 1918-30: a postscript to the Western Front *(London: Butterworth 1931), 318p.*
UNITED STATES Department of Army
  American Military Government of occupied Germany, 1918-20 *(Washington DC: 1943), 365p.*
WALKER, W
  Sketches of a Tommy on the Rhine *(London: Stockwell 1921), 88p.*

OFFICER TRAINING CORPS

BROWN, A R H
  The O.T.C. and the Great War *(London: Country Life 1915), 245p.*
OFFICERS Training Corps: a record of war service, 1914-1918 *(Cambridge: CUP 1919), 239p.*

ORIGINS OF THE WAR

ADKINS, F J
  The war: its origins and warnings *(London: Allen 1915), 227p.*
ALBERTINI, L
  The origins of the war of 1914 *(London: OUP), 3 vols.*
ALLEN, G H
  Causes of and motives for the Great War *(Philadelphia, Pa: Barrie 1915), 377p.*
ANDRASSY, G *count*
  Whose sin is the World War? *(New York: New Era 1915), unp.*
ANDRIULLI, G A
  Documents relating to the Great War *(London: Fisher Unwin 1915), 176p.*
ARCHER, W
  The thirteen days, July 23-August 4, 1914: a chronicle and an interpretation *(London: OUP 1915), 244p.*
BARNES, H E
  The genesis of the World War: an introduction to the problem of war guilt *(New York: Knopf 1929), 754p.*
BARRON, C W
  The audacious war: an examination of its causes, especially financial and economic *(London: Constable 1915), 208p.*
BARRY, W
  The world's debate: an historical defence of the Allies *(London: Hodder & Stoughton 1917), 382p.*
BEAZLEY, *Sir* C R
  The road to ruin in Europe, 1890-1914 *(London: Dent 1932), 111p.*
BECK, J M
  The evidence in the case: an analysis of the diplomatic records submitted by England, Germany, Russia and Belgium in the Supreme Court of Civilization *(New York: Putnam 1915), 258p.*
BENEDICT, C
  Six months, March-August 1914 *(New York: Benedict 1916), 88p.*
BEVAN, E R
  The method in the madness: a fresh consideration of the case between Germany and ourselves *(London: Arnold 1917), 309p.*
BLOCH, C
  The causes of the World War: an historical summary *(London: Allen & Unwin 1935), 224p.*
BODEN, J F W
  Freedom's battle: being historical essays occasioned by the Great War *(London: Simpkin Marshall 1916), 77p.*
BOGITSHEVICH, M
  Causes of the war *(New York: Lemcke 1919), 135p.*
BOSWORTH, R J B
  Italy and the approach of the First World War *(New York: St. Martin's 1983), 174p.*
BRERETON, C S H
  Who is responsible? Armageddon and after *(London: Harrap 1914), 126p.*

BURGESS, J W
  The European war, its causes, purposes and probable results *(Chicago: McClurg 1915)*, *209p.*
CARPENTER, E
  The healing of the nations and the hidden sources of their strife *(London: Allen 1915)*, *266p.*
CASSELS, L
  The Archduke and the assassin: Sarajevo, June 28th 1914 *(New York:Stein & Day 1985)*, *216p.*
CHESTERTON, G K
  Appetite of tyranny *(New York: Dodd 1915)*, *122p.*
CHITWOOD, O P
  The immediate causes of the Great War *(New York: Crowell 1917)*, *196p.*
COOK, *Sir* T A
  Kaiser, Krupp and Kultur *(New York: Scribner 1915)*, *178p.*
  The mark of the beast *(London: Murray 1917)*, *432p.*
COUDERT, F R *and others*
  Why Europe is at war *(New York: Putnam 1915)*, *179p.*
CRAMB, J A
  Germany and England *(New York: Dutton 1914)*, *152p.*
CRAMPTON, R J
  The hollow detente: Anglo–German relations in the Balkans, 1911–1914 *(London: Prior 1981)*, *255p.*
DAVENPORT, B
  The genesis of the war *(London: Putnam 1916)*, *545p.*
DAVIS, W S *and others*
  The roots of the war *(New York: Century 1918)*, *unp.*
DE BRISAY, A C B
  And then came war: outline of the European tragedy *(London: Nicholson & Watson 1937)*, *312p.*
DEDIJER, V
  The road to Sarajevo *(London: MacGibbon & Kee 1967)*, *550p.*
DICKINSON, G L
  The international anarchy, 1904-1914 *(London: Allen & Unwin 1926)*, *516p.*
DILLON, E J
  Ourselves and Germany *(London: Chapman & Hall 1916)*, *322p.*
EWART, J S
  The roots and causes of the war, 1914-1918 *(London: Hutchinson 1925)*, *2 vols.*
FAY, S
  The origins of the World War *(New York: Macmillan 1929)*, *2 vols.*
FEDERN, C
  The origins of the war *(New York: Dillingham 1915)*, *207p.*
FERNAU, H
  Because I am a German *(London: Constable 1916)*, *153p.*
FERRARA, O
  Causes and pretexts of the war *(New York: New Library 1918)*, *314p.*

FISCHER, F
War of illusions: German policies from 1911 to 1914 *(London: Chatto & Windus 1975)*, *578p.*

FITZPATRICK, *Sir* J P
The origins, causes and objects of the war *(London: Simpkin Marshall 1915)*, *124p.*

FLEMING, D F
The origins and legacies of World War I *(New York: Doubleday 1968)*, *352p.*

FREDERICK WILLIAM Crown Prince of Germany
I seek the truth: a book on responsibility for the war *(London: Faber & Gwyer 1926)*, *325p.*

GAUSS, C
Why we went to war *(New York: Scribner 1918)*, *386p.*

GEDDES, P *and* SLATER, G
Ideas at war *(London:Williams & Norgate 1917)*, *270p.*

GEISS, I *ed*
July 1914: the outbreak of the First World War *(New York: Norton 1974)*, *400p.*

GIBBONS, H A
The new map of Europe, 1911-1914 *(London: Duckworth 1914)*, *382p.*

GOOCH, G P *and* TEMPERLEY, H
British documents on the origins of the war, 1898-1914 *(London: HMSO 1927-1938)*, *13 vols.*

GORDY, W F
The causes and meaning of the Great War *(New York: Scribner 1919)*, *154p.*

GORICAR, J *and* STOWE, L B
The inside story of Austro-German intrigue; or, How the World War was brought about *(New York: Doubleday 1920)*, *301p.*

GRATACAP, L P
Europe's handicap – tribe and class *(New York: Benton 1915)*, *304p.*

GRELLING, R
J'accuse *(New York: Doran 1917-19)*, *4 vols.*

GRIEB, C K
Uncovering the forces for war *(New York: Examiner 1947)*, *118p.*

GUYOT, Y
The causes and consequences of the war *(London: Hutchinson 1916)*, *395p.*

HALDANE, R *viscount*
Before the war *(London: Cassell 1920)*, *207p.*

HARRISON, A
The Kaiser's war *(London: Allen & Unwin 1914)*, *252p.*

HART, A B
The war in Europe: its causes and results *(New York: Appleton 1914)*, *254p.*

HART, A B *and* BASSETT, J S
The great explosion: backgrounds and origins of the World War *(New York: Harper 1920)*, *vol 1.*

HEADLAM, J W
The German Chancellor and the outbreak of war *(London: Fisher Unwin 1917)*, *127p.*
History of twelve days, July 24th to August 4th, 1914 *(London: Fisher Unwin 1915)*, *436p.*

HOBBS, W H
World war and its consequences *(New York: Putnam 1919), 446p.*
HOVELACQUE, E
The deeper causes of the war *(London: Allen & Unwin 1916), 158p.*
HOWE, F C
Why war? *(New York: Scribner 1916), 366p.*
JOLL, J
The origins of the First World War *(London: Longman 1984), 240p.*
KEIGER, J R V
France and the origins of the First World War *(London: Macmillan 1983), 201p; bib.*
KELLY, M
Carlyle and the war *(Chicago: Open Court 1915), 337p.*
KENNEDY, J M
How the war began *(London: Hodder & Stoughton 1914), 187p.*
KOCH, H W
The origins of the First World War *(London: Macmillan 1972), 374p; bib.*
KYLIE, E
Who caused the war? *(London: Milford 1915), 86p.*
LAFORE, L
The long fuse: an interpretation of the origins of World War I *(London: Weidenfeld & Nicolson 1966), 282p; bib.*
LANGHORNE, R
The collapse of the concert of Europe: international politics 1890–1914 *(New York: St Martin's 1981), 137p.*
LEE, D E ed
The outbreak of the First World War: who was responsible? *(Boston, Mass: Heath 1958), 74p; bib.*
LEGGE, E
King Edward, the Kaiser and the war *(London: Grant Richards 1917), 384p.*
LICHNOWSKY, K M *prince*
The guilt of Germany for the war of German aggression *(New York: Putnam 1918), 122p.*
THE LIE of the 3rd of August 1914 *(London: Hodder & Stoughton 1917), 350p.*
LOREBURN, R T R *1st earl*
How the war came *(London: Methuen 1919), 340p.*
McLAREN, A D
Germanism from within *(New York: Dutton 1919), 383p.*
MACINTYRE, D
The Great War: causes and consequences *(Glasgow: Blackie 1979), 81p.*
MAGNUS, L A
Pros and cons in the Great War: a record of foreign opinions with a register of fact *(London: Kegan Paul 1917), 396p.*
MANSEARGH, N
Coming of the First World War: a study in the European balance 1878-1914 *(London: Longmans 1949), 257p.*
MARTEL, G
The origins of the First World War *(London: Longman 1987), 112p; bib.*

MARTI, O A
   The Anglo-German commercial and colonial rivalry as a cause of the Great War *(Boston, Mass: Stratford 1917), 97p.*

MOREL, E D
   Truth and the war *(London: National Labour 1916), 320p.*

MORRIS, C *and* DAWSON, L H
   Why the nations are at war: the causes and issues of the great conflict *(London: Harrap 1915), 407p.*

MUIR, R
   Britain's case against Germany: an examination of the historical background to the German action in 1914 *(London: Sherratt & Hughes 1914), 208p.*

NOMIKOS, E V *and* NORTH, R C
   International crisis: the outbreak of World War I *(Toronto: McGill-Queens UP 1976), 339p.*

NYSTROM, A K
   Before, during and after *(London: Heinemann 1914), 368p.*

O'REGAN, J R H
   The German war of 1914 *(London: Milford 1915), 101p.*

OXFORD UNIVERSITY Faculty of Modern History
   Why we are at War *(Oxford: 1914), 264p.*

PARKINSON, R
   The origins of World War One *(London: Wayland 1970), 128p; bib.*

PLAYNE, C E
   Bertha von Suttner and the struggle to avert the World War *(London: Allen & Unwin 1936), 248p.*
   The neuroses of the nations *(London: Allen & Unwin 1925), 468p.*

POINCARÉ, R N L *president of France*
   The origins of the war *(London: Cassell 1922), 275p.*

PRICE, W H C
   The dawn of Armageddon; or, The provocation by Serbia *(London: Simpkin Marshall 1917), 67p.*

REMAK, J
   The origins of World War I, 1871-1914 *(New York: Holt 1967), 162p; bib.*

RENOUVIN, P
   The immediate origins of the war, 28 June-4 August 1914 *(New Haven, Conn: Yale UP 1928), 395p.*

ROHL, J C G *ed*
   1914; delusion or design: the testimony of two German diplomats *(London: St. Martin's 1973), 143p.*

ROSE, J H
   The origins of the war *(Cambridge: CUP 1914), 201p.*

SCHMITT, B E
   The coming of the war, 1914 *(New York: Scribner 1930), 2 vols.*

SCHREINER, G A
   Craft sinister: a diplomatico-political history of the Great War and its causes *(New York: Stechert 1920), 422p.*

SETON-WATSON, R W
   German, Slav and Magyar: a study in the origins of the Great War *(London: Williams & Norgate 1916), 198p.*
SLADEN, D
   Germany's great lie *(London: Hutchinson 1914), 195p.*
STILWELL, A E
   To all the world (except Germany): an indictment of war, with proposals for universal peace *(London: Allen & Unwin 1915), 252p.*
TAYLOR, A J P
   War by time-table: how the First World War began *(London: Macdonald 1969), 128p.*
THROUGH terror to triumph: the declarations of British statesmen on the causes of the European war *(Edinburgh: 1914), 184p.*
TURNER, L C F
   Origins of the First World War *(London: Arnold 1970), 120p; bib.*
WILLMORE, J S
   A great crime and its moral: a connected narrative of the Great War *(New York: Doran 1919), 323p.*
WILSON, H W
   The war guilt *(London: Sampson Low 1928), 366p.*
WOODWARD, E L
   Great Britain and the German Navy *(Oxford: Clarendon 1935), 524p.*

PACIFISM

BOULTON, D
   Objection overruled *(London: MacGibbon & Kee 1967), 319p; bib.*
COULTON, G G
   The main illusions of pacifism *(Cambridge: Bowes 1916), 317p.*
   Pacifist illusions: a criticism of the Union of Democratic Control *(Cambridge: Bowes 1915), 103p.*
HARDY, G H
   Bertrand Russell and Trinity *(Cambridge: CUP 1942), 61p.*
NORDENTOFT, S
   Practical pacifism and its adversaries *(London: Allen & Unwin 1917), 213p.*
SOLANO, E J
   The pacifist lie: a book for sailors and soldiers *(London: Murray 1918), 71p.*
SWARTZ, M
   The Union of Democratic Control in British politics during the First World War *(Oxford: Clarendon 1971), 267p; bib.*
[See also CONSCIENTIOUS OBJECTORS]

PALESTINE

AARONSOHN, A
   With the Turks in Palestine *(London: Constable 1917), 124p.*

ADAMS, R E C
The modern crusaders, Palestine, October 1917-May 1918 *(London: Routledge 1920)*, *183p.*
BENTWICH, N de M
Palestine of the Jews, past, present and future *(New York: Dutton 1919), 288p.*
BLASER, B
Kilts across the Jordan: being experiences and impressions with the Second Battalion 'London Scottish' in Palestine *(London: Witherby 1926), 252p.*
BLUETT, A
With our Army in Palestine *(London: Melrose 1919), 288p.*
CANTON, W
Dawn in Palestine *(New York: Macmillan 1918), 99p.*
COLDICOTT, R
London men in Palestine, and how they marched to Jerusalem *(New York: Longmans 1919), 232p.*
ENGLE, A
The Nili spies *(London: Hogarth 1959), 245p.*
FALLS, C
Armageddon 1918 *(London: Weidenfeld & Nicolson 1964), 216p; bib.*
FINLEY, J H
A pilgrim in Palestine after its deliverance *(London: Chapman & Hall 1919), 251p.*
GOODSALL, R H
Palestine memories, 1917-1918-1925 *(Canterbury, Kent: 1925), 223p.*
IDRIESS, I L
The desert column: the classic account of the Palestine and Sinai campaign *(Ryde, Aust: Angus & Robertson 1985), 295p.*
INCHBALD, G
Camels and others *(London: Johnson 1968), 184p.*
Imperial Camel Corps *(London: Johnson 1970), 166p.*
JARVIS, C S
The back garden of Allah *(London: Murray 1939), 212p.*
JERUSALEM, its redemption and future: the great drama of deliverance *(New York: Christian Herald 1918), 227p.*
KEARSEY, A H C
The events, strategy and tactics of the Palestine campaign *(London: Rees 1928), 73p.*
The operations in Egypt and Palestine, 1914 to June 1917 *(Aldershot: Gale & Polden 1929), 88p.*
The operations in Egypt and Palestine *(Aldershot: Gale & Polden 1937), 154p.*
LOCKHART, J G
Palestine days and nights: sketches of the campaign in the Holy Land *(London: Scott 1920), 140p.*
MAGMUNN, *Sir* G F *and* FALLS, C
Military operations, Egypt and Palestine *(London: HMSO 1928-1930), 2 vols.*

MASSEY, W T
Allenby's final triumph *(London: Constable 1920), 347p.*
The desert campaign *(London: Constable 1918), 174p.*
How Jerusalem was won: being the record of Allenby's campaign in Palestine *(London: Constable 1919), 295p.*
MASTERMAN, E W G
The deliverance of Jerusalem *(London: Hodder & Stoughton 1918), 63p.*
MAXWELL, D
The last crusade *(London: Lane 1920), 144p.*
MILLS, F
Great uncle Fred's war: an illustrated diary 1917–1920 *(Whitstable, Kent: Pryor 1985), 120p.*
PATTERSON, J H
With the Judaeans in the Palestine campaign *(London: Hutchinson 1922), 279p.*
PRESTON, R M P
The Desert Mounted Corps: an account of the cavalry operations in Palestine and Syria, 1917-1918 *(London: Constable 1921), 356p.*
ROLT-WHEELER, F W
The wonder of war in the Holy Land *(New York: Lothrop 1919), 368p.*
SALAMAN, R N
Palestine reclaimed: letters from a Jewish officer *(London: Routledge 1920), 236p.*
SOMMERS, C
Temporary crusaders *(London: Lane 1919), 142p.*
WAVELL, A P
The Palestine campaign *(London: Constable 1928), 259p; bib.*
WILSON, J P
With the soldiers in Palestine and Syria *(London: SPCK 1920), 115p.*
WILSON, R H
Palestine 1917 *(Tunbridge Wells, Kent: Costello 1987), 192p.*
WINTRINGHAM, J W
With the Lincolnshire Yeomanry in Egypt and Palestine 1914–1918 *(Grimsby, Humb: Lincolnshire Life 1979), 84p.*
[See also EGYPT, LAWRENCE OF ARABIA, MESOPOTAMIA]

PARIS

ADAM, H P
Paris sees it through: a diary, 1914-1919 *(London: Hodder & Stoughton 1919), 331p.*
ALDERMAN, S M
Three Americans in Paris, Spring 1919 *(Durham, NH: Duke UP 1952), 126p.*
BARNARD, C I
Paris war days: diary of an American *(Boston, Mass: Houghton Mifflin 1914), 226p.*
CLARKE, M C
Paris waits *(London: Smith, Elder 1914), 289p.*
CORDAY, M
The Paris Front: an unpublished diary, 1914-1918 *(London: Gollancz 1933), 395p.*

GIBBONS, H A
  Paris reborn: a study in civic psychology *(New York: Century 1915), 395p.*
GRANT, M
  Verdun days in Paris *(London: Collins 1918), 239p.*
GUARD, W J
  The soul of Paris: two months in the French capital during the war of 1914 *(New York: Rogowski 1914), 150p.*
HOLT, L
  Paris in shadow: a diary 1916-17 *(London: Lane 1920), 310p.*
MACDONALD, J F
  Two towns-one city *(New York: Dodd 1918), 246p.*
MILLER, H W
  The Paris gun: the bombardment of Paris by the German long-range guns, and the great German offensives of 1918 *(London: Harrap 1930), 276p.*
ROOT, E S *and* CROCKER, E
  Over periscope pond: letters from two American girls in Paris, October 1916-January 1918 *(Boston, Mass: Houghton Mifflin 1918), 295p.*
WATSON, S N
  Those Paris years: with the world at the cross-roads *(New York: Revell 1936), 347p.*

PASSCHENDAELE

GIBBS, *Sir* P H
  From Bapaume to Passchendaele, 1917 *(London: Heinemann 1918), 384p. U.S. title:* Struggle in Flanders.
MACDONALD, L
  They called it Passchendaele: the story of the third battle of Ypres, and the men who fought it *(London: Joseph 1978), 253p.*
QUIGLEY, H
  Passchendaele and the Somme *(London: Methuen 1928), 203p.*
TERRAINE, J
  The road to Passchendaele; the Flanders offensive: a study in inevitability *(London: Cooper 1977), 365p.*
WARNER, P
  Passchendaele: the story behind the tragic victory of 1917 *(London: Sidgwick & Jackson 1987), 269p; bib.*

PEACE

AUSTRIAN, D
  Ways of war and peace *(Larchmont, NY: Stanhope-Dodge 1915), 207p.*
BALCH, E G
  Approaches to the great settlement *(New York: Huebsch 1918), 351p; bib.*
BASS, J F
  The peace tangle *(New York: Macmillan 1920), 345p.*

BECK, J M
   The reckoning: the moral aspects of the peace problem *(London: Hodder & Stoughton 1919), 223p.*
BOURNE, R S
   Towards an enduring peace: a symposium of peace proposals and program, 1914-1916 *(New York: American Association for International Conciliation 1916), 336p.*
BRAILSFORD, H N
   After the peace *(London: Parsons 1920), 185p.*
BUXTON, C R *ed*
   Towards a lasting settlement *(London: Allen & Unwin 1915), 216p.*
BUXTON, N *and* LEESE, C L
   Balkan problems and European peace *(London: Allen & Unwin 1919), 135p.*
CARSTEN, F L
   British and German radical movements in the First World War *(Berkeley, Cal: California UP 1982), 285p.*
CHERADAME, A
   Essentials of an enduring victory *(New York: Scribner 1918), 259p.*
CHESTERTON, C E
   The perils of peace *(London: Werner Laurie 1916), 239p.*
COSMOS *pseud*
   The basis of durable peace *(New York: Scribner 1917), 144p.*
CROSBY, G R
   Disarmament and peace in British politics, 1914-1919 *(London: OUP 1957), 192p; bib.*
CROZIER, A O
   Nation of nations: the way to permanent peace *(Cincinnati, Ohio: Stewart & Kidd 1915), 130p.*
DAVIS, R J
   America's view of the sequel *(London: Headley 1916), 155p.*
DAWSON, R J
   Problems of the peace *(London: Allen & Unwin 1917), 365p.*
DICKINSON, G L
   Documents and statements relating to peace proposals and war aims, December 1916-November 1918 *(London: Allen & Unwin 1919), 259p.*
DOCKRILL, M L *and* GOULD, D J
   Peace without promise: Britain and the Peace Conference 1919–23 *(Hamden, Conn: Shoestring 1981), 287p.*
ELDER, T C
   The coming crash of peace and Britain's mechanical renaissance *(London: Simpkin Marshall 1916), 149p.*
ELIOT, C W
   The road towards peace *(London: Constable 1915), 228p.*
ELSON, R T
   Prelude to war *(New York: Time-Life 1976), 216p.*
FAYLE, C E
   The great settlement *(London: Murray 1915), 309p.*
FIELDING-HALL, H
   The way to peace *(London: Hurst & Blackett 1917), 287p.*

FLETCHER, G B
The new pacific: British policy and German aims *(London: Macmillan 1917), 325p.*
FORSTER, K
The failures of peace: the search for a negotiated peace during the First World War *(Washington DC: American Council on Public Affairs 1941), 159p.*
GELFAND, L E
The inquiry: American preparations for peace *(New Haven, Conn: Yale UP 1963), 387p; bib.*
GREAT BRITAIN National Peace Council
Problems of international settlement *(London: NPC 1918), 205p.*
GREENWOOD, G A
Civilization in the melting pot *(London: Headley 1915), 111p.*
HANNAH, I C
Arms and the map: a study of nationalities and frontiers *(London: Fisher Unwin 1915), 261p.*
HEADLAM, J W
The issue: German utterances on the terms of peace *(London: Constable 1916), 166p.*
HERRON, G D
The menace of peace *(London: Allen & Unwin 1916), 118p.*
HERSHEY, B
The odyssey of Henry Ford and the great peace ship *(New York: Taplinger 1967), 212p.*
HOOVER, H C
America's first crusade *(New York: Scribner 1942), 81p.*
HOWE, F C
The only possible peace *(London: Fisher Unwin 1919), 265p.*
HUGINS, R
The possible peace: a forecast of world politics *(New York: Century 1916), 195p.*
JASTROW, M
The war and the coming peace *(Philadelphia, Pa: Lippincott 1918), 144p.*
JORDAN, D S
Ways to a lasting peace *(Indianapolis, Ind: Bobbs-Merrill 1916), 254p.*
KIRBY, A
The way of peace *(London: Methuen 1916), 130p.*
KRAFT, B S
The peace ship: Henry Ford's pacifist adventure in the First World War *(New York: Collier-Macmillan 1978), 36p.*
LANSING, R
The peace negotiations: a personal narrative *(Boston, Mass: Houghton Mifflin 1921), 328p.*
LEHMANN, J F
Germany's future with a good peace and a bad peace *(London: Darling 1918), 56p.*
LENTIN, A
Lloyd George, Woodrow Wilson and the guilt of Germany: an essay in the pre-history of appeasement *(Leicester: Leicester UP 1984), 208p.*
LIPPMAN, W
The political scene: an essay on the victory of 1918 *(London: Allen & Unwin 1919), 124p.*

McCLURE, S S
Obstacles to peace: attitude of the chief countries engaged *(London: Stanley Paul 1917)*, *442p.*

MacCORMICK, H F
Via pacis: how terms of peace can be automatically prepared while the war is still going on *(London: Allen & Unwin 1916)*, *56p.*

MacCULLUM, R B
Public opinion and the last peace *(London: OUP 1944)*, *214p.*

MacCURDY, C A
The terms of the coming peace *(London: St. Catherine 1918)*, *48p.*

MacFALL, H C
Beware the German's peace *(London: Cassell 1918)*, *151p.*

MALYYNSKI, E *count*
A short cut to a splendid peace *(London: King 1918)*, *42p.*

MARSHALL, H R
War and the ideal of peace *(New York: Duffield 1915)*, *234p.*

MATTHEWS, B
Three years' war for peace *(London: Hodder & Stoughton 1917)*, *95p.*

MLYNARSKI, F
The problems of the coming peace *(New York: Polish Book Importing 1916)*, *172p.*

MUNSTERBERG, H
Tomorrow: letters to a friend in Germany *(New York: Appleton 1916)*, *274p.*

PEACE 'Made in Germany': what Tommy and Poilu think about it *(London: Hodder & Stoughton 1917)*, *64p.*

PHILLIPSON, C
Termination of war and treaties of peace *(London: Fisher Unwin 1916)*, *486p.*

POWERS, H H
The great peace *(New York: Macmillan 1918)*, *333p.*

RIMINGTON, A W
The conscience of Europe: the war and the future *(London: Allen & Unwin 1918)*, *191p.*

ROBBINS, K
The abolition of war: the 'Peace Movement' in Britain, 1914-1919 *(Cardiff: University of Wales P 1976)*, *255p; bib.*

ROYCE, J
The hope of the great community *(New York: Macmillan 1916)*, *136p.*

SANDAY, W
In view of the end *(Oxford: Clarendon 1916)*, *89p.*

SHARTLE, S G
Spa, Versailles, Munich: an account of the Armistice Commission *(Philadelphia, Pa: Dorrance 1941)*, *136p.*

SHAW, G B
Peace conference hints *(London: Constable 1919)*, *108p.*

SHUMAKER, E E
The world crisis and the way to peace *(New York: Putnam 1915)*, *110p.*

STEIN, R
Peace through a disentangling alliance *(Washington DC: Judd & Detweller 1916)*, *72p.*

STODDARD, T L *and* FRANK, G
  Stakes of the war: summary of the various problems, claims and interests of the nations at the peace table *(New York: Century 1918), 377p; bib.*
STROMBERG, R N
  Redemption by war: the intellectuals and 1914 *(Lawrence, Kan: Regents 1982), 250p.*
T, O B I
  The Great War: a plan for peace *(London: Salmond 1915), 63p.*
TOYNBEE, A J
  The world after the peace conference *(London: Royal Inst. of Int. Affairs 1925), 91p.*
VAN DER SLICE, A
  International labor, diplomacy and peace, 1914-1919 *(Philadelphia, Pa: University of Pennsylvania P 1941), 405p.*
VEBLEN, T
  The nature of peace: an inquiry ... showing the necessity of the destruction of the German Imperial State *(New York: Macmillan 1917), 367p.*
WELLS, H G
  In the fourth year: anticipations of a world peace *(London: Chatto & Windus 1918), 156p.*
  The war that will end war *(London: Palmer 1914), 99p.*
WEYL, W E
  The end of the war *(New York: Macmillan 1918), 323p.*
WILSON, A J
  No deluding peace *(London: Investors' Review 1915), 88p.*
WILSON, W E
  The foundations of peace: a discussion on pacifism and the prevention of wars *(London: Headley 1918), 171p.*
[See also PACIFISM, TREATIES, TRIANON, VERSAILLES]

PENSIONS

BARLOW, *Sir* C A M *and* WILLIAMS, W G
  War pensions: a handbook *(London: Davey 1918), 44p.*
GERDS, D N
  The ABC of pensions *(London: Comrades of the Great War 1920), 80p.*
GLASSON, W H
  Federal military pensions in the United States *(New York: OUP 1918), 305p.*
HATTON, A P
  The pensions ABC *(London: United Newspapers 1922), 96p.*
HOGGE, J M *and* GARSIDE, T H
  War pensions and allowances *(London: Hodder & Stoughton 1918), 463p.*
MACDONALD, H T
  What is due to me?: a handy compendium of information on pensions *(London: Daily Herald 1919), 57p.*
PARRY, E A *and* CODRINGTON, *Sir* A E
  War pensions, past and present *(London: Nisbet 1918), 191p.*
PENSIONERS of the Great War *(London: Scott 1922), 63p.*

PERSHING

PERSHING, J J
  Final report of General Pershing *(Washington DC: War Department 1919), 95p.*
  My experiences in the World War *(New York: Stokes 1931), 2 vols.*
TOMLINSON, E T
  The story of General Pershing *(New York: Appleton 1919), 260p.*
VANDIVER, F E
  Black Jack: the life and times of John J. Pershing *(Texas: A & M University 1977), 2 vols; bib.*

PERSONAL NARRATIVE

ABELS, C H
  The last of the fighting four *(New York: Vantage 1968), 173p.*
ALLEN, W H
  Towards the flame *(New York: Farrar 1934), 282p.*
ASHMEAD-BARTLETT, E
  Some of my experiences in the Great War *(London: Newnes 1918), 187p.*
BACON, A F L
  Wanderings of a temporary warrior *(London: Witherby 1922), 230p.*
BARROW, *Sir* G
  The fire of life *(London: Hutchinson 1942).*
BELL, D H
  A soldier's diary of the Great War *(London: Faber 1929), 252p.*
BEMELMANS, L
  My war with the United States *(London: Gollancz 1938), 149p.*
BERNHEIM, B M
  Passed as censored *(Philadelphia, Pa: Lippincott 1918), 148p.*
BERRY, H
  Make the Kaiser dance *(New York: Doubleday 1978), 455p.*
BLOCH, M L B
  Memoirs of war 1914–15 *(Ithica, NY: Cornell 1980), 177p.*
BLUNDEN, E
  Undertones of war *(London: OUP 1956), with a new preface, 366p.*
BOND, B *ed*
  Staff officer: the diaries of Lord Moyne 1914–1918 *(London: Cooper 1987).*
BRUCE, T B
  'Missing': experiences during thirteen weeks in enemy territory disguised as a Belgian peasant *(Edinburgh: Blackwood 1930), 246p.*
BUCKLEY, H H C
  Great event: a narrative of the experiences of a young officer in the Great War *(London: Figurehead 1930), 197p.*
BUNAU-VARILLA, P
  From Panama to Verdun: my fight for France *(Philadelphia, Pa: Dorrance 1940), 277p.*

BURGOYNE, G A
  The Burgoyne diaries *(London: Harmsworth 1985), 249p.*
CALLAWAY, A B
  With packs and rifles: a story of the World War *(Boston, Mass: Meador 1939), 270p.*
CARRINGTON, C E
  A subaltern's war: being a memoir of the Great War *(New York: Arno 1972), 224p.*
CHAPMAN, G
  A passionate prodigality *(London: Nicholson & Watson 1933), 281p.*
CLAPHAM, H S
  Mud and khaki: the memories of an incomplete soldier *(London: Hutchinson 1930), 224p.*
CLARK, A
  Echoes of the Great War: the diary of the Rev. Andrew Clark, 1914–1919 *(Oxford: OUP 1985), 304p.*
CLARKE, B
  My round of the war *(London: Heinemann 1917), 303p.*
CLOVER, G
  Stop at Suzanne's and lower flights *(New York: Doran 1919), 265p.*
CRAWSHAY-WILLIAMS, E
  Leaves from an officer's note book *(London: Arnold 1917), 280p.*
CROFT, H P
  Twenty-two months under fire *(London: Murray 1917), 243p.*
CRUM, F W
  With riflemen, scouts and snipers from 1914-1919 *(Oxford: Clarendon 1921), 179p.*
CUDDEFORD, D W J
  And all for what?: some war time experiences *(London: Heath Cranton 1933), 226p.*
CUPPLES, W H
  My helpful angel flew with me *(New York: Exposition 1975), 94p.*
CUTCHINS, J A
  Amateur diplomat in the World War *(Richmond, Va: Garrett 1938), 227p.*
CUTCHLOW, W
  Tale of an old soldier *(London: Hale 1937), 286p.*
DESPATCHES from the heart *(London: Hamilton 1984), 138p.*
DOYLE, *Sir* A C
  A visit to three Fronts, June 1916 *(London: Hodder & Stoughton 1916), 78p.*
EADES, F *ed*
  The war diary and letters of Corporal Tom Eades, 1915-1917 *(Cambridge: Aids to Learning 1973), 47p.*
FARNOL, J
  Some war impressions *(London: Sampson Low 1918), 118p.*
FETTERLESS, A
  Battle days *(London: Blackwood 1918), 313p.*
FINZI, K J
  Eighteen months in the war zone *(London: Cassell 1916), 283p.*
FREEMAN, L R
  Many Fronts *(London: Murray 1918), 315p.*
FRENCH, A
  Gone for a soldier *(Kineton, Warwick: Roundwood 1972), 109p.*

GEORGE, H
  Farrier in arms *(New York: Pageant 1953), 236p.*
GIBBS, H
  Gun fodder: the diary of four years of war *(Boston, Mass: Little, Brown 1919), 313p. U.K. title:* Grey wave.
GIBBS, S
  From the Somme to the Armistice: the memoirs of Stormont Gibbs *(London: Kimber 1986), 206p*
GIRADOUX, J
  Campaigns and intervals *(Boston, Mass: Houghton Mifflin 1918), 272p.*
GORDON, A A
  Culled from a diary *(Edinburgh: Oliver & Boyd 1941), 214p.*
GURNEY, I
  War letters *(London: Hogarth 1984), 271p.*
HADLOW, H J
  The experiences of a volunteer in the First World War *(Eynsford, Kent: Hadlow nd), 134p.*
HANSON, W L
  I was there: a memoir *(Gerald, Mo: Patrice 1982), 115p.*
HARVEY, H
  A soldier's sketches under fire *(London: Sampson Low 1916), 176p.*
HENDERSON, J H
  Soldier country *(Wellington, NZ: Millword 1978), 216p.*
HOME, *Sir* A
  Diary of a World War I cavalry officer *(Tunbridge Wells, Kent: Costello 1985), 256p.*
HORNSEY, F H
  Hell on earth *(London: Chapman & Hall 1930), 244p.*
HORTON, A E
  When I became a man: private memoir of two years' overseas service *(Boston, Mass: Houghton Mifflin 1931), 248p.*
JACKSON, E B
  Fall out to the right of the road! *(White Mash, Va: McClure 1973), 506p.*
JONES, W R
  Fighting the Hun from saddle and trench *(New York: Aiken 1918), 281p.*
KETTLE, T M
  The ways of war *(London: Constable 1917), 249p.*
KIERNAN, R H
  Little brother goes soldiering *(London: Constable 1930), 136p.*
KINGSMILL, A G
  The silver badge *(Ilfracombe, Devon: Stockwell 1966), 96p.*
KRAMER, H M
  With seeing eyes: the unusual story of an observant thinker at the Front *(New York: Lothrop 1919), 397p.*
LARDNER, R W
  My four weeks in France *(Indianapolis, Ind: Bobbs-Merrill 1918), 187p.*
LAUDER, *Sir* H
  A minstrel in France *(London: Melrose 1918), 320p.*

LEVYNS, J E P
   The disciplines of war: memories of war 1914–18 *(New York : Vantage 1984)*, *173p.*
LIVEING, E G D
   Attack: an infantry subaltern's impressions of July 1, 1916 *(New York: Macmillan 1918)*, *114p.*
THE LIVING and the living dead: ruminations with a batch of war experiences, 1914-1918 *(London: Stockwell 1923)*, *206p.*
McCLINTOCK, A
   Best o'luck: how a fighting Kentuckian won the thanks of Britain's King *(New York: Grosset 1918)*, *171p.*
McCLUNG, *Mrs* N L
   Three times and out, told by Private Simmons *(Boston, Mass: Houghton Mifflin 1918)*, *247p.*
McCOY, P T *pseud*
   Kittie McCoy: an American boy with an Irish name fighting in France as a Scottish soldier *(Indianapolis, Ind: Bobbs-Merrill 1918)*, *246p.*
MELLERSH, H E L
   School boy into war *(London: Kimber 1978)*, *200p.*
MITCHELL, F
   Fred Mitchell's war story: three years in the war zone *(New York: Knopf 1918)*, *239p.*
MONTAGUE, C E
   Disenchantment *(London: Chatto & Windus 1922)*, *221p.*
MORGAN, J H
   Leaves from a field note-book *(London: Macmillan 1916)*, *308p.*
MORRISON, E J
   My experiences overseas in World War I *(New York: Vantage 1983)*, *114p.*
MUEGGE, M A
   The war diary of a square peg *(London: Routledge 1920)*, *224p.*
MUNROE, J
   Mopping up: through the eyes, of Bobbie Burns, regimental mascot *(New York: Fly 1918)*, *319p.*
MURDOCK, L B
   They also served *(New York: Carlton 1967)*, *129p.*
NESHAM, F *ed*
   Socks, cigarettes and shipwrecks *(Gloucester: Sutton 1986)*, *256p.*
NICHOLSON, M
   My experiences on three Fronts *(London: Allen & Unwin 1916)*, *288p.*
NOBLE, C
   Jugheads behind the lines *(Caldwell, Idaho: Caxton 1938)*, *208p.*
NORMAN, H N
   Tattered shuttlecock *(London: Sampson Low 1937)*, *328p.*
O'BRIEN, J
   Into the jaws of death *(New York: Dodd 1919)*, *295p.*
ODYSSEUS *pseud*
   The scene of war *(London: Blackwood 1917)*, *437p.*
OGSTON, *Sir* A
   Reminiscences of three campaigns *(London: Hodder & Stoughton 1919)*, *342p.*

PALMER, F
My years of the war *(London: Murray 1915)*, *390p.*
PARKER, E W
Into battle, 1914-1918 *(London: Longmans 1964)*, *98p.*
PEACOCK, B
Tinker's mufti: memoirs of a part-time soldier *(London: Seeley 1974)*, *214p.*
PEAT, H R
Private Peat *(London: Hutchinson 1918)*, *224p.*
PINKERTON, R D
Ladies from Hell *(New York: Century 1918)*, *254p.*
PULITZER, R
Over the Front in an aeroplane and scenes inside the French and Flemish trenches *(New York: Harper 1915)*, *159p.*
PURDOM, C B *ed*
Everyman at war: sixty personal narratives of the war *(London: Dent 1930)*, *425p.*
REDMOND, J E
Account of a visit to the Front *(London: Nelson 1916)*, *47p.*
REES, R T
A schoolmaster at war *(London: Haycock 1936)*, *123p.*
RENWICK, G
War wanderings, 1914-1916 *(London: Chapman & Hall 1916)*, *304p.*
REPINGTON, C à'C
The First World War: personal experiences *(London: Constable 1920)*, *2 vols.*
RINEHART, *Mrs* M
Kings, queens and pawns: an American woman at the Front *(New York: Doran 1915)*, *368p.*
ROBERTS, W
Memories of the war to end war, 1914-18 *(London: Lund Humphries 1974)*, *45p.*
ROBSON, S
It's old stuff now *(New York: Vantage 1976)*, *137p.*
SAINT-MANDE, W
War, wine and women *(London: Cassell 1936)*, *555p.*
SCOTT, R
A soldier's war diary *(London: Collins 1923)*, *194p.*
SHEPHARD, E
A sergeant-major's war: from Hill 60 to the Somme *(Marlborough, Wilts: Bird 1987)*, *240p.*
SLACK, C M
Grandfather's adventures in the Great War *(Ilfracombe, Devon: Stockwell 1977)*, *284p.*
SMITH, Joseph S
Over there and back in three uniforms: being the experiences of an American boy in Canadian, British and American Armies at the Front and through No-Man's-Land *(New York: Dutton 1918)*, *244p.*
SNOW, W J
Signposts of experience: World War memoirs *(Washington DC: U.S. Field Artillery Assoc. 1941)*, *317p.*

STEVENSON, W Y
  From Poilu to Yank *(Boston, Mass: Houghton Mifflin 1918), 205p.*
SWEETSER, A
  Roadside glimpses of the Great War *(London: Macmillan 1916), 282p.*
TENNANT, N
  A Saturday night soldier's war *(Aylesbury, Bucks: Kylin 1983), 128p.*
THREE personal records of the war: R. H. Mottram, John Easton, Eric Partridge *(London: Scholartis 1929), 405p.*
TROOPER *pseud*
  The four horsemen ride *(London: Davies 1935), 211p.*
VANSITTART, P *comp.*
  Voices from the Great War *(London: Cape 1981), 302p.*
VAUGHAN, E C
  Some desperate glory: the diary of a young officer, 1917 *(London: Warne 1981), 232p.*
VOIGT, F A
  Combed out *(London: Cale 1929).*
WEST, A G
  Diary of a dead officer *(London: Allen & Unwin 1919), 110p.*
WEST, W B
  The fight for the Argonne: personal experiences of a 'Y' man *(New York: Abingdon 1919), 124p.*
WESTCAR, W V L
  Big game, Boers and Boches *(London: Stanley Paul 1937), 319p.*
WILLIAMS, J E H
  One young man: the simple and true story of a clerk who enlisted in 1914 *(London: Hodder & Stoughton 1917), 173p.*
WILLIAMS, R S G
  Under the black ensign *(London: Hutchinson 1922), 238p.*
WINE, women and war: a diary of disillusionment *(London: Heinemann 1927), 307p.*
WORDEN, A F
  'Yes Daddy, but there has been another war since then' *(London: P. R. Macmillan 1961), 91p.*
YOUNG, G V
  The grace of forgetting *(London: Country Life 1953), 352p.*
ZANDER, H W
  Thirteen years of hell *(Boston, Mass: Meador 1933), 307p.*

PETAIN

RYAN, S
  Pétain the soldier *(London: Yoseloff 1969), 315p.*

PHILATELY

ARMSTRONG, D B *and* GREENWOOD, C H
  War stamps of the Allies, 1914-1920 *(London: Stamp Collecting 1920), 96p.*
FIELD, D
  Postage stamps of the Great War and after, 1914-1920 *(London: Field 1920), 150p.*
KENNEDY, A *and* CRABB, G
  The postal history of the British Army in World War I: before and after, 1903 to 1929 *(Epsom, Sy: Crabb 1977), 301p.*
WILLIAMS, L N *and* WILLIAMS, M
  The 'Propaganda' forgeries: a history and description of the Austrian, Bavarian and German stamps counterfeited by order of the British Government during the war *(London: Field 1938), 42p.*

PHILOSOPHY

ADLER, F
  The world crisis and its meaning *(New York: Appleton 1915), 232p.*
ARU-MUGAM
  The golden key to world power and the war *(London: Longmans 1915), 127p.*
BOUTROUX, E
  Philosophy and the war *(New York: Dutton 1917), 212p.*
BROWNE, J H B
  War problems *(London: Longmans 1915), 96p.*
CLAYTON, I M
  Shadow on the universe; or, The physical results of war *(London: Simpkin Marshall 1915), 150p.*
CLUTTON-BROCK, A
  Thoughts on the war *(London: Methuen 1914), 86p.*
  The ultimate belief *(London: Constable 1916), 116p.*
CRILE, G W
  A mechanistic view of war and peace *(London: Werner Laurie 1916), 115p.*
CROFT, G G
  Some 1918 reflections *(London: Simpkin Marshall 1918), 100p.*
GOULD, B A
  War thoughts of an optimist (London: Dent 1915), 200p.
GRIGGS, E H
  The soul of democracy: the philosophy of the World War *(New York: Macmillan 1918), 158p.*
HAYWARD, C W
  War and rational politics *(London: Watts 1915), 88p.*
HOLMES, E E
  The message of the soldiers *(London: Mowbray 1917), 80p.*
MITCHELL, P C
  Evolution and the war *(London: Murray 1915), 114p.*

MUIRHEAD, J H
  German philosophy in relation to the war *(London: Murray 1915), 110p.*
OMAN, J
  The war and its issues *(Cambridge: CUP 1915), 130p.*
PERRY, R B
  The present conflict of ideals *(New York: Longmans 1918), 549p.*
POLE, W T
  The Great War: some deeper issues *(London: Bell 1915), 99p.*
SLATER, G
  Peace and war in Europe *(London: Constable 1915), 122p.*
SPEARE, M E *and* NORRIS, W B
  World War issues and ideals *(Boston, Mass: Ginn 1918), 461p.*
TOYNBEE, A J
  Nationality and the war *(London: Dent 1915), 522p.*
THE WAR of democracy: statements by Allied leaders of their aims and ideals *(New York: Doubleday 1917), 441p.*

PHOTOGRAPHY

ABBOT, W J
  Pictorial history of the World War *(New York: Leslie-Judge 1919), unp.*
BALDRIDGE, C L
  I was there with the Yanks on the Western Front *(New York: Putnam 1919), unp.*
BARBER, F A *comp.*
  The horror of it *(New York: Harcourt 1932), unp.*
DAILY EXPRESS *(newspaper)*
  Covenants with death: 184 pages of photos of the First World War *(London: Daily Express 1934), 184p.*
DUNCAN-CLARK, S J
  Pictorial history of the World War *(Chicago: Walter 1919), 415p.*
FROM the first shot: a picture history of the Great War *(New York: Independent 1918), 223p.*
GILBERT, A
  World War I in photographs *(London: Orbis 1986), 192p.*
HART, A R *and others eds*
  Harper's pictorial library of the World War *(New York: Harper nd), 12 vols.*
JABLONSKI, E
  A pictorial history of World War I years *(New York: Doubleday 1979), 316p.*
KENNEDY, *Sir* A B W
  Ypres to Verdun: a collection of photographs *(London: Country Life 1921), 84p.*
LIDDLE, P
  Photo history of the Great War *(Poole, Dorset: Blandford 1987), unp.*
LIFE *(periodical)*
  The First World War *(New York: Doubleday 1965), 126p.*
MALINS, G H
  How I filmed the war *(London: Jenkins 1920), 307p.*

MOERAN, J W W
  Illustrations from the Great War *(London: R. Scott 1915), 268p.*
MORRIS, V J
  War photographs *(Azalia, Ind: Morris 1919), 252p.*
NEW YORK TIMES (Midweek pictorial)
  War of the nations: portfolio of rotogravure etchings *(New York: New York Times 1919), 528p.*
REYNOLDS, F J *and* TAYLOR, C
  Collier's new photographic history of the World War *(New York: Collier 1918), 128p.*
RUSSELL, T H
  America's war for humanity: pictorial history of the World War for liberty *(New York: Walter 1919), 514p.*
SMITH, J A
  In France with the American Expeditionary Force *(New York: Hahlo 1919), 200 pl.*
STALLINGS, L
  The First World War: a photographic history *(London: Daily Express 1933), 307p.*
SZEGEDI, S
  My war *(New York: Morrow 1932), 206p.*
UNITED STATES War Department
  Catalogue of official AEF photographs taken by the Signal Corps US Army *(Washington, DC: Govt PO 1919), 577p.*

PIGEONS

OSMAN, A H
  Pigeons in the Great War: a complete history of the Carrier Pigeon Service *(London: Racing Pigeon 1929), 58p.*

POLAND

BENSON, E F
  The white eagle of Poland *(London: Hodder & Stoughton 1918), 265p.*
BOLESLAVSKI, R
  Way of a lancer *(Indianapolis, Ind: Bobbs-Merrill 1932), 316p.*
GIBBONS, H A
  The reconstruction of Poland *(New York: Century 1917), 218p.*
MASON, J M
  The Danzig dilemma: a study in peacemaking by compromise *(Stanford, Cal: Stanford UP 1946), 377p.*
POLAND's case for independence *(London: Allen & Unwin 1916), 352p.*
ROY, J A
  Pole and Czech in Silesia *(London: Lane 1921), 212p.*
STANDING, P C
  The campaign in Russian Poland *(London: Hodder & Stoughton 1914), 185p.*

TURCZYNOWICZOWA, L
When the Prussians came to Poland: the experiences of an American woman during the German invasion (New York: Grosset 1917), 281p.
WALLSZEWSKI, K
Poland, the unknown *(New York: Doran 1919), 263p.*
WASHBURN, S
Victory in defeat: the agony of Warsaw and the Russian retreat *(New York: Doubleday 1916), 180p.*

POLICE

CITY of London Police Reserve: a record, 1914-1920 *(London: C.L.P.R. 1921), 132p.*
PRESTON-MUDDOCK, J E
'All clear': the work of the London Special Constabulary, 1914-1919 *(London: Everett 1920), 122p.*
SUB-INSPECTOR *pseud*
Two years with the 'Specials' *(London: Crowther & Goodman 1916), 68p.*

POLITICS

Addison, C
Politics from within *(London: Jenkins 1924), 2 vols.*
AITKEN, W M *1st baron Beaverbrook*
Men and power, 1917-1918 *(London: Hutchinson 1956), 448p.*
Politicians and the war, 1914–1916 *(London: Butterworth 1928–1932), 2 vols.*
ANGELL, N
The political conditions of Allied success *(London: Putnam 1918), 379p.*
War aims: the need for a Parliament of the Allies *(London: Headley 1917), 127p.*
BALDWIN, E F
The world war, how it looks to the nations involved and what it means to us *(New York: Macmillan 1914), 267p.*
BANDINI, P
About this Anglo-German war *(Genoa, Italy: 1915), 141p.*
BERGSON, H L
The meaning of the war *(London: Fisher Unwin 1915), 47p.*
BLACK, H
The cleavage of the world *(London: Hodder & Stoughton 1920), 279p.*
BRYCE, J *viscount*
The way of democracy: the Allies statement *(New York: Macmillan 1917), 441p.*
CAMERON, J
1916 – year of decision *(London: Oldbourne 1962), 240p.*
CHAMBERS, F P
The war behind the war, 1914-1918: a history of the political and civilian Fronts *(London: Faber 1939), 620p.*

COURTNEY, W L

Armageddon – and after *(London: Chapman & Hall 1914), 91p.*

CREEL, G

The war, the world and Wilson *(New York: Harper 1920), 366p.*

DAVIS, M O

The Great War and what it means to Europe *(Oxford: Clarendon 1915), 110p.*

DICKINSON, G L

The European anarchy *(London: Allen & Unwin 1916), 153p.*

DOYLE, *Sir* A C

The German war *(London: Hodder & Stoughton 1914), 152p.*

ELY, R T

World war and leadership in a democracy *(New York: Macmillan 1918), 189p.*

FYFE, H H

The making of an optimist *(London: Parsons 1921), 279p.*

GREENE, F V

Why Europe is at war *(London: Putnam 1915), 170p.*

HAYENS, H

Teuton versus Slav *(London: Collins 1914), 160p.*

HEAPS, W J

Autocracy vs. democracy *(New York: Neale 1918), 121p.*

HENDERSON, F

A new faith: a study of party politics and the war *(London: Jarrolds 1915), 113p.*

HILLIS, N D

Studies of the Great War: what each nation has at stake *(New York: Revell 1915), 272p.*

HOBHOUSE, L T

The world in conflict *(London: Fisher Unwin 1915), 104p.*

HOBSON, J A

Democracy after the war *(London: Allen & Unwin 1917), 215p.*

HODGE, H

In the wake of the war: Parliament or Imperial government *(London: Lane 1917), 234p.*

HUEFFER, F H M

Between St Dennis and St George: a sketch of three civilisations *(London: Hodder & Stoughton 1915), 297p.*

JANE, L C

The nations at war: the birth of a new era *(London: Dent 1914), 228p.*

JELLICOE, E G

Playing the game: what Mr Asquith in 'The genesis of the war' does not tell us *(London: Long 1925), 304p.*

KNIGHT, A E

World-war and after: an inquiry and a fore-cast *(London: Morgan & Scott 1915), 152p.*

LYNCH, F

The last war: a study of things present and to come *(New York: Revell 1915), 118p.*

MUIR, J R B

Political consequences of the Great war *(London: Butterworth 1930), 251p.*

NORMAN, C H

A searchlight on the European war *(London: Labour 1921), 176p.*

OGG, F A *and* BEARD, C A
National governments and the Great War *(New York: Macmillan 1919), 603p.*
OLIVER, F S
Ordeal by battle *(London: Macmillan 1915), 488p.*
PHILLIPS, L M
Europe unbound *(London: Duckworth 1916), 212p.*
PLUM, H G *and* BENJAMIN, G G
Modern and contemporary European civilization: the persisting factors of the Great War
(Philadelphia, Pa: Lippincott 1923), 413p.
ROBINSON, J J
National reconstruction: a study in practical politics and statesmanship *(London: Hurst &*
Blackett 1918), 164p.
SANDAY, W
The meaning of the war for Germany and Great Britain *(Oxford: Clarendon 1915), 124p.*
SAROLEA, C
The Anglo-German problem *(London: Jack 1915), 384p.*
SCHULE, G
Revolutions and peace treaties, 1917-1920 *(London: Methuen 1972), 258p; bib.*
SETON-WATSON, R W
Europe in the melting pot *(New York: Macmillan 1919), 400p.*
TAYLOR, A J P
Politics in wartime *(London: Hamilton 1964), 207p.*
THOMSON, G M
The twelve days: 24 July to 4 August, 1914 *(London: Hutchinson 1964), 228p; bib.*
WHETHAM, W C D
The war and the nation: a study in constructive politics *(London: Murray 1917), 320p.*
WRIGHT, H F
The constitutions of the States at war, 1914-1918 *(Washington DC: Dept. of State 1919),*
679p.
ZANGWILL, I
The war for the world *(London: Heinemann 1916), 347p.*
[See also DIPLOMATIC HISTORY]

POPPIES

MICHAEL, M B
Miracle flower: the story of the Flanders Fields memorial poppy *(Philadelphia, Pa:*
Dorrance 1941), 177p.

POSTCARDS

HOLT, I *and* HOLT, V
Till the boys come home: the picture postcards of the First World War *(London:*
Macdonald & Jane's 1977), 192p.

POSTERS

RICKARDS, M
Posters of the First World War *(London: Evelyn, Adams and Mackay 1968), unp.*
THE FIRST World War in posters *(London: Constable 1974), 72p.*

PRESS

BENNETT, I E
Editorials from the Washington Post, 1917-1920 *(Washington DC: Washington Post 1921), 584p.*
BLUMENFELD, R D
All in a lifetime *(London: Benn 1931), 276p.*
COOK, *Sir* E T
The Press in wartime *(London: Macmillan 1920), 200p.*
CORNEBISE, A E
The Stars and Stripes *(Westport, Conn: Greenwood 1984).*
GOWANS, A L
A month's German newspapers *(London: Gowans & Gray 1915), 275p.*
LE QUEUX, W
Britain's deadly peril; or, Are we told the truth? *(London: Stanley Paul 1915), 176p.*
LYTTON, N S
The Press and the General Staff *(London: Collins 1921), 231p.*
NEW YORK EVENING MAIL *(newspaper)*
The gravest 366 days: editorials *(New York: Evening Mail 1916), 622p.*
RAPPAPORT, A
The British Press and Wilsonian neutrality *(London: OUP 1951), 162p.*
SQUADS write!: a selection of the best things in prose, verse and cartoon from 'The Stars and Stripes', official newspaper of the A.E.F. *(New York: Harper 1931), 335p.*
THE STARS and Stripes: the complete file of the official newspaper of the A.E.F., 1918-1919 *(New York: Arno 1971), unp.*
SWETLAND, H M *ed*
American journalists in Europe: an account of a visit to England and France at the close of the war *(New York: United Publishers Association 1919), 115p.*
THROUGH German spectacles: an account of the Huns as they are; pictured by themselves in their own Press *(London: Nisbet 1917), 120p.*
WILLIAMS, I
Newspapers of the First World War *(Newton Abbot, Devon: David & Charles 1970), 160p.*
WILLIAMS, W
Passed by the censor: the experience of an American newspaperman in France *(New York: Dutton 1916), 270p.*
THE WIPERS Times *(London: Jenkins 1918), unp.*

PRISONERS OF WAR

AUSTIN, L J
My experiences as a German prisoner *(London: Melrose 1915), 158p.*
BATZLER-HEIM, G
Horrors of Cayenne: the experiences of a German as a French bagno-convict *(London: Coristable 1933), 206p.*
BEAUMONT, H
Old Contemptible: a personal narrative *(London: Hutchinson 1967), 224p.*
BEHIND the prison bars of Germany: a detailed record of six months' experiences in German prisons and detention camps *(London: Newnes 1915), 158p.*
THE BLACK hole of the desert: being the diary of a Yeoman signaller, one of the survivors of HMS 'Tara' *(London: Hodder & Stoughton 1916), 137p.*
BOND, R C
Prisoners grave and gay *(Edinburgh: Blackwood 1934), 290p.*
BURDICK, C B *and* MOESSNER, U
The German POW in Japan 1914–1920 *(London: Arms & Armour 1984), 128p.*
BURY, H *bishop*
My visit to Ruhleben *(London: Mowbray 1917), 81p.*
CAMERON, J S
Ten months in a German raider: a prisoner of war aboard the Wolf *(New York: Doran 1918), 168p.*
CIMINO, H
Behind the prison bars in Germany *(London: Newnes 1915), 157p.*
CLOSE, P L
A prisoner of the Germans in South West Africa *(London: Fisher Unwin 1916), 318p.*
COHEN, I
The Ruhleben prison camp: a record of nineteen months' internment *(London: Methuen 1917), 251p.*
COHEN-PORTHEIM, P
Time stood still: my internment in England, 1914-18 *(London: Duckworth 1931), 235p.*
CUMMINGS, E E
The enormous room: experiences of an American in a French concentration camp during the European war *(London: Cape 1928), 332p.*
DENNETT, C P
Prisoners of the Great War: authoritative statement of conditions in the prison camps of Germany *(Boston, Mass: Houghton Mifflin 1919), 236p.*
DEPEW, A N
Gunner Depew *(Chicago: Reilly 1918), 312p.*
DESSON, G
A hostage in Germany *(London: Constable 1917), 145p.*
DOLBEY, R V
A regimental surgeon in war and prison *(London: Murray 1917), 257p.*
DOUGLAS, J H
Captured: sixteen months as a prisoner of war *(New York: Doran 1918), 195p.*
DURNFORD, H G E
The tunnellers of Holzminden *(London: CUP 920), 196p.*

EHLERS, L
One lives to tell the tale *(London: Cape 1931), 356p.*
FALKSON, E L
A Cockney among the Reds *(Ilfracombe, Devon: Stockwell 1945), 237p.*
FOLEY, H A
Three years on active service and eight months as a P.O.W. *(Bridgewater, Som: Foley 1920), 185p.*
FORDER, A
In brigands' hands and Turkish prisons, 1914–1918 *(London: Marshall 1920), 314p.*
GIBBONS, A
A guest of the Kaiser: the plain story of a lucky soldier *(New York: McBride 1919), 189p.*
GILLILAND, H G
My German prisons: two and a half years as a prisoner of war *(London: Hodder & Stoughton 1918), 316p.*
GREEN, A
The story of a prisoner of war: more light on Wittenberg *(London: Chatto & Windus 1916), 104p.*
HALYBURTON, E *and* GOLL, R
Shoot and be damned *(New York: Covici 1932), 452p.*
HARVEY, F W
Comrades in captivity: a record of life in seven German prison camps *(London: Sidgwick & Jackson 1920), 319p.*
HENNEBOIS, C
In German hands *(London: Heinemann 1916), 254p.*
HILL, C W
The spook and the Commandant *(London: Kimber 1975), 201p.*
HOFFMAN, C
In the prison camps of Germany: a narrative of Y service among the prisoners of war *(New York: Associated P 1920), 279p.*
HOLTOM, E C
Two years' captivity in German East Africa *(London: Hutchinson 1919), 239p.*
HOPFORD, W
Twice interned: Transvaal 1901-02, Germany 1914-18 *(London: Murray 1919), 140p.*
HOPKINS, T
Prisoner of war *(London: Simpkin Marshall 1914), 188p.*
THE HORRORS of Wittenburg: official report *(London: Pearson 1916), 82p.*
IMREY, F *and* PALEN, L S
Through blood and ice *(New York: Dutton 1930), 353p.*
INTERNATIONAL RED CROSS COMMITTEE
Reports on British prison-camps in India and Burma *(London: Fisher Unwin 1917), 64p.*
Turkish prisoners in Egypt: a report *(London: Cassell 1917), 64p.*
IN the hands of the Huns: being reminiscences of a British civil prisoner of war *(London: Simpkin Marshall 1916), 95p.*
ISAACS, E V M
Prisoner of the U-90: being the personal narrative of the adventures of the only live officer of the United States Navy to be captured in the Great War *(Boston, Mass: Houghton Mifflin 1919), 184p.*

JONES, E H
The road to En-dor *(London: Lane 1919), 351p.*
KETCHUM, J D
Ruhleben: a prison camp society *(London: 0UP 1965), 397p; bib.*
KINGSMILL, H
Behind both lines *(London: Kennerley 1930), 255p.*
KUNCZ, A
Black monastery *(London: Chatto & Windus 1934), 409p.*
KURTZ, R M
Beyond no man's land *(Buffalo, NY: Foster & Stewart 1937), 151p.*
LEE, J
Captive at Carlsruhe *(London: Lane 1920), 219p.*
THE LINK: a souvenir book published by British prisoners of war interned at Doeberitz, 1914-17 *(Berlin-Schoneberg 1917), 65p.*
LUSHINGTON, R F
A prisoner with the Turks, 1915-1918 *(London: Simpkin Marshall 1923), 101p.*
MCCARTHY, D J
The prisoner of war in Germany: the care and treatment of the prisoner with a history of the development of neutral inspection and control *(London: Skeffington 1918), 256p.*
MAHONEY, H C *and* TALBOT, F A
Interned in Germany *(London: Sampson Low 1918), 287p.*
Sixteen months in four German prisons: Wesel; Sennelager; Klingelputz; Ruhleben *(London: Sampson Low 1917), 330p.*
MARKLE, C M
Yankee prisoner in Hunland *(New Haven, Conn: Whitlock 1920), 52p.*
MOLONY, W O
Prisoners and captives *(London: Macmillan 1933), 305p.*
MOYNIHAN, M *ed*
Black bread and barbed wire *(London: Cooper 1978), 186p.*
O'RORKE, B G
In the hands of the enemy *(London: Longmans 1915), 112p.*
PHILLIMORE, G W *baron*
Recollections of a prisoner of war *(London: Arnold 1930), 310p.*
POLING, D A
Huts in hell *(Boston, Mass: Christian Endeavor 1918), 214p.*
POWELL, J *and* GRIBBLE, F H
The history of Ruhleben: a record of British organization in a prison camp in Germany *(London: Collins 1919), 246p.*
PRICE, H T
Boche and Bolshevik: experiences of an Englishman in the German Army and in Russian prisons *(London: Murray 1919), 247p.*
PYE, E
Prisoner of war *(New York: Revell 1938), 202p.*
PYKE, G N
To Ruhleben - and back *(London: Constable 1916), 246p.*
ROGER, N
The victims' return *(London: Constable 1917), 134p.*

ROSSITER, I
In kultured kaptivity: life and death in Germany's prison camps and hospitals *(Indianapolis, Ind: Bobbs-Merrill 1918), 244p.*

ROXBURGH, R F
The Prisoners of War Information Bureau in London *(London: Longmans 1915), 64p.*

SLADEN, D B W
In Ruhleben: letters from a prisoner *(London: Hurst & Blackett 1917), 291p.*

SPANTON, E F
In German gaols: two years' captivity in German East Africa *(London: SPCK 1917), 111p.*

STEWART, T
Nine months as a Prisoner of War *(London: Stockwell 1933), 56p.*

STILL, J
A prisoner in Turkey *(London: Lane 1920), 250p.*

STOKER, H G
Straws in the wind *(London: Jenkins 1925), 315p.*

THORN, J C
Three years a prisoner in Germany *(Vancouver: 1919), 151p.*

TUCKER, W A
The lousier war *(London: New English Library 1974), 125p.*

VISCHER, A L
Barbed wire disease: a psychological study of the Prisoner of War *(London: Bale 1919), 84p.*

WARBURTON, E
Behind Boche bars *(London: Lane 1920), 126p.*

WARNOD, A
Prisoner of War *(London: Heinemann 1916), 172p.*

WAUGH, A
The prisoners of Mainz *(London: Chapman & Hall 1919), 274p.*

WILLIAMS, R S G
Prisoners of the Red Desert: being a history of the men of the 'Tara' *(London: Butterworth 1919), 304p.*

WILLIS, E F
Herbert Hoover and the Russian prisoners of war of World War I: a study in diplomacy and relief, 1918-1919 *(London: OUP 1951), 67p.*

WOOLLEY, C L
From Kastamuni to Kedos: being a record of experiences of prisoners of war in Turkey, 1916-1918 *(Oxford: Clarendon 1921), 179p.*

WOUNDED and a Prisoner of War *(London: Blackwood 1916), 316p.*

YEATS-BROWN, F
Caught by the Turks *(London: Arnold 1919), 220p.*

[See also ESCAPES]

PROPAGANDA

BLANKENHORN, H
Adventures in propaganda: letters from an Intelligence Officer in France *(Boston, Mass: Houghton Mifflin 1919), 167p.*

BRUNTZ, G G
Allied propaganda and the collapse of the German Empire in 1918 *(Stanford, Cal: Stanford UP 1938), 246p.*

CLAES, J
The German mole: a study of the art of peaceful penetration *(London: Bell 1915), 143p.*

CREEL, G
How we advertised America: the story of the Committee on Public Information *(New York: Harper 1920), 466p.*

GAFFNEY, T St J
Breaking the silence: England, Ireland, Wilson and the war *(New York: Liveright 1931), 358p.*

HASTE, C
Keep the home fires burning: propaganda in the First World War *(London: Lane 1977), 230p; bib.*

HOWARD, K
An author in wonderland *(London: Chatto & Windus 1919), 231p.*

LASSWELL, H D
Propaganda technique in the World War *(London: Kegan Paul 1927), 233p.*

MACLAREN, A D
Peaceful penetration *(London: Constable 1916), 224p.*

MOCK, J R *and* LARSON, C
Words that won the war: the story of the Committee on Public Information, 1917-1919 *(Princeton, NJ: Princeton UP 1939), 372p.*

PETERSON, H C
Propaganda for war: the campaign against American neutrality, 1914-1917 *(Norman, Okl: University of Oklahoma P 1939), 357p.*

PONSONBY, A A
Falsehood in wartime: containing an assortment of lies circulated during the Great War *(London: Allen & Unwin 1928), 192p.*

READ, J M
Atrocity propaganda, 1914-1919 *(New Haven, Conn: Yale UP 1941), 319p.*

SANDERS, M L *and* TAYLOR, P M
British propaganda during the First World War 1914–1918 *(London: Macmillan 1982), 320p; bib.*

SQUIRES, J D
British propaganda at home and in the United States from 1914 to 1917 *(Cambridge, Mass: Harvard UP 1935), 113p.*

STUART, *Sir* C
Secrets of Crewe House: the story of a famous campaign *(London: Hodder & Stoughton 1920), 240p.*

SUTER-LERCH, H J
Germany her own judge *(London: Allen & Unwin 1918), 128p.*

PSYCHOLOGY

HOBHOUSE, L T
The world in conflict: the psychological causes of the war *(London: Fisher Unwin 1915), 104p.*
LE BON, G
The psychology of the Great War *(London: Fisher Unwin 1916), 479p.*
MAXWELL, W N
A psychological retrospect of the Great War *(London: Allen & Unwin 1923), 191p.*
MORAN, C M *1st baron*
The anatomy of courage *(London: Constable 1945), 216p.*
ROETTER, C
The art of psychological warfare, 1914-1945 *(London: Batsford 1974), 199p. U.S. title: Psychological warfare.*
TAYLOR, G R S
The psychology of the Great War *(London: Secker 1915), 195p.*

Q SHIPS

AUTEN, H
'Q' boat adventures: the exploits of the famous mystery ships *(London: Jenkins 1919), 289p.*
CAMPBELL, G
My mystery ships *(London: Hodder & Stoughton 1928), 300p.*
CHATTERTON, E K
'Q' ships and their story *(London: Sidgwick & Jackson 1922), 276p.*
COLES, A
Slaughter at sea: the truth behind a naval war crime *(London: Hale 1986), 220p; bib.*
NOYES, A
Mystery ships: trapping the U-boats *(London: Hodder & Stoughton 1916); 181p.*
RITCHIE, C I A
Q ships *(Lavenham: Dalton 1985), 216p.*

QUAKERS

THE FRIENDS' Ambulance Unit, 1914-1919 *(London: Swarthmore 1920), 263p.*
FRIENDS and the war *(London: Headley 1914), 146p.*
THE FRIENDS' emergency work in England, 1914 to 1920 *(London: Friends' Bookshop 1933), 151p.*
FRY, A R
A Quaker adventure: the story of nine years' relief and reconstruction *(London: Nisbet 1926), 389p.*
GRAHAM, J W
War from a Quaker point of view *(London: Headley 1918), 114p.*

HOWARD, E F
Friends' service in war-time *(London: Friends' Council for International Service 1920), 48p.*
JONES, R M
A service of love in war time: American Friends' relief work in Europe, 1917-1919 *(New York: Macmillan 1920), 284p.*
STEPHENS, D O
With Quakers in France *(London: Daniel 1921), 336p.*

RAILWAYS

DARROCH, G R S
Deeds of a great railway: the London and North Western Railway Company during the war *(London: Murray 1920), 217p.*
DAVIES, W J K
Light railways of the First World War: a history of tactical rail communications on the British Fronts, 1914-18 *(Newton Abbot, Devon: David & Charles 1967), 196p; bib.*
DIXON, F H *and* PARMELEE, J H
War administration of the railways in the United States and Great Britain *(New York: OUP 1918), 155p.*
HAMILTON, J A B
Britain's railways in World War I *(London: Allen & Unwin 1967), 220p.*
HINES, W D
The war history of American railroads *(New Haven, Conn: Yale UP 1928), 327p.*
HORNIMAN, R
How to make the railways pay for the war *(London: Routledge 1919), 375p.*
KAHN, O H
Government ownership of railroads and war taxation *(New York: Kahn 1918), 50p.*
PRATT, E H
British railways and the Great War *(London: Selwyn & Blount 1921), 2 vols.*

RASPUTIN

LE QUEUX, W
The Minister of evil: the secret history of Rasputin's betrayal of Russia *(London: Cassell 1918), 253p.*
Rasputin the rascal monk *(London: Hurst & Blackett 1917), 176p.*
MARSDEN, V E
Rasputin and Russia: the tragedy of a throne *(London: Bird 1919), unp.*
OMESSA, C
Rasputin and the Russian Court *(London: Newnes 1918), 123p.*
RODZIANKO, M V
The reign of Rasputin *(London: Philpot 1927), 292p.*
VOGEL-JORGENSEN, T
Rasputin: prophet, libertine and plotter *(London: Fisher Unwin 1917), 143p.*

WILSON, C
  Rasputin and the fall of the Romanovs *(London: Barker 1964), 240p; bib.*
YOUSSOUPOFF, F F *prince*
  Rasputin *(London: Cape 1934), 256p.*
[See also NICHOLAS II, RUSSIA]

RECONSTRUCTION

AFTER victory *(London: Melrose 1917), 317p.*
AMERICA after the war *(New York: Century 1918), 208p.*
BRANFORD, V V *and* GEDDES, P
  The coming polity: a study in reconstruction *(London: Williams & Norgate 1917), 278p.*
BUCHANAN, L G
  After the war: preliminaries of reconstruction *(London: SPCK 1916), 79p.*
BUXTON, C R *and* BUXTON, D F
  The world after the war *(London: Allen & Unwin 1920), 155p.*
CHAPMAN, S J *ed*
  Labour and capital after the war *(London: Murray 1918), 290p.*
DAWSON, C W
  It might have happened to you: a study of conditions in Central Europe *(London: Lane 1921), 196p.*
THE ELEMENTS of reconstruction *(London: Nisbet 1916), 119p.*
FRIED, A H
  The restoration of Europe *(New York: Macmillan 1916), 157p.*
FRIEDMAN, E M *ed*
  American problems of reconstruction *(New York: Dutton 1918), 492p.*
  Labor and reconstruction in Europe *(New York: Dutton 1919), 216p.*
FUNNELL, H F D
  The great rebuilding: a study in political and economic reconstruction *(London: Parsons 1920), 324p.*
GARDNER, L
  The hope for society: essays on social reconstruction after the war *(London: Bell 1917), 236p.*
  Some Christian essentials of reconstruction *(London: Bell 1920), 235p.*
GIBBS, *Sir* P H
  Ten years after: a reminder *(London: Hutchinson 1924), 190p.*
HAMILTON, *Sir* I S M
  The millennium *(London: Arnold 1919), 156p.*
HARGRAVE, J
  The Great War brings it home: the natural reconstruction of an unnatural existence *(London: Constable 1919), 367p.*
HERFORD, R T
  Realities and reconstruction *(London: Lindsey 1920), 152p.*
HERSEY, H
  When the boys come home *(New York: Britton 1919), 204p.*

HILL, D J
    The rebuilding of Europe *(New York: Century 1917), 289p.*
HIRST, F W
    The consequences of the war to Great Britain *(London: OUP 1934), 311p.*
HOPKINSON, *Sir* A
    Rebuilding Britain: a survey of problems of reconstruction after the World War *(London: Cassell 1918), 192p.*
LAVELL, C F
    Reconstruction and national life *(New York: Macmillan 1919), 193p.*
LIPPINCOTT, I
    Problems of reconstruction *(New York: Macmillan 1919), 340p.*
LODGE, *Sir* O J
    The war and after *(London: Methuen 1915), 240p.*
LUGARD, *Sir* F J D
    The dual Mandate in British tropical Africa *(Edinburgh: Blackwood 1923), 643p.*
LYDE, L W
    Some frontiers of tomorrow: an aspiration for Europe *(London: Black 1915), 128p.*
MACDONALD, W
    Reconstruction in France *(London: Macmillan 1922), 349p.*
MACKINDER, H J
    Democratic ideals and reality: a study in the politics of reconstruction *(London: Constable 1919), 272p.*
MAN, H de
    The remaking of the mind: a soldier's thoughts on war and reconstruction *(London: Allen & Unwin 1920), 289p.*
MEYER, H R
    After the war *(London: Simpkin Marshall 1915), 179p.*
MILNES, A
    The economic foundations of reconstruction *(London: Macdonald & Evans 1919), 226p.*
MITRANY, D
    The effect of the war in South-Eastern Europe *(New Haven, Conn: Yale UP 1936), 282p.*
MOWRER, P S
    Balkanized Europe: a study in political analysis and reconstruction *(New York: Dutton 1921), 349p.*
NITTI, F S
    The decadence of Europe: the paths of reconstruction *(London: Fisher Unwin 1923), 279p.*
    Peaceless Europe *(London: Cassell 1922), 292p.*
    They make a desert *(London: Dent 1924), 270p.*
PEDDIE, J T
    Economic reconstruction *(London: Longmans 1918), 242p.*
PERLA, L
    What is 'National Honor': the challenge of reconstruction *(New York: Macmillan 1918), 211p.*
PHILLIPS, G C
    The land after the war: a business proposition *(London: St. Catherine 1915), 54p.*
PROBLEMS of readjustment after the war *(New York: Appleton 1915), 185p.*

PROBLEMS of reconstruction: lectures and addresses *(London: Longmans 1918), 315p.*
QUICK, H
   From war to peace: a plea for a definite policy of reconstruction *(Indianapolis, Ind: Bobbs-Merrill 1919), 278p.*
THE REBUILDING of Britain *(London: Brown 1920), 141p.*
ROBERTS, K L
   Europe's morning after *(New York: Harper 1921), 409p.*
ROGERS, L
   The problems of reconstruction, international and national *(New York: American Assoc. of International Conciliation 1919), 164p.*
SAMUEL, H
   The war and liberty and an address on reconstruction *(London: Hodder & Stoughton 1917), 128p.*
SAVIC, V R
   The reconstruction of South-Eastern Europe *(London: Chapman & Hall 1917), 280p.*
SIMONS, A M
   The vision for which we fought: a study in reconstruction *(London: Citizens Library 1919), 197p.*
SMITH, C H *and* HILL, C R
   Rising above the ruins in France: an account of progress made in the devastated areas *(New York: Putnam 1920), 247p.*
STOCKER, R D
   From warfare to welfare: essays in social reconstruction *(London: Palmer & Hayward 1916), 244p.*
TODD, E
   The new exodus *(London: Stockwell 1918), 64p.*
UNWIN, R
   The war; and what after *(Letchworth, Herts: Garden City 1915), 63p.*
VILLIERS, B
   Britain after peace: revolution or reconstruction? *(London: Fisher Unwin 1918), 263p.*
WARMAN, W H
   The soldier colonists: a plan for post-bellum emigration *(London: Chatto & Windus 1918), 191p.*
WEBB, M de P
   Britain victorious! *(London: King 1920), 157p.*
WEBB, S *and* FREEMAN, A
   Great Britain after the war *(London: Allen & Unwin 1916), 80p.*
WELLS, H G
   What is coming?: a forecast of things after the war *(London: Cassell 1916), 295p.*
WHELPLEY, J D
   Reconstruction *(New York: Funk 1925), 383p.*
ZIMMERN, A E
   Europe in convalescence *(London: Mills & Boon 1922), 309p.*

RECRUITMENT

GRIEVES, K
The politics of manpower 1914–18 *(Manchester: Manchester UP 1987), 208p.*

RED CROSS

AMES, F
American Red Cross work among the French people *(New York: Macmillan 1921), 178p.*
BAKEWELL, C M
The story of the American Red Cross in Italy *(New York: Macmillan 1920), 253p.*
BARKER, H G
The Red Cross in France *(London: Hodder & Stoughton 1916), 168p.*
BICKNELL, E P
In war's wake, 1914-1915: the Rockefeller Foundation and the American Red Cross join in civilian relief *(Washington DC: American Red Cross 1936), 276p.*
With the Red Cross in Europe, 1917-1922 *(Washington DC: American Red Cross 1938), 506p.*
BILLINGTON, M F
The Red Cross in war: woman's part in the relief of suffering *(London: Hodder & Stoughton 1914), 190p.*
BOARDMANN, M T
Under the Red Cross flag at home and abroad *(Philadelphia, Pa: Lippincott 1915), 333p.*
BOCHARSKAYA, S *and* PIER, F
They knew how to die: a narrative of the personal experiences of a Red Cross Sister on the Russian Front *(London: Davies 1931), 31lp.*
BRITISH RED CROSS SOCIETY
The Red Cross in Gloucestershire during the war *(Gloucester: 1919), 153p.*
D'ABERNON, H V *viscountess*
Red Cross and Berlin Embassy, 1915-1926 *(London: Murray 1946), 152p.*
DAVISON, H P
The American Red Cross in the Great War *(New York: Macmillan 1919): 303p.*
DEASE, A
With the French Red Cross *(New York: Kennedy 1917), 96p.*
FIFE, G B
The passing legions: how the American Red Cross met the American Army in Great Britain, the gateway to France *(New York: Macmillan 1920), 369p.*
GAINES, R L
Helping France: the Red Cross in the devastated area *(New York: Dutton 1919), 235p.*
HARRISON, C H
With the American Red Cross in France, 1918-1919 *(Chicago: Seymour 1947), 341p.*
HUNGERFORD, E
With the doughboy in France: a few chapters of an American effort *(New York: Macmillan 1920), 291p.*
LEIGH, D
The background of battle *(London: Hodder & Stoughton 1916), 255p.*

LIVINGSTON, ST C *and* STEEN-HANSEN, I
Under three flags: with the Red Cross in France *(London: Macmillan 1916), 251p.*
LUCAS, B J
Children of France and the Red Cross *(New York: Stokes 1918), 193p.*
LUCAS, E V
Outposts of mercy: the record of a visit in 1916 to the various units of the British Red Cross in Italy *(London: Methuen 1917), 60p.*
LUGARD, E A
Some impressions of the work of the British Red Cross in France *(Bombay: 1919), 63p.*
MOORE, M M
The Maple Leaf's Red Cross *(London: Skeffington 1919), 223p.*
REPORTS by the Joint War Committee and the Joint War Finance Committee of the British Red Cross Society and the Order of St John of Jerusalem in England *(London: British Red Cross Society 1921),. 823p.*
SEARS, H M
Journal of a canteen worker: a record of service with the American Red Cross in Flanders *(Boston, Mass: Sears 1919), 213p.*
SENN, A E
The Russian revolution in Switzerland, 1914-1917 *(Madison: University of Wisconsin P 1971), 250p; bib.*
SPEARING, E M
From Cambridge to Camiers under the Red Cross *(Cambridge: CUP 1917), 87p.*
TOLAND, E D
The aftermath of battle: with the Red Cross in France *(London: Macmillan 1916), 175p.*
VAN SCHAICK, J
The little corner never conquered: the story of the American Red Cross war work for Belgium *(New York: Macmillan 1922), 282p.*
VIVIAN, E C *and* HODDER-WILLIAMS, J E
The way of the Red Cross *(London: Hodder & Stoughton 1915), 290p.*
WESTERDALE, T L B
Under the Red Cross flag *(London: Kelly 1915), 170p.*
[See also RELIEF WORK, VAD]

REFERENCE BOOKS

ANDERSON, C C
War manual *(London: Fisher Unwin 1915), 2 vols.*
ARMINIUS *pseud*
From Serajevo to the Rhine: Generals of the Great War *(London: Hutchinson 1933), 287p.*
DAILY CHRONICLE *(newspaper)*
The Great War book *(London: Daily Chronicle 1914), 192p.*
DARNTON, M C
War makers and peace makers *(New York: Harper 1920), 406p.*
DE BECK, A M
The Imperial war: personalities and issues *(London: Hurst & Blackett 1916), 336p.*

De Weerd, H A
  Great soldiers of two World Wars *(New York: Norton 1941), 378p.*
Dodd, F
  Generals of the British Army *(London: Country Life 1917-18), 2 pts.*
Gardiner, A G
  War lords *(London: Dent 1915), 326p.*
Gilbert, M
  First World War atlas *(New York: Macmillan 1971), 159p.*
Guernsey, I S
  Reference history of the war *(New York: Dodd 1920), 392p.*
Haulsee, W M *and others comps*
  Soldiers of the Great War *(Washington DC: Soldiers Record nd), 3 vols.*
Johnston, C H L
  Famous Generals of the Great War *(New York: Page 1919), 310p.*
Lauzanne, S J V
  Great men and great days *(New York: Appleton 1921), 262p.*
Leland, W G *and* Mareness, N D
  Introduction to the American official sources for the economic and social history of the World War *(New Haven, Conn: Yale UP 1926), unp.*
Mudd, T B *comp*
  The Yanks were there: a chronological and documentary review of World War I *(New York: Vantage 1958), 258p.*
Nash, J E
  Nash's war manual *(London: Nash 1914), 350p.*
Natesan, G
  All about the war *(Madras: 1915), 440p.*
New War encyclopaedia and dictionary *(London: Jarrolds 1914), 94p.*
Page, A P
  'World's work': war manual of the great conflict of 1914 *(New York: Doubleday 1914), 143p.*
Parkman, M R
  Fighters for peace *(New York: Century 1919), 311p.*
Rowe, R P P
  A concise chronicle of events of the Great War *(London: P Allan 1920), 343p.*
Rowell, *Mrs* C W
  Leaders of the Great War *(New York: Macmillan 1919), 336p.*
Simonds, F H
  They won the war: sketches of Allied Generals *(New York: Harper 1931), 109p.*
The Marshall Cavendish illustrated encyclopaedia of World War One *(London: Marshall Cavendish 1984), 12 vols.*
Things to know about the war *(London: Pearson 1915), 159p.*
The Times *(newspaper)*
  The Times diary and index of the war, 1914-1918 *(London: The Times 1921), 342p.*
Two thousand questions and answers about the war *(New York: Review of Reviews 1918), 372p.*
Uncle Sam's fact book of the World War *(New York: Hammond 1918), 248p.*
The War book of facts *(London: Shaw 1914), 146p.*

WILE, F W
Who's Who in Hunland *(London: Simpkin Marshall 1916), 154p.*

REFUGEES

AUSTIN, H H
The Baqubah Refugee Camp: an account of work on behalf of the persecuted Assyrian Christians *(London: Faith 1920), 119p.*
CAHALAN, P
Belgian refugee relief in England during the Great War *(New York: Garland 1982), 552p.*
CAMPBELL, H
Belgian soldiers at home in the United Kingdom *(London: Saunders & Cullingham 1917), 95p.*
CLIERENS, F
A plain tale from Malines: the authentic story of a refugee *(Oxford: Blackwell 1914), 48p.*
FOUR years in a refugee camp: being an account of the British Government War Refugees' Camp, Earls Court, London, 1914-1919 *(London: Baynard 1920), 84p.*
JONES, F
With Serbia in exile *(New York: Century 1916), 447p.*
PITTARD, Mrs H
Victims' return *(Boston, Mass: Houghton Mifflin 1918), 134p.*
RADFORD, M
Our friends the Belgians *(London: Stockwell 1921), 103p.*
THURSTON, V
The people who run: being the tragedy of the refugees in Russia *(New York: Putnam 1916), 175p.*
WHARTON, Mrs E N ed
Book of the homeless *(New York: Scribner 1915), 154p.*

RELIEF WORK

BELL, L L
The story of the Christmas ship *(Chicago: Rand 1915), 382p.*
BINYON, L
For dauntless France: an account of Britain's aid to the French wounded and victims of war *(London: Hodder & Stoughton 1918), 387p.*
FORD, G B
Out of the ruins *(New York: Century 1919), 275p.*
GAINES, R L
The ladies of Grécourt: the Smith College Relief Unit in the Somme *(New York: Dutton 1920), 246p.*
A village in Picardy *(New York: Dutton 1918), 193p.*
HISTORY of the American Field Service in France: friends of France, 1914-1917 *(Boston, Mass: Houghton Mifflin 1920), 3 vols.*

Lovejoy, E
  The house of the good neighbor *(New York: Macmillan 1919), 218p.*
Saint-Rene Taillandier, *Mme*
  The soul of the 'C.R.B': a French view of the Hoover Relief work *(New York: Scribner 1919), 233p.*
Taggart, G *and* Winchell, W
  A Yankee Major invades Belgium: a chronicle of a merciful and peaceful mission to Europe during the World War *(New York: Revell 1917), 209p.*
[See also RED CROSS, VAD]

RELIGION

Abbott, H P A
  Religion of the Tommy: war essays and addresses *(Milwaukee, Wis: Morehouse 1918), 144p.*
Abrams, R H
  Preachers present arms: a study of the war-time attitudes and activities of the Churches and the clergy in the United States, 1914-1918 *(Philadelphia, Pa: Round Table 1933), 297p.*
Adams, J
  The great sacrifice; or, The altar-fire of war *(Edinburgh: 1915), 135p.*
Anderson, *Sir* R
  The higher criticism and the war *(London: Nisbet 1915), 165p.*
The Army and religion: an inquiry and its bearing upon the religious life of the nation *(New York: Associated P 1920), 447p.*
Ball, C R
  The war: thoughts on its religious aspects *(London: SPCK 1914), 63p.*
Ballard, F
  Britain justified: the war from the Christian standpoint *(London: Kelly 1914), 143p.*
  Christianity after the war *(London: Kelly 1916), 155p.*
Barry, F R
  Religion and the war *(London: Methuen 1915), 92p.*
Barton, W E
  Blue stars and gold; for every home that flies a service flag *(Chicago: Reilly 1918), 216p.*
Bedborough, G
  Arms and the clergy, 1914 -1918 *(London: Secular Society 1934), 109p.*
Bell, G K A
  The war and the kingdom of God *(London: Longmans 1915), 185p.*
Bernard, J H *archbishop*
  In war time *(London: Mowbray 1917), 109p.*
Borsi, G
  A soldier's confidences with God *(New York: Kennedy 1918), 362p.*
Broomhall, M
  'Mine own vineyard': personal religion and the war *(London: Morgan & Scott 1916), 81p.*
Brown, C
  The war and the Faith *(London: Morgan & Scott 1915), 145p.*

Religion

BULL, P B
Peace and war *(London: Longmans 1917), 127p.*
BUNSEN, V B
War and men's minds *(London: Lane 1919), 185p.*
BURROUGHS, E A
The fight for the future *(London: Nisbet 1916), 127p.*
CAIRNS, D S
The Army and religion *(London: Macmillan 1919), 455p.*
CAMPBELL, R J
The war and the soul *(London: Chapman & Hall 1916), 277p.*
CARPENTER, E J
Ethical and religious problems of the war *(London: Lindsey 1916), 208p.*
CHAPMAN, H B
Home truths about the war *(London: Allen & Unwin 1917), 187p.*
CLARK, C H D
God within the shadows: the Divine Hand in the First and Second Great Wars of this twentieth century *(London: Regency 1970), 171p; bib.*
CLARKE, F J
The world, the war and the Cross *(London: Allen & Unwin 1916), 91p.*
CLAYTON, P B
Letters from Flanders *(London: Longmans 1932), 176p.*
Plain tales from Flanders *(London: Longmans 1929), 168p.*
CLOW, W M
The Christian message in the light of the war *(London: Marshall 1918), 152p.*
COMMITTEE ON THE WAR AND THE RELIGIOUS OUTLOOK
Missionary outlook in the face of the war *(New York: Associated P 1920), 329p.*
Religion among American men, as revealed by a study of conditions in the Army *(New York: Associated P 1920), 155p.*
COPPING, A E
Souls in khaki: a spiritual experience among our lads in the firing line *(London: Hodder & Stoughton 1917), 195p.*
CRANANGE, D H S
The war and the unity *(London: CUP 1919), 161p.*
CROSSE, E C
The God of battles: a soldier's faith *(London: Longmans 1917), 77p.*
CUNNINGHAM, W
Christianity and politics *(London: Murray 1916), 284p.*
DAVIDSON, R T *archbishop*
'Quit you like men' *(London: SPCK 1915), 89p.*
The testing of a nation *(London: Macmillan 1919), 221p.*
DAVIS, O S
The Gospel in the light of the Great War *(Chicago: Chicago UP 1919), 219p.*
DAWSON, C W
Glory of the trenches: an interpretation *(London: Lane 1918), 141p.*
DAWSON, J
Christ and the sword: words for the war-perplexed *(London: Kelly 1916), 155p.*

DE CANDOLE, A C V
The faith of a subaltern *(London: CUP 1919), 92p.*
DENNETT, T
A better world *(New York: Doran 1920), 173p.*
DENNEY, J
War and the fear of God *(London: Hodder & Stoughton 1916), 192p.*
DRAKE, E
The universal mind and the Great War: outlines of a new religion *(London: Daniel 1916,. 100p.*
DRAWBRIDGE, C L
The war and religious ideals *(London: Longmans 1915), 151p.*
DRESSER, H W
The victorious faith: moral ideals in war time *(New York: Harper 1917), 221p.*
DUDDEN, F H
The heroic dead, and other sermons *(London: Longmans 1917), 156p.*
DUKE, J A
The religions of our Allies *(London: Hodder & Stoughton 1916), 163p.*
EDDY, S
Suffering and the war *(London: Longmans 1916), unp.*
ELPHINSTONE, M C
War and the Gospel of Christ *(London: Skeffington 1915), 150p.*
FAUNCE, W H P
Religion and war *(New York: Abingdon 1918), 188p.*
FIGGIS, J N
The will to freedom; or, The Gospel of Nietzsche and the Gospel of Christ *(London: Longmans 1917), 388p.*
FISHER, R H
A letter to you: letters addressed to our soldiers *(London: Hodder & Stoughton 1915), 57p.*
FLACK, W T
Christ on Ariadne; or, 'What I said to our soldiers' *(Cambridge, CUP 1916), 81p.*
FORSYTH, P T
The Christian ethic of war *(London: Longmans 1916), 196p.*
FOSDICK, H E
The challenge of the present crisis to Christianity *(New York: Doran 1917), 99p.*
FRIBOURG, A
Flaming crucible: the faith of the fighting men *(New York: Macmillan 1918), 185p.*
GORDON, S D
Quiet talks on the deeper meaning of the war and its relation to our Lord's return *(New York: Revell 1919), 286p.*
GORE, C
The war and the Church *(London: Mowbray 1914), 139p.*
GOUGH, A W
Repentance and strength: recollections of sermons bearing on the war and the national mission *(London: Nisbet 1916), 119p.*
GRANT, J G
The heart beneath the uniform *(London: Morgan & Scott 1917), 137p.*

GRIFFITH-JONES, E
The challenge of Christianity to a world at war *(London: Duckworth 1915)*, *264p.*
HARDIN, M D *and others*
The pulpit in war time *(Philadelphia, Pa: Presbyterian Board 1918)*, *173p.*
HENDERSON, G
The experiences of a hut leader at the Front *(Paisley, Scot: 1918)*, *145p.*
HENLEY, T
After the war: Christendom and the coming peace from an Australian point of view *(London: Hodder & Stoughton 1917)*, *52p.*
HENSON, H H
War-time sermons *(London: Macmillan 1915)*, *287p.*
HERTSLET, E L A
The cup and the sacrifice *(London: Simpkin Marshall 1915)*, *179p.*
HODGES, G
Religion in a world at war *(New York: Macmillan 1918)*, *103p.*
HOLLAND, H S
So as by fire: notes on the war *(London: Wells Gardner 1915)*, *120p.*
HUNT, J B
War, religion and science *(London: Melrose 1915)*, *144p.*
INGRAM, A F W
The Church in time of war *(London: Wells Gardner 1915)*, *330p.*
A day of God *(London: Wells Gardner 1914)*, *77p.*
Victory and after *(London: Wells Gardner 1919)*, *242p.*
IRVINE, A
God and Tommy Atkins *(London: Hutchinson 1918)*, *127p.*
JACKSON, F J F
The Faith and the war *(London: Macmillan 1915)*, *261p.*
JEFFERSON, C E
Old truths and new facts: Christian life and thinking as modified by the Great War *(New York: Revell 1918)*, *223p.*
What the war has taught us *(New York: Revell 1919)*, *238p.*
JEFFS, H
'When the lads come home': what will the Churches do with them? *(London: Johnson 1916)*, *80p.*
JONES, E G
The challenge of Christianity to a world at war *(London: Duckworth 1915)*, *245p.*
KELMAN, J
The war and preaching *(London: Hodder & Stoughton 1919)*, *286p.*
KENNEDY, G A S
The hardest part: thoughts on religion in war *(London: Hodder & Stoughton 1918)*, *205p.*
KIRK, H E
Consuming fire *(New York: Macmillan 1919)*, *183p.*
KIRKLAND, W M
The new death *(Boston, Mass: Houghton Mifflin 1918)*, *173p.*
KLEIN, F
Hope in suffering *(London: Melrose 1916)*, *317p.*

LANG, C G
The Church and the clergy at this time of war *(London: SPCK 1916), 58p.*

LEONARD, G H
They also serve *(London: Student Christian Movement 1915), 61p.*

LINDSEY, B B
The Doughboy's religion *(New York: Harper 1920), 89p.*

LLOYD THOMAS, J M
The immorality of non-resistance and other sermons of the war *(Birmingham: Cornish 1915), 126p.*

LOISY, A F
The war and religion *(Oxford: Clarendon 1915), 116p.*

MACCABE, J
The war and the Churches *(London: Watts 1915), 114p.*

MACHEN, A
War and the Christian Faith *(London: Skeffington 1918), 62p.*

MACKARNESS, C C
Faith and duty in time of war *(London: Mowbray 1916), 109p.*

MACKENZIE, W D
Christian ethics in the war *(London: Melrose 1918), 199p.*

MACKINTOSH, D C
God in a world at war *(London: Allen & Unwin 1918), 59p.*

McKIM, R H
For God and country; or, The Christian pulpit in wartime *(New York: Dutton 1918), 129p.*

MACLEAN, N *and* SCLATER, J R
God and the soldier *(London: Hodder & Stoughton 1917), 283p.*

MACNUTT, F B *ed*
The Church in the furnace: essays by seventeen temporary Church of England chaplains on active service in France and Flanders *(New York: Macmillan 1918), 464p.*

MARRIN, A
The last crusade: the Church of England in the First World War *(Durham, NC: Duke UP 1974), 303p.*

MATHEWS, B J *ed*
Christ and the world at war *(London: Clarke 1917), 191p.*

MATHEWS, S
Patriotism and religion *(New York: Macmillan 1918), 161p.*

MAUD, J P
Our comradeship with the blessed dead *(London: Longmans 1915), 96p.*

MAYHEW, D M *ed*
Lift up your hearts: a book for those whom the war has put in mourning *(London: Hodder & Stoughton 1915), 126p.*

MILLARD, F L H
Short war sermons for Good Friday and Easter *(London: Skeffington 1916), 60p.*

MOODIE, J W
700 days with the troops *(London: Marshall 1916), 60p.*

MORGAN, G C
God, humanity and the war *(London: Clarke 1914), 80p.*

MUIR, J
   War and Christian duty *(Paisley, Scot: 1916), 278p.*
MURRAY, M
   Bible prophecies and the present war *(London: Hodder & Stoughton 1916), 338p.*
   The Christian's war book *(London: Hodder & Stoughton 1914), 192p.*
MURSELL, W A
   The bruising of Belgium, and other sermons during war time *(London: Wells Gardner 1915), 276p.*
NEWTON, J F
   The sword of the spirit: Britain and America in the Great War *(London: Nisbet 1918), 246p.*
NICOLL, *Sir* W R
   Prayer in war time *(London: Hodder & Stoughton 1916), 187p.*
NURSE, E J
   Christmas time and the war *(London: Skeffington 1915), 77p.*
ORCHARD, W E
   The true patriotism, and other sermons *(London: Allen & Unwin 1918), 192p.*
OSBORNE, C E
   Religion in Europe and the world crisis *(London: Fisher Unwin 1916), 414p.*
PAGET, H L
   In the way of battle *(London: Longmans 1915), 157p.*
PATERSON, W P
   In the day of the ordeal *(London: Clarke 1917), 262p.*
PIPER, J F
   The American churches in World War I *(Athens, Ohio: Ohio UP 1985), 230p.*
PLATER, C D *ed*
   Catholic soldiers *(London: Longmans 1919), 157p.*
PLOWDEN-WARDLAW, J *and others*
   Religious reconstruction after the war *(London: Scott 1916), 153p.*
   The test of war: war addresses *(London: Scott 1916), 202p.*
PONSONBY, M
   Visions and vignettes of war *(London: Longmans 1917), 116p.*
POTTER, J H
   Discipline of war: nine addresses on the lessons of war in connection with Lent *(London: Skeffington 1915), 94p.*
   Judgment of war *(London: Skeffington 1915), 96p.*
POTTER, J H *and* WORSEY, F W
   Harvest thanksgiving in war time *(London: Skeffington 1915), 94p.*
PROCTOR, F B
   The national crisis and why the Churches fail *(London: Stockwell 1915), 218p.*
RAWSON, F L
   How to protect our soldiers; or, The practical utilisation of the power of God by right thinking *(London: Crystal 1916), 138p.*
ROLLINGS, W S
   The great assize: war studies in the light of Christian ideals *(London: Allenson 1916), 253p.*

ROSCOE, J E
    War messages to the nations *(London: Skeffington 1915), 96p.*
    War saints and subjects *(London: Skeffington 1915), 104p.*
SCLATER, J R P
    The eve of battle: addresses at Church parade *(London: Hodder & Stoughton 1915), 104p.*
SCOTT-MONCRIEFF, C E
    War thoughts for the Christian year *(London: Skeffington 1915), 124p.*
SEAVER, R W
    What of our dead in the Great War *(London: Taylor 1916), 72p.*
SELLERS, W E
    With our heroes in khaki: Christian work with our soldiers and sailors *(London: RTS 1918), 302p.*
SERVICE, W J N
    War and the peace of God *(Glasgow: 1915), 148p.*
SHILLITO, E
    The Christian year in war time *(London: Longmans 1918), 93p.*
    Through the war to the Kingdom *(London: Morgan & Scott 1915), 110p.*
SINKER, J
    The war, its deeds and lessons *(London: Skeffington 1916), 130p.*
SMITH, *Sir* G A
    The war, the nation and the Church *(London: Hodder & Stoughton 1916), 46p.*
SMYTH, J P
    God and the war *(London: Hodder & Stoughton 1915), 196p.*
    The men who died in battle *(London: Hodder & Stoughton 1916), 67p.*
SNEATH, E H
    Religion and the war *(New Haven, Conn: Yale UP 1918), 178p.*
THE SOLDIER'S companion: message of hope, comfort and love *(London: Oliphants 1916), 192p.*
SOLOVEV, V S
    War and Christianity from the Russian point of view *(London: Constable 1915), 188p.*
SPEER, R E
    The Christian man, the Church and the war *(New York: Macmillan 1918), 105p.*
STACKHOUSE, P J
    The sword of Christ and the World War *(Philadelphia, Pa: American Baptist 1917), 124p.*
STIDGER, W le R
    Star dust from the dugouts: a reconstruction book *(New York: Abingdon 1919), 236p.*
STIRES, E M
    High call *(New York: Dutton 1917), 179p.*
    The price of peace *(New York: Dutton 1919), 279p.*
TALBOT, N S
    Religion behind the Front and after the war *(London: Macmillan 1918), 125p.*
    Thoughts on religion at the Front *(London: Macmillan 1917), 91p.*
THOMAS, G
    Grapes and thorns: thoughts in war time *(London: Headley 1915), 104p.*
TITTERTON, C H
    Armageddon, or the last war *(Edinburgh: Thynne 1916), 121p.*

TOMKINS, A
    And behold we live: papers by a wounded soldier *(London: Constable 1918), 135p.*
TREVELYAN, W B
    A nation at prayer *(London: Longmans 1914), 112p.*
TUDOR-POLE, W
    Great War: some deeper issues *(London: Bell 1915), 108p.*
VANCE, J I
    Silver on the iron cross *(New York: Revell 1919), 416p.*
VEACH, R W
    The meaning of the war for religious education *(New York: Revell 1920), 254p.*
VELIMIROVIC, N
    The agony of the Church *(London: Student Christian Movement 1917), 125p.*
WACE, H
    The war and the Gospel *(Edinburgh: Thynne 1917), 247p.*
WALKER, W L
    The war, God and our duty *(London: R. Scott 1917), 113p.*
WAR and Christianity *(London: Jarrolds 1914), 73p.*
A WAR manual of prayer *(London: Longmans 1914), 63p.*
WARD, H M
    Behind the lines *(London: RTS 1918), 143p.*
WATT, L M
    The heart of a soldier *(New York: Doran 1918), 258p.*
WIGGINS, C F
    Saved as by fire *(Boston, Mass: Badger 1918), 185p.*
WILBERFORCE, A B O
    Why does not God stop the war? *(London: Elliot Stock 1915), 78p.*
WILKINSON, A B
    The Church of England and the First World War *(London: SPCK 1978), 370p.*
WILLIAMS, J H
    Lenten thoughts in war time *(London: Skeffington 1916), 130p.*
WISEMAN, F L
    The Christ of the soldier *(London: Epworth 1919), 116p.*
WOODS, E S
    Knights in armour *(London: R. Scott 1916), 64p.*
WOODS, H G
    Christianity and the war *(London: Scott 1916), 170p.*
THE WORLD in tears *(London: Hayes 1915), 91p.*
WOTHERSPOON, H J
    Some spiritual issues of the war *(London: Scott 1918), 80p.*
[See also CATHOLICISM, CHAPLAIN]

REPARATIONS

Angas, L L B
Germany and her debts: a critical examination of the reparation problem *(London: Simmonds 1923), 158p.*
Reparations, trade and foreign exchange *(London: King 1922), 351p.*

Auld, G P
The Dawes Plan and the new economics *(London: Allen & Unwin 1928), 317p.*

Baruch, B M
The making of the reparation and economic sections of the Treaty *(New York: Harper 1920), 353p.*

Bergmann, C
The history of reparations *(London: Benn 1927), 333p.*

Burnett, P M
Reparations at the Paris Peace Conference from the standpoint of the American delegation *(New York: Columbia UP 1940), 2 vols.*

Dawes, C G
A journal of reparations *(London: Macmillan 1939), 527p.*

Dawes, R C
The Dawes Plan in the making *(Indianapolis, Ind: Bobbs-Merrill 1925), 525p.*

Felix, D
Walter Rathenau and the Weimar Republic: the politics of reparations *(Baltimore: Johns Hopkins UP 1971), 210p; bib.*

Hague Conference on Reparations 1929-30
The final settlement of the reparation problems growing out of the Great War *(Worcester, Mass: 1930), 205p.*

Long, R C
The mythology of reparations *(London: Duckworth 1928), 109p.*

Macfadyean, *Sir* A
Reparations reviewed *(London: Benn 1930), 220p.*

Moulton, H G
The reparation plan *(New York: Inst. of Economics 1924), 325p.*

Moulton, H G *and* MacGuire, C E
Germany's capacity to pay *(New York: Inst. of economics 1923), 385p.*

Mousley, E O
A British brief: England's reparation victims and war debt *(London: Hutchinson 1932), 206p.*

Penson, *Sir* T H
Is Germany prosperous?: impressions gained January 1922 *(London: Arnold 1923), 124p.*

Schacht, H
The end of reparations *(London: Cape 1931), 271p.*

Trachenberg, M
Reparations in world politics: France and European economic diplomacy 1916–1923 *(Guildford, NY: Columbia UP 1980), 423p.*

Wheeler-Bennett, J W *and* Latimer, H
Information on the Reparation Settlement: being the background and history of the Young Plan and The Hague Agreements *(London: Allen & Unwin 1930), 253p.*

RICHTHOFEN

BRIGGS, R
Richthofen the Red Baron *(London: Hamilton 1968), 40p.*
BURROWS, W E
Richthofen: a true history of the Red Baron *(London: Hart-Davis 1970), 268p; bib.*
CARISELLA, P J
Who killed the Red Baron?: the final answers *(Wakefield, Mass: Daedalus 1969), 288p.*
GIBBONS, F
The red knight of Germany: Baron von Richthofen *(London: Cassell 1930), 408p.*
NOWARRA, H J *and* BROWN, K S
Von Richthofen and the flying circus *(Letchworth, Herts: Harleyford 1958), 207p.*
RICHTHOFEN, M A
The red baron *(New York: Doubleday 1969), 240p.*
The red battle flyer *(New York: McBride 1918), 222p. U.K. title:* The red air fighter.
TITLER, D M
The day the Red Baron died *(London: Ian Allan 1973), 328p.*
VIGILANT *pseud*
Richthofen, the red knight of the air *(London: Hamilton 1934), 285p.*
WRIGHT, N
The red baron *(London: Sidgwick & Jackson 1976), 120p.*
[See also FIGHTERS, GERMAN AIR FORCE]

ROOSEVELT

LODGE, H C *ed*
Selections from the correspondence of Theodore Roosevelt *(New York: 1925), 2 vols.*
ROOSEVELT, T
America and the World War *(London: Murray 1915), 277p.*
Fear God and take your own part *(London: Hodder & Stoughton 1916), 414p.*
The great adventure: present-day studies in American nationalism *(London: Murray 1919), 204p.*
Why America should join the Allies *(London: Pearson 1915), 64p.*

ROYAL AIR FORCE

ASHMORE, E B
Air defence: an account of air defence in England, 1914-1918 *(London: Longmans 1929), 179p.*
BALFOUR, H H
An airman marches *(London: Hutchinson 1933), 282p.*
BARNES, J T S
Half a life *(London: Eyre & Spottiswoode 1933), 342p.*
BLAKE, W T
'Over the ˑe': stories of the Royal Air Force *(London: Cassell 1918), 209p.*

BOTT, A
Eastern nights - and flights *(London: Blackwood 1920), 315p.*
BOWYER, C
Airmen of World War I: men of the British and Empire Air Forces in old photographs *(London: Arms & Armour Press 1975), 128p.*
BRUCE, J M
British aeroplanes, 1914-18 *(London: Putnam 1957), 742p.*
BURGE, C G *comp*
The annals of 100 Squadron *(London: Reiach 1919), 211p.*
BUSK, M
E. T. Busk, a pioneer in flight; with a short memoir of H. A. Busk *(London: Murray 1925), 167p.*
BUTLER, A S G
Plain impressions *(London: Aeroplane 1919), 95p.*
COLE, C
Royal Air Force, 1918 *(London: Kimber 1968), 256p.*
The air defence of Britain 1914–1918 *(London: Putnam 1984), 485p.*
FLIGHT *pseud*
Flying Yankee *(New York: Dodd 1918), 248p.*
FLIGHT COMMANDER *pseud*
Cavalry of the air *(London: Burrow 1918), 269p.*
FREDETTE, R H
The first Battle of Britain, 1917-1918, and the birth of the Royal Air Force *(London: Cassell 1966), 289p; bib.*
HUGHES, C E
Above and beyond Palestine: an account of the work of the East Indies and Egypt Seaplane Squadron, 1916-1918 *(London: Benn 1930), 268p.*
ILLINGWORTH, A E
'Fly papers': being leaves from the diary of a war pilot *(Newcastle-upon-Tyne: 1919), 107p.*
JOHNSTONE, E G
Naval eight: a history of No. 8 Squadron R.N.A.S.– afterwards No. 208 Squadron R.A.F. – from its formation in 1916 until the Armistice in 1918 *(London: Signal 1931), 207p.*
JONES, H A
Over the Balkans and South Russia: being the history of No. 47 Squadron Royal Air Force *(London: Arnold 1923), 176p.*
JOY-STICK *pseud*
An artistic and literary tribute to officers and men of the R.A.F. *(London: Blighty 1918), 176p.*
KINGSFORD, A R
Night raiders of the air: being the experiences of a night flying pilot *(London: Hamilton 1930), 222p.*
LEWIS, C A
Sagittarius rising *(London: Davies 1936), 331p.*
LEWIS, G H
Wings over the Somme, 1916-1918 *(London: Kimber 1976), 205p.*

LIDDLE, P
The airman's war 1914–1918 *(Poole, Dorset: Blandford 1987), 224p; bib.*
MACMILLAN, N
Into the blue *(London: Duckworth 1929), 213p.*
MARSON, T B
Scarlet and khaki *(London: Cape 1930), 225p.*
MIDDLETON, E C
Tails up: aircraft sketches *(London: Simpkin Marshall 1918), 314p.*
MONTGOMERY, D H
Down the flare path *(London: Hamilton 1937), 144p.*
MORRIS, A
First of the many: the story of Independent Force, R.A.F. *(London: Jarrolds 1968), 188p.*
MORRISS, H F
Two brave brothers, Major Lord Llanattock, Hon. C. S. Rolls *(London: James 1918), 212p.*
NIGHT HAWK, M C *pseud*
Rovers of the night sky *(London: Cassell 1919), 204p.*
PATTINSON, L A
History of 99 Squadron, Independent Force, Royal Air Force March 1918-November 1918 *(Cambridge: CUP 1920), 73p.*
REID, A C
Planes and personalities *(London: Allan 1920), 190p.*
ROCHFORD, L H
I chose the sky *(London: Kimber 1977), 224p.*
SAMSON, C R
Fights and flights *(London: Benn 1930), 372p.*
SCOTT, A J L
Sixty Squadron R.A.F.: a history *(London: Heinemann 1920), 145p.*
SMITH, A
Smithy *(London: Cape 1926), 310p.*
SPIN *pseud*
Short flights with the cloud cavalry *(London: Hodder & Stoughton 1918), 218p.*
STRANGE, L A
Recollections of an airman *(London: Hamilton 1933), 224p.*
SUTTON, H T
Raiders approach!: the fighting traditions of Royal Air Force Station Hornchurch and Sutton's Farm *(Aldershot: Gale & Polden 1956), 181p.*
TURNER, C C
The struggle in the air, 1914-1918 *(London: Arnold 1919), 288p.*
VEE, R
Flying minnows *(London: Hamilton 1935), 320p.*
WING ADJUTANT *pseud*
Over there *(London: Cassell 1918), 217p.*
Plane tales from the skies *(London: Cassell 1918), 192p.*
WINGS *pseud*
Over the German lines: the work of an artillery Squadron of the R.A.F. in France *(London: Hodder & Stoughton 1918), 184p.*

ROYAL FLYING CORPS

B, W T
The Royal Flying Corps in the war *(London: Cassell 1918), 123p.*
BARING, M
R.F.C., H.Q., 1914-1918 *(London: Bell 1920), 315p.*
BUTCHER, P E
Skill and devotion: a personal history of the famous No. 2 Squadron of the Royal Flying
Corps *(Hampton Hill, Middx: Radio Modeller 1971), 87p.*
CAMPBELL, G L
Royal Flying Corps, military wing: casualties and honours during the war of 1914-17
(London: Picture Advertising 1917), 250p,
COLE, C
Royal Flying Corps, 1915-1916 *(London: Kimber 1969), 352p.*
CONTACT *pseud*
An airman's outings *(London: Blackwood 1917), 323p.*
DEATH in the air: the war diary and photographs of a Flying Corps pilot *(London:
Heinemann 1933), 166p.*
FRY, W M
Air of battle *(London: Kimber 1974), 194p.*
FUSSELL, P *ed*
The ordeal of Alfred M. Hale: the memories of a soldier servant *(London: Cooper 1975),
185p.*
GRAHAME-WHITE, C
Heroes of the Flying Corps: a description of the work of the airmen during the early stages
of the war *(London: Frowde & Hodder 1915), 350p.*
GRINNEL-MILNE, D
Wind in the wires *(London: Hurst & Blackett 1933), 208p.*
HALL, B
In the air: three years on and above three Fronts *(London: Hurst & Blackett 1918), 128p.*
HARRIS, J N
Knights of the air: Canadian aces of World War I *(London: Macmillan 1958), 160p.*
HARVEY, W F J
'Pi' in the sky: a history of No. 22 Squadron, Royal Flying Corps and R.A.F. in the war
of 1914-1918 *(Leicester: Colin Huston 1971), 108p; bib.*
INSALL, A J
Observer: memoirs of the R.F.C., 1915-1918 *(London: Kimber 1970), 208p.*
LAMBERT, B
Combat report *(London: Kimber 1973), 224p.*
MILLER, L
The chronicles of 55 Squadron R.F.C., and R.A.F. *(London: Unwin 1919), 126p.*
MORRIS, A
Bloody April *(London: Jarrolds 1967), 208p; bib.*
NORRIS, G
The Royal Flying Corps: a history *(London: Muller 1965), 256p; bib.*
PILOT *pseud*
War flying *(London: Murray 1917), 117p.*

RIMELL, R L
   The Royal Flying Corps in World War One *(London: Arms & Armour 1985), 64p.*
TAYLOR, *Sir* G
   Sopwith Scout 7309 *(London: Cassell 1968), 177p.*
THOMPSON, *Sir* R
   The Royal Flying Corps (per ardua ad astra) *(London: Hamilton 1968), 151p.*
TIDY, D
   I fear no man: the story of No. 74 (Fighter) Squadron Flying Corps and Royal Air Force (the Tigers) *(London: Macdonald 1972), 239p.*
WHITEHOUSE, A
   The fledgling: an aerial gunner in World War I – the epic of a volunteer airman *(New York: Duell 1964), 307p.*
   Hell in the heavens: the adventures of an aerial gunner in the R.F.C. *(London: Chambers 1938), 262p.*
WING ADJUTANT *pseud*
   The Royal Flying Corps in the war *(London: Cassell 1918), 124p.*
WOOD, E
   Thrilling deeds of British airmen *(London: Harrap 1917), 317p.*
THE WORK and training of the Royal Flying Corps *(London: Illustrated London News 1918), 46p.*
[See also FIGHTERS, ROYAL AIR FORCE, VICTORIA CROSS]

ROYAL MARINES

BLUMBERG, *Sir* H E
   Britain's sea soldiers: a record of the Royal Marines during the war *(Devonport, Devon: Swiss 1927), unp.*
BRUCKSHAW, H
   The diaries of Private Bruckshaw 1915–1916 *(London: Scolar 1979), 229p; bib.*

ROYAL NAVY

BARTIMEUS *pseud*
   The Navy eternal *(London: Hodder & Stoughton 1918), 332p.*
BINGHAM, E B S
   Falklands, Jutland and the Bight *(London: Murray 1919), 155p.*
BRANDON, B
   The silent service: diary of a sailor *(Bognor Regis, Sx: New Horizon 1978), 179p.*
BRITISH vessels lost at sea, 1914-1918 *(Cambridge: Stephens 1977), 36p.*
BUCHAN, J
   A history of the British Navy during the war *(London: Nelson 1918), 360p.*
BUCHAN, W
   The log of HMS 'Bristol' 13th May 1914 till December 17th 1915 *(London: Log Series 1916), 147p.*

BUSH, E W
Bless our ship *(London: Allen & Unwin 1958), 282p.*
CARR, W G
Good hunting *(London: Hutchinson 1940), 288p.*
Hell's angels of the deep *(London: Hutchinson 1932), 288p.*
Out of the mists: great deeds of the Navy in the last war *(London: Hutchinson 1942), 176p.*
CATO, C
The Navy everywhere *(London: Constable 1917), 297p.*
The Navy in Mesopotamia, 1914 to 1917 *(London: Constable 1917), 211p.*
CHATTERTON, E K
'Severn's' saga *(London: Hurst & Blackett 1938), 288p.*
CLINKER KNOCKER *pseud*
Aye, aye, sir: a saga of the lower deck *(London: Rich & Cowan 1938), 310p.*
COPPLESTONE, B *pseud*
The secret of the Navy: what it is and what we owe to it *(London: Murray 1918), 333p;*
U.S. title: Silent watchers.
CORBETT, *Sir* J S *and* NEWBOLT *Sir* H
History of the Great War: naval operations *(London: Longmans 1920-1931), 5 vols.*
CORNFOLD, L C
The British Navy, the Navy vigilant *(New York: Macmillan 1918), 202p.*
Echoes of the Fleet *(London: Williams & Norgate 1914), unp.*
Lord High Admiral and others *(London: Williams & Norgate 1915), unp.*
Paravane adventure *(New York: Doran 1920), 278p.*
With the Grand Fleet *(London: Williams & Norgate 1915), 63p.*
CURREY, E H
How we kept the seas *(London: Nelson 1917), 180p.*
THE CURTAIN of steel: sketches of life in the Navy during the European war *(London:*
Hodder & Stoughton 1918), 248p.
DAWSON, E P
Pushing water *(London: Lane 1918), 123p.*
DEARDON, R L
Watch on deck *(London: Blackie 1934), 246p.*
DITTMAR, F J *and* COLLEDGE, J J
British warships 1914-1919 *(London: Ian Allan 1972), 336p.*
DIXON, W M
The British Navy at war *(London: Heinemann 1917), 93p.*
ETIENNE *pseud*
A naval lieutenant, 1914-1918 *(London: Methuen 1919), 260p.*
EVANS, E R G R
Keeping the seas *(London: Warne 1920), 326p.*
EXPERIENCES of a war baby *(London: Hogg 1920), 159p.*
FIELD, C
British Navy book *(London: Blackie 1915), 312p.*
FIENNES, G Y
Our Navy at war *(London: Newnes 1916), 128p.*

FILSON, A B
With Beatty in the North Sea *(Boston, Mass: Little, Brown 1921), 349p; previously published as:* With the battle cruisers.
FREEMAN, L R
To Kiel in the 'Hercules' *(London: Murray 1919), 306p.*
FROM Snotty to Sub *(London: Heinemann 1918), 142p.*
FRY, J W *and* MACMILLAN, T
The complete history of the Royal Naval Division *(Alnwick: 1919), 92p.*
GEARY, S
The Collingwood Battalion, Royal Naval Division *(Hastings, Sx: Parsons 1920), unp.*
GIBSON, C R
Ships that saved the Empire *(London: Collins 1919), 96p.*
GOLDRICK, J
The King's ships were at sea: the war in the North Sea, August 1914–Feb 1915 *(Washington, DC: Naval Inst. 1984), 356p.*
GOODCHILD, G
The last cruise of the 'Majestic' *(London: Simpkin Marshall 1917), 189p.*
GRAND FLEET days *(London: Hodder & Stoughton 1917), 250p.*
GREAT BRITAIN, Admiralty
Navy losses *(London: HMSO 1919), 36p.*
HAINSSELIN, M T
Curtain of steel *(New York: Doran 1919), 249p.*
HALL, M
Some naval yarns *(London: Hodder & Stoughton 1917), 82p.*
HALL, S K
A North Sea diary, 1914-1918 *(London: Newnes 1936), 252p.*
HALPERN, P G *ed*
The Keyes papers: vol. 1, 1914-1918 *(London: Navy Records Society 1972).*
The naval war in the Mediterranean 1914–1918 *(London: Arms & Armour 1987), 592p.*
HISLAM, P A
How we twisted the dragon's tail: the operations of the Navy against the Belgian coast *(London: Hutchinson 1918), 96p.*
HOUGH, R
The Great War at sea 1914–1918 *(Oxford: OUP 1983), 320p.*
HURD, A S
The British Fleet in the Great War *(London: Constable 1919), 216p.*
HURD, A S *and* BASHFORD, H H
Sons of Admiralty: the naval war, 1914-1918 *(London: Constable 1919), 294p; U.S. title:* Heroic record of the British Navy.
JEFFERY, J E
Servants of the guns *(London: Smith, Elder 1917), 263p.*
JELLICOE, J R *1st viscount*
The Grand Fleet, 1914-16; 1917-1918 *(London: Cassell 1919-1920), 2 vols.*
JERROLD, D
The Hawke Battalion: some personal records of four years, 1914-1918 *(London: Benn 1925), 240p.*
The Royal Naval Division *(London: Hutchinson 1923), 368p.*

KIPLING, R
The fringes of the Fleet *(London: Macmillan 1915), 70p.*
KLAXON *pseud*
H.M.S. — : sketches of life in the Navy *(Edinburgh: Blackwood 1918), 335p.*
LANG, W
A sea-lawyer's log *(London: Methuen 1919), 257p.*
LEYLAND, J
The achievement of the British Navy in the World War *(London: Hodder & Stoughton 1918), 94p.*
LIDDLE, P
The sailor's war *(Poole, Dorset: Blandford 1985), 224p.*
LOCKHART, J G
The sea our heritage *(London: Bles 1940), 219p.*
McCLEMENT, F C
Guns in paradise *(Markham, Ont: Paperjacks 1979), 252p.*
MACLEAN, A *and* POOLE, S
Fighting ships of World Wars One and Two *(London: Phoebus 1976), 255p.*
MARDER, A J
From the Dardanelles to Oran: studies of the Royal Navy in peace and war, 1915-40 *(London: OUP 1974), 320p.*
From the dreadnought to Scapa Flow: the Royal Navy in the Fisher era, 1904-1919 *(London: OUP 1964-1970), 5 vols.*
MARGERISON, J S
Action!: stories of the modern Navy *(London: Hodder & Stoughton 1917), 288p.*
The sure shield *(London: Duckworth 1917), 286p.*
MIDSHIPMAN *pseud*
From Dartmouth to the Dardanelles *(London: Heinemann 1916), 174p.*
NOBLE, E
The naval side *(London: Palmer & Hayward 1918), 279p.*
POLLEN, A H
The Navy in battle *(London: Chatto & Windus 1918), 371p.*
R, L F
Naval guns in Flanders, 1914-1915 *(London: Constable 1920), 184p.*
ROBERTS, C
A week with the Fleet: impressions from a visit to the Grand Fleet *(London: Clarke 1917), 95p.*
SCHOULTZ, G von
With the British Battle Fleet: war recollections of a Russian naval officer *(London: Hutchinson 1925), 360p.*
SMITH, A C
The seafarers *(London: Cassell 1919), 280p.*
SPARROW, G *and* ROSS, J N M
On four Fronts with the Royal Navy Division *(London: Hodder & Stoughton 1918), 260p.*
STEWART, A T *and* PESHALL, C J E
The immortal gamble and the part played in it by HMS Cornwallis *(London: Black 1917), 284p.*

SUTHERLAND, J G
  At sea with Joseph Conrad *(London: Grant Richards 1922), 150p.*
USBORNE, C V
  Blast and counterblast: a naval impression of the war *(London: Murray 1935), 293p.*
VAUX, P
  Gadgets: the work of the Navy *(London: Hodder & Stoughton 1917), 225p.*
  Sea, salt and cordite *(London: Hodder & Stoughton 1914), 190p.*
VINCENT, H
  A stoker's log *(London: Jarrolds 1929), 256p.*
WELDON, L B
  'Hard lying': Eastern Mediterranean, 1914-1919 *(London: Jenkins 1925), 256p.*
WHEELER, H F B
  Stirring deeds of Britain's sea-dogs in the Great War *(London: Harrap 1916), 347p.*
THE WORK of the Royal Naval Reserve *(London: Yachting Monthly 1918), 64p.*
YOUNG, E H
  By sea and land: some naval doings *(London: Jack 1920), 362p.*
[See also BATTLESHIPS, CORONEL, CRUISERS, DESTROYERS, JUTLAND, MINESWEEPERS, MOTOR LAUNCHES, NAVAL WARFARE, SUBMARINES]

ROYAL NAVAL AIR SERVICE

COLLYER, D *comp*
  Flying: the First World War in Kent *(Rochester, Kent: North Kent 1982), 64p.*
GAMBLE, C F S
  The story of a North Sea Air Station: being some account of the early days of the Royal Flying Corps (Naval Wing) *(London: Spearman 1967), 446p; bib.*
LIVOCK, G E
  To the ends of the air *(London: HMSO 1973), 204p.*
MOORE, W G
  Early bird *(London: Putnam 1963), 146p.*
PERRETT, B *and* LORD, A
  The Czar's British squadron *(London: Kimber 1981), 192p.*
ROSHER, H
  In the Royal Naval Air Service *(London: Chatto & Windus 1917), 148p.*
ROSKILL, S W *ed*
  The Naval Air Service, 1908-18 *(London: Navy Records Society 1969), vol 1.*

RUMANIA

CAROSSA, H
  A Roumanian diary *(London: Secker 1929), 252p.*
CLARK, C U
  United Roumania *(New York: Dodd 1932), 418p.*
FITZROY, Y
  With the Scottish nurses in Roumania *(London: Murray 1918), 165p.*

JONESCU, T
The policy of national instinct *(London: Causton 1916), 108p.*
KENNARD, *Lady* D
A Roumanian diary, 1915-1917 *(London: Heinemann 1917), 191p.*
LUPU, N
Rumania and the war *(Boston, Mass: Badger 1919), 122p.*
MAGNUS, L A
Rumania's cause and ideals *(London: Kegan Paul 1917), 179p.*
MARIE *queen of Rumania*
My country *(London: Hodder & Stoughton 1916), 69p.*
NEGULESCU, G
Rumania's sacrifice *(New York: Century 1918), 265p.*
PANTAZZI, E G
Roumania in light and shadow *(London: Fisher Unwin 1921), 279p.*
SETON-WATSON, R W
Roumania and the Great War *(London: Constable 1915), 102p.*

RUSSIA

ALEKSINSKAYA, T
With the Russian wounded *(London: Fisher Unwin 1916), 191p.*
ALEKSINSKY, G A
Russia and the Great War *(London: Fisher Unwin 1915), 357p.*
BARBER, M H
A British nurse in Bolshevik Russia, April 1916-December 1919 *(London: Fifield 1920), 64p.*
BECHOFER, C E
Russia at the crossroads *(London: Kegan Paul 1916), 210p.*
BERG, A
Latvia and Russia *(London: Dent 1920), 93p.*
BOTKIN, G
The real Romanovs *(New York: Revell 1931), 336p.*
BUCHANAN, *Sir* G
My mission to Russia *(Boston, Mass: Little, Brown 1923), unp.*
BUCHANAN, M
Petrograd, the city of trouble, 1914-1918 *(London: Collins 1918), 262p.*
COXWELL, C F
Through Russia in war time *(London: Fisher Unwin 1917), 312p.*
DADISHKILIANI, K *princess*
Princess in uniform *(London: Bell 1934), 301p.*
DAWE, R E
A memoir of an English governess in Russia 1914-1917 *(Chichester, Sx: Bishop Otter College 1973), 45p.*
DE WINDT, H
Russia as I know it *(London: Chapman & Hall 1917), 240p.*

DILLON, E J
The eclipse of Russia *(London: Dent 1918), 427p.*
DOBSON, C *and* MILLER, J
The day we almost bombed Moscow: the Allied war in Russia 1918–1920 *(London: Hodder & Stoughton 1986), 288p.*
DOROSHEVITCH, V
The way of the Cross: a picture of the Russian fugitives after the German invasion of Aug.-Sept. 1915 *(London: Constable 1916), 140p.*
DREW, A N
Russia: a study *(London: Simpkin Marshall 1918), 188p.*
FARBMAN, M S
Russia and the struggle for peace *(London: Allen & Unwin 1918), 188p.*
FLORINSKY, M
The end of the Russian Empire *(London: OUP 1931), 272p.*
FRASER, J F
Russia of today *(London: Cassell 1915), 298p.*
FROM a Russian diary, 1917-1920 *(London: Murray 1921), 266p.*
THE GAME of diplomacy *(London: Hutchinson 1918), 256p.*
GARSTIN, D
Friendly Russia *(London: Unwin 1915), 248p.*
GIBSON, W J
Wild career: my crowded years of adventure in Russia and the Near East *(London: Harrap 1935), 288p.*
GILLIARD, P
Thirteen years at the Russian Court: a personal record of the last years and death of Nicholas II and his family *(London: Hutchinson 1921), 304p.*
GRAHAM, S
Russia and the world: a study of the war *(London: Cassell 1915), 260p.*
Russia in 1916 *(London: Cassell 1917), 179p.*
GRONSKY, P P
The war and the Russian Government *(New Haven, Conn: Yale UP 1929), 331p.*
HARPER, F M
Runaway Russia *(New York: Century 1918), 321p.*
HEYKING, A *baron*
Problems facing Russia *(London: King 1918), 235p.*
HOARE, *Sir* S J G
The fourth seal: the end of a Russian chapter *(London: Heinemann 1930), 377p.*
HOWE, *Mrs* S E
Real Russians *(Philadelphia, Pa: Lippincott 1918), 240p.*
HUBBACK, J
Russian realities: being impressions gathered during recent journeys to Russia *(London: Lane 1915), 296p.*
KADOMTSEV, B
The Russian collapse *(London: Roworth 1918), 48p.*
KETTLE, M
The Allies and the Russian collapse, March 1917–March 1918 *(London: Deutsch 1979), 288p.*

KING, H S
Russia during the war *(London: King 1919), 57p.*
KON, S
The cost of the war to Russia *(New Haven, Conn: Yale UP 1932), 219p.*
LIDDELL, R S
Actions and reactions in Russia *(London: Chapman & Hall 1917), 227p.*
LIEVEN, D C B
Russia and the origins of the First World War *(London: Macmillan 1983), 213p; bib.*
LINCOLN, W B
Passage through Armageddon: the Russians in war and revolution 1914–1918 *(New York: Simon & Schuster 1986), 557p.*
LOBANOV-ROSTOVSKY, A
Grinding mill: reminiscences of war and revolution in Russia, 1913-1920 *(New York: Macmillan 1935), 387p.*
MARCOSSAN, I F
The rebirth of Russia *(London: Lane 1917), 196p.*
MARYE, G T
Nearing the end in Imperial Russia *(Philadelphia, Pa: Dorrance 1929), 479p.*
MERRY, W M
Two months in Russia, 1914 *(Oxford: Blackwell 1916), 202p.*
MOORE, F
The chaos in Europe: a consideration of the political destruction that has taken place in Russia *(New York: Putnam 1919), 192p.*
MURRAY, M
Russian advance *(London: Hodder & Stoughton 1914), 192p.*
PARES, *Sir* B
The fall of the Russian monarchy *(London: Cape 1939), 512p.*
PIERCE, *Mrs* R
Trapped in black Russia: letters, June-Nov. 1915 *(Boston, Mass: Houghton Mifflin 1918), 149p.*
THE RED archives: Russian State papers and other documents relating to the years 1915-1918 *(London: Bles 1929), 320p.*
ROOT, E
The United States and the war: the mission to Russia *(Cambridge, Mass: Harvard UP 1918), 362p.*
RUSSIA Foreign Office
How the war began: being the diary of the Russian Foreign Office from the 3rd to the 20th – old style – of July 1914 *(London: Allen & Unwin 1925), 122p.*
RUSSIAN diary of an Englishwoman, Petrograd, 1915-1917 *(New York: McBride 1919), 228p.*
SAROLEA, C
Europe's debt to Russia *(London: Heinemann 1916), 251p.*
SAZONOV, S D
Fateful years, 1909-16 *(London: Cape 1928), 327p.*
SHKLOVSKII, V B
A sentimental journey: memoirs, 1917-1922 *(Ithaca, NY: Cornell UP 1970), 304p.*

SHUMSKY-SOLOMONOV, K M
Russia's part in the World War *(New York: Russian Information Bureau 1920), 47p.*
SIEGELBAUM, L H
The politics of industrial mobilization in Russia 1914–1917: a study of war-industry committees *(New York: St Martin's 1984), 312p.*
SIMPSON, J Y
The self-discovery of Russia *(London: Constable 1916), 240p.*
STEPHENS, W ed
The soul of Russia *(London: Macmillan 1916), 324p.*
STIEVE, F
Isvolsky and the World War *(London: Allen & Unwin 1926), 254p.*
THOMPSON, D C
Donald Thompson in Russia *(New York: Century 1918), 353p.*
From Czar to Kaiser: the betrayal of Russia *(New York: Doubleday 1918), 200p.*
WASHBURN, S
On the Russian Front in World War I: memoirs of an American correspondent *(New York: Speller 1982), 332p.*
WILSON, M
Baltic assignment: British submarines in Russia 1914–1919 *(London: Cooper & Secker & Warburg 1985), 243p; bib.*
WITTE, S *count*
Memoirs *(New York: Doubleday 1921), 445p.*

RUSSIAN ARMY

BELLEGARDE, S de
The Russian soldier *(London: Mowbray 1917), 71p.*
BRUSILOV, A A
A soldier's note-book, 1914-1918 *(London: Macmillan 1930), 340p.*
FARMBOROUGH, F
Nurse at the Russian Front: a diary, 1914-18 *(London: Constable 1974), 422p.*
GOLOVIN, N N
The Russian Army in the World War *(New Haven, Conn: Yale UP 1931), 287p.*
The Russian campaign of 1914 *(Fort Leavenworth, Kansas: General Staff School 1933), unp.*
IRONSIDE, *Sir* E
Tannenberg: the first thirty days in East Prussia *(London: Blackwood 1925), 316p.*
KNOX, *Sir* A
With the Russian Army, 1914-1917 *(London: Hutchinson 1921), 2 vols.*
LIDDELL, R S
On the Russian Front *(London: Simpkin Marshall 1916), 273p.*
LONG, R E C
Colors of war *(New York: Scribner 1915), 306p; U.K. title:* A book of the Russian campaign.
MACCORMICK, R R
With the Russian Army *(London: Macmillan 1915), 306p.*

MORSE, J
An Englishman in the Russian ranks *(London: Duckworth 1915), 337p.*
MURRAY, M
The Russian advance *(London: Hodder & Stoughton 1914), 192p.*
PARES, *Sir* B
Day by day with the Russian Army *(London: Constable 1915), 287p.*
ROUSTAM-BEK, B
Russia in arms: a story of the Czar's troops *(London: Nisbet 1916), 197p.*
RUTHERFORD, W
The Russian Army in World War I *(London: Gordon & Cremonesi 1975), 303p.*
WARTH, R D
The Allies and the Russian Revolution, from the fall of the monarchy to the peace of Brest-Litovsk *(London: CUP 1954), 294p; bib.*
WASHBURN, S
The Russian campaign, April to August 1915 *(London: Melrose 1915), 347p.*
Field notes from the Russian Front, June to September, 1916 *(London: Curtis Brown 1916-1917), 3 vols.*
[See also BREST-LITOVSK, GERMAN ARMY, HISTORY]

RUSSIAN CAMPAIGN (ALLIED)

BRADLEY, J
Allied intervention in Russia, 1917-1920 *(London: Weidenfeld & Nicolson 1968), 251p; bib.*
ELLIS, C H
The Trans-Caspian episode, 1918-1919 *(London: Hutchinson 1963), 176p; bib.*
KINDALL, S G
American soldiers in Siberia *(New York: R. Smith 1945), 251p.*
MACLAREN, R
Canadians in Russia, 1918-1919 *(Toronto: Macmillan 1976), 301p.*
MAYNARD, *Sir* C
The Murmansk venture *(London: Hodder & Stoughton 1928), 334p.*
MOORE, J R *and other eds*
History of the American expedition fighting the Bolsheviki: campaigning in North Russia, 1918-1919 *(Hillsdale, Mich: Polar Bear 1920), 303p.*
SILVERLIGHT, J
The victor's dilemma: Allied intervention in the Russian civil war *(London: Barrie & Jenkins 1970), 392p; bib.*
STRAKHOVSKY, L I
Intervention in Archangel: the story of Allied intervention and Russian counter-revolution in North Russia, 1918-1920 *(Princeton, NJ: Princeton UP 1944), 336p.*

RUSSIAN NAVY

GRAF, H
 The Russian Navy in war and revolution from 1914 up to 1918 *(New York: Kolands 1923)*, *223p.*
GREGER, R
 The Russian Fleet, 1914-1917 *(London: Ian Allan 1972), 176p.*
MAKHOV, A
 Smell of smoke *(London: Duckworth 1936), 314p.*

RUSSIAN REVOLUTION

ANET, C *pseud*
 Through the Russian revolution *(London: Hutchinson 1917), 353p.*
BERKMAN, A
 The Russian tragedy *(Orkney: Cienfuegos 1976), 112p.*
DORR, R L
 Inside the Russian revolution *(New York: Macmillan 1917), 248p.*
FARBMAN, M S
 The Russian revolution and the war *(London: Headley 1917), 46p.*
GANKIN, *Mrs* O *and* FISHER, H H
 Bolsheviks and the World War: the origins of the Third International *(Stanford, Cal: Stanford UP 1940), 856p.*
GERMANY Auswartiges Amt
 Germany and the revolution in Russia, 1915-1918: documents from the archives of the German Foreign Ministry *(London: OUP 1958), 157p.*
GILBREATH, O
 Russia in travail *(London: Murray 1918), 315p.*
GOURKO, B
 Memories and impressions of war and revolution in Russia *(London: Murray 1918),420p.*
 U.S. title: War and revolution in Russia, 1914-1917.
GRAEVENITZ, P *baron*
 From autocracy to Bolshevism *(London: Allen & Unwin 1918), 128p.*
JONES, S
 Russia in revolution: being the experiences of an Englishman in Petrograd during the upheaval *(London: Jenkins 1917), 289p.*
KANTAKUZEN, J
 Revolutionary days *(New York: Arno 1970), 411p.*
KEEP, J L H
 The Russian revolution: a study in mass mobilization *(London: Weidenfeld & Nicolson 1976), 614p; bib.*
KERENSKY, A F
 The crucifixion of liberty *(London: Barker 1934), 368p.*
 The prelude to Bolshevism: the Kornilov rebellion *(London: Unwin 1919), 318p.*
LEVINE, I D
 The Russian revolution *(London: Lane 1917), 248p.*

LITVINOFF, M
The Bolshevik revolution: its rise and meaning *(London: British Socialist Party 1918)*, *54p.*

LUKOMSKI, A S
Memoirs of the Russian revolution *(New York: Wilson 1922), 255p.*

MOOREHEAD, A
The Russian revolution *(London: Collins & Hamilton 1958), 320p; bib.*

OLGIN, M J
The soul of the Russian revolution *(New York: Holt 1917), 423p.*

POLLOCK, F J
War and revolution in Russia: sketches and studies *(London: Constable 1918), 280p.*

POOLE, E
The village: Russian impressions *(New York: Macmillan 1918), 302p.*

PRICE, M P
My reminiscences of the Russian revolution *(London: Allen & Unwin 1921), 402p.*
War and revolution in Asiatic Russia *(London: Allen & Unwin 1918), 296p.*

RADZIWILL, C *princess*
Russia's decline and fall: the secret history of a great debacle *(London: Cassell 1918), 256p. U.S. title:* Rasputin and the Russian revolution.

RANSOME, A
Adventures in Russia *(London: Methuen 1918), unp.*
The revolution in Russia *(London: Methuen 1917), unp.*

RAPPOPORT, A S
Pioneers of the Russian revolution *(London: Stanley Paul 1918), 308p.*

ROSS, E A
Russia in upheaval *(London: Fisher Unwin 1918), 367p.*

RUSSELL, C E
Unchained Russia *(New York: Appleton 1918), 323p.*

SAROLEA, C
The Russian revolution and the war *(London: Allen & Unwin 1917), 100p.*

STEBBING, E P
From Czar to Bolshevik *(London: Lane 1918), 337p.*

TROTSKY, L
History of the Russian revolution *(London: Gollancz 1933-1934), 3 vols in 1.*

TYRKOVA-WILLIAMS, Mrs A
From liberty to Brest-Litovsk: the first year of the Russian revolution *(London: Macmillan 1919), 538p.*

ULAM, A B
The Bolsheviks *(New York: Macmillan 1965), 785p. U.K. title:* Lenin and the Bolsheviks.

VANDERVELDE, E
Three aspects of the Russian revolution *(London: Allen & Unwin 1918), 281p.*

WELLS, H G
Russia in the shadows *(London: Hodder & Stoughton 1920), 153p.*

WILTON, R
Russia's agony *(New York: Dutton 1919), 357p.*

SALONIKA

DAVIS, R H
  With the French in France and Salonika *(London: Duckworth 1916), 240p.*
FEDDEN, M
  Sister's quarters: Salonika *(London: Grant Richards 1921), 221p.*
LAKE, H
  In Salonika with our Army *(London: Melrose 1917), 287p.*
MANN, A J
  The Salonika Front *(London: Black 1920), 196p.*
OWEN, H C
  Salonika and after *(London: Hodder & Stoughton 1919), 295p.*
PACKER, C
  Return to Salonika *(London: Cassell 1964), 164p.*
PALMER, A W
  The gardeners of Salonika *(London: Deutsch 1965), 286p; bib.*
SALONIKA memories, 1915-1919 *(North Greenford, Middx: Salonika Reunion Association 1969), 65p.*
SELIGMAN, V J
  The Salonika side-show *(London: Allen & Unwin 1919), 256p.*
TAPP, A G
  Stories of Salonika and the new crusade *(London: Drane's 1922), 128p.*
WARD PRICE, G
  The story of the Salonika Army *(London: Hodder & Stoughton 1917), 298p.*
[See also BALKANS, GREECE]

SALVATION ARMY

BOOTH, E C *and* HILL, G L
  The war romance of the Salvation Army *(Philadelphia, Pa: Lippincott 1919), 356p.*
BOOTH, M
  With the B.E.F. in France *(London: Salvation Army 1916), 120p.*

SARAJEVO

DEDIJER, V
  The road to Sarajevo *(London: MacGibbon & Kee 1967), 550p*
GILFORD, H
  The Black Hand at Sarajevo *(Indianapolis, Ind: Bobbs-Merrill 1975), 176p.*
SETON-WATSON, R W
  Sarajevo: a study in the origins of the Great War *(London: Hutchinson 1926), 303p.*
[See also AUSTRIA, HUNGARY, ORIGINS]

SCANDINAVIA

MORRIS, I N
From an American Legation: Sweden, 1914-1922 *(New York: Knopf 1923), 287p.*
OSSIANILSSON, K G
Who is right in the World War? *(London: Fisher Unwin 1917), 95p.*
SWEDEN, Norway, Denmark and Iceland in the World War *(New Haven, Conn: Yale UP 1930), 593p.*
[See also DENMARK, NEUTRALS, NORWAY]

SCAPA FLOW

BROWN, M
Scapa Flow: the reminiscences of men and women who served in Scapa Flow in the two World Wars *(London: Allen Lane 1968), 264p.*
BURROWS, C W
Scapa and a camera: pictorial impressions of five years spent at the Grand Fleet Base *(London: Country Life 1921), 144p.*
COUSINS, G
The story of Scapa Flow *(London: Muller 1965), 209p; bib.*
MUNRO, D J
Scapa Flow: a naval retrospect *(London: Sampson Low 1932), 244p.*
REUTER, L von
Scapa Flow: the account of the greatest scuttling of all time *(London: Hurst & Blackett 1940), 153p.*
[See also GERMAN NAVY, ROYAL NAVY]

SCARBOROUGH

A GERMAN crime: bombardment of Scarborough *(Scarborough, Yorks: 1915), 32p.*
MILLER, F
Under German shell-fire: the Hartlepools, Scarborough and Whitby *(West Hartlepool: Martin 1915), 159p.*
MOULD, D
Remember Scarborough 1914! *(Nelson, Lancs: Hendon 1978), 48p.*

SCIENCE

ASHFORD, B K
A soldier in science *(London: Routledge 1934), 425p.*
POULTON, E B
Science and the Great War *(Oxford: Clarendon 1915), 47p.*
YERKES, R M *ed*
New world of science: its development during the war *(New York: Century 1920), 443p.*

SECRET SERVICE

ASTON, *Sir* G G
Secret service *(London: Faber 1930), 316p.*

BARTON, G
Celebrated spies and famous mysteries of the Great War *(Boston, Mass: Page 1919), 345p.*

BAUERMEISTER, A
Spies break through: memoirs of a German secret service officer *(London: Constable 1934), 184p.*

BERNDORFF, H R
Espionage *(London: Nash & Grayson 1930), 254p.*

BLACKER, L V S
On secret patrol in high Asia *(London: Murray 1922), 302p.*

BLAIR, D *and* DAND, C H
Russian hazard: the adventures of a British secret service agent in Russia *(London: Hale 1937), 288p.*

BOUCARD, R
Revelations from the secret service: the spy on two Fronts *(London: Hutchinson 1929), 173p.*

CARL, E
One against England: the death of Lord Kitchener and the plot against the British Fleet *(London: Jarrolds 1935), 288p.*

COOK, G
Missions most secret *(London: Harwood-Smart 1976), 186p; bib.*

COULSON, T
Queen of spies, Louise de Bettignies *(London: Constable 1935), 385p.*

DE HALSALLE, H
Who goes there?: being an account of the secret service adventures of 'Ex-Intelligence' during the Great War of 1914-1918 *(London: Hutchinson 1927), 253p.*

DESGRANGES, P
In the enemy's country *(London: Hutchinson 1931), 256p.*

ECKE, H
Four spies speak *(London: Hamilton 1933), 179p.*

ENGLE, A
Nili spies *(London: Hogarth 1959), 245p.*

EVERITT, N
British secret service during the Great War *(London: Hutchinson 1920), 320p.*

FELSTEAD, S T *comp*
German spies at bay: being an actual record of German espionage in Great Britain during the years 1914-1918 *(London: Hutchinson 1920), 288p.*

THE GERMAN spy system from within *(London: Hodder & Stoughton 1914), 204p.*

GOLTZ, H von der
My adventures as a German secret service agent *(London: Cassell 1918), 275p.*

GOWENLOCK, T R
Soldiers of darkness *(New York: Doubleday 1937), 285p.*

GROUNDSELL, F
The lunatic spy *(London: Jarrolds 1935), 288p.*
HAVARD, R A
Portland spy *(London: Stanley Paul 1939), 255p.*
HILL, G A
Dreaded hour *(London: Cassell 1936), 280p.*
Go spy the land: being the adventures of I.K.8 of the British secret service *(London: Cassell 1932), 283p.*
HOLST, B P
My experiences with spies in the Great European War *(Boone, Iowa: Holst 1916), 222p.*
HOUGH, E
Web: a revelation of patriotism *(Chicago: Reilly & Lee 1919), 511p.*
HOY, H C
40 O.B.; or How the war was won *(London: Hutchinson 1932), 287p.*
JAMESON, *Sir* W
The eyes of the Navy: a biographical study of Admiral Sir Reginald Hall *(London: Methuen 1955), 212p.*
JENSSEN, C *baroness*
I spy!: sensational disclosures of a British secret service agent *(London: Jarrolds 1930), 286p.*
JOHNSON, T M
Our secret war: true American spy stories, 1917-1919 *(Indianapolis, Ind: Bobbs-Merrill 1929), 340p. U.K. title:* Secret war.
Without censor: new light on our greatest war battles *(Indianapolis, Ind: Bobbs-Merrill 1928), 411p.*
JONES, J P
The German secret service in America *(Toronto: Small 1918), 340p.*
The German spy in America *(London: Hutchinson 1917), 256p.*
K-7 *pseud*
Spies at war *(New York: Appleton 1934), 312p.*
KALEDIN, V R
K. 14-O.M.66: adventures of a double spy *(London: Hurst & Blackett 1934), 288p.*
LADOUX, G
Marthe Richard the skylark *(London: Cassell 1932), 250p.*
LANDAU, H
All's fair: the story of the British secret service behind the German lines *(New York: Putnam 1934), 329p.*
Enemy within: the inside story of German sabotage in America *(New York: Putnam 1937), 323p.*
Secrets of the White Lady *(New York: Putnam 1935), 314p.*
Spreading the spy net: the story of a British spy director *(London: Jarrolds 1938), 284p.*
LE QUEUX, W
German spies in England: an exposure *(London: Stanley Paul 1915), 224p.*
LINCOLN, I T T
Revelations of an international spy *(New York: McBride 1916), 323p.*
LOCKHART, *Sir* R B H
Memoirs of a British agent *(London: Putnam 1932), 355p.*

MACKENNA, M
I was a spy *(London: Queenway 1934), 316p.*
My master spy: a narrative of war-time secret service *(London: Jarrolds 1936), 287p.*
Spies I knew *(London: Jarrolds 1933), 287p.*
A spy was born *(London: Jarrolds 1935), 255p.*

MACKENZIE, E M C
First Athenian memories *(London: Cassell 1931), 401p.*
Greek memories *(London: Chatto & Windus 1939), 455p.*

MY secret service *(London: Jenkins 1916), 214p.*

NEWMAN, B
Inquest of Mata Hari *(London: Hale 1956), 191p.*
Spy *(London: Gollancz 1935), 288p.*

NICOLAI, W
The German secret service *(London: Stanley Paul 1924), 298p.*

REDIER, A
The story of Louise de Bettignies *(London: Hutchinson 1926), 251p.*

RICHER, M
I spied for France *(London: Long 1935), 288p.*

RINTELEN, F von
The dark invader: wartime reminiscences of a German naval intelligence officer *(London: Dickson 1933), 287p.*

RUSSELL, C E
Adventures of the D.C.L. Department of Criminal Investigation *(New York: Doubleday 1924), 280p.*

SCHWEIN, E E
Combat intelligence: its acquisition and transmission *(Washington DC: Infantry Journal 1936), 125p.*

SETH, R
The spy who wasn't caught *(London: Hale 1966), 189p; bib.*

SILBER, J C
The invisible weapons *(London: Hutchinson 1932), 298p.*

SNOWDEN, N
Memoirs of a spy: adventures along the Eastern Fronts *(London: Jarrolds 1934), 282p.*

SPERRY, E E *and* WEST, M M
German plots and intrigues in the United States during the period of our neutrality *(New York: Committee on Public Information 1918), 64p.*

STEINHAUER, C
Steinhauer, the Kaiser's master spy *(London: Lane 1930), 356p.*

STRAWBRIDGE, A
Suspect: the war story of a young artist accused of espionage *(London: Heinemann 1936), 374p.*

STROTHER, F
Fighting Germany's spies: a revelation of German intrigue in America *(New York: Doubleday 1918), 275p.*

STUART, *Sir* C
Secrets of Crewe House: the story of a famous campaign *(London: Hodder & Stoughton 1920), 253p.*

THOMSON, *Sir* B H
  The Allied secret service in Greece *(London: Hutchinson 1931), 288p.*
THULIEZ, L
  Condemned to death *London: (Methuen 1934), 241p.*
TOYNE, J
  Win time for us *(New York: Longmans 1962), 241p.*
TUNNEY, T J
  Throttled!: the detection of the German and anarchist bomb plotters *(Boston Mass: Small 1919), 277p.*
TUOHY, F
  The secret corps *(London: Murray 1920), 289p.*
VIGILAN, T *pseud*
  Secrets of modern spying *(London: Hamilton 1930), 298p.*
VILLE, J B de
  Back from Belgium: a secret history of three years within the German lines *(New York: Fly 1918), 268p.*
VOSKA, E V *and* IRWIN, W H
  Spy and counterspy *(New York: Doubleday 1940), 322p.*
WADE, A G
  'Counterspy!' *(London: Stanley Paul 1938), 287p.*
WELDON, L B
  'Hardlying': Eastern Mediterranean, 1914-1918 *(London: Jenkins 1925), 246p.*
WILD, M
  Secret service on the Russian Front *(London: Bles 1932), 324p.*
WILLIAMS, A R
  In the claws of the German eagle *(New York: Dutton 1917), 273p.*
WOODHALL, E T
  Spies of the Great War: adventures with the Allied secret service *(London: Long 1932), 251p.*
YARDLEY, H O
  American black chamber *(London: Faber 1934), 266p.*

SERBIA

ADAMS, J C
  Flight in winter *(Princeton, NJ: Princeton UP 1942), 281p.*
ASKEW, A *and* ASKEW, C
  The stricken land *(London: Nash 1916), 378p.*
BERRY, J
  The story of a Red Cross visit in Serbia *(London: Churchill 1916), 292p.*
BURGESS, A
  The lovely sergeant *(London: Heinemann 1963), 183p.*
CORBETT, E
  Red Cross in Serbia, 1915-1919: a personal diary of experiences *(Banbury, Oxon: Cheney 1964), 186p.*

DAVIES, E C
A farmer in Serbia *(London: Methuen 1916), 248p.*
DEARMER, M
Letters from a field hospital *(London: Macmillan 1915), 186p.*
DEVINE, A
Off the map: the suppression of Montenegro *(London: Chapman & Hall 1921), 47p.*
DOWNER, E B
The highway of death *(Philadelphia, Pa: Lippincott 1916), 209p.*
FARNHAM, R S
A nation at bay: what an American woman saw and did in suffering Serbia *(Indianapolis, Ind: Bobbs-Merrill 1918), 229p.*
GORDON-SMITH, G
From Serbia to Jugoslavia: Serbia's victories, reverses and final triumph *(New York: Putnam 1920), 360p.*
Through the Serbian campaign: the great retreat of the Serbian Army *(London: Hutchinson 1916), 319p.*
JONES, F
With Serbia into exile: an American's adventures with the Army that cannot die *(New York: Century 1916), 447p.*
KARAGORGEVIC, A *princess*
For the better hour and the resurrection of Serbia *(London: Constable 1917), 155p.*
KRUNICH, M
Serbia crucified *(Boston, Mass: Houghton Mifflin 1918), 304p.*
LAFFAN, R G D
Guardians of the gate: historical lectures on the Serbs *(Oxford: Clarendon 1918), 299p.*
MACLAREN, E S
Elsie Inglis, the woman with the torch *(London: SPCK 1920), 80p.*
MARKOVIC, L
Serbia and Europe, 1914-1920 *(London: Allen & Unwin 1920), 355p.*
MATTHEWS, C
Experiences of a woman doctor in Serbia *(London: Mills & Boon 1916), 246p.*
PRICE, C
Serbia's part in the war: the political and military story of the Austro-Serbian campaign *(London: Simpkin Marshall 1918), vol I.*
REISS, R A
The kingdom of Serbia: infringements of the rules of war committed by the Austro-Bulgaro-Germans *(London: Allen & Unwin 1919), 128p.*
SANDES, F
An English woman-sergeant in the Serbian Army *(London: Hodder & Stoughton 1916), 242p.*
STANLEY, M M
My diary in Serbia *(London: Simpkin Marshall 1915), 128p.*
STEBBING, E P
At the Serbian Front in Macedonia *(London: Lane 1917), 245p.*
STOBART, M A
The flaming sword in Serbia and elsewhere *(London: Hodder & Stoughton 1916), 325p.*

VELIMIROVIC, N
Serbia in light and darkness *(London: Longmans 1916), 160p.*
WALSHE, D
With the Serbs in Macedonia 1916-1918 *(London: Lane 1920), 278p.*
WARREN, W
Montenegro: the crime of the Peace Conference *(New York: Brentano 1922), 64p.*
WYNNE, M
An English girl in Serbia *(London: Collins 1916), 215p.*
YOUNG, A D
A subaltern in Serbia, and some letters from the Struma Valley *(London: Dranes 1922), 126p.*
[See also BALKANS, MACEDONIA, SARAJEVO]

SHIPBUILDING

HURLEY, E N
The bridge to France: on the work of the U.S. Shipping Board *(Philadelphia, Pa: Lippincott 1927), 338p.*
MATTOX, W C
Building the emergency fleet *(Cleveland, Ohio: Penton 1920), 279p.*
SMITH, J R
The influence of the Great War on shipping *(New York: OUP 1919), 357p.*
UNITED STATES Bureau of Yards & Docks
Activities of the Bureau, 1917-1918 *(Washington DC: 1921), 522p.*

SIBERIA

BRANDSTROM, E
Among prisoners of war in Russia and Siberia *(London: Hutchinson 1929), 284p.*
COLEMAN, F
Japan moves North: the story of the struggle for Siberia *(London: Cassell 1918), 187p.*
U.S. title: Japan or Germany.
DWINGER, E E
The Army behind barbed wire: a Siberian diary *(London: Allen & Unwin 1930), 341p.*
FLEMING, P
The fate of Admiral Kolchak *(London: Hart-Davis 1963), 253p; bib.*
MORLEY, J W
The Japanese thrust into Siberia, 1918 *(London: OUP 1957), 395p.*
SWANLJUNG, C
Men and monsters: on the treatment of German prisoners in Siberia *(London: Lane 1928), 315p.*

UNTERBERGER, B M
America's Siberian expedition, 1918-1920: a study of national policy *(London: CUP 1956), 271p; bib.*
[See also JAPAN, PRISONERS OF WAR, RUSSIA, RUSSIAN CAMPAIGN (ALLIED), RUSSIAN REVOLUTION]

SOCIALISM

BOUDIN, L B
Socialism and war *(New York: New Review 1916), 267p.*
BROWNE, J H B
War problems *(London: Longmans 1915), 96p.*
COLE, G D H
Labour in war time *(London: Bell 1915), 316p.*
CONNOLLY, J
A Socialist and war, 1914-1916 *(London: Lawrence & Wishart 1941), 125p.*
CORNFORD, L C
The secret of consolation *(London: Williams & Norgate 1916), 168p.*
FAINSOD, M
International socialism and the World War *(New York: Octagon 1966), 238p.*
GOMPERS, S
American labor and the war *(New York: Doran 1919), 377p.*
HENDERSON, A
The aims of Labour *(London: Headley 1918), 108p.*
HUMPHREY, A W
International socialism and the war *(London: King 1915), 176p.*
HUTTON, J E
Welfare and housing: a practical record of war-time management *(London: Longmans 1918), 192p.*
IRWIN, W
Men, women and war *(London: Constable 1915), 192p.*
LA CHESNAIS, P G
The Socialist Party in the Reichstag and the declaration of war *(London: Fisher Unwin 1915), 128p.*
LENSCH, P
Three years of world revolution *(London: Constable 1918), 220p.*
MORSE, A D
Civilisation and the World War *(Boston, Mass: Ginn 1919), 222p.*
POSTGATE, R W
The International during the war *(London: The Herald 1918), 168p.*
POWELL, L P *and* CURRY, C M
The world and democracy *(Chicago: Rand 1919), 553p.*
RUSSELL, B *earl*
Principles of social reconstruction *(London: Allen & Unwin 1916), 250p.*

STANSKY, P
  The Left and war: the British Labour Party and World War I *(London: OUP 1969), 335p;*
  bib.
WALLING, W E
  The Socialists and the war: a documentary statement of the position of the Socialists of
  all countries *(New York: Holt 1915), 512p.*
THE WAR and democracy (London: Macmillan 1914), 384p.
WORSFOLD, W B
  The war and social reform: an endeavour to trace the influence of the war as a reforming
  agency *(London: Murray 1919), 248p.*
[See also POLITICS]

SOCIOLOGY

LEED, E J
  No man's land: combat and identity in World War I *(Cambridge: CUP 1981), 257p; bib,*

SOMME

AITKEN, A
  Courage past: a duty done *(Glasgow: Aitken 1971), 159p.*
BUCHAN, J
  The battle of the Somme *(London: Nelson 1916), 264p.*
DAWSON, A J
  Somme battle stories *(London: Hodder & Stoughton 1916), 246p.*
DUGMORE, A R
  When the Somme ran red *(New York: Doran 1918), 285p.*
EDMUNDS, G B
  Somme memories: memoirs of an Australian artillery driver, 1916-1919 *(Ilfracombe,
  Devon: Stockwell 1955), 43p.*
EYRE, G E M
  Somme harvest: memories of a P.B.I. in the summer of 1916 *(London: Jarrolds 1938),
  255p.*
FARRAR-HOCKLEY, A
  The Somme *(London: Batsford 1964), 224p; bib.*
GARDNER, B
  The big push: a portrait of the Battle of the Somme *(London: Cassell 1961), 177p; bib.*
GIBBS, *Sir* P H
  The battles of the Somme *(London: Heinemann 1917), 336p.*
GILES, J
  The Somme: then and now *(Folkstone, Kent: Bailey 1977), 140p; bib.*
GLADDEN, E N
  The Somme, 1916: a personal account *(London: Kimber 1974), 200p.*
THE GREAT advance: tales from the Somme battlefield told by wounded officers and men
  on their arrival at Southampton from the Front *(London: Cassell 1916), 182p.*

HARRIS, J
The Somme: death of a generation *(London: Hodder & Stoughton 1966), 128p; bib.*
HUGHES, C
Mametz: Lloyd George's 'Welsh Army' at the battle of the Somme *(Gerards Cross, Bucks: Orion 1982), 160p; bib.*
LEWIS, G H
Wings over the Somme, 1916-1918 *(London: Kimber 1976), 205p.*
MACDONAGH, M
The Irish at the Front *(New York: Doran 1916), 197p. U.K. title:* The Irish on the Somme.
MACDONALD, L
Somme *(London: Joseph 1983), 336p; bib.*
MARK VII *pseud*
A subaltern on the Somme in 1916 *(London: Dent 1927), 241p.*
MARTIN, C
Battle of the Somme *(London: Wayland 1973), 128p; bib.*
MASEFIELD, J
The battle of the Somme *(London: Heinemann 1919), 96p.*
The old Front line; or The beginning of the battle of the Somme *(London: Heinemann 1917), 128p.*
MIDDLEBROOK, M
The first day on the Somme, 1 July 1916 *(London: Lane 1971), 365p; bib.*
NORMAN, T
The hell they called High Wood: the Somme 1916 *(London: Kimber 1984), 256p.*
ORR, P
The road to the Somme: men of the Ulster Division tell their story *(Belfast: Blackstaff 1987), 256p; bib.*
PALMER, F
With the new Army on the Somme: my second year of the war *(London: Murray 1917). 348p.*
PLOWMAN, M
A subaltern on the Somme *(London: Dent 1927)*
ROBINSON, H P
The turning point: the battle of the Somme *(London: Heinemann 1917), 291p.*
ROGERSON, S
Twelve days *(London: Barker 1933), 172p.*
SIR Douglas Haig's great push: the battle of the Somme; illustrated by 700 official photographs *(London: Hutchinson 1917), 396p.*
THE SOMME *(Miltown, NJ: Michelin 1919), 2 vols.*
THOMAS, W B
With the British on the Somme *(London: Methuen 1917), 285p.*
VEDETTE pseud
The adventures of an ensign: personal experiences with the Guards on the Somme *(London: Blackwood 1917), 348p.*

SONGS

ADCOCK, A S T J
Songs of the World War *(London: Palmer & Hayward 1916), 78p.*
BLACKALL, C W
Songs from the trenches *(London: Lane 1915), 59p.*
BROPHY, J *and* PARTRIDGE, E
The long trail: what the British soldier sang and said in the Great War, 1914-1918 *(London: Deutsch 1965), 239p; previously published as:* Songs and slang of the British soldier.
GIBBONS, H A *comp*
Songs from the trenches: the soul of the A.E.F. *(New York: Harper 1918), 206p.*
GIRAUD, S L *ed*
Songs that won the war *(London: Daily Express 1930), 96p.*
MACGILL, P
Soldier songs *(London: Jenkins 1917), 120p.*
NETTLEINGHAM, F T *ed*
More Tommy's tunes *(London: Erskine Macdonald 1918), 98p.*
Tommy's tunes *(London: Erskine Macdonald 1917), 91p.*
NILES, J J
Singing soldiers *(New York: Scribner 1927), 171p.*
Songs my mother never taught me *(New York: Macaulay 1935), 227p.*
PARTRIDGE, E *and* BROPHY, J *eds.*
Songs and slang of the British soldier 1914–1918 *(London: Partridge 1931), 3rd ed.*
PEAT, F E *and* SMITH, L O *comps*
Legion airs: songs of over there and over here *(New York: Feist 1932), 144p.*
RUTHVEN, G
Songs for the Army and Navy *(London: Nisbet 1916), 70p.*
SKEYHILL, T
Soldier songs from Anzac *(London: Fisher Unwin 1916), 63p.*
SOLDIER poets: songs of the fighting men *(London: Macdonald 1916), 105p.*
SONGS and sonnets for England in war time: being a collection of lyrics by various authors inspired by the Great War *(London: Lane 1914), 110p.*
YORK, D *ed*
Mud and stars: an anthology of World War songs and poems *(New York: Holt 1931), 301p.*
[See also LANGUAGE*]*

SOUTH AFRICA

ALPORT, A C
The lighter side of war: experiences of a South African civilian in uniform *(London: Hutchinson 1934), 290p.*
ARMSTRONG, H C
Grey steel: a study in arrogance [J. C. Smuts] *(London: Barker 1938), 405p.*

BUCHAN, J
The history of the South African Forces in France *(London: Nelson 1920), 404p.*
The story of the South African Brigade *(London: Nelson 1921), 189p.*
CLOSE, P L
A prisoner of the Germans in South West Africa *(London: Fisher Unwin 1916), 318p.*
COOPER, F H
Khaki crusaders: with the South African artillery in Egypt and Palestine *(Cape Town: 1919), 92p*
DESMORE, A J B
With the 2nd Cape Town thro' Central Africa *(Cape Town: 1920), 100p.*
DIFFORD, L D
The story of the 1st Battalion Cape Corps, 1915-1919 *(Cape Town: 1921), 448p.*
DOITISH, E
The First Springbok prisoner in Germany *(London: McBride 1917), 127p.*
FRENNSEN, G
Peter Moor: a narrative of the German campaign in South West Africa *(London:Constable 1914), 256p.*
HAY, S
History of the R.N.V.R., South Africa Division *(Cape Town: 1920), 193p.*
KENNEDY, J
Sun, sand and sin *(London: Hodder & Stoughton 1916), 142p.*
LEVI, N
Character sketch of General the Right Hon. J. C. Smuts *(London: Longmans 1917), 310p.*
MACMILLAN, W M
A South African student and soldier: Harold Edward Howse *(Cape Town: 1920), 99p.*
MILLER, W
With the Springboks in Egypt *(London: Hodder & Stoughton 1916), 148p.*
O'CONNOR, J K
The Afrikaner rebellion; South Africa today: an exposure of German intrigue in South Africa *(London: Allen & Unwin 1915), 116p.*
RAINER, P W
African hazard *(London: Murray 1940), 287p.*
RAYNER, W S
How Botha and Smuts conquered German South West Africa: a full record of the campaign *(London: Simpkin Marshall 1916), 299p.*
ROBINSON, J P K
With Botha's Army in German South-West Africa *(London: Allen & Unwin 1916), 158p.*
SAMPSON, P J
The capture of De Wet: an account of the South African rebellion *(London: Arnold 1915), 274p.*
STANDAERT, E H G
The Belgian mission to the Boers *(New York: Doran 1918), 286p.*
THE UNION of South Africa and the Great War, 1914-1918 *(Pretoria, SA: Government Printing & Stationery Office 1924), 230p.*
WARWICK, G W
We band of brothers *(Cape Town: Timmins 1962), 211p.*

WHITTALL, W
  With Botha and Smuts in Africa *(London: Cassell 1917), 279p.*
  [See also BOTHA, EAST AFRICA, EGYPT, PALESTINE]

SOUTH AMERICA

KIRKPATRICK, F A
  South America and the war *(London: CUP 1918), 79p.*

SOUTH EAST ASIA

MILLS, C
  A strange war: Burma, India and Afghanistan 1914–1919 *(Gloucester: Sutton 1987),*
  224p.

SPAIN

GOMEZ CARILLO, E
  In the heart of the tragedy *(London: Hodder & Stoughton 1918), 153p.*
MELGAR, F M
  Germany and Spain: the views of a Spanish Catholic *(London: Fisher Unwin 1916), 192p.*

SPIES [see SECRET SERVICE]

STATISTICS

GREAT BRITAIN War Office
  Statistics of the military efforts of the British Empire during the Great War 1914–1920
  (London: HMSO 1922), 880p.

STORIES

ADCOCK, A St J
  In the firing line: stories of the war by land and sea *(London: Hodder & Stoughton 1914),*
  192p.
BEST stories of the 1914 European war *(New York: Ogilvie 1914), 122p.*
BRENT, R *ed*
  Great war stories: true adventures of fighting men in 2 World Wars *(New York: Barth-*
  olomew House 1957), 188p.
CANDLER, E
  The years of chivalry: war sketches and stories *(London: Simpkin Marshall 1916), 308p.*

CAPART, G P
  Blue devil of France: epic figures and stories of the Great War, 1914-1918 *(New York: Watt 1918), 198p.*
CONGDON, D *ed*
  Combat: World War I *(New York: Dial 1964), 426p.*
COOK, G
  None but the valiant: stories of war at sea *(London: Hart-Davis 1972), 153p; bib.*
  Wings of glory: stories of air adventures *(London: Hart-Davis 1971), 151p.*
DAWSON, A J
  Back to Blighty *(London: Hodder & Stoughton 1917), 231p.*
  The great advance *(London: Cassell 1916), 183p.*
DIEBOLD, B L *comp*
  Book of good deeds, 1914-1918 *(New York: Farrar 1933), 309p.*
DURELL, J C V
  Whizzbangs and Woodbines: tales from the Western Front *(London: Hodder & Stoughton 1918), 197p.*
FIFTY amazing stories of the Great War *(London: Odhams 1936), 767p.*
FOREMAN, T
  Whizzbangs: true episodes of the war *(London: Dranes 1921), 96p.*
FOSTER, S N
  Plain tales from the war *(London: Collins 1914), 256p.*
FRAZER, E
  Old Glory and Verdun, and other stories *(New York: Duffield 1918), 303p.*
GREAT War adventures: true tales of fighting men *(London: World's Work 1932), 176p.*
GRIBBLE, L *comp*
  Great war adventures *(London: Barker 1966), 192p.*
HARPER, C G
  Overheard at the Front: stories of the war *(London: Iliffe 1915), 110p.*
HARVEY, H E
  Battle-line narratives, 1915-1918 *(London: Brentano 1928), 255p.*
HAYNES, H *ed*
  The Victory adventure book *(London: Collins 1916), unp.*
HEILGERS, L
  Somewhere in France *(London: Dryden 1915), 194p.*
HERRIES, J W
  Tales from the trenches *(London: Hodge 1915), 114p.*
HOLMES, R
  My police court friends with the colours *(Edinburgh: Blackwood 1915), 368p.*
LATZKO, A
  Men in battle *(London: Cassell 1918), 237p.*
MACKENZIE, D A
  From all the Fronts *(New York: Stokes 1918), 199p.*
MACMUNN, *Sir* G F
  The King's pawns: being Empire stories of the World War *(London: Sheldon 1930), 217p.*
MEDLEY, A
  A material medley *(London: Partridge 1931), 361p.*

MILLS, A H
With my Regiment from the Aisne to La Bassée *(London: Soldiers' Tales of the Great War 1915), 231p.*

MILNE, J
The war stories of Private Thomas Atkins *(London: Daily Chronicle 1914), 192p.*

MINCHIN, J H C
Great short stories of the war: England, France, Germany, America *(London: Eyre & Spottiswoode 1930), 983p.*

MORE war adventures on land, sea and in the air *(London: World's Work 1932), 176p.*

MOUDIE, W
The crown of honour: being stories of heroism from the Great War *(London: Clarke 1931), 239p.*

NEWBOLT, *Sir* H J
Tales of the Great War *(London: Longmans 1916), 294p.*

NEWMAN, B *and* EVANS, I O
Anthology of Armageddon *(London: Archer 1935), 454p.*

PARROTT, *Sir* J E
The path of glory: heroic stories of the Great War *(London: Nelson 1921), 304p.*

PETER *pseud*
Trench yarns for subalterns and others *(London: Cassell 1916), 136p.*

RICHARDS, C
Tales of the Great War *(London: Bell 1931), 274p.*

ROOSEVELT, T
Rank and file: true stories of the Great War *(New York: Scribner 1928), 279p.*

SAPPER *pseud*
Lieutenant and others: tales from the Front *(London: Hodder & Stoughton 1915), 184p.*

SELLERS, W E
With our fighting men *(London: RTS 1915), 216p.*

TALLENTS, S G
The starry pool and other tales *(London: Constable 1918), 181p.*

TRUE stories of the Great War *(New York: Review of Reviews 1917), 6 vols.*

WARR, C L
Unseen hosts: stories of the Great War *(London: Gardner 1916), 268p.*

WHITE, M
Alive to tell the tale: a selection of true personal narratives by survivors and eye-witnesses of outstanding episodes of the Great War *(London: World's Work 1940), 96p.*

WHITEHOUSE, A
Epics and legends of the First World War *(London: Muller 1964), 352p; bib.*

WILSON, R
The post of honour: stories of daring deeds in the Great War *(London: Dent 1917), 159p.*

WOOD, W
In the line of battle: soldiers' stories of the war *(London: Chapman & Hall 1916), 316p.*

WOOLLCOTT, A
The command is forward: tales of the A.E.F. battlefields as they appeared in the Stars and Stripes *(New York: Century 1919), 304p.*

WREN, P C
Stepsons of France: true tales of the French Foreign Legion *(London: Murray 1918), 269p.*

STRATEGY

BARNETT, C
  The swordbearers: studies in Supreme Command in the First World War *(London: Eyre & Spottiswoode 1963), 387p; bib.*
BLANCHON, G
  The new warfare *(London: Harrap 1917), 254p.*
CRUTTWELL, C R M
  The role of British strategy in the Great War *(London: CUP 1936), 99p.*
ELLISON, *Sir* G F
  The perils of amateur strategy, as exemplified by the attack on the Dardanelles fortress in 1915 *(London: Longmans 1926), 152p.*
FRENCH, D
  British strategy and war aims 1914–1916 *(London: Allen & Unwin 1986), 312p; bib.*
GARDINER, J B W *and* YBARRA, T Y
  How the war was lost and won: the grand strategy of the High Commands *(New York: Harper 1920), unp.*
GARSIA, C
  A key to victory: a study in war planning *(London: Eyre & Spottiswoode 1940), 328p.*
GOOCH, J
  The plans of war: the General Staff and British military strategy *(London: Routledge & Kegan Paul 1974), 348p; bib.*
GUINN, P
  British strategy and politics, 1914-1918 *(Oxford: Clarendon 1965), 359p; bib.*
HANKEY, M P A *1st baron*
  The Supreme Command, 1914-1918 *(London: Allen & Unwin 1961), 2 vols.*
HUNT, B *and* PRESTON, A *eds*
  War aims and strategic policy in the Great War *(London: Croom Helm 1977), 1 vol.*
JOHNSON, D W
  Topography and strategy in the war *(New York: Holt 1917), 211p.*
LIDDELL HART, H B
  Reputations: sketches of military commanders in the European war *(London: Murray 1928), 327p.*
  Through the fog of war *(London: Faber 1938), 366p.*
MACFALL, C H C
  Germany at bay *(London: Cassell 1917), 319p.*
MACPHERSON, W L
  Strategy of the Great War: a study of its campaigns and battles in their relation to Allied and German military policy *(New York: Putnam 1929), 417p.*
MAURICE, *Sir* F B
  Lessons of Allied co-operation: naval, military and air, 1914-1918 *(London: OUP 1942), 195p.*
NEAME, P
  German strategy in the Great War *(London: Arnold 1923), 132p.*
PIERREFEU, J
  Plutarch lied *(London: Grant Richards 1924), 304p.*

THE POMP of power: a criticism of the Allied conduct of the European war and the Peace *(London: Hutchinson 1922), 360p.*

POWERS, B D
Strategy without slide-rule: British air strategy 1914–1919 *(London: Croom Helm 1976), 300p.*

PULESTON, W D
High Command in the World War *(New York: Scribner 1934), 331p.*

RITTER, G
The Schlieffen plan: critique of a myth *(London: Wolff 1958), 195p.*

SARGENT, H H
The strategy on the Western Front, 1914-1918 *(Chicago: McClurg 1920), 261p.*

SMYTH, *Sir* J
Leadership in battle, 1914-1918: commanders in action *(Newton Abbot, Devon: David & Charles 1975), 191p; bib.*

Snyder, J L
The ideology of the offensive: military decision making and the disasters of 1914 *(Ithiaca, NY: Cornell 1984), 267p.*

SOUZA, C de *count*
Germany in defeat: a strategic history of the war *(New York: Dutton 1919), 231p.*

SPEARS, E L
Prelude to victory *(London: Cape 1939), 640p.*

THOMPSON, P A
Lions led by donkeys: showing how victory in the Great War was achieved by those who made the fewest mistakes *(London: Werner Laurie 1927), 317p.*

WOODS, W S
Colossal blunders of the war *(London: Allen & Unwin 1930), 274p.*

WRIGHT, P E
At the Supreme War Council *(London: Nash 1921), 201p.*

STRETCHER BEARERS

DUNHAM, F
The long carry: the journal of a stretcher bearer, 1916-18 *(Oxford: Pergamon 1970), 231p.*

DUPUY, G M
The stretcher-bearer *(Oxford: Clarendon 1915), 138p.*

HAIGH, R H *and* TURNER, P W *eds*
The long carry: the journal of stretcher bearer Frank Dunham 1916–1918 *(Oxford: Pergamon 1970).*

L, R A
Letters of a Canadian stretcher bearer *(Boston, Mass: Little, Brown 1918), 288p.*

NEWTON, J H
A stretcher bearer's diary: three years in France with the 21st Division *(London: Stockwell 1932), 79p.*

SUBMARINES

ABBOT, W J
Aircraft and submarines *(New York: Putnam 1918), 388p.*
BISHOP, F
The story of the submarine *(New York: Century 1916), 211p.*
BRODIE, C G
Forlorn hope 1915: the submarine passage of the Dardanelles *(London: Frederick Books 1956), 91p.*
CARR, W G
By guess and by God: the story of the British submarines in the war *(London: Hutchinson 1930), 288p.*
COOK, W V
Grey fish *(New York: Stokes 1920), 303p.*
DOMVILLE-FIFE, C W
Submarines, mines and torpedoes in the war *(London: Hodder & Stoughton 1915), 192p.*
Submarine warfare of today *(London: Seeley 1920), 303p.*
EVERITT, D
The K boats: a dramatic first report on the Navy's most calamitous submarines *(London: Harrap 1963), 206p; bib.*
FAYLE, C E
Seaborne trade *(New York: Longmans 1920-24), 3 vols.*
GRAY, E
A damned un-English weapon: the story of British submarine warfare, 1914-18 *(London: Seeley 1971), 259p; bib.*
HAY, M F
Secrets of the submarine *(London: Skeffington 1918), 123p.*
HOAR, A
The submarine torpedo-boat *(London: Crosby Lockwood 1917), 210p.*
JAMESON, *Sir* W
The most formidable thing: the story of the submarine from its earliest days to the end of World War I *(London: Hart-Davis 1965), 280p; bib.*
JONES, T M
Watchdogs of the deep: life in a submarine during the Great War *(Sydney: Angus & Robertson 1935), 224p.*
KLAXON *pseud*
The story of our submarines *(London: Blackwood 1919), 297p.*
LAKE, S
The submarine in war and peace: its developments and possibilities *(Philadelphia, Pa: Lippincott 1918), 314p.*
MASTERS, D
'I.D': new tales of the submarine war *(London: Eyre & Spottiswoode 1935), 296p.*
MILLHOLLAND, R
Splinter fleet of the Otranto Passage *(Indianapolis, Ind: Bobbs-Merrill, 1936), 307p.*
MOFFAT, A W
Maverick Navy *(Middletown, Conn: Wesleyan UP 1976), 157p.*

NEWBOLT, *Sir* H J
Submarine and anti-submarine *(London: Longmans 1918), 312p.*
SMITH, G
Britain's clandestine submarines, 1914-1918 *(New Haven, Conn: Yale UP 1964), 155p.*
TALBOT, F A
Submarines, their mechanism and operation *(London: Heinemann 1915), 284p.*
THOMPSON, T B
Take her down: wartime adventures of U.S. submarine L-9 *(New York: Sheridan 1942), 313p.*
WHEELER, H F B
War in the underseas *(London: Harrap 1919), 319p.*
WHITEHOUSE, A
Subs and submariners *(New York: Doubleday 1961), 416p; bib.*
WILSON, H W
Hush; or, The hydrophone service *(London: Mills & Boon 1920), 188p.*
WILSON, M
Baltic assignment: British submarines in Russia 1914–1919 *(London: Cooper & Secker & Warburg 1985), 243p.*

SURVIVORS (SEA)

JOHNSON, E H
Torpedoed in the Mediterranean *(New York: Ogilvie 1918), 128p.*
Y *pseud*
Odyssey of a torpedoed transport *(Boston, Mass: Houghton Mifflin 1918), 217p.*

SUVLA BAY

HARGRAVE, J
At Suvla Bay *(London: Constable 1916), 181p.*
The Suvla Bay landing *(London: Macdonald 1964), 266p; bib.*
JUVENIS, *pseud*
Suvla Bay and after *(London: Hodder & Stoughton 1916), 169p.*
[See also DARDANELLES, GALLIPOLI]

SWITZERLAND

EARLE, M R
A backwater of war: being letters from Switzerland, September to December 1914 *(London: Headley 1915), 126p.*
HAUSER, K
Swiss internment of prisoners of war *(New York: Columbia UP 1917), 154p.*
PICOT, H P
The British interned in Switzerland *(London: Arnold 1919), 212p.*

RUFENER, L A
The economic position of Switzerland during the war *(Washington DC: Bureau of Foreign & Domestic Commerce 1919), 88p.*

TACTICS

ANDERSON, C C
War manual *(London: Fisher Unwin 1916), 4 vols.*
BECA, *Colonel*
A study of the development of infantry tactics *(London: Allen & Unwin 1915), 148p.*
CASSERLEY, G
Tactics for beginners *(London: Hodder & Stoughton 1916), 188p.*
LYNCH, G
War wire *(London: Bird 1916), 88p.*
SLEEMAN, J L
First principles of tactics and organization *(Aldershot: Gale & Polden 1915), 162p.*
TACTICIAN *pseud*
The Battalion in attack *(London: Forester Groom 1916), 56p.*
[See also TANKS, TRENCH WARFARE]

TANKS

BARTHOLOMEW, E
First World War tanks *(Aylesbury, Bucks: Shire 1986), unp.*
FITZIMONS, B *ed*
Tanks and weapons of World War I *(London: Phoebus 1973), 160p.*
FLETCHER, D
Landships: British tanks in the First World War *(London: HMSO 1984), 60p.*
FOOT, S
Three lives *(London: Heinemann 1934), 355p.*
FOSTER, W
The tank, its birth and development *(Lincoln: 1920), 90p.*
JONES, R E
The fighting tanks since 1916 *(Old Greenwich, Conn: We 1969), 325p.*
LIDDELL HART, B H
The tanks: the history of the Royal Tank Regiment *(London: Cassell 1959), vol. I.*
MITCHELL, F
Tank warfare: the story of the tanks in the Great War *(London: Nelson 1933), 312p.*
STERN, *Sir* A G
Tanks, 1914-1918 *(London: Hodder & Stoughton 1919), 297p.*
TANK tales *(New York: Funk 1919), 213p.*
[See also BRITISH ARMY (ROYAL TANK CORPS), CAMBRAI, MEMOIRS: Sir E.W. SWINTON]

TAXATION

LANGDON, A M
  The Excess Profits Duty and Excess Mineral Rights Duty *(London: Stevens & Haynes 1916), 102p.*
LAWRENCE, F W P
  A levy on capital *(London: Allen & Unwin 1918), 94p.*
MONTGOMERY, R M *and* ALLEN, W
  Excess Profits Duty and Excess Mineral Rights Duty *(London: Butterworth 1919), 136p.*
SNELLING, W E
  Excess Profits including Excess Mineral Rights Duty *(London: Pitman 1917), 327p.*
SPICER, E E *and* PEGLER, E C
  The Excess Profits Duty *(London: Lynch 1920), 224p.*
SUTCLIFFE, R J
  Excess Profits Duty and the cases decided thereon *(London: Stevens 1919), 168p.*

TECHNOLOGY

TERRAINE, J
  White heat: the new warfare 1914–18 *(London: Sidgwick & Jackson 1982), 352p.*

TOC H

CLAYTON, P T B
  Letters from Flanders *(London: Centenary 1932), 175p.*
  Tales of Talbot House: everyman's club in Poperinghe and Ypres *(London: Chatto & Windus 1919), 169p.*

TRADE UNIONS

FYFE, T A
  Employers and workmen, 1915-1917 *(London: Hodge 1918), 364p.*
RAMSAY, A
  The terms of industrial peace *(London: Constable 1917), 155p.*
WEBB, S
  The restoration of Trade Union conditions *(London: Nisbet 1917), 109p.*
[See also SOCIALISM]

TRAINING

CASSERLY, G
  A manual of war training for the new armies and volunteers *(London: Hodder & Stoughton 1916), 192p.*

CODDINGTON, F J O
The young officer's guide to military law *(Aldershot: Gale & Polden 1916), 126p.*
'COMMANDER' *pseud*
Hints and tips for members of the O.T.C. *(London: Forster Groom 1915), 48p.*
COOKE, F G
Scouting by night *(Aldershot: Gale & Polden 1916), 59p.*
The value of observation in war *(Aldershot: Gale & Polden 1916), 45p.*
HALE, *Sir* L
What to observe and how to report it *(London: Rees 1916), 70p.*
HORNBY, M L
How to march *(London: Rees 1915), 52p.*
'INSTRUCTOR' *pseud*
Rapid training of recruits: a practical scheme *(Aldershot: Gale & Polden 1916), 178p.*
JACKSON, L E S
The why and wherefore of indirect laying: a simple explanation for officers, N.C.O.'s and men *(London: Forster Groom 1915), 52p.*
LINGS, H C
Musketry lectures for officers and Non-Commissioned officers *(Aldershot: Gale & Polden 1915), 106p.*
MACALISTER, D A
Field gunnery: a practical manual *(London: Murray 1915), 136p.*
MACGILL, P
The amateur army: the experiences of a soldier in the making *(London: Jenkins 1915), 122p.*
MAIS, S P B
An English course for army candidates *(London: Sidgwick & Jackson 1915), 194p.*
MAKING of a soldier; or, How the lad went away *(London: Simpkin Marshall 1916), 128p.*
MORRIS, A
The musketry teacher: a complete guide for instructors of musketry *(Aldershot: Gale & Polden 1915), 152p.*
NEW army in the making *(London: Kegan Paul 1915), 80p.*
ROUSE, S
Practical notes for machine-gun drill and training *(London: Forster Groom 1916), 82p.*
TILNEY, W A
Rapid night-marching made easy *(London: Stanford 1915), unp.*
WALSH, H P
On taking bearings: a simple treatise on bearings *(London: Murray 1915), 62p.*
WHEN I join the ranks: what to do and how to do it *(Aldershot: Gale & Polden 1916), 122p.*
WINGFIELD, W J R
Lectures to Cavalry subalterns of the new armies *(London: Forster Groom 1915), unp.*

TRANSCASPIA

ELLIS, C H
The Transcaspian episode 1918–19 *(London: Hutchinson 1963), 176p; bib.*

TRANSPORTATION

GLEAVES, A
  History of the Transport Service: adventures and experiences of United States transports and cruisers in the World War *(New York: Doran 1921), 284p.*
HENNIKER, A M
  Transportation on the Western Front, 1914–1918 *(London: HMSO 1937), 531p.*
WILGUS, W J
  Transporting the A.E.F., in Western Europe, 1917–1918 *(New York: OUP 1931), 612p.*
WYATT, H M
  Motor transports in war *(New York: Doran 1915), 192p.*
[See also BRITISH ARMY (ROYAL ARMY SERVICE CORPS), MERCHANT NAVY, RAILWAYS, SHIPBUILD-ING]

TREATIES

ALMOND, N *and* LUTZ, R H *eds*
  The Treaty of St. Germain: a documentary history of its territories and political clauses *(Stanford, Cal: Stanford UP 1935), 712p.*
COCKS, F S
  The secret treaties and understandings *(London: Union of Democratic Control 1918), 94p.*
GREAT BRITAIN Foreign Office
  Treaty of Peace between the Allied and Associated Powers and Austria *(London: HMSO 1919).*
  Treaty of Peace between the Allied and Associated Powers and Bulgaria *(London: HMSO 1920).*
  Treaty of Peace between the Allied and Associated Powers and Germany, with amendments and other Treaty engagements *(London: HMSO 1925), 441p.*
  Treaty of Peace between the Allied and Associated Powers and Hungary *(London: HMSO 1920).*
  Treaty of Peace between the Allied and Associated Powers with Turkey *(London: HMSO 1920).*
MILLER, D H
  The Peace Pact of Paris: a study of the Briand-Kellogg Treaty *(New York: Putnam 1928), 287p.*
MOLONY, W O
  Nationality and the Peace Treaties *(London: Allen & Unwin 1934), 278p.*
NELSON, H I
  Land and power: British and Allied policy on Germany's frontiers, 1916-19 *(London: Routledge & Kegan Paul 1963), 402p.*
NICOLSON, *Sir* H
  Peacemaking, 1919 *(London: Methuen 1964), 378p.*
SANGER, C P *and* NORTON H T J
  England's guarantee to Belgium and Luxemburg, with the full text of the Treaties *(London: Allen & Unwin 1915), 162p.*

SCOTT , A P
An introduction to the Peace Treaties *(Chicago: Chicago UP 1920), 292p.*
[See also BREST-LITOVSK, TRIANON, VERSAILLES]

TRENCH WARFARE

ASHWORTH, T
Trench warfare 1914–1918: the live and let live system *(London: Macmillan 1980), 266p.*
BERTRAND, G *and* SOLBERT, O N
Tactics and duties for trench fighting *(New York: Putnam 1918), unp.*
CAMMAERTS, E
The adoration of the soldiers *(London: Longmans 1916), 55p.*
DAWSON, C
The glory of the trenches *(London: Lane 1918), 158p.*
DOLDEN, A S
Cannon fodder: an infantryman's life on the Western Front 1914–18 *(Poole, Dorset: Blanford 1980), 185p.*
ELLIS, J
Eye-deep in hell: life in the trenches, 1914-1918 *(London: Fontana 1977), 214p.*
HOLDEN, M
War in the trenches *(London: Wayland 1973), 96p.*
HOLMES, R D
A Yankee in the trenches *(Boston, Mass: Little, Brown 1918), 214p.*
HOOBLER, D *and* HOOBLER, T
The trenches: fighting on the Western Front in World War I *(New York:Putnam 1978), 191p.*
HOULIHAN, M
World War I: trench warfare *(London: Ward Lock 1974), 144p; bib.*
LLOYD, A
The war in the trenches *(London: Hart-Davis, MacGibbon 1976), 200p; bib.*
MARKS, T P
The laughter goes from life: in the trenches of the First World War *(London: Kimber 1977) 190p.*
MESSENGER, C
Terriers in the trenches: the Post Office Rifles at war 1914–1918 *(Chippenham, Wilts: Picton 1982), 170p.*
Trench fighting, 1914-18 *(New York: Ballantine 1972), 160p; bib.*
MORGAN, H
Life among the sandbags *(London: Hodder & Stoughton 1916), 123p.*
REDMOND, W
Trench pictures from France *(London: Melrose 1917), 185p.*
RUTLEDGE, S
Pen pictures from the trenches *(Toronto: Briggs 1918), 125p.*
SAPPER *pseud*
No man's land *(London: Hodder & Stoughton 1917), 328p.*

SMITH, J S
　Trench warfare: by an American serving with the British Army *(New York: Dutton 1917)*, *144p.*
TALES of a dug-out (London: George 1915), 122p.
[See also DARDANELLES, FLANDERS, GALLIPOLI, WESTERN FRONT]

TRIANON

BETHLEN, I *count*
　The Treaty of Trianon and European peace *(London: Longmans 1934)*, *187p.*
BIRINYI, L K
　Why the Treaty of Trianon is void *(Grand Rapids, Mich: Simmons 1938)*, *246p.*
DEAK, F
　Hungary at the Paris Peace Conference: the diplomatic history of the Treaty of Trianon *(New York: Columbia UP 1942)*, *594p.*
HARMSWORTH, H S *1st viscount Rothermere*
　My campaign for Hungary *(London: Eyre & Spottiswoode 1939)*, *222p.*
MACARTNEY, C E
　Hungary and her successors: the Treaty of Trianon and its consequences, 1919-1937 *(London: Royal Institute of International Affairs 1937)*, *504p.*

TURKEY

AHMAD AMIN
　Turkey in the Great War *(New Haven, Conn: Yale UP 1930)*, *310p.*
ARMSTRONG, H C
　Grey Wolf: Mustapha Kemal *(London: Barker 1932)*, *352p.*
BENSON, E F
　Crescent and Iron Cross *(London: Hodder & Stoughton 1918)*, *268p.*
BRAY, N N E
　Shifting sands *(London: Unicorn 1934)*, *312p.*
CASTLE, W T F
　Grand Turk *(London: Hutchinson 1943)*, *170p.*
CEMAL, P
　Memories of a Turkish statesman, 1913-1919 *(New York: Arno 1973)*, *302p.*
DONOHOE, M H
　With the Persian Expedition *(London: Arnold 1919)*, *276p.*
DUNSTERVILLE, L C
　The adventures of Dunsterforce *(London: Arnold 1920)*, *323p.*
EINSTEIN, L
　Inside Constantinople: a diplomatist's diary during the Dardanelles Expedition, April-September, 1915 *(London: Murray 1917)*, *291p.*
EMIN, A
　Turkey in the World War *(New Haven, Conn: Yale UP 1930)*, *310p.*

FRENCH, F J F
From Whitehall to the Caspian *(London: Odhams 1921), 255p.*
HAR DAYAL
Forty-four months in Germany and Turkey, February 1915 to October 1918 *(London: King 1920), 103p.*
HELMREICH, P C
From Paris to Sèvres: the partition of the Ottoman Empire at the Peace Conference of 1919-1920 *(Columbus, Ohio: Ohio State University P 1974), 376p.*
HOWARD, H N
The partition of Turkey: a diplomatic history, 1913-1923 *(Norman, Okl: University of Oklahoma P 1931), 486p.*
JABOTINSKY, V
Turkey and the war *(London: Fisher Unwin 1917), 264p.*
JASTROW, M
The war and the Baghdad railway: the story of Asia Minor and its relation to the present conflict *(Philadelphia, Pa: Lippincott 1918), 160p.*
MORGENTHAU, H
Ambassador Morgenthau's story *(New York: Doubleday 1918), 407p.*
Secrets of the Bosphorus *(London: Hutchinson 1918), 275p.*
NOGALES, R de
Four years beneath the Crescent *(New York: Scribner 1926), unp.*
OSTROROG, L *count*
The Turkish problem *(London: Chatto & Windus 1918), 225p.*
PHILLIPSON, C *and* BUXTON, N
The question of the Bosphorus and Dardanelles *(London: Stevens & Haynes 1917), 280p.*
SANDERS, L *von*
Five years in Turkey *(Washington DC: Naval Institute 1927), 326p.*
SANDES, E W C
Tales of Turkey *(London: Murray 1924), 173p.*
SCHREINER, G A
From Berlin to Baghdad: behind the scenes in the Near East *(New York: Harper 1918), 370p.*
STUERMER, H
Two war years in Constantinople *(London: Hodder & Stoughton 1917), 308p.*
WARFIELD, W
The gate of Asia: a journey from the Persian Gulf to the Black Sea *(New York: Putnam 1917), 374p.*
WOOLF, L S
The future of Constantinople *(London: Allen & Unwin 1917), 109p.*
YEATS-BROWN, F C C
Caught by the Turks (New York: Macmillan 1920), 239p.
[See also DARDANELLES, GALLIPOLI, MESOPOTAMIA]

U-BOATS

AJAX *pseud*
The German pirate, his methods and record *(London: Pearson 1918), 120p.*

ARCHER, W
The pirate's progress: a short history of the U-Boat *(London: Chatto & Windus 1918), 96p.*

BATEMAN, C T
U-Boat devilry *(London: Hodder & Stoughton 1918), 192p.*

CHATTERTON, E K
Beating the U-Boats, 1917-1918 *(London: Hurst & Blackett 1943), 172p.*
Fighting the U-Boats, 1914-1916 *(London: Hurst & Blackett 1942), 216p.*

CLARK, W B
When the U-Boats came to America *(Boston, Mass: Little, Brown 1929), 359p.*

CLOSE, A
I accuse!: the fate of 212 U-Boats *(Ilford, Essex: 1930), 97p.*

COLES, A
Three before breakfast: a true and dramatic account of how a German U-Boat sank three British cruisers in one desperate hour *(Havant, Hants: Mard 1979), 192p.*

DIARY of a U-Boat commander *(London: Hutchinson 1920), 288p.*

FROST, W
German submarine warfare: a study of its methods and spirit *(New York: Appleton 1918), 243p.*

GIBSON, R H *and* PRENDERGAST, M
The German submarine war, 1914-1918 *(London: Constable 1931), 438p.*

GRANT, R M
U-Boats destroyed: the effect of anti-submarine warfare, 1914-1918 *(London: Putnam 1964), 172p; bib.*
U-Boat intelligence, 1914-1918 *(London: Putnam 1969), 192p; bib.*

GRAY, E
The killing time: the U-Boat war, 1914-18 *(London: Seeley 1972), 280p; bib.*

HASHAGEN, E
The log of a U-Boat commander *(London: Putnam 1931), 277p.*

JAMES, H J
German subs in Yankee waters: First World War *(New York: Gotham House 1940), 208p.*

JELLICOE, J R *1st earl*
The submarine peril: the Admiralty policy in 1917 *(London: Cassell 1934), 240p.*

KOENIG, P
The voyage of the 'Deutschland' *(London: Pearson 1917), 126p.*

NEUREUTHER, C *and* BERGEN, C
U-Boat stories: narratives of German U-Boat sailors *(London: Constable 1931), 207p.*

NOYES, A
Open boats *(London: Blackwood 1917), 136p.*

PRESTON, A
U-Boats *(London: Arms & Armour 1978), 192p.*

SPIEGEL, A C *von*
U-Boat 202: the war diary of a German submarine *(London: Melrose 1919), 170p; U.S. title:* The adventures of U-202.

THOMAS, L J
Raiders of the deep: tales of German submarine raids *(London: Heinemann 1929), 363p.*
The sea devil's fo'c'sle *(London: Heinemann 1930), 300p.*
UNITED STATES Office of Naval Records
German submarine activities on the Atlantic coast of the United States and Canada *(Washington DC: 1920), 163p.*
[See also GERMAN NAVY, MERCHANT NAVY, Q SHIPS]

UNIFORMS

DE FALLS, W C
Army and Navy information, uniforms, organization, arms and equipment of the warring Powers *(New York: Dutton 1917), 195p.*
MOLLO, A
Army uniforms of World War I: European and United States armies and aviation forces *(Poole, Dorset: Blandford 1977), 219p.*
WILKINSON, F
World War I weapons and uniforms *(London: Ward Lock 1978), 128p.*

UNITED STATES (general)

ABBOT, W J
The United States in the Great War *(New York: Leslie-Judge 1919), 296p.*
ADDAMS, J
Peace and bread in time of war *(New York: Macmillan 1922), 257p.*
AMERICANS in the Great War *(Milltown, NJ: Michelin Tire 1920), 3 vols.*
AYRES, L P
The war with Germany: a statistical summary *(Washington DC: War Dept. 1919), 154p.*
BAILEY, T A
The policy of the United States toward the neutrals, 1917-1918 *(Baltimore: Johns Hopkins UP 1942), 520p.*
BASSETT, J S
Our war with Germany: a history *(New York: Knopf 1919), 386p.*
BENSON, A L
Inviting war to America *(New York: Huebsch 1916), 190p.*
BLUM, J M
Joe Tumulty and the Wilson era *(Boston, Mass: Houghton Mifflin 1951), 337p.*
BOURNE, R S
War and the intellectuals: essays, 1915-1919 *(New York: Harper 1964), 198p; previously published as:* Untimely papers.
BROWNE, P E
Uncivil war *(New York: Doran 1918), 186p.*
BULLARD, R L
Personalities and reminiscences of the war *(London: Heinemann 1925), 347p.*

BURGESS, J W
America's relations to the Great War *(Chicago: McClurg 1916), 209p.*
CHAFEE, Z
Freedom of speech *(New York: Harcourt 1920), 431p.*
CHERADAME, A
Essentials of an enduring victory *(New York: Scribner 1918), 259p.*
United States and Pangermania *(New York: Scribner 1918), 170p.*
CHURCHILL, M S
You who can help: Paris letters of an American Army officer's wife, August 1916-January 1918 *(Boston, Mass: Small 1918), 296p.*
CLARK, J M
The costs of the World War to the American people *(New Haven, Conn: Yale UP 1931), 316p.*
COAR, J F
Democracy and the war *(London: Putnam 1918), 138p.*
CRIGHTON, J C
Missouri and the World War, 1914-1917: a study in public opinion *(Columbus, Mo: University of Missouri P 1947), 199p.*
DAWSON, W J
The father of a soldier: sketches of life during the European war *(London: Lane 1918), 197p.*
DE SUMICHRAST, F C
Americans and Britons *(London: Duckworth 1915), 388p.*
DUPUY, R E
Five days to war, April 2-6, 1917 *(Harrisburg, Pa: Stackpole 1967) 192p.*
DUPUY, W A
Uncle Sam fighter *(New York: Stokes 1919), 304p.*
FITZGERALD, W G
America's day: studies in light and shade *(New York: Dodd 1919), 425p.*
FROTHINGHAM, T G
The American reinforcement in the World War *(London: Heinemann 1927), 388p.*
FULLERTON, W M
The American crisis and the war *(London: Constable 1916), 137p.*
GENTHE, C V
American war narratives, 1917-1918: a study and bibliography *(New York: Lewis 1969), 194p.*
GOULD, B A
The greater tragedy, and other things *(New York: Putnam 1916), 189p.*
GREENE, F V
Our first year in the Great War *(New York: Putnam 1918), 127p.*
H, S R *and* M, J F
Sixty American opinions on the war *(London: Fisher Unwin 1915), 165p.*
HALLGREN, M A
Tragic fallacy: a study of America's war policies *(New York: Knopf 1937), 474p.*
HALLOWELL, J M
Spirit of Lafayette *(New York: Doubleday 1918), 101p.*

HARBORD, J G
America in the Great War *(Boston, Mass: Houghton Mifflin 1933), 111p.*
HAY, I *pseud*
Getting together *(London: Hodder & Stoughton 1917), 86p.*
Last million: how they invaded France – and England *(Boston, Mass: Houghton Mifflin 1919), 202p.*
HOBBS, W H
World war and its consequences *(New York: Putnam 1919), 446p.*
JANTZEN, S
Hooray for peace, hurrah for war: the United States during World War I *(New York: Knopf 1972), 327p.*
JOHNSON, D W
Plain words from America *(London: Hodder & Stoughton 1917), 48p.*
JOHNSON, W F
America and the Great War for humanity and freedom *(Philadelphia, Pa: Winston 1917), 352p.*
JOHNSTON, R M
First reflections on the campaign of 1918 *(New York: Holt 1920), 79p.*
KELLER, P
States of belonging: German-American intellectuals and the First World War *(Cambridge, Mass: Harvard 1979), 324p.*
KELLY, Mrs F
What America did *(New York: Dutton 1919), 343p.*
KELLY, M
American bias in the war *(New York: Lemcke 1922), 272p.*
KENNEDY, D M
Over here: the First World War and American society *(New York: OUP 1980), 404p; bib.*
KNIGHT, W A
War time over here *(Boston, Mass: Pilgrim 1918), 139p.*
LARSON, S
Labor and foreign policy: Gompers, the A.F.L., and the First World War, 1914-18 *(Rutherford: Fairleigh Dickinson UP 1975), 176p; bib.*
LAVINE, A L
Circuits of victory *(New York: Doubleday 1921), 634p.*
LEE, G S
We: a confession of faith for the American people during and after the war *(London: Curtis Brown 1916), 728p.*
LOCHNER, L P
America's Don Quixote: Henry Ford's attempt to save Europe *(London: Kegan Paul 1924), 240p.*
McLAUGHLIN, A C
America and Britain *(New York: Dutton 1919), 221p.*
MACMASTER, J B
The United States in the World War, 1918-1920 *(New York: Appleton 1920), 2 vols.*
MARCH, P C
The nation at war *(New York: Doubleday 1932), 407p.*

MARRIN, A
The Yanks are coming: the United Satets in the First World War *(New York: Atheneum 1986), 248p.*

MOCK, J R *and* LARSON, C
Words that won the war: the story of the Committee on Public Information, 1917-1919 *(Princeton, NJ: Princeton UP 1939), 372p.*

MOORE, S T
America and the World War: a narrative of the part played by the United States from the outbreak to peace *(New York: Greenberg 1937), 309p.*

MORSE, E W
Vanguard of American volunteers in the fighting lines and humanitarian service, August 1914-April 1917 *(New York: Scribner 1918), 281p.*

MUNSTERBERG, H
The peace and America *(New York: Appleton 1915), 275p.*
The war and America *(New York: Appleton 1915), 209p.*

OKIE, H P
America and the German peril *(London: Heinemann 1915), 198p.*

O'LAUGHLIN, J C
Imperilled America *(Chicago: Reilly 1916), 264p.*

O'MALLEY, F W
War-whirl in Washington *(New York: Century 1918), 298p.*

PALMER, F
Our gallant madness *(New York: Doubleday 1937), 320p.*
With our faces in the light: America's spirit in this war *(London: Murray 1917), 105p.*

PAXON, F L
American democracy and the World War *(Boston, Mass: Houghton Mifflin 1939), 2 vols.*

REILLY, H J
America's part in the European war *(New York: Cosmopolitan 1928), 326p.*

REQUIN, E J
America's race to victory *(New York: Stokes 1919), 211p.*

RIDDER, H
Hyphenations: collection of articles on the World War *(New York: Schmetterling 1915), 268p.*

ROGERS, L
America's case against Germany *(New York: Dutton 1917), 264p.*

ROOSEVELT, T
America and World War *(London: Murray 1915), 296p.*
Average Americans *(New York: Putnam 1920), 252p.*
Fear God and take your own part: the United States and the war *(London: Hodder & Stoughton 1916), 414p.*

RYLY, T W
A little group of wilful men: a study of Congressional-Presidential authority *(London: Kennikat 1975), 198p; bib.*

SCHERER, J A B
A nation at war *(New York: Doran 1918), 285p.*

SELDES, G V
The United States and the war *(London: Allen & Unwin 1917), 148p.*

SLOSSON, P W
The great crusade and after, 1914-1928 *(New York: Macmillan 1930), 486p.*
SMITH, A S
America at home: impressions of a visit in war time *(London: Oliphants 1920), 182p.*
SMITH, D M
The great departure: the United States and World War I 1914-1920 *(New York: Wiley 1965), 221p; bib.*
War and depression; America, 1914-1939 *(St. Charles, Mo: Forum 1974), 215p.*
SOULSBY, L H M
The America I saw in 1916-1918 *(London: Longmans 1920), 205p.*
SQUIERS, A L
One hundred per cent American *(New York: Doran 1918), 398p.*
SQUIRES, C W
Munsterberg and militarism checked *(Toronto: Briggs 1915), 241p.*
STEIN, R M
M-Day, the first day of war *(New York: Harcourt 1936), 398p.*
STEINER, E A
The confession of an hyphenated American *(New York: Revell 1916), 63p.*
SYNON, M
My country's part *(New York: Scribner 1918), 142p.*
TAFT, R W H
The United States and peace *(London: Murray 1914), 182p.*
TRASK, D F
The United States in the Supreme War Council: American war aims and inter-Allied strategy 1917–1918 *(Westport, Conn: Greenwood 1978), 244p.*
World War I at home: readings on American life, 1914-1920 *(New York: Wiley 1970), 212p.*
USHER, R G
Pan-Americanism: a forecast of the clash between the U.S., and Europe's victor *(New York: Century 1915), 466p.*
WALKER, J B
America fallen!: the sequel to the European war *(London: Putnam 1915), 158p.*
THE WAR from this side *(Philadelphia, Pa: Lippincott 1916), 2 vols.*
WARD, F W
Between the big parades *(New York: Waterbury 1932), 284p.*
WELSH, D
The USA in World War I *(New York:Galahad 1982), 64p.*
WHITE, J W
America and Germany: a textbook of the war *(London: Fisher Unwin 1915), 551p.*
America's arraignment of Germany *(London: Harrap 1915), 143p.*
WHITRIDGE, F W
One American's opinion of the European war: an answer to Germany's appeals *(New York: Dutton 1915), 100p.*
WILKINSON, S
Government and the war *(New York: McBride 1918), 268p.*

WILLOUGHBY, W F
Government organization in war time and after: a survey of the Federal civil agencies created for the prosecution of the war *(New York: Appleton 1919), 370p.*

WILSON, H R
The education of a diplomat *(London: Longmans 1938), 224p.*

WOOD, E F
The writing on the wall: the nation on trial *(New York: Century 1916), 208p.*

THE WORLD'S peril: America's interest in the war *(Princeton, NJ: Princeton UP 1917), 245p.*

ZOOK, G F
America at war: a series of illustrated lectures on American war activities *(Washington DC: Committee on Public Information 1918), 9 vols.*

UNITED STATES (American-Germans)

CHILD, C J
The German-Americans in politics, 1914-1917 *(Madison: University of Wisconsin P 1939), 193p.*

HAGEDORN, H
Where do you stand?: an appeal to Americans of German origin *(New York: Macmillan 1918), 126p.*

LUEBKE, F C
Bonds of loyalty: German-Americans and World War I *(De Kalb, Ill: Northern Illinois UP 1974), 366p.*

OHLINGER, G
Their true faith and allegiance: the position of the German-Americans in the United States *(New York: Macmillan 1916), 124p.*

SKAGGS, W H
German conspiracies in America *(London: Fisher Unwin 1915), 332p.*

WILE, F W
The German-American plot: a record of a great failure *(London: Pearson 1915), 128p.*

WITTKE, C
German-Americans and the World War: with special emphasis on Ohio's German language Press *(Columbus, Ohio: Ohio State Archives Society 1936), 223p.*

UNITED STATES (intervention)

BAKER, N D
Why we went to war *(New York: Harper 1936), 199p.*

BASS, H J *comp*
America's entry into World War I: submarines, sentiment, or security? *(New York: Holt 1964), 122p; bib.*

BECK, J M
The war and humanity: the ethics of the war and the attitude and duty of the United States *(New York: Putnam 1917), 397p.*

BULLARD, A
Mobilising America *(New York: Macmillan 1917), 129p.*
CASTLE, W R
Wake up, America *(New York: Dodd 1916), 111p.*
CHAMBERLAIN, T G
Why we fought *(New York: Macmillan 1919), 93p.*
COHEN, W I
The American revisionists: the lessons of intervention in World War I *(Chicago: Chicago UP 1967), 252p.*
CROWELL, B *and* WILSON, R F
How America went to war: our mobilization and control of industry and natural resources *(New Haven, Conn: Yale UP 1921), 6 vols.*
GRATTAN, C H
Why we fought *(New York: Vanguard 1929), 453p.*
HAGEDORN, H
The bugle that woke America: the saga of Theodore Roosevelt's last battle for his country *(New York: Day 1940), 223p.*
MARTIN, E S
Diary of a nation: the war and how we got into it *(New York: Doubleday 1917), 407p.*
MILLIS, W
Road to war: America 1914-1917 *(London: Faber 1935), 466p.*
SMITH, D M *ed*
American intervention, 1917 *(Boston, Mass: Houghton Mifflin 1960), 260p.*
SPENCER, S R *jr*
Decision for war, 1917: the Laconia sinking and the Zimmerman telegram as key factors in the public reaction against Germany *(West Ringge, NH: R. R. Smith 1953), 109p.*
TANSILL, C C
America goes to war *(Boston, Mass: Little, Brown 1938), 731p.*

UNITED STATES (neutrality)

BALDWIN, J M
American neutrality: its cause and cure *(New York: Putnam 1916), 139p.*
BORCHARD, E M
Neutrality for the United States *(New York: AMS 1973), 461p.*
GIFFIN, F C
Six who protested: radical opposition to the First World War *(Port Washington, Conn: Kennikat 1977), 158p.*
MAY, E R
The World War and American isolation, 1914-1917 *(London: OUP 1959), 482p; bib.*
NICHOLSON, J S
The neutrality of the United States in relation to the British and German Empires *(London: Macmillan 1915), 92p.*
PETERSON, H C
Propaganda for war: the campaign against American neutrality, 1914-1917 *(Norman, Okl: Oklahoma UP 1939), 357p.*

SEYMOUR, C
American neutrality, 1914-1917: essays on the causes of American intervention in the World War *(New Haven, Conn: Yale UP 1935), 187p.*

STEPHEN, S I *pseud*
Neutrality: the crucifixion of public opinion *(Chicago: Open Court 1916), 227p.*

UNITED STATES ARMY (preparedness)

ANGELL, N
The dangers of half-preparedness: a plea for a declaration of American policy *(New York: Putnam 1916), 129p.*

CROZIER, W
Ordnance and the World War: a contribution to the history of America's preparedness *(New York: Scribner 1920), 292p.*

FINNEGAN, J P
Against the specter of a dragon: the campaign for American military preparedness, 1914-1917 *(Westport, Conn: Greenwood 1975), 253p.*

FORD, J L
Waitful watching; or, Uncle Sam and the fight in Dame Europa's school *(New York: Stokes 1916), 56p.*

FREEMAN, W
Awake! U.S.A. *(New York: Doran 1916), 453p.*

HORNADAY, W T
Awake! America: object lessons and warnings *(New York: Moffat 1918), 197p.*

HUIDEKOPER, F L
The military unpreparedness of the United States: a history of American Land Forces from Colonial times until June 1, 1915 *(London: Macmillan 1915), 735p.*

HULL, W I
Preparedness: the American versus the military programme *(New York: Revell 1916), 271p.*

KELLOR, F A
Straight America: a call to national service *(New York: Macmillan 1916), 193p.*

KIMBALL, W W
Our question of questions: arm or disarm? *(Washington DC: Navy 1917), 131p.*

MAXIM, H
Defenceless America *(London: Hodder & Stoughton 1915), 251p.*

MULLER, J W
The A B C of national defence: what the Army and Navy would have to do in war, why they would have to do it, and what they need for successful performance *(New York: Dutton 1915), 215p.*

WHEELER, H D
Are we ready?: a study of the preparedness for war in the United States of America *(Boston, Mass: Houghton Mifflin 1915), 227p.*

UNITED STATES ARMY (general)

ABBEY, E A
An American soldier: letters *(Boston, Mass: Houghton Mifflin 1918), 173p.*
ADAMS, R E C
Modern crusaders *(New York: Dutton 1920), 183p.*
ALBERTINE, C
The Yankee doughboy *(Boston, Mass: Branden 1968), 306p.*
ALDRICH, M
When Johnny comes marching home *(Boston, Mass: Small 1919), 286p.*
ALEXANDER, R
Memories of the World War, 1917-1918 *(New York: Macmillan 1931), 309p.*
AMERINE, W H
Alabama's own in France *(New York: Eaton & Gettinger 1919), 416p.*
BALDWIN, H
Holding the line *(Chicago: McClurg 1918), 305p.*
BARNES, J F
The genesis of the American First Army *(Washington DC: Army War College 1929), 81p.*
BEAMISH, R J *and* MARCH, F A
America's part in the World War *(Philadelphia, Pa: Winston 1919), 608p.*
BELTON, J *and* ODELL, E G
Hunting the Hun *(New York: Appleton 1918), 269p.*
BERRY, H
Make the Kaiser dance: living memories of the doughboy *(New York: Arbor 1984), 455p.*
BROUN, H
The A.E.F.: with General Pershing and the American Forces *(New York: Appleton 1918), 297p.*
BULLARD, R L *and* REEVES, E
American soldiers also fought *(New York: Longmans 1936), 118p.*
BUTTERS, H A
Harry Butters: life and war letters *(New York: Lane 1917), 297p.*
CANNONEERS *pseud*
The cannoneers have hairy ears: a diary of the Front lines *(New York: Sears 1927), 337p.*
CARSTAIRS, C
A generation missing: a personal record of the European war *(London: Heinemann 1930), 208p.*
CHAMBRUN, J A *and* MARENCHES, C de
The American Army in the European conflict *(New York: Macmillan 1919), 436p.*
CHASE, J C
Soldiers all: portraits and sketches of the men of the A.E.F. *(New York: Doran 1920), 475p.*
COBB, I S
The glory of the coming: what mine eyes have seen of Americans in action *(London: Hodder & Stoughton 1919), 463p.*
CLARK, G W *ed*
S.S.U.503 of the U.S. Army Ambulance service with the French Army *(Philadelphia, Pa: Clark 1921), 60p.*

COWAN, S K
Sergeant York and his people *(New York: Funk 1922), 292p.*
CRAWFORD, C
Six months with the Sixth Brigade *(Kansas City: Barnett 1928), 220p.*
DAWES, C G
A journal of the Great War *(Boston, Mass: Houghton Mifflin 1921), 2 vols.*
DAWSON, C W
Out to win: the story of America in France *(London: Lane 1918), 196p.*
The unknown soldier *(New York: Doubleday 1929), 60p.*
DE CASTELBLED, M *comp*
History of the A.E.F. *(Miami, Fla: De Castelbled 1937), 172p.*
DE VARILA, O
The first shot for liberty: the story of an American who went over with the first Expeditionary Force *(Philadelphia, Pa: Winston 1918), 223p.*
DICKINSON, J
The building of an Army: a detailed account of legislation, administration and opinion in the United States, 1915-1920 *(New York: Century 1922), 298p.*
DICKMAN, J T
The great crusade: a narrative of the World War *(New York: Appleton 1927), 313p.*
ELY, D
Dinsmore Ely: one who served *(Chicago: McClurg 1919), 215p.*
EMMETT, C
Give way on the right: serving with the A.E.F. in France during the war *(San Antonio: Naylor 1934), 302p.*
FERGUSSON, R M
With the American Army in France: diary of a lecture tour *(Paisley, Scot: 1919), 63p.*
FORD, B
Fighting Yankees overseas *(Boston, Mass: McPhail 1919), 259p.*
FORD, T
Cheer-up letters from a Private with Pershing *(New York: Clode 1918), 192p.*
FREIDEL, F B
Over there: the story of America's first great overseas crusade *(Boston, Mass: Little, Brown 1964), 385p.*
GIBSON, P
Battering the Boche *(New York: Century 1918), 120p.*
GLEASON, A H
Our part in the Great War *(New York: Burt 1911), 338p.*
GLEASON, A H *and* GLEASON, H H
Golden lads: eye-witnesses' stories of the European war *(New York: Century 1916), 262p.*
GRASTY, C H
Flashes from the Front *(New York: Century 1918), 306p.*
HARBORD, J G
The American Army in France, 1917-1919 *(Boston, Mass: Little, Brown 1936), 632p.*
Leaves from a war diary *(New York: Dodd 1931), 407p.*
HARRISON, H S
When I come back: memoir of an American soldier *(London: Constable 1920), 62p.*

HAY, I *pseud*
All in it: K (I) carries on *(New York: Grosset 1918), 238p.*
HERZOG, S J
Fightin' Yanks *(Stanford, Conn: Herzog 1922), 116p.*
HOEHLING, A A
Fierce lambs *(Boston, Mass: Little, Brown 1960), 210p.*
HOLMES, R D
A Yankee in the trenches *(Boston, Mass: Little, Brown 1918), 214p.*
HOPKINS, N M
Over the threshold of war: personal experiences *(Philadelphia, Pa: Lippincott 1918), 375p.*
JOHNSON, T M
Without censor: new light on our greatest World War battles *(Indianapolis, Ind: Bobbs-Merrill 1928), 411p.*
JOHNSON, T M *and* PRATT, F
The lost Battalion *(Indianapolis, Ind: Bobbs-Merrill 1938), 338p.*
JUDY, W
A soldier's diary: a day-by-day record in the World War *(Chicago: Judy 1930), 216p.*
KEHOE, T J
Fighting mascot: the true story of a boy soldier *(New York: Dodd 1918), 237p.*
LAWRENCE, J D
Fighting soldier: the American Expeditionary Force in 1918 *(Boulder, Col: Colorado 1985), 165p.*
LONERGAN, T C
It might have been lost!: a chronicle from alien sources of the struggles to preserve the national identity of the A.E.F. *(New York: Putnam 1929), 327p.*
LOOMIS, E L *comp*
History of the 304th Ammunition train *(Boston, Mass: Badger 1920), 244p.*
MACBRIDE, H W
The Emma Gees *(Indianapolis, Ind: Bobbs-Merrill 1918), 219p.*
MCCORMICK, R R
The Army of 1918 *(New York: Harcourt 1920), 276p.*
MACQUARRIE, H
How to live at the Front: tips for American soldiers *(Philadelphia, Pa: Lippincott 1917), 269p.*
MACVEACH, E C
The Yankee in the British zone *(New York: Putnam 1920), 418p.*
MACK, A J
Shellproof Mack: an American's fighting story *(Boston, Mass: Small 1918), 224p.*
MARCOSSON, L F
S.O.S.: America's miracle in France *(London: Lane 1919), 346p.*
MILLER, W H
The boys of 1917: famous American heroes of the World War *(Boston, Mass: Page 1939), 452p.*
MORIAE, E
A soldier of the Legion *(Boston, Mass: Houghton Mifflin 1916), 128p.*

MORRIS, C
Heroes of the Army *(Philadelphia, Pa: Lippincott 1919), 354p.*
OTTOSEN, P H
Trench artillery, A.E.F.: the personal experiences of lieutenants and captains of artillery who served with trench mortars *(Boston, Mass: Lothrop 1931), 367p.*
PALMER, F
America in France: the story of the making of an Army *(London: Murray 1919), 378p.*
Our greatest battle – the Meuse–Argonne *(New York: Dodd 1919), 629p.*
POWELL, E A
The Army behind the Army *(New York: Scribner 1919), 470p.*
Fighting in Flanders *(New York: Grosset 1918), 231p.*
PUGH, I E *and* THAYER, W F
Forgotten fights of the A.E.F.: seven battlefront maps *(Boston, Mass: Roxburgh 1921), 141p.*
RIGGS, A S
With three Armies on and behind the Western Front *(Indianapolis, Ind: Bobbs-Merrill 1918), 303p.*
ROGERS, H
World War I through my sights *(San Rafael, Cal: Presidio 1977), 268p.*
SKILLMAN, W R
A.E.F., who they were! what they did! how they did it! *(Philadelphia, Pa: Jacobs 1920), 231p.*
STALLINGS, L
The Doughboys: the story of the A.E.F., 1917-1918 *(New York: Harper 1963), 405p; bib.*
STERNE, E
Over the seas for Uncle Sam *(Cleveland, Ohio: Britton 1918), 264p.*
STONE, E
Battery B thru the fires of France *(Los Angeles, Cal: Wayside 1919), 242p.*
STRINGFELLOW, J S
Hell! no! this and that: a narrative of the Great War *(Boston, Mass: Meador 1936), 362p.*
SWAN, C J
My company *(Boston, Mass: Houghton Mifflin 1918), 263p.*
THOMAS, L J
This side of hell: Dan Edwards, adventurer *(London: Long 1933), 255p.*
Woodfill of the Regulars: a true story of adventure from the Arctic to the Argonne *(London: Heinemann 1930), 325p.*
THOMAS, S
The history of the A.E.F. *(New York: Doran 1920), 540p.*
UNITED STATES Army War College
Order of battle of the United States Land Forces in the World War: American Expeditionary Force *(Washington DC: 1931), 451p.*
UNITED STATES War Department
Battle participation of organizations of the American Expeditionary Force in France, Belgium and Italy, 1917-1918 *(Washington DC: 1920), 106p.*
U.S. Army in the World War, 1917-1918 *(Washington DC: 1948), 17 vols.*
VAN EVERY, D
The A.E.F. in battle *(New York: Appleton 1928), 385p.*

WALDO, F L
America at the Front *(New York: Dutton 1918), 170p.*
WATERS, W W
B.E.F. (i.e. Bonus Expeditionary Force): the whole story of the Bonus Army *(New York: Day 1933), 288p.*
WERNER, M R
'Orderly!' *(London: Cape 1930), 214p.*
WERSTEIN, I
The lost battalion *(New York: Norton 1966), 191p.*
WHEELER, C
Letters from an American soldier to his father *(Indianapolis, Ind: Bobbs-Merrill 1918), 113p.*
WOOLLCOTT, A
The command is forward: tales of the A.E.F., battlefields *(New York: Century 1919), 304p.*
WRENTMORE, E L
In spite of hell: a factual story of incidents that occurred during World War I *(New York: Greenwich 1958), 193p.*
YOAKUM, C S *and* YERKES, R M
Mental tests in the American Army *(London: Sidgwick & Jackson 1920), 303p.*
YORK, A C
Sergeant York: his own life story and war diary *(New York: Doubleday 1928), 309p.*

UNITED STATES ARMY (Divisions)

SCIPIO, L A
With the Red Hand division *(Silver Springs, Md: Roman 1985), 175p.*
BENWELL, H A
History of the Yankee Division *(Cornhill: 1919), 283p.*
SIBLEY, F P
With the Yankee Division in France *(Boston, Mass: Little, Brown 1919), 365p.*
WASHBURN, S
One of the Y.D. (Yankee Division) *(Boston, Mass: Houghton Mifflin 1919), 163p.*
MILLER, H R
First Division *(Pittsburgh, Pa: Crescent 1920), 49p.*
SECOND Division, American Expeditionary Force in France *(New York: Hillman 1937), 412p.*
SOCIETY OF THE FIFTH DIVISION
Official history of the Fifth Division, United States Army *(Washington DC: 1919), 423p.*
UNITED STATES Department of War
Records of the World War Field Orders, 1918: 5th Division *(Washington DC: 1921), 175p.*
FELL, E T *comp*
History of the Seventh Division, United States Army, 1917-1919 *(Philadelphia, Pa: 7th Division Officers Association nd), 261p.*

FORBES, *Lady* H E
Saga of the Seventh Division *(London: Lane 1920), 74p.*
GEORGE, A E *and* COOPER, E H
Pictorial history of the Twenty-sixth Division, United States Army *(Boston, Mass: Ball 1920), 320p.*
TAYLOR, E G
New England in France, 1917-1919: a history of the Twenty-sixth Division, United States Army *(Boston, Mass: Houghton Mifflin 1920), 325p.*
O'RYAN, J F
Story of the 27th Division *(New York: Wynkoop Crawford 1922), 2 vols.*
PROCTOR, H G
Iron Division, National Guard of Pennsylvania in the World War [28th Division] *(Philadelphia, Pa: Winston 1919), 296p.*
BOWEN, W S
Source book: operations of the 29th Division, East of the Meuse River, October 8th to 30th, 1918 *(Fort Monroe, Va: Coast Artillery Journal nd), 2 vols.*
CUTCHINS, J A *and* STEWART, G S
History of the Twenty-ninth Division; Blue and Grey, 1917-1919 *(Philadelphia, Pa: Stewart 1921), 493p.*
MURPHY, E A *and* THOMAS, R S
Thirtieth Division in the World War *(Lepanto, Ark: Old Hickory 1937), 342p.*
WISCONSIN WAR HISTORY COMMITTEE
32nd Division in the World War *(Milwaukee, Wis: 1920), 319p.*
HUIDEKOPER, F L
The history of the 33rd Division, American Expeditionary Force *(Springfield, Ill: 1921), 4 vols.*
CARTER, R L
Pictorial history of the 35th Division *(St. Louis: Carter 1933), unp.*
KENAMORE, C
From Vanquois Hill to Exermont: a history of the 35th Division of the United States Army *(St. Louis: Guard 1919), 435p.*
CHASTAINE, B H
Story of the 36th: the experiences of the 36th Division in the World War *(Oklahoma City: Harford 1920), 291p.*
KOONS, J F
Billets and bullets of 37 Division *(Cincinnati: Bacharach 1919), 217p.*
HISTORY of the Fortieth (Sunshine) Division *(Los Angeles, Cal: Hutson 1920), 179p.*
BROWN, W J
Child Yank over the Rainbow Division, 1918 [42nd Division] *(Largo, Fla: Aero-Medical 1975), 289p.*
LANGILLE, L
Men of the Rainbow [42nd Division] *(Chicago: Langille 1933), 203p.*
REILLY, H J
Americans all; the Rainbow at war: official history of the 42nd Rainbow Division in the war *(Columbus, Ohio: Heer 1936), 888p.*
TOMPKINS, R S
Story of the Rainbow Division *(New York: Bonn & Liveright 1919), 264p.*

SMALL, G W *comp*
Story of the Forty-seventh *(Mount Washington, Md: Small 1919), 200p.*
DUFFY, F P
Father Duffy's story: life and death with the fighting Sixty-ninth *(New York: Doran 1920), 382p.*
HOGAN, M J
The Shamrock Battalion of the Rainbow: a story of the 'Fighting' Sixty-ninth *(New York: Appleton 1919), 279p.*
CROSBY, P L
Between shots: with the 77th Division in France *(New York: Harper 1919), 94p.*
McKEOGH, A
Victorious 77th Division (New York's Own) in the Argonne fight *(New York: Eggers 1919), 30p.*
MEEHAN, T F *ed*
History of the Seventy-eighth Division in the World War, 1917-18-19 *(New York: Dodd 1922), 243p.*
PICTORIAL history of the 78th Division in France *(New York: Cochrane 1920), 55p.*
HISTORY of the Seventy-ninth Division, A.E.F. during the World War, 1917-1919 *(Lancaster, Pa: Steinman 1922), 510p.*
OFFICIAL history of 82nd Division, American Expeditionary Force: All American Division *(Indianapolis, Ind: Bobbs-Merrill 1920), 310p.*
88TH Division in the World War of 1914-1918 *(Wynkorp: Hallenbeck Crawford 1919), 236p.*
LARSON, E J D *comp*
Memoirs of France and the Eighty-eighth Division *(St. Paul, Minn: 1920), 173p.*
ENGLISH, G H *jr*
History of the 89th Division, United States Army *(Denver, Co: War Society of the 89th Division 1920), 511p.*
STORY of the 91st Division *(San Mateo, Cal: 91st Division 1919), 177p.*

UNITED STATES ARMY (Infantry)

PATCH, J D
A soldier's war: the 1st Infantry Division, A.E.F., 1917-1918 *(Corpus Christi, Tex: Patch 1966), 171p.*
POLLARD, J E
Forty-seventh Infantry: a history, 1917-1918 *(Columbus, Ohio: Pollard 1920), 183p.*
MABRY, G *comp*
Recollections of a recruit: an official history of the Fifty-fourth United States Infantry *(New York: Schilling 1919), 237p.*
FRANCIS, A T
History of the 71st Regiment *(New York: Joyce 1919), 900p.*
SUTLIFFE, R S *comp*
Seventy-first New York in the World War *(New York: 71st Infantry 1922), 522p.*
YOUNG, R S
Over the top with the 80th, 1917–1919 *(Washington DC: Young 1935), 156p.*

HENDERSON, A P
Ninety-first: the first at Camp Lewis *(Tacoma, Wash: Bass, 1918), 510p.*
SHORT history and illustrated roster of the 105th Infantry, Army of the United States *(Chicago: Stern 1918), 117p.*
SHORT history and illustrated roster of the 106th Infantry, Army of the United States *(Chicago: Stern 1918), 119p.*
JACOBSON, G F *comp*
History of the 107th Infantry, United States Army *(New York: Jacobson 1920), 546p.*
SHORT history and illustrated roster of the 107th Infantry, Army of the United States *(Chicago: Stern 1918), 56p.*
SHORT history and illustrated roster of the 108th Infantry, Army of the United States *(Chicago: Stern 1918), 117p.*
SHORT history and illustrated roster of the 110th Infantry, Army of the United States *(Chicago: Stern 1918), 134p.*
COOPER, G W
Our second battalion: the accurate and authentic history of the Second Battalion, 111th Infantry *(Pittsburgh, Pa: Second Bn. 1920), 299p.*
SHORT history and illustrated roster of the 111th Infantry, Army of the United States *(Chicago: Stern 1918), 134p.*
SHORT history and illustrated roster of the 112th Infantry, Army of the United States *(Chicago: Stern 1918), 136p.*
REYNOLDS, F C *ed*
115th Infantry, United States Army in the war *(Baltimore: Read-Taylor 1920), 241p.*
CONWAY, C B *and* SHUFORD, G A *comps*
History of the 119th Infantry, 60th Brigade, 30th Division, United States Army *(Wilmington, NC: Chamber of Commerce 1920), 140p.*
WALKER, J O *and others*
Official history of the 120th Infantry, 3rd North Carolina, 30th Division from August 5, 1917 to April 17th, 1919 *(Lynchburg, Va: Bell 1919), 56p.*
SCHMIDT, P W
Co.C, 127 Infantry in the World War: a story of the 32nd Division *(Sheboygan, Wis: Press 1919), 189p.*
HATERIUS, C E *comp*
Reminiscences of the 137th U.S. Infantry *(Topeka, Kan: Crane 1919), 256p.*
KENAMORE, C
Story of the 139th Infantry *(St. Louis: Guard 1920), 167p.*
JOHNSON, R N
Heaven, hell or Hoboken *(Cleveland: Johnson 1919), 198p.*
ROBB, W E
The price of our heritage: in memory of the heroic dead of the 168 Infantry *(Des Moines, Io: Robb 1919), 417p.*
TABER, J H
Story of the 168th Infantry *(Iowa: Iowa State Historical Society 1925), 2 vols.*
TIEBOUT, F B
History of the 305th Infantry *(New York: Tiebout 1919), 432p.*

RAINSFORD, W K
From Upton to the Meuse with the Three Hundred and Seventh Infantry *(New York: Appleton 1920), 297p.*

MILES, L W
History of the 308th Infantry, 1917–1919 *(New York: Putnam 1927), 357p.*

COLONNA, B A
History of Company B, 311th Infantry in the World War *(New York: Stiles 1922), 113p.*

THORN, H C *jr*
History of 313th U.S. Infantry, Baltimore's Own *(Wynkoop: Hallenbeck Crawford 1920), 77p.*

HERR, C R
Company F history, 319th Infantry *(Sommerville, NJ: Unionist Gazette 1920), 103p.*

JOHNSON, C W
History of the 321st Infantry *(Columbia, SC: Bryan 1919), 201p.*

COMPANY log, 332nd Infantry, A.E.F., from September 7, 1917–May 2, 1919 *(Cleveland, Ohio: Britton 1920), 75p.*

LETTAU, J L
In Italy with the 332nd Infantry *(Youngstown, Ohio: Lettau 1921), 76p.*

FISKE, P M *ed*
History of the Three Hundred Fiftieth Regiment of the U.S. Infantry, Eighty-eighth Division American Expeditionary Force *(Cedar Rapids, Io: Laurance 1920), 235p.*

ROSS, W O *and* SLAUGHTER, D L *comps*
With the 351st in France *(Baltimore: Afro-American 1919), 52p.*

BURTON, H H *ed*
600 days' service: a history of the 361st Infantry Regiment of the United States Army *(Portland, Ore: Kanzier 1921), 276p.*

HEYWOOD, C D
Negro combat troops in the World War: the story of the 371st Infantry *(Worcester, Mass: Commonwealth 1929), 310p.*

AMERICAN ARMY (Engineers)

PARSONS, W B
The American Engineers in France (New York: Appleton 1920), 429p.

TOMLIN, R K
American engineers behind the battle lines in France *(New York: McGraw Hill 1918), 91p.*

BOUGHTON, V T
History of the Eleventh Engineers, United States Army, Feb 3, 1917-May 8, 1919 *(Plainfield, NJ: Boughton 1926), 539p.*

HENDERSON, R G *ed*
History of the Fourteenth Engineers, United States Army, from May, 1917 to May, 1919 *(Boston, Mass: Atlantic 1923), 195p.*

HISTORY of the Twenty-sixth Engineers (Water Supply Regiment) in the World War *(New York: Angell, Goulds 1920), 258p.*

HISTORY of the 27th Engineers, United States Army, 1917-1919 *(Broadway, NY: The Association 1920), 94p.*

STORY of E Company, 101st Engineers, 26th Division *(Boston, Mass: The Company 1919)*, *152p.*

WEAVER, F N *and* SANBORN, P N

Story of F Company, 101st Regiment U.S. Engineers *(Boston, Mass: Metcalf 1924), 174p.*

SULLIVAN, W P *and* TUCKER, H S *comps*

History of the 105th Regiment of Engineers; Divisional Engineers of the Old Hickory (30th) Division *(New York: Doran 1919), 466p.*

WEAVER, E J

Three Hundred and First Engineers: a history, 1917-1919 *(Boston, Mass: Houghton Mifflin 1920), 310p.*

ROTH, J P C *and* WHEELER, R L *comps*

History of Company E, 303rd Engineers of the 78th Division, 1917-1919 *(Rochester, NY: Roth 1919), 224p.*

OFFICIAL history of the Three Hundred and Fourth Engineers Regiment, Seventy-ninth Division, U.S.A. during the World War *(Philadelphia, Pa: 304th Engineers 1920), 415p.*

AMERICAN ARMY (Field Artillery)

BEING the story of a light field artillery battery from Illinois during the World War *(Chicago: Gunthrop-Warren 1930), 257p.*

DUFF, J L

The Eleventh Field Artillery *(Dijon, France: 1919), 214p.*

BACON, W J *ed*

History of the Fifty-fifth Field Artillery Brigade, 1917, 1918, 1919 *(Memphis, Tenn: Bacon 1920), 335p.*

CUTLER, F M

55th Artillery (C.A.C.) in the American Expeditionary Force, France 1918 *(Worcester, Mass: Commonwealth 1920), 413p.*

HARLOW, R F

Trail of the 61st: a history of the 61st Field Artillery Brigade during the World War, 1917-1919 *(Oklahoma City: Harlow 1920), 231p.*

BEING the narrative of Battery A, of the 101st Field Artillery *(Boston, Mass: Loomis 1919), 269p.*

CARTER, R G

101st Field Artillery, A.E.F., 1917-1919 *(Boston, Mass: Houghton Mifflin 1940), 305p.*

SHORT history and photographic record of the 101st Field Artillery 1917 *(Cambridge, Mass: University P 1918), 60p.*

SHORT history and photographic record of the 102nd Field Artillery 1918 *(Cambridge, Mass: University P 1918), 58p.*

SIROIS, E D *and* McGINNIS, W

Smashing through the World War with fighting battery C, 102nd Field Artillery, Yankee Division, 1917, 1918, 1919 *(Lawrence, Mass: Sirois 1919), 176p.*

KERNAN, W F *and* SAMSON, H T

History of the 103rd Field Artillery (Twenty-sixth Division) A.E.F. World War, 1917-1919 *(Providence, RI: Marine Corps of Artillery 1937), 255p.*

BUCKLEW, L L *comp*
Orphan Battery and operations, 128th U.S. Field Artillery *(Cleveland, Ohio: Bucklew 1921), 115p.*

KIRTLEY, L E *ed*
Liaison, a history of Regimental Headquarters Company, One Hundred Thirty-fourth U.S. Field Artillery *(Dayton, Ohio: Otterbein 1919), 145p.*

RED Guidon (Soixante Quinze): being a complete illustrated history of B Battery, 134th Field Artillery from 1915 to 1919 *(Akron, Ohio: Red Guidon Association 1920), 234p.*

WITT, F R
Riding to war with 'A': a history of Battery 'A' of the 135th Field Artillery *(Cleveland, Ohio: Witt 1919), 186p.*

COFFIN, L *and* SANDERS, C H *comps*
History of the Third Field Artillery, Ohio National Guard, which served through the World War, 1917-1919, as the 136th Field Artillery, U.S.A. *(Cincinnati, Ohio: Mitchell 1928), 458p.*

MOORHEAD, R L
Story of the 139th Field Artillery, American Expeditionary Force *(Indianapolis, Ind: Bobbs-Merrill 1920), 468p.*

CLAY, H K *and* DAVIS, P M
History of Battery C, 148th Field Artillery, American Expeditionary Force *(Colorado Springs, Col: Davis & Clay 1919), 300p.*

COLLINS, L L
History of the 151st Field Artillery, Rainbow Division *(St. Paul: Minnesota Historical Society 1924), 427p.*

RUSSELL, R M
151st Field Artillery Brigade *(Cornhill: 1919), 50p.*

302ND FIELD ARTILLERY ASSOCIATION
302nd Field Artillery, United States Army *(Cambridge, Mass: Lane 1919), 172p.*

GLASS, J *and others*
Story of Battery D, 304th Field Artillery, September 1917 to May 1919 *(New York: Commanday-Roth 1919), 112p.*

HOWARD, J M
Autobiography of a Regiment: a history of the 304th Field Artillery in the World War *(Morristown, NJ: Howard 1920), 310p.*

CAMP, C W
History of the 305th Field Artillery *(New York: Doubleday 1919), 361p.*

MCCARTHY, W E
Memories of the 309th Field Artillery *(Rochester, NY: Connolly 1920), 193p.*

BACHMAN, W E
Delta of the triple elevens: the history of Battery D, 311th Field Artillery, United States Army, American Expeditionary Force *(Hazleton, Pa: Bachman 1920), 143p.*

HISTORY of the 313th Field Artillery, United States Army *(New York: Cowell 1920), 299p.*

HISTORY of the 322nd Field Artillery *(New Haven, Conn: Yale UP 1920), 511p.*

RIGGS, M H *and* PLATT, R H
History of Battery F, 323 Field Artillery *(Cleveland, Ohio: Dempsey 1920), 154p.*

ASHBURN, T Q
History of the 324th Field Artillery, United States Army *(New York: Doran 1920), 141p.*

ALLEN, W M *ed*
The 331st Field Artillery, United States Army, 1917-1919 *(Dixon, Ill: Rogers 1919), 509p.*

UNITED STATES ARMY (Machine Gunners)

BAKER, L S
Company history: the story of Company B, 106th Machine Gun Battalion, 27th Division, United States Army *(Published by the Company: 1920), 135p.*
KUHN, W R *ed*
Narrative of Company A, 106th Machine Gun Battalion, 27th Division, United States Army in the Great War *(New York: Patterson 1919), 144p.*
WESTOVER, W
Suicide Battalion: experiences in a United States Machine Gun Battalion *(New York: Putnam 1929), 278p.*
WHITNEY, S
Squadron A in the Great War, 1917-1918, including a narrative of the 105th Machine Gun Brigade *(New York: Squadron A Association 1923), 464p.*

UNITED STATES ARMY (Air Division)

ARCHIBALD, N S
Heaven high, hell deep, 1917-1918 *(London: Heinemann 1935), 352p.*
BINGHAM, H
An explorer in the Air Service *(New Haven, Conn: Yale UP 1920), 260p.*
CAMPBELL, G F
Soldier of the sky *(Chicago: Davis 1918), 232p.*
CARVER, L M *and others*
Ninetieth Aero Squadron, American Expeditionary Force: a history of its activities during the World War *(Hinsdale, Ill: Greist 1920), 91p.*
DRAKE, V
Above the battle: experiences of an airman *(New York: Appleton 1918), 322p.*
FITCH, W S
Wings in the night *(Boston, Mass: Jones, Marshall 1938), 302p.*
GENET, E
War letters: the First American aviator killed flying the Stars and Stripes *(New York: Scribner 1918), 330p.*
HAINES, D H
Dragon flies: a tale of the Flying Service *(Boston, Mass: Houghton Mifflin 1919), 299p.*
HART, P G
History of the 135th Aero Squadron from July 25 to November 11, 1918 *(Chicago: Hart 1939), 178p.*
HARTNEY, H E
Up and at 'em *(Harrisburg, Pa: Stackpole 1940), 360p. U.K. title:* Wings over France.

HUDSON, J T
  Hostile skies: a combat history of the American Air Service in World War I *(Syracuse, NY: Syracuse UP 1968), 338p.*
KEEZER, W S
  Men of the Twentieth *(Manhattan, Kan: Aerospace 1974), unp.*
MARSH, H R
  Nine-nine lives: the amazing adventures of Charles Veil *(London: Bles 1934), 316p.*
MOLTER, B A
  Knights of the air *(New York: Appleton 1918), 243p.*
MORSE, D P
  History of the 50th Aero Squadron *(New York: Blanchard 1920), 94p.*
RICKENBACKER, E V
  Fighting the flying circus *(New York: Doubleday 1965), 296p.*
ROBERTS, E M
  A flying fighter: an American above the lines in France *(New York: Harper 1918), 338p.*
SPRINGS, E W
  War birds: the diary of an unknown aviator *(London: Hamilton 1931), 166p.*
SUETER, M F
  Airmen or Noahs: fair play for our airmen *(New York: Putnam 1928), 448p.*
TAYLOR, W P *and* IRVIN, F L *comps*
  Francis L. Spike Irvin's war diary, and the history of the 148th Aero Squadron Aviation Section *(Manhattan, Kan: Aerospace 1974), unp.*
TOULMIN, H A
  Air service, American Expeditionary Force, 1918 *(New York: Van Nostrand 1927), 388p.*
WALCOTT, S
  Above the French lines: letters of Stuart Walcott, American aviator *(Princeton, NJ: Princeton UP 1918), 93p.*

UNITED STATES MARINES

ABBOT, W J
  Soldiers of the sea: the story of the United States Marine Corps *(New York: Dodd 1918), 315p.*
CATLIN, A W
  'With the help of God, and a few Marines': the U.S. Marine Corps during the European war *(London: Curtis Brown 1919), 425p.*
COWING, K F *comp*
  'Dear folks at home ...': the glorious story of the U.S. Marines in France *(Boston, Mass: Houghton Mifflin 1919), 288p.*
HEMRICK, L E
  Once a Marine *(New York: Carlton 1968), 195p.*
HISTORY of the Third Battalion Sixth Regiment, United States Marines *(Hillsdale, Mich: Akers 1919), 130p.*
MACCLELLAN, E N
  The U.S. Marine Corps in the World War *(Washington DC: 1920), 108p.*

RENDINELL, J E *and* PATTULLO, G
One man's war: the diary of a leatherneck *(New York: Sears 1928), 177p.*
SUSKIND, R
The battle of Belleau Wood: the Marines stand fast *(London: Collier-Macmillan 1964), 86p; bib.*
THOMASON, J W
Fix bayonets!: experiences with the 1st Battalion, 5th Regiment, U.S. Marine Corps in France, 1917-18 *(New York: Scribner 1926), 245p.*
WISE, F M
A Marine tells it to you *(New York: Sears 1929), 365p.*

UNITED STATES NAVY

ABBOT, W J
Blue jackets of 1918: the story of the work of the American Navy in the World War *(New York: Dodd 1921), 311p.*
BATTEY, G M *jr*
70,000 miles on a submarine destroyer; or, The Reid boat in the World War *(Atlanta, Ga: Battey 1920), 448p.*
BESTON, H B
Full speed ahead: tales from the log of a correspondent with our Navy *(New York: Doubleday 1919), 254p.*
COLLINS, F A
Naval heroes of today *(New York: Century 1918), 285p.*
DANIELS, J
The Navy and the nation: war-time addresses *(New York: Doran 1919), 348p.*
HUSBAND, J
On the coast of France: the story of the United States Naval Force in French waters *(Chicago: McClurg 1919), 127p.*
A Year in the Navy *(Boston, Mass: Houghton Mifflin 1919), 180p.*
KAUFFMAN, R W
Our Navy at work: the Yankee Fleet in French waters *(Indianapolis, Ind: Bobbs-Merrill 1918), 258p.*
KITTREDGE, T B
Naval lessons of the Great War *(New York: Doubleday 1921), 472p.*
LEIGHTON, J L
Simsadus: London: the American Navy in Europe *(New York: Holt 1920), 169p.*
MILLHOLLAND, R
The splinter fleet of the Otranto Barrage *(Indianapolis, Ind; Bobbs-Merrill 1936), 307p.*
MORRIS, C
Heroes of the Navy in America *(Philadelphia, Pa: Lippincott 1919), 347p.*
NEESER, R W
Our Navy and the next war *(New York: Scribner 1915), 205p.*
PAINE, R D
First Yale Unit: a story of Naval Aviation, 1916-1919 *(Locust Valley, Li: Davison 1920), 2 vols.*

PERRY, L
Our Navy in the war *(New York: Scribner 1918), 279p.*
SCOTT, L N
Naval Consulting Board of the United States *(Washington DC: 1920), 288p.*
SILVERSTONE, P
U.S. Warships of World War I *(London: Ian Allan 1970), 304p.*
SIMS, W S *and* HENDRICK, B J
Victory at sea *(New York: Doubleday 1920), 410p.*
UNITED STATES Bureau of Ordnance
Navy Ordnance activities, 1917-1918 *(Washington DC: 1920), 323p.*
UNITED STATES Navy Department
The Medical Department of the United States Navy with the Army and Marine Corps in France in World War I: its functions and employment *(Washington DC: Bureau of Medicine and Surgery 1947), 322p.*
UNITED STATES NAVY DEPARTMENT Bureau of Navigation
Officers and enlisted men of the United States Navy who lost their lives during the World War, April 6, 1917–November 11, 1918 *(Washington, DC: Dept. of the Navy 1920), 812p.*
WHITAKER, H
Hunting the German shark: the American Navy in the underseas war *(New York: Century 1918), 310p.*

VAD (Voluntary Aid Detachment)

BOWSER, T
The story of British V.A.D. work in the Great War *(London: Melrose 1917), 300p.*
DE LISLE, A
Leaves from a V.A.D.'s diary *(London: Elliot Stock 1922), 109p.*
DENT, O
A V.A.D. in France *(London: Grant Richards 1917), 349p.*
WHITSED, J de K
Come to the cook-house door!: a V.A.D. in Salonika *(London: Joseph 1932), 185p.*
THE WORK of V.A.D. London during the war *(London: Allen & Unwin 1920), 96p.*
[See also RED CROSS, RELIEF WORK]

VATICAN [see Catholicism]

VENIZELOS

GIBBONS, H A
Venizelos: a study *(Boston, Mass: Houghton Mifflin 1920), 384p.*
KEROFILAS, C
Eleftherios Venizelos: his life and work *(London: Murray 1915), 216p.*

PRICE, C
  Venizelos and the war: a sketch of personalities and politics *(London: Simpkin Marshall 1917), 200p.*
  [See also GREECE]

VERDUN

THE BATTLE of Verdun, 1914-1918 *(Milltown, NJ: Michelin Tire 1920), 111p.*
BLOND, G
  Verdun *(New York: Macmillan 1964), 250p.*
BRITTAIN, H E
  To Verdun from the Somme *(London: Lane 1917), 160p.*
BURKE, K
  The white road to Verdun *(London: Hodder & Stoughton 1916), 127p.*
CAMPBELL, G F
  Verdun to the Vosges: impressions of the war on the fortress frontier of France *(London: Arnold 1916), 335p.*
DUGARD, H
  The battle of Verdun *(London: Hutchinson 1916), 287p.*
GENEVOIX, M
  Neath Verdun *(London: Hutchinson 1916), 309p.*
HEIN, A
  In the hell of Verdun *(London: Cassell 1930), 372p.*
HERMANNS, W
  The holocaust: from a survivor of Verdun *(New York: Harper 1972), 141p.*
HORNE, A
  The price of glory: Verdun, 1916 *(London: Macmillan 1962), 372p; bib.*
JUENGER, E
  The storm of steel *(London: Chatto & Windus 1929), 319p.*
LAMBIE, M
  Verdun experiences *(Washington DC: Courant 1945), 79p.*
PETAIN, H P B
  Verdun *(London: Mathews & Marrot 1930), 254p.*
  [See also FRANCE (ARMY), PETAIN]

VERSAILLES

BARTLETT, V
  Behind the scenes at the Peace Conference *(London: Allen & Unwin 1919), 208p.*
BEADON, R H
  Some memories of the Peace Conference *(London: Williams 1933), 294p.*
BEER, G L
  African questions at the Paris Peace Conference *(New York: Macmillan 1923), 628p.*
BIRDSALL, P
  Versailles twenty years after *(London: Allen & Unwin 1941), 350p.*

BONSALS, S
Unfinished business *(London: Joseph 1944), 283p.*
CARRIÉ, R A
Italy at the Paris Peace Conference *(New York: Columbia UP 1938), 575p.*
DAWSON, W H
Germany under the Treaty *(London: Allen & Unwin 1933), 421p.*
DILLON, E J
The Peace Conference *(London: Hutchinson 1919), 439p.*
EBRAY, A
A Frenchman looks at the peace *(London: Kegan Paul 1927), 267p.*
ELCOCK, H J
Portrait of a decision: the Council of Four and the Treaty of Versailles *(London: Eyre & Spottiswoode 1972), 386p; bib.*
FABRE-LUCE, A
The limitations of victory *(London: Allen & Unwin 1926), 367p.*
GARNERIN DE MONTGELAS, M M *count*
The case for the Central Powers: an impeachment of the Versailles verdict *(London: Allen & Unwin 1925), 255p.*
THE GERMAN Treaty text *(London: Hodder & Stoughton 1920), 302p.*
GOLDBERG, G
The peace to end peace: the Paris Peace Conference of 1919 *(New York: Harcourt 1969), 221p.*
HANKEY, M P A *1st baron*
The supreme control at the Paris Peace Conference, 1919: a commentary *(London: Allen & Unwin 1963), 207p.*
HARRIS, H W
The peace in the making *(London: Swarthmore 1919), 246p.*
HASKINS, C H *and* LORD, R H
Some problems of the Peace Conference *(Cambridge, Mass: Harvard UP 1920), 307p.*
HEADLAM-MORLEY, *Sir* J
A memoir of the Paris Peace Conference, 1919 *(London: Methuen 1972), 230p.*
HENIG, R
Versailles and after, 1919–1933 *(London: Methuen 1984), 50p; bib.*
HERRON, G D
The defeat in victory: a criticism of the work of the Peace Conference *(London: Palmer 1921), 225p.*
HOUSE, E M *and* SEYMOUR, C
What really happened at Paris: the story of the Peace Conference, 1918-1919 *(London: Hodder & Stoughton 1921), 528p.*
HUDDLESTONE, S
Peace-making at Paris *(London: Fisher Unwin 1919), 240p.*
JESSOP, T E
The Treaty of Versailles: was it just? *(London: Nelson 1942), 167p.*
KING, J C
Foch versus Clemenceau: France and German dismemberment 1918-19 *(London: OUP 1960), 137p; bib.*

LANSING, R
   The Big Four, and others of the Peace Conference *(London: Hutchinson 1922)*, *212p.*
   The Peace negotiations: a personal narrative *(London: Constable 1921)*, *298p.*
LEDERER, I J *comp*
   The Versailles settlement: was it foredoomed to failure? *(Boston, Mass: Heath 1960)*, *116p; bib.*
LUCKAU, A
   The German delegation and the Paris Peace Conference *(New York: Columbia UP 1941)*, *522p.*
MARSTON, F S
   The Peace Conference of 1919: organization and procedure *(London: OUP 1944)*, *276p.*
MAYER, A J
   Politics and diplomacy of peacemaking: containment and counter-revolution at Versailles, 1918-1919 *(London: Weidenfeld & Nicolson 1968)*, *918p; bib.*
MONTGOMERY, B G de
   Versailles: a breach of agreement *(London: Methuen 1932)*, *144p.*
MYERS, D P
   The Treaty of Versailles and after: annotations of the text of the Treaty *(Washington DC: US Dept. of State 1947)*, *1018p.*
NICOLSON, H G
   Peacemaking, 1919 *(London: Constable 1933)*, *378p.*
NOBLE, G B
   Policies and opinions at Paris, 1919 *(New York: Macmillan 1935)*, *465p.*
NOWAK, C F
   Versailles *(London: Gollancz 1928)*, *287p.*
PARKERSON, J T
   Looking back to glory *(Paris: 1933)*, *244p.*
THE PEACE Conference – and after *(London: Macmillan 1919)*, *77p.*
SCHIFF, V
   The Germans at Versailles, 1919 *(London: Williams & Norgate 1930)*, *208p.*
SEYMOUR, C
   Letters from the Paris Peace Conference *(New Haven, Conn: Yale UP 1965)*, *289p.*
SHOTWELL, J T
   At the Paris Peace Conference *(New York: Macmillan 1937)*, *444p.*
   What Germany forgot *(New York: Macmillan 1940)*, *152p.*
SIMONDS, F H
   How Europe made peace without America *(London: Heinemann 1927)*, *407p.*
STEGEMANN, H
   The mirage of Versailles *(London: Allen & Unwin 1928)*, *360p.*
STEPHENS, W E
   Revisions of the Treaty of Versailles *(New York: Columbia UP 1939)*, *285p.*
TARDIEU, A
   The truth about the Treaty *(Indianapolis, Ind: Bobbs-Merrill 1921)*, *473p.*
TEMPERLEY, H W V *ed*
   A history of the Peace Conference of Paris *(London: Frowde 1920-21)*, *5 vols.*

THE TREATY of Peace between the Allied and Associated Powers and Germany, the protocol annexed thereto, the Agreement respecting the military occupation of the territories of the Rhine, and the Treaty between France and Great Britain *(London: HMSO 1919), 453p.*
TREATY of Peace with Germany *(New York: Brooklyn Daily Eagle 1919), 263p.*
THE TREATY of Versailles: the essential text and amendments *(London: Peace 1940), 127p.*
THE TREATY of Versailles and after *(London: Allen & Unwin 1935), 192p.*
UNITED STATES Department of State
The Treaty of Versailles and after: annotations of the text of the Treaty *(Washington, DC: US Govt PO 1943), 1018p.*
WEGERER, A von
A refutation of the Versailles war guilt *(New York: Knopf 1930), 386p.*

VICTORIA CROSS

ASGHAR-ALI, Sardar
Our heroes of the Great War: a record of the V.C.'s won by the Indian Army during the Great War *(Bombay: 1922), 119p.*
BARNETT, G
V.C.'s of the air *(London: Burrow 1918), 36p.*
BOWYER, C
For valour: the air V.C.s *(London: Kimber 1978), 548p; bib.*
Albert Ball V.C. *(London: Kimber 1977), 208p; bib.*
BOYLE, W H D
Gallant deeds: being a record of the circumstances under which the Victoria Cross, Conspicuous Gallantry, or Albert Medal were won by Petty Officers, Non-Commissioned Officers and men of the Royal Navy, Royal Marines and the Reserve Forces *(Portsmouth: 1930), 61p.*
BRISCOE, W A
The boy hero of the air: Captain Albert Ball, V.C. *(London: Milford 1921), 108p.*
CONGREVE, B
Armageddon road: a V.C's diary 1914–1916 *(London:Kimber 1982), 223p.*
CORNWELL, J
The story of John Travers Cornwell, V.C. 'boy-1st class.' *(London: Hodder & Stoughton, nd), 79p.*
HARDY, M
Hardy, V.C.: an appreciation of Theodore Bayley Hardy *(London: Skeffington 1920), 94p.*
HAWKER, T M
Hawker, V.C.: the biography of the late Major L. G. Hawker *(London: Mitre 1965), 253p.*
JAMESON, *Sir* W
Submariners V.C. *(London: Davies 1962), 208p; bib.*
JOHNS, W E
Air V.C.'s *(London: Hamilton 1935), 181p.*
KIERNAN, R H
Captain Albert Ball, V.C. *(London: Hamilton 1933), 198p.*
LEASK, G A
V.C. heroes of the war *(London: Harrap 1917), 300p.*

A MEMOIR and some letters of Frank Maxwell, V.C. *(London: Murray 1921), 239p.*
POLLARD, A O
   Fire-eater: the memoirs of a V.C. *(London: Hutchinson 1932), 278p.*
ROBERTS, T G *ed*
   Thirty Canadian V.C's, 23rd April 1915 to 30th March 1918 *(London: Skeffington nd), 96p.*
WONDERFUL stories: winning the V.C. in the Great War *(New York: Dutton 1918), 280p.*

VIMY RIDGE

McKEE, A
   Vimy Ridge *(London: Souvenir 1966), 242p.*
MACKSEY, K
   The shadow of Vimy Ridge *(London: Kimber 1965), 264p; bib.*
   Vimy Ridge *(New York: Ballantine 1972), 160p; bib.*
WOOD, H F
   Vimy *(London: Macdonald 1967), 186p; bib.*
[See also CANADIAN ARMY]

WALES

DOBBINS, E Ll
   South Wales as the chief industrial centre of the United Kingdom: her part in the great victory war *(Cardiff: 1922), 266p.*
MORGAN, J V
   The war and Wales *(London: Chapman & Hall 1916). 412p.*
NICHOLSON, I *and* WILLIAMS, T Ll
   Wales: its part in the war *(London: Hodder & Stoughton 1919), 260p.*

WAR CORRESPONDENTS

ADAM, G
   Behind the scenes at the Front *(London: Chapman & Hall 1915), 239p.*
ASHTON, H
   First from the Front *(London: Pearson 1914), 168p.*
BENNETT, E A
   Over there: war scenes on the Western Front *(London: Methuen 1915), 192p.*
CABLE, B
   Action Front *(New York: Dutton 1916). 295p.*
   Between the lines *(New York: Dutton 1915), 258p.*
CROZIER, E
   American reporters on the Western Front, 1914-1918 *(New York: OUP 1959), 299p; bib.*

FLEUROT, A D
Through war to revolution: the experiences of a newspaper correspondent *(London: Lane 1931), 242p.*
FORTESCUE, G
At the Front with three Armies *(London: Melrose 1915), 272p.*
Front line and deadline: the experiences of a war correspondent *(New York: Putnam 1937), 310p.*
Russia, the Balkans and the Dardanelles *(London: Melrose 1915), 286p.*
GIBBS, *Sir* P
The war dispatches *(London: Gibbs & Phillips 1964), 409p.*
GREEN, H
The log of a non-combatant *(Boston, Mass: Houghton Mifflin 1915), 168p.*
GREENWALL, H J
Scoops: being leaves from the diary of a special correspondent *(London: Stanley Paul 1923), 287p.*
IRWIN, W
The Latin at war: visits to the French and Italian Fronts *(London: Constable 1917), 295p.*
A Reporter at Armageddon: letters from the Front and behind the lines of the Great War *(New York: Appleton 1918), 354p.*
JEFFRIES, J M N
Front everywhere *(London: Hutchinson 1936), 298p.*
PALMER, F
With my own eyes *(London: Jarrolds 1934), 350p.*
POWELL, E A
Slanting lines of steel *(New York: Macmillan 1933), 307p.*
PRICE, J M
On the path of adventure *(London: Lane 1919), 244p.*
ROSS, M *and* ROSS, N
Light and shade in war *(London: Arnold 1916), 291p.*
RUHL, A
Antwerp to Gallipoli: a year of war on many Fronts *(London: Allen & Unwin 1916), 304p.*
[See also CENSORSHIP, PRESS]

WAR CRIMES

ANDLER, C
'Frightfulness' in theory and practice *(London: Fisher Unwin 1916), 182p.*
BALLARD, F
Plain truths versus German lies: documents *(London: Kelly 1915), 146p.*
BLAND, J O P
Germany's violations of the laws of war, 1914-15 *(London: Heinemann 1915), 381p.*
BOOTH, J B
The gentle cultured German, the road-hog of Europe *(London: Grant Richards 1915), 199p.*
THE CRIMES of Germany *(London: The Field 1916), 106p.*

DER SARKISS, K
Journey to the light *(Chicago: Adams 1969), 253p.*
GERMAN atrocities: Official book of the German atrocities; Report of the Belgian, French and Russian Commissions of enquiry *(London: Pearson 1915), 176p.*
HILLIS, N D
Blot on the Kaiser's 'scutcheon *(New York: Revell 1918), 193p.*
German atrocities; their nature and philosophy: studies in Belgium and France during July and August 1917 *(New York: Revel 1918), 160p.*
LE QUEUX, W
German atrocities: a record of shameless deeds *(London: Newnes 1914), 128p.*
MACCAS, L
German barbarism: a neutral's indictment *(London: Hodder & Stoughton 1916), 228p.*
MARSHALL, L
Horrors and atrocities of the Great War *(Philadelphia, Pa: Winston 1915), 320p.*
MIRMAN, L
Their crimes *(London: Cassell 1917), 64p.*
MORGAN, J H
German atrocities: an official investigation *(London: Fisher Unwin 1916), 128p.*
REPORT on the atrocities committed by the Austro-Hungarian Army during the first invasion of Serbia *(London: Simpkin Marshall 1916), 204p.*
TOYNBEE, A J
German terror in France: an historical record *(New York: Doran 1917), 220p.*
The Western question in Greece and Turkey: a study in the contact of civilisation *(New York: Fertig 1970), 408p.*
WAR on hospital ships *(New York: Harper 1918), 47p.*
WHERE the German Army has passed *(London: Daily Chronicle 1915), 66p.*

WAR DEBTS

COE, F E
We have paid enough: Europe's message to America *(London: Simpkin Marshall 1932), 129p.*
DEXTER, P *and* SEDGWICK, J H
The war debts: an American view *(New York: Macmillan 1928), 173p.*
FRASURE, C M
British policy on war debts and reparations *(Philadelphia, Pa: Dorrance 1940), 188p.*
HOLLANDER, J H
War borrowing: a study of Treasury certificates of indebtedness of the United States *(New York: Macmillan 1919), 215p.*
LLOYD, W
European war debts and their settlement *(New York: McClelland 1934), 88p.*
MOULTON, H G *and* POZVOLSKY, L
War debts and world prosperity *(Washington DC: Brookings Institute 1932), 498p.*
World war debts settlement *(London: Allen & Unwin 1927), 448p.*

MOUNTSIER, R
Our eleven million dollars: Europe's debt to the United States *(New York: Seltzer 1922)*, *149p.*

PEABODY, F W *and* COE, F E
Honour or dollars? *(Sydney: 1928), 86p.*

REID, L J
Britain and the war debts *(London: Jenkins 1933), 108p.*

RICHARDSON, D
Will they pay?: a primer of the war debts *(Philadelphia, Pa: Lippincott 1933), 169p.*

SIMONDS, F H
America must cancel: an American reviews war-debts *(London: Hamilton 1933), 95p.*

UNITED STATES Senate Committee on the judiciary
Loans to foreign governments: rdsume of the laws under which loans were made ... during and since the war, and the main features of the loans *(Washington DC: 1921), 388p.*

WAR TRIALS

ADAM, G
Treason and tragedy: an account of French war trials *(London: Cape 1929), 253p.*

MULLINS, C
The Leipzig trials: an account of the war criminals' trials and a study of German mentality *(London: Witherby 1921), 238p.*

WEAPONS [see ARMS AND ARMOUR]

WEST AFRICA

GORGES, E H
The Great War in West Africa *(London: Hutchinson 1930), 284p.*

MOBERLY, F J
Military operations, Togoland and the Cameroons, 1914-1916 *(London: HMSO 1931), 469p.*

WESTERN FRONT

ADAMS, J B P
Nothing of importance: at the Front, Oct. 1915 to June 1916 *(London: Methuen 1917), 308p.*

ASHMEAD BARTLETT, E
From the Somme to the Rhine *(London: Lane 1921), 205p.*

BANTING, D R *and* EMBLETON, G A
The Western Front, 1914-1918 *(London: Almark 1974), 80p; bib.*

BARBER, G
My diary in France *(Liverpool: Young 1917), 88p.*

BEHREND, A
As from Kemmel Hill: an adjutant in France and Flanders, 1917 and 1918 *(London: Eyre & Spottiswoode 1963), 176p.*

BROWN, M
Tommy goes to war *(London: Dent 1978), 272p.*

BUMBLE BEE *pseud*
The Salient, the Somme and Arras: leaves from the diary of ... *(London: Palmer & Sutton 1919), 106p.*

CAMPBELL, P J
The ebb and flow of battle *(London: Hamilton 1917), 167p.*
In the cannon's mouth *(London: Hamilton 1977), 317p.*

CARRINGTON, C E
Soldier from the wars returning *(London: Hutchinson 1965), 287p.*

CHUTE, A H
The real Front *(New York: Harper 1918), 308p.*

CLARK, A
The donkeys *(London: Hutchinson 1961), 216p; bib.*

COWLEY, R
1918; the gamble for victory: the greatest attack of World War I *(New York: Macmillan 1964), 90p; bib.*

DANE, E
The battle of the rivers *(London: Hodder & Stoughton 1914), 208p.*
Hacking through Belgium *(London: Hodder & Stoughton 1914), 176p*

DAVIS, R H
Somewhere in France *(London: Duckworth 1916), 232p.*
With the Allies *(London: Duckworth 1915), 240p.*

DAWSON, C W
Living bayonets: a record of the last push *(London: Lane 1919), 212p.*

FALLS, C
Military operations, France and Belgium, 1917: the German retreat to the Hindenburg Line and the battle of Arras *(London: Macmillan 1940), 3pts.*

FENNAH, A
Retaliation 1914-1918 *(London: Houghton 1935), 184p.*

FOLEY, H A
Three years on active service and eight months as a prisoner-of-war *(Bridgwater, Som: 1920), 185p.*

FORTESCUE, G
At the Front with three Armies *(London: Melrose 1915), 271p.*

GANSSER, E B
On the battle fields of France in 1918 *(Grand Rapids, Mich: Gansser1958), 166p.*

GAULD, H D
The truth from the trenches: experiences in France, 1916-18 *(London: Stockwell 1927), 305p.*

GOWLAND, J S
War is like that *(London: Hamilton 1933), 239p.*

GRAVES, A F

The turn of the tide: continuation of the long retreat *(London: Murray 1916), 52p.*

GRAY, F

The confessions of a Private *(London: OUP 1920), 202p.*

GREGORY, H

Never again: a diary of the Great War *(London: Stockwell 1934), 141p.*

GRIFFITH, L W

Up to Mametz *(London: Faber 1931), 238p.*

HILL, J A S

The Front line and beyond: a diary of 1917-18 *(London: Houghton 1930), 80p.*

HITCHCOCK, F C

'Stand to': a diary of the trenches, 1915-18 *(London: Hurst & Blackett 1937), 358p.*

HOPE, T S

The winding road unfolds *(London: Putnam 1937), 349p.*

HORNE, A

Death of a generation: from Neuve Chapelle to Verdun and the Somme *(London: Macdonald 1970), 128p; bib.*

HORNUNG, E W

Notes of a camp-follower on the Western Front *(London: Constable 1919), 260p.*

IGGLESDEN, C

Out there: impressions of a visit to the Western Front *(London: Long 1916), 158p.*

INGPEN, R

The fighting retreat to Paris *(New York: Doran 1914), 192p.*

JONES, N H

The war walk: a journey along the Western Front *(London: Hale 1983), 234p; bib.*

KEARSEY, A H C

Notes on the campaign in France, 1914, from the beginning of hostilities until the end of the battle of the River Aisne *(London: Sifton Praed 1926), 64p.*

1915 campaign in France: the battles of Aubers Ridge, Festubert and Loos *(Aldershot: Gale & Polden 1930), 99p.*

LAFFIN, J

On the Western Front: soldiers' stories from France and Flanders 1914–1918 *(Gloucester: Sutton 1985), 277p.*

LEWIS, P W

Blasting and bombardiering *(London: Eyre & Spottiswoode 1937), 312p.*

LIVEING, E G D

Attack: an infantry subaltern's impressions *(London: Heinemann 1918), 86p.*

MACNAIR, W

Blood and iron: impressions from the Front in France and Flanders *(London: Seeley 1916), 310p.*

MARTIN, B

Poor bloody infantry: a subaltern on the Western Front 1916–1917 *(London: Murray 1987), 192p.*

MATTHEWS, E C

A subaltern in the field *(London: Heath Cranton 1920), 63p.*

MIDDLEBROOK, M
The Kaiser's battle; 21 March 1918: the first day of the German Spring offensive *(London: Allen Lane 1978), 431p; bib.*

MILES, W
Military operations, France and Belgium, 1916: 2nd July 1916 to the end of the battle of the Somme *(London: MacMillan 1938), 2 vols.*

MILNE, J
News from 'Somewhere' *(London: Chapman & Hall 1915), 240p.*

MINDER, C F
The man's war: the day-by-day record of an American Private on the Western Front *(New York: Payson 1931), 368p.*

MOORE, W
See how they ran: the British retreat of 1918 *(London: Cooper 1970), 256p.*

MUSGRAVE, G C
Under four flags for France *(New York: Appleton 1918), 363p.*

NETTLETON, J
The anger of the guns: an infantry officer on the Western Front *(London: Kimber 1979), 206p.*

NICHOLSON, W N
Behind the lines *(London: Cape 1939), 320p.*

NOBBS, G
Englishman, Kamerad!: right of the British line *(London: Heinemann 1918), 210p.*

PEIXOTTO, E C
American Front in France *(New York: Scribner 1919), 230p.*

POUND, R
The lost generation *(London: Constable 1964), 288p; bib.*

POWELL, E A
Vive La France: the Western Front, 1915-16 *(London: Heinemann 1916), 270p.*

PRIVATE No. 940 *pseud*
'On the remainder of your Front' *(London: Harrison 1917), 156p.*

QUEX *pseud*
Push and the return push *(London: Backwood 1919), 331p.*

RAWLINSON, A
Adventures on the Western Front, August 1914-June 1915 *(London: Melrose 1925), 315p.*

RHYS, E
The roar of battle: scenes and episodes of war *(London: Jarrolds 1914), 286p.*

RICHARDS, F
Old soldiers never die *(London: Faber 1933), 324p.*

ROBINSON, H R
Belated comments on a great event: the German offensive in the Spring of 1918 *(London: Williams & Norgate 1932), 112p.*

RUFFIN, H *and* TUDESQ, A
Brother Tommy: the British offensive on the Western Front, January to June 1917 *(London: Fisher Unwin 1918), 160p.*

RUSSELL, H
Slaves of the war lords: experiences in France, 1916-18 *(London: Hutchinson 1928), 287p.*

SHAW, K E
Jottings from the Front: impressions and experiences *(London: Allen & Unwin 1918), 183p.*

SMITH, Aubrey
Four years on the Western Front: being the experiences of a ranker in the London Rifle Brigade *(London: Odhams 1922), 409p.*

SMITH, Gene
Still quiet on the Western Front: fifty years later *(New York: Morrow 1965), 108p.*

SPARROW, A A H
The land-locked lake *(London: Barker 1932), 317p.*

SPEARS, E L
Liaison 1914: a narrative of the great retreat *(London: Heinemann 1930), 597p.*

TERRAINE, J
The road to Passchendaele; the Flanders Offensive: a study in inevitability *(London: Cooper 1977), 365p.*
The Western Front, 1914-1918 *(London: Hutchinson 1964), 231p.*

TIPLADY, T
The kitten in the crater, and other fragments from the Front *(London: Kelly 1917), 182p.*

TUCKER, J F
Johnny get your gun: a personal narrative of the Somme, Ypres and Arras *(London: Kimber 1978), 207p.*

WARD, M A
Fields of victory *(London: Hutchinson 1919), 260p.*

WATT, L
In France and Flanders with the fighting men *(London: Hodder & Stoughton 1917), 220p.*

WHITEHAIR, C W
Out there *(New York: Appleton 1918), 248p.*

WILLIAMS, A
Experiences of the Great War; Artois, St Mihiel, Meuse-Argonne *(Roanoke, Va: Williams 1919), 197p.*

WYNNE, G C
If Germany attacks: the battle in depth in the West: lessons from the Western Front, 1915-17 *(London: Faber 1940), 343p.*

X, BOMBARDIER *pseud*
So this was war!: the truth about the Western and Eastern Fronts revealed *(London: Hutchinson 1930), 224p.*

[See also ARMIES OF INDIVIDUAL COUNTRIES, FLANDERS, INDIVIDUAL BATTLES, INDIVIDUAL MEMOIRS, PERSONAL NARRATIVES]

WILSON, WOODROW

ARCHER, W
The peace President: a brief appreciation *(London: Hutchinson 1918), 125p.*

ARNETT, A M
Claude Kitchin and the Wilson war policies *(Boston, Mass: Houghton Mifflin 1937)*, *341p.*
BAILEY, T A
Woodrow Wilson and the great betrayal *(New York: Macmillan 1945), 429p.*
Woodrow Wilson and the lost peace *(New York: Macmillan 1944), 381p.*
BAKER, R S
Woodrow Wilson and world settlement *(London: Heinemann 1923), 3 vols.*
Woodrow Wilson: life and letters *(New York: Doubleday 1927-1939), 8 vols.*
BECK, J M
The passing of the new freedom: a criticism of President Wilson *(New York: Doran 1920)*, *174p.*
CREEL, G
Wilson and the issues *(New York: Century 1916), 167p.*
DANIELS, J
The Wilson era *(Chapel Hill, NC: University of North Carolina P 1944-1946), 2 vols.*
DEVLIN, P A *baron*
Too proud to fight: Woodrow Wilson's neutrality *(London: OUP 1974), 731p; bib.*
DODD, W E
Woodrow Wilson and his work *(London: Simpkin Marshall 1920), 385p.*
DOS PASSOS, J
Mr Wilson's war *(New York: Doubleday 1962), 517p.*
FERRELL, R H
Woodrow Wilson and World War I *(New York: Harper 1985), 346p.*
FIFIELD, R H
Woodrow Wilson and the Far East: the diplomacy of the Shantung question *(New York: Crowell 1952), 383p.*
HERRON, G D
Woodrow Wilson and the world's peace *(New York: Kennerley 1917), 173p.*
HOOVER, H C
The ordeal of Woodrow Wilson *(London: Museum 1958), 318p; bib.*
HOOVER, H C *and* WILSON, W
The Hoover-Wilson wartime correspondence, Sept. 24, 1914 to Nov. 11, 1918 *(Ames, Iowa: Iowa State UP 1974), 297p.*
HOUSTON, D F
Eight years with Wilson's Cabinet, 1913-1920 *(London: Heinemann 1926), 2 vols.*
JONES, C S
President Wilson: the man and his message *(London: Rider 1918), 79p.*
LAWRENCE, D
The true story of Woodrow Wilson *(New York: Doran 1924), 368p.*
LINK, A S
Wilson the diplomatist: a look at his major foreign policies *(Baltimore: Johns Hopkins UP 1957), 165p.*
MAMATEY, V S
The United States and East Central Europe, 1914-1918: a study in Wilsonian diplomacy and propaganda *(Princeton, NJ: Princeton UP 1957), 431p; bib.*

MARTIN, L W
  Peace without victory: Woodrow Wilson and the British Liberals *(New Haven, Conn: Yale UP 1958), 230p.*
NOTTER, H
  The origins of the foreign policy of Woodrow Wilson *(Baltimore: Johns Hopkins UP 1937), 698p.*
PRESIDENT Wilson from an English point of view *(New York: Stokes 1917), unp.*
RAPPAPORT, A
  The British Press and Wilson neutrality *(Stanford, Cal: Stanford UP 1951), 162p.*
ROBINSON, E E *and* WES, V J
  The foreign policy of President Wilson, 1913-1917 *(New York: Macmillan 1917), 428p.*
ROZWENC, E C *and* LYONS, T
  Realism and idealism in Wilson's peace program *(Boston, Mass: Heath 1965), 104p; bib.*
SCHWABE, K
  Woodrow Wilson, revolutionary Germany and peace-making 1918–1919 *(Chapel Hill, NC: North Carolina UP 1985), 565p.*
SEYMOUR, C
  Woodrow Wilson and the World War *(New Haven, Conn: Yale UP 1920), 382p.*
TUMULTY, J P
  Woodrow Wilson as I know him *(London: Heinemann 1921), 553p.*
VIERECK, G S
  The strangest friendship in history: Woodrow Wilson and Colonel House *(London: Duckworth 1932), 375p.*
WHITE, W A
  Woodrow Wilson *(Boston, Mass: Houghton Mifflin 1924), 527p.*
WILSON, T W
  America and freedom: the statements of President Wilson on the war *(London: Allen & Unwin 1917), 76p.*
  Messages and papers *(New York: Doran 1924), 2 vols.*
  This man was right: Woodrow Wilson speaks again *(London: W H Allen 1943), 64p.*
  War addresses of Woodrow Wilson *(Boston, Mass: Ginn 1918), 161p.*
YOUNG, E W
  The Wilson administration and the Great War *(Boston, Mass: Badger 1922), 466p.*
[See also FOURTEEN POINTS, VERSAILLES]

WOMEN

ATKINS, T
  The letters of Thomasina Atkins *(London: Hodder & Stoughton 1918), 251p.*
BARTON, E M
  Eve in khaki: the story of the Women's Army at home and abroad *(London: Nelson 1918), 200p.*
BEGBIE, H
  The Queen's net: true stories of all sorts and conditions of women saved from the war flood of suffering, privation and despair *(London: Hodder & Stoughton 1915), 300p.*

BILLINGTON, M F
  The roll-call of serving women *(London: RTS 1915), 227p.*
BLATCH, *Mrs* H
  Mobilizing woman-power *(New York: Woman's P 1918), 195p.*
BRAYBON, G
  Women workers in the First World War: the British experience *(London: Croom Helm 1981), 224p.*
CAINE, T H H
  Our girls: their work for the war *(London: Hutchinson 1916), 127p.*
CARR, K
  Women who dared: heroines of the Great War *(London: Partridge 1920), 284p.*
CHURCHILL, *Lady* R
  Woman's work in war-time *(London: Pearson 1915), 244p.*
CLARKE, I C
  American women and the World War *(New York: Appleton 1918), 544p.*
CONDELL, D *and* LIDDIARD, J
  Working for victory?: images of women in the First World War 1914–1918 *(London: Routledge 1987).*
CREED, L
  A woman's experiences in the Great War *(London: Fisher Unwin 1915), 297p.*
DAGGETT, *Mrs* M
  Women wanted: the story written in blood red letters on the horizon of the great World War *(New York: Doran 1918), 384p.*
FITCH, R L
  Madame France *(New York: Woman's P 1919), 189p.*
FRASER, H
  Women and war work *(Chicago: Shaw G Arnold 1918), 308p.*
GEORGE, S
  Woman's world-wide work with war *(London: Power 1915), 63p.*
GREAT BRITAIN War Office
  Women's war work in maintaining the industries and export trade of the United Kingdom *(London: HMSO 1916), 93p.*
GREENWALD, M W
  Women, war and work: the impact of World War I on women workers in the United States *(Westport, Conn: Greenwood 1980), 309p.*
GREIG, G A
  Women's work on the land *(London: Jarrolds 1916), 48p.*
GREVILLE, F E *countess of Warwick*
  A woman and the war *(London: Chapman & Hall 1916), 245p.*
GRIBBLE, F
  Women in war *(London: Sampson Low 1916), 350p.*
HOCKIN, O
  Two girls on the land: wartime on a Dartmoor farm *(London: Arnold 1918), 158p.*
JAMES, B R
  For God, for country, for home: a story of the first national organization of American women for war service *(New York: Putnam 1920), 260p.*

JESSE, F T
The sword of Deborah: first-hand impressions of the British Women's Army in France *(London: Heinemann 1919), 135p.*

LAWRENCE, D
Sapper Dorothy Lawrence, the only English woman soldier, late Royal Engineers *(London: Lane 1919), 191p.*

LLOYD, G
An Englishwoman's adventures in the German lines *(London: Pearson 1914), 128p.*

MACLAREN, B
Women of the war *(London: Hodder & Stoughton 1917), 148p.*

MARWICK, A
Women at war, 1914-1918 *(London: Fontana 1977), 177p.*

MILITARISM versus feminism *(London: Allen 1915), 68p.*

MITCHELL, D
Women on the warpath: the story of the women of the First World War *(London: Cape 1966), 400p.*

ONIONS, M
A woman at war: being experiences of an Army Signaller in France in 1917-1919 *(London: Daniel 1929), 63p.*

PENNANT, V B D
Under the searchlight: a record of a great scandal *(London: Allen & Unwin 1922), 463p.*

SALMOND, *Lady* M M
Bright armour: memories off our years of war *(London: Faber 1935), 251p.*

SILLARS, S
Women in World War I *(London: Macmillan 1987), 113p; bib.*

SMITH, Annie S
As others see her: an Englishwoman's impressions of the American woman in war time *(Boston, Mass: Houghton Mifflin 1919), 182p.*

STONE, G *ed*
Women war workers *(London: Harrap 1917), 320p.*

TWEEDIE, E B
Women and soldiers *(London: Lane 1918), 192p.*

USBORNE, H M
Women's work in wartime *(London: Werner Laurie 1917), 174p.*

VAUGHAN, *Dame* H C
Service with the Army *(London: Hutchinson 1942), 168p.*

WALTERS, E W
Heroines of the World War *(London: Kelly 1916), 222p.*

WEST, *Mrs* J C
Women's war work *(London: Pearson 1916), 159p.*

WILTSHER, A
Most dangerous women: feminist peace campaigners of the Great War *(London: Pandora 1985), 263p; bib.*

WOLSELEY, F G *viscountess*
Women and the land *(London: Chatto & Windus 1916), 229p.*

WOMEN helpers of their nation *(London: Skeffington 1916), 108p.*

[See also CANTEENS, DEPORTATIONS, HOSPITALS, MUNITIONS, NURSES AND NURSING]

YMCA

BARRETT, *Sir* J W
The war work of the Y.M.C.A. in Egypt *(London: Lewis 1919), 212p.*
BISHOP, C W
The Canadian Y.M.C.A. in the Great War: the official record *(Toronto: 1924), 446p.*
COPPING, A E
Tommy's triangle: first hand impressions of the Y.M.C.A.'s war activities *(London: Hodder & Stoughton 1917), 189p.*
DELAND, M
Small things: an account of the American Y.M.C.A. in France *(New York: Appleton 1919), 325p.*
FEDDEN, M
From an Abbeville window, 1918-19 *(Bristol: Arrowsmith 1922), 140p.*
GIBBONS, H D
A little gray home in France: experiences with the American Y.M.C.A. *(New York: Century 1919), 258p.*
MACLEAN, J K *and* REDDLE, T W
The Y.M.C.A. with the colours *(London: Marshall 1915), 123p.*
MAYO, K
'That damn Y': a record of overseas service *(Boston, Mass: Houghton Mifflin 1920), 432p.*
RED triangle girl in France *(New York: Doran 1918), 168p.*
SHORTALL, K
A 'Y' girl in France *(Boston, Mass: Badger 1919), 80p.*
STEVENSON, B G
Betty Stevenson, Y.M.C.A.: a memoir, with her letters from France *(London: Longmans 1920), 295p.*
TOLD in the huts: the Y.M.C.A. gift book *(London: Jarrolds 1916), 236p.*
WARREN, H C
With the Y.M.C.A. in France; or, Souvenirs of a secretary *(New York: Revell 1919), 160p.*
YAPP, *Sir* A
The romance of the Red Triangle *(London: Hodder & Stoughton 1918), 195p.*

YPRES

BOYD, W
With a field ambulance at Ypres *(New York: Doran 1915), 110p.*
BRICE, B *comp*
The battle book of Ypres *(London: Murray 1927), 273p; bib.*
BUTLER, P R
A galloper at Ypres, 1914 *(London: Fisher Unwin 1920), 276p.*
CAMPBELL, P J
In the cannon's mouth *(London: Hamilton 1979), 146p.*
CAREW, T
Wipers *(London: Hamilton 1974), 230p; bib.*

COLEMAN, F A
   With cavalry in 1915: the British trooper in the trench line through the second battle of Ypres *(London: Sampson Low 1916), 302p.*
COLUMBAN, *Dame* M
   The Irish nuns at Ypres: an episode of the war *(London: Smith, Elder 1915), 220p.*
DAVIS, H W C
   The battle of Ypres-Armentières *(London: Milford 1915), 59p.*
FARRAR-HOCKLEY, A
   Death of an Army *(London: Barker 1967), 195p; bib.*
FLOYD, T H
   At Ypres with Bert Dunkley of the 2/5th Lancashire Fusiliers *(London: Lane 1920), 234p.*
GILES, J
   The Ypres Salient *(London: Cooper 1970), 229p.*
GLADDEN, N
   Ypres, 1917: a personal account *(London: Kimber 1967), 192p.*
HUNTER, J T
   Hell at Ypres *(San Antonio, Cal: Naylor 1934), 209p.*
IRWIN, W
   Men, women and war, includes the splendid story of Ypres *(London: Constable 1916), 200p.*
MACDONALD, L
   They called in Passchendaele: the story of the third battle of Ypres and the men who fought it *(London: Joseph 1978), 253p.*
MACLEAN, A M
   With the Gordons at Ypres *(Paisley, Scot: Gardner 1916), 70p.*
MACNAGHTEN, A
   'Missing': an account of the efforts made to find an officer of the Black Watch, reported 'missing' on 29th October 1914 during the first battle of Ypres *(Bala, Wales: Dragon 1970), 62p.*
MOTTRAM, R H
   Through the Menin Gate *(London: Chatto & Windus 1932), 259p.*
THE PILGRIMS' guide to the Ypres Salient *(London: Talbot House 1920), 91p.*
POLLARD, H B C
   The story of Ypres *(New York: MacBride 1917), 63p.*
PULTENEY, *Sir* W P *and* BRICE, B
   Immortal Salient: an historical record and complete guide for pilgrims to Ypres *(London: Ypres League 1925), 89p.*
WILLSON, B
   In the Ypres Salient: the Canadian fighting, June 2-16, 1916 *(London: Simpkin Marshall 1916), 79p.*
   Ypres, the holy ground of British arms *(Bruges, Belgium: 1920), 83p.*
THE WIPERS Times: a complete facsimile of the famous World War One trench newspaper *(London: Davies 1973), 377p.*
WOMBELL, P
   Battle, Passchendaele 1917 *(London: Travelling Light 1980), 148p.*
YPRES and the battle of Ypres *(Milltown, NJ: Michelin Tire 1920), 138p.*
YPRES before and after the Great War *(Liege: Benard 1927), 154p.*

YPRES 1914: an official account, published by order of the German General Staff
(London: Constable 1919), 160p.
[See also BRITISH ARMY, CANADIAN ARMY, FLANDERS, WESTERN FRONT]

YUGOSLAVIA

BAILEY, W F
The Slavs of the war zone *(London: Chapman & Hall 1916), 278p.*
DJORDJEVIC, D ed
The creation of Yugoslavia 1914–1918 *(Santa Barbara, Cal: American Bib. Centre 1980), 228p.*
LEDERER, I J
Yugoslavia at the Paris Peace Conference: a study in frontier making *(New Haven, Conn: Yale UP 1963), 351p; bib.*
REYNOLDS, R
My Slav friends *(London: Mills & Boon 1916), 320p.*
TAYLOR, A H E
The future of the Southern Slavs *(London: Fisher Unwin 1917), 326p.*
VOSNJAK, B
A bulwark against Germany *(London: Allen & Unwin 1917), 270p.*
[See also BALKANS, SERBIA]

ZEEBRUGGE

BELL, J K
The glory of Zeebrugge and the 'Vindictive' *(London: Chatto & Windus 1918), 63p.*
CAMPBELL, A B
Zeebrugge: St George's Day, 1918 *(London: OUP 1940), 40p.*
CARPENTER, A F B
The blocking of Zeebrugge *(London: Jenkins 1922), 295p.*
FERRABY, H C
The immortal story of Zeebrugge and Ostend *(London: Gieves 1920), 48p.*
KEYES, Sir R J B
Ostend and Zeebrugge, April 23-May 10, 1918: the despatches of Vice-Admiral Sir Roger Keyes and other narratives of the operations *(London: Milford 1919), 224p.*
PITT, B
Zeebrugge, St George's Day, 1918 *(London: Cassell 1958), 237p.*
WARNER, P
The Zeebrugge raid *(London: Kimber 1978), 238p.*

ZEPPELINS

CAMPBELL, E
Zeppelins: the past and the future *(St. Albans, Herts: 1918), 43p.*

DUDLEY, E
Monsters of the purple twilight: the true story of the life and death of the Zeppelins, first menace from the skies *(London: Harrap 1960), 218p.*
GRAVES, A K
Zeppelins and the German war machine *(London: Werner Laurie 1915), 24p.*
HEARNE, R P
Zeppelins and super-Zeppelins *(London: Lane 1916), 182p.*
INGLEBY, H
The Zeppelin raid in West Norfolk *(London: Arnold 1915), 31p.*
LEHMANN, E A *and* MINGOS, H
The Zeppelins: the development of the airship, with the story of the Zeppelin air raids in the World War *(New York: Sears 1927), 329p.*
MARBEN, R
Zeppelin adventures *(London: Hamilton 1932), 232p.*
POOLMAN, K
Zeppelins over England *(London: Evans 1960), 224p.*
RIMELL, R
Zeppelin! a battle for air supremacy in World War I *(London: Conway 1984), 256p.*
ROBINSON, D H
The Zeppelin in combat: a history of the German Naval Airship Division, 1912-1918 *(London: Foulis 1962), 417p; bib.*
TREUSCH VON BUTTLAR BRANDENFELS, H
Zeppelins over England *(London: Harrap 1931), 231p.*
WHITEHOUSE, A
The Zeppelin fighters *(New York: Doubleday 1966), 290p; bib.*
WRIGHT, C E
The fate of Zeppelin L32 *(Billericay, Essex: Chanticleer 1978), 24p.*

ZIMMERMAN

TUCHMAN, B W
The Zimmerman telegram *(New York: Viking 1958), 244p; bib.*
[See also SECRET SERVICE, UNITED STATES INTERVENTION]

AUTHOR INDEX

Aaronsohn, A., *With the Turks in Palestine*, 202

Abbey, E. A., *An American soldier*, 298

Abbot, W. J., *Aircraft and submarines*, 3, 280; *Blue jackets of 1918*, 311; *Pictorial history of the World War*, 217; *Soldiers of the sea*, 310; *The United States in the Great War*, 290

Abbott, G. F., *Greece and the Allies, 1914-1922*, 126; *Turkey, Greece and the Great Powers*, 80

Abbott, H. P.A., *Religion of the Tommy*, 237

Abbott-Brown, C., *How to do it*, 54

Abels, C. H., *The last of the fighting four*, 210

Abhayasuriya, S., *Ceylon and the war*, 69

Abraham, J. J., *My Balkan log*, 21

Abrams, R. H., *Preachers present arms*, 237

Ackermann, C. W., *Germany the next Republic*, 115

Adam, G., *Behind the scenes at the Front*, 317; *Treason and tragedy*, 320

Adam, H. P., *Paris sees it through*, 204

Adam, Mme J., *The schemes of the Kaiser*, 150

Adams, A. H., *The Lusitania crime and the escape of the Orduna*, 162

Adams, J., *The great sacrifice; or, The altar-fire of war*, 237

Adams, J. B. P., *Nothing of importance*, 34, 320

Adams, J. C., *Flight in winter*, 267

Adams, J. W. B., *A pedagogue's fatigues*, 89

Adams, R. E. C., *The modern crusaders*, 203, 298

Adams, R. J. & Poirier, P. P., *The conscription controversy in Great Britain 1900-18*, 75

Adcock, A. St. J., *Australasia triumphant*, 14; *In the firing line*, 275; *Seeing it through*, 30; *Songs of the World War*, 273

Addams, J., *Peace and bread in time of war*, 290

Adderley, H. A., *The Warwickshire Yeomanry in the Great War*, 55

Addison, C., *Four and a half years*, 171; *Politics from within, 1911-1918*, 219

Addison, J. T., *The story of the first Gas Regiment*, 114

Adkins, F. J., *The war; its origins and warnings*, 197

Adler, F., *The world crisis and its meaning*, 216.

Adler, M., *Prayer book for Jewish sailors and soldiers*, 148

Africanus, *The Prussian lash in Africa*, 1

Agate, J. E., *The letters of a temporary officer in the Army Service Corps*, 54

Ah Kow, A., *William McKenzie . . . Anzac Padre*, 15

Ahmad Amin, *Turkey in the World War*, 287

Ainsworth, R. B., *The story of the 6th Battalion, the Durham Light Infantry, France April 1915-November 1918*, 44

Aitken, A., *Courage past: duty done*, 271

Aitken A. C., *Gallipoli to the Somme*, 190

Aitken, W. M., *Canada in Flanders, 63; Men and power*, 219; *Politicians and the war*, 219

Ajax, *The German pirate, his methods and record*, 115, 289

Albert I., *The war diaries of Albert I, King of the Belgians*, 171

Albertine, C., *The Yankee doughboy*, 298

Albertini, L., *The origins of the war of 1914*, 197

Alderman, S. M., *Three Americans in Paris, Spring 1919*, 204

Aldington. R., *Lawrence of Arabia*, 153

Aldrich, M., *A hilltop on the Marne*, 163; *On the edge of the war zone*, 8; *Peak of the load*, 163; *When Johnny comes marching home*, 298

Aldridge, O. M., *The retreat from Serbia through Albania*, 21

Aleksinskaya, T., *With the Russian wounded*, 255

Aleksinsky, G. A., *Russia and the Great War*, 255

Alexander, A. C. B., *Jutland*, 149

Alexander, H. M., *On two Fronts*, 112, 141

Alexander, R., *The cruise of the raider Wolf*, 125

Alexander, Robert, *Memories of the World War, 1917-1918*, 298

Alexandra, *Letters of the Tsaritsa to the Tsar*, 192

Alington, A. F., *The lamps go out*, 128

Allan, A., *Armageddon! before and after*, 194

Allen, G. H., *Causes of and motives for the Great War*, 197; *The Great War*, 128

Allen, H. T., *My Rhineland journal*, 196; *The Rhineland occupation*, 196

Allen, H. W., *The unbroken line*, 108

Allen, J. E., *The war debt and how to meet it*, 97

Allen, S. S., *2/Auckland, 1918*, 190

Allen, T., *The tracks they trod*, 186

Allen, W., *Our Italian Front*, 147

Allen, W. H., *Towards the flame*, 210

Allen, W. M., *The 331st Field Artillery, United States Army, 1917-1919*, 309

Allinson, S., *The Bantams*, 34

Allinson, R. S., *The surgeon probationer*, 165

Allison, W., *The monocled mutineer*, 185

Almond, N. & Lutz, R. H., *The Treaty of St. Germain*, 285

Alport, A. C., *The lighter side of war*, 273; *Malaria and its treatment in the line and at the base*, 165

Alting, J. H. and Buning, W., *Effect of the war upon the Colonies*, 128

Altsheler, J. A., *The hosts of the air*, 194

American Heritage, *The American Heritage history of World War I*, 128

Amerine, W. H., *Alabama's own in France*, 298

Ames, F., *American Red Cross work among the French people*, 233

Anderson, A. L. K., *The unbreakable coil*, 52

Anderson, A. T., *War services of the 62nd West Riding Divisional Artillery*, 57

Anderson, B. M., *Effects of the war on money, credit and banking in France*, 97

Anderson, C. C., *War manual*, 234, 282

Anderson, I. W., *Zigzagging*, 138

Anderson, Sir R., *The higher criticism and the war*, 237

Andler, C., *'Frightfulness' in theory and practice*, 318

Andrassy, J., *Diplomacy and the war*, 80; *Whose sin is the World War?*, 197

Andrews, W. L., *Haunting years*, 35

Andriulli, G. A., *Documents relating to the Great War*, 197

Anet, C., *Through the Russian revolution*, 260

Angas, L. L. B., *Germany and her debts*, 245; *Reparations, trade and foreign exchange*, 245

Angeli, D., *Sword and Plough*, 147

Angell, N., *The dangers of half-preparedness*, 297; *The Peace Treaty and the economic chaos of Europe*, 87; *The political conditions of Allied success*, 219; *Prussianism and its destruction*, 115; *War aims*, 219; *The world's highway*, 143

Annunzio, G, d', *The rally*, 100

Apex, *The uneasy triangle*, 196

Applin, A., *Admiral Jellicoe*, 148

Apponyi, A., *Justice for Hungary*, 140

Aquila, *With the cavalry in the West*, 55

Archer, W., *The peace President*, 324; *The pirate's progress*, 289; *The thirteen days, July 23-August 4, 1914*, 197

Archibald, N. S., *Heaven high, hell deep, 1917-1918*, 309

Arminius, *From Sarajevo to the Rhine*, 234

Armitage, F. P., *Leicester, 1914-1918*, 30

Armstrong, D. B. & Greenwood, C. H., *War stamps of the Allies, 1914-1920*, 216

Armstrong, E. H., *The crisis of Quebec, 1914-1918*, 61

Armstrong, G. G., *Our ultimate aim in the war*, 30

Armstrong H. C., *Grey steel*, 273; *Grey wolf*, 287; *On the run*, 91

Armstrong, J. W. S., *War and treaty legislation, 1914-1922*, 153

Armstrong, W. J. M., *My first week in Flanders*, 100

Arnaud, R., *Tragedie bouffe*, 108

Arnett, A. M., *Claude Kitchin and the Wilson policies*, 325

Arnold, G., *Sister Anne! Sister Anne!*, 192

Arnoux, A., *The European war*, 129

Arthur, Sir G. C. A., *The life of Lord Kitchener*, 151; *Lord Haig*, 127; *The story of the Household Cavalry*, 55

Aru-Mugam, *The golden key to world power and the war*, 216

Ascoli, D., *The Mons Star*, 183

Asghar-Ali, S., *Our heroes of the Great War*, 316

Ash, B., *The last dictator*, 177

Ash, E. L., *Nerve in wartime*, 165

Ashbee, C. R., *The American League to enforce peace*, 155

Ashburn, T. Q., *History of the 324th Field Artillery United States Army* 308

Ashford, B. K., *A soldier in science*, 263

Ashley, R. S., *War diary of Private ...*, 47

Ashmead Bartlett, E., *Ashmead Bartlett's despatches from the Dardanelles*, 76; *From the Somme to the Rhine*, 320; *Some of my experiences in the Great War*, 210; *The uncensored Dardanelles*, 76

Ashmore, E. B., *Air defence*, 246

Ashton, H., *First from the Front*, 317

Ashurst, G., *My bit*, 47

Ashwell, L., *Modern troubadours*, 91

Ashworth, T., *Trench warfare 1914–1918*, 286

Askew, A. & Askew, C., *The stricken land*, 267

Aspinall-Oglander, C. F., *Official history of the Great War; Military operations: Gallipoli*, 112

Asprey, R. B., *The first battle of the Marne*, 163

Asquith, H. H., *The genesis of the war*, 14; *The great shell shortage*, 14; *Memories and reflections*, 14

Assher, B., *A nomad under arms*, 57

Aston, *Sir* G. G., *The biography of the late Marshal Foch*, 102; *The Great War of 1914-1918*, 129; *Secret service*, 264; *The triangle of terror in Belgium*, 24

Atkins, T., *The letters of Thomasina Atkins*, 326

Atkinson, C. F., *Dictionary of English and French military terms*, 79; *Dictionary of English and German military terms*, 79

Atkinson, C. T., *The Devonshire Regiment, 1914-1918*, 44; *The history of the South Wales Borderers, 1914-1918*, 52; *The Queen's Own Royal West Kent Regiment, 1914-1919*, 49; *The Royal Hampshire Regiment*, 66; *The Seventh Division 1914-1918*, 40

Atteridge, A. H., *The first phase of the Great War*, 129; *History of the 17th-Northern-Division*, 40; *Marshal Ferdinand Foch*, 102; *The second phase of the Great War*, 129; *The world wide war: first stage*, 129

Augé-Laribé, M., *Agriculture and food supply in France during the war*, 2

Auld, G. P., *The Dawes Plan and the new economics*, 245

Auld, S. J. M., *Gas and flame in modern warfare*, 114

Austin, H. H., *The Baqubah Refugee Camp*, 236

Austin, L. J., *My experiences as a German prisoner*, 223

Austrian, D., *Ways of war and peace*, 205

Auten H., *'Q' boat adventures*, 228

Ayres, L. P., *The war with Germany*, 290

Ayscough, J., *French windows*, 70, 104

Azan, P. J. L., *Warfare of today*, 91

B. B., *Over there*, 22

B, W. T., *Plane tales from the skies*, 3; *The Royal Flying Corps in the war*, 249

Bachman, W. E., *Delta of the triple elevens*, 308

Bacon, A. F. L., *Wanderings of a temporary warrior*, 210

Bacon, *Sir* R. H. S., *The concise story of the Dover Patrol*, 83; *The Dover Patrol, 1915-1917*, 83; *The Jutland scandal*, 149; *Life of Lord Fisher*, 172

Bacon, W. S., *Sky fighters of World War I*, 95

Bacon, W. J., *History of the Fifty-Fifth Field Artillery Brigade, 1917, 1918, 1919*, 307

Badcock, G. E., *History of the transport services of the Egyptian Expeditionary Force*, 54, 90

Badley, J. H., *Education after the war*, 89

Baerlein, H. P. B., *The march of the seventy thousand*, 76

Baggs, T. A., *Back from the Front*, 100

Bagnold, E., *A diary without dates*, 138, 192

Bailey, T. A., *The policy of the United States toward the neutrals, 1917-1918*, 80, 290; *Woodrow Wilson and the great betrayal*, 325; *Woodrow Wilson and the lost peace*, 325

Bailey, T. A. and Ryan, P. B., *The Lusitania disaster*, 162

Bailey, W. F., *The Slavs of the war zone*, 331

Baillie, W., *History in prophecy*, 194

Bainbridge, W. S., *Report on medical and surgical developments of the war*, 165

Bairnsfather, B., *Bullets and billets*, 66; *From mud to mufti*, 66

Baker, C. W., *Government control and operation of industry in Great Britain and the United States during the World War*, 142

Baker, G., *The soul of a skunk*, 74

Baker, J. A., *A leader of men*, 171

Baker, L. S., *Company history*, 309

Baker, N. D., *Frontiers of freedom*, 1; *Why we went to war*, 295

Baker, P. S., *Animal war heroes*, 9

Baker, R. S., *Woodrow Wilson*, 325; *Woodrow Wilson and world settlement*, 325

Bakewell C. M., *The story of the American Red Cross in Italy*, 233

Balch, E. G., *Approaches to the great settlement*, 205

Baldridge, C. L., *I was there with the Yanks on the Western Front*, 217

Baldwin, E. F., *The world war, how it looks to the nations involved*, 219; *The world war: a sketch of the different nations*, 129

Baldwin, H., *Holding the line*, 298

Baldwin, H. W., *World War I*, 129

Baldwin, J. M., *American neutrality*, 296; *France and the war*, 104

Baldwin, M., *Canteening overseas, 1917-1919*, 66

Bales, P. G., *The history of the 1/4th Battalion, Duke of Wellington's Regiment, 1914-1918*, 53

Balfour, A. J., *Essays, speculative and political*, 21

Balfour, H. H., *An airman marches*, 246

Balfour, M., *The Kaiser and his times*, 150

Ball, C. R., *The war*, 237

Ballard, F., *Britain justified*, 237; *Christianity after the war*, 237; *Plain truths versus German lies*, 115, 318

Bandini, P., *About this Anglo-German war*, 219

Bane, S. L. & Lutz, R. H., *Blockade of Germany after the Armistice, 1918-1919*, 28

Bandholtz, H. H., *An undiplomatic diary*, 140

Bang, J. P., *Hurrah and hallelujah*, 115

Banker, M. S., *My beloved Armenia*, 10

Banks, A., *A military atlas of the First World War*, 163

Banks, T. M. & Chell, R. A., *With the 10th Essex in France*, 45

Banse, E., *Germany, prepare for war*, 129

Banting, D. R. & Embleton, G. A., *The Western Front, 1914-1918*, 320

Barbeau, A. E. & Henri, F., *The unknown soldiers*, 188

Barber, C. H., *Besieged in Kut and after*, 152

Barber, F. A., *The horror of it*, 217

Barber, G., *My diary in France*, 321

Barber, M. H., *A British nurse in Bolshevik Russia*, 255

Barbusse, H., *Under fire*, 108

Barclay, C. N., *Armistice 1918*, 11

Barclay, Sir T., *New methods of adjusting international disputes and the future*, 155

Baring, M., *R.F.C., H.Q., 1914-1918*, 249

Barker, A. J., *The neglected war*, 178; *Townshend of Kut*, 152

Barker, E., *War letters from the living dead man*, 194

Barker, Ernest, *A confederation of the nations*, 155

Barker, H. G., *The Red Cross in France*, 233

Barker, J. E., *Economic statesmanship*, 87; *Foundations of Germany*, 115; *The great problems of British statesmanship*, 80

Barlow, Sir C. A. M. & Williams, W. G., *War pensions*, 209

Barnard, C. I., *Paris war days*, 204

Barnes, A. F., *The story of the 2/5th Battalion, Gloucestershire Regiment, 1914-1918*, 45

Barnes, H. E., *The genesis of the World War*, 197

Barnes, J. F., *The genesis of the American First Army*, 298

Barnes, J. T. S., *Half a life*, 246

Barnes, R. M., *The British Army of 1914*, 35

Barnett, C., *The swordbearers*, 278; *The Great War*, 129

Barnett, G., *V.C.'s of the air*, 316.

Barnett, G. H., *With the 48th Division in Italy*, 42

Barr, J. C., *Home service*, 35

Barrett, Sir J. W., *The war work of the Y.M.C.A. in Egypt*, 329

Barrett, Sir J. W. & Deane, P. E., *The Australian Army Medical Corps in Egypt, 1914-1915*, 15

Barrett, W. E., *The first war planes*, 3

Barrie, A., *War underground*, 181

Barrie, J. M., *Echoes of the war*, 93

Barron, C. W., *The audacious war*, 197; *War finance*, 97; *A world re-making; or, Peace finance*, 87

Barron, E. A., *Deeds of Heroism and Daring*, 111

Barrow, Sir G., *The fire of life*, 171, 210

Barry, F. R., *Religion and the war*, 237

Barry, W., *The world's debate*, 197

Bartholomew, E., *First World War tanks*, 282

Bartimeus, *The Navy eternal*, 250

Bartlett, C. P. O., *Bomber pilot, 1916-1918*, 29

Bartlett, V., *Behind the scenes at the Peace Conference*, 313; *Mud and khaki*, 101

Bartlett, W. T., *The world's crisis in the light of prophecy*, 194

Barton, E. M., *Eve in khaki*, 326

Barton, G., *Celebrated spies and famous mysteries of the Great War*, 264

Barton, W. E., *Blue stars and gold*, 237

Baruch, B. M., *The making of the reparation and economic sections of the Treaty*, 245

Bass, H. J., *America's entry into World War I*, 295

Bass, J. F., *The peace tangle*, 205

Bassett, J., *The home front 1914–1918*, 15

Bassett, J. S., *Lost fruits of Waterloo*, 155; *Our war with Germany*, 290

Bassompierre, A. de, *The night of August 2-3, 1914 at the Belgian Foreign Office*, 24

Batchelor, J., *Fighting aircraft of World War One and Two*, 95; *Fighting ships of World War One and Two*, 185

Bateman, C. T., *U-boat devilry*, 177, 289

Bates, J. V., *Our Allies and enemies in the Near East*, 187

Battey, G. M., *70,000 miles on a submarine destroyer*, 311

Battine, C., *Military history of the war: the campaign of 1914*, 129

Baty, T. & Morgan, J. H., *War*, 143

Batzler-Heim, G., *Horrors of Cayenne*, 223

Bauermeister, A., *Spies break through*, 264

Baumont, M., *The fall of the Kaiser*, 150

Baunville, J., *Italy and the war*, 145

Bausman, F., *Let France explain*, 104

Bavin, W. D., *Swindon's war record*, 30

Baxter, A., *We will not cease*, 74

Bayly, H. W., *Triple challenge; or, War, whirligigs and windmills*, 165

Bayne, J. B., *Bugs and bullets*, 165

Baynes, E. H., *Animal heroes of the Great War*, 9

Baynes, J., *Morale*, 189

Beadon, R. H., *Some memories of the Peace Conference*, 313

Beaman, A., *The squadroon*, 70

Beamish, R. J. & March, F. A., *America's part in the World War*, 198

Bean, C. E. W., *Anzac to Amiens*, 15; *The Australian Imperial Force in France, 1916*, 16; *The Australians in France and the story of Anzac*, 16; *Gallipoli mission*, 112; *Gallipoli correspondent*, 112; *Letters from France on the achievements of the Australian Imperial Force in 1916*, 16; *The official history of Australia in the war of 1914-1918*, 15; *Two men I knew*, 16

Beatson, A. M., *The motor-bus in war*, 54

Beauchamp, P., *Fanny goes to war*, 193

Beauman, A. B., *With the 38th in France and Italy*, 41

Beaumont, H., *Old Contemptible*, 223

Beaumont, J. C. H., *The British Mercantile Marine during the war*, 177

Beazley, *Sir* C. R., *The road to ruin in Europe, 1890-1914*, 197

Beca, *Colonel*, *A study of the development of infantry tactics*, 282

Bechhofer, C. E., *Russia at the crossroads*, 255

Beck, J. M., *The evidence in the case*, 197; *The passing of the new freedom*, 325; *The reckoning*, 206; *The war and humanity*, 295

Becke, A. F., *The order of battle of Divisions*, 35; *The Royal Regiment of Artillery at Le Cateau, Wednesday 26th August, 1914*, 57

Becker, J. J., *The Great War and the French people*, 104

Beckett, F. W. & Simpson, K., *A nation in arms*, 35

Bedborough, G., *Arms and the Clergy, 1914-1918*, 237

Bedford, C. W., *Legs eleven*, 16

Beer, G. L., *African questions at the Paris Peace Conference*, 313

Beesly, P., *Room 40*, 143

Begbie, H., *On the side of the angels*, 194; *The Queen's net*, 326

Begg, R., *Surgery on trestles*, 165

Behrend, A. F., *As from Kemmel Hill*, 321; *Make me a soldier*, 112; *Nine days*, 57

Belknap, R. R., *Yankee mining squadron; or, Laying the North Sea mine barrage*, 181

Bell, A. D., *Sergeant Richardson's war*, 16

Bell, D. H., *A soldier's diary of the Great War*, 210

Bell, E. P., *The British censorship*, 69

Bell, G. K. A., *The war and the kingdom of God*, 237

Bell, G. M. L., *The Arab war*, 178

Bell, J., *We did not fight*, 74

Bell, J. J., *Little grey ships*, 78

Bell, J. K., *The glory of Zeebrugge and the 'Vindictive'*, 331

Bell, L. L., *The story of the Christmas ship*, 236

Bell, R. W., *Canada in war paint*, 61

Bell, W., *A scavenger in France*, 104

Bellairs, C. W., *The battle of Jutland*, 149

Bellegarde, S. de, *The Russian soldier*, 258

Belloc, J. H. P., *A general sketch of the European war*, 129; *The two maps of Europe and some aspects of the Great War*, 129

Belmont, F., *A crusader of France*, 108

Belton, J. & Odell, E. G., *Hunting the Hun*, 298

Bemelmans, L., *My war with the United States*, 210

Beneckendorff und Hindenburg, P., *Out of my life*, 128

Benedict, B., *History of the Great War*, 129

Benedict, C., *Six months, March-August 1914*, 197

Benes, E., *My war memoirs*, 171

Benn, W. W., *In the side shows*, 3

Bennett, E. A., *Liberty*, 30; *Over there, war scenes on the Western Front*, 317

Bennett, G., *The battle of Jutland*, 149; *Coronel and the Falklands*, 75; *Naval battles of the first World War*, 185

Bennett, I. E., *Editorials from 'The Washington Post'*, 222

Bennett, J. J., *The Dover Patrol*, 84

Bennett, S. G., *The 4th Canadian Mounted Rifles, 1914-1919*, 63

Bensen, W., *Hindenburg's soldier*, 122

Benson, A. L., *Inviting war to America*, 290

Benson, E. F., *Crescent and Iron Cross*, 115, 287; *The white eagle of Poland*, 218

Benson, *Sir* I., *The man with the donkey*, 112

Benson, R., *State credit and banking during the war and after*, 97

Benson, S. C., *'Back from Hell'*, 165

Benstead, C. R., *The Fifth Army fell back*, 39

Bent, J., *From training camp to fighting line*, 35

Bentinck, H. D., *The letters of Major Henry Bentinck*, 156

Bentwich, N. de M., *Palestine of the Jews, past, present and future*, 203

Benwell, H. A., *History of the Yankee Division*, 302

Beraud-Villars, J. M. E., *Notes on a lost pilot*, 107

Berden, L., *Pictures of ruined Belgium*, 24

Berdinner, H. F., *With the heavies in Flanders*, 57

Berg, A., *Latvia and Russia*, 255

Berger, M., *Germany after the Armistice*, 115; *The ordeal by fire*, 108; *Secret of the Marne*, 163

Bergmann, C., *The history of reparation*, 245

Bergson, H. L., *The meaning of the war*, 219

Berkeley, R., *The history of the Rifle Brigade in the war of 1914-1918*, 49

Berkman, A., *The Russian tragedy*, 260

Bernard, J. H., *In war time*, 237

Berndorff, H. R., *Espionage*, 264

Bernheim, B. M., *Passed as censored*, 210

Bernstorff, J. von, *My three years in America*, 172

Berrie, G., *Morale*, 16

Berry, H., *Make the Kaiser dance*, 210, 298

Berry, J., *The story of a Red Cross visit in Serbia*, 267

Berry, J. M., *European history foretold*, 194

Bertie, F. L., *The diary of Lord Bertie of Thame, 1914-1918*, 172

Bertrand, A., *The victory of Lorraine*, 101

Bertrand, G. & Sombert, O. N., *Tactics and duties for trench-fighting*, 286

Beston, H. B., *Full speed ahead*, 311

Bethlen, I., *The Treaty of Trianon and European peace*, 287

Bethman-Hollweg, T., *Reflections on the World War*, 172; *Seven war speeches*, 172

Betts, E., *The bagging of Baghdad*, 178

Bevan E. R., *German social democracy during the war*, 115; *German war aims*, 115; *The method in the madness*, 115, 197

Bevan, T., *With Haig at the Front*, 127

Beveridge, A. J., *What is back of the war*, 129

Beveridge, Sir W. H., *British food control*, 103

Bewsher, F. W., *History of the 51st (Highland) Division, 1914-1918*, 42

Bewsher, P., *'Green balls'*, 29

Bibikoff, M., *Our Indians at Marseilles*, 141

Bickerstaff-Drew, F., *John Ayscough's letters to his mother during 1914, 1915 and 1916*, 156

Bickersteth, J. B., *History of the 6th Cavalry Brigade, 1914-1919*, 55

Bicknell, E. P., *In war's wake, 1914-1915*, 233; *With the Red Cross in Europe, 1917-1922*, 233

Biddle, C. J., *Fighting airman*, 95; *Way of an eagle*, 3

Bidwells, S., *Gunners at war*, 57

Bigelow, G. L., *Liege on the line of march*, 159

Bigwood, G., *The Lancashire fighting Territorials in Gallipoli*, 35, 112

Bill, C. A., *The 15th Battalion Royal Warwickshire Regiment (2nd Birmingham Bn.) in the Great War*, 51

Billington, M. F., *The Red Cross in war*, 233; *The roll-call of serving women*, 193, 327

Binding, R. G., *A fatalist at war*, 122

Bing, A. M., *War-time strikes and their adjustment*, 142

Bingham, A., *Handbook of the European war*, 27

Bingham, E. B. S., *Falklands, Jutland and the Bight*, 250

Bingham, H., *Explorer in the air service*, 3, 309

Binyon, R. L., *For dauntless France*, 165, 236

Bird, W. D., *A chapter of misfortunes*, 178

Birdsall, P., *Versailles twenty years after*, 313

Birinyi, L. K., *The tragedy of Hungary*, 140; *Why the Treaty of Trianon is void*, 287

Birmingham, G. A., *A Padre in France*, 70

Bishop, C. W., *The Canadian Y.M.C.A. in the Great War*, 329

Bishop, F., *The story of the submarine*, 280

Bishop, H. C. W., *A Kut prisoner*, 152

Bishop, W. A., *The courage of early morning*, 95; *Winged warfare*, 95

Black, D., *Red Dust*, 8

Black, E. G., *I want one volunteer*, 63

Black E. W., *Hospital heroes*, 138

Black, H., *The cleavage of the world*, 219

Black, J., *Around the guns*, 57

Black Tab, *On the road to Kut*, 179

Blackall, C. W., *Songs from the trenches*, 273

Blackburn, C. J., *How the Manx fleet helped in the Great War*, 145

Blackburn, D., *The martyr nurse*, 68

Blackburne, H. W., *This also happened on the Western Front*, 70

Blackburne, L. E., *Lieut. Col. C. H. Blackburne*, 172

Blacker, L. V. S., *On secret patrol in high Asia*, 264

Blackledge, W. J., *The legion of marching madmen*, 178

Blackwell, E. & Axe, E. C., *Romford to Beirut*, 57

Blair, D. & Dand, C. H., *Russian hazard*, 264

Blake, W. T., *'Over there'*, 246

Blakeslee, G. H., *The problems and lessons of the war*, 181

Blanchon, G., *The new warfare*, 278

Bland, J. O. P., *Germany's violations of the laws of war*, 318

Blankenhorn, H., *Adventures in propaganda*, 227

Blaser, B., *Kilts across the Jordan*, 203

Blatch, *Mrs* H., *Mobilizing woman-power*, 327

Blatchford, R., *General von Sneak*, 115; *The war that was pretold*, 194

Blaxland, G., *Amiens, 1918*, 9

Blenkinsop, Sir L. J. & Rainey, J. W., *Veterinary services*, 54, 165

Blick, G., *The 1/4 Battalion, Wiltshire Regiment, 1914-19*, 53

Blicq, A. S., *Norman Ten Hundred*, 50

Bloch, C., *The causes of the World War*, 197

Bloch, M. L. B., *Memoirs of war 1914–1915*, 210

Blocksidge, W., *An Anzac muster*, 16

Bloem, W., *The advance from Mons, 1914*, 183

Blond, G., *The Marne*, 163; *Verdun*, 313

Bluecher, E. M., *An English wife in Berlin*, 115

Bluett, A., *With our Army in Palestine*, 203

Blum, J. M., *Joe Tumulty and the Wilson era*, 290

Blumberg, Sir H. E., *Britain's sea soldiers*, 250

Blumenfeld, R. D., *All in a lifetime*, 222

Blumenthal, D., *Alsace-Lorraine*, 7

Blunden, E., *Undertones of war*, 210

Boardman, M. T., *Under the Red Cross flag at home and abroad*, 233

Bocharskaya, S. & Pier, F., *They knew how to die*, 233

Boden, J. F. W., *Freedom's battle*, 197

Bodley, J. E. C., *Romance of the battle-line in France*, 22, 181

Bogart, E. L., *Direct and indirect costs of the great World War*, 97; *War costs and their financing*, 97

Bogitschevich, M., *Causes of the war*, 197

Boleslavski, R., *Way of a lancer*, 218

Bolwell, F. A., *With a Reservist in France*, 40

Bond, A. R., *Inventions of the Great War*, 91

Bond, B., *Staff Officer*, 210

Bond, F. B., *The hill of vision*, 194

Bond, R. C., *The history of the King's Own Yorkshire Light Infantry in the Great War*, 47; *Prisoners grave and gay*, 223

Bone, D. W., *Merchantmen-at-arms*, 177

Bone, M., *War Drawings*, 12; *The Western Front*, 12; *With the Grand Fleet*, 12

Bonsal, S., *Unfinished business*, 314

Booth, A. H., *The true book about the First World War*, 129

Booth, E. C. & Hill, G. L., *The war romance of the Salvation Army*, 262

Booth, J. B., *The gentle cultured German, the road-hog of Europe*, 318

Booth, M., *With the B.E.F. in France*, 262

Boraston, J. H. & Bax, C. E., *The Eighth Division in war*, 40

Borchard, E. M., *Neutrality for the United States*, 296

Bordeaux, H., *The deliverance of the captives*, 104; *Georges Guynemer, knight of the air*, 95; *The last days of Fort Vaux*, 104

Borden, M., *The forbidden zone*, 193

Borden, Sir R. L., *The war and the future*, 61

Borer, M. C., *The First World War*, 129

Borsi, G., *A soldier's confidences with God*, 237

Bosworth, R. J. B., *Italy and the approach of the First World War*, 197

Botkin, G., *The real Romanovs*, 255

Bott, A. J., *Eastern Flights*, 91; *Eastern nights – and flights*, 247

Boucard, R., *Revelations from the Secret Service*, 264

Boudin, L. B., *Socialism and war*, 270

Boughton, V. T., *History of the Eleventh Engineers, U.S. Army*, 306

Boullier, J. A., *Jottings by a gunner and chaplain*, 70

Boulnois, H. M., *Some soldiers and little Mamma*, 104

Boulton, D., *Objection overruled*, 202

Bourcier, E., *Under German shells*, 108

Bourne, R. S., *Towards an enduring peace*, 206; *War and the intellectuals*, 290

Boutroux, E., *Philosophy and the war*, 216

Bowden, S. H., *The history of the Australian Comforts Fund*, 15

Bowen, E., *Knights of the air*, 95

Bowen, W. S., *Source book: operations of the 29th Division*, 303

Bowley, A. L., *The effect of the war on the external trade of the United Kingdom*, 142; *Prices and wages in the U.K., 1914-1920*, 87; *Some economic consequences of the Great War*, 87

Bowser, T., *The story of British V.A.D. work in the Great War*, 312

Bowyer, C., *Airmen of World War I*, 247; *Albert*

Ball, V.C., 95; *For valour*, 316; *Sopwith Camel*, 95

Boyd, W., *With a Field Ambulance at Ypres*, 329

Boyle, J. F., *The Irish Rebellion of 1916*, 144

Boyle, R. C., *Record of the West Somerset Yeomanry, 1914-19*, 55

Boyle, W. H. D., *Gallant deeds*, 316

Boylston, H. D., *'Sister'*, 193

Bracq, J. C., *The provocation of France*, 108

Bradbridge, E. U., *Record of the 59th Division, 1915-1918*, 42

Braddon, R., *The siege*, 152

Bradford, M., *A hospital letter writer in France*, 138

Bradley, A. O., *Back of the Front in France*, 8

Bradley, J., *Allied intervention in Russia*, 259

Bradley, S., *More adventures of an A.D.C.*, 35

Bragg, Sir W. L., *Artillery survey in the First World War*, 58

Brailsford, H. N., *Across the blockade*, 115; *After the peace*, 206; *A League of Nations*, 155; *The war of steel and gold*, 87

Braithwaite, W. S. B., *Story of the Great War*, 129

Brandes, G., *The world at war*, 93

Brandon, B., *The silent service*, 250

Brandstrom, E., *Among prisoners-of-war in Russia and Siberia*, 269

Branford, V. V. & Geddes, P., *The coming polity*, 230

Bray, N. N. E., *A Paladin of Arabia*, 179; *Shifting Sands*, 179, 287

Braybon, G., *Women workers in the First World War*, 327

Brazier, R. H. & Sandford, E., *Birmingham and the Great War*, 30

Brehm, B., *That was the end*, 30

Brennan, A., *Pope Benedict XV and the war*, 68

Brent, P., *T. E. Lawrence*, 154

Brent, R., *Great War stories*, 275

Brereton, C. B., *Tales of three campaigns*, 190

Brereton, C. S. H., *Who is responsible?*, 197

Brereton, F. S., *The Great War and the R.A.M.C.*, 53

Brewer, D. C., *Rights and duties of neutrals*, 189

Brice, B., *The battle book of Ypres*, 329

Bridge, F. M., *A short history of the Great World War*, 129

Bridges, R., *The immortal dawn*, 112

Bridges, Sir, T., *Alarms and excursions*, 172; *On land and sea at the Dardanelles*, 76

Bridie, J., *Some talk of Alexander*, 187

Briggs, M. S., *Through Egypt in wartime*, 90

Briggs, R., *Richthofen the Red Baron*, 246

Bringolf, H., *I have no regrets*, 104

Briscoe, W. A., *The boy hero of the air*, 316

Briscoe, W. A. & Stannard, H. R., *Captain Ball, V.C.*, 95

British Museum Dept. of Printed Books, *Subject Index of Books Relating to the European War 1914-1918*, 27

British Red Cross Society, *The Red Cross in Gloucestershire during the war*, 233; *The work of V.A.D. (London) during the war*, 312

Britnieva, M., *One woman's story*, 165

Brittain, H. E., *To Verdun from the Somme*, 313

Broca, A. & Ducroquet, J., *Artificial limbs*, 165

Brockington, W. A., *Elements of military education*, 89

Brocklebank, H. C. R., *Tenth Cruiser Squadron Northern Patrol*, 76

Brodie, C. G., *Forlorn Hope, 1915*, 76, 280

Broinowski, L., *Tasmania's war record*, 15

Brookes, E., *Destroyer*, 79

Brooks, A., *As I saw it*, 109

Brook-Shepherd, G., *November 1918*, 129; *Royal sunset*, 129

Broomhall, M., *'Mine own vineyard'*, 237

Brophy, J., *The five years*, 129

Brophy, J. & Partridge, E., *The long trail*, 153, 273

Broughton, U. H., *The British Empire at war*, 59

Broun, H., *The A.E.F. with General Pershing and the American Forces*, 298

Brown, A. R. H., *The O.T.C. and the Great War*, 196

Brown, C., *The war and the faith*, 237

Brown, Cyril, *Germany as it is today*, 115

Brown, D., *Constantine; King and traitor*, 126; *In the heart of German intrigue*, 21, 115, 126

Brown, J., *Turkish days and ways*, 16

Brown, Mabel, W., *Neuropsychiatry and the war*, 166

Brown, Malcolm, *Scapa Flow*, 263; *Tommy goes to war*, 321

Brown, M. & Seaton, S., *Christmas truce*, 11

Brown, Warren J., *Child Yank over the Rainbow Division, 1918*, 303

Brown, William S., *My war diary, 1914-1919*, 187

Brown, W. Sorley, *War record of the 4th Battalion King's Own Scottish Borderers and Lothian and Border Horse*, 46

Browne, D. G., *The tank in action*, 54

Browne, J. H. B., *War problems*, 216, 270

Browne, K. M., *'Pot luck'*, 179

Browne, P. E., *Uncivil war*, 290

Brownlow, C. A. L., *The breaking of the storm*, 57

Brownlow, K., *The war, the west and the wilderness*, 97

Brownrigg, Sir D. E. R., *Indiscretions of the Naval censor*, 69

Bruce, C., *Humour in tragedy*, 138

Bruce, E. S., *Aircraft in war*, 3

Bruce, H. A., *Politics and the Canadian Army Medical Corps*, 61

Bruce, J. M., *Britain's first warplanes*, 3; *British aeroplanes, 1914-18*, 247; *War planes of the First World War*, 3

Bruce, T. B., *'Missing'*, 210

Bruckshaw, H., *The diaries of ...*, 250

Brugger, S. M., *Australians and Egypt 1914–1918*, 16

Bruntz, G. G., *Allied propaganda and the collapse of the German Empire in 1918*, 227

Brusilov, A. A., *A soldier's note-book, 1914-1918*, 258

Bruun, G., *Clemenceau*, 73

Bryan, J. H., *Ambulance 464*, 8

Bryan W. J. & Bryan, M., *The memoirs of William Jennings Bryan*, 172

Bryce, J., *Essays and addresses in war time*, 93; *The way of democracy*, 219

Buchan, J., *The battle of Jutland*, 149; *The battle of the Somme*, 271; *Days to remember*, 59; *A history of the British Navy during the war*, 250; *A history of the Great War*, 129; *The history of the South African Forces in France*, 274; *The long road to victory*, 129; *Naval episodes of the Great War*, 185; *Nelson's history of the war*, 130; *The story of the South African Brigade*, 274

Buchan W., *The log of HMS Bristol*, 76, 250

Buchanan, A., *Three years of war in East Africa*, 84, 188

Buchanan, Sir G. C., *My mission to Russia*, 255; *The tragedy of Mesopotamia*, 179

Buchanan, L. G., *After the war*, 230

Buchanan, M., *Petrograd, the city of trouble*, 255

Bucher, G., *In the line, 1914-1918*, 122

Buckell, A. C., *The greatest war*, 1

Buckland, C. S. B., *The 25th Army Brigade, R.G.A. on the Western Front in 1918*, 57

Bucklew, L. L., *Orphan Battery and operations, 128th U.S. Field Artillery*, 308

Buckley, H. H .C., *Great event*, 210

Buckrose, J. E., *War time in our street*, 30

Buffin, C., *Brave Belgians*, 24

Bugnet, *Commandant, Foch talks*, 102

Buist, H. M., *Aircraft in the German war*, 3

Buley, E. C., *Glorious deeds of Australasians in the Great War*, 16

Bulkley, M. E., *Bibliographical survey of contemporary sources for the economic and social history of the war*, 27

Bull, P. B., *Peace and war*, 238

Bullard, A., *The diplomacy of the Great War*, 80; *Mobilising America*, 296

Bullard, R.L., *Personalities and reminiscences of the war*, 290

Bullard, R. L. & Reeves, E., *American soldiers also fought*, 298

Bullitt, E. D., *An uncensored diary from the Central Empires*, 19

Bullock, D., *Allenby's war*, 7

Bulow, B. von, *Memoirs*, 172

Bulygin, P. & Kerensky, A., *The murder of the Romanovs*, 192

Bumble Bee, *The Salient, the Somme and Arras*, 321

Bunau-Varilla, P., *From Panama to Verdun*, 210

Bunbury, W. J., *A diary of an officer with the 4th Northumberland Fusiliers, 1915*, 48

Bunselmeyer, R. E., *The cost of the war, 1914-1918*, 30

Bunsen, V. B. de, *War and men's minds*, 238

Burge, C. G., *The annals of 100 Squadron*, 247

Burdick, C. B., *The frustrated raider*, 125

Burdick, C. B. & Moessner, U., *The German P.O.W. in Japan 1914–1920*, 223

Burgess, A., *The lovely sergeant*, 267

Burgess, J. W., *America's relations to the Great War*, 291; *The European War*, 198

Burgoyne, G. A., *The Burgoyne diaries*, 211

Burian von Rajecz, S., *Austria in dissolution*, 19

Burk, K., *Britain, America and the sinews of war*, 87

Burke, K., *Little heroes of France*, 104; *The white road to Verdun*, 313

Burke-Gaffney, J. J., *The story of the King's Regiment, 1914-18*, 47

Burne, A. H., *Mesopotamia*, 179; *Some pages from the history of 'Q' Battery, R.H.A. in the Great War*, 57

Burnell, F. S., *Australia versus Germany*, 189

Burnet, J., *Higher education and the war*, 89

Burnett, P. M., *Reparation at the Paris Peace Conference*, 245

Burrage, A., *War is war*, 35

Burroughs, E. A., *The fight for the future*, 238
Burrows, A. R., *The 1st Battalion, the Faugh-a-Ballaghs, Irish Fusiliers in the Great War*, 50
Burrows, C. W., *Scapa and a camera*, 263
Burrows, J. W., *The Essex Regiment, 1st Battalion*, 45; *The Essex Regiment, 2nd Battalion (56th) (Pompadours)*, 45
Burrows, W. E., *Richthofen*, 246
Burt, R. A., *British cruisers in World War One*, 76; *British destroyers in World War One*, 79
Burton, F. N., *The war diary, 1914-1918 of 10th Service Battalion, Royal Welch Fusiliers*, 51
Burton, H. H., *600 days' service*, 306
Burton, O. E., *The Auckland Regiment*, 190; *Silent Division*, 190
Bury, H., *Here and there in the war area*, 70; *My visit to Ruhleben*, 223
Busch, T., *Secret service unmasked*, 69
Bush, E. W., *Bless our ship*, 251; *Gallipoli*, 112
Busk, M., *E. T. Busk, a pioneer in flight*, 247
Buswell, L., *Ambulance No. 10*, 8
Butcher, P. E., *Skill and devotion*, 249
Butler, A. G., *The official history of the Australian Medical Services in the war of 1914-1918*, 16
Butler, A. S. G., *Plain impressions*, 247
Butler, N. M., *A world in ferment*, 1
Butler, P. R., *A galloper at Ypres*, 329
Butler, T., *Boche land before and during the war*, 115
Butters, H. A., *Harry Butters*, 298
Butterworth, H. M., *Letters written in the trenches near Ypres between May and September 1915*, 190
Buxton, A. R., *Andrew R. Buxton*, 172
Buxton, C. R., *Towards a lasting settlement*, 206
Buxton C. R. & Buxton, D. F., *The world after the war*, 230
Buxton, L., *The black sheep of the Balkans*, 21
Buxton, N. & Buxton, C. R., *The war and the Balkans*, 21
Buxton, N. & Leese, C. L., *Balkan problems and European peace*, 206
Bygott, J., *Two soldier brothers*, 177
Byrne, A. E., *Official history of the Otago Regiment NZEF in the Great War 1914–1918*, 190
Byrne, J. R., *New Zealand artillery in the field, 1914-18*, 190
Byron, M., *How to save cookery*, 103
Bywater, H. C., *Cruisers in battle*, 76; *Their secret purposes*, 185

C., *The Yeomanry Cavalry of Worcestershire,*

1914-22, 55
C, F., *On safari*, 84
Cababe, M., *The freedom of the seas*, 143
Cable, B., *Action front*, 317; *Between the lines*, 317; *Doing their bit*, 184; *Grapes of wrath*, 181
Cadenhead, J. F., *The Canadian Scottish*, 63
Caffret, K., *Farewell Leicester Square*, 60
Cahalan, P., *Belgian refugee relief in England during the Great War*, 236
Caine, T. H. H., *The drama of the three hundred and sixty-five days*, 130; *Our girls*, 327
Cairns, D. S., *The Army and religion*, 238
Calder, K. J., *Britain and the origins of the new Europe*, 80
Calhoun, F. S., *Power and principle*, 80
Call, A. P., *Neves and the war*, 166
Callaway, A. B., *With packs and rifles*, 211
Callaway, R. F., *Letters from two Fronts*, 156
Callin, R. W., *When the lantern of hope burned low*, 48
Callwell, *Sir* C. E., *Experiences of a dug-out*, 172; *The Dardanelles*, 76; *Field Marshal Sir Henry Wilson*, 177; *The life of Lieut.-General Sir Stanley Maude*, 174
Cambridge, T. R., *In the land of the Turkana*, 2
Cameron, J., *1914*, 130; *1916 – year of decision*, 219
Cameron, J. S., *Ten months in a German raider*, 125, 223
Cameron, K., *History of No. 1 General Hospital, Canadian Expeditionary Force, 1914-1919*, 63
Cammaerts, E., *The adoration of the soldiers*, 286; *Through the iron bars*, 24
Camp C. W., *History of the 305th Field Artillery*, 308
Campbell, A., *Crieff in the Great War*, 30
Campbell A. B., *Zeebrugge: St. George's Day, 1918*, 331
Campbell, C. & Wood, J. W., *Aces and aircraft of World War I*, 3
Campbell E., *Zeppelins*, 331
Campbell G., *My mystery ships*, 228
Campbell, G. F., *Soldier of the sky*, 3, 309; *Verdun to the Vosges*, 313
Campbell, G. L., *Royal Flying Corps, military wing*, 249
Campbell, H., *Belgian soldiers at home in the United Kingdom*, 24, 236
Campbell, Henry, *The law of war and contract*, 153
Campbell, P., *Back of the Front*, 166, 193
Campbell P. J., *The ebb and flow of battle*, 321; *In*

the cannon's mouth, 321, 329

Campbell, R. J., *The war and the soul*, 238; *With our troops in France*, 70

Campbell, R. W., *The mixed division*, 181

Campbell, W. W., *East Africa by motor lorry*, 84

Camus, J., *Physical and occupational re-education of the maimed*, 166

Cana, F. R., *The Great War in Europe*, 130

Canby, H. S., *Education by violence*, 93

Canada, Dept. of Agriculture, *Production and thrift*, 2

Canada Dept. of Secretary of State, *Copies of Proclamation Orders*, 61

Canada Field Comforts Commission, *With the First Canadian contingent*, 63

Canada Munitions Resources Commission, *Final Report*, 184

Candler, E., *The long road to Baghdad*, 179; *The years of chivalry*, 181, 275

Cannell, W. O., *Fighting types*, 12

Canning, J., *Living history, 1914*, 130

Cannoneers, *The cannoneers have hairy ears*, 298

Canton, W., *Dawn in Palestine*, 203

Capart, G. P., *Blue devil of France*, 276

Capek, T., *Bohemia under Hapsburg misrule*, 76

Capel, A., *Reflections on victory and a project for the federation of governments*, 181

Caraman, E., *Daughter of the Euphrates*, 10

Carbery, A. R. D., *The New Zealand Medical Service in the Great War*, 166

Carew, T., *The vanished Army*, 60; *Wipers*, 329

Carey, B., *Leaves from the diary of a Catholic Chaplain in the Great World War*, 70

Carey, G. V. & Scott, H. S., *An outline history of the Great War*, 130

Carisella, P. J., *Who killed the Red Baron?*, 246

Carl, E., *One against England*, 264

Carnbee, G. T., *War memories and sketches*, 70

Carnegie, D., *History of munitions supply in Canada*, 184

Carnegie Endowment for International Peace, *Diplomatic documents*, 80

Carossa, H., *A Roumanian diary*, 254

Carpenter, A. F. B., *The blocking of Zeebrugge*, 331

Carpenter, E. J., *Ethical and religious problems of the war*, 238; *The healing of the nations and the hidden sources of their strife*, 198

Carr, C. D. A., *From chauffeur to Brigadier*, 54

Carr, K., *Women who dared*, 327

Carr, W., *A time to leave the ploughshares*, 57

Carr, W. G., *Brass hats and bell-bottomed trousers*, 127; *By guess and by God*, 280; *Good hunting*, 251; *Hell's angels of the deep*, 251; *Out of the mists*, 251

Carrel, A. & Dehelly, G., *The treatment of infected wounds*, 166

Carrel, F., *Impressions of war*, 63

Carrie, R. A., *Italy at the Paris Peace Conference*, 314

Carrington, C. E., *Soldier from the wars returning*, 321; *A subaltern's war*, 211; *The war record of the 1/5th Battalion The Royal Warwickshire Regiment*, 51

Carstairs, C., *A generation missing*, 298

Carsten, F. L., *British and German radical movements in the First World War*, 206; *War against war*, 115

Carter, B. R., *Another part of the platform*, 144

Carter, F. L., *The conflagration in Europe*, 190

Carter, H., *The control of the drink trade*, 84; *Industrial reconstruction*, 142

Carter, Robert L., *Pictorial history of the 35th Division*, 303

Carter, Russell, G., *101st Field Artillery, A.E.F., 1917-1919*, 307

Cartmell, H., *For remembrance*, 30

Carver, L. M., *Ninetieth Aero Squadron, A.E.F.*, 309

Carver, T. N., *Government control of the liquor business in Great Britain and the United States*, 84

Casalis, A. E., *A young soldier of France and of Jesus Christ*, 156

Case, C. M., *Non-violent coercion*, 75

Cassar, G. H., *The French and the Dardanelles*, 77; *Kitchener, architect of victory*, 151; *The tragedy of Sir John French*, 110

Cassel, G., *Money and foreign exchange after 1914*, 98

Cassels, L., *The archduke and the assassin*, 198

Casserly, G., *A manual of war training for the new armies and volunteers*, 283; *Tactics for beginners*, 282

Cassells, J., *With the Black Watch, 1914*, 43

Casson, S., *Steady drummer*, 162

Castle, A. & Castle, E., *Little hours in great days*, 30

Castle, H. G., *Fire over England*, 3

Castle, W. R., *Wake up, America*, 296

Castle, W. T. F., *Grand Turk*, 287

Casualty, *Contemptible*, 60

Catchpool, T. C., *On two Fronts*, 8, 74

Catellani, E. L., *Italy and Austria at war*, 145

Catlin, A. W., *'With the help of God and a few Marines'*, 310

Catling, A. H., *The Kaiser under the searchlight*, 150

Cato, C., *The Navy everywhere*, 251; *The Navy in Mesopotamia, 1914 to 1917*, 251

Cator, D., *In a French military hospital*, 138

Catto, A., *With the Scottish troops in France*, 35

Caunter, J. A. L., *13 days*, 91

Cavell, E., *Nurse Cavell*, 68

Cavill, H. W., *Imperishable Anzacs*, 16

Celarié, H., *Slaves of the Huns*, 78

Cemal, P., *Memories of a Turkish statesman, 1913-1919*, 287

Centurion, *Gentlemen at arms*, 35

Chafee, Z., *Freedom of speech*, 291

Challand, G., *From genocide to resistance*, 10

Chamberlain, H. S., *The ravings of a renegade*, 115

Chamberlain, T. G., *Why we fought*, 296

Chamberlain, W. J., *A C.O. in prison*, 74

Chambers, F. P., *The war behind the war*, 219

Chambers, H. R., *United States submarine chasers in the Mediterranean, Adriatic, and the attack on Durazzo*, 79

Chambrun, J. A. & Marenches, C., *The American Army in the European conflict*, 298

Chambry, R., *The truth about Louvain*, 161

Champneys, A. C., *Tekel; the Papacy and the war*, 68

Chandos, O. L., *From peace to war*, 46

Chapin, H., *Soldier and dramatist*, 156

Chaplain, A., *Vermelles*, 70

Chapman, G., *A passionate prodigality*, 211; *Vain glory*, 181

Chapman, H. B., *Home truths about the war*, 238

Chapman, S. J., *Labour and capital after the war*, 230

Chapman-Houston, W. D. M., *General Sir John Cowans, the Quarter-Master-General of the Great War*, 172

Chapple, J. M., *'We'll stick to the finish!'*, 181

Charlton, P., *Australians on the Somme Pozieres 1916*, 16

Charlton, R. & Lascot, F. R., *Edith Cavell*, 68

Charrington, H. V. S., *The 12th Royal Lancers in France*, 55

Charteris, J., *At G.H.Q.*, 35; *Field Marshal Earl Haig*, 127

Charteris, N. K., *Some lectures and notes on machine guns*, 11

Chartres, J. S., *Judicial interpretations of the Munitions of War Acts*, 153; *The Munitions of War Acts, 1915 and 1916*, 153

Chase, H. L., *The 2/1st London Field Ambulance*, 8

Chase, J. C., *Soldiers all*, 298

Chastaine, B-H., *Story of the 36th Division in the World War*, 303

Chatterton, E. K., *The auxiliary patrol*, 183; *Beating the U-boats*, 289; *The big blockade*, 28; *Dardanelles dilemma*, 77; *Fighting the U-Boats*, 289; *Gallant gentlemen*, 185; *The 'Konisberg' adventure*, 125; *'Q' ships and their story*, 228; *Seas of adventures*, 185; *The sea-raiders*, 125; *'Severn's' saga*, 251

Cheradame, A., *Essentials of an enduring victory*, 206, 291; *The Pangerman plot unmasked*, 115; *United States and Pangermania*, 291

Chesterton, C. E., *The perils of peace*, 206; *The Prussian hath said in his heart*, 115

Chesterton, G. K., *The Crimes of England*, 30; *The Barbarism of Berlin*, 116; *Appetite of tyranny*, 198

Chevrillon, A., *Britain and the war*, 31

Chidgey, H. T., *Black square memories*, 51

Child, C. J., *The German-Americans in politics, 1914-1917*, 295

Childs Sir W., *Episodes and reflections*, 172

Chirol, Sir V., *The Egyptian problem*, 90

Chisholm, C., *Sir John French*, 111

Chitwood, O. P., *The immediate causes of the Great War*, 198

Christy, J. & Shamburger, P., *Aces and planes of World War I*, 3

Church, J. R., *The doctor's part*, 166

Church, L. F., *Story of Alsace-Lorraine*, 7

Churchill, M. S., *You who can help*, 291

Churchill, Lady R., *Woman's work in wartime*, 327

Churchill, W. S., *Traveller in wartime*, 72; *The world crisis, 1911-1918*, 72

Churchwoman, *The chariots of God*, 194

Churton, W. A. V., *War record of the 1/5th (Earl of Chester's) Battalion, the Cheshire Regiment*, 44

Chute, A. H., *The real Front*, 321

Cimino, H., *Behind the prison bars in Germany*, 223

City of London Police Reserve, *A record*, 219

Claes, J., *The German mole*, 227

Clapham, H. S., *Mud and khaki*, 211

Clapp, E. J., *Economic aspects of the war*, 87

Clark, A., *The donkeys*, 321

Clark, Alan, *Aces high*, 3; *Suicide of the Empires*, 86

Clark, Andrew, *Echoes of the Great War*, 211

Clark, Arthur T., *To Baghdad with the British*, 179

Clark, C. H. D., *God within the shadow*, 238

Clark, C. U., *United Roumania*, 254

Clark, G. S., *S.S.U. 503 of the U.S. Army Ambulance service with the French Army*, 298

Clark, J. M., *The costs of the World War to the American people*, 291

Clark, W. B., *When the U-boats came to America*, 289

Clarke, A. H. F., *To Kiel in the German Raider Wolf*, 125

Clarke, A. O. T., *Transport and sport in the Great War period*, 31

Clarke, B., *My round of the war*, 211

Clarke, F. J., *The world, the war and the Cross*, 238

Clarke, I. C., *American women and the World War*, 327

Clarke, M. C., *Paris waits*, 204

Clarkson, G. B., *Industrial America in the World War*, 142

Claxton, W. J., *The Mastery of the air*, 3

Clay, H. K. & Davis, P. M., *History of Battery C, 148th Field Artillery, A.E.F.*, 308

Clayton, I. M., *Shadow on the universe; or, The physical results of war*, 216

Clayton, P. T. B., *Letters from Flanders*, 238, 283; *Plain tales from Flanders*, 238; *Tales of Talbot House*, 283

Clemenceau, G. E. B., *France facing Germany*, 73; *Grandeur and misery of victory*, 73

Clierens, F., *A plain tale from Malines*, 236

Clifford, G. R., *My experiences as an aviator in the World War*, 3

Clifford, Sir H. C., *The Gold Coast Regiment in the East African campaign*, 126

Clifford, W. G., *The ex-soldier, by himself*, 83, 94

Clinker Knocker, *Aye, aye, sir*, 251

Close, A., *I accuse!*, 289

Close, P. L., *A prisoner of the Germans in South-West Africa*, 223, 274

Clover, G., *Stop at Suzanne's and lower flights*, 211

Clow, W. M., *The Christian message in the light of war*, 238

Clutton-Brock, A., *Thoughts on the war*, 216; *The ultimate belief*, 216

Clymer, G., *History of the U.S. Base Hospital No. 6*, 138

Coar, J. F., *Democracy and the war*, 291

Cobb, I. S., *The glory of the coming*, 298; *The red glutton*, 122

Cobb, R., *French and German, German and French*, 104

Coblentz, P., *The silence of Sarrail*, 109

Cocks, F. S., *The secret treaties and understandings*, 285

Coddington, F. J. O., *The young officer's guide to military law*, 284

Codman, C. R., *Contact*, 3

Coe, F. E., *We have paid enough*, 319

Coffin, L. & Sanders, C. H., *History of the Third Field Artillery, Ohio National Guard (136th F.A. Regiment, U.S. Army)*, 308

Cohen, I., *The Ruhleben prison camp*, 223

Cohen, W. I., *The American revisionists*, 296

Cohen-Portheim, P., *Time stood still*, 223

Coldicott, R., *London men in Palestine*, 203

Cole, C., *McCudden, V.C.*, 95; *Royal Air Force, 1918*, 247; *Royal Flying Corps, 1915-1916*, 249

Cole, Christopher, *The air defence of Britain 1914–1918*, 247

Cole, G. D. H., *Labour in the coal-mining industry*, 142; *Labour in war time*, 270; *Trade Unionism and munitions*, 184; *Workshop organization*, 142

Coleman, F. A., *From Mons to Ypres with French*, 111, 183; *Japan moves North*, 269; *With cavalry in 1915*, 55, 330

Coleridge, J. D., *The Grand Fleet*, 12

Coles, A., *Slaughter at sea*, 228; *Three before breakfast*, 289

Coller, F. H., *A State trading adventure*, 103

Collett, H. B., *The 28th; a record of war service with the A.I.F.*, 16

Collie, Sir J., *The management of neurasthenia and allied disorders contracted in the Army*, 166

Collier, B., *Brasshat*, 177

Colliers, *History of the war*, 130

Collin, C. C. R., *War against war and the enforcement of peace*, 93

Collings, J., *The Great War*, 183

Collins, F. A., *Naval heroes of to-day*, 311

Collins, J., *Italy re-visited, 1917-1918*, 145

Collins, L. L., *History of the 151st Field Artillery, Rainbow Division*, 308

Collison, C. S., *The 11th Royal Warwicks in*

France, 1915-16, 51

Collman, C. A., *The war plotters of Wall Street*, 98

Collyer, D., *Flying*, 254

Collyer, J. J., *The South Africans*, 84

Colonna, B. A., *History of Company B, 311th Infantry in the World War*, 306

Columban, Dame M., *The Irish nuns at Ypres*, 330

Colwill, R. A., *Through hell to victory*, 44

'Commander', *Hints and tips for members of the O.T.C.*, 284

Commentitius, *The Great War for the greater peace*, 194

Committee on the war and religious outlook, *Missing outlook*, 238; *Religion among American men*, 238

Condell, D. & Liddiard. J., *Working for victory?*, 327

Congdon, D., *Combat; World War I*, 276

Congreve, B., *Armageddon road*, 316

Connolly, J., *A socialist and war, 1914-1916*, 270

Connolly, J. B., *U-boat hunters*, 79

Connors, J. F., *Albatross*, 95

Consett, M. W., *The triumph of un-armed forces, 1914-18*, 28

Contact, *An airman's outings*, 249; *Cavalry of the clouds*, 3

Conway, C. B. & Shuford, G. A., *History of the 119th Infantry, 60th Brigade, 30th Division, U.S. Army*, 305

Cook, Sir E. T., *The Press in war-time*, 222

Cook, G., *Break out!*, 92; *Missions most secret*, 264; *None but the valiant*, 276; *Wings of glory*, 276

Cook, Sir T. A., *Kaiser, Krupp and Kultur*, 198; *Kultur and catastrophe*, 116; *The last lap*, 181; *The mark of the beast*, 198

Cook, W. V., *Grey fish*, 280

Cooke, C. H., *Historical records of the 16th Battalion. Northumberland Fusiliers. 1914-1918*, 49; *Historical records of the 19th Service Battalion Northumberland Fusiliers (Pioneers)*, 49

Cooke, F. G., *Scouting by night*, 284; *The value of observation in war*, 284

Coolidge, A. C., *The origins of the Triple Alliance*, 130

Coombs, R. E. B., *Before endeavours fade*, 22

Coop, J. O., *Short guide to the battlefields*, 22; *The story of the 55th Division*, 42

Cooper, B., *The Tenth (Irish) Division in Gallipoli*, 40

Cooper, Bryan, *The ironclads of Cambrai*, 61; *Tank battles of World War I*, 54

Cooper, D., *Haig*, 127

Cooper, F. H., *Khaki crusaders*, 274

Cooper, G. W., *Our second battalion (111th Infantry, U.S. Army)*, 305

Cooper, H. E. H., *The battle of the Falkland Isles*, 94

Coppard, G., *With a machine gun to Cambrai*, 53, 61

Coppens de Houlthulst, W., *Days on the wing*, 108

Copping, A. E., *Souls in khaki*, 238; *Tommy's Triangle*, 329

Copplestone, B., *The secret of the Navy*, 251

Corbett, E., *Red Cross in Serbia, 1915-1919*, 267

Corbett, E. C., *The Worcestershire Regiment*, 53

Corbett, Sir J. S. & Newbolt, Sir H., *History of the Great War; naval operations*, 185, 251

Corbett-Smith. A., *The Marne - and after*, 163; *The retreat from Mons*, 183

Corcoran, A. P., *Daredevil of the Army*, 78

Corday, M., *The Paris Front*, 204

Cornebise, A. E., *The stars and stripes*, 222

Cornet-Auquier, A., *Soldier unafraid*, 109

Cornford, L. C., *The British Navy, the Navy vigilant*, 251; *Echoes from the Fleet*, 251; *Lord High Admiral and others*, 251; *The merchant seaman in war*, 177; *Paravane adventure*, 181, 251; *The secret of consolation*, 270; *With the Grand Fleet*, 251

Cornwell, J., *The story of John Travers Cornwell, V.C.*, 316

Corrigall, D. J., *History of the Twentieth Canadian Battalion (Central Ontario Regiment) C.E.F.*, 63

Corrigan, J. P., *Tin ensign*, 181

Cosens, M., *Lloyd George's munition girls*, 184

Cosgrove, E. C., *Canada's fighting pilots*, 62

Cosmos, *The basis of durable peace*, 206

Costello, J. & Hughes, T., *Jutland, 1916*, 149

Costello, L. W. & O'Sullivan, R., *The Profiteering Act, 1919*, 153

Coudert, F. R., *Why Europe is at war*, 198

Couhat, J. L., *French warships of World War I*, 110

Coulson, T., *Mata Hari*, 164; *Queen of spies. Louise de Bettignies*, 264

Coulton, G. G., *The case for compulsory military service*, 75; *The main illusions of pacifism*, 202; *Pacifist illusions*, 202

Courtney, W. L., *Armageddon - and after*, 220

Cousins, G., *The story of Scapa Flow*, 263

Cowan, J., *The Maoris in the Great War*, 190

Cowan, S. K., *Sergeant York and his people*, 299

Cowie, J. S., *Mines, minelayers and minelaying*, 181

Cowing, K. F., *'Dear folks at home . . .'*, 310

Cowland, W. S., *Some account of the 10th and 12th Battalions, the Hampshire Regiment, 1914-1918*, 46

Cowles, V., *The last Tsar and Tsarina*, 192

Cowley, R., *1918: the gamble for victory*, 321

Coxon, S. W., *Dover during the dark days*, 84

Coxwell, C. F., *Through Russia in war time*, 255

Coyle, E. R., *Ambulancing on the French Front*, 8

Crafer, T. W., *A prophet's visions and the war*, 194

Cram, R. A., *Heart of Europe*, 24

Cramb, J. A., *Germany and England*, 198

Cramm, R., *The first five hundred*, 63

Crampton, R. J., *The hollow detente*, 198

Cranage, D. H. S., *The war and unity*, 238

Craster, J. M., *'Fifteen rounds a minute'*, 46

Cravath, P. D., *Great Britain's part*, 35

Craven, D., *Peninsula of death*, 113

Crawford, C., *Six months with the Sixth Brigade*, 299

Crawshay-Williams, E., *Leaves from an officer's note book*, 211

Creed, L., *A woman's experiences in the Great War*, 327

Creel, G., *How we advertised America*, 227; *The war, the world and Wilson*, 220; *Wilson and the issues*, 325

Creighton, O., *With the 29th Division in Gallipoli*, 70, 113

Creswick, P., *Kent's care for the wounded*, 166

Crighton, J. C., *Missouri and the World War*, 291

Crile, G. W., *A mechanistic view of war and peace*, 216

Croft, G. G., *Some 1918 reflections*, 216

Croft, H. P., *Twenty-two months under fire*, 211

Croft, W. D., *Three years with the 9th Division*, 40

Croisilles, H., *The flaming sword of France*, 104

Croney, P., *Soldier's luck*, 45

Crookenden, A., *The history of the Cheshire Regiment in the Great War*, 44

Crosby, G. R., *Disarmament and peace in British politics 1914-19*, 206

Crosby, P. L., *Between shots; with the 77th Division in France*, 304; *That rookie from the 13th Squad*, 67

Crosland, T. W. H., *Find the angels*, 194

Cross, J., *Christendom's impending doom*, 194

Crosse, E. C., *The defeat of Austria*, 40; *The god of battles*, 238

Crowe, J. H. V., *General Smuts' campaign in East Africa*, 85

Crowell, B., *American munitions, 1917-1918*, 184

Crowell, B. & Wilson, R. F., *How America went to war*, 296

Crowell, J. F., *Government war contracts*, 87

Croy, M. de, *War memoirs*, 172

Crozier, A. O., *Nation of nations*, 206

Crozier, E., *American reporters on the Western Front*, 317

Crozier F. P., *A brass-hat in No Man's Land*, 35; *The men I killed*, 35

Crozier W., *Ordnance and the World War*, 297

Crum, F. W., *With riflemen, scouts and snipers from 1914-1919*, 211

Crundall, E. D., *Fighter pilot on the Western Front*, 95

Crutchley, C. E., *Machine-gunner, 1914-18*, 53

Cruttwell, C. R. M. F., *A history of the Great War*, 130; *The role of British strategy in the Great War*, 278; *The war service of the 1/4 Royal Berkshire Regiment (T.F.)*, 50

Cuddeford, D. W. J., *And all for what?*, 211

Culbertson, W. S., *Commercial policy in war time and after*, 87

Culling, E. V. H., *Arms and the woman*, 66

Cumming, H. R., *A Brigadier in France, 1917-18*, 35

Cummings, E. E., *The enormous room*, 223

Cummins, S. L., *Studies of influenza in hospitals of the British Armies in France, 1918*, 166

Cuneo, J. R., *Winged Mars*, 3

Cunningham, W., *Christianity and politics*, 238

Cunnington, S., *The world in arms, 1914-1918*, 130

Cupples, W. H., *My helpful angel flew with me*, 211

Currey, E. H., *How we kept the sea*, 251

Currie, J. A., *'The Red Watch' (1st Canadian Division)*, 63

Curry, F. C., *From the St. Lawrence to the Yser with the 1st Canadian Brigade*, 63

Curtin, D. T., *Edge of the quicksands*, 116; *The land of deepening shadow; Germany 1916*, 116

Cushing, H., *From a surgeon's journal, 1915-1918*, 166

Cutchins, J. A., *Amateur diplomat in the World*

War, 211

Cutchins, J. A. & Stewart, G. S., *History of the Twenty-ninth Division, Blue and Grey*, 1917-1919, 303

Cutchlow, W., *Tale of an old soldier*, 211

Cutlack, F. M., *Australian Flying Corps in the Western and Eastern theatres of war, 1914-1918*, 15; *The Australians*, 16

Cutler, F. M., *55th Artillery (C.A.C.) in the A.E.F. France*, 307

Cutler, G. R., *Of battles long ago*, 8

Cuttriss, G. P., *'Over the top' with the Third Australian Division*, 16

Cuvru-Margot, H., *Beyond the Marne, Quincy, Hulry, Voisins, before and during the battle*, 164

Czernin, O., *In the World War*, 172

D, F., *The war and the prophets*, 194

D'Abernon, H. V., *Red Cross and Berlin Embassy, 1915-1926*, 233

D'Acosta, U., *Peace problems in economics and finance*, 87

Dadishkiliani, K., *Princess in uniform*, 255

Dafoe, J. W., *Over the Canadian battlefields*, 63

Daggett, Mrs M., *Women wanted*, 327

Daily Chronicle, *The Great War book*, 234

Daily Express, *Covenants with death*, 217

Dalbiac, P. H., *History of the 60th Division – 2/2nd London Division*, 42

Dalton, H., *With British guns in Italy*, 147

Dampierre, J. de, *German imperialism and international law*, 143

Dane, E., *The battle of the rivers*, 321; *The battles in Flanders from Ypres to Neuve Chapelle*, 101; *British campaigns in Africa and the Pacific*, 2; *British campaigns in the Nearer East*, 179, 187; *Hacking through Belgium*, 101, 321

Daniell, D. S., *World War I*, 130

Daniels, J., *The Navy and the nation*, 311; *The Wilson era*, 3, 325

Dark, S., *The glory that is France*, 104; *Thou art the man*, 116

Darling, J. C., *The 20th Hussars in the Great War*, 55

Darlington, Sir H. C., *Letters from Helles*, 16, 77

Darnton, M. C., *War makers and peace makers*, 234

Darroch, G. R. S., *Deeds of a great railway*, 229

D'Auvergne, E. B. F., *An ABC guide to the Great War*, 130

Davenport, B., *The genesis of the war*, 198; *A*

history of the Great War to Aug. 1915, 130; *What the British Empire is doing in the war*, 59

Davenport, C. B. & Love, A. G., *Army anthropology*, 166

David, D., *The 1914 campaign August–October 1914*, 130

Davidson, G., *The incomparable 29th and the 'River Clyde'*, 41

Davidson, Sir J., *Haig: master of the field*, 127

Davidson, R. T., *'Quit you like men'*, 238; *The testing of a nation*, 238

Davies, D. W., *A Welshman in Mesopotamia*, 179

Davies, E. C., *A farmer in Serbia*, 268; *Ward tales*, 138

Davies, Emlyn, *Taffy went to war*, 51

Davies, G. C., *World War I aeroplanes*, 3

Davies, Hugh, *The compassionate war*, 49

Davies, Sir J., *The Prime Minister's Secretariat, 1916-1920*, 31

Davies, W. J. K., *Light railways of the First World War*, 229

Davis, A. H., *Extracts from the diary of a Tommy*, 35

Davis, Arthur N., *The Kaiser as I know him*, 150

Davis, H. W. C., *Battles of the Marne and Aisne*, 23; *Battle of Ypres-Armentieres*, 23, 330

Davis, M. O., *The Great War and what it means to Europe*, 220

Davis, O. S., *The Gospel is the light of the Great War*, 238

Davis, R. H., *Somewhere in France*, 321; *With the Allies*, 321; *With the French in France and Salonika*, 109, 262

Davis, R. J., *America's view of the sequel*, 206

Davis, W. S., *The roots of the war*, 198

Davison, H. P., *The American Red Cross in the war*, 233

Davray, H. D., *Lord Kitchener*, 151; *Through French eyes*, 31

Davson, H. M., *The history of the 35th Division in the Great War*, 41; *Memoirs of the Great War*, 57; *The story of 'G' Troop, Royal Horse Artillery*, 57

Dawbarn, C., *France at bay*, 104; *Joffre and his Army*, 109, 149

Dawe, R. E., *A memoir of an English governess in Russia*, 255

Dawes, C. G., *A journal of the Great War*, 299; *A journal of reparations*, 245

Dawes, R. C., *The Dawes Plan in the making*, 245

Dawson, A. J., *Back to Blighty*, 276; *For France*, 109; *The great advance*, 276; *Somme battle sto-*

ries, 271

Dawson, C. W., *Glory of the trenches*, 238, 286; *It might have happened to you*, 230; *Khaki courage*, 156; *Living bayonets*, 321; *Out to win*, 299; *The Unknown soldier*, 299

Dawson, E. P., *Pushing water*, 251

Dawson, J., *Christ and the sword*, 238

Dawson, L., *Flotillas*, 79

Dawson, N. P., *Good soldier*, 156

Dawson, R. J., *Problems of the peace*, 206

Dawson, W. B., *The close of the present age in the light of the periods predicted in prophecy*, 194

Dawson, W. H., *After-war problems*, 94; *Germany under the Treaty*, 314

Dawson, W. J., *The father of a soldier*, 291

Day, H. C., *An Army Chaplain*, 70; *A Cavalry Chaplain*, 70; *Macedonian memories*, 162

Day, K. H., *Camion cartoons*, 67

Day, S. R., *Round about Bar-le-Duc*, 105

Deak, F., *Hungary at the Paris Peace Conference*, 287; *The Hungarian-Rumanian land dispute*, 140

Dean, A. D., *Our schools in wartime - and after*, 89

Dearborn, F. M., *American homeopathy in the World War*, 166

Dearden, H., *Medicine and duty*, 166; *Time and chance*, 166

Deardon, R. L., *Watch on deck*, 251

Dearle, N. B., *Dictionary of official wartime organisations*, 79; *Economic chronicle of the Great War for Britain and Ireland, 1914-1919*, 87; *Labour cost of the World War to Great Britain*, 98

Dearmer, M., *Letters from a field hospital*, 268

Dease, A., *With the French Red Cross*, 233

De Bary, R., *The international king*, 155

De Beaufort, J. M., *Behind the German veil*, 116

De Beck, A. M., *The Imperial war*, 234

De Brisay, A. C. D., *And then came war*, 198

De Candole, A. C. V., *The faith of a subaltern*, 239

De Castelbled, M., *History of the A.E.F.*, 299

Dedijer, V., *The road to Sarajevo*, 198, 262

De Falls, W. C., *Army and Navy Information*, 290

De Halsalle, H., *Who goes there?*, 264

Delage, E., *The tragedy of the Dardanelles*, 77

Deland, M., *Small things*, 329

De Lisle, A., *Leaves from a V.A.D.'s diary*, 312

De Logne, S., *The Straits impregnable*, 77

Delorme, E., *War surgery*, 166

Dempsey, J. J. & Joy, W. L., *Storms over the Danube*, 140

Denham, H. M., *Dardanelles*, 77

Denison, H. P., *The Lord in his temple*, 194

Dennett, C. P., *Prisoners of the Great War*, 223

Dennett, T., *A better world*, 239

Denney, J., *War and the fear of God*, 239

Denny, W. J., *The Diggers*, 16

Dent, O., *A V.A.D. in France*, 312

Depew, A. N., *Gunner Depew*, 57, 223

De Pratz, C., *A Frenchwoman's notes on the war*, 105

De Pree, H. D., *The Battle of Cambrai*, 61

Derby, R., *'Wade in, Sanitary!'*, 166

Der Sarkiss, K., *Journey to the light*, 319

Desagneau, H., *A French soldier's war diary*, 109

De Saint Dalmas, H. G., *The time of the end of the 'Weeks' of Daniel*, 195

Desgranges, P., *In the enemy's country*, 264

Desmore, A. J. B., *With the 2nd Cape Corps thro' Central Africa*, 274

Desson, G., *A hostage in Germany*, 223

Destrée, J., *Britain in arms*, 31; *The deportation of Belgian workmen*, 78

Destrée, J. & Dupierreux, R., *To the Italian Armies*, 147

De Sumichrast, F. C., *Americans and Britons*, 291

De Varila, O., *The first shot for liberty*, 299

Devas, D., *From a cloister to camp*, 70

Devenish, G. W., *A subaltern's share in the war*, 156

Devine, A., *Off the map*, 268

Devlin, P. A., *Too proud to fight*, 325

Dewar, G. A. B., *The great munition feat, 1914-1918*, 184

Dewar, G. A. B. & Boraston, J. H., *Sir Douglas Haig's command*, 127

De Weerd, H. A., *Great soldiers of two World Wars*, 235

De Windt, H., *Russia as I know it*, 255

Dexter, M., *In the soldier's service*, 193

Dexter, P. & Sedgwick, J. H., *The war debts*, 319

Dickinson, G. L., *The choice before us*, 155; *Documents and statements relating to peace proposals and war aims*, 206; *The European anarchy*, 220; *The international anarchy, 1904-1914*, 198

Dickinson, J., *The building of an Army*, 299

Dickman, J. T., *The great crusade*, 299

Dicksee, L. R., *Business methods and the war*, 87

Dickson, M. R., *The food front in World War I*, 103

Dickson, W. E. R., *East Persia; a backwater of the Great War*, 187

Dickson, W. K., *War records of the 2nd City of Edinburgh Battery, First Lowland Brigade - C Battery, 86th Army Brigade*, 43

Diebold, B. L., *Book of good deeds, 1914-1918*, 276

Dieppe, C., *As it was*, 16

Difford, L. D., *The story of the 1st Battalion Cape Corps*, 274

Digby, E., *Tips for padres*, 70

Dillon, E. J., *The eclipse of Russia*, 256; *From the Triple to the Quadruple Alliance*, 145; *Ourselves and Germany*, 198; *The Peace Conference*, 314; *A scrap of paper*, 80

Dilnot, F., *Lloyd George*, 160

Dinesen, T., *Merry hell!*, 63

Dinning, H., *By-ways on service*, 17; *Nile to Aleppo*, 179

Dittmar, F. J. & Colledge, J. J., *British Warships*, 251

Dixon, A. M., *Canteeners*, 66

Dixon, F. H. & Parmelee, J. H., *War administration of the railways in the United States and Great Britain*, 229

Dixon, T. B., *The enemy fought splendidly*, 124

Dixon, W. M., *The British Navy at war*, 251; *The fleets behind the Fleet*, 177

Djordjevic, D., *The creation of Yugoslavia 1914-1918*, 331

Dobbins, E. Ll., *South Wales as the chief industrial centre of the United Kingdom; her part in the great victory war*, 317

Dobson, C. & Miller, J., *The day we almost bombed Moscow*, 256

Doc., *Letters from somewhere*, 54

Dockrill, M. & Gould, D. J., *Peace without promise*, 206

Dod, T. A., *Notes on the present age*, 195

Dodd, Mrs A. B., *Heroic France*, 105

Dodd, F., *Generals of the British Army*, 235

Dodd, W. E., *Woodrow Wilson and his work*, 325

Doitsh, E., *The first Springbok prisoner in Germany*, 274

Dolden, A. S., *Cannon fodder*, 286

Dolbey, R. V., *A Regimental surgeon in war and prison*, 166, 223; *Sketches of the East African campaign*, 85

Domelier, H., *Behind the scenes at German Headquarters*, 122

Dommett, W. E., *Aeroplanes and airships*, 3

Domville-Fife, C. W., *Submarines, mines and torpedoes in the war*, 280; *Submarine warfare of today*, 280

Donald, Sir R., *The tragedy of Trianon*, 140

Donnell, A., *Letters of an Australian Army Sister*, 17

Donohoe, M. H., *With the Persian Expedition*, 287

Dooly, W. G., *Great weapons of World War I*, 11

Dopson F. W., *The 48th Divisional Signal Company in the Great War*, 58

Dorling, H. T., *Ribbons and medals of the Great War*, 165; *Swept channels*, 181

Dorling, S., *Ribbons and medals*, 165

Doroshevitch, V., *The way of the Cross*, 256

Dorr, Mrs R., *A soldier's mother in France*, 105

Dorr, R. L., *Inside the Russian revolution*, 260

Dos Passos, J., *Mr. Wilson's war*, 325

Doty, M. Z., *Short rations*, 116

Doughty, H., *An actor-soldier, Henry Doughty*, 157

Douglas, J. H., *Captured*, 223

Douglas, Sholto, *Years of combat*, 172

Douglass, G. N., *Alone*, 145

Douie, C. O. G., *The weary road*, 35

Doull, D., *With the Anzacs in Egypt*, 90

Downer, E. B., *The highway of death*, 268

Doyle, Sir A. C., *The British campaigns in France and Flanders*, 35; *The German war*, 220; *A visit to three Fronts, June 1916*, 211

Drake, E., *The universal mind and the Great War*, 239

Drake, V., *Above the battle*, 4, 309

Drawbridge, C. L., *The war and religious ideals*, 239

Dresser, H. W., *The victorious faith*, 239

Drew, A. N., *Russia*, 256

Drew, G. A., *Canada's fighting airmen*, 62

Drew, H. T. B., *The war effort of New Zealand*, 190

Driggs, L. La. T., *Heroes of aviation*, 4

Droste, C. L., *Germany's Golgotha*, 116; *The Lusitania case*, 162

Drumont, Mme E. A., *A French mother in war time*, 105

Drury, W. E., *Camp follower*, 70

Duchesne, A. E., *Democracy and the Empire*, 59

Duckers, J. S., *Handed over*, 74

Ducray, C., *Clemenceau*, 73

Dudden, F. H., *The heroic dead, and other sermons*, 239

Dudgeon, L. S., *Studies of bacillary dysentery occurring in the British Forces in Macedonia*, 166

Dudley, E., *Monsters of the purple twilight*, 332

Duff, J. L., *The Eleventh Field Artillery*, 307
Duffy, F. P., *Father Duffy's story*, 304
Dugard, H., *The battle of Verdun*, 313
Dugdale, G., *'Langemarck' and 'Cambrai'*, 35
Dugmore, A. R., *When the Somme ran red*, 271
Duguid, A. F., *Official history of the Canadian Forces in the Great War*, 63
Duhamel, G., *The new book of martyrs*, 138
Duhem, J., *The question of Alsace-Lorraine*, 7
Duke, J. A., *The religions of our Allies*, 239
Dulles, E. L., *The French franc, 1914-1918*, 98
Dumba, C., *Memoirs of a diplomat*, 172
Duncan, G. S., *Douglas Haig as I knew him*, 127
Duncan, J., *With the Church Lad's Brigade Battalion in France*, 35
Duncan, W., *How I escaped from Germany*, 92
Duncan-Clark, S. J., *Pictorial history of the World War*, 217
Duncan-Clark, S. J. & Plewman, W. R., *Pictorial history of the Great War: Canada*, 62
Dundas, H. L. N., *Henry Dundas, Scots Guards* 51
Dunham, F., *The long carry*, 279
Dunn, E. A., *Three Anzacs in the war*, 17
Dunn, J. C., *The war the infantry knew 1914–1919*, 51
Dunsany, E. J., *Unhappy far off things*, 105
Dunsterville, L. C., *The adventures of Dunsterforce*, 179, 287
Du Parcq, H., *David Lloyd George*, 160
Dupont, M., *In the field, 1914-1915*, 109
Dupuy, G. M., *The stretcher-bearer*, 279
Du Puy, R. E., *Five days to war, April 2-6, 1917*, 291
Dupuy, T. N., *The military history of World War I*, 130
Dupuy, W. A., *Uncle Sam fighter*, 291
Durand, Sir H. M., *The Thirteenth Hussars in the Great War*, 55
Durell, J. C. V., *Whizbangs and Woodbines*, 276
Durham, M. E., *Twenty years of Balkan tangle*, 21
Durnford, H. G. E., *The tunnellers of Holzminden*, 92, 223
Dwinger, E. E., *The Army behind barbed wire*, 269
D'ydewalle, C., *Albert and the Belgians*, 24
Dyer, H. G., *Ma Te Reinga*, 190
Dyer, R. E. H., *The raiders of the Sarhad*, 187
Dyson, W., *Australia at war*, 17, 67; *Kultur cartoons*, 67; *War cartoons*, 67

Eades, F., *The war diary and letters of Corporal Tom Eades*, 211
Earle, E. G., *History of the 20th Divisional artillery 1914-18*, 40
Earle, M. R., *A backwater of war*, 281
Eastman, M., *Understanding Germany*, 94
Easum, C. V., *Half-century of conflict*, 130
Eaton, W. D. & Read, H. C., *A complete history of the World War*, 130
Eberle, M., *World War I and the Weimar artists*, 12
Eberle, V. F., *My sapper venture*, 58
Ebray, A., *A Frenchman looks at the peace*, 314
Ecke, H., *Four spies speak*, 264
Eddy, S., *Suffering and the war*, 239
Eden, A., *Another world 1897–1917*, 130
Eder, M. D., *War shock; the psycho-neuroses in war*, 166
Edgeworth, F. Y., *Currency and finance in the time of war*, 98
Edleston, R. H., *Italian neutrality*, 145, 189
Edmonds, C., *A subaltern's war*, 36; *T. E. Lawrence*, 154
Edmonds, Sir J. E., *Military operations of the British Army in the Western theatre of war, 1914-1918*, 36; *A short history of World War I*, 130
Edmonds, Sir J. E. & Davies, H. R., *Military operations: Italy, 1915-19*, 130, 147
Edmunds, G. B., *Somme memories*, 271
Edsall, E. W., *The coming scrap of paper*, 88
Edwards, H. I. P., *The Sussex Yeomanry and the 16th Battalion, Royal Sussex Regiment, 1914-1919*, 56
Edwards, J. H., *The life of David Lloyd George*, 160
Egan, E. F., *The war in the cradle of the world*, 179
Egan, M. F., *Ten years near the German frontier*, 116
Egerton, W. A., *Contraband of war*, 143
Ehlers, L., *One lives to tell the tale*, 224
Einstein, L., *Inside Constantinople*, 287; *A prophecy of the war, 1913-1914*, 195
Eisenmenger, A., *Blockade*, 28
Elcock, H. J., *Portrait of a decision*, 314
Elder, T. C., *The coming crash of peace and Britain's mechanical renaissance*, 206
Eley, C. V. A., *How to save a big ship from sinking, even though torpedoed*, 177
Elgood, P. G., *Egypt and the Army*, 90
Eliot, C. W., *The road towards peace*, 206
Ellice, A., *War diary and letters*, 157

Eliot, G. F. S., *War history of the 5th Battalion, King's Own Scottish Borderers*, 46

Elliot, H., *Snapshots of valor*, 111

Elliot, W. R., *The Second Twentieth (2/20 Battalion, London Regiment)*, 47

Elliott, S. E., *Wooden crates and gallant pilots*, 4

Ellis, Alec., *Public libraries and the First World War*, 159

Ellis, A. D., *The story of the Fifth Australian Division*, 17

Ellis, C., *The 4th-Denbighshire-Battalion, Royal Welch Fusiliers in the Great War*, 51

Ellis, C. H., *The Transcaspian episode*, 259, 284

Ellis, C. W. & Ellis, A. W., *The Tank Corps*, 54

Ellis, F. D., *The tragedy of the Lusitania*, 162

Ellis, H., *Essays in war time*, 94

Ellis J., *Eye-deep in hell*, 286

Ellis, John, *The social history of the machine gun*, 11

Ellison, Sir G. F., *The perils of amateur strategy, as exemplified by the attack on the Dardanelles fortress in 1915*, 278

Ellison, W., *Escaped!*, 92

Elphinstone, M . C., *War and the Gospel of Christ*, 239

Elson, R. T., *Prelude to war*, 206

Eltzbacher, P., *Germany's food: can it last?*, 103

Ely, D., *Dinsmore Ely*, 299

Ely, R. T., *World war and leadership in a democracy*, 220

Emin, A., *Turkey in the World War*, 287

Emmett, C., *Give way on the right*, 299

Empey, A. G., *From the fire step*, 36; *'Over the top'*, 36

Engall, J. S., *A subaltern's letters, 1915-16*, 157

Engle, A., *The Nili spies*, 203, 264

English, G. H., *History of the 89th Division, U.S. Army*, 304

Erichsen, E., *Forced to fight*, 78

Errington, F. H. L., *The Inns of Court Officer Training Corps during the Great War*, 55

Erzberger, M., *League of Nations*, 155

Escouflaire, R. C., *Ireland an enemy of the Allies?*, 144

Esher, R., *Journals and letters*, 172; *The tragedy of Lord Kitchener*, 151

Esposito, V. J., *A concise history of World War I*, 130

Essame, H., *The battle for Europe, 1918*, 130

Essen, L van der, *The invasion and the war in Belgium from Liege to the Yser*, 24; *A short account of the German invasion and occupation of Belgium*, 24

Etienne, *A Naval Lieutenant, 1914-1918*, 251

Ettighoffer, P. C., *Tovarish*, 92

Evans, E. J., *The escaping club*, 92

Evans, E. R. G. R., *Keeping the seas*, 84, 251

Evans, Sir G., *Tannenberg, 1410 and 1914*, 86

Evans, H. K. D., *The 4th (Queen's Own) Hussars in the Great War*, 56

Evans, J. W. & Harding, G. L., *Entertaining the American Army*, 91

Evans, M. St. H., *Going across; or, With the 9th Welch in the Butterfly Division*, 53

Evans, R., *A brief outline of the campaign in Mesopotamia*, 179

Evening Mail, *Gravest 366 days*, 222

Everest, J. H., *The first battle of the tanks; Cambrai*, 61

Everett, S., *World War I*, 130

Everitt, D., *The K boats*, 280

Everitt, N., *British secret service during the Great War*, 264

Ewart, J. S., *The roots and causes of the war, 1914-1918*, 198; *Scots Guard*, 51

Ewart, W. H. G., *When Armageddon came*, 94

Ewing, J., *History of the 9th-Scottish Division, 1914-1919*, 40; *The Royal Scots, 1914-1919*, 50

Ewing, W., *From Gallipoli to Baghdad*, 179

Eydoux-Demains, M., *In a French hospital*, 138

Eye-witness, *Narrative of the war from the Marne to Neuve Chapelle*, 101

Eyre, G. E. M., *Somme harvest*, 271

Fabre-Luce, A., *The limitations of victory*, 314

Fainsod, M., *International socialism and the World War*, 270

Fair, F., *Momentous events*, 195

Fairclough, J. E. B., *The First Birmingham Battalion in the Great War*, 51

Fairlie, J. A., *British war administration*, 31

Fa-Iz Al-Ghusain, *Martyred Armenia*, 10

Falconer, R. A., *German tragedy and its meaning for Canada*, 62

Falkenhayn, E. G., *General Headquarters, 1914-1916 and its critical decisions*, 122

Falkson, E. L., *A Cockney among the Reds*, 224

Fallon, D., *The big fight: Gallipoli to the Somme*, 113, 130

Falls, C., *Armageddon*, 7, 203; *Caporetto*, 66; *The First World War*, 131; *The history of the first seven Battalions, the Royal Irish Rifles in the Great War*, 50; *History of the Thirty-Sixth (Ulster) Division*, 41; *Military operations,*

France and Belgium, 1917, 321; *Military operations, Macedonia,* 162; *War books,* 27

Farbman, M. S., *Russia and the struggle for peace,* 256; *The Russian revolution and the war,* 260

Farmborough, F., *Nurse at the Russian Front,* 258; *Russian Album,* 166

Farnham, R. S., *A nation at bay,* 268

Farnol, J., *Great Britain at war,* 31; *Some war impressions,* 211

Farrar, L. L., *The short war illusion,* 116

Farrar-Hockley, A., *Death of an Army,* 330; *Goughie,* 126; *The Somme,* 271

Farré, H., *Sky fighters of France,* 4

Farrell, F. A., *The 51st Division war sketches,* 42

Farrer, R. J., *The void of war,* 157

Farrow, E. S., *American guns in the war with Germany,* 184

Farrow, T. & Crotch, W. W., *How to win the war,* 98

Farwell, B., *The Great War in Africa 1914–1918,* 2

Faunce, W. H. P., *Religion and war,* 239

Fawcett, H. W. & Hooper, G. W., *The fighting at Jutland,* 149

Far, Sir S., *The War Office at war,* 36

Fay, Sidney, *The origins of the World War,* 198

Fayle, C. E., *The great settlement,* 206; *History of the Great War: seaborne trade,* 177, 280

Fedden, M., *From an Abbeville window,* 329; *Sister's quarters: Salonika,* 262

Federn, C., *The origins of the war,* 198

Fedyshyn, P. S., *Germany's drive to the East and Ukranian revolution, 1917-1918,* 116

Feilding, R., *War letters to a wife,* 157

Feldman, G. D., *Army, industry and labor in Germany, 1914-1918,* 116; *German Imperialism, 1914-1918,* 116

Felix, D., *Walter Rathenau and the Weimar Republic,* 245

Fell, E. T., *History of the Seventh Division, U.S. Army,* 302

Felstead, S. T., *Edith Cavell,* 68; *German spies at bay,* 264; *Under the German heel,* 25

Fendall, C. P., *The East African Field Force,* 85

Fenn, C. R., *Middlesex to wit,* 138

Fennah, A., *Retaliation 1914-1918,* 321

Fenton, N., *Shell shock and its aftermath,* 167

Ferguson, D., *History of the Canterbury Regiment, N.Z.E.F.,* 190

Fergusson, R. M., *With the American Army in France,* 299

Fernau, H., *Because I am a German,* 198; *The coming democracy,* 116

Ferraby, H. C., *The immortal story of Zeebrugge and Ostend,* 331

Ferrara, O., *Causes and pretexts of the World War,* 198

Ferree, B., *The bombardment of Reims,* 109

Ferrell, R. H., *Woodrow Wilson and World War I,* 325

Ferrero, G., *Europe's fateful hour,* 146

Ferro, M., *The Great War, 1914-1918,* 131

Fest, W., *Peace or partition,* 80

Fetherstonhaugh, R. C., *No. 3 Canadian General Hospital (McGill),* 63; *24th Battalion, C.E.F. Victoria Rifles,* 63

Fetterless, A., *Battle days,* 211

Fevyer, W. H., *The Distinguished service Medal 1914–20,* 111

Fiebeger, G. J., *World War,* 131

Field, C., *British Navy book,* 251

Field, D., *Postage stamps of the Great War and after,* 216

Field, G. L., *The First World War,* 131

Fielding-Hall, H., *The field of honour,* 111; *The way to peace,* 206

Fiennes, G., *Our Navy at war,* 251

Fife, G. B., *The passing legions,* 233

Fifield, R. H., *Woodrow Wilson and the Far East,* 325

Figgis, J. N., *The will to freedom,* 239

Filgate, J. V. M., *History of the 33rd Divisional Artillery in the war,* 41

Filson, A. B., *With Beatty in the North Sea,* 252

Finch, G. A., *The Treaty of Peace with Germany in the United States Senate,* 80

Findlay, J. M., *With the 8th Scottish Rifles, 1914-1919,* 52

Fink, C., *The Genoa conference,* 114

Finley, J. H., *A pilgrim in Palestine after its deliverance,* 203

Finnegan, J. P., *Against the specter of a dragon,* 297

Finnemore, J., *A Boy Scout with the Russians,* 29

Finzi, K. J., *Eighteenth months in the war zone,* 211

Fisch, M. H., *Selected papers of Robert C. Binckley,* 172

Fischer, F., *Germany's aims in the First World War,* 116; *War of illusions,* 199; *World power or decline,* 116

Fish, C. R., *American diplomacy,* 80

Fisher, D. F., *Day of glory,* 167

Fisher, J. A., *Memories and records*, 172

Fisher, J. J., *History of the Duke of Wellington's West Riding Regiment during the first three years of the Great War*, 53

Fisher, R. H., *A letter to you*, 239

Fisk, H. E., *French public finance in the Great War and today*, 98

Fiske, P. M., *The Inter-Ally debt*, 98; *History of the Three Hundred Fiftieth Regiment of the U.S. Infantry Eighty Eight Division, A.E.F.*, 306

Fitch, R. L., *Madame France*, 327

Fitch, W. S., *Wings in the night*, 4, 309

Fitz-Gerald, W. G., *America's day*, 291

Fitzpatrick, Sir J. P., *The origins, causes and objects of the war*, 199

Fitzroy, Y., *With the Scottish nurses in Roumania*, 254

Fitzsimons, B., *Heraldry and regalia of war*, 91; *Tanks and weapons of World War I*, 282; *War planes and air battles of World War I*, 4; *Warships and sea battles of World War I*, 185

Fitzwilliams, D. C. L., *A nursing manual for nurses and nursing orderlies*, 193

Flack, W. T., *Christ on Ariadne; or 'What I said to our soldiers'*, 239

Fleming, A., *How to see the battlefields*, 22

Fleming, D. F., *The origins and legacies of World War I*, 199

Fleming, J. A., *The last voyage of His Majesty's Hospital Ship 'Britannic'*, 140

Fleming, P., *The fate of Admiral Kolchak*, 269

Fletcher, C. B., *The new Pacific*, 207

Fletcher, C. R. L., *The Great War*, 131

Fletcher, D., *Landships*, 282

Fleurot, A. D., *Through war to revolution*, 318

Flier, M. J. van der, *War finances in the Netherlands*, 98

Flight, Flying Yankee, 247

Flight Commander, *Cavalry of the air*, 247

Florez, C. de, *No. 6: a few pages from the diary of an ambulance driver*, 8

Florinsky, M., *The end of the Russian Empire*, 256

Floto, I., *Colonel House in Paris*, 80, 140

Flower, N., *The history of the Great War*, 131

Flowers, M., *What every American should know about the war*, 131

Floyd, T. H., *At Ypres with Bert Dunkley of the 2/5th Lancashire Fusiliers*, 330

Foakes-Jackson, F. J., *The faith and the war*, 94

Foch, F., *The memoirs of Marshal Foch*, 102

Foley, H. A., *Scrap book of the 7th Battalion Somerset L.I.*, 52; *Three years on active service and eight months as a prisoner-of-war*, 224, 321

Foley, J., *The boilerplate war*, 54

Folks, H., *The human costs of the war*, 182

Fonck, R., *Ace of aces*, 108

Fontaine, A., *French industry during the war*, 142

Foot, S., *Three lives*, 282

Forbes, Lady H. E., *Saga of the Seventh Division*, 40, 303

Ford, B., *Fighting Yankees overseas*, 299

Ford, G. B., *Out of the ruins*, 236

Ford, J. L., *Waitful watching; or, Uncle Sam and the fight in Dame Europa's school*, 297

Ford, T., *Cheer-up letters from a Private with Pershing*, 299

Forder, A., *In brigands' hands and Turkish prisons, 1914-1918*, 224

Foreman, T., *Whizz bangs*, 276

Formby, C. W., *The soul of England; or, A great Empire at the cross roads*, 31

Forrester, J. & Watson, C., *Argyll and Sutherland Highlanders, 9th battalion Dunbartonshire men*, 43

Forster, K., *The failures of peace*, 207

Forsyth, P. T., *The Christian ethic of war*, 239

Fortescue, G., *At the Front with three Armies*, 318, 321; *France bears the burden*, 105; *Front line and deadline*, 318; *Russia, the Balkans and the Dardanelles*, 86, 318; *What of the Dardanelles?*, 77

Forty, G., *A photo history of armoured cars in two World Wars*, 11

Fosdick, H. E., *The challenge of the present crisis to Christianity*, 239

Foster, H. C., *At Antwerp and the Dardanelles*, 9

Foster, S. N., *Plain tales from the war*, 276

Foster, W., *The tank, its birth and development*, 282

Foulkes, C. H., *'Gas!'*, 43

Fox, E. L., *Behind the scenes in warring Germany*, 116; *William Hohenzollern & Co.*, 116

Fox, F., *The agony of Belgium*, 25; *The British Army at War*, 36; *The Royal Inniskillin Fusiliers*, 50; *History of the Royal Gloucestershire Hussars*, 56

Fox, M. S., *'Corporals all'*, 59

Fox, R., *Lenin*, 156

Fox, R. F., *Physical remedies for disabled soldiers*, 167

Fox, R. J., *Revelation on revelation and these latter days*, 195; *Unexpected tidings of the war*,

195
Foxwell, A. K., *Munition lasses*, 184
France, A., The path of glory, 105
France: Ministry of Foreign Affairs, *The deportation of women and girls from Lille*, 78; *Germany's violation of the laws of war*, 105, 143
Ministry of War, *French official view of the first six months of the war*, 131
Francis, A. T., *History of the 71st Regiment*, 304
Francis Joseph, *Emden*, 90
Franklin, J. H., *In the track of the storm*, 105
Fraser, E. & Gibbons, J., *Soldier and sailor words and phrases*, 153
Fraser, H., *Women an d war work*, 327
Fraser, J. F., *Deeds that will never die*, 111; *Russia of to-day*, 256
Fraser, T. N., *With Lancashire lads and field guns in France*, 58
Frasure, C. M., *British policy on war debts and reparations*, 319
Frazer, E., *Old Glory and Verdun and other stories*, 276
Frederick William, *I seek the truth*, 199
Fredette, R. H., *The first Battle of Britain, 1917-1918, and the birth of the Royal Air Force*, 247
Freeman, L. R., *Many fronts*, 211; *Seahounds*, 79; *To Kiel in the 'Hercules'*, 252
Freeman, W., *Awake! U.S.A.*, 297
Freidel, F. B., *Over there*, 299
Freiwald, L., *Last days of the German Fleet*, 124
French, A., *Gone for a soldier*, 211
French, D., *British strategy and war aims 1914–1916*, 278
French, E. G., *French replies to Haig*, 111
French, F. J. F., *The Kitchener-French dispute*, 111; *From Whitehall to the Caspian*, 288
French Gunner, *General Joffre*, 149
French, Sir J. D. P., *The despatches of Lord French*, 111; *1914*, 111; *Some war diaries addresses and correspondence*, 111
Frennsen, G., *Peter Moor*, 274
Freulich, R., *Soldiers in Judea*, 148
Freytag-Loringhoven, H. F., *Deductions from the World War*, 116
Fribourg, A., *Flaming crucible*, 239
Fried, A. H., *The restoration of Europe*, 230
Friedel, V. H., *The German school as a war nursery*, 116
Friedman, E. M., *American problems of reconstruction*, 230; *Labor and reconstruction in Europe*, 230
Friends, Society of, *The Friends' Ambulance Unit*,

1914-1919, 228; *Friends and the war*, 228
Frost, G. H., *Munitions of war*, 184
Frost, H. H., *The battle of Jutland*, 149
Frost, L. M., *Fighting men*, 63
Frost W., *German submarine warfare*, 289
Frothingham, T. G., *The American reinforcement in the World War*, 291; *Guide to the military history of the World War*, 131; *The Naval history of the World War*, 185; *A true account of the battle of Jutland*, 149
Fry, A. R., *A Quaker adventure*, 228
Fry, J. W. & Macmillan, T., *The complete history of the Royal Naval Division*, 252
Fry, W. M., *Air of battle*, 249
Fryer, E. R. M., *Reminiscences of a Grenadier*, 46
Fryer, P., *The men from Greenwood*, 52
Funderburk, T. R., *The early birds of war*, 95
Funcken, L. & Funcken, F., *The First World War (arms and uniforms)*, 91
Fuehr, A., *The neutrality of Belgium*, 25
Fuller, J. F. C., *Memoirs of an unconventional soldier*, 173; *Tanks in the Great War*, 55
Fullerton, G. S., *Germany today*, 116
Fullerton, W. M., *The American crisis and the war*, 291
Funnell, H. F. D., *The great rebuilding*, 230
Fussell, P., *The Great War and modern memory*, 31
Fussell, P., *The ordeal of Alfred M. Hale*, 249
Fyfe, H. H., *The making of an optimist*, 220
Fyfe, T. A., *Employers and workmen, 1915-1917*, 283

G., *The last lap of the European war*, 131
G., H. L., *Meanwhile*, 157
Gaell, R., *Priests in the firing line*, 70
Gaffney, T. St. J., *Breaking the silence*, 227
Gains, R. L., *Helping France*, 233; *The ladies of Grécourt*, 236; *A village in Picardy*, 236
Gajda, P. A., *Postscript to victory*, 81
Galet, E. H., *Albert King of the Belgians in the Great War*, 25
Gallatin, A. E., *Art and the Great War*, 12
Gallishaw, J., *Trenching at Gallipoli*, 113
Galsworthy, J., *A sheaf: papers on the European war*, 94
Galtrey, S., *The horse and the war*, 56
Gamble, C. F. S., *The story of a North Sea Air Station*, 254
Gammage, W. L., *The broken years*, 17
Gankin, Mrs. O. & Fisher, H. H., *Bolsheviks and the World War*, 260

Gansser, E. B., *On the battle fields of France in 1918*, 321

Ganterbein, J. W., *The doctrine of continuous voyage*, 143

Gardam, *Seventy years after 1914–1918*, 62

Gardiner, A. G., *War Lords*, 235

Gardiner, J. B. W., *German plans for the next war*, 117

Gardiner, J. B. W. & Ybarra, T. Y., *How the war was lost and won*, 278

Gardner, B., *Allenby*, 7; *The big push*, 271; *German East Africa*, 85

Gardner, L., *The hope for society*, 230; *Some Christian essentials of reconstruction*, 230

Garey, E. B., *American guide book to France and its battlefields*, 22

Garner, J. W., *International law and the Great War*, 144; *Prize law during the World War*, 144

Garnerin de Montgelas, M. M., *The case for the Central Powers*, 314

Garnett, R., *Kenneth Gordon Garnett*, 173

Garrett, P. W., *Government control over prices*, 98

Garsia, C., *A key to victory*, 278

Garstin, D., *Friendly Russia*, 256

Garvin, J. L., *The coming of the Great War*, 131; *Economic foundations of peace*, 88

Gates, H. L., *The auction of souls*, 10

Gatzke, H. W., *Germany's drive to the West*, 117

Gauld, H. D., '*Scotland yet!*', 36; *The truth from the trenches*, 321

Gaunt, F., *The immortal first (B.E.F.)*, 60

Gauss, C., *Why we went to war*, 199

Gay, H. N., *Italy's great war, and her national aspirations*, 146

Geare, W. D., *Letters of an Army Chaplain*, 70

Geary, S., *The Collingwood Battalion, Royal Naval Division*, 252

Geddes, P. & Slater, G., *Ideas at war*, 199

Gee, A. E. & Shaw, A., *A record of D245 Battery*, 58

Geffroy, G., *Clemenceau*, 73

Geisinger, F. J., *History of the U.S. Army Base Hospital No. 45 in the Great War*, 138

Geiss, I., *July 1914*, 131, 199

Gelfand, L. E., *The inquiry*, 207

Genet, E., *An American for Lafayette*, 108; *War letters*, 309

Genevoix, M., *Neath Verdun*, 313

Genthe, C. V., *American war narratives, 1917-1918*, 291

George, A. E. & Cooper, E. H., *Pictorial history of the Twenty-sixth Division, U.S. Army*, 303

George, H., *Farrier in arms*, 212

George, S., *Woman's world-wide work with war*, 327

Georgevitch, T. R., *Macedonia*, 162

Geoghegan, S., *The campaigns and history of the Royal Irish Regiment*, 50

Gephart, W. F., *Effects of the war upon insurance*, 143

Gerard, Sir J. W., *My four years in Germany*, 117, 173

Gerds, D. N., *The ABC of pensions*, 209

Gerlache de Gomery, A., *The unconquerable soul*, 25

Germains, V. W., *The Kitchener Armies*, 36; *The tragedy of Winston Churchill*, 73; *The truth about Kitchener*, 151

Germany: Auswartiges Amt., *The German Army in Belgium*, 122; *German White Book concerning the responsibility of the authors of the war*, 117; *Germany and the revolution in Russia*, 260 Naturalversammlung, *Official German documents relating to the World War*, 117

Gerring, C., *A record of the early Volunteer Movement and of the Notts Volunteer Regiment (The Sherwood Foresters), 1914-1919*, 52

Gervis, H., *Arms and the doctor*, 167

Geshev, L. E., *The Balkan League*, 21

Gibbins, H. A., *The blackest page of modern history*, 10

Gibbon F. P., *The 42nd Division, 1914-1918*, 41

Gibbon, M., *Inglorious soldier*, 54

Gibbon, P., *The triumph of the Royal Navy*, 124

Gibbons, Arthur, *A guest of the Kaiser*, 224

Gibbons, F., *The red knight of Germany*, 246

Gibbons, H. A., *France and ourselves*, 105; *The new map of Europe, 1911-1914*, 199; *Paris reborn*, 205; *The reconstruction of Poland*, 218; *The reconstruction of the Near East*, 187; *Songs from the trenches*, 273; *Venizelos*, 312

Gibbons, H. D., *A little gray home in France*, 329

Gibbons, S. R. & Morican, P., *World War One*, 131

Gibbons, T., *With the 1/15th Essex in the East*, 45

Gibbs, A. H., *The grey wave*, 13

Gibbs, H., *Gun fodder*, 212

Gibbs, Sir P. H., *The battles of the Somme*, 271; *From Bapaume to Passchendaele*, 101, 205; *Open warfare: from Cambrai to the Marne*, 61; *Realities of war*, 182; *The soul of the war*, 131; *Ten years after*, 230; *The war dispatches*, 318; *The way to victory*, 131

Gibbs, S., *From the Somme to the Armistice*, 212

Gibson, A. H. & Kirkaldy, A. W., *British finance, 1914-1921*, 98

Gibson, C. R., *Ships that saved the Empire*, 252

Gibson, H., *A diplomatic diary*, 25

Gibson, L. & Harper, J. E. T., *The riddle of Jutland*, 149

Gibson, M., *Spotlight on the First World War*, 131

Gibson, P., *Battering the Boche*, 299

Gibson, R. H., *Three years of naval warfare*, 185

Gibson, R. H. & Prendergast, M., *The German submarine war, 1914-1918*, 289

Gibson, W. J., *Wild career*, 256

Gide, C., *Effects of the war upon French economic life*, 105

Gies, J., *Crisis 1918*, 131

Giffin, F. C., *Six who protested*, 296

Gilbert, A., *World War I in photographs*, 217

Gilbert, C., *American financing of World War I*, 98

Gilbert, M., *First World War atlas*, 235: *Winston Churchill, 1914-1916; 1917-1922*, 73

Gilbert, V., *The romance of the last crusade*, 7

Gilbreath, O., *Russia in travail*, 260

Gilchrist, J. W. S., *An aerial observer in World War I*, 4

Giles, J., *The Somme: then and now*, 271; *The Ypres Salient*, 330

Gilford, H., *The black hand at Sarajevo*, 262

Gill, C. C., *Naval power in the war*, 185; *What happened at Jutland*, 150

Gill, C. C. & Stevens, W. O., *The war on the sea*, 185

Gill, D. & Dallas, G., *The unknown army*, 36

Gill, E. W. B., *War, wireless and wangles*, 113

Gillespie, A. D., *Letters from Flanders*, 101, 157

Gilliard, P., *Thirteen years at the Russian Court*, 256

Gilliland, H. G., *My German prisons*, 224

Gillon, S. A., *The K.O.S.B. in the Great War*, 46; *Story of the 29th Division*, 41

Ginsburg, B. W., *War speeches. 1914-1917*, 1

Giradoux, J., *Campaigns and intervals*, 212

Giraud, S. L., *Ghosts in the Great War, and true tales of haunted houses*, 195; *Songs that won the war*, 273

Gladden, E. N., *Across the Piave*, 147; *The Somme, 1916*, 271; *Ypres, 1917*, 330

Glass, J., *Story of Battery O, 304th Field Artillery*, 308

Glasson, W. H., *Federal military pensions in the U.S.*, 209

Glazebrook, G. P., *Canada at the Paris Peace Conference*, 62

Gleason, A. H., *Inside the British Isles*, 31; *Our part in the Great War*, 299; *With the first war ambulance in Belgium*, 8

Gleason, A. H. & Gleason, H. H., *Golden lads*, 299

Gleaves, A., *History of the Transport Service*, 285

Gleichen, A. E. W., *The doings of the Fifteenth Infantry Brigade*, 43

Gleichen, *Lady H., Contacts and contrasts*, 193

Glen, D., *In the steps of Lawrence of Arabia*, 154

Glubb, *Sir J. B., Into battle*, 173

Goerlitz, W., *History of the German General Staff, 1657-1945*, 123

Goldberg, G., *The peace to end peace*, 314

Goldrick, J., *The King's ships were at sea*, 252

Goldsmid, C. H., *Diary of a liaison officer in Italy*, 147

Goldsmith, R., *A League to enforce peace*, 155

Golovin, N. N., *The Russian Army in the World War*, 258; *The Russian campaign of 1914*, 86, 258

Goltz, H. von der, *My adventures as a German secret agent*, 264

Gomez Carrillo, E., *Among the ruins*, 105; *In the heart of the tragedy*, 275

Gompers, S., *American labor and the war*, 270

Gooch, G. P., *Recent revelations of European diplomacy*, 81

Gooch, G. P. & Temperley, H., *British documents on the origins of the war, 1898-1914*, 199

Gooch, J., *The plans of war*, 278

Goodchild, G., *Behind the barrage*, 13; *Blinded soldiers and sailors gift book*, 83; *The last cruise of the 'Majestic'*, 252

Goodsall, R. H., *Palestine memories, 1917-1918-1925*, 203

Goodspeed, D. J., *The German wars, 1914-1945*, 131; *Ludendorff*, 161; *The road past Vimy*, 63

Gordon, A. A., *Culled from a diary*, 212

Gordon, G., *An intepreter of war*, 195

Gordon, G. S., *Mons and the retreat*, 183

Gordon, H., *The unreturning Army*, 13

Gordon, J. & Gordon, C. J., *The luck of thirteen*, 21

Gordon, M. H., *Cerebrospinal fever*, 167

Gordon, S. D., *Quiet talks on the deeper meaning of the war*, 239

Gordon-Smith, G., *From Serbia to Jugoslavia*, 268; *Mons and the retreat*, 183; *Through the Serbian campaign*, 268

Gordon, *Mrs* W., *A woman in the Balkans*, 21

Gordy, W. F., *The causes and meaning of the Great War*, 199

Gore, C., *The League of Nations*, 155; *The war and the Churches*, 239

Gore-Browne, F., *The effect of the war on commercial engagements*, 88

Gorges, E. H., *The Great War in West Africa*, 320

Goricar, J. & Stowe, L. B., *The inside story of Austro-German intrigue*, 199

Gorman, E., *With the 22nd Battalion A.I.F.*, 17

Gorman, J. T., *With Lawrence to Damascus*, 154

Goss, L., *A Border Battalion: the history of the 7/8th Battalion, K.O.S.B.*, 47

Gosse, E., *Inter Arma*, 94

Gosse, P., *Memoirs of a camp follower*, 167

Got, A., *The case of Miss Cavell*, 69

Gottlieb, W. W., *Studies in secret diplomacy during the First World War*, 81

Gough, A., *Repentance and strength*, 239

Gough, *Sir* H. de la P., *The Fifth Army*, 39; *The March retreat*, 39; *Soldiering on*, 173

Gould, B. A., *The greater tragedy, and other things*, 291; *War thoughts of an optimist*, 216

Gould, L. M., *From British Columbia to Baiseux*, 64

Gourko, B., *Memories and impressions of war and revolution in Russia*, 260

Gow, K., *Letters of a soldier*, 157

Gowans, A. L., *A month's German newspapers*, 222

Gowenlock, T. R., *Soldiers of darkness*, 264

Gower, M. F., *Six weeks at the war*, 193

Gowland, J. S., *War is like that*, 321

Grady, H. F., *British war finance, 1914-1919*, 98

Graebner, T. C., *Prophecy and the war*, 195

Graevenitz, P., *From autocracy to Bolshevism*, 260

Graf, H., *The Russian Navy in war and revolution*, 260

Graham, J. G., *Gallipoli diary*, 113

Graham, J. W., *Conscription and conscience*, 74, 75; *War from a Quaker point of view*, 228

Graham, M. W., *The controversy between the United States and the Allied governments respecting neutral rights and commerce*, 144

Graham, S., *The challenge of the dead*, 36, 182; *A Private in the Guards*, 46; *Russia and the world*, 256; *Russia in 1916*, 256

Grahame-White, C., *Heroes of the Flying Corps*, 249

Grahame-White, C. & Harper, H., *Aircraft in the Great War*, 4

Grain, H. W. W., *The 16th (Public School) Service Battalion*, 48

Grant, Allan, *The real Colonel House*, 175

Grant, A G., *Letters from Armageddon*, 157

Grant, D. F., *History of 'A' Battery, 84th Army Brigade, R.F.A.*, 43

Grant, D. P., *The 1/4th Hallamshire Battalion, York and Lancaster Regiment, 1914-1919*, 53

Grant, J. G., *The heart beneath the uniform*, 239

Grant, M., *Verdun days in Paris*, 205

Grant, R., *S.O.S. Stand to! three years' experience with the First Canadian Division in the European war*, 64

Grant, Robert, *Their spirit*, 31, 105

Grant, Robert M., *U-boats destroyed*, 289; *U-boat intelligence, 1914-1918*, 289

Granville, W. & Kelly, R., *Inshore heroes*, 183

Grasshoff, R., *The tragedy of Belgium*, 25

Grasty, C. H., *Flashes from the front*, 299

Gratacap, L. P., *Europe's handicap*, 199

Grattan, C. H., *Why we fought*, 296

Gratz, G. & Schueller, R., *The economic policy of Austro-Hungary during the war in its external relations*, 19

Graves, A. F., *The turn of the tide*, 322

Graves, A. K., *The red secrets of the Hohenzollerns*, 117; *Zeppelins and the German war machine*, 332

Graves, H. S., *Lost diary (First Canadian Corps)*, 64

Graves, R. P., *Lawrence of Arabia and his world*, 154

Graves, Robert, *Goodbye to all that*, 173; *Lawrence and the Arabs*, 154

Gray, A., *The upright sheaf*, 117

Gray, Edwyn, *A damned un-English weapon*, 280; *The killing time*, 289

Gray, E. M., *Belgium under the German sword*, 25

Gray F., *The confessions of a Private*, 322

Gray, H. B. & Turner, S., *Eclipse or Empire*, 89

Gray, H. L., *War time control of industry*, 142

Gray, T., *Hospital days in Rouen*, 138

Grayson, B. L., *Russian American relations in World War I*, 81

Grazebrook, R. M., *The Gloucestershire Regiment*, 45

Great Britain: Admiralty, *Merchant shipping losses*, 177; *Narrative of the battle of Jutland*, 150; *Navy losses*, 252;

Board of Agriculture & Fisheries, *Fisheries in*

the Great War, 100

British Association, *Credit, industry and the war*, 98; *Industry and finance*, 98; *Labour, finance and the war*, 98

Committee of Imperial Defence, *History of the Great War based on official documents: Principal events, 1914-1918*, 72, 131

Foreign Office, *Collected diplomatic documents relating to the outbreak of the European war*, 81; *Great Britain and the European crisis*, 31; *The Great War and how it came*, 31; *The outbreak of the war 1914-18*, 31; *Reply of the Belgian Ministries of Justice and Foreign Affairs to the German White Book of the 10th May, 1915*, 25; *The Second Belgian Grey Book*, 25; *The Treaty of Peace between the Allied & Associated Powers and Germany*, 285; *The Treaty of Peace between the Allied & Associated Powers and Austria*, 285; *The Treaty of Peace between the Allied & Associated Powers and Hungary*, 285; *The Treaty of Peace between the Allied & Associated Powers and Bulgaria*, 285; *The Treaty of Peace between the Allied & Associated Power and Turkey*, 285

Imperial War Museum, *War pictures*, 12

Ministry of Information, *Chronology of the war*, 72; *War paintings and drawings by British artists*, 12

Ministry of Munitions, *History of the Ministry of Munitions*, 184

National Council for Civil Liberties, *British freedom, 1914-1917*, 31

National Peace Council, *Problems of international settlement*, 207

Tariff Commission, *The war and British economic policy*, 88

War Office, *Battle honours awarded for the Great War*, 36; *Battle of the Aisne, 13-15th Sept. 1914*, 7; *Battle of the Marne, 8th-10th Sept. 1914*, 164; *French-English Dictionary*, 79; *Handbook of the German Army in war*, 123; *A review of new Orders, Decorations and Gallantry Medals instituted by H.M. during the war, 1914-1920*, 165; *Report of enquiry into "shell shock"*, 167; *Statistics of the military effort of the British Empire during the Great War*, 59; *Women's war work in maintaining the industries and export trade of the United Kingdom*, 327

Grebler, L., *The cost of the World War to Germany and to Austria-Hungary*, 88

Green, A., *The story of a prisoner-of-war*, 224

Green, F. C., *The Fortieth: a record of the 40th Battalion, A.I.F.*, 17

Green, Horace, *The log of a non-combatant*, 318

Green, Howard, *The British Army in the First World War*, 36

Green, J., *News from No Man's Land*, 17, 77

Greene, F. V., *Our first year in the Great War*, 291; *Why Europe is at war*, 220

Greenwald, M. W., *Women, war and work*, 327

Greenwall, H. J., *Scoops*, 318

Greenwell, G. H., *An infant in arms*, 157

Greenwood, G. A., *Civilization in the melting pot*, 207

Greger, R., *Austro-Hungarian warships of World War I*, 19; *The Russian Fleet, 1914-1917*, 260

Gregory, H., *Never again*, 322

Gregory, R., *Walter Hines Page: Ambassador to the Court of St. James's*, 175

Grelling, R., *Belgian documents*, 25; *J'accuse*, 199

Greig, G. A., *Women's work on the land*, 327

Greville, F. E., *A woman and the war*, 327

Grew, E. S., *Field Marshal Lord Kitchener*, 151; *The Great War*, 131

Grey, C. G., *Tales of the flying services*, 4

Grey, E., *Twenty-five years, 1892-1916*, 126

Grey, W. E., *The 2nd City of London Regiment (Royal Fusiliers) in the Great War*, 50; *With the French Eastern Army*, 109

Gribble, F. H., *In Luxemburg in war time*, 162; *Women in war*, 327

Gribble, L., *Heroes of the fighting RAF*, 96; *Great War adventures*, 276

Grider, J. M., *War birds*, 4

Grieb, C. K., *Uncovering the forces for war*, 199

Grierson, F. D., *The ABC of military law*, 144; *Illusions and realities of the war*, 182

Grieve, W. G. & Newman, B., *Tunnellers*, 59

Grieves, K., *The politics of manpower*, 233

Griff, *Surrendered: some naval war secrets*, 185

Griffith, L. W., *Up to Mametz*, 322

Griffith-Jones, E., *The challenge of Christianity to a world at war*, 240

Griffiths, W. R., *The Great War*, 132

Griggs, E. H., *The soul of democracy*, 216

Grimshaw, D., *Indian cavalry officer 1914–15*, 141

Grimwade, F. C., *The war history of the 4th Battalion, the London Regiment (Royal Fusiliers), 1914-1919*, 50

Grinnell-Milne, D., *An escaper's log*, 92; *Wind in the wires*, 249

Grondijs, L. H., *The Germans in Belgium*, 25

Gronsky, P. P., *The war and the Russian Government*, 256

Groom, W. H. A., *Poor bloody infantry*, 36

Grotius, H., *The freedom of the seas*, 144

Groundsell, F., *The lunatic spy*, 265

Grove, E. W. H., *Gunshot injuries of bones*, 167

Groves, H., *Toronto does her 'Bit'*, 62

Grow, M. C., *Surgeon Grow*, 167

Grumbach, S., *Germany's annexionist aims*, 117

'G.S.O.', *G.H.Q. (Montreuil-sur-Mer)*, 36

Guard, W. J., *The soul of Paris*, 205; *The spirit of Italy*, 146

Guernsey, I. S., *Reference history of the war*, 235

Guerrier, E., *We pledged allegiance*, 103

Guichard, L., *The naval blockade, 1914-1918*, 28

Guinn, P., *British strategy and politics, 1914-1918*, 31, 278

Gullett, Sir H. S., *The Australian Imperial Force in Sinai and Palestine, 1914-1918*, 17

Gullett, Sir H. S. & Barrett, C. L., *Australia in Palestine*, 17

Gurney, G., *Five down and glory*, 96; *Flying aces of World War I*, 96

Gurney, I., *War letters*, 212

Guttersen, G., *Granville tales and tail spins from a flyer's diary*, 4

Guyot, Y., *The causes and consequences of the war*, 199

Gwatkin-Williams, Mrs, *In the hands of the Senussi*, 90

Gwynn, S., *The letters and friends of Sir Cecil Spring-Rice*, 176

H, S. R. & M, J. F., *Sixty American opinions on the war*, 291

Haber, L. F., *The poisonous cloud*, 114

Hacobian, A. P., *Armenia and the war*, 10

Haddow, G. W. & Grosz, P. M., *The German giants*, 121

Hadjich, T. D., *The world's war cartoons*, 67

Hadlow, H. J., *The experiences of a volunteer in the First World War*, 212

Hafkesbrink, H., *Unknown Germany*, 117

Hagedorn, H., *The bugle that woke America*, 296; *Where do you stand?*, 295

Hague Conference, *The final settlement of the reparation problems*, 245

Hahn, J. E., *The Intelligence Service within the Canadian Corps, 1914-1918*, 64

Haig, Countess, *The man I knew*, 127

Haig, Sir D., *The private papers of Douglas Haig, 1914-1919*, 127; *Sir Douglas Haig's despatches, 1915-1919*, 127

Haig-Brown, A. R., *The O.T.C. and the Great War*, 55

Haigh, R., *Life in a tank*, 55

Haigh R. H. & Turner, P. W., *The long carry*, 279

Haines, D. H., *Dragon flies*, 309

Hainsselin, M. T., *Curtain of steel*, 252

Halasi, O., *Belgium under the German heel*, 25

Haldane, E. S., *The British nurse in peace and war*, 193

Haldane, Sir J. A. L., *A Brigade of the old Army 1914*, 43

Haldane, M. M., *A history of the Fourth Battalion the Seaforth Highlanders*, 52

Haldane, R. B., *Autobiography*, 173; *Before the war*, 199

Hale, Sir L., *What to observe and how to report*, 284

Hale, Walter, *By motor to the firing line*, 12

Hale, William B., *American rights and British pretensions on the seas*, 88

Hales, A. G., *Where angels fear to tread*, 146

Halevy, E., *The world crisis of 1914-1918*, 132

Hall, A. D., *Agriculture after the war*, 2

Hall, B., *In the air*, 249

Hall, B. & Niles, J. J., *One man's war: the story of the Lafayette Escadrille*, 108

Hall, H., *British archives and the sources for the history of the World War*, 27

Hall, J. A., *The law of naval warfare*, 144

Hall, J. N., *High adventure*, 4; *Kitchener's mob*, 36

Hall, J. N & Nordhoff, C. B., *Lafayette Flying Corps*, 108

Hall, J. R., *The desert hath pearls*, 187

Hall, L. J., *The Inland Water Transport in Mesopotamia*, 179

Hall, M., *Some naval yarns*, 252

Hall, N. S., *Balloon buster*, 22

Hall, S. K., *A North Sea diary, 1914-1918*, 252; *The war at sea, 1914-1918*, 185

Hall, W. G., *The green triangle (2/5th Battalion Sherwood Foresters)*, 52

Hall, W. H., *Near East*, 187

Hallam, G. H., *Notes on the war*, 132

Hallgren, M. A., *Tragic fallacy*, 291

Halliday, E. M., *The ignorant Armies*, 10

Hallion, R., *Rise of the fighter aircraft*, 96

Hallowell, J. M., *Spirit of Lafayette*, 291

Hallowes, F. S., *Mothers of men and militarism*, 31

Halpern, P. G., *The Keyes papers: vol I, 1914-1918*, 252; *The naval war in the Mediterranean*, 252

Halsey, F. W., *The Literary Digest history of the World War*, 132

Halter, H., *Finland breaks the Russian chains*, 100

Halyburton, E. & Goll, R., *Shoot and be damned*, 224

Hamelius, P., *The siege of Liege*, 159

Hamilton, C., *Senlis*, 105

Hamilton, D. E., *How the fight was won*, 132

Hamilton, E. W., *The first seven Divisions*, 39, 101; *The soul of Ulster*, 145

Hamilton, I. B. M., *The happy warrior*, 173

Hamilton, *Sir* I. S. M., *Gallipoli diary*, 113; *Ian Hamilton's despatches from the Dardanelles*, 77; *Ian Hamilton's final despatches*, 77; *The millennium*, 230

Hamilton, J. A. B., *Britain's railways in World War I*, 229

Hamilton, *Lady* M. L., *Three years or the duration*, 184

Hamilton, R. G. A., *The war diary of the Master of Belhaven*, 173

Hammerton, *Sir* J. A., *The Great War: I was there!*, 132; *Popular history of the Great War*, 132; *The war illustrated*, 132; *Wrack of war*, 22

Hammond, E. W., *History of the 11th Light Horse Regiment*, 17

Hammond, J. M., *A living witness*, 157

Hammond, M. B., *British labor conditions and legislation during the war*, 142

Hamon, A. F., *Lessons of the World War*, 182

Hampshire, A. C., *The blockaders*, 28

Hanak, H., *Great Britain and Austria-Hungary during the First World War*, 81; *How diplomats make war*, 81

Hanbury-Williams, *Sir* J., *The Emperor Nicholas II as I knew him*, 192

Hand-Newton, C. T. A., *A physician in peace and war*, 190

Hanes, E. L., *Minds and nerves of soldiers*, 167

Hankey, D., *The beloved captain*, 94; *A student in arms*, 157

Hankey, M. P. A., *The Supreme Command, 1914-1918*, 278; *The Supreme Control at the Paris Peace Conference, 1919*, 314

Hanman, E. F., *Twelve months with the Anzacs*, 17

Hanna, H. S., *The pals of Suvla Bay*, 113

Hanna, H. S. & Lauck, W., *Wages and war*, 88

Hannah, I. C., *Arms and the map*, 207

Hannula, J. O., *Finland's war of independence*, 100

Hansen, H., *The adventures of the Fourteen Points*, 104

Hanson, J. M., *World War through the telebinocular*, 132

Hanson, W. L., *I was there*, 212

Hanssen, H. P., *Diary of a dying Empire*, 20, 117

Harbord, J. G., *The American Army in France, 1917-1919*, 299; *America in the Great War*, 292; *Leaves from a war diary*, 299

Harbottle, G., *Civilian soldier 1914–1919*, 36

Hardach, G., *The First World War*, 88, 132

Har Dayal, *Forty-four months in Germany and Turkey*, 117, 288

Harden, E. S., *An American Poilu*, 109

Harden, H. S. S., *Faenza Rest Camp*, 193

Hardie, M., *Our Italian front*, 147

Hardie, M. & Sabin A. K., *War posters issued by belligerent and neutral nations, 1914-1919*, 12

Hardin, M. D., *The pulpit in war time*, 240

Harding, G. P., *Escape fever*, 92

Hardy, E. J., *The British soldier*, 36

Hardy, G. H., *Bertrand Russell and Trinity*, 202

Hardy, G. M. G., *The Fourteen Points and the Treaty of Versailles*, 104

Hardy, J. L., *I escape*, 92

Hardy, M., *Hardy, V.C.*, 316

Hardy, S. J., *History of the Royal Scots Greys — the Second Dragoons, 1914-1919*, 56; Hargrave, J., *At Suvla Bay*, 281; *The Great War brings it home*, 230; *The Suvla Bay landing*, 281

Harington, *Sir* C., *Plumer of Messiner*, 175; *Tim Harington looks back*, 173

Harlow, R. F., *Trail of the 61st*, 307

Harmaja, L., *Effects of the war on economic and social life in Finland*, 100

Harmer, M., *The forgotten hospital*, 167

Harmon, F. S., *Keep 'em rolling*, 109

Harmsworth, A. C. W., *At the war*, 173

Harmsworth, H. S., *My campaign for Hungary*, 287

Harper, C. G., *Overheard at the Front*, 276

Harper, F. M., *Runaway Russia*, 256

Harper, J. E. T., *The truth about Jutland*, 150

Harper, R. W. E., *Singapore mutiny*, 141

Harris, H., *The Irish Regiments in the First World War*, 36, 46

Harris, H. W., *The peace in the making*, 314

Harris, J. N., *The Somme: death of a generation*, 272; *Knights of the air*, 249

Harris, W., *Nerve injuries and shock*, 167

Harrison, A., *The Kaiser's war*, 199

Harrison, C. H., *With the American Red Cross in France*, 223

Harrison, F., *The German peril*, 117

Harrison, H. S., *When I come back*, 299

Harrison, M., *The stolen lands*, 7

Harrison, M. C. C., *Within four walls*, 92

Hart, A. B., *America at war*, 28; *Problems of re-adjustment after the war*, 182; *The war in Europe*, 199

Hart, A. B. & Bassett, J. S., *The great explosion*, 199

Hart, A. R., *Harper's pictorial library of the World War*, 217

Hart, P. G., *History of the 135th Aero Squadron*, 309

Hartill, L. R., *Men are like that*, 10

Hartney, H. E., *Up and at 'em*, 4, 309

Harvey, F. W., *Comrades in captivity*, 224

Harvey, H., *A soldier's sketches under fire*, 12, 212

Harvey, H. E., *Battle-line narratives, 1915-1918*, 276

Harvey, W. F. J., *'P' in the sky (No. 22 Squadron, R.F.C. & R.A.F)*, 249

Hase, G., *Kiel and Jutland*, 150

Hashagen, E., *The log of a U-boat commander*, 289

Haskins, C. H. & Lord, R. H., *Some problems of the Peace Conference*, 314

Haslam, A. D., *Cannon fodder*, 36

Haslett, E., *Luck on the wing*, 4

Haste, C., *Keep the home fires burning*, 227

Hastings, H. D. & Parker, P., *War planes in battle dress, 1914-1918*, 4

Hastings, S., *First aid for the trenches*, 167

Hatch, F. H., *The iron and steel industry of the United Kingdom under war conditions*, 142

Haterius, C. E., *Reminiscences of the 137th U.S. Infantry*, 305

Hatt, C. W., *The future of the disabled soldier*, 83

Hatton, A. P., *The pensions ABC*, 209

Hatton, S. F., *The yarn of a yeoman (Middlesex Yeomanry)*, 56

Hau, G. W., *War echoes; or, Germany and Austria in the crisis*, 117

Haulsee, W. M., *Soldiers of the Great War*, 235

Haupt-Heydemarck, G., *Double-decker C 666*, 121; *Flying Section 17*, 121; *War flying in Macedonia*, 121

Hauser, K., *Swiss internment of prisoners of war*, 281

Havard, R. A., *Portland spy*, 265

Hawker, T. M., *Hawker, V.C.*, 316

Hawkins, F., *From Ypres to Cambrai*, 36

Haworth, C., *March to Armistice, 1918*, 43

Hay, I., *All in it*, 300; *Carrying on after the first hundred thousand*, 36; *The first hundred thousand*, 36; *Getting together*, 292; *Last million*, 292; *The ship of remembrances*, 21

Hay, M. F., *Secrets of the submarine*, 280

Hay, S., *History of the R.N.V.R. South African Division*, 274

Haydon, W., *Canada and the war*, 62

Haydens, H., *Teuton versus Slav*, 220; *Midst shot and shell in Flanders*, 64

Hayes, C. J. H., *A brief history of the Great War*, 132

Hayes, G. P., *World War I*, 132

Hayes, J., *The Eighty-Fifth in France and Flanders*, 64

Hayes, R. A., *Secretary Baker at the Front*, 171

Haynes, H., *The Victory adventure book*, 276

Hays, H. M., *Cheerio!*, 167

Hayward, C. W., *War and rational politics*, 216

Hayward, V., *HMS Tiger at bay*, 24

Hazen, C. D., *Alsace-Lorraine under German rule*, 7

Hazlehurst, C., *Politicians at war*, 160

Head, C. O., *A glance at Gallipoli*, 113; *No great shakes*, 37

Headlam, C., *History of the Guards Division in the Great War*, 40

Headlam, J. W., *The German Chancellor and the outbreak of war*, 199; *History of twelve days. July 24th to August 4th, 1914*, 199; *The issue*, 207

Headlam-Morley, Sir J., *A memoir of the Paris Peace Conference*, 314

Heaps, W. J., *Autocracy versus democracy*, 220

Hearne, R. P., *Zeppelins and super-Zeppelins*, 332

Heath, A. G., *Letters of A. G. Heath*, 157

Hecht, G. J., *The war in cartoons*, 67

Hedin, S. A., *With the German Armies in the West*, 123

Heilgers, L., *Somewhere in France*, 276

Hein, A., *In the hell of Verdun*, 313

Heinz, M., *Loretto*, 123

Helmreich, P. C., *From Paris to Sèvres*, 288

Hemrick, L. E., *Once a Marine*, 310

Henderson, A. P., *Ninety-first*, 305

Henderson, Arthur, *The aims of Labour*, 270

Henderson, E. F., *Germany's fighting machine*, 117

Henderson, F., *A new faith*, 220

Henderson, G., *The experiences of a hut leader at the Front*, 240

Henderson, H. D., *The Cotton Control Board*, 142

Henderson, J. H., *Soldier country*, 132, 212

Henderson, K., *Letters to Helen*, 157

Henderson, R. G., *History of the Fourteenth Engineers, U.S. Army*, 306

Hendrick, B. J., *Life and letters of Walter H. Page*, 175

Henig, R., *Versailles and after 1919–1933*, 314

Henley, T., *After the war*, 240

Hennebois, C., *In German hands*, 224

Henniker, A. M., *Transportation on the Western Front*, 285

Henriques, J. Q., *War history of the 1st Battalion, Queen's Westminster Rifles, 1914-1918*, 49

Henson, H. H., *War-time sermons*, 240

Herbert, A. N. H., *Mons, Anzac and Kut*, 183

Herbert, A. P., *The secret battle*, 77

Herdman, T., *Some geographical factors in the Great War*, 132

Herford, R. T., *Realities and reconstruction*, 230

Hermanns, W., *The holocaust*, 313

Hermes, *The hornets*, 4

Herr, C. R., *Company F history, 319th Infantry, U.S. Army*, 306

Herrick, R., *The world decision*, 105

Herries, J. W., *Tales from the trenches*, 276

Herringham, *Sir* W. P., *A physician in France*, 167

Herron, G. D., *The defeat in the victory*, 314; *The menace of peace*, 207; *Woodrow Wilson and the world's peace*, 325

Hersey, H., *When the boys come home*, 230

Hershey, B., *The odyssey of Henry Ford and the great peace ship*, 207

Hertslet, E. L. A., *The cup and the sacrifice*, 240

Hervey, H. E., *Cage-birds*, 92

Hervier, P-L., *The super-Huns*, 117

Herwig, H. H., *Biographical dictionary of World War I*, 79

Herzog, S. J., *Fightin' Yanks*, 300

Hesketh-Prichard, H., *Sniping in France*, 37

Heuvel, J. van den, *Slave raids in Belgium*, 78

Hewett, S. H., *A scholar's letters from the Front*, 157

Heyking, A., *Problems facing Russia*, 256

Heywood, C. D., *Negro combat troops in the World War*, 188, 306

Hibbard, B. H., *Effects of the Great War upon agriculture in the United States and Great Britain*, 2

Hibben, P., *Constantine I and the Greek people*, 126

Hickey, D. E., *Rolling into action*, 55

Hickey, D. & Smith, G., *Seven days to disaster*, 162

Hickling, H., *Sailor at sea*, 173

Hicks, W. J., *The command of the air*, 4

Higgins, A. P., *Armed merchant ships*, 144; *Defensively-armed merchant ships and submarine war-fare*, 144

Higgins, T., *Winston Churchill and the Dardanelles*, 73

Higonnet, M., *Behind the lines*, 132

Hilditch, A. N., *Battle sketches, 1914-15*, 23; *Coronel and the Falkland Islands*, 75; *The stand at Liege*, 159

Hill, C. W., *The spook and the Commandant*, 92, 224

Hill, D. J., *Impressions of the Kaiser*, 151; *The rebuilding of Europe*, 231

Hill, G. A., *Dreaded hour*, 265; *Go spy the land*, 265

Hill, J. A. S., *The Front line and beyond*, 322

Hill, W. T., *The martyrdom of Nurse Cavell*, 69

Hillgruber, A., *Germany and the two world wars*, 117

Hillis, N. D., *Blot on the Kaiser's 'scutcheon*, 319; *German atrocities*, 319; *Studies of the Great War*, 220

Hines, W. D., *The war history of American railroads*, 229

Hinkson, K., *Life in the occupied area*, 196

Hinsley, F. H., *British foreign policy under Sir Edward Grey*, 31

Hirschfeld, M. & Gaspar, A., *Sexual history of the World War*, 183

Hirst, F. W., *The consequences of the war to Great Britain*, 231; *The political economy of the war*, 88

Hirst, F. W. & Allen, J. E., *British war budgets*, 98

Hirst, L., *Coronel and after*, 75

His, W., *German doctor at the Front*, 167

Hiscock, E., *The bells of Hell go ting-a-ling*, 50

Hislam, P. A., *How we twisted the dragon's tail*, 252

Historicus, *The 'Lusitania' case*, 162

Hitchcock, F. C., *'Stand to'*, 322

Hoar, A., *The submarine torpedo-boat*, 280

Hoare, E., *Palestine, Russia and the present war*,

195

Hoare, R. J., *World War One*, 132

Hoare, Sir S. J. G., *The fourth seal: the end of a Russian chapter*, 256

Hoare, Stephen, *Fighting in World War I*, 132

Hobbs, W. H., *World war and its consequences*, 200, 292

Hobhouse, Mrs H., *I appeal to Caesar*, 74

Hobhouse, L. T., *The world in conflict*, 220, 228

Hobley, L. F., *The First World War*, 132

Hobson, J. A., *Democracy after the war*, 220

Hockin, O., *Two girls on the land*, 327

Hodder-Williams, R., *Princess Patricia's Canadian Light Infantry*, 64

Hodge, H., *In the wake of the war*, 220

Hodges, G., *Memoirs of an old balloonatic*, 22

Hodges, G., *Religion in a world at war*, 240

Hodges, Geoffrey, *The Carrier Corps*, 85

Hodges, T. O., *Short history of the Great War for young people*, 132

Hodson, J., *The soul of a soldier*, 182

Hody, E. H., *With the mad 17th to Italy*, 54

Hoehling, A. A., *Fierce lambs*, 300; *The Great War at sea*, 186; *Lonely command*, 90; *The whisper of eternity*, 69

Hoffman, C., *In the prison camps of Germany*, 224

Hoffmann, M., *War diaries and other papers*, 173

Hoffmann, O. F. C., *The war of lost opportunities*, 123

Hogan, Mrs G. F., *Experiences of a dinki di R.R.C. nurse*, 17

Hogan, M. J., *The Shamrock Battalion of the Rainbow*, 304

Hogg, I. V., *Gas*, 114; *The guns, 1914-18*, 13; *The machine-gun*, 11

Hogg, I. V. & Thurston, L. F., *British artillery weapons and ammunition, 1914-1918*, 13

Hogg, I. V. & Weeks, J., *Military small arms of the twentieth century*, 11

Hogg, J. M. & Garside, T. H., *War pensions and allowances*, 209

Hoggson, N. F., *Just behind the Front in France*, 105

Hogue, O., *Love letters of an Anzac*, 17; *Trooper Bluegum at the Dardanelles*, 77

Holden, M., *War in the trenches*, 286

Holland, H., *So as by fire*, 240

Holland, W. L., *Final call to arms; or, Armagaddon*, 182

Hollander, J. H., *War borrowing*, 98, 319

Holley, I. B., *Ideas and weapons*, 4, 11

Holloway, W. H., *Northamptonshire and the Great War*, 31

Holme, C., *The war depicted by our distinguished British artists*, 12

Holmes, E. E., *The message of the soldiers*, 216

Holmes, Edmond, *The nemesis of docility*, 117

Holmes, R., *My police court friends with the colours*, 276

Holmes, R. D., *A Yankee in the trenches*, 286, 300

Holst, B. P., *My experiences with spies in the great European war*, 265

Holt, I. & Holt, V., *Till the boys come home*, 221

Holt, L., *Paris in shadow*, 205

Holtom, E. C., *Two years' captivity in German East Africa*, 224

Home, Sir A., *Diary of a World War I cavalry officer*, 212

Hoobler, D. & Hoobler, T., *An album of World War I*, 132; *The trenches*, 286

Hook, F. A., *Merchant adventurers, 1914-1918*, 177

Hooper, F. H., *These eventful years*, 132

Hoover, H. C., *America's first crusade*, 207; *The ordeal of Woodrow Wilson*, 325

Hoover, H. C. & Wilson, W., *The Hoover-Wilson wartime correspondence*, 325

Hope, A., *The new German-testament*, 117

Hope, T. S., *The winding road unfolds*, 322

Hopford, W., *Twice interned*, 224

Hopkins, C. P., *'National Service' of British Merchant Seamen*, 178

Hopkins, J. C., *Canada at war, 1914-1918*, 62

Hopkins, N. M., *Over the threshold of war*, 300

Hopkins, T., *Prisoners of war*, 275

Hopkinson, Sir A., *Rebuilding Britain*, 231

Hopkinson, E. C., *1st Battalion, the East Lancashire Regiment, August and September 1914*, 44

Hopper, J. M., *Medals of honor*, 73

Hordern, C., *Military operations in East Africa*, 85

Horn, D., *The German naval mutinies of World War I*, 124, 185

Horn, T., *Lancer dig in*, 164

Hornaday, W. T., *Awake! America*, 297

Hornby, M. L., *How to march*, 284

Horne, A., *Death of a generation*, 322; *The price of glory: Verdun, 1916*, 313

Horne, C. F. & Austin, W. F., *Great events of the Great War*, 132

Horniman, R., *How to make the railways pay for the war*, 229

Hornsey, F. H., *Hell on earth*, 212

Hornung, E. W., *Notes of a camp-follower on the Western Front*, 322

Horton, A. E., *When I become a man*, 212

Horvath, J., *Responsibility of Hungary for the war*, 140

Hough, E., *Web*, 265

Hough, R. A., *The battle of Jutland*, 150; *Former naval person*, 73; *The Great War at sea 1914–1918*, 252; *The pursuit of Admiral von Spee*, 75

Houghton, M., *In the enemy's country*, 118

Houlihan, M., *World War I: trench warfare*, 286

House, E. M., *The intimate papers of Colonel House*, 140

House, E. M. & Seymour, C., *What really happened at Paris*, 314

Housman, L., *War letters of fallen Englishmen*, 157

Houston, D. F., *Eight years with Wilson's Cabinet, 1913-20*, 325

Houtte, P. van, *The Pan-Germanic crime*, 25

Hovelacque, E., *The deeper causes of the war*, 200

Hovell, H., *Rebel prophets and 'Assassins Anglais'*, 74

Hovre Fr. de, *German and English education*, 89

Howard, E. F., *Friends' service in war-time*, 229

Howard, H. N., *The partition of Turkey*, 288

Howard, J. M., *Autobiography of a Regiment (304th Field Art.)*, 308

Howard, K., *An author in wonderland*, 227

Howe, F. C., *The only possible peace*, 207; *Why war?*, 200

Howe, M. A. D., *The Harvard Volunteers in Europe*, 167

Howe, R. W., *Mata Hari*, 164

Howe, Mrs S. E., *Real Russians*, 256

Howland, C. R., *Military history of the World War*, 133

Howell, R., *Phillip Howell*, 37

Howson, G., *Handbook for the limbless*, 83

Hoy, H.C., *40 O.B.; or How the war was won*, 265

Hoyt, E. P., *The Army without a country*, 76; *Disaster at the Dardanelles*, 77; *Defeat at the Falklands*, 124; *The elusive seagull*, 124; *The fall of Tsingtao*, 72; *The Germans never lost*, 124; *Ghost of the Atlantic*, 125; *Guerilla*, 85; *The Karlsruhe affair*, 124; *Kreuzerkrieg*, 124; *The last cruise of the 'Emden'*, 91; *The raider Wolf*, 125

Huard, F. W., *My home in the field of honour*, 164

Hubatsch, W., *Germany and the Central Powers in the World War*, 118

Hubback, J., *Russian realities*, 256

Huberich, C. & King, R., *The prize code of the German Empire, as in force July 1, 1915*, 118

Huddleston, S., *Peace-making at Paris*, 314; *Poincaré*, 175

Hudson, J. J., *Hostile skies*, 310

Hudson, S., *War-time silhouettes*, 182

Hudson, W. J., *Billy Hughes in Paris*, 81

Hueffer, F. H. M., *Between St. Dennis and St. George*, 220

Hughes, B. & Banks, H. S., *War surgery from firing line to base*, 167

Hughes, C. E., *Above and beyond Palestine*, 247

Hughes, Colin, *Mametz*, 272

Hughes, F. K., *A short history of the 49th West Riding and Midland Division*, 42

Hugins, R., *Germany misjudged*, 118; *The possible peace*, 207

Huguet, V. J. M., *Britain and the war*, 31

Huidekoper, F. L., *The history of the 33rd Division, A.E.F.*, 303; *The military unpreparedness of the United States*, 297

Hull, A. J., *Surgery in war*, 167

Hull, W. I., *Preparedness*, 297

Humphrey, A. W., *International socialism and the war*, 270

Humphrey, F., *The experiences of a temporary C.F.*, 70

Hungerford, E., *With the Doughboy in France*, 233

Hunt, B. & Preston, A., *War aims and strategic policy in the Great War*, 278

Hunt, E. T. E., *War bread*, 25

Hunt, J. B., *War, religion and science*, 240

Hunt, M. S., *Nova Scotia's part in the World War*, 62

Hunter, F. T., *Beatty, Jellicoe, Sims and Rodman*, 186

Hunter, J. T., *Hell at Ypres*, 330

Hunton, Mrs A. D. & Johnson, K. M., *Two colored women with the A.E.F.*, 188

Hurd, A. S., *The British Fleet in the Great War*, 252; *The Fleets at war*, 186; *The German Fleet*, 124; *Italian sea-power and the Great War*, 147; *A Merchant Fleet at war*, 178; *The Merchant Navy*, 178; *Ordeal at sea*, 178

Hurd, A. S. & Bashford, H. H., *Sons of Admiralty*, 252

Hurd, A. S. & Bywater, H. C., *From Heligoland to Keeling Island*, 186

Hurd, A. S. & Hurd, P. H., *New Empire partnership*, 59

Hurd, P. H., *The fighting Territorials*, 37

Hurgronje-Snouk, C., *The holy war, made in Germany*, 179

Hurley, E. N., *The bridge to France*, 269

Hurst, Sir A. F., *Medical diseases of war*, 167

Hurst, G. B., *With the Manchesters in the East*, 48

Hurst, S. C., *The silent cities*, 69

Hurwitz, S. J., *State intervention in Great Britain*, 31

Husband, J., *On the coast of France*, 311; *A year in the Navy*, 311

Hussey, A. H., *Narrative of the 5th Divisional artillery 1914-1918*, 40

Hussey, A. H. & Inman, D. S., *The Fifth Division in the Great War*, 40

Hutchinson, W., *Doctor in war*, 168

Hutchison, G. S., *Machine-Guns*, 53; *Pilgrimage*, 22; *The Thirty-Third Division in France and Flanders, 1915-1919*, 41; *Warrior*, 37

Hutton, I. E., *With a woman's unit in Serbia, Salonika and Sebastopol*, 138

Hutton, J. E., *Welfare and housing*, 270

Hyde, H. E., *The international solution*, 155; *The two roads*, 155

Hyde, H. M., *Solitary in the ranks*, 154

Hyde, R., *Passport to Hell*, 190

Hyndman, H. M., *Georges Clemenceau*, 73

Hyndson, J. G. W., *From Mons to the first battle of Ypres*, 101

Idriess, I., *Desert column*, 17, 203; *Lurking death*, 179

Igglesden, C., *Out there*, 322

Illingworth, A. E., *'Fly papers'*, 247

Imbrie, R. W., *Behind the wheel of a war ambulance*, 8

Immelmann, F., *Immelmann, the eagle of Lille*, 121

Imperial War Museum, *A concise catalogue of paintings, drawings and sculpture of the First World War*, 12

Imrey, F. & Palen, L. S., *Through blood and ice*, 224

Imrie, A., *Fokker fighters*, 121; *German air aces of World War I*, 121; *German fighter units June 1917-1918*, 121

Imrie, A., *The German Army Air Service*, 121

Inchbald, G., *Camels and others*, 203; *Imperial Camel Corps*, 203

Index Medicus, *War Supplement*, 168

Ingleby, H., *The Zeppelin raid in West Norfolk*, 332

Inglefield, V. E., *History of the Twentieth (Light) Division*, 41

Inglis, B., *Roger Casement*, 67

Ingpen, R., *Fighting retreat to Paris*, 101, 322

Ingram, A. F. W., *The Church in time of war*, 240; *A day of God*, 240; *Rebuilding the walls*, 32; *Victory and after*, 240

Innes, J. R., *Flash spotters and sound rangers*, 59

Insall, A. J., *Observer: memoirs of the R.F.C.*, 249

Instructor, *Rapid training of recruits*, 284

International Red Cross, *Reports on British prison camps*, 224; *Turkish prisoners in Egypt*, 224

Ireland, M. W., *The medical department of the United States Army in the World War*, 168

Ironside, Sir W. E., *Archangel, 1918-1919*, 10; *Tannenberg*, 86, 258

Irvine, A., *God and Tommy Atkins*, 240

Irving, J., *Coronel and the Falklands*, 75; *The smoke screen of Jutland*, 150

Irwin, W., *The Latin at war*, 147, 318; *Men, women and war*, 270, 330; *A reporter at Armageddon*, 318

Isaacs, E. V. M., *Prisoners of the U-90*, 224

Isselin, H., *The battle of the Marne*, 164

Italy: Army Commando Supremo, *The battle of the Piave*, 147

Jablonski, E., *The knighted skies*, 4; *A pictorial history of World War I years*, 217

Jabotinsky, V., *Turkey and the war*, 288

Jack, J. L., *General Jack's diary, 1914-1918*, 174

Jackson, E. B., *Fall out to the right of the road!*, 212

Jackson, F. J. F., *The faith and the war*, 240

Jackson, L. E. S., *The why and wherefore of indirect laying*, 284

Jackson, R., *Fighter pilots of World War I*, 96

Jacobson, G. F., *History of the 107th Infantry, U.S. Army*, 305

Jaffe, L. S., *The decision to disarm Germany*, 83

Jamal, *Pasha, Memories of a Turkish statesman*, 174

James, B. R., *For God, for country, for home*, 327

James, E. A., *British Regiments 1914-1918*, 37; *A record of the battles and engagements of the British Armies in France and Flanders, 1914-18*, 37

James, F. H., *Faraway campaign (Afghanistan)*, 1

James, H. J., *German subs in Yankee waters: First World War*, 289

James, R. R., *Gallipoli*, 113
James, S. B., *The man who dared*, 74
Jameson, *Sir* W., *The eyes of the Navy*, 173, 265; *The most formidable thing*, 280; *Submarines, V.C.*, 316
Jamie, J. P. W., *'The 177th Brigade'*, 43
Jane, F. T., *All about the German Navy*, 124
Jane, L. C., *The action off Heligoland, August 1914*, 128; *The nations at war*, 220
Jannasch, L., *German militarism at work*, 118
Jantzen, S., *Hooray for peace, hurrah for war*, 292
Jarves, *Mrs* E. D., *War days in Brittany*, 105
Jarvis, C. S., *The back garden of Allah*, 203
Jastrow, M., *The war and the Baghdad railway*, 288; *The war and the coming peace*, 207
Jefferson, C. E., *Old truths and new facts*, 240; *What the war has taught us*, 240; *What the war is teaching*, 182
Jeffery, J. E., *Servants of the guns*, 252
Jeffries, J. M. N., *Front everywhere*, 318
Jeffs, H., *'When the lads come home'*, 240
Jellicoe, E. G., *Playing the game*, 220
Jellicoe, *Sir* J. R., *The battle of Jutland Bank*, 150; *The crisis of the naval war*, 148, 186; *The Grand Fleet 1914-1918*, 252; *The Jellicoe papers*, 148; *The submarine peril*, 289
Jenkin, A., *A tank driver's experiences*, 55
Jenkins, B. A., *Facing the Hindenburg Line*, 128
Jenkins, R., *Asquith*, 14
Jennings, M. J., *Australia in the Great War*, 15
Jenssen, C., *I spy!*, 265
Jephson, *Lady* H. J., *A war-time journal: Germany 1914*, 118
Jerrold, D., *The Hawke Battalion*, 252; *The Royal Naval Division*, 252; *The war on land, 1914-1918*, 133
Jerrold, L., *France today*, 105
Jerrold, W., *Earl Kitchener of Khartoum*, 151; *Field Marshal Sir John French*, 111
Jervis, H. S., *The 2nd Munsters in France*, 50
Jesse, F. T., *The sword of Deborah*, 328
Jessel, *Sir* H. M., *The story of Romsey Remount Depot*, 56
Jessop, T. E., *The Treaty of Versailles*, 314
Jeze, G., *The war finance of France*, 98
Joatamon, *A mug in Mesopotamia*, 179
Jobson, A., *Via Ypres: story of the 39th Divisional Field Ambulance*, 8
Joffre, J. J. C., *Memoirs*, 149
Johannet, R., *Pan-Germanism versus Christendom*, 118

John Bull, *John Bull's diary of the war*, 133
Johns, W. E., *Air V.C.'s*, 316; *Fighter planes and aces*, 96
Johnson, C. W., *History of the 321st Infantry*, 306
Johnson, D. W., *Battlefields of the World War*, 22; *Plain words from America*, 292; *Topography and strategy in the war*, 278
Johnson, E. H., *Torpedoed in the Mediterranean*, 281
Johnson, H. J. T., *Vatican diplomacy in the World War*, 68
Johnson, O. M., *The spirit of France*, 105
Johnson, R. M., *29th Divisional Artillery war record and honours book*, 41
Johnson, R. N., *Heaven, hell or Hoboken*, 305
Johnson, Severance, *Enemy within*, 106
Johnson, Stanley C., *The medals of our fighting men*, 165
Johnson, T. M., *Our secret war*, 265; *Without censor*, 265, 300
Johnson T. M. & Pratt, F., *The lost Battalion*, 300
Johnson, W. F., *America and the Great War for humanity and freedom*, 292
Johnston, A., *At the Front*, 157
Johnston, C. H. L., *Famous Generals of the Great War*, 235
Johnston, *Sir* H., *The black man's part in the war*, 188
Johnston, M. A. B. & Yearsley, K. D., *Four-fifty miles to freedom*, 92
Johnston, R. M., *First reflections on the campaign of 1918*, 292; *General Foch*, 102
Johnstone, E. G., *Naval eight (No. 8 Squadron, R.N.A.S.)*, 247
Joll, J., *The origins of the First World War*, 200
Jones, B. & Howell, B., *Popular arts of the First World War*, 13
Jones, B. D., *The diary of a Padre at Suvla Bay*, 71
Jones, B. E., *Workshop hints for munition workers*, 184
Jones, C. S., *London in war-time*, 160; *President Wilson*, 325; *W. T. Stead and the war*, 195
Jones, E. G., *The challenge of Christianity to a world at war*, 240
Jones, E. H., *The road to En-dor*, 92, 225
Jones, F., *With Serbia in exile*, 236, 268
Jones, H. A., *The official history of the war in the air*, 4; *Over the Balkans and South Russia*, 247; *Sir Walter Raleigh and the air history*, 4
Jones, H. P. M., *War letters of a public school boy*, 157
Jones, J. I. T., *An air-fighter's scrap-book*, 96;

King of air fighters, 96

Jones, Jefferson, *The fall of Tsingtao*, 72

Jones, John P., *The German secret service in America, 1914-18*, 265; *The German spy in America*, 162, 265

Jones, M., *The dance of death*, 13

Jones, N., *The origins of strategic bombing*, 29

Jones, Nigel, H., *The war walk*, 322

Jones, R. E., *The fighting tanks since 1916*, 282

Jones, Robert, *Injuries of the joints*, 168

Jones, Rufus M., *A service of love in war time*, 229

Jones, S., *Russia in revolution*, 260

Jones, T. M., *Watchdogs of the deep*, 280

Jones, W. R., *Fighting the Hun from saddle and trench*, 212

Jonescu, T., *The policy of national instinct*, 255

Jordon, D. S., *Ways to lasting peace*, 207

Jorgensen, J., *False witness*, 25, 78; *The war pilgrim*, 78

Jose, A. W., *The Royal Australian Navy, 1914-1918*, 19

Joynt, W. D., *Saving the Channel ports*, 17

Joy-Stick, *An artistic and literary tribute to officers and men of the R.A.F.*, 247

Judson, H., *Edith Cavell*, 69

Judy, A., *A soldier's diary*, 300

Juenger, E., *Copse 125*, 123; *The storm of steel*, 123, 313

Jukes, G., *Carpathian disaster*, 86

Juvenis, *Suvla Bay and after*, 281

K-7, *Spies at war*, 265

Kadomtsev, B., *The Russian collapse*, 256

Kahn, A., *Life of General Joffre*, 149

Kahn, E. L., *The neglected majority*, 13

Kahn, O. H., *Government ownership of railroads and war taxation*, 229; *Reflections of a financier*, 98; *Right above race*, 118

Kaledin, V. R., *K.14-OM.66: adventures of a double spy*, 265

Kaltenbach, F. W., *Self-determination, 1919*, 111

Kannengiesser, H., *The campaign in Gallipoli*, 113

Kantakuzen, J., *Revolutionary days*, 260

Karagorgevic, A., *For the better hour and the resurrection of Serbia*, 268

Karolyi, M., *Fighting the world*, 140, 174

Kassowitz, K. E., *Around the world on fire*, 20

Kauffman, R. W., *In the moment of time*, 25; *Our Navy at work*, 311

Kautsky, C., *The guilt of William Hohenzollern*, 151

Kautz, J. I., *Trucking to the trenches*, 157

Kayaloff, J., *The battle of Sardarabad*, 68

Keable, R., *Standing by*, 182

Kearsey, A. H. C., *The battle of Amiens, 1918*, 9; *The events, strategy and tactics of the Palestine campaign*, 203; *1915 campaign in France*, 322; *Notes and comments on the Dardanelles campaign*, 77; *Notes and lectures on the campaign in Mesopotamia*, 179; *Notes on the campaign in France, 1914*, 322; *The operations in Egypt and Palestine, 1914-17*, 187, 203; *A study of the strategy and tactics of the East Prussian campaign*, 86; *A study of the strategy and tactics of the Mesopotamia campaign*, 179

Keating, J. & Lavery, F., *Irish heroes in the war*, 43

Keay, J., *The spy who never was*, 164

Keegan, J., *The face of battle*, 23; *Opening moves: August 1914*, 25, 101

Keeling, E. H., *Adventures in Turkey and Russia*, 92, 152

Keeling, F. H., *Keeling's letters and recollections*, 158

Keep, J. L. H., *The Russian revolution*, 260

Keezer, W. S., *Men of the Twentieth*, 310

Kehoe, T. J., *Fighting mascot*, 300

Keiger, J. F. V., *France and the origins of the First World War*, 200

Keir, Sir J. L., *A soldier's eye-view of our Armies*, 37

Keith, A. B., *War government of the British Dominions*, 60

Keith, E. A., *My escape from Germany*, 92

Keith-Falconer, A. W., *The Oxfordshire Hussars in the Great War*, 56

Keller, C., *The power situation during the war*, 142

Keller, P., *States of belonging*, 292

Kellogg, C., *Mercier, the fighting Cardinal of Belgium*, 174

Kellogg, V. L., *Fighting starvation in Belgium*, 25; *Germany in the war and after*, 118; *Herbert Hoover*, 173

Kellogg, W. G., *The conscientious objector*, 74

Kellor, F. A., *Straight American*, 297

Kelly, D. V., *39 months with the 'Tigers' (the 110th Infantry Brigade), 1915-1918*, 47

Kelly, Mrs F., *What America did*, 292

Kelly, M., *American bias in the war*, 292; *Carlyle and the war*, 200

Kelly, S. P., *Pictorial review of 1916*, 87

Kelman, J., *The war and preaching*, 240

Kemp, P. K., *H.M. Destroyers*, 79; *The Stafford-shire Yeomanry (Q.O.R.R.) in the First and Second World Wars*, 56

Kempe, H., *Participation*, 15

Kenamore, C., *From Vanquois Hill to Exermont (35th Division, U.S. Army)*, 303; *Story of the 139th Infantry*, 305

Kennan, G. F., *The fateful alliance*, 81

Kennard, *Lady* D., *A Roumanian diary, 1915-1917*, 255

Kennedy, A. & Crabb, G., *The postal history of the British Army in World War I*, 216

Kennedy, *Sir* A. B. W., *Ypres to Verdun*, 217

Kennedy, David M., *Over here*, 292

Kennedy, E. J., *With the immortal Seventh Division*, 40

Kennedy, G. A. S., *The hardest part: thoughts on religion in war*, 240; *Rough talks by a Padre*, 71

Kennedy, J., *Sun, sand and sin*, 274

Kennedy, J. McF., *The campaign round Liege*, 159; *How the nations waged war*, 133; *How the war began*, 200

Kennedy, T. C., *The hound of conscience*, 75

Kennedy, W. A., *As Britons see it*, 32

Kensit, J. A., *Rome behind the Great War*, 68

Kerensky, A. F., *The catastrophe*, 174; *The crucifixion of liberty*, 260; *The prelude to Bolshevism*, 260

Kernan, W. F. & Samson, H. T., *History of the 103rd Field Artillery*, 307

Kernek, S. J., *Distractions of peace during war*, 81

Kerofilas, C., *Eleftherios Venizelos*, 312

Kerr, M., *Land, sea and air*, 174

Kerr, S. E., *The lions of Marash*, 10

Kerr, S. P., *What the Irish Regiments have done*, 37

Kerr, W. B., *Arms and the maple leaf*, 64; *Historical literature on Canada's participation in the Great War*, 62; *Shrieks and crashes*, 64

Kershaw, A., *The first war planes*, 5

Kessler, H., *Germany and Europe*, 118

Ketchum, J. D., *Ruhleben; a prison camp society*, 225

Kettle, M., *The Allies and the Russian collapse*, 256

Kettle, T. M., *The ways of war*, 212

Keyes, *Sir* R. J. B., *The fight for Gallipoli*, 113; *Ostend and Zeebrugge*, 331

Keynes, J. M., *The economic consequences of the peace*, 88; *A revision of the Treaty*, 88

Kiernan, R. H., *Captain Albert Ball, V.C.*, 316;

Little brother goes soldiering, 212

Kiernan, T. J., *British war finance and the consequences*, 99

Kilduff, P., *Germany's last knight of the air*, 122

Kilpatrick, J. A., *Atkins at war*, 158

Kimball, W. W., *Our question of questions; arm or disarm?*, 297

Kincaid-Smith, M., *The 25th Division in France and Flanders*, 41

Kindall, S. G., *American soldiers in Siberia*, 259

King, D. W., *L.M.8046*, 109

King, H. B., *7th (S) Battalion, Northamptonshire Regiment*, 48

King, H. S., *Russia during the war*, 257

King, J. C., *The First World War*, 133; *Foch versus Clemenceau*, 314; *Generals and politicians*, 106

Kingham, W. R., *London gunners*, 58

Kingsford, A. R., *Night raiders of the air*, 247

Kingsford, C. L., *The story of the Royal Warwickshire Regiment*, 51

Kingsmill, A. C., *The silver badge*, 212

Kingsmill, H., *Behind both lines*, 225

Kinney, C. & Titler, D. M., *I flew a Camel*, 96

Kipling, R., *France at war*, 106; *The fringes of the Fleet*, 253; *The Irish Guards in the Great War*, 46; *The new army in training*, 37; *Sea warfare*, 186

Kiraly, B. K. & Dreisziger, F., *East Central European society in World War I*, 86

Kirby, A., *The way of peace*, 207

Kirby, D., *War, peace and revolution*, 133

Kirk, H. E., *Consuming fire*, 240

Kirkaldy, A. W., *Industry and finance*, 88; *Labour, finance and the war*, 88

Kirkland W. M., *The new death*, 240

Kirkpatrick, F. A., *South America and the war*, 153, 275

Kirschstein, A. J., *Lullaby of guns*, 86

Kirtley, L. E., *Liaison*, 308

Kitchen, M., *The silent dictatorship*, 118

Kittredge, T. B., *Naval lessons of the Great War*, 311

Klaxon, *H.M.S.—*, 253; *The story of our submarine*, 280

Klein, D., *With the Chinks*, 72

Klein, F., *Diary of a French Army Chaplain*, 71; *Hope in suffering*, 240

Kluck, A. von, *The march on Paris, and the battle of the Marne*, 164

Knapp, G. H., *The tragedy of Bitlis*, 10

Knappen, T. M., *Wings of war*, 2

Knight, A. E., *World War and after*, 220

Knight, E. F., *The Harwich Naval Forces*, 128; *The Union-Castle and the war, 1914-1919*, 178

Knight, F., *'Brother Bosch'*, 92

Knight, G. F., *A knight of the air*, 96

Knight, W. A., *War-time over here*, 292

Knight, W. S. M., *History of Britain during the Great War*, 32; *History of the great European war*, 133

Knightley, P., *Lawrence of Arabia*, 154

Knightley, P. & Sampson C., *The secret lives of Lawrence of Arabia*, 154

Knott, G. H., *The trial of Sir Roger Casement*, 67

Knott, Sir A., *With the Russian Army, 1914-1917*, 258

Knox, R. A., *Patrick Shaw-Stewart*, 176

Knyvett, R. H., *'Over there' with the Australians*, 17

Kobayashi, U., *The basic industries and social history of Japan, 1914-1918*, 148

Koch, H. W., *The origins of the First World War*, 200

Koch, T. W., *Books in war*, 159

Kock, N., *Blockade and jungle*, 85, 186

Kocka, J., *Facing total war*, 118

Koehl, H., *Airman's escape*, 92

Koenig, P., *The voyage of the 'Deutschland'*, 124, 289

Koeppen, E., *Higher Command*, 123

Kolbe, P. R., *Colleges in war time and after*, 89

Kon, S., *The cost of the war to Russia*, 257

Koons, J. F., *Billets and bullets of 37 Division*, 303

Kopp, G., *Two lone ships; 'Goeben' and 'Breslau'*, 124

Koss, S. E., *Lord Haldane*, 173, *Asquith*, 14

Kraft, B. S., *The peace ship*, 207

Kramer, H. M., *With seeing eyes*, 212

Krause, C. L., *What is the German nation dying for?*, 118

Kreisler, F., *Four weeks in the trenches*, 174

Krippner, M., *The quality of mercy*, 168

Krist, G., *Prisoner in the Forbidden Land*, 92

Krunich, M., *Serbia crucified*, 268

Kuhn, W. R., *Narrative of Company A, 106th Machine-gun Battalion, 27th Division, U.S. Army*, 309

Kuncz, A., *Black monastery*, 225

Kunz, A., *Civil servants and the politics of inflation in Germany, 1914–1924*, 118

Kurenberg, J. von, *The Kaiser*, 151

Kurtz, R. M., *Beyond no man's land*, 275

Kylie, E., *Who caused the war?*, 200

L. R. A., *Letters of a Canadian stretcher bearer*, 279

La Barre, G., *Captive of the Kaiser*, 26

La Chesnais, P. G., *The Socialist Party in the Reichstag and the declaration of war*, 270

Ladoux, G., *Marthe Richard the skylark*, 265

La Fargue, T. E., *China and the World War*, 72

Laffan, R. G. D., *Guardians of the gates*, 268

Laffin, J., *Damn the Dardanelles*, 77; *Letters from the Front*, 158; *On the Western Front*, 322

Lafond, G., *Covered with mud and glory*, 109

Lafore, L., *The long fuse*, 200

Lagarde, L. A., *Gunshot injuries*, 168

Lake, H., *Campaigning in the Balkans*, 21; *In Salonika with our Army*, 262

Lake, S., *The submarine in war and peace*, 280

Lambert, A., *Over-the-top*, 46

Lambert, B., *Combat report*, 249

Lambert, R. C., *The Parliamentary history of conscription in Great Britain*, 75

Lambie, M., *Verdun experiences*, 313

La Motte, E. N., *Backwash of war*, 138, 168; *Peking dust*, 72

Lancaster, G. H., *Prophecy, the war, and the Near East*, 195

Lanchester, F. W., *Aircraft in warfare*, 5

Landau, H., *All's fair*, 265; *Enemy within*, 265; *Secrets of the White Lady*, 265; *Spreading the spy net*, 265

Landrieux, M., *The cathedral of Reims*, 106

Lane, F. K., *The American spirit*, 1

Lang, C. G., *The church and the clergy at this time of war*, 241

Lang, W., *A sea-lawyer's log*, 253

Langdon, A. M., *The Excess Profits Duty and Excess Mineral Rights Duty*, 283

Lange, F. W. & Berry, W. T., *Books on the Great War*, 28

Langenhove, F., *The growth of a legend*, 26

Langer, W. L., *Gas and flame in World War I*, 114; *With E of the First Gas*, 114

Langhorne, R., *The collapse of the concert of Europe*, 200

Langille, L., *Men of the Rainbow (42nd Division)*, 303

Langmaid, K. J. R., *The approaches are mined*, 181; *The blind eye*, 186; *The sea raiders*, 125

Langner, L. & White, W. W., *Basic patent and trade-mark laws of the principal belligerent Powers*, 142

Lansing, R., *The Big Four and others of the Peace Conference*, 315; *The peace negotiations*, 207, 315; *War memoirs*, 174

Lapradelle, A., *War letters from France*, 106

Lardner, R. W., *My four weeks in France*, 212

Larson, E. J. D., *Memoirs of France and the 88th Division*, 304

Larson, S., *Labor and foreign policy: Gompers, the AFL and the First World War*, 292

Lasswell, H. D., *Propaganda technique in the World War*, 227

Latham, B., *A Territorial soldier's war*, 37

Latter, J. C., *The history of the Lancashire Fusiliers, 1914-1918*, 47

Latzko, A., *Men in battle*, 276

Lauck, W., *The cost of living and the war*, 88

Lauder, Sir H., *A minstrel in France*, 212

Laughlin, C.E., *Foch the man*, 102; *The martyred towns of France*, 106

Laughlin, J. L., *Credit of the nations*, 99

Lauriat, C. E., *Lusitania's last voyage*, 162

Lauzanne, S. J., *Fighting France*, 106; *Great men and great days*, 235

Lavell, C. F., *Reconstruction and national life*, 231

Lavery, F., *Irish heroes in the war*, 37

Lavine, A. L., *Circuits of victory*, 292

Lavington, H., *Psychical phenomena and the war*, 195

Law, H. A., *Why is Ireland at war?*, 145

Lawley, Sir, A., *A message from Mesopotamia*, 180

Lawrence, David, *The true story of Woodrow Wilson*, 325

Lawrence, Dorothy, *Sapper Dorothy Lawrence*, 59, 328

Lawrence F. W. P., *A levy on capital*, 283

Lawrence, J. D., *Fighting soldier*, 300

Lawrence, T. E., *Evolution of a revolt*, 154; *The letters of T. E. Lawrence*, 154; *Secret despatches from Arabia*, 154; *Seven pillars of wisdom*, 154; *T. E. Lawrence to his biographers*, 154

Lawson, Sir A., *War blindness at St. Dunstan's*, 168

Lawson, D., *Great air battles*, 5

Lawson, H. S., *Letters of a headmaster soldier*, 158

Lawson, J. B., *A Cameronian officer*, 44

Lawson, J. C., *Tales of Aegean intrigue*, 126, 187

Lawson, W. R., *British war finance, 1914-15*, 99

Laytham, J. H., *Chronicles of the 20th Light Railway Train Crews Company, Royal Engineers, 1917-1919*, 59

Leary, L. P., *New Zealanders in Samoa*, 190

League of Nations, *Agricultural Production in Continental Europe*, 2

Leask, G. A., *Golden deeds of heroism*, 112; *V.C. heroes of the war*, 316

Le Bas, Sir H., *The Lord Kitchener memorial book*, 152

Le Bon, G., *The psychology of the Great War*, 228

Lecomte, G., *Georges Clemenceau, the Tiger of France*, 73

Lederer, I. J., *The Versailles settlement*, 315; *Yugoslavia at the Paris Peace Conference*, 331

Lee, A. G., *No parachute*, 96; *Open cockpit*, 96

Lee, D. E., *Europe's crucial years*, 81; *The outbreak of the First World War*, 200

Lee, G. S., *We*, 292

Lee, J., *Captive at Carlsruhe*, 225

Lee, J. A., *Todmorden and the Great War*, 32

Leed, E. J., *No man's land*, 271

Leeds, H., *Edith Cavell*, 69

Leeson, C., *The child and the war*, 72

Leete, A., *The Bosch book*, 67

Le Fleming, H. M., *ABC warships of World War I*, 186

Legard, Sir J. D., *The North Riding of Yorkshire Volunteers, 1914-19*, 37

Legg, S., *Jutland*, 150

Legge, E., *King Edward, the Kaiser and the war*, 200; *The public and private life of Kaiser Wilhelm II*, 151

Le Goffic, C., *Dixmude*, 83; *General Foch at the Marne*, 164

Lehmann, E. A. & Mingos, H., *The Zeppelins*, 332

Lehmann, J. F., *Germany's future with a good peace and a bad peace*, 207

Leigh, D., *The background of battle*, 233

Leigh, H., *Planes of the Great War*, 5

Leigh, M. S., *The Punjab and the war*, 141

Leighton, J. L., *Simsadus; London*, 311

Lejars, F., *Urgent surgery*, 168

Leland, F. W. G., *With the M. T. in Mesopotamia*, 180

Leland, W. G. & Mareners, N. D., *Introduction to the official sources for the economic and social history of the World War*, 235

Lelean, P. S., *Sanitation in war*, 168

Leng, W. St. Q., *S.S.A.10.*, 8

Lensch, P., *Three years of world revolution*, 270

Lentin, A., *Lloyd George, Woodrow Wilson and the guilt of Germany*, 207

Leonard, G. H., *They also serve*, 241

Leoning, C. C., *Military aeroplanes*, 5

Le Queux, W., *Britain's deadly peril*, 32, 222; *Devil's spawn*, 146; *German atrocities*, 319; *German spies in England*, 265; *The Minister of evil*, 229; *Rasputin the rascal monk*, 229; *The secret shame of the Kaiser*, 151; *The war of the nations*, 133

Le Roux, R. C. H., *On the field of honor*, 109

Lescaboura, A. C., & Bird, J. M., *The inventive and industrial triumphs of the war*, 142

Leslie, H. W., *'The Royal Mail' war book*, 178

Le Sueur, G., *Germany's vanishing colonies*, 118

L'Etang, H., *The pathology of leadership*, 168

Lettau, J. L., *In Italy with the 332nd Infantry*, 306

Lettow-Vorbeck, P. E., *East African campaigns*, 85; *My reminiscences of East Africa*, 85

Levey, J. H., *Lectures to Regimental officers on the Western campaign*, 37

Levi, N., *Character sketch of General the Right Hon. J. C. Smuts*, 274

Levine, I. D., *The Russian Revolution*, 260

Levinger, L. J., *A Jewish Chaplain in France*, 148

Levison, L., *The Jewish problem and the World War*, 148

Levyns, J. E. P., *The disciplines of war*, 213

Lewin, E., *The German road to the East*, 118

Lewis, C. A., *Sagittarius rising*, 247

Lewis, G. H., *Wings over the Somme*, 247, 272

Lewis P. W., *Blasting and bombardiering*, 322

Lewis, T. E., *Twelve months in an Army hospital*, 139

Lewis, Thomas, *The soldier's heart and the effort syndrome*, 168

Lewys, G., *Charmed American*, 109

Leyland, J., *The achievement of the British Navy in the World War*, 253

Libert De Flemalle, G., *Fighting with King Albert*, 26

Lichnowsky, K. M., *The guilt of Germany for the war of German aggression*, 200; *Heading for the abyss*, 118

Liddell Hart, H. B., *Foch the man of Orleans*, 102; *History of the World War*, 133; *Memoirs*, 174; *The real war*, 133; *Reputations*, 278; *The tanks*, 282; *'T. E. Lawrence' in Arabia and after*, 154; *Through the fog of war*, 278; *The war in outline*, 133

Liddell, R. S., *Action and reaction in Russia*, 257; *On the Russian front*, 258; *The Track of the war*, 26

Liddle, P., *The airman's war 1914–1918*, 248;

British social and military experience in the First World War, 32; *Gallipoli*, 113; *Men of Gallipoli*, 113; *Photohistory of the Great War*, 217; *The sailor's war*, 253; *Testimony of war 1914–1918*, 133

Liebknecht, K. P., 'The future belongs to the people', 118

Lieven, D. C. B., *Russia and the origins of the First World War*, 257

LIFE, *The First World War*, 217

Liggett, H., *A.E.F., ten years ago in France*, 159; *Commanding an American Army*, 159

Lincoln, I. T. T., *Revelations of an international spy*, 265

Lincoln, W. B., *Passage through Armageddon*, 257

Lindsay, J. H., *The London Scottish in the Great War*, 48

Lindsey, B. B., *The Doughboy's religion*, 241

Lings, H. C., *Musketry lectures for officers and N.C.O.'s*, 284

Link, A. S., *Wilson the diplomatist*, 325; *Wilson: the struggle for neutrality, 1914-1915*, 81

Lintier, P., *My 75*, 28, 13, 109

Lippincott, I., *Problems of reconstruction*, 231

Lippman, W., *The political scene*, 207

Lipson, E., *Europe, 1914-1939*, 133

Lissa, N. R., *War-time cookery*, 103

Litman, S., *Prices and price control in Great Britain and the United States during the world War*, 88

Little, A. W., *From Harlem to the Rhine*, 188

Littlefair, M., *An English girl's adventures in hostile Germany*, 118

Litvinoff, M., *The Bolshevik revolution*, 261

Liveing, E. G. D., *Attack*, 213, 322

Livermore, B., *Long 'un*, 49

Livesay, J. F. B., *Canada's hundred days; from Amiens to Mons, 1918*, 64

Livingston, St. C. & Steen-Hansen, I., *Under three flags*, 234

Livock, G. E., *To the ends of the air*, 254

Lloyd, A., *The war in the trenches*, 286

Lloyd, E. M. H., *Experiments in state control at the War Office and Ministry of Food*, 103

Lloyd, G., *An Englishwoman's adventures in the German lines*, 328

Lloyd George, D., *The great crusade*, 160; *Through terror to triumph*, 160; *The truth about reparations and war debts*, 160; *The truth about the peace treaties*, 160; *War memoirs*, 160

Lloyd, Ll., *Lice and their menace to man*, 168

Lloyd, T., *The blazing trail of Flanders*, 101

Lloyd Thomas, J. M., *The immorality of non-resistance*, 241

Lloyd, W., *European war debts and their settlement*, 319

Lobanov-Rostovsky, A., *Grinding mill*, 257

Lochner, L. P., *America's Don Quixote*, 293

Lock, B. S., *Right against might*, 133

Locke, C. R. L., *The fighting 10th*, 17

Lockhart, J. G., *Palestine days and nights*, 203; *The sea our heritage*, 253

Lockhart, Sir R. B. H., *Memoirs of a British agent*, 265

Lodge, H. C., *Selections from the correspondences of Theodore Roosevelt*, 246; *Senate and the League of Nations*, 155; *War addresses, 1915-1917*, 1

Lodge, Sir O. J., *The war and after*, 231

Logan, L., *On the King's service*, 37

Loisy, A. F., *The war and religion*, 241

London Committee of Deputies of the British Jews, *The Peace Conference, Paris*, 148

Lonergan, T. C., *It might have been lost!*, 300

Long, P. W., *Other ranks of Kut*, 152

Long, R. C., *The mythology of reparations*, 245

Long, R. E. C., *Colors of war*, 258

Longbottom, F. W., *Chester in the Great War*, 32

Longmore, C., *The old Sixteenth (16th Battalion, A.I.F.)*, 18

Longstaff, F. V. & Atteridge, A. H., *The book of the machine-gun*, 11

Longstreet, S., *The canvas falcons*, 5

Lonnroth, E., *Lawrence of Arabia*, 154

Loomis, E. L., *History of the 304th Ammunition Train*, 300

Lord, J. R., *The story of the War Hospital, Epsom*, 139

Loreburn, R. T. R., *How the war came*, 200

Loti, P., *War*, 182

Lovejoy, E., *The house of the good neighbor*, 237

Low, S. J. M., *Italy in the war*, 146; *Spirit of the Allied nations*, 133

Lowe, C. E. B., *Siege Battery 94 during the World War*, 13

Lowe, C. J. & Dockrill, M., *The mirage of power*, 32

Lowe, T. A., *The Western battlefields*, 22

Lowe, W. D., *War history of the 18th (S) Battalion, Durham Light Infantry*, 44

Loyson, P. H., *The gods in battle*, 182

Luard, K. E., *Unknown warriors*, 193

Lucas, B. J., *Children of France and the Red Cross*, 234

Lucas, Sir C. P., *The Empire at war*, 60; *The Gold Coast and the war*, 126

Lucas, E. V., *Outposts of mercy*, 234

Lucas, J., *The world fight for freedom*, 133

Lucas, J. S., *Austro-Hungarian Infantry 1914-18*, 20

Lucchi, L., *By the waters of Fiume*, 100

Luckau, A., *The German delegation and the Paris Peace Conference*, 315

Lucy, J., *There's a devil in the drum*, 183

Ludendorff, E., *The General Staff and its problems*, 161; *My war memoirs*, 161

Ludwig, E., *Austria-Hungary and the war*, 20; *Hindenburg and the saga of the German revolution*, 128; *Wilhelm Hohenzollern*, 151

Luebke, F. C., *Bonds of loyalty*, 295

Lugard, E., *An Emperor's madness*, 118

Lugard, E. A., *Some impressions of the work of the British Red Cross in France*, 234

Lugard, Sir F. J. D., *The dual Mandate in British tropical Africa*, 231

Luke, C. H., *The war and the parting of the ways*, 60

Lukomski, A. S., *Memoirs of the Russian revolution*, 261

Lupu, N., *Rumania and the war*, 255

Lushington, R. F., *A prisoner with the Turks, 1915-1918*, 225

Lussu, E., *Sardinian Brigade*, 147

Lutz, H., *Lord Grey and the World War*, 127

Luxford, J. H., *With the machine gunners in France and Palestine*, 190

Lyddon, W. G., *British war missions to the United States, 1914-1918*, 88

Lyde, L. W., *Some frontiers of tomorrow*, 231

Lynch, F., *The last war*, 220

Lynch, G., *War wire*, 282

Lynch, J. W., *Princess Patricia's Canadian Light Infantry*, 64

Lynd, R., *If the Germans conquered England*, 94

Lynk, M. V., *Negro pictorial review of the Great World War*, 188

Lyon, L., *Pomp of power*, 133

Lytton, N. S., *The Press and the General Staff*, 69, 222

M, D. R., *A silver lining (Glasgow Highlanders in France*, 45

MacAlister, D. A., *Field gunnery*, 284

McAuley, M. E., *Germany in war time*, 119

MacBride, H. W., *The Emma Gees*, 300

McBride, H. W., *Riflemen went to war*, 64

MacCabe, J., *Georges Clemenceau*, 73; *The soul of Europe*, 182; *Treitsche and the Great War*, 119; *The war and the churches*, 241

MacCall, R., *Roger Casement*, 67

McCarthy, D. E., *The Irish in the Great War*, 145

McCarthy, D. J., *The prisoner of war in Germany*, 225

McCarthy, Dudley, *Gallipoli to the Somme*, 18

McCarthy, W. E., *Memories of the 309th Field Artillery*, 308

Macartney, C. E., *Hungary and her successors*, 287

MacClellan, E. N., *The U.S. Marine Corps in the World War*, 310

McClellan, G. B., *The heel of war*, 133

McClement, F. G., *Guns in paradise*, 253

McClintock, A., *Best o' luck*, 213

McClung, N. L., *Next of kin*, 62; *Three times and out*, 213

McClure, S. S., *Obstacles to peace*, 208

Macclure, W. K., *Italy's part in the war*, 146

McCombe, J. & Menzies, A. F., *Medical service at the Front*, 168

McConnell, J. R., *Flying for France*, 108

McCormick, D., *The mystery of Lord Kitchener's death*, 152

McCormick, F., *The menace of Japan*, 148

MacCormick, H. F., *Via pacis*, 208

McCormick, R. R., *The Army of 1918*, 300; *With the Russian Army*, 258

McCoy, P. T., *Kittie McCoy*, 213

McCudden, J. T. B., *Flying fury*, 96

MacCullum, R. B., *Public opinion and the last peace*, 208

MacCurdy, C. A., *The terms of the coming peace*, 208

MacCustra, L., *Gallipoli days and nights*, 113

McDermott, F., *Confessions of an old soldier*, 37

McDill, J. R., *Lessons from the enemy*, 168

MacDonagh, M., *In London during the Great War*, 160; *The Irish at the Front*, 37; *The Irish on the Somme*, 37, 272

MacDonald, H. T., *What is due to me?*, 209

MacDonald, J. F., *Two towns – one city; Paris – London*, 205

Macdonald, J. N., *A political escapade*, 100

Macdonald, L., *1914*, 133; *Somme*, 272; *The roses of no man's land*, 168; *Tey called it Passchendaele*, 205, 330

Macdonald, M., *Some experiences in Hungary, Aug. 1914-Jan. 1915*, 141; *Under the French flag*, 109

Macdonald, W., *Reconstruction in France*, 231

McDougall, G., *A nurse at the war*, 193

MacEchern, D., *The sword of the North*, 37

MacEntee, G. L., *Italy's part in winning the World War*, 146; *Military History of the World War*, 133

MacFadyean, Sir A., *Reparations reviewed*, 245

MacFall, H. C., *Beware the German's peace*, 208; *Germany at bay*, 119, 278

MacFarlane, C. W., *The economic basis of an enduring peace*, 88

MacGill, P., *The amateur Army*, 284; *The Diggers*, 18; *The great push*, 161; *The red horizon*, 161, 182; *Soldier songs*, 273

McGuinness, F., *Observe the sons of Ulster marching towards the Somme*, 84

McGuire, J. K., *The King, the Kaiser and Irish freedom*, 145; *What would Germany do for Ireland?*, 145

Macin.osh, J. C., *Men and tanks*, 55

Macintyre, D., *Fighting ships and seamen*, 186; *Jutland*, 150; *Canada at Vimy*, 64

MacIntyre, Duncan, *The Great War*, 200

Mackarness, C. C., *Faith and duty in time of war*, 241

Mackay, H., *Journal of small things*, 106

McKee, A., *The friendless sky*, 5; *Vimy Ridge*, 317

MacKenna, M., *I was a spy*, 266; *My master spy*, 266; *Spies I knew*, 266; *A spy was born*, 266

MacKenzie, C. N., *The tale of a trooper*, 191

MacKenzie, D., *The Sixth Gordons in France and Flanders*, 45

Mackenzie, Donald A, *From all the Fronts*, 276; *Heroes and heroic deeds of the Great War*, 112; *The story of the Great War*, 133

Mackenzie, E. M. Compton, *First Athenian memories*, 266; *Gallipoli memories*, 113; *Greek memories*, 266

McKenzie, F. A., *Canada's day of glory*, 64; *The Irish rebellion*, 145; *Through the Hindenburg Line*, 64, 128

Mackenzie, J., *Number 4 Canadian Hospital*, 64

Mackenzie, K. W., *The story of the 17th Battalion, A.I.F. in the Great War*, 18

MacKenzie, R. T., *Reclaiming the maimed*, 168

Mackenzie, S. S., *The Australians at Rabaul*, 18

Mackenzie, W. D., *Christian ethics in the World War*, 241

McKeogh, A., *Victorious 77th Division*, 304

McKernan, M., *Padre*, 71

McKim, R. H., *For God and country; or, The*

Christian pulpit in wartime, 241

Mackinder, *Sir* H. J., *Democratic ideals and reality*, 231; *The World War and after*, 133

Mackinnon, I., *Garroot*, 187

Mackintosh, D. C., *God in a world at war*, 241

Mackintosh, E. W., *War, the liberator*, 182

McLaren, A. D., *Germanism from within*, 119, 200; *Peaceful penetration*, 227

Maclaren, B., *Women of the war*, 328

Maclaren, E. S., *Elsie Inglis, the woman with the torch*, 268

Maclaren, R., *Canadians in Russia, 1918-1919*, 259

McLaughlin, A. C., *America and Britain*, 292

McLauglin, R., *The escape of the Goeben: prelude to Gallipoli*, 124

Maclean, A. M., *With the Gordons at Ypres*, 330

MacLean, A. & Poole, S., *Fighting ships of World War One and Two*, 253

Maclean, H., *Albuminuria and war nephritis among British troops in France*, 168

MacLean, J. K. & Reddle, T. W., *The Y.M.C.A. with the colours*, 329

MacLean, N. & Sclater, J. R., *God and the soldier*, 241

Maclennan, R. W., *The ideals and training of a flying officer*, 62

MacLeod, G. H., *The blight of kultur*, 119

MacMaster, J. B., *The United States in the World War*, 292

Macmillan, H., *Winds of change*, 174

Macmillan, N., *Into the blue*, 248; *Offensive patrol*, 5; *Tales of two air wars*, 5

Macmillan, W. M., *A South African student and soldier*, 274

McMullen, F. & Evans, J., *Out of the jaws of Hunland*, 92

Macmunn, *Sir* G. F., *The King's pawns*, 276

Macmunn *Sir* G. F. and Falls, C., *Military operations, Egypt and Palestine*, 203

Macmurtrie, D. C., *The disabled soldier*, 83

Macnabb, V. J., *Europe's ewe-lamb*, 94

Macnair, W., *Blood and iron*, 322

MacNaghten, A., *"Missing"*, 330

Macnaughtan, *Mrs* S., *My war experiences in two continents*, 168; *A woman's diary of the war*, 26, 193

McNicol, N. G., *Thirty-seventh (37th Battalion, A.I.F.)*, 18

McNish, R., *Iron Division*, 40

Macnutt, F. B., *The Church in the furnace*, 241

Macphail, *Sir* A., *Official history of the Canadian Forces in the Great War; Medical Services*, 64

Macpherson, *Sir* W. G., *History of the Great War; Medical Services*, 168

Macpherson, W. L., *Short history of the Great War*, 134; *Strategy of the Great War*, 278

Macquarrie, H., *How to live at the Front*, 300

Macqueen, J. M., *Our war*, 169

Macscotch, *pseud, Fighter pilot*, 96

Macveagh, E. G. & Brown, L. D., *Yankee in the British zone*, 32, 300

Macvey, F. L., *The financial history of Great Britain, 1914-1918*, 99

Maanen-Helmer, E., *The Mandates system in relation to Africa and the Pacific Islands*, 163

Mabry, G., *Recollections of a recruit (54th U.S. Infantry)*, 304

Maccas, L., *German barbarism*, 119, 319

Mach, E. von, *Germany's point of view*, 119

Machar, J. S., *The jail*, 20

Machen, A., *The angels of Mons*, 195; *War and the Christian faith*, 241

Mack, A. J., *Shellproof Mack*, 300

Mack, J. E., *A Prince of our disorder*, 154

Mack, L., *A woman's experiences in the Great War especially in Antwerp and Brussels*, 26

Mackie, D. M., *Forfar and District in the war*, 32

Macksey, K., *The shadow of Vimy Ridge*, 317; *Vimy Ridge*, 317

Maeterlinck, M., *The Burgomaster of Stilemonde*, 84; *The wrack of the storm*, 26

Maeztu, R. de, *Authority, liberty and function in the light of the war*, 94

Magan, P. T., *The Vatican and the war*, 68

Maglic, K., *The dandy Hun*, 20

Magnes, J. L., *Russia and Germany at Brest-Litovsk*, 30

Magnus, L. A., *Pros and cons in the Great War*, 200; *Rumania's cause and ideals*, 255; *The third great war in relation to modern history*, 134; *The West Riding Territorials in the Great War*, 53

Magnus, P., *Kitchener*, 152

Mahoney, H. C. & Talbot, F. A., *Interned in Germany*, 144, 225; *Sixteen months in four German prisons*, 225

Mair, C., *Britain at war 1914–1919*, 32

Mais, S. P. B., *An English course for Army candidates*, 284; *A Public School in war time*, 89

Majendie, V. H. B., *A history of the 1st Battalion the Somerset Light Infantry, July 1st, 1916-1918*, 52

Makhov, A., *Smell of smoke*, 260

Makins, G. H., *Gunshot injuries of the arteries*, 169

Malcolm, I. Z., *Scraps of paper*, 106; *War pictures behind the lines*, 139

Malden, R. H., *The battle of Jutland, May 31st, 1916*, 150

Malherbe, F. de, *The flame that is France*, 106

Malins, G. H., *How I filmed the war*, 217

Mallet, C., *Impressions and experiences of a French trooper*, 109

Mallock, W. H., *Capital, war and wages*, 99

Malthus, C., *Anzac*, 191

Malynski, E., *A short cut to a splendid peace*, 208

Mamatey, V. S., *The United States and East Central Europe, 1914-18*, 325

Man, H. de, *The remaking of the mind*, 231

Manchester Guardian, History of the war, 1914-15, 134

Manion, R. J., *A surgeon in arms*, 169

Manley, W. F., *Galaxy of coming events*, 195

Mann, A. J., *The Salonika Front*, 262

Mannock, E., *The personal diary of Major Edward 'Mick' Mannock*, 96

Mansergh, P. N. S., *The coming of the first World War*, 200

Mansfield, W., *Day to day, 1914-1915*, 174

Manteyer, G. de, *Austria's peace offer, 1916-1917*, 20

Mantoux, E., *Carthaginian peace; or, The economic consequences of Mr. Keynes*, 88

Manwaring, G. B., *If we return*, 158

Mappin, G. E., *Can we compete?*, 88

Marben, R., *Zeppelin adventures*, 332

March, F. A., *History of the World War*, 134

March, P. C., *The nation at war*, 292

Marcosson, L. F., *The business of war*, 54; *The rebirth of Russias* 257; *S.O.S. America's miracle in France*, 300; *The war after the war*, 88

Marden, T. O., *A short history of the 6th Division*, 40

Marder, A. J., *Fear God and dread nought*, 172; *From the Dardanelles to Oran*, 253; *From the dreadnought to Scapa Flow*, 253

Margerison, J. S., *Action!*, 253; *The sure shield*, 253

Marie, *Queen of Rumania, My Country*, 255

Mark VII, *A subaltern on the Somme in 1916*, 272

Markham, V. R., *A woman's watch on the Rhine*, 196

Markland, R., *The glory of Belgium*, 26

Markle, C. M., *Yankee prisoner in Hunland*, 225

Markovic, L., *Serbia and Europe, 1914-1919*, 268

Marks, T. P., *The laughter goes from life*, 286

Marr, H. C., *Psychoses of the war*, 169

Marr, J. L., *The 142nd Heavy Battery, R.G.A.*, 58

Marran, Albert, *The Yanks are coming*, 293

Marrin, A., *The last crusade*, 241

Marsden, V. E., *Rasputin and Russia*, 229

Marsh, H. R., *Nine-nine lives*, 310

Marshall-Cornwall, Sir J., *Foch as military commander*, 102; *Haig as military commander*, 127

Marshall, H. R., *War and the ideal of peace*, 208

Marshall, L., *Horrors and atrocities of the Great War*, 319; *The story of Europe and the nations at war*, 134; *World War*, 134

Marshall, S. L. A., *World War I*, 134

Marshall, Sir W. R., *Memories of four Fronts*, 174, 180

Marson, T. B., *Scarlet and khaki*, 248

Marston, F. S., *The Peace Conference of 1919*, 315

Martel, G., *The origins of the First World War*, 200

Marti, O. A., *The Anglo-German commercial and Colonial rivalry as a cause of the Great War*, 201

Martin, A. A., *A surgeon in khaki*, 169

Martin, A. G., *Mother country-Fatherland*, 123

Martin, B., *Poor bloody infantry*, 322

Martin, C., *Battle of the Somme*, 272

Martin, E. S., *Diary of a nation*, 296; *The war week by week as seen from New York*, 134

Martin, J., *Captivity and escape*, 93

Martin, L. W., *Peace without victory*, 326

Martin-Nicholson, *Sister, My experiences on three Fronts*, 193

Martin, P. A., *Latin America and the war*, 153

Marwick, A., *The deluge*, 32; *Women at war, 1914-1918*, 328

Marye, G. T., *Nearing the end in Imperial Russia*, 257

Masaryk, T. G., *The making of a State*, 174

Masefield, J., *The battle of the Somme*, 272; *Gallipoli*, 113; *John Masefield's letters from the Front 1915-1917*, 158; *The old Front Line; or, The beginning of the battle of the Somme*, 272; *St. George and the dragon*, 182

Mason, D. M., *Monetary policy, 1914-1918*, 99

Mason, E. W., *Made free in prison*, 74

Mason, H. M., *High flew the falcons*, 108

Mason, J. M., *The Danzig dilemma*, 218

Mason, M. & Furr, A., *An American Negro soldier with the Red Hand of France*, 188

Massart, J., *Belgians under the German eagle*, 26; *The secret Press in Belgium*, 26

Massey, W. T., *Allenby's final triumph*, 204; *The desert campaign*, 90, 204; *How Jerusalem was won*, 204

Massie, R., *Nicholas and Alexandra*, 192

Masterman, C. F. G., *England after the war*, 32

Masterman, E. W. G., *The deliverance of Jerusalem*, 204

Masters, D., *'I.D.'*, 280

Masters, J., *Fourteen eighteen*, 134

Mather, W. D., *"Muckydonia, 1917–1918"*, 163

Mathews, S., *Patriotism and religion*, 241

Matthews, B. J., *Christ and the world at war*, 241; *Three years' war for peace*, 208

Matthews, C., *Experiences of a woman doctor in Serbia*, 268

Matthews, E. C., *A subaltern in the field*, 322; *With the Cornwall Territorials on the Western Front*, 37

Mattox, W. C., *Building the emergency fleet*, 269

Maud, C. E., *My French year*, 106

Maud, J. P., *Our comradeship with the blessed dead*, 241

Maude, A. H., *The 47th London Division, 1914-1919*, 42

Maunsell, M. C., *English-French and French-English military and naval technical dictionary*, 79; *English-Italian, Italian-English artillery and naval technical terms*, 79

Maurice, Sir F. B., *The Armistices of 1918*, 11; *Forty days in 1914*, 134; *Haldane*, 173; *The last four months*, 134; *Lessons of Allied co-operation*, 278; *The life of General Lord Rawlinson of Trent*, 175; *The Maurice case*, 38

Mawson, T. H., *An Imperial obligation*, 83

Maxim, H., *Defenceless America*, 297

Maximilian Alexander, F. W., *The memoirs of Prince Max of Baden*, 174

Maxwell, D., *A dweller in Mesopotamia*, 13; *The last crusade*, 13, 204

Maxwell, G. A., *Swan song of a rustic moralist*, 174

Maxwell, G. S., *The motor launch patrol*, 183; *The Naval Front*, 186

Maxwell, J., *Hell's bells and Mademoiselles*, 18

Maxwell-Lefroy, H., *Measures for avoidance and extermination of flies, mosquitoes, lice and other vermin*, 169

Maxwell, W. N., *A psychological retrospect of the Great War*, 228

May, A. J., *The passing of the Hapsburg Monarchy, 1914-1918*, 20

May, E. R., *Signal Corporal (2nd London Irish Rifles)*, 47; *The World War and American isolation, 1914-1917*, 296

Mayer, A. J., *Politics and diplomacy of peace making*, 315

Mayhew, D. M., *Lift up your hearts*, 241

Maynard, Sir C., *The Murmansk venture*, 259

Mayo, K., *Soldiers what next!*, 94; *'That damn Y'*, 329

Mayo, M., *Trouping for the troops*, 91

Maze, P., *A Frenchman in khaki*, 110

Meakin, W., *The Fifth North Staffords and the North Midland Territorials (46th and 59th Divisions)*, 48

Medley, A., *A martial medley*, 276

Meehan, T. F., *History of the Seventy-eighth Division in the World War*, 304

Megerdichian, E., *From Turkish toils*, 10

Meinertzhagen, R., *Army Diary, 1899-1926*, 174

Melas, G. M., *Ex-King Constantine and the war*, 126

Melgar, F. M., *Germany and Spain*, 275

Mellersh, H. E. L., *School boy into war*, 213

Mendelssohn-Bartholdy, A., *The war and German society*, 119

Menne, B., *Armistice and Germany's food supply, 1918-19*, 28, 119

Menpes, M., *Lord Kitchener*, 152

Menzies, J. H., *Canada and the war*, 62

Mercier, D. J., *Cardinal Mercier's own story*, 174; *A shepherd among wolves*, 26; *The voice of Belgium*, 26

Merewether, J. W. B. & Smith, Sir F., *The Indian Corps in France*, 141

Meriwether, L., *The war diary of a diplomat*, 106

Merrill, W., *A college man in khaki*, 14

Merritt, W. H., *Canada and National Service*, 62

Merry, W. M., *Two months in Russia, 1914*, 257

Merton, J., *Love letters under fire*, 158

Mesopotamia Commission, *Report*, 180

Messenger, C., *Terriers in the trenches*, 286; *Trench fighting, 1914-18*, 286

Messenger, F. M., *World war, four horses of Revelation*, 195

Metchim, D. B., *Our own history of the war; from a South London view*, 160

Meyer, E. L., *'Hey! Yellowbacks!'*, 74

Meyer, H. R., *After the war*, 231

Meyers, J., *The wounded spirit*, 154

Michael, M. B., *Miracle flower*, 221

Middlebrook, M., *The first day on the Somme, 1 July, 1916*, 272; *The Kaiser's battle*, 123, 151, 323

Middlemas, K., *Command the far seas*, 75

Middleton, E. C., *Glorious exploits of the air*, 5; *The Great War in the air*, 5; *Tails up*, 248; *The way of the air*, 5

Middleton, Sir T. H., *Food production in war*, 103

Midshipman, *From Dartmouth to the Dardanelles*, 253

Milan, R., *Vagabonds of the sea*, 110

Miles, H., *Untold tales of war-time London*, 160

Miles, H. E., *Economy in war time; or, Health without meat*, 103

Miles, L. W., *History of the 308th Infanry, 1917-1919*, 306

Miles, W., *Military operations, France and Belgium 1917; the battle of Cambrai*, 61; *Military operations, France and Belgium 1916; the Battle of the Somme*, 323

Millar, R., *Kut; the death of an Army*, 152

Millar, W. C., *From Thunder Bay through Ypres with the fighting 52nd (Canada)*, 64

Millard, F. L. H., *Short war sermons for Good Friday and Easter*, 241

Millard, O. E., *Burgomaster Max*, 26; *Uncensored*, 26

Millard, S., *I saw them die*, 193

Millard, T. F. F., *Democracy and the Eastern question*, 95

Miller, C., *Battle for the bundu*, 85

Miller, D. H., *The Peace Pact of Paris*, 285

Miller, E., *Camps, tramps and trenches*, 191

Miller, F., *Under German shell-fire*, 263

Miller, H. R., *First Division*, 302

Miller, H. W., *The Paris gun*, 205

Miller, J. M. & Canfield, H. S., *The people's war book*, 134

Miller, K., *Kelly Miller's history of the World War for human rights*, 188

Miller, L., *The chronicles of 55 Squadron, R.F.C. and R.A.F.*, 249

Miller W., *With the Springboks in Egypt*, 274

Miller, W. H., *The boys of 1917*, 300; *Sea fighters*, 186

Millet, P., *Comrades in arms*, 110

Millholland, R., *The plinter fleet of the Otranto Barrage*, 280, 311

Millioud, M., *The ruling caste and frenzied trade in Germany*, 119

Millis, W., *Road to war; America 1914-1917*, 296

Mills, A. H., *Hospital days*, 139; *With my Regiment from the Aisne to La Bassée*, 7, 277

Mills, C., *A strange war*, 275

Mills, F., *Great Uncle Fred's war*, 204

Mills, J. S., *David Lloyd George; War Minister*, 160

Milne, Sir A. B., *The flight of the 'Goeben' and the 'Breslau'*, 124

Milne, D. G., *The escaper's log*, 93

Milne, J., *Footprints of the 114th Leicestershire Regiment, August 1914 to November 1918*, 47; *News from 'Somewhere'*, 323; *A new tale of two cities*, 160; *The war stories of Private Thomas Atkins*, 277

Milnes, A., *The economic foundations of reconstruction*, 231

Minchin, J. H. C., *Great short stories of the war*, 277

Minder, C. F., *The man's war*, 323

Minor, R. C., *A republic of nations*, 155

Mirman, L., *Their crimes*, 319

Missen, L. R., *The history of the 7th Services Battalion, Prince of Wales's North Staffordshire Regiment, 1914-1919*, 48

Mitchell, C. van S., *With a military ambulance in France, 1914-1915*, 8

Mitchell, D., *Women on the warpath*, 328

Mitchell, F., *Tank warfare*, 282; *Tried and tempted in every shape and form*, 106

Mitchell, Fred, *Fred Mitchell's war story*, 213

Mitchell, G. D., *Backs to the wall*, 18

Mitchell, P. C., *Evolution and the war*, 216

Mitchell, W., *Memoirs of World War I*, 175

Mitrany, D., *The effect of the war in South-Eastern Europe*, 231

Mitton, G. E., *The cellar-house of Pervyse*, 169

Mixter, G. W. & Emmons, H. H., *U.S. Army aircraft production facts*, 2

Mlynarski, F., *The problems of the coming peace*, 208

Moberly, F. J., *Military operations; the 'campaign in Mesopotamia*, 180; *Military operations; Togoland and the Cameroons*, 320

Mock, J. R., *Censorship, 1917*, 69

Mock, J. R. & Larson, C., *Words that won the war*, 227, 293

Mocsy, I. J., *The effects of World War I*, 141

Moeran, J. W. W., *Illustrations from the Great War*, 218

Moffat, A. W., *Maverick Navy*, 280

Mokveld, L., *The German fury in Belgium*, 26

Molesworth, Sir G. L., *Democracy and war*, 32

Mollo, A., *Army uniforms of World War I*, 290

Molony, C. V., *'Invicta'; with the first Battalion the Queen's Own Royal West Kent Regiment in the Great War*, 49

Molony, W. O., *Nationality and the Peace Treaties*, 285; *Prisoners and captives*, 225

Molter, B. A., *Knights of the air*, 96, 310

Monash, *Sir J., The Australian victories in France in 1918*, 18; *War letters*, 18

Money, R. R., *Flying and soldiering*, 5

Montague, C. E., *Disenchantment*, 213; *Notes from Calais Base*, 60

Montgomery, *Sir A. A., The story of the Fourth Army in the battle of the hundred days*, 39

Montgomery, B. G. de, *Versailles*, 315

Montgomery, D. H., *Down the flare path*, 248

Montgomery, R. M. & Allen, W., *Excess Profits Duty and Excess Mineral Rights Duty*, 283

Montgomery-Moore, C., *That's my bloody plane*, 5

Moodie, J. W., *700 days with the troops*, 241

Moodie, W., *The crown of honour*, 277

Moody, R. S. H., *Historical records of the Buffs East Kent Regiment*, 44

Moon, E. R. P., *Four weeks as acting Commandant at the Belgian Field Hospital*, 139

Moore, A. B., *The mounted riflemen in Sinai and Palestine*, 191

Moore, E. C., *What the war teaches about education*, 90

Moore, F., *The chaos in Europe*, 257

Moore, Geoffrey, *Kitchener's pioneers*, 48

Moore, H. C., *Under Jellicoe's command*, 148

Moore, Howard W., *Plowing my own furrow*, 75

Moore, J. R., *History of the American Expedition fighting the Bolsheviki*, 259

Moore, M. M., *The maple leaf's Red Cross*, 234

Moore, S. T., *America and the World War*, 293

Moore, W., *Notes on the operations of the B.E.F.*, 60

Moore, William, *See how they ran*, 323; *The thin yellow line*, 169

Moore, W. G., *Early bird*, 254

Moorehead, A., *Gallipoli*, 113; *The Russian revolution*, 261

Moorhead, R. L., *Story of the 139th Field Artillery, A.E.F.*, 308

Moran, C. M., *The anatomy of courages*, 228

More, J. N., *With Allenby's crusaders*, 180

Morel E. D., *Truth and the war*, 201

Morgan, G. C., *God, humanity and the war*, 241

Morgan, H., *Life among the sandbag*, 286

Morgan, J. H., *German atrocities*, 319; *Leaves from a field note book*, 213

Morgan, J. V., *The war and Wales*, 317

Morgenthau, H., *Ambassador Morgenthau's story*, 175, 288; *Secrets of the Bosphorus*, 288

Moriæ, E., *A soldier of the Legion*, 300

Morison, F., *War on great cities*, 5

Morison, R. & Richardson, W. G., *Abdominal injuries*, 169; *Bipp treatment of war wounds*, 169

Morley, J. W., *The Japanese thrust into Siberia, 1918*, 269

Morris, A., *The musketry teacher*, 284

Morris, Alan, *The balloonatics*, 22; *Bloody April*, 249; *First of the many*, 248

Morris, C., *Heroes of the Army, in America*, 301; *Heroes of the Navy, in America*, 311

Morris, C. & Dawson, L. H., *Why the nations are at war*, 201

Morris, I. N., *From an American Legation, Sweden, 1914-1922*, 263

Morris, J., *The German air raids on Great Britain, 1914-1918*, 32, 122

Morris, K., *A great soldier of the Empire (Botha)*, 29; *Louis Botha; or, Through the great thirst land*, 29

Morris, V. J., *War photographs*, 218

Morrison, A. D., *Summarised war diary of the 7th Battalion Argyll & Sutherland Highlanders*, 43

Morrison, D., *The Great War 1914–18*, 134

Morrison, E. J., *My experiences overseas in World War I*, 213

Morrison, H. C., *World war in prophecy*, 195

Morrison, M. A., *Sidelights on Germany*, 119

Morriss, H. F., *Bermondsey's 'Bit' in the Greatest War*, 160; *Two brave brothers, Major Lord Llan gattock, and Hon. C. S. Rolls*, 176, 248

Morrissey, A. M., *The American defense of neutral rights, 1914-17*, 144

Morrow, E., *Iron in the fire*, 18

Morrow, I. F. D., *The peace settlement in the German-Polish borderlands*, 111

Morse, A. D., *Civilisation and the World War*, 270

Morse, D. P., *History of the 50th Aero Squadron*, 310

Morse, E. W., *Vanguard of American volunteers in the fighting lines and in humanitarian service, 1914-1917*, 293

Morse, J., *An Englishman in the Russian ranks*, 259

Mortane, J., *Guynemer, the ace of aces*, 96; *Spe-*

cial missions of the air, 5

Moseley, S. A., *The truth about the Dardannelles*, 77

Mosley, L., *Duel for Kilimanjaro*, 85

Moss, J. A. & Howland, H. S., *America in battle*, 22

Mottram, R. H., *Journey to the Western Front, twenty years after*, 23; *Ten years ago*, 11; *Through the Menin Gate*, 330

Mould, D., *Remember Scarborough*, 263

Mould, D. H., *American newsfilm*, 97; *Black bread and barbed wire*, 225; *God on our side*, 71; *Greater love*, 158

Moulton, H. F., *The business man's guide to the Peace Treaty*, 88

Moulton, H. G., *The reparation plan*, 245

Moulton, H. G. & MacGuire, C. E., *Germany's capacity to pay*, 245

Moulton, H. G. & Pozvolsky, L., *War debts and world prosperity*, 319; *World war debt settlement*, 319

Mountsier, R., *Our eleven million dollars*, 320

Mousa, S., *T. E. Lawrence*, 154

Mousley, E. O., *A British brief*, 245; *The secrets of a Kuttite*, 152

Mowrer, P. S., *Balkanised Europe*, 231

Moynihan, M., *A place called Armageddon*, 158; *People at war, 1914-1918*, 32

Mudd, T. B., *The Yanks were there*, 235

Muecke, H. von, *The 'Ayesha'*, 125

Muegge, M. A., *The war diary of a square peg*, 213

Muehlon, W., *Dr. Muehlon's diary*, 182

Muhlhauser, G. H. P., *Small craft*, 184

Muhlon, W., *Vandal of Europe*, 119

Muir, J., *War and Christian duty*, 242; *Years of endurance*, 169

Muir, R. B., *Britain's case against Germany*, 201; *Political consequences of the Great War*, 220

Muir, W., *The happy hospital*, 139; *Observations of an orderly in an English war hospital*, 139

Muirhead, F., *Belgium and the Western Front, British and American*, 23

Muirhead, J. H., *German philosophy in relation to the war*, 217

Mullendore, W. C., *History of the United States Food Administration, 1917-1919*, 103

Muller, G. A. von, *The Kaiser and his court*, 119

Muller, J. W., *The ABC of national defence*, 297

Mullins, C. F., *The Leipzig trials*, 320; *Shocked and disillusioned*, 32

Mumby, F. A., *The Great World War*, 134

Munby, J. E., *A history of the 38th Division*, 41

Mundy, P. C. D., *History of the 1/1st Hants Royal Horse Artillery during the Great War*, 58

Munro, D. J., *Convoys, blockades and mystery towers*, 28; *Scapa Flow*, 263

Munro, I. S., *Youth of yesteryear*, 38

Munro, R., *From Darwinism to Kaiserism*, 119

Munroe, J., *Mopping up*, 213

Munson, K., *Aircraft of World War I*, 5; *Bombers, 1914-1919*, 29

Munsterberg, H., *The Peace and America*, 293; *Tomorrow*, 208; *The war and America*, 293

Munthe, A., *Red Cross and Iron Cross*, 169

Murdock, L. B., *They also served*, 213

Mure, A. H., *With the incomparable 29th*, 41

Murphy, C. C. R., *The history of the Suffolk Regiment, 1914-1927*, 52

Murphy, E. A. & Thomas, R. S., *Thirtieth Division in the World War*, 303

Murphy, J. K., *Wounds of the thorax in war*, 169

Murray, A. C., *At close quarters*, 81

Murray, Sir A. J., *Sir Archibald Murray's despatches, June 1916-June 1917*, 90, 187

Murray, A. M., *The 'Fortnightly' history of the war*, 134

Murray, F., *Women as Army surgeons*, 169

Murray, G., *Faith, war and policy*, 94

Murray, J., *Call to arms*, 38; *Gallipoli as I saw it*, 113

Murray, M., *Bible prophecies and the plain man*, 195; *Bible prophecies and the present war*, 242; *The Christian's war book*, 242; *Drink and the war, from the patriotic point of view*, 84; *The Russian advance*, 86, 257, 259

Mursell, W. A., *The bruising of Belgium*, 242

Musciano, W. A., *Eagles of the Black Cross*, 122

Musgrave, G. C., *Under four flags for France*, 323

Musman, R., *The First World War*, 134

Mussolini, B., *My diary, 1915-1917*, 175

Myers, C. S., *Shell shock in France, 1914-1918*, 169

Myers, D. P., *The Treaty of Versailles and after*, 315

Myron, P., *Our Chinese chances through Europe's war*, 72

Nabokov, K., *The ordeal of a diplomatist*, 81, 175

Nadel, H., *Down the red lane*, 110

Na Im, Bey, *The memoirs of Na Im Bey*, 10

Napier, H. D., *The experiences of a military attaché in the Balkans*, 21

Nash, D., *German infantry, 1914-1918*, 123

Nash, J. E., *Nash's war manual*, 235

Nasmith, G. G., *Canada's sons and Great Britain in the World War*, 62; *On the fringe of the great fight*, 64, 169

Natesan, G., *All about the war*, 235

Nathan, M., *The influence of war on contracts and other liabilities*, 153

Naumann, F., *Central Europe*, 20

Navarro, A. de, *France afflicted; France serene*, 106; *The Scottish women's hospital at the French Abbey of Royaumont*, 139

Neame, P., *German strategy in the Great War*, 278

Neave, D. L., *Remembering Kut*, 152

Needham, M. M., *Shall angels weep again?*, 106

Neeser, R. W., *Our Navy and the next war*, 311

Negulescu, G., *Rumania's sacrifice*, 255

Neill, J. C., *The New Zealand Tunnelling Company, 1915-19*, 191

Neilson, K., *Strategy and supply*, 81

Nekludoff, A., *Diplomatic reminiscences before and during the World War, 1911-1917*, 81

Nelson, H. I., *Land and power*, 285

Nesham, F., *Stocks, cigarettes and shipwrecks*, 213

Nettleingham, F. T., *More Tommy's tunes*, 273; *Tommy's tunes*, 273

Nettleton, J., *The anger of the guns*, 323

Neumann, G. P., *The German Air Force in the Great War*, 122

Neureuther, C. & Bergen, C., *U-Boat stories*, 289

Neutral, *In Germany today*, 119

Neville, J. E. H., *The war letters of a light infantryman*, 158

Nevinson, C. R. W., *British artists at the Front*, 13; *The Great War fourth year*, 13; *Modern war paintings*, 13

Nevinson, H. W., *The Dardanelles campaign*, 77; *Last changes last chances*, 175

Newbigin, M. I., *Geographical aspects of Balkan problems in their relation to the great European war*, 21

Newbolt, Sir, H., *A Naval history of the war 1914-1918*, 186; *Book of the thin red line*, 38; *Submarine and anti-submarine*, 281; *Tales of the Great War*, 277

Newman, B., *Inquest of Mata Hari*, 266; *Spy*, 266

Newman, B. & Evans, I. O., *Anthology of Armageddon*, 277

Newton, J. F., *Preaching in London*, 160; *The sword of the spirit*, 242; *A stretcher bearer's diary*, 279

Newton, L. W., *The story of the 12th. (A.I.F.)*, 18

Newton, W. D., *Undying story. (B.E.F.)*, 60

New York American Jewish Committee, *The Jews in the eastern war zone*, 148

New York Times, *War of the nations*, 218

New Zealand Expeditionary Force, *The Great War*, 191; *List of casualties*, 191

Nicholas, *prince of Greece, Political memories, 1914-1917*, 175

Nichols, G. H. F., *The 18th Division in the Great War*, 40

Nicholson, Sir C. L. & Macmullen, H., *History of the East Lancashire Regiment in the Great War*, 45

Nicholson, G. W. L., *Official history of the Canadian Army in the First World War*, 65

Nicholson, I. & Williams, T. Ll., *Wales; its part in the war*, 317

Nicholson, J. S., *The neutrality of the US*, 296; *War finance*, 99

Nicholson, M., *My experiences on three fronts*, 213

Nicholson, W. N., *Behind the lines*, 323

Nicol, G., *Uncle George*, 163, 175

Nicol, Sir W. R., *Prayer in war time*, 242

Nicolai, W., *The German secret service*, 266

Nicolas, R., *Campaign diary of a French Officer*, 110

Nicolson, H. G., *Peacemaking, 1919*, 285, 315

Niemoller, M., *From U-boat to concentration camp*, 119

Niezychowski, A., *The cruise of the Kronprinz Wilhelm*, 125

Night Hawk, M. C., *Rovers of the night sky*, 248

Niles, J. J., *Singing soldiers*, 273; *Songs my mother never taught me*, 273

Nippold, O., *The awakening of the German people*, 119

Nitti, F. S., *The decadence of Europe*, 231; *Peaceless Europe*, 231; *They make a desert*, 231

Noakes, A., *Distant drum*, 38

Nobbs, G., *Englishman, Kamerad!*, 323

Noble C., *Jugheads behind the lines*, 213

Noble, E., *The naval side*, 253

Noble, G. B., *Policies and opinions at Paris, 1919*, 315

Noble, W., *With a Bristol fighter squadron*, 96

Noel, L., *Louvain, 891-1914*, 161

Nogales, R. de, *Four years beneath the Crescent*, 288

Nolan, S., *Nolan's Gallipoli*, 113

Nomikos, E. V. & North, R. C., *International crisis; the outbreak of World War I*, 201

Nordentoft, S., *Practical pacifism and its adversaries*, 202

Norman, A., *The great air war*, 5

Norman, C. H., *A searchlight on the European war*, 220

Norman, H. N., *Tattered shuttlecock*, 213

Norman, T., *The hell they called High Wood*, 272

Norris, G., *The Royal Flying Corps*, 249

North, J., *Gallipoli*, 113

Norway, Mrs H., *The Sinn Fein rebellion as I saw it*, 145

Notestein, W. & Stoll, E. E., *Conquest and Kultur*, 119

Nothomb, P., *The barbarians in Belgium*, 26

Notter, H., *The origins of the foreign policy of Woodrow Wilson*, 326

Nowak, C. F., *The collapse of Central Europe*, 134; *Versailles*, 315

Nowarra, H. J. & Brown, K. S., *Von Richthofen and the flying circus*, 246

Noyes, A., *The accusing ghost of justice for Casement*, 68; *Mystery ships*, 228; *Open boats*, 289

Noyes, A. D., *Financial chapters of the war*, 99; *The war period of American finance*, 99

Noyes, F. W., *Stretcher bearers – at the double!*, 65

Nunn, W., *Tigris gunboats*, 2180

Nurse, E. J., *Christmas time and the war*, 242; *Prophecy and the war*, 195

Nutting, A., *Lawrence of Arabia*, 154

Nyrop, K., *Imprisonment of the Ghent professors Paul Fredericq and Henri Pirenne*, 26

Nystrom, A. K., *Before, during and after*, 201

O, F. O., *With the guns*, 14

Oakeshott, E., *The blindfold game; 'The Day' at Jutland*, 150

Oates, W. C., *The Sherwood Foresters in the Great War*, 52

O'Brian, A. L., *No glory*, 139

O'Brien, J., *Into the jaws of death*, 213

O'Brien, P. A., *Outwitting the Hun*, 93

O'Connor, J. K., *The Afrikaner rebellion*, 274

O'Connor, M. D., *Air aces of the Austro-Hungarian Empire 1914–1918*, 20

O'Connor, T. P., *T.P.'s journal of great deeds of the Great War*, 112

Oduinets, D. M., *Russian schools and Universities in the World War*, 90

Odysseus, *The scene of war*, 213

Ogg, F. A. & Beard, C. A., *National governments and the World War*, 221

Ogilvie, D. D., *The Fife and Forfar Yeomanry*, 56

Ogston, Sir A., *Reminiscences of three campaigns*, 213

Ohlinger, G., *Their true faith and allegiance*, 295

O'Kavanagh, J., *Gethsemane of a little child and its sequel in Louvain*, 161

O'Kie, H. P., *America and the German peril*, 293

O'Laughlin, J. C., *Imperilled America*, 293

Olden, A. C. N., *Western cavalry in the war*, 18

Oldmeadow, E., *Home cookery in war time*, 103

Olgin, M. J., *The soul of the Russian revolution*, 261

Oliver, F. S., *The anvil of war*, 158; *Ordeal by battle*, 221

O'Malley, F. W., *War-whirl in Washington*, 293

Oman, J., *The war and its issues*, 217

Omessa, C., *Rasputin and the Russian Court*, 229

Ommanney, C. H., *The war history of the 1st Northumbrian Brigade, R.F.A.*, 43

Ommundsen, H. & Robinson, E. H., *Rifles and ammunition, and rifle shooting*, 11

O'Neill, H. C., *A history of the war*, 134; *The Royal Fusiliers in the Great War*, 50; *The war in Africa, 1914-1917*, 2; *The war in the Far East, 1914*, 95

Onions, M., *A woman at war*, 328

Open University, *World War I*, 134

Oppenheim, L., *The League of Nations and its problems*, 156

Orchard, W. E., *The true patriotism*, 242

Orcutt, P. D., *White road of mystery*, 8

O'Regan, J. R. H., *The German war of 1914*, 201

Orex, *Three chevrons*, 38

Orgill, D., *German armour*, 156

Orlando, V. E., *War speeches*, 146

Orpen, Sir W., *An onlooker in France*, 13, 175

O'Rorke, B. G., *In the hands of the enemy*, 225

Orr, P., *The road to the Somme*, 272

Orth, S. P., *The Imperial impulse*, 119

O'Ryan, J. F., *Story of the 27th Division*, 303

Osborn, E. B., *The new Elizabethans*, 175

Osborne, C. E., *Religion in Europe and the world crisis*, 242

Osborne, J. M., *The voluntary recruiting movement in Britain 1914–1916*, 32

Osburn, A. C., *Unwilling passenger*, 169

O'Shaughnessy, E. L., *My Lorraine journal*, 106

Osman, A. H, *Pigeons in the Great War*, 218

Ossian-Nilsson, K. G., *Militarism at work in Belgium and Germany. Who is right in the World War?*, 26, 263

Ostrorog, L., *The Turkish problem*, 288

Ostrovosky, E., *Eve of dawn*, 164

Osuntokun, A., *Nigeria in the First World War*, 192

Oswald, O. C. W., *How some wheels went round*, 58

O'Toole, T., *The way they have in the Army*, 38

Ottosen, P. H., *Trench artillery, A.E.F.*, 301

Oughton, F., *The aces*, 5

Owen, E., *Glory departing*, 134

Owen, H. C., *Salonika and after*, 262

Owen, W., *Selected letters*, 158

Oxenham, J., *High altars*, 23

P, E., *The hidden side of war*, 195

Packer, C., *Return to Salonika*, 262

Packer, S., *Prussia's bid for world power*, 120

Pagan, A. W., *Infantry; an account of the Gloucestershire Regiment during the war*, 45

Page, A., *War and alien enemies*, 153

Page, A. P., *'World's Work' war manual of the great conflict*, 235

Page, E., *Escaping from Germany*, 93

Page Geoffrey, *Shadows from wire*, 18

Page, M. E., *Africa and the First World War*, 2

Page, T. N., *Italy and the World War*, 146

Paget, H. L., *In the way of battle*, 242; *Records of the raids*, 161

Paine, R. D., *Corsair in the war zone*, 186; *The fighting fleets*, 79; *First Yale Unit*, 311

Paish, Sir G., *A permanent League of Nations*, 156

Paleologue, G. M., *An Ambassador's memoirs, 1914-1917*, 175

Palles, A. A., *Greece's Anatolian venture – and after*, 126

Palmer, A., *The warlord of the First Reich*, 151

Palmer, A. W., *The gardeners of Salonika*, 262

Palmer, F., *America in France*, 301; *My years of the war*, 214; *Newton D. Baker*, 171; *Our gallant madness*, 293; *Our greatest battle - the Meuse-Argonne*, 301; *With my own eyes*, 318; *With our faces in the light*, 293; *With the new Army on the Somme*, 272

Panichas, G. A., *Promise of greatness*, 134

Pankhurst, E. S., *The Home Front*, 32

Pantazzi, E. G., *Roumania in light and shadow*, 255

Papazian, B. S., *The tragedy of Armenia*, 10

Pares, Sir B., *Day by day*, 259; *The fall of the Russian monarchy*, 257; *The League of Nations and other questions of peace*, 156; *My Russian memoirs*, 175

Parfit, J. T., *Serbia to Kut*, 187

Parker, A. C., *The diaries of Parker Pasha*, 180

Parker, E., *Hesketh Pritchard*, 175

Parker, Ernest W., *Into battle, 1914-1918*, 214

Parker, Sir G., *The world in the crucible*, 134

Parker, Peter, *The old lie*, 33

Parkerson, J. T., *Looking back to glory*, 315

Parkinson, R., *The origins of World War One*, 201

Parkman, M. R., *Tormented warrior*, 161; *Fighters for peace*, 235

Parmalee, M., *Blockade and sea power*, 28

Parmiter, G. de C., *Roger Casement*, 68

Parrott, Sir J. E., *The path of glory*, 277

Parry, E. A. & Codrington, Sir A. E., *War pensions, past and present*, 209

Parson, E. C., *Flight into hell*, 108

Parsons, E. B., *Wilsonian diplomacy*, 81

Parsons, W. B., *The American Engineers in France*, 306

Partridge, E. & Brophy, J., *Songs and slangs of the British soldier 1914–1918*, 273

Passelecq, F., *Truth and travesty*, 26

Patch, J. D., *A soldier's war; the 1st Infantry Division, A.E.F.*, 304

Paterson, W. P., *In the day of the ordeal*, 242

Patterson, A. T., *Jellicoe*, 148

Patterson, J. E., *A war-time voyage*, 178

Patterson, J. H., *With the Judaeans in the Palestine campaign*, 204; *With the Zionists in Gallipoli*, 113

Pattinson, L. A., *History of the 99 Squadron Independent Force, R.A.F., March 1918-November 1918*, 248

Paxon, F. L., *American democracy and the World War*, 293

Peabody, F. W. & Coe, F. E., *Honour or dollars?*, 320

Peacock, B., *Tinker's mufti*, 214

Peake, A. S., *Prisoners of hope*, 74

Pearce, B., *How Haig saved Lenin*, 134

Pearce, C. E., *War up to date*, 11

Pearl, C., *Anzac newsreel*, 18

Pearman, D. G., *The Imperial Camel Corps with Colonel Lawrence, and Lawrence and the Arab revolt*, 154

Pearse, H. W. & Sloman, H. S., *History of the East Surrey Regiment*, 45

Pearson, G. E., *The escape of a Princess Pat*, 93

Pease, H., *History of the Northumberland Hussars Yeomanry, 1819-1919*, 56

Peat, F. E. & Smith, L. O., *Legion airs*, 273

Peat, H. R., *Private Peat*, 214

Peddie, J. T., *British industry and the war*, 142; *Economic reconstruction*, 231

Peel, *Mrs* C. D. E., *How we lived then, 1914-1918*, 33

Peel, D. C. S., *A year in public life*, 33

Peel, S. C., *O.C. Bedfordshire Yeomanry*, 56

Peixotto, E. C., *American Front in France*, 323

Pellatt, T., *Public school education and the war*, 90

Pemberton, T. J., *Gallipoli today*, 114

Pendo, S., *Aviation in the cinema*, 97

Penhallow, D. P., *Military surgery*, 169

Pennant, V. B. D., *Under the searchlight*, 328

Pennell, J., *Pictures of war work in America*, 13; *Pictures of war work in England*, 13

Penson, *Sir* T. H., *Is Germany prosperous?*, 245

Perfect, C. T., *Hornchurch during the Great War*, 33

Perkins, A. M., *Between battles at a Base in France*, 71

Perla, L., *What is 'National Honour?'*, 231

Perrett, B. & Lord, A., *The Czar's British squadron*, 254

Perris, G. H., *The battle of the Marne*, 164; *Campaign of 1914 in France and Belgium*, 101; *Germany and the German Emperor*, 120

Perry, L., *Our navy in the war*, 312

Perry, R. B., *The present conflict of ideals*, 217

Pershing, J. J., *Final report of General Pershing*, 210; *My experiences in the World War*, 210

Petain, H. P. B., *Verdun*, 313

Peter, *Trench yarns for subalterns and others*, 277

Peterson, H. C., *Propaganda for war*, 227, 296

Peterson, H. C. & Fite, G. C., *Opponents of war, 1917-1918*, 74

Petre, F. L., *The Scots Guards in the Great War*, 51

Petre, M. D., *Reflections of a non-combatant*, 74

Phelan, J. A., *Aircraft and flyers of the first World War*, 5

Philip, A. J., *Rations, rationing and food control*, 103

Phillimore, G. W., *Recollections of a prisoner of war*, 225

Phillips, G. C., *The land after the war*, 231

Phillips, W. A., *The revolution in Ireland, 1906-1923*, 145

Phillips, W. C., *The loss of H.M.S. 'Hampshire' and the death of Lord Kitchener*, 152

Phillipps, L. M., *Europe unbound*, 221

Phillipson, C., *Alsace-Lorraine*, 7; *International law and the Great War*, 144; *Termination of war and Treaties of peace*, 208

Phillipson, C. and Buxton, N., *The Queen of the Bosphorus and Dardanelles*, 288

Phocas-Cosmetatos, S. P., *The tragedy of Greece*, 126

Pick, R., *The last days of Imperial Vienna*, 20

Pickford, P., *War record of the 1/4th Battalion Oxfordshire & Buckinghamshire Light Infantry*, 49

Pickhard, M. F. S., *France in war time, 1914-1915*, 106

Picot, H. P., *The British interned in Switzerland*, 281

Pierce, *Mrs* R., *Trapped in black Russia*, 257

Piermarini, *What I saw in Berlin and other European capitals during wartime*, 120

Pierrefeu, J. De, *French Headquarters, 1915-1918*, 110; *Plutarch lied*, 278

Piggott, *Sir* F., *The neutral merchant in relation to the law of contraband of war and blockade*, 144

Pigou A. C., *The disorganization of commerce and finance*, 99; *The economy and finance of the war*, 99

Pilot, *War flying*, 249

Pilsudski, J., *The memories of a Polish revolutionary and soldier*, 175

Pimlott, J., *The First World War*, 134

Pinkerton, R. D., *Ladies from hell*, 214

Piper, J. F., *The American churches in World War I*, 242

Pirie-Gordon, H., *A brief record of the advance of the Egyptian Expeditionary Force*, 90

Pitt, B., *Coronel and Falkland*, 76; *1918: the last act*, 135; *Zeebrugge, St. George's Day, 1918* 331

Pitt, W. O., *Italy and the unholy alliance*, 146

Pittard, *Mme* H., *Victims' return*, 236

Plater, C. D., *Catholic soldiers*, 242

Platoon Commander, *Hospital days*, 139

Platt, F. C., *Great battles of World War I (in the air)*, 5

Playne, C. E., *Bertha von Suttner and the struggle to avert the World War*, 201; *Britain holds on, 1917, 1918*, 33; *The neuroses of the nations*, 201; *Society at war, 1914-1916*, 33

Plivier, T., *Kaiser's coolies*, 124

Plowden-Wardlaw, J., *Religious reconstruction*

after the war, 242; *The test of war*, 1, 242

Plowman, C. F. & Dearden, W. F., *Fighting the fly peril*, 169

Plowman, M., *A subaltern on the Somme*, 272

Plueschow, G., *My escape from Donington Hall, preceded by an account of the siege of Kiao-Chow in 1915*, 72, 93

Plum, H. G. & Benjamin, G. G., *Modern and contemporary European civilization*, 221

Plummer, M., *With the first Canadian contingent*, 65

Plumridge, J. H., *Hospital ships and ambulances*, 140

Pochhammer, H., *Before Jutland: Coronel and the battle of the Falklands*, 76

Poincaré, R., *The memoirs of Raymond Poincaré*, 175; *The origins of the war*, 201

Pole, W. T., *The Great War*, 217

Poling, D. A., *Huts in hell*, 225

Pollard, A. F., *The Commonwealth at war*, 60; *A short history of the Great War*, 135

Pollard, A. O., *Fire-eater*, 317

Pollard, A. W., *Two brothers*, 175

Pollard, H. B. C., *The story of Ypres*, 330

Pollard, J. E., *Forty-seventh Infantry, U.S. Army*, 304

Pollen, A. H., *The great gunnery scandal*, 150; *The Navy in battle*, 253

Pollock, F. J., *War and revolution in Russia*, 261

Ponsonby, A. A., *Falsehood in wartime*, 227

Ponsonby, C., *The Buffs, 1914-1919*, 44

Ponsonby, Sir F., *The Grenadier Guards in the Great War*, 46

Ponsonby, M., *Visions and vignettes of war*, 242

Poole, E., *The village: Russian impressions*, 261

Pooley, A. M., *Japan at the cross roads*, 148; *Secret memoirs of Count Tadasu Hayashi*, 173

Poolman, K., *Armed merchant cruisers*, 178; *Zeppelins over England*, 332

Pootle, F. A., *Stretchers*, 139

Poseck, M. von, *German cavalry in Belgium and France, 1914*, 123

Postgate, R. W., *The International during the war*, 270

Potter, J. H., *Discipline of war*, 242; *Judgment of war*, 242

Potter, J. H. & Worsey, H. W., *Harvest thanksgiving in war time*, 242

Poulton E. B., *The life of Ronald Poulton*, 175; *Science and the Great War*, 263

Pound, R., *The lost generation*, 323

Powell, E. A., *The Army behind the Army*, 301;

Fighting in Flanders, 101, 301; *Slanting lines of steel*, 318; *Vive la France*, 323; *With the Italians*, 147

Powell, J. & Gribble, F. H., *The history of Ruhleben*, 225

Powell, L. P. & Curry, C. M., *The world and democracy*, 270

Power, Sir d'A., *Wounds in war*, 169

Powers, B. D., *Strategy without slide-rule*, 279

Powers, H. H., *The great peace*, 208

Powles, C. G., *The history of the Canterbury Mounted Rifles, 1914-1919*, 191; *The New Zealanders in Sinai and Palestine*, 191

Powys, J. C., *The menace of German culture*, 120

Poy, *Poy's War cartoon*, 67

Poynter, A., *The coming war*, 142

Prasad, Y. D., *The Indian Muslims and World War I*, 141

Pratt, A., *The judgment of the Orient*, 95

Pratt, E. H., *British railways and the Great War*, 229

Prentice, S., *Padre*, 71

Presland, J., *Deedes Bey*, 172

Preston, A., *Battleships of World War I*, 24; *U-Boats*, 289

Preston, R. M. P., *The Desert Mounted Corps*, 56, 204

Preston-Muddock, J. E., *'All clear'*, 219

Pribram, A. F., *Austrian foreign policy, 1908-1918*, 20

Price, C., *Serbia's part in the war*, 268; *Venizelos and the war*, 313

Price, H. T., *Boche and Bolshevik*, 226

Price, J. M., *On the path of adventure*, 318; *Six months on the Italian Front, 1915-1916*, 147

Price, M. P., *Diplomatic history of the war*, 81; *My reminiscences*, 261; *War and revolution*, 261

Price, T., *Crucifiers and crucified*, 75

Price, W. H. C., *The dawn of Armageddon; or, The provocation of Serbia*, 201; *Venizelos and the war*, 126; *With the Fleet in the Dardanelles during the campaign in the Spring of 1915*, 77

Priestley, R. E., *Breaking the Hindenburg Line*, 42; *The Signal Service in the European war*, 59

Priestman, E. Y., *With a Baden-Powell scout in Gallipoli*, 114

Prince, M., *The creed of Deutschtum*, 120

Prinzing, F., *Epidemics resulting from wars*, 169

Prior, R., *Churchill's "World crisis" as history*, 135

Private No. 940, *'On the remainder of our Front'*, 323

Proctor, F. B., *The national crisis and why the Churches fail*, 242

Proctor, H. G., *Iron Division; National Guard of Pennsylvania in the World War*, 303

Protheroe, E., *Lord Kitchener*, 152; *A noble woman (Edith Cavell)*, 69; *Edith Cavell*, 69

Protheroe, G. W., *Catalogue of war publications*, 28

Pryse, G. S., *Four days*, 106

Puaux, R., *Marshal Foche*, 102

Pugh I. E. & Thayer, W. F., *Forgotten fights of the A.E.F.*, 301

Pugsley, C., *Gallipoli*, 114

Puleston, W. D., *High Command in the World War*, 279

Pulitzer, R., *Over the Front in an aeroplane, and scenes inside the French and Flemish trenches*, 6, 214

Pull, E., *The munition worker's handbook*, 184

Pulteney, Sir W. P. & Brice, B., *Immortal Salient*, 330

Purdom, C. B., *Everyman at war*, 214

Pye, E., *Prisoner of war*, 225

Pyke, E. L., *Desperate Germany*, 120

Pyke, G. N., *To Ruhleben - and back*, 225

Pyke, H. R., *Law of contraband of war*, 144

Pym, T. W. & Gordon, G., *Papers from Picardy*, 71

Quex, *Pushed and return push*, 323

Quick, H., *From war to peace*, 232

Quigley, H., *Passchendaee and the Somme*, 205

R, L. F., *Naval guns in Flanders, 1914-1915*, 101, 253

Radclyffe, R., *The war and finance*, 99

Radford, M., *Our friends the Belgians*, 236

Radiguet, R., *The making of a modern Army, and its operation in the field*, 110

Radziwill, C., *Nicholas II*, 192; *Russia's decline and fall*, 261

Rae, H., *Maple leaves in Flanders fields*, 65

Rae, J., *Conscience and politics*, 75

Raemaekers, L., *America in the war*, 67; *Raemaeker's cartoons*, 67

Rafbird *Zooms and spins*, 6

Raimes, A. L., *The Fifth Battalion, the Durham Light Infantry*, 44

Rainer, P. W., *African hazard*, 274

Rainsford, W. K., *From Upton to the Meuse with the Three Hundred and Seventh Infantry*, 306

Raleigh, Sir W. A., *England and the war*, 1; *The war in the air*, 6

Ramsay, A., *The terms of industrial peace*, 283

Ramsay, A. M., *Injuries of the eyes, nose, throat and ears*, 170

Ramsey, A. R. J. & Weston, H. C., *A manual of explosives*, 184

Randolph, J. A., *The call of Belgium and other war area articles*, 26

Randolph, W., *French churches in the war zone*, 106

Ransome, A., *Adventures in Russia*, 261; *The revolution in Russia*, 261

Rappaport, A., *British Press and Wilsonian eutrality*, 189, 222, 326

Rappoport, A. S., *Pioneers of the Russian revolution*, 261

Ravage, M. E., *The Jew pays*, 149

Rawling, L. B., *Surgery of the head*, 170

Rawlinson, A., *Adventures in the Near East*, 187; *Adventures on the Western Front*, 323; *The defence of London, 1915-1918*, 161

Rawson, F. L., *How to protect our soldiers*, 242; *How the war will end*, 195

Rawson, G., *Earl Beatty*, 24

Raymond, A., *Intimate Prussia*, 120

Raymond, E., *Tell England*, 101

Rayner, W. S., *How Botha and Smuts conquered German South West*, 274

Read, H. E., *In retreat*, 39

Read, J. M., *Atrocity propaganda, 1914-19*, 227

Reckitt, H. J., *V.R.76*, 139

Recouly, R., *Foch*, 102; *Marshal Foch*, 102

Redier, A., *Comrades in courage*, 110; *The story of Louise de Bettignies*, 266

Redlich, J., *Austrian war government*, 20

Redmayne, Sir R. A. S., *The British coal-mining industry during the war*, 73

Redmond, J. E., *Account of a visit to the Front*, 214

Redmond, W., *Trench pictures from France*, 286

Redmond-Howard, L. G., *Sir Roger Casement*, 68; *Six days of the Irish Republic*, 145

Reece, R. H., *Night bombing with the Bedouins*, 29

Reed, J., *The war in Eastern Europe*, 86

Rees, R. T., *A schoolmaster at war*, 214

Reeves, L. C., *Australians in action in New Guinea*, 189

Reid, A. C., *Planes and personalities*, 248

Reid, F., *Footslogging in East Africa*, 85

Reid, L. J., *Britain and the war debts*, 320

Reilly, H. J., *Americans all; the Rainbow at war*, 303; *America's part in the European war*, 293

Reiners, L., *The lamps went out in Europe*, 135

Reiss, R. A., *The kingdom of Servia*, 268

Reith, J. C. W., *Wearing spurs*, 176

Reitz, D., *Trekking on*, 85

Remak, J., *The origins of World War I, 1871-1914*, 201

Reault, L., *First violations of International Law by Germany*, 144

Rendinell, J. E. & Pattullo, G., *One man's war*, 311

Renouvin, P., *The forms of war government in France*, 106; *The immediate origins of the war, 28 June-4 August 1914*, 201

Renwick, G., *War wanderings, 1914-1916*, 214

Repington, C. à C., *The First World War*, 135, 214

Requin, E. J., *America's race to victory*, 293

Reuter, L. von, *Scapa Flow*, 263

Revell, A., *British fighter units, Western Front 1917-18*, 96; *The vivid air*, 96

Reventlow, E., *The vampire of the Continent*, 33

Reynardson, H. B., *Mesopotamia 1914-1915*, 180

Reynolds, F. C., *115th Infantry, U.S. Army in the World War*, 305

Reynolds, F. J. & Churchill, A. L., *World's War events recorded by statesmen, commanders, historians and by men who fought or saw the great campaign*, 135

Reynolds, F. J. & Taylor, C., *Collier's new photographic history of the World War*, 218

Reynolds, Q. J., *They fought for the sky*, 6

Reynolds, R., *My Slav friends*, 331

Rhys, E., *The roar of the battle*, 323

Ribbons, I., *Tuesday 4 August 1914*, 135

Rice, P. S., *American crusader at Verdun*, 9

Richards, C., *Tales of the Great War*, 277

Richards, F., *Old soldiers never die*, 51, 323

Richards, I., *A sketch-map history of the Great War and after, 1914-1935*, 135

Richards, V., *Portrait of T. E. Lawrence*, 154

Richardson, D., *Will they pay?*, 320

Richardson, E. H., *British war dogs*, 9

Richardson, E. M. E., *Remembrance wakes*, 33

Richardson, G., *The Great War and Canadian society*, 62

Richer, M., *I spied for France*, 266

Richter, L., *Family life in Germany under the blockade*, 28

Richthofen, M. A., *The red baron*, 246; *Red battle flyer*, 246

Rickard, Mrs L., *The story of the Munsters at Etreux*, 50, 101; *The story of the Munsters at Festubert, Rue de Bois and Hulluch*, 101

Rickards, M., *Posters of the First World War*, 222

Rickards, M. & Moody, M., *The First World War*, 135

Rickenbacker, E. V., *Fighting the flying circus*, 96, 310

Riddell, E. P. A. & Clayton, M. C., *The Cambridgeshires, 1914-1919*, 44

Riddell, G. A., *Lord Riddell's war diary*, 176

Ridder, H., *Hyphenations*, 293

Riggs, A. S., *With three Armies on and behind the Western Front*, 301

Riggs, M. H. & Platt, R. H., *History of Battery F, 325 Field Artillery*, 308

Rimbaud, I., *In the whirlpool of war*, 110

Rimell, R. L., *Air war over Great Britain 1914-1918*, 33; *The German Army Air Service*, 122; *The Royal Flying Corps*, 250; *Zeppelin!*, 332

Rimington, A. W., *The conscience of Europe*, 208

Rinehart, Mrs M., *Kings, queens and pawns*, 214

Rintelen, F. von, *The dark invader*, 266

Rion, G., *The diary of a French Private*, 110

Riste, O., *The neutral Ally*, 189

Ritchie, C. I. A., *Q ships*, 228

Ritchie, H., *The 'Navicert' system during the World War*, 29

Ritchie, M., *With Botha in the field*, 29

Ritter, G., *The Schlieffen plan*, 123, 279

Rivet, C., *The last of the Romanoffs*, 192

Robb, W. E., *The price of our heritage*, 305

Robbins, K., *The abolition of war*, 208; *The First World War*, 135; *Sir Edward Grey*, 127

Roberts, A. A., *The poison war*, 114

Roberts. C., *A week with the Fleet*, 253

Roberts, C. G. D., *Canada in Flanders*, 65

Roberts, E. H. G., *The story of the '9th' King's in France*, 47

Roberts, E. M., *A flying fighter*, 96, 310

Roberts, K. L., *Europe's morning after*, 232

Roberts, T. G., *Thirty Canadian V.C.'s 23rd April 1915 to 30th March 1918*, 317

Roberts, W., *Memories of the war to end war*, 214

Robertson, B., *Air aces of 1914-1918 war*, 96; *Bombing colours*, 61

Robertson, C. J. M., *Britain versus Germany*, 120; *The Germans*, 120

Robertson, J., *With the Cameliers in Palestine*, 191

Robertson, W., *Middlesborough's effort in the Great War*, 33

Robertson, Sir W., *From Private to Field Marshal*, 176; *The life story of the Chief of the*

Imperial General Staff, 176; *Soldiers and states-men, 1914-1918*, 135, 176

Robinson, B., *Cartoons of the war*, 67

Robinson, D. H., *The Zeppelin in combat*, 332

Robinson, E., *Lawrence*, 154; *Lawrence the rebel*, 154

Robinson, E. E. & West, V. J., *The foreign policy of President Wilson*, 326

Robinson, H. P., *The turning point*, 272

Robinson, H. R., *Belated comments on a great event*, 323

Robinson, J. J., *National reconstruction*, 221

Robinson, J. P. K., *With Botha's Army in German South-West Africa*, 274

Robinson, W. H., *Hun likely!*, 67; *The saintly Hun*, 67; *Some 'frightful' war pictures*, 67

Robinson, W. J., *My fourteen months at the Front*, 9

Robson, L. L., *The first A.I.F.* 18

Robson, S., *It's old stuff now*, 214

Robson, W. A., *Aircraft in war and peace*, 6

Roch, W. F., *Mr Lloyd George and the war*, 160

Rochford, L. H., *I chose the sky*, 248

Rodd, Sir J. R., *Social and diplomatic memories, 1902-1919*, 176

Roddie, W. S., *Peace patrol*, 120

Rodzianko, M. V., *The reign of Rasputin*, 229

Roetter, C., *The art of psychological warfare, 1914-1945*, 228

Roger, N., *The victims' return*, 225

Rogers, H., *World War I through my sights*, 301

Rogers, L., *America's case against Germany*, 293; *The problems of reconstruction, international and national*, 232

Rogerson, S., *The last of the ebb*, 7; *Twelve days*, 272

Rohan, J., *Rags; the story of a dog who went to war*, 9

Rohl, J. C. G., *1914; delusion or design*, 201

Rohold, S. B., *The war and the Jew*, 149

Roland, P., *Boy scout*, 30

Rolland, R., *Above the battle*, 107; *The forerunners*, 182

Rollings, W. S., *The great assize*, 242

Rolls, C. S., *Steel chariots in the desert*, 155

Rolt-Wheeler, R. W., *Wonder of war at sea*, 186; *Wonder of war in the Holy Land*, 204; *World War for liberty*, 135

Roosevelt, K., *War in the Garden of Eden*, 180

Roosevelt, T., *America and the World War*, 246, 293; *Average Americans*, 293; *Fear God and take your part*, 246, 293; *The great adventure*, 246; *Rank and file*, 277; *Why America should join the Allies* 246

Root, E., *United States and the war*, 257

Root, E. S. & Crocker, M., *Over periscope pond*, 205

Rorie, D., *A medico's luck in the war*, 170

Roscoe, J. E., *War messages to the nation*, 243; *War saints and subjects*, 243

Rose, G. K., *The story of the 2/4th Oxfordshire and Buckinghamshire Light Infantry*, 49

Rose, H. W., *Brittany patrol*, 186

Rose, J. H., *The origins of the war*, 201

Rosen, A. & Martin, P., *Canadian Expeditionary Force military cap badges of World War I*, 65

Rosher, H., *In the Royal Naval Service*, 254

Rosinski, H., *The German Army*, 123

Roskill, S. W., *The Naval Air Service*, 254

Ross, E. A., *Russia in upheaval*, 261

Ross, J., *The myth of the digger*, 18

Ross, M. & Ross, N., *Light and shade in war*, 18, 318

Ross, N., *Noel Ross and his work*, 176

Ross-of-Bladensburg, Sir J. F. G., *The Cold-stream Guards, 1914-1918*, 44

Ross, R. B., *The Fifty-first in France*, 42

Ross, Stewart, *Lloyd George and the First World War*, 160

Ross, W. A., *My colored Battalion*, 188

Ross, W. O. & Slaughter, D. L., *With the 351st in France*, 306

Rossiter, I., *In kultured kaptivity*, 226

Roth, J. J., *World War I*, 135

Roth, J. P. C. & Wheeler, R. L., *History of Company E, 303rd Engineers of the 78th Division, 1917-1919*, 307

Roth, P. B., *Notes on military orthopaedics*, 170

Rothenstein, J., *British artists and the war*, 13

Rothwell, V. H., *British war aims and peace diplomacy, 1914-1918*, 33

Rouges, J. des V., *Bourru; soldier of France*, 110

Roujon, I., *Battles and bivouacs*, 110

Rounds, O. M., *Buck Privates on Parnassus*, 159

Rouse, S., *Practical notes for machine-gun drill and training*, 284

Roussy, G. & L'Hermitte, J., *Psychoneuroses of war*, 170

Roustam-Bek, B., *Russia in arms*, 259

Rouvier, J., *Present day warfare*, 91

Rowe, E., *2nd County of London (Westminster Dragoons) Yeomanry*, 56

Rowe, J. G., *A popular history of the Great War*, 135

Rowe, J. P., *Letters from a World War I aviator*, 6

Rowe, R. P. P., *A concise chronicle of events of the Great War*, 235

Rowell, Mrs C. W., *Leaders of the Great War*, 235

Rowlands, D. H., *For the duration; the story of the Thirteenth Battalion The Rifle Brigade*, 50

Rowson, J. W., *Bridport and the Great War*, 33

Roxburgh, R. F., *The prisoners of war information bureau in London*, 226

Roy, J. A., *Pole and Czech in silesia*, 218

Royce, J., *The hope of the great community*, 208

Rozwenc, E. C. & Lyons, T., *Realism and idealism in Wilson's peace program*, 326

Rudin, H. R., *Armistice, 1918*, 11

Rudkin, M. S., *Inside Dover, 1914-1918*, 33

Rufener, L. A., *The economic position of Switzerland during the war*, 282

Ruffin, H. & Tudesq, A., *Brother Tommy*, 110, 323; *The square jaw*, 38

Ruge, F., *Scapa Flow, 1919*, 124

Ruhl, A., *Antwerp to Gallipoli*, 318

Rule, E. J., *Jacka's mob*, 18

Rumbold, *Sir* H., *War crisis in Berlin, July-August 1914*, 120

Russell, A., *The machine gunner*, 53; *With the Machine Gun Corps from Grantham to Cologne*, 53

Russell, B. A. W., *Justice in war time*, 153; *Principles of social reconstruction*, 270

Russell, C. E., *Adventures of the D.C.L. Department of Criminal Investigation*, 266; *Unchained Russia*, 261

Russell, F. M., *The Saar*, 82

Russell, G. W. E., *The spirit of England*, 33

Russell, H., *Slaves of the war lords*, 324

Russell, R. M., *151st Field Artillery Brigade*, 308

Russell, T. H., *America's war for humanity*, 218

Russenholt, E. S., *Six thousand Canadian men (44th Battalion, Canadian Infantry, 1914-1919)*, 65

Russia Foreign Office, *How the war began*, 257

Rutherford, V. H., *Commonwealth or Empire?*, 60

Rutherford, W., *The Russian Army in World War I*, 259

Ruthven, G., *Songs for the Army and Navy*, 273

Rutledge, S., *Pen pictures from the trenches*, 286

Ryan, S., *Pétain, the soldier*, 215

Rye, J. B. & Groser, H. G., *Kitchener in his own words*, 152

Ryy, T. W., *A little group of wilful men*, 293

St. John, I., *A journey in wartime*, 107

Sabatier, P., *A Frenchman's thoughts on the war*, 107

Sacre, *Sidelights*, 67

Sadler, W. S., *Long heads and round heads*, 120

Sage, W. N. & Rush, E. E., *World war for democracy*, 135

Saillens, R., *The soul of France*, 107

Saint-Mande, W., *War, wine and women*, 214

Saint-Rene Taillandier, *Mme*, *The soul of the 'C.R.B.'*, 237

Salaman, R. N., *Palestine reclaimed*, 204

Salandra, A., *Italy and the Great War*, 146

Salmond, *Lady* M. M., *Bright armour*, 328

Salter, J. A., *Allied shipping control*, 178; *Slave of the lamp*, 176

Sampson, F. J., *The capture of De Wet*, 274; *The conquest of German East Africa*, 85

Sams, H. A., *The Post Office of India in the Great War*, 141

Samson, C. R., *Fights and flights*, 248

Samuel, H., *The war and liberty*, 232

Sanday, W., *In view of the end*, 208; *The meaning of the war for Germany and Great Britain*, 33, 221

Sanders, L. von, *Five years in Turkey*, 288

Sanders, M. L. & Taylor, P. M., *British propaganda during the First World War 1914–1918*, 227

Sanderson, J. D., *Behind enemy lines*, 135

Sandes, E. W. C., *In Kut and captivity with the Sixth Indian Division*, 152; *Tales of Turkey*, 288

Sandes, F., *An English woman-sergeant in the Serbian Army*, 268

Sandilands, H. R., *The 23rd Division, 1914-1919*, 41

Sandilands, J. W. & Macleod, N., *The history of the 7th Battalion, Queen's Own Cameron Highlanders*, 49

Sanger, C. P. & Norton, H. T. J., *England's guarantee to Belgium and Luxemburg*, 285

Sansom, N. J., *Letters from France, June 1915-July 1917*, 158

Sapper, *Lieutenant and others*, 277; *No man's land*, 286

Sargeaunt, B. E., *The Isle of Man and the Great War*, 145

Sargent, H. H., *The strategy on the Western Front, 1914-1918*, 279

Sarolea, C., *The Anglo-German problem*, 221;

The curse of the Hohenzollern, 120; *Europe's debt to Russia*, 257; *German problems and personalities*, 120; *How Belgium saved Europe*, 26; *The murder of Nurse Cavell*, 69; *The Russian revolution and the war*, 261

Sassoon, S. L., *Memoirs of an infantry officer*, 176; *Siegfried's journey, 1916-1920*, 176

Savage, R., *Allenby of Armageddon*, 7

Savic, V. R., *The reconstruction of South-Eastern Europe*, 232

Sazonov, S. D., *Fateful years. 1909-1916*, 257

Schacht, H., *The end of reparations*, 245

Schaffer, R., *The United States in World War I*, 28

Scheer, R., *Germany's High Seas Fleet*, 124

Scherer, J. A. B., *A nation at war*, 293

Schiff, V., *The Germans at Versailles*, 315

Schmalenberg, P., *German raiders*, 125

Schmidt, P. W., *Co.C., 127 Infantry in the World War*, 305

Schmitt, B. E., *The coming of the war, 1914*, 201

Schmitt, B. E. & Vedeler, H. C., *The world in the crucible*, 135

Schoen, W. E. von, *The memoirs of an Ambassador*, 176

Schoonmaker, E. D., *World storm and beyond*, 135

Schoultz, G. von, *With the British Battle Fleet*, 253

Schreiner, G. A., *Craft sinister*, 201; *From Berlin to Baghdad*, 288; *The iron ration*, 20, 29

Schroeder, H., *An airman remembers*, 122

Schubert, P. & Gibson, L., *Death of a fleet, 1917-1919*, 124

Schule, G., Revolution and Peace Treaties, 1917-1920, *221*

Schuler, P. F. E., *Australia in arms*, 18

Schwabe, K., *Woodrow Wilson, revolutionary Germany and peace-making 1918–1919*, 326

Schwabe, W. S. & Guedalla, P., *Effect of war on Stock Exchange transactions*, 99

Schwien, E. E., *Combat intelligence*, 266

Scipio, L. A., *With the Red Hand Division*, 302

Sclater, J. R. P., *The eve of battle*, 243

Scott, *Sir* A. B. & Brumwell, P. M., *History of the 12th (Eastern) Division in the Great War*, 40

Scott, A. J. L., *Sixty squadron R.A.F.*, 248

Scott, A. P., *An introduction to the Peace Treaties*, 286

Scott, E., *Australia during the war*, 15

Scott, E. J., *Scott's official history of the American Negro in the World War*, 188

Scott, F. G., *The Great War as I saw it*, 62

Scott, F. J., *Records of the Seventh Dragoon Guards during the Great War*, 56

Scott, J. B., *A survey of international relations between the United States and Germany. Aug. 1. 1914 to April 6, 1917*, 82

Scott, L. N., *Naval Consulting Board of the United States*, 312

Scott, R., *A soldier's war diary*, 214

Scott, W. R., *Economic problems of peace after war*, 89

Scott-Moncrieff, C. E., *War thoughts for the Christian year*, 243

Scrivenor, J. B., *Brigade signals*, 54

Scrymgeour, J. T., *Blue eyes*, 18

Scudamore, T. V., *A short history of the 7th Battalion, C.E.F.*, 65

Scurr, J., *Casting the silver bullets*, 99

Sears, H. M., *Journal of a canteen worker*, 234

Seaver, R. W., *What of our dead in the Great War*, 243

Secrett, T., *Twenty five years with Earl Haig*, 127

Sedgwick, F. R., *The Great War in 1914*, 135

Seeger, A., *Letters and diary of Alan Seeger*, 158

Seely, J. E. B., *Adventure*, 176; *My Horse Warrior*, 38

Seibert, W. A., *A trip to Germany during wartime*, 120

Seldes, G. V., *The United States and the war*, 293

Seligman, V. J., *Macedonian musings*, 163; *The Salonika side-show*, 262

Sellers, W. E., *With our fighting men*, 277; *With our heroes in khaki*, 243

Selote, F., *Through a lens darkly*, 120

Senn, A. E., *The Russian revolution in Switzerland 1914-1917*, 234

Senn C. H., *Meals without meat*, 103

Sergeant, E. S., *Shadow-shapes*, 139

'Sergeant-Major R.A.M.C.', *With the R.A.M.C. in Egypt*, 54

Service, W. J. N., *War and the peace of God*, 243

Seth, R., *Caporetto; the scapegoat battle*, 66; *The spy who wasn't caught*, 266

Seton, *Sir* B. G. & Grant, J., *The pipes of war*, 38

Seton-Watson, R. W., *The Balkans. Italy and the Adriatic*, 21; *Europe in the melting pot*, 221; *German, Slav and Magyar*, 202; *The rise of nationality in the Balkans*, 21; *Roumania and the Great War*, 255; *Sarajevo*, 262; *Treaty revision and the Hungarian frontiers*, 141

Severn, M., *The Gambardier*, 14

Seymour, C., *American diplomacy during the World War*, 82; *American neutrality, 1914-*

1917, 297; *The diplomatic background of the war, 1870-1914*, 82; *Letters from the Paris Peace Conference*, 315; *Woodrow Wilson and the World War*, 326

Shackleton, C. W., *East African experiences, 1916*, 85

Shahbaz, Y. H., *Rage of Islam*, 180

Shakespear, J., *Historical records of the 18th (Service) Battalion, Northumberland Fusiliers (Pioneers)*, 49; *A record of the 17th and 32nd Service Battalions, Northumberland Fusiliers, N.E.R. Pioneers*, 49; *The Thirty-Fourth Division, 1915-1919*, 41

Shanafelt, G. W., *The secret enemy*, 20

Shankland, P. & Hunter, A., *Dardanelles patrol*, 77

Sharp, W. G., *The war memoirs of W. G. Sharp, American Ambassador to France*, 176

Shartle, S. G., *Spa, Versailles, Munich*, 208

Shaw, G. B., *Peace Conference hints*, 208

Shaw, K. E., *Jottings from the Front*, 324

Shaw, W. A., *Currency credit and the Exchanges during the Great War and since, 1914-1926*, 99

Sheahan, H., *A volunteer*, 110

Sheip, H., *Handbook of the European war*, 135

Sheldon-Williams, R. F. L., *Canadian Front in France and Flanders*, 65

Shelton, A. C., *On the road from Mons with an Army Service Corps Train*, 54

Shephard, E., *A sergeant major's war*, 38, 214

Shermer, D. R., *World War I*, 135

Sherren, W., *The rights of the Ex-Service man and woman*, 94

Sherriff, R. C., *Journey's end*, 84

Sherson, C., *Townshend of Chitral and Kut*, 152

Sherwood, R. E., *Waterloo Bridge*, 84

Shillito, E., *The Christian year in war time*, 243; *Through the war to the kingdom*, 243

Shipley, A. E., *Minor horrors of war*, 170; *More minor horrors*, 170

Shipley, A. M., *The officers and nurses of Evacuation Eight*, 170

Shirley, R., *Prophecies and omens of the Great War*, 196

Shirras, G. F., *Some effects of the war on gold and silver*, 99

Shively, G. J., *Record of the S.S.U. 585, Yale Ambulance Unit with the French Army, 1917-1919*, 9

Shklovsakii, V. B., *A sentimental journey*, 257

Shortall, K., *A 'Y' girl in France*, 329

Shorthouse, W. J. T., *Sport and adventure in Africa*, 2

Shotwell, J. T., *At the Paris Peace Conference*, 315; *What Germany forgot*, 315

Shub, D., *Lenin*, 156

Shukman, H., *Lenin and The Russian revolution*, 156

Shumaker, E. E., *The world crisis and the way to peace*, 208

Shumsky-Solomonov, K. M., *Russia's part in the World War*, 258

Shumway, H. L., *War in the desert*, 155

Sibley, F. P., *With the Yankee Division in France*, 302

Sibley, J. R., *Tanganyikan guerrilla*, 85

Siegelbaum, L. H., *The politics of industrial mobilization in Russia 1914–17*, 258

Siepman, H., *Echo of the guns*, 58

Silas, E., *Crusading at Anzac, anno domini 1915*, 77

Silber, J. C., *The invisible weapons*, 266

Silberstein, G. E., *The troubled alliance*, 120

Sillars, S., *Women in World War I*, 328

Silverlight, J., *The victor's dilemma*, 259

Silverman, D. P., *Reconstructing Europe after the Great War*, 136

Silverstone, P., *U.S. Warships of World War I*, 312

Simkins, P., *Air fighting 1914–18*, 6

Simonds, F. H., *America must cancel*, 320; *The greatest war, the second phase; from the fall of Antwerp to the second battle of Ypres*, 101; *History of the World War*, 136; *How Europe made peace without America*, 315; *They won the war*, 235

Simons, A. M., *The vision for which we fought*, 232

Simplex, *Instruction on the Lewis automatic machine gun*, 11

Simpson, C., *Lusitania*, 162; *The ship that hunted itself*, 66

Simpson, C. R., *History of the Lincolnshire Regiment, 1914-1918*, 47

Simpson, F., *The Cheshire Regiment; or, 22nd Regiment of Foot*, 44

Simpson, J. Y., *The self-discovery of Russia*, 258

Simpson, K., *The Old Contemptibles*, 60

Sims, E. H., *Fighter tactics and strategy*, 96

Sims, W. S. & Hendrick, B. J., *Victory at sea*, 312

Sinclair, M., *A journal of impressions*, 9, 27, 170

Siney, M. C., *The Allied blockade of Germany, 1914-1916*, 29

Singh, S. N., *The King's Indian Allies*, 141

Sinker, J., *The war, its deeds and lessons*, 243

Sirois, E. D. & McGinnis, W., *Smashing through the World War with fighting Battery C, 102nd Field Artillery*, 307

Sixsmith, E. K. G., *Douglas Haig*, 127

Skaggs, W. H., *German conspiracies in America*, 295

Skeyhill, T., *Soldier songs from Anzac*, 273

Skillman, W. R., *A.E.F., who they were! what they did! and how they did it!*, 301

Slack, C. M., *Grandfather's adventures in the Great War*, 214

Slade, G. H., *Two sticks*, 83

Sladen, D., *From boundary rider to Prime Minister*, 174; *Germany's great lie*, 202

Sladen, D. B. W., *In Ruhleben*, 226

Slater, G., *Peace and war in Europe*, 217

Slater, Guy, *My warrior sons*, 158

Sleeman, J. L., *First principles of tactics and organization*, 282

Slosson, P. W., *The great crusade and after, 1914-1928*, 294

Slowe. P. & Wood, R., *Fields of death*, 23

Small, G. W., *Story of the Forty-seventh*, 304

Smart, H. C., *Australia in the Great War*, 15

Smith, Alexander, *Smithy*, 248

Smith, Annie S., *America at home*, 294; *An Englishwoman's home*, 33; *As others see her*, 328

Smith, Arthur, C., *The seafarers*, 253

Smith, Aubrey, *Four years on the Western Front*, 324

Smith, Charles A., *New words self-defined*, 153

Smith, C. H. & Hill, C. R., *Rising above the ruins in France*, 232

Smith, D. M., *American intervention, 1917*, 296; *The great departure*, 294; *War and depression, America, 1914-1939*, 294

Smith, F. B., *Observations in France*, 107

Smith, F. E., *The Destruction of Merchant Ships*, 178; *My American visit*, 172

Smith, Gaddis, *Britain's clandestine submarines, 1914-1918*, 281

Smith, Gene, *Still quiet on the Western Front*, 324

Smith Sir G. A., *Our common conscience*, 1; *The war, the nation and the Church*, 243

Smith, G. E. & Pear, T. H., *Shell shock and its lessons*, 170

Smith, G. V., *The Bishop of London's visit to the Front*, 71

Smith, H. H., *How to pay for the war by developing the latent resources of the Empire*, 99

Smith, James, *The City of Aberdeen Royal Field Artillery, 157th Brigade*, 58

Smith, Joseph, R., *The influence of the Great War on shipping*, 178, 269

Smith, Joseph S., *Over there and back in three uniforms*, 214; *Trench warfare*, 287

Smith, Jules A., *In France with the A.E.F.*, 218

Smith, L. B. & Collings, H. T., *The economic position of Argentine during the war*, 89

Smith, L. N., *Four years out of life*, 139, 170

Smith, Munroe, *Militarism and statecraft*, 120

Smith, Myron J., *World War I in the air*, 6, 28

Smith, Patsy A., *The Anzacs*, 19

Smith, Richard, S., *A subaltern in Macedonia and Judaea, 1916-17*, 163

Smith, Rodney, *Your boys*, 38

Smith, Sir S., *The real German rivalry*, 89

Smith T. F. A., *The soul of Germany*, 120; *What Germany thinks*, 120

Smithers, A. J., *Sir John Monash*, 19

Smithers, Alan, J., *Wonder aces of the air*, 97

Smyth, Sir J., *Leadership in battle, 1914-1918*, 279

Smyth, J. P., *God and the war*, 243; *The men who died in battle*, 243

Sneath, E. H., *Religion and the war*, 243

Snell, A. E., *The C.A.M.C.*, 65

Snelling, W. E., *Excess profits, including Excess Mineral Rights Duty*, 283

Snow, C. D. & Kral, J. J., *German trade and the war*, 89

Snow, W. J., *Signposts of experience*, 214

Snowden, N., *Memoirs of a spy*, 266

Snyder, J. L., *The ideology of the offensive*, 279

Snyder, L. L., *Historic documents of World War I*, 136

Society of the Fifth Division, *Official History*, 302

Solano, E. J., *The pacifist lie*, 202

Solomon S. J., *Strategic camouflage*, 61

Solovev, V. S., *War and Christianity from the Russian point of view*, 243

Sommers, C., *Temporary crusaders*, 38, 204; *Temporary heroes*, 38

Somerset, W. H. B., *On the Western Front, 1/3rd Battalion, Monmouthshire Regiment*, 48

Sommer, D., *Haldane of Cloan*, 173

Sommerville, F., *Present day Paris and the battlefields*, 23

Somville, G., *The road to Liege*, 27

Sonne, H. C., *The City; its finance, July 1914-July 1915 and the future*, 99

Sorley, C. H., *Letters from Germany and the*

Army, 158; *The letters of Charles Sorley*, 158

Soulsby, L. H. M., *The America I saw in 1916-1918*, 294

Souter, G., *Lion and Kangaroo*, 15

Southard, E. E., *Shell-shock and other neuropsychiatric problems*, 170

Southern, L. J. C., *The Bedfordshire Yeomanry in the Great War*, 56

Souttar, H. S., *A surgeon in Belgium*, 170

Souza, C. de, *Germany in defeat*, 136, 279

Spaight, J. M., *Aircraft in war*, 6

Spanton, E. F., *In German gaols*, 85, 226

Sparling, R. A., *History of the 12th Service Battalion, York & Lancaster Regiment*, 53

Sparrow, A. A. H., *The Landlocked lake*, 324

Sparrow, G. and Ross, J. N. M., *On four fronts*, 253

Sparrow, W. S., *The fifth Army in March 1918*, 39

Speakman, M. A. V., *Memories*, 139

Speare, M. E. & Norris, W. B., *World War issues and ideals*, 217

Spearing, E. M., *From Cambridge to Camiers under the Red Cross*, 234

Spears, E. L., *Liaison, 1914*, 136, 324; *Prelude to victory*, 279; *Two men who saved France*, 110

Speer, R. E., *The Christian man, the Church and the war*, 243

Spencer, F., *Battles of a bystander*, 20

Spencer, S. R., *Decision for war, 1917*, 296

Spender, H., *Herbert Henry Asquith*, 14

Spender, J. A. & Asquith, C., *Life of Herbert Henry Asquith, Lord Oxford and Asquith*, 14

Speranza, G. C., *Diary, Italy, 1915-1919*, 146

Sperry, E. E. & West, M. M., *German plots and intrigues in the United States during the period of our neutrality*, 266

Spicer, E. E. & Pegler, E. C., *The Excess Profits Duty*, 283

Spicer, L. D., *Letters from France, 1915–1918*, 158

Spiegel, A. C. von, *U-Boat 202*, 289

Spin, *Short flights with the cloud cavalry*, 248

Spindler, K., *Gun running for Casement in the Easter rebellion, 1916*, 68

Sprague, F. M., *Made in Germany*, 120

Springer, L., *Some aspects of financial and commercial after-war conditions*, 99

Springs, E. W., *Above the bright blue sky*, 6; *War birds*, 310

Spurr, F. C., *Some Chaplains in khaki*, 71

Squiers, A. L., *One hundred per cent American*, 294

Squire, J. E., *Medical hints for the use of medical officers temporarily employed with troops*, 170

Squires, C. W., *Munsterberg and militarism checked*, 294

Squires, J. D., *British propaganda at home and in the United States from 1914-1917*, 227

Stacke, H. F., *The Worcestershire Regiment in the Great War*, 53

Stackhouse, P. J., *The sword of Christ and the world war*, 243

Stallings, L., *The Doughboys*, 301; *The first World War*, 218

Stallybrass, W. T. S., *A society of States; or, Sovereignty, independence and equality in a League of Nations*, 156

Stamp, Sir J. C., *Taxation during the war*, 99

Standaert, E. H. G., *The Belgian Mission to the Boers*, 274

Standing, P. C., *The campaign in Russian Poland*, 86, 218

Stanley, A. A., *College man in khaki*, 158

Stanley, F. C., *The history of the 89th Brigade 1914-1918*, 43

Stanley, M. M., *My diary in Siberia*, 268

Stansky, P., *The Left and war*, 271

Stark, R., *Wings of war*, 6, 122

Starr, L., *The war story of Dillwyn Parrish Starr*, 176

Stearns, G., *From Army camps and battlefields*, 158

Stebbing, E. P., *At the Serbian Front in Macedonia*, 268; *From Czar to Bolshevik*, 261

Steege, K. R., *We of Italy*, 147

Steele, H., *The Canadians in France, 1915-1918*, 65

Stegemann, H., *The mirage of Versailles*, 315

Stein, H., *Government price policy in the United States during the World War*, 89

Stein, Hermann, *A War Minister and his work*, 176

Stein, R., *Peace through a disentangling alliance*, 208

Stein, Rose M., *M-Day, the first day of war*, 294

Steiner, E. A., *The confession of a hyphenated American*, 294

Steinhauer, G., *Steinhauer, the Kaiser's master spy*, 266

Stephen, A. C., *An Australian in the R.A.F.*, 19

Stephen, S. I., *Neutrality*, 297

Stephens, D. O., *With Quakers in France*, 229

Stephens, F. J. & Maddocks, G., *The organization and uniforms of the Imperial German Army,*

1900-1918, 123

Stephens, J., *The insurrection in Dublin*, 145

Stephens, W., *The book of France*, 107; *The France I knew*, 102; *The soul of Russia*, 258

Stephens, W. E., *Revisions of the Treaty of Versailles*, 315

Stern, *Sir* A. G., *Tanks, 1914-1918*, 282

Sterne, E., *Over the seas for Uncle Sam*, 301

Steuart, R. H. J., *March, kind comrade*, 71

Stevens, F. E., *The battle story of the Hampshire Regiment*, 46

Stevenson, B. G., *Betty Stevenson, YMCA*, 329

Stevenson, D., *French war aims against Germany*, 82

Stevenson, W. Y., *From Poilu to Yank*, 215

Stewart, A. T. & Peshall, C. J. E., *The immortal gamble and the part played in it by HMS 'Cornwallis'*, 253

Stewart, D., *T. E. Lawrence*, 155

Stewart, H., *The New Zealand Division, 1916-1919*, 191

Stewart, H. A., *From Mons to Loos*, 54

Stewart, H. L., *Nietzsche and the ideals of modern Germany*, 120

Stewart, J. & Buchan, J., *The Fifteenth (Scottish) Division, 1914-1919*, 40

Stewart P. & Evans, A., *Nerve injuries and their treatment*, 170

Stewart, T., *Nine months as a prisoner-of-war*, 226

Stidger, W. Le R., *Star dust from the dugouts*, 243

Stieve, F., *Isvolsky and the World War*, 258

Stilgebauer, E., *Ship of death*, 162

Still, J., *A prisoner in Turkey*, 226

Stillwell, A. E., *The great plan*, 99; *To all the world (except Germany)*, 202

Stimson, J. C., *Finding themselves*, 139, 193

Stires, E. M., *High call*, 243; *The price of peace*, 243

Stirling J., *The Territorial Divisions, 1914-1918*, 40

Stobart, M. A., *The flaming sword in Serbia and elsewhere*, 268

Stockbridge, F. P., *Yankee ingenuity in the war*, 91

Stocker, R. D., *From warfare to welfare*, 232

Stoddard, F. R., *War time France*, 107

Stoddard, T. L. & Frank, G., *Stakes of the war*, 209

Stoffa, P., *Round the world to freedom*, 93

Stoker, H. G., *Straws in the wind*, 226

Stokesbury, J. L., *A short history of World War I*, 136

Stoll, O., *The people's credit*, 99

Stone, E., *Battery B thru the fires of France*, 301

Stone, G., *Women war workers*, 328

Stone, G. F. & Wells, C., *Bristol and the Great War*, 33

Stone, N., *The Eastern Front, 1914-1917*, 86

Storrs, *Sir* R. H. A., *Lawrence of Arabia*, 155

Story, H. H., *History of the Cameronians (Scottish Rifles) 1910-1933*, 44

Story, S., *The Memoirs of Ismail Kemal Bey*, 174

Stowell, E. C., *The diplomacy of the war of 1914*, 82

Strakhovsky, L. I., *Intervention at Archangel*, 259

Strange, L. A., *Recollections of an airman*, 248

Strawbridge, A., *Suspect*, 266

Street, G. S., *At home in the war*, 33

Stringfellow, J. S., *Hell! No! this and that*, 301

Stromberg, R. N., *Redemption by war*, 209

Strong, A. T., *Australia and the war*, 15

Strong, R., *Diary of an English resident in France*, 107; *Trench fever*, 170; *Typhus fever*, 170

Strother, J., *Fighting Germany's spies*, 266

Struve, P. B., *Food supply in Russia during the World War*, 103

Stuart, *Sir* C., *Secrets of Crewe House*, 227, 266

Student, *pseud, The Gallipoli campaign*, 114

Studholme, J., *New Zealand Expeditionary Force*, 191

Stuermer, H., *Two war years in Constantinople*, 288

Stumpf, R., *War, mutiny and revolution in the German Navy*, 124

Sub-Inspector, *Two years with the 'Specials'*, 219

Sueter, M. F., *Airmen or Noahs*, 310

Sulley, H., *Is it Armageddon?*, 196

Sullivan, A., *Aviation in Canada, 1917-1918*, 62

Sullivan, E. J., *The Kaiser's garland*, 67

Sullivan, W. P. & Tucker, H. S., *History of the 105th Regiment of Engineers*, 307

Sulzbach, H., *With the German guns*, 14

Summers, A. & Mangold, T., *The file on the Tsar*, 192

Summerskill, M., *China, on the Western Front*, 72

Sunderland, J. T., *Rising Japan*, 148

Surface, F. M., *The grain trade during the World War*, 103

Suskind, R., *The battles of Belleau Wood*, 311

Sutcliffe, R. J., *Excess Profits Duty, and the cases decided thereon*, 283

Sutcliffe, R. S., *Seventy-first New York in the*

World War, 304

Suter-Lerch, H. J., *Germany her own judge*, 120, 227

Sutherland, D., *War diary of the Fifth Seaforth Highlanders, 51st (Highland) Division*, 52

Sutherland, J. G., *At sea with Joseph Conrad*, 254

Sutherland, L. W. and Ellison, N., *Aces and kings*, 6

Sutton, H. T., *Raiders approach!*, 248

Swan, C. J., *My Company*, 301

Swanljung, C., *Men and monsters*, 269

Swart, P. C., *England in war-time*, 33

Swartz, M., *The Union of Democratic Control in British politics during the First World War*, 202

Swayne, M. L., *In Mesopotamia*, 180

Sweetser, A., *Roadside glimpses of the Great War*, 215

Swetland, H. M., *American journalists in Europe*, 222

Swetland, M. J. & Swetland, L., *These men; for conspicuous bravery above and beyond the call of duty*, 112

Swettenham, J. A., *To seize the victory; the Canadian Corps in World War I*, 65

Swinton, Sir E. D., *Eye-witness*, 38, 176; *Twenty years after*, 23

Swope, H. B., *Inside the German Empire in the third year of the war*, 121

Sydenham, G., *India and the war*, 141

Sykes, C., *Wassmuss, 'the German Lawrence'*, 180

Sykes, Sir F., *From many angles*, 176

Synge, M. B., *The story of the world at war*, 136

Synon, M., *My country's part*, 294

Synton, E., *Tunnellers all*, 59

Szajkowski, Z., *The attitude of American Jews to World War I*, 149

Szegedi, S., *My war*, 218

T, O. B. L., *The Great War*, 209

Taber, J. H., *Story of the 168th Infantry*, 305

Tactician, *The Battalion in attack*, 282

Taffrail, *Endless story*, 79; *A little ship*, 79

Taft, R. W. H., *The United States and peace*, 294

Taggart, G. & Winchell, W., *Yankee Major invades Belgium*, 237

Talbot, F. A, *Aeroplanes and dirigibles of war*, 6; *Submarines*, 281

Talbot, H., *After the day*, 121

Talbot, K. R. R., *A subaltern's odyssey*, 38

Talbot, N. S., *Religion behind the Front and after*, 243; *Thoughts on religion at the Front*, 243

Tallents, H., *The Sherwood Rangers Yeomanry in the Great War*, 56

Tallents, S. G., *The starry pool*, 277

Tansill, C. C., *America goes to war*, 296

Tapp, A. G., *Stories of Salonika and the new crusade*, 262

Tardieu, A., *The truth about the Treaty*, 315

Taslauanu, O. C., *With the Austrian Army in Galicia*, 20

Tayler, H., *A Scottish nurse at work*, 193

Taylor, A. H. E., *The future of the Southern Slavs*, 331

Taylor, A. A., *The first World War*, 136

Taylor, A. J. P., *The first World War*, 136; *Politics in wartime*, 221; *The struggle for mastery in Europe, 1848-1918*, 136; *War by time-table*, 202

Taylor, E. G., *New England in France, 1917-1919*, 303

Taylor, F. A. J., *The bottom of the barrel*, 53

Taylor, Sir Gordon, *Sopwith Scout 7309*, 97, 250

Taylor, G. R. S., *The psychology of the Great War*, 228

Taylor, G. W., *The boy with the guns*, 14

Taylor, H. A., *Good-bye to the battlefields*, 23

Taylor, I. E., *Angels, Saints and Bowmen at Mons*, 196

Taylor, W. & Diack, P., *Student and sniper-sergeant*, 173

Taylor, W. P. & Irvin, F. L., *Francis L. Spike Irvin's war diary and the history of the 148th Aero Squadron*, 310

Teichman, O., *Diary of a Yeomanry M.O.*, 170

Temperley, H. W. V., *A history of the Peace Conference of Paris*, 315

Tennant, J. E., *In the clouds above Baghdad*, 187

Tennant, N., *A Saturday night soldier's war*, 215

Tennant, R. J., *Red herrings of 1918*, 33

Terraine, J., *Douglas Haig*, 127; *The Great War, 1914-1918*, 136; *Impacts of war, 1914-1918*, 33; *Mons*, 183: *The road to Passchendaele*, 205, 324; *The Western Front*, 324; *To win a war*, 136; *White heat*, 283

Terry, C. S., *The battle of Jutland Bank, May 31-June 1, 1916*, 150

Thayer, W. R., *The collapse of superman*, 121; *Germany versus civilization*, 121; *Volleys from a non-combatant*, 182

Therese, J., *With Old Glory in Berlin*, 93

Thetford, O. G., *Camouflage '14-'18 aircraft*, 61

Thetford, O. G. & Riding, E. J., *Aircraft of the 1914-1918 war*, 6

Thomas, A., *A life apart*, 38

Thomas, B. & Williams, W., *One hundred war cartoons*, 67

Thomas, C., *They also served*, 93

Thomas, E. W., *Bivouac and baobab*, 85

Thomas, G., *Grapes and thorns*, 243

Thomas, L. L., *Lauterbach of the China Sea*, 125; *Raiders of the deep*, 290; *The sea-devil's fo'c'sle*, 290; *This side of hell*, 301; *With Lawrence in Arabia*, 155; *Woodfill of the Regulars*, 301

Thomas, S., *The history of the A.E.F.*, 301

Thomas, Sir W. B., *Events of the Great War*, 136; *With the British on the Somme*, 272

Thomason, J. W., *Fix bayonets!*, 311

Thompson, B., *Four months in Italy in wartime*, 146

Thompson, C. W., *Records of the Dorset Yeomanry, 1914-1919*, 56

Thompson, D. C., *Donald Thompson in Russia*, 258; *From Czar to Kaiser*, 258

Thompson, E. J., *The Leicestershires beyond Baghdad*, 47

Thompson, G., *War memories and sketches*, 71

Thompson, J. H., *The harvest of war*, 62

Thompson, P. A., *Lions led by donkeys*, 279

Thompson, Sir R., *The Royal Flying corps*, 250

Thompson, R. J., *England and Germany in the war*, 121

Thompson, R. R., *The Fifty-Second (Lowland) Division, 1914-1918*, 42

Thompson, T., *Coming dawn*, 9

Thompson, T. B., *Take her down*, 281

Thomson, Sir B. H., *The Allied secret service in Greece*, 267

Thomson, C. B., *Old Europe's suicide*, 136

Thomson, G. M., *The twelve days; 24 July to 4 August, 1914*, 221

Thomson, P. D., *The Gordon Highlanders*, 46

Thorburn, A. D., *Amateur gunners*, 58

Thorn, H. C., *History of the 313th U.S. Infantry, Baltimore's Own*, 306

Thorn, J. C., *Three years a prisoner in Germany*, 226

Thornhill, C. J., *Taking Tanganyika*, 86

Thornton, G., *With the Anzacs in Cairo*, 19, 71

Thorp, C. H., *A handful of Ausseys*, 19

Thouman, R., *The First World War*, 136

302nd Field Artillery Association, *302nd Field Artillery*, 308

Thuliez, L., *Condemned to death*, 267

Thurburn, R. G., *A record of battle honours for the Great War, 1914–1919*, 39

Thurlow, E. G. L., *The pill-boxes of Flanders*, 101

Thurston, H., *The war and the prophets*, 196

Thurston, V., *Field hospital and flying column*, 139; *The hounds of war unleashed*, 87, 170; *The people who run*, 236

Thwing, C. F., *American colleges and Universities in the Great War*, 90

Tiarks, H. C., *Eternal certainties; or, The war, the world, and the future*, 196

Tidy, D., *I fear no man*, 250

Tiebout, F. B., *History of the 305th Infantry*, 305

Tierce, A., *Between two fires*, 93

Tilley, E. H., *The loud echo of thunder*, 136

Tilney, W. A., *Rapid night-marching made easy*, 284

Tilton, M., *The grey Battalion*, 19

The Times, *Documentary history of the war*, 136; *The Times diary and Index of the war*, 235; *The Times history of the war*, 136

Tiplady, T., *The Cross at the Front*, 71; *The kitten in the crater*, 324; *The soul of the soldiers*, 71

Tippett, E. J., *Who won the war?*, 158

Tirpitz, A. P. von, *My memoirs*, 176

Titler, D. M., *The day the red baron died*, 246

Titterton, C. H., *Armageddon, or the last war*, 243

Tiveychoc, A., *There and back*, 19

Todd, E., *The new Exodus*, 232

Todd, R. M., *Sopwith Camel Fighter ace*, 97

Toland, E. D., *The aftermath of battle*, 234

Toland, J. W., *No man's land*, 136

Tomkins, A., *And behold we live*, 244

Tomlin, R. K., *American Engineers behind the battle lines in France*, 306

Tomlinson, E. T., *The story of General Pershing*, 210

Tompkins, R. S., *Story of the Rainbow Division*, 303

Tonnies, F., *Warlike England as seen by herself*, 33

Topham, A., *Memories of the Kaiser's Court*, 151

Topley, W. W. C., *A report on the probable proportion of enteric infections among undiagnosed febrile cases invalided from the Western Front*, 170

Topp, C. B., *The 42nd Battalion, C.E.F., Royal Highlanders of Canada in the Great War*, 65

Torossian, S., *From Dardanelles to Palestine*, 180, 187

Toulmin, H. A., *Air service, A.E.F.*, 310

Towne, C. H., *The Balfour visit, and the significance of the Conferences in the United States in 1917*, 21; *Shaking hands with England*, 34, 107

Townshend, *Sir* C. V. F., *My campaign in Mesopotamia*, 180

Toynbee, A. J., *Armenian atrocities*, 11; *The Belgian deportations*, 78; *The German terror in Belgium*, 27; *German terror in France*, 107, 319; *Nationality and the war*, 217; *The treatment of Armenians in the Ottoman Empire*, 25; *The Western questions in Greece and Turkey*, 319; *The world after the Peace Conference*, 209

Toyne, J., *Win time for us*, 267

Trachenberg, M., *Reparations in world politics*, 245

Tracy, C. D., *Revolver shooting in war*, 12

Trapmann, A. H., *The Greeks triumphant*, 126

Trask, D. F., *World War I at home*, 294

Trayes, F. G., *Five months on a German raider*, 125

Treadway, J. D., *The falcon and the eagle*, 20

Treusch von Buttlar Brandenfels, H., *Zeppelins over England*, 332

Trevelyan, G. M., *Grey of Fallodon*, 127; *Scenes from the Italian war*, 147; *The war and European revolution in relation to history*, 136

Trevelyan, W. B., *A nation at prayer*, 244

Treves, *Sir* F. & Goodchild, G., *Made in the trenches*, 13

Trew, H. F., *Botha treks*, 29

Triana, S. P., *Some aspects of the war*, 94

Trooper, *The four horsemen ride*, 215

Trotsky, L., *History of the Russian revolution*, 261

Trotter, A., *The great world drama*, 196

Trotter, W., *Instincts of the herd in peace and war, 1916-19*, 182

Trounce, H. D., *Fighting the Boche underground*, 181

Trumpener, U., *Germany and the Ottoman Empire, 1914-1918*, 121

Trythall, A. J., *'Boney' Fuller*, 173

Tschuppik, C., *Ludendorff*, 161

Tubby, A. H., *A consulting surgeon in the Near East*, 171

Tuchman, B. W., *August 1914*, 101; *The Zimmerman telegram*, 332 ·

Tucker, A. B., *The battle glory of Canada*, 65

Tucker J. F., *Johnny get your gun*, 324

Tucker, W. A., *The lousier war*, 277

Tudor-Pole, W., *The Great War*, 244

Tumulty, J. P., *Woodrow Wilson as I know him*, 326

Tunney, T. J., *Throttled!*, 267

Tuohy, F., *The crater of Mars*, 136; *Occupied, 1918-1930*, 196; *The secret corps*, 267

Turczynowiczowa, L., *When the Prussians came to Poland*, 219

Turner, C. C., *The struggle in the air, 1914-1918*, 248

Turner, L. C. F., *Origins of the first World War*, 202

Turner, P. W., *Not for glory*, 39

Turnor, C., *Our food supply*, 103

Tweedie, E. B., *Women and soldiers*, 328

Twells, J. H., *In the prison city; Brussels 1914-1918*, 27

Tweney, C. F., *Dictionary of naval and military terms*, 80

Tyndale-Biscoe, J., *Gunner subaltern*, 159

Tyng, S. T., *The campaign of the Marne, 1914*, 164

Tyrkova-Williams, A., *From liberty to Brest-Litovsk*, 261

Tytler, N. F., *Field guns in France*, 14

Udet, E., *Ace of the Black Cross*, 122

Ulam, A. B., *The Bolsheviks*, 261

Ulanoff, S. M., *Illustrated history of World War I in the air*, 136

United States: American Battle Monuments Commission, *American Armies and battlefields in Europe*, 23

Army War College, *Order of battle of the United States Land Forces in the World War*, 301

Bureau of Labor Statistics, *British industrial experience during the war*, 142

Bureau of Ordnance, *Navy Ordnance activities, 1917-1918*, 312

Bureau of Yards & Docks, *Activities of the Bureau of Yards & Docks, 1917-1918*, 260

Department of Army, *American Military Government of Occupied Germany, 1918-1920*, 196; *United States Army in the World War, 1917-1919*, 301

Department of State, *Declarations of war*, 82; *Neutrality proclamations*, 189; *The Treaty of Versailles and after*, 316

Department of War, *The Allied Armies under Marshal Foch in the Franco-Belgian theater of operations*, 102; *Battle participation of organizations of A.E.F. in France, Belgium and Italy, 1917-1918*, 301; *Congressional Medal of Honor, the Distinguished Service Cross, and the Distinguished Service Medal issued by the War Dept. since April 6, 1917 up to and includ-*

ing Nov. 11th, 1919, 74; Histories of 251 Divisions of the German Army which participated in the War, 1914-1918, 123; Records of the World War Field Orders, 1918 Fifth Division, 302; A report on the activities of the War Department in the fields of industrial relations during the war, 142; Statement concerning the treatment of conscientious objectors in the Army, 75

Division of Negro Economics, The Negro at work during the World War and during reconstruction, 188

National War Labor Board, National War Labor Board, 143

Navy Department, Bureau of Navigation officers and enlisted men who lost their lives during the World War, April 6, 1917–November 11, 1918, 312; Medical Department, 312

Office of Naval Records, German submarine activities on the Atlantic Coast of the United States and Canada, 290; Northern Barrage and other mining activities, 181; Northern Barrage; taking up the mines, 181

Senate Committee on the Judiciary, Loans to foreign Governments, 320

Special Diplomatic Mission to Russia, America's message to the Russian people, 82

Tariff Commission, Japan; trade during the war, 148

War Department, Catalogue of official AEF photographs taken by the Signal Corps, US Army, 218

Unterberger, B. M., America's Siberian Expedition, 1918-1920, 270

Unwin, R., The war; and what after, 232

Urquart, H. M., History of the 16th Battalion, the Canadian Scottish, C.E.F. in the Great War, 66

Usborne, C. V., Blast and counterblast, 254; Smoke on the horizon, 171

Usborne, H. M., Women's work in war time, 328

Usher, R. G., Pan-Americanism, 294; The story of the Great War, 136; The winning of the war, 182

Vanamee, M. C., Vanamee; a biography of Parker Vanamee, 177

Vance, J. I., Silver on the Iron Cross, 244

Vandenbosch, A., The neutrality of the Netherlands during the World War, 189

Vanderlip, F. A., What happened to Europe, 89

Van Der Slice, A., International labor, diplomacy and peace, 1914-19, 209

Van Der Vat, D., The grand scuttle, 124; The last corsair, 125; The ship that changed the world, 125

Vandervelde, E., Three aspects of the Russian revolution, 261

Vandiver, F. E., Black Jack, 210

Van Dyke, H., Fighting for peace, 189

Van Every, D., The A.E.F. in battle, 301

Van Schaick, J., The little corner never conquered, 234

Vansittart, P., Voices from the Great War, 215

Van Vorst, M., War letters of an American woman, 159

Van Zile, E. S., A game of empires, 137

Vast, H., A little history of the Great War, 137

Vaughan, E. C., Some desperate glory, 39, 215

Vaughan, G. E. M., The flight of Mariette, 27

Vaughan, Dame H. C., Service with the Army, 328

Vaux, P., Gadgets; the work of the Navy, 254; Sea, salt and cordite, 254

Veach, R. W., The meaning of the war for religious education, 244

Veblen, T., The nature of peace, 209

Vedder, E. H., The medical aspects of chemical warfare, 171

Vedette, The adventures of an Ensign, 272; Britain and Armageddon, 34

Vee, R., Flying minnows, 248

Velimirovic, N., The agony of the Church, 244; Serbia in light and darkness, 269

Venkata-Narasayya, T. K., The war and the British Raj, 141

Verhaeren, E., Belgium's agony, 27

Vernède, R. E., Letters to his wife, 159

Verner, R. H. C., The battle cruisers at the action of the Falkland Islands, 95

Verroy, C., The European war, 137

Viereck, G. S., As they saw us, 137; The strangest friendship in history, 326; Woodrow Wilson and Colonel House, 140

Vigilant, French war birds, 108; German war birds, 122; Richthofen, the red knight of the air, 246; Secrets of modern spying, 267

Vigness, P. G., The neutrality of Norway in the World War, 192

Villard, O. G., Germany embattled, 121

Villari, L., The Macedonian campaign, 1915-1919, 163; The war on the Italian Front, 147

Ville, J. B. de, Back from Belgium, 267

Villiers, B., Britain after peace, 232

Vince, C., England in France, 42

Vincent, C. P., The politics of hunger, 29

Vincent, H., *A stoker's log*, 254

Vischer, A. L., *Barbed wire disease*, 226

Visscher, C. de, *Belgium's case*, 27

Vivian, A. P. G., *The Phantom Brigade; or The Contemptible adventurers*, 60

Vivian, E. C. H., *With the R.A.M.C. at the Front*, 54; *With the Scottish Regiments at the Front*, 39

Vivian, E. C. H. & Hodder-Williams, J. E., *The way of the Red Cross*, 234

Vivian, H., *Italy at war*, 146

Viviani, R., *As we see it; France and the truth about war*, 107

Vizetelly, E. A., *The true story of Alsace-Lorraine*, 8

Vizetelly, F. H., *The soldiers service dictionary of English and French terms*, 80

Vogel-Jorgensen, T., *Rasputin*, 229

Voigt, F. A., *Combed out*, 215

Volk, K. W., *Buddies in Budapest*, 141

Voska, E. V. & Irwin, W. H., *Spy and counterspy*, 267

Vosnjak, B., *A bulwark against Germany*, 331; *A dying Empire*, 20

Voss, V., *Flying minnows*, 97

Vredenburg, E., *West and East with the E.F.C. canteens*, 66

Waagenaar, S., *The murder of Mata Hari*, 164

Wace, H., *The war and the Gospel*, 244

Waddington, M. K., *My war diary*, 107

Wade, A., *The war of the guns*, 14

Wade, A. G., *'Counterspy!'*, 267

Wade, W. L., *The aeroplane in the Great War*, 6

Wadsworth, W. W., *War diary of the 1st West Lancashire Brigade, R.F.A.*, 58

Wagger, *Battery flashes*, 14

Waite, F., *The New Zealanders at Gallipoli*, 191

Wakefield, H. R., *A fortnight at the Front*, 71

Walbrook H. M., *Hove and the Great War*, 34

Walcott, S., *Above the French lines*, 6, 310

Waldeyer-Hartz, H., *Admiral Franz von Hipper*, 173

Waldo, F. L., *America at the Front*, 302

Waldstein, Sir C., *What Germany is fighting for*, 121

Walker, G. G., *The Honourable Artillery Company in the Great War*, 46

Walker, H. F. B., *A doctor's diary in Damaraland*, 171

Walker, J. B., *America fallen!*, 294

Walker, J. O., *Official history of the 120th Infantry, 3rd North Carolina, 30th Division*, 305

Walker, W., *Sketches of a Tommy on the Rhine*, 196

Walker, W. L., *The war, God and our duty*, 244

Wall, A. G. N., *Letters of an airman*, 15

Wall, W. W., *The war and our financial fabric*, 100

Wallace, C., *From jungle to Jutland*, 150

Wallace, Sir C. S., *War surgery of the abdomen*, 171

Wallace, Sir C. S. & Fraser, J., *Surgery at a casualty clearing station*, 171

Wallace, E., *Heroes all*, 112; *Kitchener's Army and the Territorial Forces*, 39; *Standard history of the war*, 137

Wallace, M., *Pilots of World War I*, 97

Wallace, W. K., *Greater Italy*, 146

Walling, W. E., *The Socialists and the War*, 271

Wallszewski, K., *Poland the unknown*, 219

Walmsley, L., *Flying and sport in East Africa*, 86

Walsh, C., *Mud, songs and blighty*, 34

Walsh, H. P., *On taking bearings*, 284

Walshe, D., *With the Serbs in Macedonia, 1916-1918*, 269

Walters, E. W., *Heroic airmen and their exploits*, 6; *Heroines of the World War*, 328

Walworth, Arthur, *Wilson and his peacemakers*, 82

Walworth, A. C., *America's moment; 1918*, 82

Wannamaker, O. D., *With Italy in her final war of liberation*, 146

Warburton, E., *Behind Boche bars*, 226

Ward, C. H. D., *The 56th Division - 1st London Territorial Division*, 42; *History of the 53rd (Welsh) Division*, 42; *History of the Welsh Guards*, 52; *Regimental records of the Royal Welch Fusiliers*, 51; *The 74th (Yeomanry) Division in Syria and France*, 42; *The Welsh Regiment of Foot Guards, 1915-1918*, 53

Ward, F. W., *Between the big parades*, 294

Ward, F. W., *The 23rd Battalion Royal Fusiliers*, 50

Ward H., *Mr. Poilu*, 110

Ward, Mrs H., *England's effort*, 34; *Towards the goal*, 34

Ward, H. M., *Behind the lines*, 244

Ward, J., *With the 'Die Hards' in Siberia*, 48

Ward, L. W., *The motion picture goes to war*, 97

Ward, M. A., *Fields of victory*, 324

Ward Price, G., *The story of the Salonika Army*, 262

Warfield, W., *The gate of Asia*, 288

Warman, W. H., *The soldier colonists*, 232

Warne, F. J., *The workers at war*, 143

Warner, P., *The battle of Loos*, 161; *Passchendaele*, 205; *The Zeebrugge raid*, 331

Warnod, A., *Prisoner of war*, 226

Warr, C. L., *Echoes of Flanders*, 39, 102; *Unseen hosts*, 277

Warren, H. C., *With the Y.M.C.A. in France*, 329

Warren, *Mrs M. R., The white flame of France*, 107

Warren, W., *Montenegro*, 269

Warth, R. D., *The Allies and the Russian revolution*, 82, 259

Warwick, G. W., *We band of brothers*, 274

Washburn, Slater, *One of the Y.D. (Yankee Division)*, 302

Washburn, Stanley, *Field notes from the Russian Front*, 87, 259; *On the Russian front*, 258; *The Russian campaign, April to August 1915*, 87, 259; *Victory in defeat*, 219

Watchman, *Rome and Germany*, 68; *Rome and the war*, 68

Waters, W. W., *B.E.F. (i.e. Bonus Expeditionary Force)*, 302

Watkins, G. S., *Labor problems and the labor administration in the United States during the World War*, 143

Watkins, O. S., *With French in France*, 71, 111

Watson, A. S., *The flashing sword and its significance*, 196

Watson, S. N., *Those Paris years*, 205

Watson, W. H. L., *Adventures of a despatch rider*, 78; *A company of tanks*, 55

Watt, L. M., *The heart of a soldier*, 244; *In France and Flanders with the fighting men*, 71, 324; *In the land of war*, 71

Watt, R. M., *Dare call it treason*, 185

Wauchope, A. G., *History of the Black Watch–Royal Highlanders, 1914-1918*, 43

Waugh, A., *The prisoners of Mainz*, 226

Wavell, Sir A. P., *Allenby*, 7; *The Palestine campaign*, 204

Waxweiler, E., *Belgium and the Great Powers*, 27; *Belgium neutral and loyal*, 27

Weaver, E. J., *Three Hundred and First Engineers*, 307

Weaver, F. N. & Sanborn, P. N., *Story of F. Company, 101st Regiment, U.S. Engineers*, 307

Webb, C., *In time of war*, 1

Webb, M. de P., *Britain victorious!*, 232

Webb, Sidney, *How to pay for the war*, 100; *The restoration of Trade Union conditions*, 283

Webb, S. & Freeman, A., *Great Britain after the war*, 232

Webber, J. J., *178 Siege Battery R.G.A. France, 1916-1918*, 58

Weber, F. G., *Eagles on the Crescent*, 82

Weber, W. H. F., *A Field Artillery group in battle*, 58

Webster, R. G., *The awakening of an Empire*, 60

Weetman, W. C. C., *The Sherwood Foresters in the Great War*, 52

Wegerer, A. von, *A refutation of the Versailles war guilt*, 316

Weintraub, S., *A stillness heard round the world*, 137

Weldon, L. B., *'Hardlying'*, 254, 267; *In the fourth year*, 209

Wells, H. G., *Russia in the shadows*, 261; *The war of the future*, 137; *The war that will end war*, 209; *What is coming?*, 232

Wells, W. B. & Marlowe, N., *A history of the Irish rebellion of 1916*, 145

Welsh, D., *The USA in World War I*, 294

Wenzel, M & Cornish, J., *Auntie Mabel's war*, 171

Werner, J., *Knight of Germany; Oswald Boelcke. German ace*, 122

Werner, M. R., *'Orderly'*, 302

Wernstein, I., *The lost battalion*, 302; *The many faces of World War I*, 137

Wesselitsky, G. de, *The German peril and the Grand Alliance*, 121

West, A. F., *War and education*, 90

West, A. G., *Diary of a dead officer*, 215

West, *Mrs J. C., Women's war work*, 328

West, Rachel, *The Department of State on the eve of the First World War*, 82

West, R. J., *A guide to the battlefields of the Western Front*, 23

West, W. B., *The fight for the Argonne*, 215

Westcar, W. V. L., *Big game, Boers and Boches*, 215

Westerdale, T. L. B., *Messages from Mars*, 71; *Under the Red Cross flag*, 234

Wester-Wemyss, R., *The Navy in the Dardanelles campaign*, 78

Westman, S. K., *Surgeon with the Kaiser's Army*, 123

Weston, C. H., *Three years with the New Zealanders*, 191

Westover, W., *Suicide battalions*, 309

Wetterle, L'Abbe F., *Behind the scenes in the Reichstag*, 121

Weyl, W. E., *The end of the war*, 209

Whalen, R. W., *Bitter wounds*, 121

Wharton, *Mrs* E. N., *Book of the homeless*, 236; *Fighting France, from Dunkerque to Belfort*, 107

Whates, H. R., *Midland Regiments in France*, 39

Wheatley, D., *Officer and temporary gentleman, 1914-1919*, 177

Wheeler, C., *Letters from an American soldier to his father*, 302

Wheeler, C., *Memorial record of the Seventh (Service) Battalion, the Oxfordshire and Buckinghamshire Light Infantry*, 49

Wheeler, H. D., *Are we ready?*, 297

Wheeler, H. F. B., *Daring deeds of merchant seamen in the Great War*, 178; *Stirring deeds of Britain's sea-dogs in the Great War*, 254; *War in the underseas*, 281

Wheeler, W. R., *China and the World War*, 72

Wheeler-Bennett, J. W., *Brest-Litovsk*, 30; *Hindenburg—wooden titan*, 128

Wheeler-Bennett, J. W. & Latimer, H., *Information on the Reparation Settlement*, 245

Whelpley, J. D., *Reconstruction*, 232

Whetham, W. C. D., *The war and the nation*, 221

Whinyates, R., *Artillery and trench mortar memories, 32nd Division*, 41

Whitaker, H., *Hunting the German shark*, 312

Whitaker, J. P., *Under the heel of the Hun*, 107

White, A., *Is the Kaiser insane?*, 151

White, B., *The currency of the Great War*, 100

White, C. M., *The Gotha summer*, 34

White, F., *Mandates*, 163

White, John, *With the Cameronians in France*, 44

White, J. W., *America and Germany*, 137, 294; *America's arraignment of Germany*, 294

White, M., *Alive to tell the tale*, 277

White, Stephen., *The origins of detente*, 114

White, *Sir* T., *The story of Canada's war finance*, 100

White, T. W., *Guests of the unspeakable*, 15

White, W. A., *Woodrow Wilson*, 326

White, W. L., *Records of the East Yorkshire Volunteer Force*, 45

Whitehair, C. W., *Out there*, 324

Whitehouse, A., *Epics and legends of the First World War*, 277; *The fledgling*, 250; *Decisive battles of the First World War*, 6; *Hell in the heavens*, 250; *Heroes of the sunlit skies*, 6; *Subs and submariners*, 281; *The years of the sky kings*, 6; *The Zeppelin fighters*, 97, 332

Whitehouse, J. H., *Belgium in war*, 27

Whitlock, B., *Belgium under the German occupation*, 27

Whitman, S., *The war on German trade*, 89

Whitmore, F. D. H., *The 10th Royal Hussars and the Essex Yeomanry during the war*, 57

Whitney, S., *Squadron A in the Great War (105th M.G. Brigade)*, 309

Whitridge, F. W., *One American's opinion of the European war*, 294

Whitsed, J. de K., *Come to the cook-house door!*, 312

Whittall, W., *With Botha and Smuts in Africa*, 2, 275

Whitton, F. E., *History of the 40th Division*, 41; *The history of the Prince of Wales's Leinster Regiment, Royal Canadians*, 66; *The Marne campaign*, 164

Whyte, A. G. & Elder, T. G., *The underwar*, 89

Whyte, G. H., *Glimpses of the Great War*, 159

Wibberley, T., *War-time farming*, 2

Widner, E. J., *Military observation balloons*, 22

Wiggins, C. F., *Saved as by fire*, 244

Wight, O. B., *On active service with Base Hospital 46, U.S. Army*, 139

Wilberforce, A. B. O., *Why does not God stop the war?*, 244

Wild, M., *Secret service on the Russian Front*, 267

Wile, F. W., *The assault*, 34; *Explaining the Britishers*, 34; *The German-American plot*, 295; *Who's Who in Hunland*, 236

Wilgus, W. J., *Transporting the A.E.F. in Western Europe, 1917-19*, 285

Wilkie, A. H., *Official war history of the Wellington Mounted Rifles Regiment, 1914-1919*, 191

Wilkins, G. H., *Australian war photographs*, 15

Wilkins, H. T., *Mysteries of the Great War*, 182

Wilkinson, A. B., *The Church of England and the First World War*, 244

Wilkinson, F., *Cavalry and Yeomanry badges of the British Army, 1914*, 91; *World War I weapons and uniforms*, 12, 290

Wilkinson, N. L., *The Dardanelles*, 13, 78

Wilkinson, S., *Lighter than air*, 22

Wilkinson, Spenser, *August, 1914*, 137; *Government and the war*, 294

Willcocks, *Sir* J., *With the Indians in France*, 141

Willcox, W. T., *The 3rd (King's Own) Hussars in the Great War*, 57

Willert, *Sir* A., *The road to safety*, 82

William II, *Emperor of Germany, Letters to the Tsar*, 151; *My memoirs*, 151

Williams, A. F. B., *The campaigns of 1917*, 137;

Raising and training the new Armies, 39
Williams, Albert R., *In the claws of the German eagle,* 267
Williams, Ashby, *Experiences of the Great War,* 324
Williams, C., *Sidelights on Negro soldiers,* 188
Williams, G. V., *With our Army in Flanders,* 102
Williams, H. R., *Comrades of the great adventure,* 19; *The gallant company,* 19
Williams, H. S. & Williams E. H., *Modern warfare,* 91
Williams, I., *Newspapers of the First World War,* 222
Williams, John, *The Home Fronts; Britain, France and Germany, 1914-1918,* 137; *Mutiny, 1917,* 185
Williams, J. E. H., *One young man,* 215
Williams, J, H., *Lenten thoughts in war time,* 244
Williams, L. N. & Williams, M., *The 'Propaganda' forgeries,* 216
Williams, R. F. L., *The Canadian Front in France and Flanders,* 66
Williams, R. S. G., *Prisoners of the Red Desert,* 226; *Under the Black Ensign,* 215
Williams, W., *Passed by the censor,* 222
Williamson, B., *'Happy days' in France and Flanders with the 47th and 48th Divisions,* 42
Williamson, H., *The wet Flanders Plain,* 102
Willis, E. F., *Herbert Hoover and the Russian prisoners of war of World War I,* 226
Willis, I. C., *England's Holy War,* 34
Willmore, J. S., *A great crime and its moral,* 202; *The story of King Constantine as revealed in the Greek White Book,* 126
Willoughby, W. F., *Government organization in war time and after,* 295
Willson, B., *From Quebec to Piccadilly,* 66; *In the Ypres Salient,* 66, 330; *Ypres, the holy ground of British arms,* 330
Wilmer, W. H., *Aviation medicine in the A.E.F.,* 171
Wilsher, L., *Britain in World War I,* 34
Wilson, A. J., *No deluding peace,* 209
Wilson, Sir A. T., *Loyalties, Mesopotamia, 1914-1917,* 180; *Mesopotamia, 1917-1920,* 180
Wilson, C., *Rasputin and the fall of the Romanovs,* 230
Wilson, E. B., *The memoirs of Mrs. Woodrow Wilson,* 177
Wilson, G. M., *Fighting tanks,* 55
Wilson, H. R., *The education of a diplomat,* 295
Wilson, H. W., *Battleships in Action,* 24; *The war guilt,* 202; *Hush,* 281
Wilson, H. W. & Hammerton, J. A., *The Great War,* 137
Wilson, John, *Hamp,* 84
Wilson, J. P., *With the soldiers in Palestine and Syria,* 204
Wilson, L., *The incredible Kaiser,* 151
Wilson, Michael, *Baltic assignment,* 258, 281
Wilson, P. W., *The unmaking of Europe,* 137
Wilson, R., *The post of honour,* 277
Wilson, Robert H., *Palestine, 1917,* 204
Wilson, S. J., *The Seventh Manchester, July 1916 to March 1918,* 48
Wilson, Trevor, *The myriad forces of war,* 34, 137
Wilson, T. W., *America and freedom,* 326; *Messages and papers,* 326; *This man was right,* 326; *War addresses of Woodrow Wilson,* 326
Wilson, W. E., *The foundations of peace,* 209
Wilton, R., *Last days of the Romanoffs,* 192; *Russia's agony,* 261
Wiltsher, A., *Most dangerous women,* 328
Winchester, B., *Beyond the tumult,* 93
Windischgraetz, L. A., *My memoirs,* 177
Wind Adjutant, *Over there,* 248; *Plane tales from the skies,* 248; *The Royal Flying Corps in the war,* 250
Wingfield, W. J. R., *Lectures to cavalry subalterns of the new Armies,* 284
Wingfield-Stratford, E. C., *The harvest of victory, 1918-1926,* 137
Wings, *Over the German lines,* 248
Winnifrith, D. P., *The Church in the fighting line,* 71
Winslow, C. D., *With the French Flying Corps,* 108
Winstone, H. V. F., *Leachman,* 180
Winter, D., *Death's men,* 39, 137; *The first of the few,* 97
Winter, J. M., *The Great War and the British people,* 34
Wintringham, J. W., *With the Lincolnshire Yeomanry in Egypt and Palestine 1914–1918,* 204
Wisbkin, H. W., *A short history of the 39th (Deptford) Divisional artillery 1915–1918,* 41
Wisconsin War History Committee, *32nd Division in the World War,* 303
Wise, F. M., *A Marine tells it to you,* 311
Wise, J. C., *Turn of the tide,* 164
Wiseman, F. L., *The Christ of the soldier,* 244
Wister, O., *Neighbours henceforth,* 107; *The Pentecost of calamity,* 121
Withers, H., *War and Lombard Street,* 100; *War-*

time financial problems, 100

Withington, R., *In occupied Belgium*, 27

Witkop, P., *German students' war letters*, 123

Witt, F. R., *Riding to war with 'A'; a history of Battery A, of the 135th Field Artillery*, 308

Witte, S., *Memoirs*, 258

Wittke, C., *German-Americans and the World War*, 295

Wohl, R., *The generation of 1914*, 137

Wolfe, H., *Labour supply and regulation*, 143

Wolff, H. W., *Rural reconstruction*, 34

Wolff, L., *In Flanders fields; the 1917 campaign*, 102

Wolff, T., *Eve of 1914*, 121

Wolseley, F. G., *Women and the land*, 328

Wombell, P., *Battle, Passchendaele 1917*, 330

Wood, E., *Thrilling deeds of British airmen*, 250

Wood, E. F., *The notebook of an Attaché*, 82; *The writing on the wall*, 295

Wood, Graham, *I was there*, 86

Wood, H. F., *Vimy*, 317

Wood, L., *The history of the First World War*, 137

Wood, Walter, *The fisherman in war-time*, 100; *In the line of battle*, 277

Wood, W. de B., *The history of the King's Shropshire Light Infantry in the Great War*, 47

Wood, W. J., *With the 5th Glo'sters at home and overseas from 3rd August, 1914 to 21st March, 1918*, 45

Woodhall, E. T., *Spies of the Great War*, 267

Woodhouse, E. J. & Woodhouse, C. G., *Italy and the Jugoslavs*, 146

Woodhouse, J. and Embleton, G., *The war in the air*, 6

Woods, E. S., *Knights in armour*, 244

Woods, H. C., *Cradle of the war; the Near East and Pan-Germanism*, 187

Woods, H. G., *Christianity and war*, 244

Woods, W. S., *Colossal blunders of the war*, 279

Woodward, D., *The collapse of power; mutiny in the High Seas Fleet*, 125

Woodward, David R., *America and World War I*, 28

Woodward, E. L., *Great Britain and the German Navy*, 202

Woodward, Sir Ll., *Great Britain and the war of 1914-1918*, 34

Woolf, L. S., *The framework of a lasting peace*, 156; *The future of Constantinople*, 288

Woollard, C. L. A., *With the Harwich Naval Forces*, 128

Woollcombe, R., *The first tank battle; Cambrai 1917*, 61

Woollcott, A., *The command is forward*, 277, 302

Woolley, C. L., *From Kastamuni to Kedos*, 226

Worden, A. F., *'Yes Daddy, but there has been another war since then'*, 215

Worsfold, W. B., *The war and social reform*, 271

Wotherspoon, H. J., *Some spiritual issues of the war*, 244

Wray, W. F., *Across France in war time*, 107

Wren, E., *Randwick to Hargicourt; history of the 3rd Battalion, A.I.F.*, 19

Wren, J., *The great battles of World War I*, 23

Wren. P. C., *Stepsons of France*, 277

Wrench, Sir J. E. L., *Struggle, 1914-1920*, 34

Wrentmore, E. L., *In spite of hell*, 302

Wright, Sir A. E., *Wound infections and some new methods*, 171

Wright, C. E., *The Fate of Zeppelin L.32*, 332

Wright, H. F., *The constitutions of the States at war*, 221

Wright, N., *The red baron*, 246

Wright, P. E., *At the Supreme War Council*, 279

Wright, P. L., *The First Buckinghamshire Battalion, 1914-1919*, 49

Wright, P. Q., *Mandates under the League of Nations*, 163

Wright, S. S., *Of that fellowship (Gallipoli)*, 114

Wrigley, C., *Lloyd George and the British Labour Movement*, 184

Wurtzburg, C. E., *The history of the 2/6th Battalion, 'The King's' (Liverpool Regiment), 1914-1919*, 47

Wyall, E., *The History of the Somerset Light Infantry*, 52

Wyatt, H. M., *Motor transports in war*, 285

Wyllie, W. L., *More sea fights of the Great War, including the battle of Jutland*, 150

Wyllie, W. L. & Wren, M. F., *Sea fights of the Great War*, 186

Wylly, H. C., *The Border Regiment in the Great War*, 43; *The 1st and 2nd Battalions, the Sherwood Foresters in the Great War*, 52; *The Green Howards in the Great War*; 46; *History of the 1st and 2nd Battalions, the Leicestershire Regiment in the Great War*, 47; *Neill's 'Blue Caps', 1st Battalion, the Royal Dublin Fusiliers*, 50

Wyndham, H., *Soldiers on service*, 39

Wynn, A. H. W., *Ambush*, 86

Wynn, W., *Revelation in the light of the war and modern events*, 196

Wynne, C. W., *If Germany attacks*, 138, 324

Wynne, M., *An English girl in Serbia*, 269

Wyrall, E., *The Die-Hards (Middlesex Regiment) in the Great War*, 48; *The East Yorkshire Regiment in the Great War*, 45; *Europe in arms*, 138; *The Gloucestershire Regiment in the war*, 45; *The history of the Fiftieth Division, 1914-1919*, 42; *The history of the King's Regiment (Liverpool)*, 47; *The history of the 19th Division, 1914-1918*, 40; *The history of the Second Division, 1914-1918*, 40; *The history of the 62nd (West Riding) Division*, 42; *The 17th-S-Battalion, Royal Fusiliers, 1914-1918*, 50; *The history of the Somerset Light Infantry*, 42; *The West Yorkshire Regiment in the war, 1914-1918*, 53

X, *Bombardier, So this was war!*, 324

X, *Captain, With Winston Churchill at the Front*, 73

X, P. L., *The spider's web*, 102

Y, *The odyssey of a torpedoed tramp*, 178, 281

Yapp, *Sir A., The romance of the Red Triangle*, 329

Yardley, H. O., *American black chamber*, 267

Yardley, M., *Backing into the limelight*, 155

Yates, L. A. R., *United States and French security, 1917-1921*, 82

Yates, L. K., *The woman's part*, 184

Yealland, L. R., *Hysterical disorders of warfare*, 171

Yeats-Brown, F. C., *Caught by the Turks*, 226, 288; *Golden Horn*, 188

Yeo, *Soldier men*, 39

Yerkes, R. M., *New world of science*, 263

Yerta, G. and Yerta, M., *Six Women and the invasion*, 27

Yoakum, C. S. and Yerkes, R. M., *Mental tests in the American army*, 302

York, A. C., *Sergeant York*, 302

York, D., *Mud and stars*, 273

Young, A. B. F., *With the battle cruisers*, 76

Young, A. D., *A subaltern in Serbia*, 269

Young, E. H., *By sea and land*, 254

Young, E. W., *The Wilson administration and the Great War*, 326

Young, F. B., *Marching on Tanga*, 86

Young, G., *Nationalism and war in the Near East*, 82

Young, G. W., *The grace of forgetting*, 215

Young, G. W. W., *From the trenches*, 102

Young, *Sir H., The independent Arab*, 180

Young, H. F., *Prince Lichnowsky and the Great War*, 174

Young, J., *With the 52nd Division in three continents*, 42

Young, R. S., *Over the top with the 80th, 1917-1919*, 304

Youssoupoff, F. F., *Rasputin*, 230

Zagorsky, S. O., *State control of industry in Russia during the war*, 143

Zanardi Landi, C. F. M., *Is Austria doomed?*, 20

Zander, H.W., *Thirteen years in hell*, 215

Zangwill, I., *The war for the world*, 221

Zeman, Z. A. B., *The break-up of the Habsburg Empire*, 20; *A diplomatic history of the First World War*, 83

Zhabotinsky, V. E., *The story of the Jewish Legion*, 149

Zimmermann, E., *The German Empire of Central Africa as the basis of a new German world-policy*, 121

Zimmern, A. E., *Europe in convalescence*, 232

Zimmern, H., *Italian leaders of to-day*, 146

Zook, G. F., *America at war*, 295

SUBJECT INDEX

Addresses and Speeches 1
Afghanistan 1
Africa 1-2
Agriculture 2
Aircraft Production 2
Air warfare 3-7
Aisne 7
Allenby 7
Alsace-Lorraine 7-8
Ambulances 8-9
Amiens 9
Animals 9
Anthology 9
Antwerp 9
Arabia *see* Mesopotamia
Archangel 10
Armenia 10-11
Armistice 11
Arms and Armour 11-12
Arras 12
Art and Artists 12-13
Artillery 13-14
Asquith 14
Atrocities *see* War Crimes
Australia 14-15
Australian Air Force 15
Australian Army 15-19
Australian Navy 19
Austria 19-20

Balfour 21
Balkans 21
Balloons 22
Battlefields 22-3
Battles 23
Battleships 24
Beatty 24
Belgium 24-7
Bibliographies 27-8
Blockade 28-9
Bombers 29
Botha 29
Boy Scouts 29-30

Brest-Litovsk 30
Britain 30-4
British Army
  (general) 34-9
  Fourth Army 39
  Fifth Army 39
  Divisions 39-42
  Brigades 43
  Regiments 43-53
  Corps 53-5
  Cavalry 55-7
  Royal Artillery 57-8
  Royal Engineers 58-9
British Empire 59-60
British Expeditionary Force 60

Calais 60
Cambrai 61
Camouflage 61
Canada 61-2
Canadian Air Force 62
Canadian Army 63-6
Canteens 66
Caporetto 66
Carmania 66
Cartoons 66-7
Casement 67-8
Catholicism 68
Caucasus 68
Cavell 68-9
Cemeteries 69
Censorship 69
Ceylon 69
Chaplains 70-1
Children 72
China 72
Chronologies 72
Churchill 72-3
Clemenceau 73
Coal 73
Conferences *see* under name
Congressional
  Medal of Honor 73-4

Conscientious Objectors 74-5
Conscription 75
Coronel 75-6
Cruisers 76
Czecho-Slovakia 76

Dardanelles 76-8
Denmark 78
Deportations 78
Despatch Riders 78
Destroyers 78-9
Dictionaries 79-80
Diplomatic History 80-3
Disabled Ex-Servicemen 83
Disarmament 83
Dixmude 83
Dover patrol 83-4
Drama 84
Drink 84

East Africa 84-6
Eastern Europe 86-7
Easter Rising 87
Economics 87-9
Education 89-90
Egypt 90
Emden 90-1
Entertainment 91
Equipment 91
Escapes 91-3
Espionage *see* Search Service
Essays 93-4
Ex-Servicemen 94

Falkland Islands 94-5
Far East 95
Fighters 95-7
Films 97
Finance 97-100
Finland 100
Fishing 100
Fiume 100

Flanders 100-2
Flying Boats 102
Foch 102
Food 103
Fort Vaux 104
Fourteen Points 104
France 104-7
French Air Force 107-8
French Army 108-10
French Navy 110
French (Sir John) 110-11
Frontiers 111

Gallantry 111-12
Gallipoli 112-14
Gas Warfare 114
Genoa 114
Germany 115-21
German Air Force 121-2
German Army 122-3
German Navy 124-5
German Surface Raiders 125
Gold Coast 126
Gough 126
Greece 126
Grey 126-7

Haig 127
Harwich 127-8
Heligoland Bight 128
Hindenburg 128
Hindenburg Line 128
History 128-38
Holland see Netherlands
Hospitals 138-9
Hospital Ships 140
House (Colonel) 140
Hungary 140-1

India 141
Indian Army 141
Industry 142-3
Insurance 143
Intelligence 143
International Law 143-4
Internment 144
Ireland 144-5
Isle of Man 145
Italy 145-6
Italian Army 147
Italian Front 147
Italian Navy 147

Japan 148
Jellicoe 148
Jews 148-9
Joffre 149
Jutland 149-50

Kaiser Wilhelm II 150-1
Kitchener 151-2
Kut 152

Language 153
Latin America 153
Law 153
Lawrence of Arabia 153-5
League of Nations 155-6
Lenin 156
Letters 156-9
Libraries 159
Liège 159
Liggett 159
Lloyd George 160
London 160-1
Loos 161
Louvain 161
Ludendorff 161
Lusitania 162
Luxemburg 162

Macedonia 162-3
Mandates 163
Maps 163
Marne 163-4
Mata Hari 164
Medals 165
Medical 165-71
Mediterranean 171
Memoirs 171-7
Merchant Navy 177-8
Mesopotamia Campaign 178-80
Mines and Minesweeping 181
Miscellaneous Writings 181-2
Missionaries 183
Mons 183
Morals 183
Motor Launches 183-4
Munitions 184
Mutinies 185

Naval Warfare 185-6
Near East 186-8
Negroes 188
Netherlands 189

Neutrals 189
Neuve Chapelle 189
New Guinea 189
New Zealand 190-1
Nicholas II Tsar 192
Nigeria 192
Norway 192
Nurses and Nursing 192-4

Occult 194-6
Occupation 196
Officer Training Corps 196
Origins of the War 197-202

Pacifism 202
Palestine 202-4
Paris 204-5
Passchendaele 205
Peace 205-9
Pensions 209
Pershing 210
Personal Narrative 210-15
Pétain 215
Philately 216
Philosophy 216-17
Photography 217-18
Pigeons 218
Poland 218-19
Police 219
Politics 219-21
Poppies 221
Postcards 221
Posters 222
Press 222
Prisoners of War 223-6
Propaganda 227
Psychology 228

Q Ships 228
Quakers 228-9

Railways 229
Rasputin 229-30
Reconstruction 230-2
Recruitment 233
Red Cross 233-4
Reference Books 234-6
Refugees 236
Relief Work 236-7
Religion 237-44
Reparations 245
Richthofen 246

Roosevelt 246
Royal Air Force 246-8
Royal Flying Corps 249-50
Royal Marines 250
Royal Navy 250-4
Royal Naval Air Service 254
Rumania 254-5
Russia 255-8
Russian Army 258-9
Russian Campaign
  (Allied) 259
Russian Navy 260
Russian Revolution 260-1

Salonika 262
Salvation Army 262
Sarajevo 262
Scandinavia 263
Scapa Flow 263
Scarborough 263
Science 263
Secret Service 264-7
Serbia 267-9
Shipbuilding 269
Siberia 269-70
Socialism 270-1
Sociology 271
Somme 271-2
Songs 273
South Africa 273-5
South America 275
South East Asia 275
Spain 275
Spies see Secret Service

Statistics 275
Stories 275-7
Strategy 278-9
Stretcher Bearers 279
Submarines 280-1
Survivors (sea) 281
Suvla Bay 281
Switzerland 281-2

Tactics 282
Tanks 282
Taxation 283
Technology 283
Toc H 283
Trade Unions 283
Training 283-4
Transcaspia 284
Transportation 285
Treaties 285-6
Trench Warfare 286-7
Trianon 287
Turkey 287-8

U-Boats 289-90
Uniforms 290
United States
  (general) 290-5
  American-Germans 295
  Intervention 295-6
  Neutrality 296-7
  Preparedness 297
United States Army
  (general) 298-302
  Divisions 302-4

Infantry 304-6
Engineers 306-7
Artillery 307-9
Machine Gunners 309
Air Division 309-10
United States Marines 310-11
United States Navy 311-12

VAD 312
Vatican see Catholicism
Venizelos 312-13
Verdun 313
Versailles 313-16
Victoria Cross 316-17
Vimy Ridge 317

Wales 317
War Correspondents 317-18
War Crimes 318-19
War Debts 319-20
War Trials 320
Weapons see Arms and Armour
West Africa 320
Western Front 320-4
Wilson (Woodrow) 324-6
Women 326-8

YMCA 328
Ypres 329-31
Yugoslavia 331

Zeebrugge 331
Zeppelins 331-2
Zimmerman 332

INDEX OF TITLED BOOKS ONLY

Achievement of France, 104
After two years, 1
After victory, 230
America after the War, 230
America in the Great War, 290
Amiens before and during the war, 9
Ancient Babylon and modern Germany, 194
Anzac book, 112
Anzac memories, 112
The Army and religion, 237
The Battle of Verdun, 313
Battlefields of World War, I 22
Behind the Prison bars, 223
Being the narrative of Battery A., 307
Being the story of a light field artillery battery, 307
Belgium and Germany, 24
Best stories of the 1914 European war, 275
The Blackhole of the desert, 223
A book of Belgian gratitude, 24
A book of British heroes, 111
Brief history of the 30th Division, 41
A brief record of the advance of the Egyptian Expeditionary Force under General Allenby, 7
British medicine in the war, 165
British universities and the war, 89
British vessels lost at sea, 177, 250
The campaign of the British Army in Mesopotamia 1914–18, 179
Canada in khaki, 63
Canadian Jews in World War I, 61
Can Germany win?, 115
Catholics of the British Empire, 68
Cavalry combat, 55
Chaplains in council, 70
Collections and recollections, 58
Company log, 306
Complete history of the coloured soldier in the war, 188
Cost of the World War, 98
The crimes of Germany, 318
Croydon in the war, 31
The curtain of steel, 251

Dardanelles, 77
Death in the air, 249
Declaration of London, 185
Deeds that thrill the Empire, 111
Despatches from the heart, 211
Diary of a nursing sister on the Western Front, 193
Diary of a U-Boat commader, 289
Diplomatic correspondence between the U.S. and Germany August 1914–April 1917, 80, 143
88th Division in the World War, 304
The elements of reconstruction, 230
The Empire and the future, 59
England's financial supremacy, 98
Escapers all, 92
Experiences of a war baby, 251
The fall of the Romanoffs, 192
Field ambulance sketches, 8
Fields and battlefields, 22
Fifty amazing stories of the Great War, 276
The 54th Infantry Brigade, 43
Fifty thousand miles on a hospital ship, 140
Fighting Australia, 17
Financial mobilization for war, 98
The first World War in posters, 222
Fleets of the World 1915, 185
Four years in a refugee camp, 236
French yellow book, 105
Friends of France, 8
Frightfulness in retreat, 105
From a Russian diary, 256
From dug-out to billet, 157
From Snotty to Sub, 252
From the first shot, 217
Further recollections of the 107th Field Company, 59
Fusilier bluff, 187
The game of diplomacy, 256
German atrocities, 319
A German crime – Scarborough, 263
A German deserter's war experience, 122
German war proclamations, 117
Germans at Louvain, 161
The German white book, 117, 122

Germany's great lie, 117
The German spy system, 264
The German Treaty text, 314
Germany's war mania, 117
Germany, Turkey and Armenia, 10
The golden horseshoe, 41
Grand Fleet days, 252
The great advance, 271
Great battles of the Great War, 23
Great speeches of the War, 1
Great War adventures, 276
The Greek Army and the recent Balkan offensive, 126
Handbook to Belgium and the battlefields, 22
Happy though wounded, 138
High explosive shell, 184
History of the American Field Service in France, 236
History of the 15th Infantry Brigade, 1914–1919, 43
History of the 50th Infantry Brigade, 43
History of the 520th, 59
History of the 40th (Sunshine), 303
History of the 79th Division, AEF, 304
History of the 3rd Battalion Sixth Regiment, 310
History of the 313th Field Artillery, 308
History of the 322nd Field Artillery, 308
History of the 26th Engineers, 306
History of the 27th Engineers, 306
History of the World War, 132
Honours and Awards of the Old Contemptibles, 112
The horrors of Wittenburg, 224
India and the war, 141
India's services in the war, 141
In the fire of the furnace, 109
In the hands of the Hun, 224
In the whirlpool of the races, 183
Iron times with the Guards, 37
The Italian Green Book, 146
Italy and the war, 146
J'Accuse, 118
Jerusalem, its redemption and future, 203
King Albert's book, 25
The last of the war lords, 151
Letters of a soldier, 109
Letters from a French hospital, 139
The lie of the 3rd August 1914, 200
Lille before and during the war, 106
The link, 225
List of officers and men serving in the first Canadian contingent with the B.E.F. 1914, 64

The living and the dead, 213
Lloyd George and the War, 160
Machine gunners pocket book, 11
Making of a soldier, 284
The Marne battlefields 1914, 164
Marshall Cavendish illustrated encyclopaedia of World War I, 235
A Memoir and some letters of Frank Maxwell, 317
Militarism versus feminism, 328
Military medical manuals, 169
Mirrors of Downing Street, 32
More war adventures on land, sea and in the air, 277
Mr. Punch's history of the Great War, 67
My secret service, 266
Netherlands and the World War, 189
Neutrality, Its history, economics and law, 189
New Army in the making, 284
New England aviators, 13
New War encyclopaedia and dictionary, 235
New Zealand at the Front, 191
Nominal roles of officers, non-commissioned officers and men, 65
Nursing adventures, 193
The Occupation of the Rhineland, 196
Officers Training Corps: a record of war service, 196
Officers who died in the Great War 1914–1919, 38
Official history of the 304th Engineers Regiment, 307
Official list of casualties to members of the Canadian Expeditionary Force, 65
Official names of the battles and other engagements, 23
On the Anzac trail, 191
Our gallant Guards, 112
Our heroic Highlanders, 112
Out of their own mouths, 119
The Peace Conference and after, 315
Peace 'Made in Germany', 208
Pen pictures of British battles, 23
Pensioners of the Great War, 209
Pictorial history of the 78th Division in France, 304
The Pilgrims' guide, 330
Poland's case for independence, 218
The Pomp of Power, 279
Posters of World War I and World War II, 12
Practical guide to the British war area in France and Belgium, 23

President Wilson from an English point of view, 326

Problems of readjustment after the war, 231

Problems of reconstruction, 232

Proceedings of the Brest-Litovsk Peace Conference, 30

Proceedings on a formal investigation into the Lusitania, 162

The rebuilding of Britain, 232

Recalled to life, 83

The Red archives, 257

Red Guidon, 308

Red Triangle girls in France, 329

Regimental history of a New Zealand Cyclist Corps, 191

Regimental nicknames and traditions of the British Army, 38

Reminiscent sketches 1914–1919, 193

Report on the atrocities, 319

Reports by the Joint War Committee, 234

Rheims and the battle for its possession, 106

Royal Artillery War Commemoration, 58

Rural Scotland during the war, 33

Russian diary of an Englishwoman, 257

Russian public finance complore title?, 99

Salonika memories, 262

Second division, 302

Service medals, ribbons, badges and flags, 165

Shell shocks, 191

Short history and illustrated roster (105, 106, 107, 108, 110, 111, 112 Infantries), 305

Short history of the 19th (Western) Division, 40

Short history and photographic record of the Field Artillery (101 + 102), 307

A simple prayer book for soldiers, 68

Sir Douglas Haig's great push, 272

Sir Edward Grey, 127

Soldier poets, 273

Soldier's companion, 243

The Somme, 272

Songs and sonnets for England, 273

A souvenir of the battlefields pilgrimage August 1928, 23

Squads write, 222

The Stars and Stripes, 222

The story of the Anzacs, 19

Story of the East Company, 101st Engineers, 307

Story of the 91st Division, 304

Story of the Sixty-ninth Canadian Field Artillery, 65

Sweden, Norway, Denmark and Iceland in the World War, 189, 263

Tale of a casualty clearing station, 170

Tale of a Territorial, 38

Tales of a dug-out, 287

Tank tales, 282

A temporary gentleman in France, 158

The Tenedos Times, 79

Texts of the Russian 'Peace', 30

Things to know about the war, 235

Thirty Canadian V.C.'s, 65

Three personal records of the war, 215

Thrilling deeds of valour, 112

Through German spectacles, 222

Through terror to triumph, 202

Told in the huts, 329

Towards the Goal, 34

Treaty of Peace, 316

Treaty of Peace with Germany, 316

Treaty of Versailles, 316

Treaty of Versailles and after, 316

True stories of the Great War, 277

Twelve months with the Australian Expeditionary Force, 19

Two Battles of the Marne, 164

'Two Eleven' 58

Two thousand questions and answers about the war, 235

Two World Wars

Two years captivity in German East Africa, 86

Uncensored letters of a canteen girl, 66

Uncensored letters from the Dardanelles, 78

Uncle Sam's fact book of the World War, 235

The Union of South African and the Great War, 274

Unknown soldiers, 65

War addresses for Catholic pulpit and platform, 68

War and Christianity, 244

War and democracy, 217, 271

War book of facts, 235

The wards in wartime, 139

War Finance Acts 1914 to 1917, 100

The war from this side, 294

War in the air, 6

A war manual of prayer, 244

War of 1914, 27

War nurse's diary, 139, 194

War on hospital ships, 319

Washington and Berlin, 82

When I joined the ranks, 284

Where the German Army has passed, 319

Why Germany capitulated on Nov. 11th, 1918, 137

Why we are at war, 34, 201

Wine, women and war, 215

The Wipers Times, 222, 330

With a Highland Regiment in Mesopotamia 1916–17, 180

Women helpers of their nations, 328

Wonderful stories, 317

Work of the Royal Engineers, 59

The work of the Royal Navy Reserve, 254

The work and training of the Royal Flying Corps, 250

The World Crisis by Winston Churchill, 73

The World in tears, 244

The world's peril, 295

Wounded and a P.O.W., 226

Ypres 1914, 330

Ypres before and after the Great War, 330